Get Your
Degree Online

Get Your Degree Online

Matthew L. Helm and April Leigh Helm

McGRAW-HILL

New York   San Francisco   Washington, D.C.   Auckland   Bogotá
Caracas   Lisbon   London   Madrid   Mexico City   Milan
Montreal   New Delhi   San Juan   Singapore
Sydney   Tokyo   Toronto

McGraw-Hill

A Division of The McGraw·Hill Companies

    4 5 6 7 8 9 0   AGM/AGM   6 5 4 3 2 1

0-07-135713-0

Printed and bound by Quebecor/Martinsburg.

McGraw-Hill books are available at special quantity discounts to use as
premiums and sales promotions, or for use in corporate training
programs. For more information, please write to the Director of Special
Sales, Professional Publishing, McGraw-Hill, Two Penn Plaza, New York,
NY 10121-2298. Or contact your local bookstore.

 This book is printed on recycled, acid-free paper containing a
minimum of 50% recycled de-inked fiber.

Contents

INTRODUCTION

Background on Distance Learning

Just What is Distance Learning

Simply put, distance learning is the delivery of education in which the instructor and students are not in the same classroom. It builds on the idea that students are learning all the time—you don't have to be sitting in a classroom listening to an instructor deliver a lecture about a particular topic to learn about that topic. As with traditional higher education, students can take distance learning courses for self-improvement, certification, or to earn a degree.

While online distance learning programs are, of course, a modern phenomenon, distance learning has a much longer history. Today's distance learning programs have their roots in the correspondence courses of the late 1800s in the United States. In Europe, Africa, and Asia, distance learning dates back even further. Some of the earliest U.S. correspondence programs were offered from land-grant institutions which were trying to reach an agricultural population that couldn't afford to leave their work behind to attend college on a campus. They used postal systems to send course materials to students in rural communities. The students would complete and return assignments through the mail. While this concept of correspondence courses has continued to the present, distance learning has grown and taken on new and combined forms as technological advances were made.

In the 1920s, some schools began enhancing and expanding upon their correspondence courses with the use of radio. They would broadcast lectures over the radio to supplement the written course materials that they would still distribute using mail. As America moved from radio to television in the 1950s, so did distance learning broadcasting. Schools started broadcasting the lectures on closed circuit and public television while continuing to use mail-based correspondence for texts and assignments. As times and technology continued to change, they moved to broadcasting on dedicated cable channels and through the use of audio- and video-tapes. From the 1960s until the 1990s, many distance learning programs used combinations of delivery methods—primarily television-based delivery for the lecture portion of a course and written materials transmitted through the postal service.

In the 1980s, as computers gained popularity, several colleges and universities began experimenting with virtual delivery of courses. They tried different ways to use the computer in distance learning. But it wasn't until the 1990s, when the Internet gained acceptance into peoples' homes, that the idea really caught on. Online distance learning took off as more and more schools began tailoring their programs to use computers and the Internet.

The first program to offer courses solely through distance learning—the University of the State of New York's External Degree Program—was founded in 1971. The program was quite popular and has grown over the years. Granted a charter by the New York State Board of Regents in 1998, it's now a private institution known as Regents College. Another modern innovator in distance learning was Nova University, which lead the way in computer-based distance learning. Building on a UNIX-based network, Nova began offering distance learning courses that used computers as a delivery method over 15 years ago.

What is Online Distance Learning?

Online distance learning is a term we apply to any distance learning course that is delivered via computer and has two or more Internet-based components. The Internet is a system of computer networks joined together by high-speed data lines, and electronic mail (e-mail), scheduled Internet Relay Chat, and the World Wide Web are considered Internet-based components to online distance learning courses.

Electronic mail consists of messages that are sent from one person to another electronically over the Internet. It is also called e-mail. In online distance learning, it is often used as the method of communication among students and between the student and instructor. It can also be used for submitting course assignments.

Internet Relay Chat is a network providing channels or areas (called chat rooms) where you can log in and participate (using chat software) in real-time discussions about various topics. It is also called IRC or chat. In online distance learning, the course instructor may hold chat sessions where class participants can discuss readings, virtual lectures, or just about anything course-related.

The *World Wide Web* (also known as the Web) is a system for viewing and using multimedia documents on the Internet. Web documents are created in HyperText Markup Language (HTML) and are interpreted by Web browsers (software that enables you to view HTML). In online distance learning, instructors can create Web sites to deliver lectures, assignments, and tests, as well as message boards where students can share information and questions. Students can also search the Web for online databases to use on assignments.

At first glance, online distance learning resembles education through correspondence courses. This shouldn't be surprising—after all they are, in essence, an outgrowth of correspondence courses and involve a delivery method that isn't face-to-face with the instructor of a course. However, upon closer examination, you'll see that online courses are actually more like traditional classes or a hybrid of traditional and correspondence courses. For many courses, instructors post assignments (readings, lectures to watch, projects, etc.) via the Web or e-mail, and students have a certain amount of time in which to work on or complete them outside of class. Upon completing an assignment, the student submits it—usually via e-mail. Then all of the students are expected to log-on to the Web (to a particular chat room or discussion board) at a given time to discuss assignments—this gives the students direct interaction with each other and immediate feedback from the instructor. And many of the online distance learning programs adhere to the same academic schedule as their traditional counterparts—they are based on semester or quarter terms.

Can You Earn a Degree or Certificate Online?

The level of degree or certificate that you can earn through online distance learning depends on the school and particular field in which you want to study. There are programs available for degrees at the Associate, Baccalaureate, Master, and Doctorate levels, as well as professional certificate programs and Continuing Education Units.

- *Associate's degree*—An Associate's degree is awarded to a student upon the successful completion of a two-year program of study. Typically, it requires that the student pass courses totaling 60 credit hours, with a minimum number of courses being in a particular field. It usually takes a student two years of full-time enrollment to complete an Associate's degree.

- *Baccalaureate or Bachelor's degree*—To earn a Bachelor's degree, a student is usually required to successfully complete at least 120 credit hours of coursework. Typically, 60 credit hours of the 120 must be upper-division courses related to the student's major. It usually takes a student four or five years of full-time enrollment to complete a Bachelor's degree.
- *Master's degree*—A Master's degree is a graduate degree awarded to a student upon successful completion of a post-baccalaureate program. The number of credits or units that a student must complete, and the amount of time that it takes, depends entirely upon the graduate program.
- *Doctorate or Doctoral degree*—This is the highest degree awarded by colleges and universities in the United States. The requirements for the degree vary depending on the institution and field of study. Typically, it requires a dissertation or a comprehensive examination during the final phases of the program. And it usually takes around four years to complete.
- *Certificate*—A certificate is a document validating that a student has completed particular courses of student in his/her field of expertise.
- *Continuing Education Unit (CEU)*—This is a standard measurement for a student's participation in a continuing education program. Generally, these programs apply to fields that require certification or licensure. One unit is equal to ten contact hours of participation in a qualified course.

Is a Degree Earned Through Distance Learning Credible?

The degree you earn is as credible as the institution from which you earn it. This means if you choose a quality school, then a degree you earn through distance learning will be just as credible as a traditional degree in the same major from the same school. Chapter 5 provides more detailed information about selecting a school.

Is Distance Learning for You?

Who are Distance Learning Students?

Distance learning students are people from all walks of life who want to further their educations but cannot commit to an on-campus program for one reason or another.

According to a 1998 survey by the Education Commission of the States, the average distance learning student is over 25 years of age, employed, and has some previous college experience. Over half of the distance learning students are female. And distance learners have proven to be highly motivated and disciplined in their studies.

What are the Advantages of Online Education?

There are several advantages to taking courses online instead of in a traditional classroom. Here are a few:

- Taking online courses from home doesn't require commuting. This saves you time and money—time that you don't have to spend in the car and money that you don't have to spend on gas and car maintenance.
- You can complete most of the coursework for online classes when it's convenient for you. Most online courses are asynchronous, which means you don't have to attend a lecture at a particular place and time. You can review what would traditionally be lecture material and work on assignments before or after

work, during your lunch hour, or after the kids have gone to bed—whenever it best fits your schedule.

- Being able to take classes from home and working on assignments on your own schedule enable you to be home with your kids. This can save you childcare costs.
- Online courses address physical accessibility issues that some disabled persons and senior citizens encounter when taking traditional classes. You don't have to worry about gaining access to a campus building or being forced to sit in uncomfortable desks for one or more hours at a time. Instead, you access the course materials from home through your computer. The furniture you use is your own so it's most likely comfortable. And you have the luxury of being able to get up and stretch whenever you need to do so without interrupting an entire classroom full of students.

Is Online Distance Learning for You?

If you want to earn a certificate or degree, or simply to enhance your work skills and experience, but you find yourself unable to attend traditional courses for one reason or another then online distance learning may be just the thing for you.

You may be a parent who works full-time and doesn't want to give up what little time you have with your kids to commute to campus and sit through a lecture. Or you may have child care issues that are preventing you from enrolling. You might be a disabled or retired person who finds it challenging to get to a location where traditional courses are offered. Or you may live in a rural area and can't bear the thought of driving a couple of hours or more just to take a class. Online distance learning addresses all of these problems with traditional courses. It doesn't require a commute to an-

other location and, for the most part, you can work on courses at your convenience.

And there are financial incentives for wanting to complete a degree or further advance your education, whether it's online or off-line. The U.S. Census Bureau reports that in 1997, the average amount that a male with a high school diploma earned was $32,611; while the average earnings of a male with a Bachelor's degree was $44,832. The average earnings for a female with only a high school diploma was $22,656, while a female with a Bachelor's degree earned $37,319. Earnings potential for both genders continued to increase by each level of higher education.

Convenience and financial rewards are appealing reasons to pursue an online degree. However, there are a few things to consider about yourself. Do you have personal characteristics that will help you succeed if you take courses online?

- You need to be committed to your pursuit of a certificate or degree. Just because a course is offered online doesn't mean it's going to be easier than its traditional counterpart. In fact, many online courses have been proven to be more rigorous and challenging than their off-line equivalents.
- You really need to be highly motivated. There will be times when you feel like you're all alone, with no one to turn to for advice or feedback. You'll have to keep your end goal in mind and have the drive to continue on.
- It will help if you're well organized and disciplined. You'll have to make yourself study for exams and complete assignments, just as you would if you were taking a traditional course. This means you'll have to schedule your time judiciously.
- You need to be a self-directed learner because you'll be handling much of your course planning and scheduling yourself. You may even be required to prepare and adhere to a learn-

ing contract, which is a legal document you and your school's representative agree to that outlines your educational goals, how you intend to meet them, and how your progress will be evaluated.

- You need access to a computer that meets certain requirements. If you don't have a computer at home, you may be able to use one where you work.
- It also helps if you actually enjoy sitting in front of your computer, working alone for relatively long periods of time (a couple of hours at a time).

What Technology Do You Need to Participate in Online Education?

The key to taking courses online is to be online. This means accessing the Internet and its various resources using a computer and some sort of connection, most likely using a modem and telephone line. Schools have different technological requirements for their online courses so you'll need to contact the school directly to get a specific list. However, most programs don't require that you be an expert in the field of computers—as long as you have some basic computing skills (knowledge of e-mail and the Web, and the appropriate software), you have the skills necessary. Some schools even offer orientation courses to prepare you for their online courses and the technology you'll be using.

Here is a list of some general, technological requirements that most online programs of study have in common.

- *Computer*—While all online education requires a computer, you'll need to contact the school for specific equipment recommendations (speed, memory, and accessories).
- *Modem or other connection to the internet*— If your computer is not directly connected to

the Internet, you will need to have a modem so that you can access information on the Internet via a telephone line. A modem allows your computer to talk to other computers through the telephone line. They can be internal (inside your computer) or external (plugged into one of your computer's serial ports).

- *Printer*—Although you'll submit most of your assignments electronically over the Internet, many schools recommend having a printer for your own use and in case you need to submit something in paper form.
- *Speakers and a sound card*—A sound card is an internal device on your computer that allows you to hear any kind of sound file that plays on your computer. If lectures for your online course are delivered as real-time video over the Internet, you'll need a sound card and speakers to hear them.
- *Internet Service Provider* (ISP)—This is a company or organization that provides you with access to the Internet through a dial-up (telephone) or direct connection. America Online is an example of an Internet Service Provider.
- *Software*—You will need various types of software: a word processor, a Web browser, an electronic mail program, and a program to participate in chat rooms, just to name a few.

Finding the Right School

Who Offers Online Distance Learning?

You can find distance learning courses offered by various types of organizations at all levels of education—from Kindergarten through 12th grade classes offered by school districts, to employment or military training offered by industry and the Armed Forces. So who is offering collegiate-level certificate and degree programs online? Colleges and universities offer most of the online programs of study that you'll find. Many of them are the same colleges and universities that offer traditional, on-campus programs. Additionally, there are some state-established distance learning systems or consortia that consist of two or more colleges or universities working with each other to deliver online courses and programs of study. And we're seeing more involvement in online distance learning from corporations. It is important to note that most of the corporate-sponsored distance learning programs are restricted to company employees, so we have not provided details about them in this book.

What is Accreditation and Why is it Important?

Accreditation is formal recognition, or a guarantee of sorts, that an entire school or one of its programs of study meets certain standards and provides quality education. In the United States, schools and/or programs of study may be accredited by one of six regional agencies, a specialized accrediting agency, or a state agency. In Canada, the government regulates all of the schools within a province.

There are larger organizations that recognize accrediting agencies, giving them validation, much as the accrediting agencies validate the schools. Two such organizations are the U.S. Department of Education and the Council for Higher Education Accreditation (CHEA). As you probably suspect, the U.S. Department of Education is the arm of the federal government that loosely oversees all education in the United States. The Council for Higher Education Accreditation is a voluntary organization that helps set policy in higher education and acts as a clearinghouse on accreditation. In Canada, this service is provided by the Association of Universities and Colleges of Canada.

There are six regional accrediting agencies that are recognized by the U.S. Department of Education and CHEA. They are all identified below. All are equally authoritative and recognize each other as such. This means schools accredited by one regional accrediting agency recognize degrees earned through schools accredited by another regional accrediting agency. And each lists or has a searchable database of the schools that it accredits on its Web site.

- *Middle States Association of Colleges and Schools*—accredits schools in Delaware, District of Columbia, Maryland, New Jersey, New York, Pennsylvania, Puerto Rico, and the Virgin Islands; 3624 Market Street, Philadelphia PA 19104; (215) 662-5606; http://www.msache.org.
- *New England Association of Schools and Colleges*—accredits schools in Connecticut, Maine, Massachusetts, New Hampshire, Rhode Island, and Vermont; 209 Burlington Road, Bedford MA 07130; (781) 271-0022; http://www.neasc.org.
- *North Central Association of Colleges and Schools*—accredits schools in Arizona, Arkansas, Colorado, Illinois, Indiana, Iowa, Kansas, Michigan, Minnesota, Missouri, Nebraska, New Mexico, North Dakota, Ohio, Oklahoma, Utah, and Washington; 30 North LaSalle, Suite 2400, Chicago IL 60602; (800) 621-7440 or (312) 263-0456; http://www.ncacihe.org.
- *Northwest Association of Schools and Colleges*—accredits schools in Alaska, Idaho, Montana, Nevada, Oregon, Utah, and Washington; 11130 NE 33rd Place, Suite 120, Bellevue WA 98004; (425) 827-2005; http://www.cocnasc.org (under construction); and NASC's Commission on Schools can be contacted at 1910 University Drive, Boise ID 83725; (208) 334-3210 or at www2.idbsu.edu/nasc.

- *Southern Association of Colleges and Schools*—accredits schools in Alabama, Florida, Georgia, Kentucky, Louisiana, Mississippi, North Carolina, South Carolina, Tennessee, Texas, and Virginia; 1866 Southern Lane, Decatur GA 30033; (404) 679-4500; http://www.sacscoc.org.
- *Western Association of Schools and Colleges*—accredits schools in California, Hawaii, and Guam; http://www.wascweb.org; WASC's Accrediting Commission for Community and Junior Colleges can be contacted at 3402 Mendocino Avenue, Santa Rosa CA 95403; (707) 569-9177; and WASC's Accrediting Commission for Senior Colleges and Universities can be reached at 985 Atlantic Avenue, Suite 100, Alameda CA 94501; (510) 748-9001.

In addition to the regional accrediting agencies, the U.S. Department of Education and CHEA recognize some other accreditation organizations. One such agency that you'll encounter quite a bit when looking at distance learning programs is the Distance Education and Training Council (DETC). The DETC is the oldest non-governmental agency in the United States that accredits distance learning schools. You can contact DETC online at http://www.detc.org or by mail at 1601 18th Street NW, Washington D.C. 20009. They can also be reached by phone, at (202) 234-5100.

We recommend that you look up the accrediting agency of any school that you are seriously considering taking courses through. Just because a school states that it is accredited by a particular organization doesn't necessarily mean that the organization itself is recognized as trustworthy or, in some cases, even legitimate.

For full lists of the accrediting agencies that the U.S. Department of Education and CHEA recognize, visit http://www.ed.gov/offices/OPE/Students/Accred.html and/or http://www.chea.org/Directories/index.html.

What Should You be Wary of?

Pursuing a certificate or degree is not a process to be taken lightly. This is your education we're talking about. And you probably want the best education possible, right? While you can use this book to identify potential schools and programs of study, there will come a time when you need to research further on your own. Here's a checklist of questions to ask of the schools you are considering.

- Is the school accredited? Is the program of study accredited? *Remember that accreditation by one of the six regional accrediting agencies is a formal recognition that a school provides a quality education. If the school is not accredited by one of the six regional agencies, be sure to check with CHEA or the U.S. Department of Education to see if the accrediting agency is real and recognized.*
- How many online courses does the school offer? *Generally, the more online courses that a school offers, the more experienced it is. This means you have a better chance of getting instructors who know what they're doing technologically.*
- How long has the school been offering courses online? *You know the old saying—practice makes perfect. The more experience a school and its instructors have had, the better the chances that they've ironed out any kinks in their virtual courses.*
- What are the demographics of students taking courses online? *If you have special concerns and want students who can relate specifically to your situation, then you'll probably want to look for a program where the other students enrolled share similarities with you. This may make the learning process easier for you.*
- What is the student to instructor ratio? *If a class is too large, it may become unmanageable, especially if everyone logs online at the same time and tries to participate in a course-related*

chat. Additionally, if there is a large number of students, it may be difficult or even impossible to get personal attention from the instructor.

- What are the direct costs to take courses from the school? *You'll want to know exactly what you can expect to pay for your courses. Ask specifically about tuition, fees, and supplies.*
- What is the school's refund policy? *It's a good thing to know ahead of time whether you'll get some or all of your money back should you need to withdraw from a course.*
- What kinds of financial aid are available to you? *This is a very important question if you haven't planned financially for your college education. You want to find out what types of aid are available (grants, scholarships, loans), what their sources are (federal, state, institutional), and whether you meet the eligibility criteria.*
- Does the school accept transfer credits? What are its requirements for transferring credits? *If you've earned credits from another school, be sure to inquire whether you can transfer them to count toward the degree or certificate you now wish to pursue. Transferring credits can save you from having to take duplicate courses.*
- Does the school accept test credits? What are its testing policies? *Find out which, if any, standardized tests you must take to be admitted. Also, inquire whether you can test out of certain courses.*
- Does the school require you to spend any time on campus? *This is an important question. Many distance learning programs require you to spend at least a little time on campus— for an orientation, examinations, or other reasons. Find out when you're expected to be in-residence and for how long so you can begin making arrangements (travel, accommodations, etc.) as soon as possible.*
- What are the student services that will be available to you if you enroll? Particularly, will you have online access to library resources? *Many colleges offer tutorial services, career planning, and general counseling to stu-*

dents on-campus. Find out if these same services are available to you, as a distance learning student. Also, ask whether there's a reference librarian you can contact if you need resources or information from the library on-campus.

- What are the time limits within which you must complete a program of study? *Before you embark on your educational adventure, you should want to know about how long it's going to take. Knowing whether it's going to take three years of commitment to your computer or five years will help you in your planning.*
- What is the drop-out rate for the program you're interested in? *If the program you're interested in has a high drop-out rate, then it's a pretty good indication there are problems with it. Try to avoid such a program in order to save yourself grief (and possibly money) in the long run.*
- What is the graduation rate for that program? *This question is somewhat related to the preceding one—if the program you're interested in has a high graduation rate, then the chances are that it's a program in which most students who are enrolled are pleased. This is a good kind of program to watch for.*
- What are the job-placement rates for graduates of the program you're interested in? *This is especially important if you're pursuing a highly-specialized degree. You want some assurance that you'll be able to find a job or advancement in your field of expertise upon graduation. If the job-placement rate is low for a particular program, then that's usually a pretty good sign that there's no need for people with that degree or even that the program is not respected within the field.*
- How will lectures be conducted—on the Web, on video, or by some other method? *You need to know this in order to plan for equipment. If lectures are delivered on the Web, then you need just your computer, a sound card, speakers, and a Web browser. But if lec-*

tures will arrive on videotape, then you need to make sure you have a VCR and television in addition to your computer.

- How will you be expected to submit assignments and collaborate with other students—via a Web page, electronic mail, chat, or through some other method? *The answers to these questions will help you plan for coursework and give you a head start familiarizing yourself with the method of interaction prior to entering the courses.*

It doesn't hurt to ask the program of study for a list of references. This way you can contact former students directly to get their opinions of the program and better prepare yourself.

Additionally, it's a good idea to check with the Better Business Bureau in the area where the school is located and the Attorney General's office in the state where the school is located to see if there are any complaints (and, if so, how many) filed against the school. A number of unresolved complaints against a school is a pretty clear signal that the school's reputation is questionable and you may want to consider another institution.

Applying to Programs and Earning Credits

How do You Apply to a School?

Each of the entries in this book includes some information about admissions and applying but it's always a good idea to contact the school directly to get the most up-to-date admissions requirements and application procedures. In general, you'll be required to submit a completed application, an application fee, an essay about your intentions and goals, a current resume, letters of recommendation, official transcripts for any college courses you've already completed, and official copies of standardized

test scores (if a particular standardized test is required for the program you're applying to).

The specific requirements you'll have to fulfill vary from school to school, and even between programs of study, so it's important that you read the directory entries in this book carefully and contact the school directly if you have additional questions. In general, here are the minimum requirements by level of degree:

- *Undergraduate programs*—Undergraduate programs are those in which you can earn an Associate's degree or Bachelor's degree. To be admitted to an undergraduate program, you generally have to be a high school graduate or have a General Education Development (GED) certificate (equivalent to a high school diploma). Also, most schools require that you take either the Scholastic Aptitude Test (SAT) or American College Testing (ACT) assessment.
- *Graduate or Professional programs*—Graduate programs are those in which you earn an advanced degree, such as a Master's or Doctoral degree. To be admitted to a Master's program, usually you're required to have a Bachelor's degree. A Master's degree is generally required for admittance to a Doctoral degree program. (However, there are some Doctoral degree programs that require only a Bachelor's degree.) Whether you are required to take a standardized test to gain admission depends upon the graduate program.
- *Certificate programs*—Generally you must have a certain amount of work experience related to the field in which the certificate is issued in order to participate in these programs. Some advanced certificate programs require you to have a Bachelor's degree as well.

Are You Required to Take a Standardized Test?

There are several standardized tests available, and which one (if any) is required when applying to a particular program of study depends on the level of certificate/degree (undergraduate, graduate, or professional) and the field of the program (such as business, education, or engineering). Since testing requirements vary by school and by program, contact the schools that interest you to determine their testing requirements before you register to take any of the tests. Below is a list of the most common standardized tests and information about them.

- *College Level Examination Program (CLEP)*— The CLEP offers general and subject-specific tests to assess knowledge at the undergraduate level. Schools award credits to students with passing scores, allowing the tests to fulfill course requirements in particular fields. They are offered in paper form and must be taken at a testing site where a proctor oversees the examination. You can get more information at http://www.collegeboard.org/clep/html/index001.html, or by writing to clep@ets.org or CLEP, P.O. Box 6600, Princeton NJ 08541-6600. Or you can call them at (609) 771-7865.
- *Scholastic Aptitude Test (SAT)*—The SAT is generally required for students applying to undergraduate programs. The general test assesses your potential or aptitude for college study, and costs $23.50. In addition to the general test, there are subject-specific tests. You can get more information by visiting http://www.sat.org or by calling (609) 771-7600.
- *American College Testing (ACT) Assessment*— The ACT is another test that is generally required for students applying to certain undergraduate programs. It assesses your educational development and aptitude for college by testing your abilities in English, mathematics, reading, and science. The test costs $22 if you take it in the United States (except in Florida, where it costs $25), or $37 if you take it outside of the United States.

You can get more information at http://www.act.org or by calling (319) 337-1000.
- *Graduate Record Examination (GRE)*—The GRE is usually required for admission to all non-business graduate programs. The general test assesses your analytical, quantitative, and verbal skills. It is offered in paper and electronic forms, and the cost is $99 (if you test in the United States, U.S. Territories, or Puerto Rico) or $125 (if you test anywhere else). In addition to the general test, there are subject-specific tests and writing assessments available for additional fees. You can get more information from the Educational Testing Service at http://www.gre.org, or by writing to gre-info@ets.org or GRE, Educational Testing Service, P.O. Box 6000, Princeton NJ 08541-6000. Or you can call them at (609) 771-7670.
- *Graduate Management Admission Test (GMAT)*—The GMAT is generally required for graduate level business and administration programs. It tests your analytical, mathematical, and verbal abilities. It is offered in an electronic form and costs $165 (if you test in the United States, U.S. Territories, or Puerto Rico) or $210 (if you test anywhere else). You can get more information from the Educational Testing Service at http://www.gmat.org, or by writing to gmat@ets.org or to GMAT, Educational Testing Service, 225 Phillips Boulevard, Princeton NJ 08628-7435. Or you can call them at (609) 771-7330.
- *Miller Analogies Test (MAT)*—Some schools require the MAT for applicants to graduate programs in psychology and related fields. It tests your ability to reason using analogies and is offered in paper form. For more information, contact the Psychological Corporation, MAT, 555 Academic Court, San Antonio TX 78204-2408 or visit the MAT Web site at http://www.hbtpc.com/mat/. Or call 1-800-622-3231.
- *Test of English as a Foreign Language (TOEFL)*—Most schools require students

whose first language is something other than English to take this test for any program of study. It tests your ability to comprehend written and spoken English, and is offered in a paper form. Generally, you'll be required to score above a 500 to be considered for admission but some schools require a higher minimum than 500. You can get more information from the Educational Testing Service at http://www.toefl.org, or by writing to toefl@ets.org or TOEFL, P.O. Box 6151, Princeton NJ 08541-6151. Or you can call them at (609) 771-7760.

What is Credit and How Do You Earn It?

A credit is a unit that measures progress toward a certificate or degree. Credits are usually based on the number of hours per week that it takes to complete a particular course over a specified period of time.

There are four ways in which you can earn credits.

- *Take a course for credit.* By successfully completing a course (either traditionally or online), you may earn a certain number of credits.
- *Life experience.* Many schools will allow you to submit a portfolio detailing your experiences in life. A board will review your portfolio and award you credits based on your experiences and the relevance they have to the degree or certificate that you seek. For more information about creating and maintaining a portfolio, see "What is a portfolio?" and "What should you include in a portfolio?"
- *Military or other professional training.* Some schools will award you credits toward your degree for the training courses you completed in the military or for your job. However, it is important to note that often the

courses have to be relevant to the degree you are seeking.
- *Examination.* Most institutions will allow you to "test out of" certain core or basic courses. You take an examination about a particular subject and, if you successfully pass that exam, the school gives you credit for it. You should contact a school directly to find out if it allows students to earn credits by taking examinations and, if so, where and when testing takes place.

Can You Transfer Credits from One School to Another?

Whether you can transfer credits from one school to another depends entirely on the schools involved. Some schools form partnerships (also called articulation agreements) guaranteeing that they'll accept credits earned at or through the other schools that participate in the partnership. Other schools accept transfer credits from various schools regardless of any formal agreement with them. To find out whether the school you would like to enroll in will accept the credits you earned at another institution, you should contact the school directly.

What are Credit Banks?

Credit banks are institutions that enable you to consolidate into one transcript some or all of the credits that you earned at various schools, as well as credits for examinations, on-the-job training, work experience, volunteer activities, and other life experiences. You must complete an application for the credit bank, pay a fee for the services, and submit a portfolio (see "What is a portfolio?" in this chapter). Administrators at the credit bank then review your application and portfolio to determine which courses to count and which experiences to award credit for. Then they create a new, single transcript reflecting all of these credits. You can use the consolidated transcript to support your application to another school (most colleges offering distance learning recognize credit bank transcripts) or for employment purposes.

Two of the best-known credit banks in the United States are at Regents College and Thomas Edison State College. Each provides specific information on its Web site regarding the application process and documents to include in your portfolio. For more information:

Regents College Credit Bank
7 Columbia Circle
Albany NY 12203
http://www.regents.edu/098.htm
crbank@regents.edu

Thomas Edison State College
Portfolio Assessment
Trenton NJ 08608
http://www.tesc.edu/ways_to_earn_degree/
portf.html
info@tesc.edu

What is a Portfolio?

A portfolio is a collection of documents, transcripts, and work-samples that you can use to support an application for admission or when requesting life-experience credits, as well as for job applications and interviews. It is intended to reflect your knowledge and experience in a particular area. Many schools that offer distance learning will perform a portfolio assessment allowing you to earn credits for your past work and life experiences outside of a classroom, and some even award credits that you can transfer to other colleges (see "What are credit banks?" in this chapter).

What Should You Include in a Portfolio?

Your portfolio should include anything you feel is directly relevant to the goal you are seeking—whether your goal is a certificate, degree, or particular job. Academic transcripts, copies of awards, a resume including work experience and volunteer activities, and samples of your work or writings are all items that you should consider including in your portfolio. When using a portfolio for academic purposes (admission to a program or to earn credits for life experience), it is a good idea to check with the school before creating it. This way you can ensure that you include items that address particular requirements of the school.

Costs and Financial Aid

What Does it Cost to Take Online Courses?

The direct costs for taking online courses depend entirely upon the school and are not necessarily less than the costs for taking traditional, in-classroom courses. In general, you can expect to pay charges for tuition, some fees, course materials, and any equipment or supplies you're going to need. For specific cost information, see the program entries in this book or contact a school directly.

What is Financial Aid and is it Available?

Financial aid is assistance meant to help you pay for school. Some schools allow students taking distance learning courses online to have financial aid, and others do not. You'll need to contact any school you're interested in to see what their specific financial aid policies and requirements are for students taking online courses. Additionally, the types and sources of financial aid can vary from school to school.

Most financial aid programs fall into two categories:

1. grants and scholarships, and
2. self-help financial aid.

Grants and scholarships are types of financial aid that you don't have to repay under normal circumstances. If you withdraw from a course or fail to maintain eligibility by successfully meeting certain criteria, you may be required to repay part or all of a grant or scholarship, depending on the particular award's rules. Some grants and scholarships are based on financial need (see more in "What is financial need?" in this chapter), while others are academic-based or awarded on your personal characteristics or traits.

Self-help financial aid consists of student loans and work-study programs. Loans are types of assistance that you have to repay after you complete your degree or if you leave school for a certain amount of time or longer. Generally, student loans have lower interest rates than other kinds of loans and some don't require interest-payments while you are in school. Work-study programs (in which the school helps you get a job so you can use the money to pay your education-related expenses) are not generally available to distance learning students as they require the qualifying students to be on-campus.

How Do You Apply for Financial Aid?

The first thing you should do is contact the school you plan to attend to get information about the financial aid programs they offer and any forms that you must complete in order to apply. Most schools require you to complete a Free Application for Federal Student Aid (FAFSA) and submit it to the federal processor. Some require an additional, institutional application for aid.

Most schools have deadlines by which you must apply for financial aid. Many of these deadlines are in the spring of the year in which you plan to begin taking courses in the fall. However, for online courses that don't necessarily fit a semester or quarter schedule, the dates may vary. You should contact the school directly to inquire about application deadlines.

Free Application for Federal Student Aid (FAFSA)

The FAFSA is a form published by the U.S. Department of Education that collects all sorts of information about you, your family (parents or spouse and children, depending on your age and marital status), and your financial circumstances. The federal processor uses all of the information you provide on the FAFSA in a prescribed formula to calculate the amount that you (and your family) should reasonably be able to pay toward your education. This amount is called your Expected Family Contribution (EFC).

After the federal processor has finished working with your FAFSA, it sends you a Student Aid Report (SAR). This SAR reflects all of the information you provided on your FAFSA and shows your resulting EFC. The federal processor also sends electronic versions of the SAR to the school you plan to attend and the agency that oversees most state-awarded financial aid. The school and state agency use the information on the SAR to determine your eligibility for financial aid that is awarded on the basis of financial need (see more in "What is financial need?" in this chapter).

You must complete a FAFSA for each year you want to be considered for financial aid. New FAFSAs are available in January. For example, the 2000-01 FAFSA became available in January 2000 and should be used to apply for financial aid for academic terms beginning in the 2000-01 school year. FAFSAs are available in paper and electronic (Web-based and on diskette) forms, and are readily available at colleges, universities, high schools, and public libraries.

Institutional Application

There are some schools that require you to complete and submit to the school's financial aid office an institutional application. (The majority of these require the institutional application in addition to a FAFSA.) Most institutional applications collect information about financial resources that the FAFSA doesn't ask about (home equity, certain types of property and investments, and so forth), as well as information about your personal interests. School personnel use the information you provide to identify your level of financial need (see more in "What is financial need? in this chapter) and the interest- and achievement-based scholarships for which you qualify.

What is Financial Need?

Financial need is not necessarily the amount of money that you think you'll need to take courses. Rather, it is the difference between the cost to attend a school and the amount that you (and your family) can reasonably be expected to pay toward your education. Most institutions that participate in federal financial aid programs use this standard formula to calculate financial need:

> Cost of attendance
> − *Expected Family Contribution* (*EFC*)
> = Financial Need

Financial aid personnel use financial need as a target amount to try to meet with the various resources that are available at a particular school. Typically, they try to award grants and scholarships first, then loans to cover the remaining financial need.

What are the Sources of Financial Aid?

There are several sources of financial aid: governments (federal, state, and local), companies, non-profit organizations, individuals, and the schools and programs of study themselves.

Federal

- **Federal Pell Grants**—Federal Pell Grants are awards to undergraduate students who have a certain level of financial need. The amount varies between $100 and $4000 per year, depending on the level of funding that the overall program receives, as well as depending on your precise financial need, cost of attendance, and whether you're enrolled on a full- or part-time basis.
- **Supplemental Education Opportunity Grants (SEOG)**—Federal SEOG awards are for undergraduate students who have the greatest financial need and the amount you receive depends on the school's awarding policies for the funds. Generally, the amount varies between $100 and $4000.
- **Federal Work-Study**—Federal Work-Study is a program in which the school helps students find jobs to earn money to pay for education-related expenses. Students enrolled in distance learning programs usually are not eligible for Federal Work-Study because of the need for the student to be able to work on-campus or near campus.
- **Stafford and Direct Loans**—Money for low-interest loans makes up the majority of federal financial aid. Federal Stafford Loans (also called Federal Family Education Loans) and Federal Direct Loans (also called William D. Ford Loans) are quite similar, except that the source of funding for a Stafford Loan is a private lender and the source for a Direct Loan is the U.S. government. If the school you're attending participates in the Direct Loan program, you apply for a loan through the school. If it participates in the Stafford Loan program, you apply for a loan through a bank, credit union, or other lender. A school can only participate in one of the two programs.

There are three types of loans under both the Stafford and Direct Loan programs—subsidized student loans, unsubsidized student loans, and Parents' Loan for Undergraduate Students (PLUS) loans. The interest on *subsidized loans* is deferred until after you graduate or otherwise leave school for a certain period of time. Your eligibility for a subsidized loan depends on your financial need, and the maximum amount you can borrow in a given year depends on your year in school. *Unsubsidized loans* are not awarded based on financial need and you are responsible for the interest on them from the time the money is disbursed to you. You can choose to let the interest accumulate while you are in school, but it is capitalized—meaning the interest is added to the principal on your loan periodically and you then must pay interest on the capitalized amount (principal plus interest). The total amount you can borrow under an unsubsidized loan in a year depends on your year in school and cost of attendance.

If you are an undergraduate student under the age of 24, your parents may be eligible to borrow a *PLUS loan* to pay your educational expenses. The amount your parents may borrow depends on your cost of attendance and the total amount of other financial aid you are receiving. To determine whether your parents are eligible, they will be subject to a credit check. Additionally, repayment of a PLUS loan begins 60 days after the final disbursement of the loan is made to your parents regardless of your status in school at that time.

- **Federal Perkins Loans**—Federal Perkins Loans are low-interest loans awarded to students with the greatest financial need. The amount you can borrow depends on the awarding policies of the school. The interest is deferred until you begin repayment on the loan after you graduate or your enrollment drops below part-time.

- **Tax Benefits**—Although saving taxes and tax credits may not seem like financial aid, they are forms of financial assistance to help with educational expenses. There are Individual Retirement Accounts (IRAs) that you can withdraw funds from without being penalized if the money is used toward college costs. And depending on your situation, there are exclusions you can take advantage of when filing your taxes, as well as the Hope and Lifetime Learning tax credit programs (giving you a credit of up to $1500). For more information about tax benefits, visit the U.S. Department of Education's Tax Benefits for Higher Education Web page at http://www.ed.gov/offices/OSFAP/Students/taxcuts/index.html.

State Grants, Scholarships, and Loans

The types of financial aid available from a state vary. So do the eligibility requirements to receive state-funded grants, scholarships, and loans. Each state has at least one agency that oversees state-funded assistance programs. You should contact this agency to find out what exactly is available and how to apply. The U.S. Department of Education lists all of these state agencies on its Web site at http://www.ed.gov/offices/OPE/Students/other.html.

Institutional Grants, Scholarships, and Loans

Colleges and universities typically have a variety of financial aid programs that they fund and oversee themselves. The application and awarding criteria for these programs depend entirely on the types of aid and the policies and procedures of the offices that handle them. To find out what's available and how to apply for institutional funds, you'll need to contact the school's financial aid office.

Private Industry

- **Corporate tuition benefits**—Many companies offer tuition-assistance to employees who wish to take courses or complete certificates/degrees in a field directly related to their work. This assistance comes in the form of partial- or full-reimbursement of tuition and fees. Some companies will even pay for your course materials, such as books and software. To find out if the company you work for offers tuition benefits and what the eligibility requirements are, you should contact the human resources office.
- **Scholarships**—There are numerous scholarships available from private sources, and the application requirements and awarding criteria vary immensely. Some are intended to award students for academic achievement, while others are awarded based on interests and affiliations.
- **Loans**—Some financial institutions offer private loans for educational purposes. The borrowing and repayment requirements for these loans differ, depending on the lender and type of loan. However, most of these loans have higher interest rates than the government-backed student loans. Thus, we recommend you pursue student loans first, and use private loans as a last resort.

Military Benefits

There are various financial aid programs available through different branches of the U.S. Armed Forces, and the requirements and benefits of each are diverse. Additionally, some states offer aid on the basis of military service or Veteran status. Your best bet to find out about specific military benefits is to contact the educational benefits officer in your unit (if you are on active or reserve duty), the Department of Veterans Affairs (if you are a Veteran or dependant of a Veteran), the state scholarship agency, and the school you plan to attend.

Where Can You get More Information about Financial Aid for which You Might be Eligible?

We recommend that you first visit the U.S. Department of Education's student financial aid Web pages at http://www.ed.gov/finaid.html. Also, you should check with the financial aid office of the school you plan to attend—visit their Web site or give them a call to find out about application procedures and programs they participate in.

After you have a general sense of the types of aid offered through your school, check out some of the online scholarship search services. While they are called scholarship searches, most of them provide information about all sorts of financial aid, not just scholarships. Two of these online services are FastWEB (http://www.studentservices.com/fastweb) and Embark.com (http://www.embark.com). We recommend that you steer away from any scholarship search services (online or otherwise) that want you to pay for their services—many of these firms take your money, then send you the same list of financial aid sources that you can get from one of the free, online search services. Even more frustrating are the few that take your money, then send you information only about the federal student financial aid programs, particularly student loans.

DIRECTORY OF INSTITUTIONS AND PROGRAMS

ALGONQUIN COLLEGE

General Contact Information

1385 Woodroffe Avenue
Nepean, Ontario Canada K2G 1V8

Phone: (613) 727-4723
FAX: (613) 727-7632
E-mail: regof1@algonquinc.on.ca
WWW: www.algonquinc.on.ca/

Online Learning Information

1385 Woodroffe Avenue
Nepean, Ontario Canada K2G 1V8

Phone: (613) 727-4723
FAX: (613) 727-7727
E-mail: distance@algonquinc.on.ca
WWW: www.algonquinc.on.ca/distance/main.html

Institution Background

Founded: 1958
Type of Institution: Private
Accreditation: Government of Ontario

Financial Aid: Algonquin College administers the Ontario Student Assistance Program, which provides student loans to eligible persons.

Individual Courses: 170 courses

Registration: You can register for online courses offered by Algonqun College via mail, phone, fax, online, or in person.

Programs

Accounting

Degree Offered: Certificate

Program Web Address: www.algonquinc.on.ca/distance/certfs.html

Program Background: This program is designed for students who want a thorough accounting education or who are looking for career advancement.

Application Requirements: To register in this program, you must be 19 years of age or older, or possess an Ontario Secondary School Diploma (or equivalent) if you're 18 years old or younger. You may be required to complete prerequisite courses. You must submit proof of your successful completion of an approved degree or diploma program.

Completion Requirements: You must successfully complete 12 courses (nine required courses and three electives) for this certificate.

Example Course Titles: Some of the course titles in this program include Accounting I, Accounting II, Intermediate Accounting I, Intermediate Accounting II, and Taxation I.

Program Contact: Algonquin College
Off-Campus Learning, Woodroffe Campus
C101-1385 Woodroffe Avenue
Nepean, Ontario K2G 1V8
(613) 727-4723 ext. 7098
(613) 727-7727
distance@algonquinc.on.ca

Applied Management

Degree Offered: Certificate

Program Web Address: www.algonquinc.on.ca/distance/certfs.html

Program Background: The Applied Management Certificate is designed to introduce students to basic management concepts and principles. Students learn skills and knowledge needed to oversee personnel administration.

Application Requirements: To register in this program, you must be 19 years of age or older, or possess an Ontario Secondary School Diploma (or equivalent) if you're 18 years old or younger. You may be required to complete prerequisite courses. You must submit proof of your successful completion of an approved degree or diploma program.

Completion Requirements: You must successfully complete four compulsory courses and two elective courses. If you have completed approved courses under the Canadian Forces Community College Network, you may be exempt from the electives. Please contact your local coordinator on base.

Example Course Titles: Some of the course titles in this program include Human Resource Management, Training and Development, and Management Principles.

Program Contact: Algonquin College
Off-Campus Learning, Woodroffe Campus
C101-1385 Woodroffe Avenue
Nepean, Ontario K2G 1V8
(613) 727-4723 ext. 7098
(613) 727-7727
distance@algonquinc.on.ca

Bookkeeping

Degree Offered: Certificate

Program Web Address: www.algonquinc.on. ca/distance/certfs.html

Program Background: The Bookkeeping Certificate Program is designed for students who are currently employed as bookkeepers or accounting clerks who possess little or no formal training, or for those students who are seeking a career change in as short a time as possible.

Application Requirements: To register in this program, you must be 19 years of age or older, or possess an Ontario Secondary School Diploma (or equivalent) if you're 18 years old or

younger. You may be required to complete prerequisite courses. You must submit proof of your successful completion of an approved degree or diploma program.

Completion Requirements: You must successfully complete six courses—four of which are available online.

On Campus Requirements: You are required to take two courses on campus.

Example Course Titles: Some of the course titles in this program include Accounting I, Accounting II, and Taxation I.

Program Contact: Algonquin College
Off-Campus Learning
Woodroffe Campus
C101-1385 Woodroffe Avenue
Nepean, Ontario K2G 1V8
(613) 727-4723 ext. 7098
(613) 727-7727
distance@algonquinc.on.ca

Business Studies

Degree Offered: Certificate

Program Web Address: www.algonquinc.on. ca/distance/certfs.html

Program Background: This program is designed to meet the needs of students seeking a broad background in all aspects of business administration, rather than a specialization in one particular area. It is suited to students preparing for careers in organizations with on-the-job training programs, or to those who plan to operate their own business. Students will develop skills in accounting, communication, microcomputers, and an awareness of management, marketing, economics, business law and more.

Application Requirements: To register in this program, you must be 19 years of age or older, or possess an Ontario Secondary School Diploma (or equivalent) if you're 18 years old or younger. You may be required to complete prerequisite courses. You must submit proof of your successful completion of an approved degree or diploma program.

Completion Requirements: You must successfully complete 12 courses (eight compulsory core courses and four in your major subject) for this certificate.

Example Course Titles: Some of the course titles in this program include Accounting, Introduction to Microeconomics, English, Business Law, Management Principles, Marketing Principles, and Quantitative Methods.

Program Contact: Algonquin College
Off-Campus Learning, Woodroffe Campus
C101-1385 Woodroffe Avenue
Nepean, Ontario K2G 1V8
(613) 727-4723 ext. 7098
(613) 727-7727
distance@algonquinc.on.ca

Commercial Gardener

Degree Offered: Certificate

Program Web Address: www.algonquinc.on.ca/distance/certfs.html

Program Background: This program provides students with a basic understanding of horticulture science.

Application Requirements: To register in this program, you must be 19 years of age or older, or possess an Ontario Secondary School Diploma (or equivalent) if you're 18 years old or younger. You may be required to complete prerequisite courses. You must submit proof of your successful completion of an approved degree or diploma program.

Completion Requirements: You must successfully complete 15 compulsory courses and three elective courses.

Example Course Titles: Some of the course titles in this program include Basic Botany and Hardy Perennials for Gardens.

Program Contact: Algonquin College
Off-Campus Learning, Woodroffe Campus
C101-1385 Woodroffe Avenue
Nepean, Ontario K2G 1V8
(613) 727-4723 ext. 7098
(613) 727-7727
distance@algonquinc.on.ca

Computer Information Systems

Degree Offered: Certificate

Program Web Address: www.algonquinc.on.ca/distance/certfs.html

Program Background: This program provides students with the necessary training for an entry level position as a business applications programmer. Students learn various programming languages, systems analysis, database systems, data communications, and good program design.

Application Requirements: To register in this program, you must be 19 years of age or older, or possess an Ontario Secondary School Diploma (or equivalent) if you're 18 years old or younger. You may be required to complete prerequisite courses. You must submit proof of your successful completion of an approved degree or diploma program.

Completion Requirements: You must successfully complete 14 courses for this certificate.

Example Course Titles: Some of the course titles in this program include Introduction to Cobol Programming, Intermediate Cobol Programming, Accounting, Computer Programming (C++), and File Processing Using Cobol Programming.

Program Contact: Algonquin College
Off-Campus Learning, Woodroffe Campus
C101-1385 Woodroffe Avenue

Nepean, Ontario K2G 1V8
(613) 727-4723 ext. 7098
(613) 727-7727
distance@algonquinc.on.ca

Human Resource Management

Degree Offered: Certificate

Program Web Address: www.algonquinc.on.
ca/distance/certfs.html

Program Background: Students earn a certificate by successfully completing a 12-course program learning basic skills in the areas of personnel administration, human resource planning, job analysis, interviewing, compensation and benefits, personnel testing, performance appraisal, industrial relations, and collective bargaining.

Additionally, students in this program can earn credits toward the C.H.R.P. designation of the Human Resources Professionals Association of Ontario.

Application Requirements: To register in this program, you must be 19 years of age or older, or possess an Ontario Secondary School Diploma (or equivalent) if you're 18 years old or younger. You may be required to complete prerequisite courses. You must submit proof of your successful completion of an approved degree or diploma program.

Completion Requirements: You must successfully complete seven core compulsory courses and five electives to obtain this certificate.

Example Course Titles: Some of the course titles include Management Principles, Industrial Relations, Human Resource Management, and Compensation Management.

Program Contact: Off-Campus Learning
Woodroffe Campus
Algonquin College
C101-1385 Woodroffe Avenue
Nepean, Ontario K2G 1V8

(613) 727-4723 ext. 7098
(613) 727-7727
distance@algonquinc.on.ca

Information Technology

Degree Offered: Certificate

Program Web Address: www.algonquinc.on.
ca/distance/certfs.html

Program Background: Proficiency in the Windows environment and in using the corresponding software is the focus of this certificate program at Algonquin College. Courses are designed to teach students how to use the most up-to-date technology.

Application Requirements: You must be 19 years or older or, if you're 18 years or less, you must have an Ontario Secondary School diploma or equivalent. Some courses in the program may have course prerequisites that you are expected to meet.

Completion Requirements: You must successfully complete six courses for this certificate.

System Requirements: You need to have a computer with an Internet account through an Internet Service Provider.

Example Course Titles: Some of the course titles in this program include Getting to Know Windows 3.1, Windows 95, Introduction to Computers, File Management, WordPerfect 8, MS Word for Windows, MS Access, and MS Excel.

Program Contact: Algonquin College
Off-Campus Learning
Woodroffe Campus
C101-1385 Woodroffe Avenue
Nepean, Ontario K2G 1V8
(613) 727-4723 ext. 7098
(613) 727-7727
distance@algonquinc.on.ca

Internet Multimedia Software

Degree Offered: Certificate

Program Web Address: www.algonquinc.on. ca/distance/certfs.html

Program Background: Algonquin College's certificate program in Internet Multimedia Software focuses on preparing students for careers in Web development. Students learn how to create Web pages that are interactive and secure, and that use multimedia. To this end, they learn how to develop Java Applets and powerful Windows applications.

Application Requirements: To register in this program, you must be 19 years of age or older, or possess an Ontario Secondary School Diploma (or equivalent) if you're 18 years old or younger. You may be required to complete prerequisite courses. You must submit proof of your successful completion of an approved degree or diploma program.

Completion Requirements: You must successfully complete ten courses for this certificate.

Example Course Titles: Some of the course titles for this program include Windows 95, Desktop Publishing—Corel WordPerfect or Microsoft Word, Developing Web Pages Using Multimedia, HTML Introduction, and Internet Essentials.

Program Contact: Algonquin College
Off-Campus Learning
Woodroffe Campus
C101-1385 Woodroffe Avenue
Nepean, Ontario K2G 1V8
(613) 727-4723 ext. 7098
(613) 727-7727
distance@algonquinc.on.ca

Management Studies

Degree Offered: Certificate

Program Web Address: www.algonquinc.on. ca/distance/certfs.html

Program Background: This program exposes students to basic concepts and principles of management. Students develop decision-making and problem-solving skills by exploring leadership, motivation, and communications. Students are able to apply management theory to real situations through case studies.

Application Requirements: To register in this program, you must be 19 years of age or older, or possess an Ontario Secondary School Diploma (or equivalent) if you're 18 years old or younger. You may be required to complete prerequisite courses. You must submit proof of your successful completion of an approved degree or diploma program.

Completion Requirements: You must successfully complete 12 courses to earn this certificate.

Example Course Titles: Some of the course titles in this program include Management Principles, Management Operations, Human Resource Management, Industrial Relations, Accounting, Business Report Writing, and Introduction to Microeconomics.

Program Contact: Algonquin College
Off-Campus Learning
Woodroffe Campus
C101-1385 Woodroffe Avenue
Nepean, Ontario K2G 1V8
(613) 727-4723 ext. 7098
(613) 727-7727
distance@algonquinc.on.ca

Marketing

Degree Offered: Certificate

Program Web Address: www.algonquinc.on. ca/distance/certfs.html

Program Background: This program is designed to give students a foundation in marketing principles. It emphasizes that the customer should be the focus of business, and students are able to apply what they are learning to current business problems.

Application Requirements: To register in this program, you must be 19 years of age or older, or possess an Ontario Secondary School Diploma (or equivalent) if you're 18 years old or younger. You may be required to complete prerequisite courses. You must submit proof of your successful completion of an approved degree or diploma program.

Completion Requirements: You must successfully complete six courses to earn this certificate.

Program Contact: Algonquin College
Off-Campus Learning
Woodroffe Campus
C101-1385 Woodroffe Avenue
Nepean, Ontario K2G 1V8
(613) 727-4723 ext. 7098
(613) 727-7727
distance@algonquinc.on.ca

Marketing Management

Degree Offered: Certificate

Program Web Address: www.algonquinc.on. ca/distance/certfs.html

Program Background: This program is designed for students who are responsible for making marketing decisions in business. It is built on the premise that long-term flexibility and profits are the best reflection of management personnel and their abilities to think critically and act ethically.

Application Requirements: To register in this program, you must be 19 years of age or older, or possess an Ontario Secondary School Diploma (or equivalent) if you're 18 years old or younger. You may be required to complete prerequisite courses. You must submit proof of

your successful completion of an approved degree or diploma program.

Completion Requirements: You must successfully complete six courses for this certificate.

Example Course Titles: Some of the course titles in this program include Accounting, Management Principles, and English.

Program Contact: Algonquin College
Off-Campus Learning
Woodroffe Campus
1385 Woodroffe Avenue
Nepean, Ontario K2G 1V8
(613) 727-4723 ext. 7098
(613) 727-7727
distance@algonquinc.on.ca

Materials Management

Degree Offered: Certificate

Program Web Address: www.algonquinc.on. ca/distance/certfs.html

Program Background: Algonquin College's certificate program in materials management was designed to prepare students for effective management in any supply chain function. Students learn about acquiring, using, and disposing of materials, including finished goods and after-sales service management. They develop skills and a comprehensive understanding of current principles and techniques that they can apply to their jobs in production planning, material planning, capacity planning, master scheduling, inventory management, production control, purchasing, traffic, logistics, service parts management, warehousing, or distribution.

Application Requirements: You must be 19 years or older or, if you're 18 years or less, you must have an Ontario Secondary School diploma or equivalent. Some courses in the program may have course prerequisites that you are expected to meet.

Completion Requirements: You must successfully complete 13 courses to earn this certificate.

Example Course Titles: Some of the course titles in this program include Management Principles, Quantitative Methods, and Management Operations.

Program Contact: Algonquin College
Off-Campus Learning
Woodroffe Campus
1385 Woodroffe Avenue
Nepean, Ontario K2G 1V8
(613) 727-4723 ext. 7098
(613) 727-7727
distance@algonquinc.on.ca

Retail Management

Degree Offered: Certificate

Program Web Address: www.algonquinc.on.ca/distance/certfs.html

Program Background: The purpose of the Retail Management Certificate is to help students develop particular skills and attitudes that are conducive to managing and operating a successful business. The program is appropriate for students who are presently employed in the retail industry and those who want to open their own retail business.

Application Requirements: You must be 19 years or older or, if you're 18 years or less, you must have an Ontario Secondary School diploma or equivalent. Some courses in the program may have course prerequisites that you are expected to meet.

Completion Requirements: You must successfully complete six courses (five are required and one is an elective).

Example Course Titles: Some of the course titles in this program include Accounting, Management Principles, and English.

Program Contact: Algonquin College
Off-Campus Learning
Woodroffe Campus
C101-1385 Woodroffe Avenue
Nepean, Ontario K2G 1V8
(613) 727-4723 ext. 7098
(613) 727-7727
distance@algonquinc.on.ca

Starting and Operating Your Business

Degree Offered: Certificate

Program Web Address: www.algonquinc.on.ca/distance/certfs.html

Program Background: This program is designed to lead prospective small-business people and potential entrepreneurs in a logical and sequential way through the conceptual stages involved in setting up a business of their own. Students get an increased awareness of small business ownership as a viable alternative to traditional employment, and they learn practical applications of business management and financial skills. Students learn about accounting, business finance, computers, marketing, and writing a business plan.

Application Requirements: You must be 19 years or older or, if you're 18 years or less, you must have an Ontario Secondary School diploma or equivalent. Some courses in the program may have course prerequisites that you are expected to meet.

Completion Requirements: You must successfully complete six courses for this certificate.

Program Contact: Algonquin College
Off-Campus Learning
Woodroffe Campus
C101-1385 Woodroffe Avenue
Nepean, Ontario K2G 1V8
(613) 727-4723 ext. 7098
(613) 727-7727

distance@algonquinc.on.ca

Teaching and Training of Adults

Degree Offered: Certificate

Program Web Address: www.algonquinc.on.ca/distance/certfs.html

Program Background: This certificate program prepares teachers of adults to respond to the needs of their students with a variety of strategies and methods that facilitate learning.

Application Requirements: You must be 19 years or older or, if you're 18 years or less, you must have an Ontario Secondary School diploma or equivalent. Some courses in the program may have course prerequisites that you are expected to meet.

Completion Requirements: You must successfully complete five courses for this certificate.

Example Course Titles: Some of the course titles in this program include Adult Learning, Adults with Learning Disabilities, Curriculum Development, Instructional Techniques, and Assessment and Evaluation.

Program Contact: Algonquin College
Off-Campus Learning
Woodroffe Campus
C101-1385 Woodroffe Avenue
Nepean, Ontario K2G 1V8
(613) 727-4723 ext. 7098
(613) 727-7727
distance@algonquinc.on.ca

AMERICAN COLLEGE OF PREHOSPITAL MEDICINE

General Contact Information

7552 Navarre Parkway, Suite 1
Navarre, Florida 32566-7312

Phone: (800) 735-2276
FAX: (800) 350-3870
E-mail: admit@acpm.edu
WWW: www.acpm.edu

Online Learning Information

365 Canal Street, Suite 2300
New Orleans, Louisiana 70130-3870

Phone: (800) 735-2276
FAX: (800) 350-3870
E-mail: admit@acpm.edu
WWW: www.acpm.edu

Institution Background

The American College of Prehospital Medicine was started in an attempt to address the need for flexible higher education for Emergency Medical Services professionals.

Founded: 1991
Type of Institution: Proprietary
Accreditation: Distance Education and Training Council

Online Course Background: All of the American College of Prehospital Medicine's courses have an online component (electronic mail) and three courses are entirely Internet based. The American College of Prehospital Medicine launched its distance education course in basic Emergency Medical Technology during late 1999. The course combines Internet resources with two weekend seminars, and leads to a certificate.

Online Course Offered: 30

Online Students Enrolled: 150

Special Programs/Partnerships: The American College of Prehospital Medicine has several articulation agreements with other institutions and organizations.

Services Offered to Students: Active American College of Prehospital Medicine students and associates have access to the Library Information Resource Network.

Financial Aid: Students who are serving in the military or are veterans of the Armed Forces may be eligible for financial aid through the Military Tuition Assistance program, DANTES, and Veterans benefits. Any student may be eligible for student loans through Sallie Mae. Also the American College of Prehospital Medicine has internal financing for tuition costs.

Individual Undergraduate Courses: You can pursue any of the courses offered by the American College of Prehospital Medicine without enrolling in a degree-seeking program.

Registration: You can register for courses by mail.

Programs:

Emergency Medical Services

Degree Offered: Associate of Science/Bachelor of Science

Program Web Address: www.acpm.edu

Online Program Started: 1991

Students Enrolled: 120

Degrees Awarded: 40

Application Requirements: You must be a high school graduate and have some EMT-Basic or equivalent training.

Completion Requirements: You must successfully complete 60 semester hours for the associate's degree, or 120 semester hours for the bachelor's degree.

Time for Completion: You have up to four years for either degree.

On Campus Requirements: There are no on-campus requirements.

System Requirements: You should have a computer with a CD-ROM drive and Internet access.

Program Contact: Dr. Richard A. Clinchy
The American College of Prehospital Medicine
7552 Navarre Parkway, Suite 1
Navarre, Florida 32566-7312
(800) 735-2276
(800) 350-3870
admit@acpm.edu

AMERICAN INSTITUTE FOR COMPUTER SCIENCES

General Contact Information

2101 Magnolia Avenue, Suite 207
Birmingham, Alabama 35205

Phone: (800) 729-2427 (within the United States)
(205) 323-6191 (outside of the United States)
FAX: (205) 328-2229
E-mail: admiss@aics.edu
WWW: www.aics.edu/

Online Learning Information

2101 Magnolia Avenue, Suite 207
Birmingham, Alabama 35205

Phone: (800) 729-2427 (within the United States)
(205) 323-6191 (outside of the United States)
FAX: (205) 328-2229
E-mail: admiss@aics.edu
WWW: www.aics.edu/

Institution Background

The American Institute for Computer Sciences offers undergraduate and graduate distance learning programs in computer science and information systems.

Founded: 1988
Type of Institution: Private
Accreditation: Alabama State Department of Education; World Association of Colleges and Universities

Online Course Background: This school offers all of its courses online and has since it began in 1988.

Financial Aid: The American Institute for Computer Sciences offers a tuition payment plan. Spouses, family members, and co-workers of current students are eligible for tuition reductions.

Registration: You can register for courses via mail and fax.

Programs

Computer Science

Degree Offered: Bachelor of Science

Program Web Address: www.aics.edu/catalog/cscurriculum.html

Program Background: The goal of this program is to produce knowledgeable graduates who have a broad understanding of computer science with a particular emphasis on software development. The courses are designed around texts and interactive learning technologies that meet this goal and are well suited for distance study.

Application Requirements: You must be a high school graduate or have an equivalent certificate (GED).

Completion Requirements: You must successfully complete 40 to 60 credit hours (10 to 15 courses) for this degree.

Time for Completion: You have up to eight years to complete this degree.

On Campus Requirements: There are no on-campus requirements.

Example Course Titles: Some of the course titles in this program include Introduction to Computer Programming, Intermediate Computer Programming, Data Structures, Discrete Mathematics, Computer Organization, Software Engineering, Programming Language, Theory of Computation, Computer Architecture, Operating Systems, Windows Programming Using Visual Basic, Concepts of Java, Visual C++, Algorithm Design and Analysis, Artificial Intelligence, Database Systems, and Data Communications and Networking.

Program Contact: Director of Admissions
American Institute for Computer Sciences
2101 Magnolia Avenue, Suite 207
Birmingham, Alabama 35205
(800) 729-AICS
(205) 328-2229
admiss@aics.edu

Computer Science

Degree Offered: Master of Science

Program Web Address: www.aics.edu/newcampus/prospective/index.html

Program Background: This program provides students with a fundamental understanding of theoretical and applied computer science. This allows students to begin exploring special topics and state-of-the-art subjects, and prepares them for advanced positions in industry application, development and research.

Application Requirements: You must have a Bachelor's degree in computer science or a related discipline.

Completion Requirements: You must successfully complete 40 to 60 credit hours (10 to 15 courses).

Time for Completion: You have up to eight years to complete this program.

On Campus Requirements: There are no on-campus requirements.

Example Course Titles: Some of the course titles in this program include Algorithm Design and Analysis, Advanced Concepts of Programming Languages, Advanced Concepts of Operating Systems, Concepts of Communication Networks, Concepts of Database Systems, Concepts of Artificial Intelligence, Concepts of Software Engineering, Concepts of Compiler Design, and Concepts of Parallel Processing.

Program Contact: Director of Admissions
American Institute for Computer Sciences
2101 Magnolia Avenue, Suite 207
Birmingham, Alabama 35205
(800) 729-AICS
(205) 328-2229
admiss@aics.edu

Information Systems

Degree Offered: Bachelor of Science

Program Web Address: www.aics.edu/catalog/iscurriculum.html

Program Background: The Information Systems program at the American Institute for Computer Sciences (AICS) is designed for students who want a broad knowledge of information systems as they are used in organizational settings. It focuses on basic theory and design of computers, techniques of programming, systems analysis and design, and practical applications of information systems. Courses are delivered via texts, CD-ROMs, and online labs that aid a student's understanding of computer hardware and software, information systems and their applications, and the impact of information systems on society.

This program is intended for students who have graduated from high school, are experienced and comfortable with computers, are interested in computer applications as used in business, have a desire to learn information systems in a rigorous way, and are self-motivated and capable of working with less direct supervision. Some of the objectives of the program are to enable students to develop practical analytical and interpersonal skills, provide knowledge and ability to develop creative solutions, and prepare students for careers in the information systems segments of business, industry, government, and education.

Application Requirements: You must be a high school graduate or have satisfactorily completed the General Educational Development (GED) requirement.

Completion Requirements: You must have a total of 120 semester hours in order to receive this degree and you can complete it on an accelerated (degree completion) or standard schedule. To participate in the accelerated schedule, you must earn a minimum of 40 to 60 credit hours by successfully completing 10 to 15 courses in this program, and you must transfer up to 80 credit hours from another college and/or receive up to 30 credit hours for life and work experience. If you transfer previous college credit or receive credit for life and work experience, most of the 40 to 60 credit hours you earn in the program will be in your area of major concentration: computer science or information systems. You will have 24 months to complete your degree and you must maintain a grade point average of 2.0 or higher.

If you transfer less than 60 credit hours or receive less than 60 credit hours for your life and work experience, or you wish to work on your degree in a more self-paced manner, AICS recommends that you enroll in the standard Bachelor of Science program. You still must have 120 credit hours to graduate and you attain credits by successfully completing courses through AICS, transferring them from other schools, receiving them for life and work experience, or a combination of all three methods. Also you must still maintain a grade point average of 2.0. But instead of having to complete your degree in two years, you have up to eight years to do so.

If you're interested in transferring credit to AICS from another institution, it's important to know that AICS recognizes credits from other institutions for comparable courses in the core curriculum, and all transfers are subject to a review of your official transcripts. To receive credit for courses in your area of concentration, you must submit a course outline and syllabus in addition to your transcripts. There is no charge for credits transferred from other institutions.

If you're interested in receiving credit for life and work experience, you have to submit information based on AICS's Life and Work Experience Assessment Guidelines. These guidelines are designed especially for adult students who have established and achieved professional goals. Your experience need not be computer related, however. AICS awards credits toward the completion of the core curriculum.

Time for Completion: If you enroll in the degree completion program, you have two years to complete your degree. If you enroll in the standard program, you have up to eight years to complete this degree.

On Campus Requirements: There are no on-campus requirements for this program.

Example Course Titles: Some of the course titles for this program include Introduction to Operating Systems and Programming, Visual Basic, Introduction to Computer Programming, Internet Navigation, Network and Database Administration, Expert Systems and Artificial Intelligence, Business on the Internet, and Information Systems Strategy and Policy.

Program Contact: Director of Admissions
American Institute for Computer Sciences
2101 Magnolia Avenue, Suite 207

Birmingham, Alabama 35205
(800) 729-AICS
(205) 328-2229
admiss@aics.edu

AMERICAN MILITARY UNIVERSITY

General Contact Information

9104-P Manassas Drive
Manassas Park, Virginia 20111

Phone: (703) 330-5398 ext. 111
FAX: (703) 330-5109
E-mail: amugen@amunet.edu
WWW: www.amunet.edu

Online Learning Information

Office of Admissions
9104-P Manassas Drive
Manassas Park, Virginia 20111

Phone: (703) 330-5398 ext. 111
FAX: (703) 330-5109
E-mail: amugen@amunet.edu
WWW: www.amunet.edu

Institution Background

The American Military University was started in 1993 by a retired U.S. Marine Corps Major, James P. Etter. Designed to provide military personnel with additional educational opportunities beyond the training they receive in the Armed Forces, the University also addresses the need to consolidate or transfer knowledge they gain in the service to count toward an academic degree.

Founded: 1993
Type of Institution: Private
Accreditation: Distance Education and Training Council

Online Students Enrolled: 1,800

Financial Aid: Military personnel may be eligible for financial aid through the Defense Activity for Non-Traditional Education Support (DANTES), Veterans benefits, federal and state aid programs, and tuition reimbursement programs through employers. American Military University has technology grants to help students pay for needed computer equipment and a merit-scholarship program. Also, the American Military University offers a tuition payment plan. For more information about the University administered scholarship, grants, and tuition payment plan, visit AMU's Web site.

Programs

Military Studies

Degree Offered: Bachelor of Arts

Program Web Address: www.amunet.edu/ucurriculum.htm

Program Background: Students enrolled in the Bachelor of Arts program in Military Studies can major in Military History (American or World), Intelligence Studies, or Military Management.

Application Requirements: American Military University considers the following criteria in determining whether to admit a student: a student's aptitude test scores (ACT, SAT, or ASVAB), occupational and professional achievement, civilian training and experience, military education and training, military experience, and recommendations.

Completion Requirements: You must successfully complete 120 semester hours for this degree. Of these 120 semester hours, you must earn at least 30 at American Military University and you must achieve a minimum grade point average of 2.0.

Example Course Titles: Some of the course titles in this program include Basic Computer Applications, Advanced Computer Applications, Proficiency in Writing, Effectiveness in Writing, Managing Performance, Statistics, American Literature from the Civil War to the Present, and World Civilization Before 1650.

Program Contact: American Military University
9104-P Manassas Drive
Manassas Park, Virginia 20111
(703) 330-5398 ext. 105
admissions@amunet.edu

Military Studies

Degree Offered: Master of Arts

Program Web Address: www.amunet.edu/gcurriculum.htm

Program Background: Students can focus their program of study in one of these areas of military studies: land warfare, naval warfare, air warfare, unconventional warfare, intelligence, defense management, and Civil War studies.

Application Requirements: You must have a Bachelor's degree from an accredited college or university and a minimum grade point average of 2.7 during your last 60 undergraduate semester hours. You need to submit an application, official transcripts, and a letter of recommendation.

American Military University considers the following criteria in determining whether to admit a student: a student's aptitude test scores (GRE or GMAT), occupational and professional achievement, civilian training and experience, military education and training, military experience, and recommendations.

Completion Requirements: You must successfully complete 36 semester hours (which consists of 12 courses and a comprehensive final examination) and achieve a minimum grade point average of 3.0 for this degree. Of the 36 semester hours, at least 21 must be earned through American Military University.

Example Course Titles: Some of the course titles in this program include Air Power, History of Military Aviation, Air War in Europe in WWII, The Air War in Korea, Civil War Strategy and Tactics, Civil War Command and Leadership, and Communications in Warfare.

Program Contact: American Military University
9104-P Manassas Drive
Manassas Park, Virginia 20111
(703) 330-5398 ext. 105
admissions@amunet.edu

ARIZONA STATE UNIVERSITY

General Contact Information

University Drive and Mill Avenue
Tempe, Arizona 85287-0501

Phone: (480) 965-9011
FAX: (480) 965-1371
E-mail: info@asu.edu
WWW: www.asu.edu

Online Learning Information

Distance Learning Technology
P.O. Box 872904
Tempe, Arizona 85287-2904

Phone: (602) 965-6738
FAX: (602) 965-1371
E-mail: distance@asu.edu

Institution Background

Arizona State University is a leading research and teaching institution with an extended campus that goes beyond physical boundaries to provide access to credit and degree programs through innovative delivery technologies.

Founded: 1885
Type of Institution: Public
Accreditation: North Central Association of Colleges and Schools

Online Course Background: Arizona State University has been offering courses online since 1996 and currently offers complete degree programs, as well as individual courses, online.

Online Course Offered: 43

Online Students Enrolled: 531

Special Programs/Partnerships: Arizona State University, in partnership with the University of Arizona and Northern Arizona University, offers a Master of Engineering degree program.

Services Offered to Students: Online students have access to the University's library and bookstore, as well as access to technical support and advising.

Financial Aid: For information about the types of financial aid available and awarding criteria, you'll need to visit their Web site or contact the school's financial aid office directly.

Individual Undergraduate Courses: ASU offers individual undergraduate courses in the following fields: accounting, algebra, business, communication, conflict resolution, dance, education, English, geography, history, humanities, paleography, physics, plant biology, psychology, nursing, statistics, and stress management.

Individual Graduate Courses: ASU offers individual graduate courses in the following fields: conflict resolution, education, engineering, paleography, and stress management.

Registration: You can register for courses via phone or in person.

Programs

Education

Degree Offered: Master of Education

Program Web Address: cionline.asu.edu

Online Program Started: 1999

Students Enrolled: 14

Program Background: This program's objective is to develop professional educators who know how to integrate theory, practice, and technology in the classroom. Students must demonstrate advanced levels of knowledge, skills, and understanding in the course content areas and technology.

Application Requirements: You need to complete an application and submit it with a $45 application fee, letter of intent, summary of your professional experience, three letters of recommendation, and two copies of official transcripts from each institution of higher education that you've attended.

Completion Requirements: You must successfully complete 30 credit units, including a culminating Applied Project, to earn this degree.

Time for Completion: You have up to five years to complete this program.

System Requirements: You must have a personal computer with a Pentium or PowerPC processor running Windows 95/98 or a Macintosh with a PowerPC processor running MacOS 7.5.5 or higher, 32 MB of RAM, a 28.8 kbps modem (or faster), a sound card and speakers, a word processor capable of saving files in rich text format (RTF), a Web browser capable of supporting Java and Javascript, and an Internet Service Provider.

Example Course Titles: Some of the course titles in this program include New Media and Curriculum Presentation, Teacher as Re-searcher, Theory and Methods in Web-based Instruction, Instructional Models of Teaching and Technology, Performance Assessment and Post Modern Media, and Communication and HyperTechnology.

Program Contact: Dr. Michael G. Flemister
Farmer Hall
Box 2011
Tempe, Arizona 85287-2011
(480) 965-4962
(480) 965-4942
mothership@asu.edu

Engineering

Degree Offered: Master of Engineering

Program Web Address: TriUniv.engr.arizona.edu

Online Program Started: 1999

Students Enrolled: 10

Completion Requirements: You must successfully complete 30 credit hours, including three hours in applied engineering or mathematics and three hours in engineering management/business. You are also required to take a final examination.

Time for Completion: You have up to six years to complete this program.

On Campus Requirements: There are no on-campus requirements.

Program Contact: Director, Master of Engineering
College of Engineering
Arizona State University
Tempe, Arizona 85287
(480) 965-1726
m.eng@asu.edu

ATHABASCA UNIVERSITY

General Contact Information

1 University Drive
Athabasca, Alberta, Canada T9S 3A3

Phone: (780) 675-6111
FAX: (780) 675-6384
E-mail: auinfo2@athabascau.ca
WWW: www.athabascau.ca

Online Learning Information

Information Centre
1 University Drive
Athabasca, Alberta, Canada T9S 3A3

Phone: (800) 788-9041 (toll-free number North America only)
FAX: (403) 675-6145
E-mail: auinfo@athabascau.ca
WWW: www.athabascau.ca

Institution Background

Athabasca University (AU) is recognized nationally and internationally as a leader in distance education. Its mission is to remove barriers to higher education and increase opportunities for adults living in Canada, the United States, or Mexico. AU has been offering distance learning courses since its creation in 1970, and has served over 130,000 students. Currently, more than 17,000 students are enrolled in Athabasca's courses each year.

Founded: 1970
Type of Institution: Public
Accreditation: The Government of Alberta

Online Course Offered: over 400

Online Students Enrolled: 17,000

Special Programs/Partnerships: AU has numerous collaborative programs and/or transfer arrangements with a variety of organizations. Some of these include ACCESS TV, Alberta Distance Ed & Training Association (ADETA), Calgary Police Service, CKUA Radio Network, École Secondaire Beaumont Composite High School, Labour College of Canada, Laurentian University, National Institute of Multimedia Education, Nortel Corporation, Northern Alberta Post-Secondary Institution Society (NAPSIS), Tokyo Accounting Centre, University of Alberta, University of Maryland-University College, and the Big Country Educational Consortium.

Services Offered to Students: Student support services include advisors, telephone tutors, access for students with disabilities, computer services help desk, library information desk and online services, access to the Ombuds, student and alumni associations, and access to the academic appeals committee.

Financial Aid: As an AU student, you may be eligible to receive scholarships and student loans. For more information about financial aid, visit AU's Web site.

Individual Undergraduate Courses: AU offers individual undergraduate courses in the following fields: Administrative Studies, Accounting, Administration, Anthropology, Art History, Astronomy and Astrophysics, Biology, Chemistry, Communications, Computers and Management Information Systems, Computer Science, Criminal Justice, Economics, Education, Educational Psychology, English, English as a Second Language, Environmental Studies, Finance, French, Geography, Geology, German, Health, Health Administration, History, Humanities, Industrial Relations, Labor Studies, Legal Studies, Management Science, Marketing, Mathematics, Music, Native Studies, Nursing, Nutrition, Organizational Behavior, Philosophy, Physics, Political Science, Psychology, Public Administration, Religious Studies, Small Business Management, Social Science, Sociology, Spanish, Taxation, and Women's Studies.

Individual Graduate Courses: AU offers individual graduate courses in Distance Education and Business Administration.

Registration: You can register for courses via mail, phone, e-mail, and the World Wide Web.

Programs

Administration

Degree Offered: Bachelor of Administration

Program Web Address: www.athabascau.ca/main/procrs.htm

Degrees Awarded: 65

Program Background: This program is designed to provide students with the conceptual, critical, and practical knowledge and skills needed to succeed and advance in the many competitive fields of management and administration. All students complete a common core set of courses and choose one of the following five concentrations: Health Administration, Industrial Relations, Management, Organization, or Public Administration.

Application Requirements: You must be 18 years or older to apply for admission to Athabasca University. Athabasca has a year round admission and an open-door policy. You can apply through a touchtone phone service, or by mail, fax, or the World Wide Web. To use the Automated Touchtone Registration and Withdrawal Service, you need to call one of the following numbers: Athabasca area (780) 675-6100; Edmonton area (780) 421-8700; Calgary area (403) 263-6465; or other parts of Canada or the United States (800) 788-9041.

Program Restrictions: At times courses may be temporarily unavailable because they have reached the enrollment capacity or because materials are temporarily depleted. It is your responsibility to call and confirm the current status of a course or program.

Completion Requirements: You must successfully complete 90 credits for this degree—24 from core courses and 66 from concentration and optional courses.

Time for Completion: Students have six months to complete most three- or four-credit courses, and 12 months to complete a six-credit course.

On Campus Requirements: Some of the courses require a lab component. You are responsible for contacting the course instructor for more information about lab fees, registration, and lab schedules.

System Requirements: You should have a personal computer with a 166 MHz Pentium processor running Windows 95/98/NT, 16 MB RAM, 1 GB free hard drive space, a 256-color monitor (800×600 SVGA), a 28.8 kpbs or faster modem, a 3.5″ floppy drive, a 12× CD-ROM drive, an Internet Service Provider, and a printer.

Example Course Titles: Some of the course titles in this program include Accounting Managers of Not-for-Profit Organizations, Accounting for Managers, Introductory Financial Accounting, Administrative Principles, Writing in Organizations, Introductory Composition, and Interpersonal Communications in Management.

Program Contact: Athabasca University
1 University Drive
Athabasca, Alberta T9S 3A3
(780) 675-6100
(780) 675-6384
auinfo2@athabascau.ca

Accounting

Degree Offered: Certificate

Program Web Address: www.athabascau.ca/html/programs/u_cert/acct

Application Requirements: Please see the appropriate Web site for information about this program and its application requirements.

Program Contact: auinfo2@athabascau.ca

Administration

Degree Offered: Certificate

Program Web Address: www.athabascau.ca/html/programs/u_cert/admn.htm

Application Requirements: Please see the appropriate Web site for information about this program and its application requirements.

Program Contact: (800) 788-9041
auinfo2@athabascau.ca

Advanced Accounting

Degree Offered: Certificate
Program Web Address:www.athabascau.ca/html/programs/u_cert/acct

Application Requirements: Please see the appropriate Web site for information about this program and its application requirements.

Program Contact: Information Centre
Athabasca University
(800) 788-9041
auinfo2@athabscau.ca

Advanced Nursing Practice

Degree Offered: Advanced Graduate Diploma in Advanced Nursing Practice

Program Web Address: www.athabascau.ca/html/programs/grad/agd_nu

Program Background: This program prepares nurses to assume a broader role in providing health care services to clients of all ages in the community. It integrates theory and clinical practice focusing on advanced community nursing practice and nurse practitioner functions. Students prepare to deliver extended health services including diagnosis and treatment of common health concerns and advanced community health services, including community assessment and development. Courses cover applying concepts of primary health care, community health, and extended health services with clients throughout the lifespan, from a perspective of promoting the health of individuals and communities.

The courses in this program are delivered through a combination of print-based and on-line methods.

Application Requirements: You should be a graduate of a nursing degree program. If you do not meet this requirement, but you are a registered nurse who has earned a minimum of 54 credits toward a Bachelor's degree and has completed courses in health assessment and community-based nursing, you can be considered for admission. In addition to the educational requirements, you should have at least two years of professional nursing experience.

You need to submit an application with an application fee, three letters of recommendation, a current resume, official transcripts from each college or university you've attended, proof of your nursing registration/license, and proof of certification in BCLS. All of the documents you submit must conform to the American Psychological Association (APA) publication format.

Completion Requirements: You must successfully complete two courses each year in order to remain active in the program.

Time for Completion: You have up to five years to complete this program.

On Campus Requirements: Some courses have a practicum component. Please contact the school directly for more information.

System Requirements: You should have a personal computer with a Pentium processor, color monitor, CD-ROM drive, 16 MB RAM (minimum), 1 MB free disk space, a floppy disk drive, mouse, 28.8 MB baud modem, Windows 95, printer, and an Internet connection. The school prefers Microsoft Word as the word processor.

Example Course Titles: Some of the course titles for this program include Foundations of Advanced Nursing Practice, Advanced Nursing Practice: Women's Health: Pregnancy/Newborn, Advanced Nursing Practice: Infants to School-age Child, Advanced Nursing Practice: Adolescents and Adults, Advanced Nursing Practice: Older Adult, and Comprehensive Advanced Nursing Practice.

Program Contact: Centre for Nursing and Health Studies
Athabasca University
1 University Drive
Athabasca, Alberta T9S 3A3
(780) 675-6300
(780) 675-6468
cherylb@athabascau.ca

Anthropology

Degree Offered: Bachelor of Arts in Anthropology

Program Background: The courses in this program are studies in human diversity. Some of the topics include culture, environment, patterns of social organization, religion, the family, marriage, economics, human origin, the arts, and linguistics.

Completion Requirements: You must successfully complete 120 credit hours for this degree.

Example Course Titles: Some of the course titles in this program include Faces of Culture: An Introduction to Cultural Anthropology, Physical Anthropology and Archaeology, History of Anthropology, Language and Culture, Ethnography: Principles in Practice, and Archaeology: Principles in Practice.

Bachelor of Arts

Degree Offered: Bachelor of Arts

Program Background: Students may choose to major in Anthropology, Canadian Studies, English, French, History, Humanities, Information Systems, Labor Studies, Psychology, Sociology, and Women's Studies.

Completion Requirements: You must successfully complete 90 credit hours for the three-year program and 120 credits for the four-year program.

Example Course Titles: Some of the course titles in this program include Global Environmental Change: The Scientific and Social Issues, Psychology as a Natural Science, Cognitive Psychology, and Learning.

Bachelor of Professional Arts

Degree Offered: Bachelor of Professional Arts

Program Background: This Bachelor of Professional Arts program is designed for students who have completed an approved two-year diploma or equivalent from a college or institute of technology. Students can choose to major in Communication Studies or Criminal Justice.

Completion Requirements: You must successfully complete 120 credit hours for this degree.

Example Course Titles: Some of the course titles in this program include Introduction to Computing and Information Systems, Accessing Information, Introductory Composition, Critical Thinking, and Professional Ethics.

Bachelor of Science

Degree Offered: Bachelor of Science

Application Requirements: You should have an approved science-oriented technical diploma from a college or institution of technology to apply for this program. This program is designed to allow students to continue studies towards a science degree from either the technician or technologist level.

Completion Requirements: You must successfully complete 120 hours for this degree.

Example Course Titles: Some of the course titles in this program include Introduction to Statistics, Introduction to Calculus I, Linear Algebra I, Introduction to Computing and Information Systems, Introductory Composition, Historical Foundations of Modern Science, Professional Ethics, and Scientific Reasoning.

Business Administration

Degree Offered: Bachelor of Administration in Administration

Program Background: This program results in a focused and professional bachelor's degree in administration and management. Students learn problem-solving, critical thinking, and communications skills. The program builds on the skills and knowledge that students acquire in a two- or three-year career or professional diploma program. Students who have this diploma will receive up to 66 credits towards the three-year, 90-credit Bachelor of Administration degree program.

Application Requirements: You must have a two- or three-year professional or career diploma from an accredited college or technical institute. You may be awarded up to 60 credits towards this 90-credit degree.

Completion Requirements: You must successfully complete 90 credits for this degree.

Example Course Titles: Some of the course titles in this program include Accounting for Managers of Not-for-Profit Organizations, Accounting for Managers, Introductory Financial Accounting, Administrative Principles, Writing

in Organizations, and Introductory Composition.

Business Administration

Degree Offered: Bachelor of Administration in Health Administration

Program Background: This program provides students with the professional knowledge base and practical skills they need in today's rapidly changing field of health administration.

Completion Requirements: You must successfully complete 90 credits for this degree.

Example Course Titles: Some of the course titles in this program include Economics of Health, Community Health Planning, The Organization of the Canadian Health Care System, Health Policy in Canada, Introduction to Epidemiology, Organizational Behaviour, Professional Ethics, and Research Methods in the Social Sciences.

Business Administration—Agriculture

Degree Offered: Master of Business Administration—Agriculture

Program Web Address: www.mbaagri. uoguelph.ca/

Program Background: This program combines the agricultural/food program of the University of Guelph with Athabasca's electronic delivery system, enabling students to study from home or work and earn their Master's degree in Business Administration. Students have the opportunity to work with other agri-business professionals and take advantage of their vast knowledge and expertise.

Application Requirements: You must have your Bachelor's degree or the equivalent and a minimum grade point average of a B during the last two years of your undergraduate study. You also must have three years of experience operating a commercial farm or business, or in a managerial position within an organization. You should be willing to spend 20-25 hours per week on this program of study, as well as be prepared to spend a week in residence at the University of Guelph.

You need to complete an application and submit it with a $100 application fee (payable to the University of Guelph), a resume, a letter of intent, two letters of recommendation, and official transcripts from each college or university that you've attended. If you are an international student, you also must submit certification of your proficiency in English (TOEFL, British Council, or MELAB.)

Time for Completion: You have up to six years to complete this degree program.

On Campus Requirements: You are required to spend one week in residence at the University of Guelph.

System Requirements: You must have a personal computer with a Pentium processor running Windows 95/98/NT, a CD-ROM drive, 1 GB of free hard drive space, 16 MB RAM, a 28.8 baud modem (or faster), and an Internet Service Provider.

Example Course Titles: Some of the course titles for this program include Thinking About Strategy, Managing Markets, Human Resources Management, Operations and Decision Making, Financial Management, Managerial Accounting, Advanced Diploma Comprehensive Examination, Managing in the Agri-Food Policy Environment, Financing Agriculture and Agribusiness, and Managing Risk.

Program Contact: University of Guelph/Athabasca University
Room 221, MacLachlan Building
Guelph, Ontario N1G 2W1

(888) 622-2474
(519) 767-1510
information@mbaagri.uoguelph.ca

Canadian Studies

Degree Offered: Bachelor of Arts in Canadian Studies

Completion Requirements: You must successfully complete 120 credits for this degree. Of this 120, 60 credits must be earned through courses designated as your major courses. And of that 60, 30 credits must be senior level courses (including a minimum of 12 credits at the 400 level). You must earn at least nine credits in each of four of these areas: Canadian History, Canadian Literature, Canadian Geography, Canadian Native and Ethnic Studies, and Canadian Politics and Government.

Additionally you must meet a language requirement in one of three ways: read French at a level consistent with the usual requirements of a junior French language course, speak fluently one of Canada's Native languages (for example, Cree or Inuktitut), or read one of Canada's Aboriginal languages (Cree or Inuktitut) at a level consistent with the usual requirements of a first-year university language course.

Example Course Titles: Some of the course titles in this program include Introduction to Canadian Literature, The Literature of Work, Native Literature in Canada, Modern Canadian Theatre, Canadian History to 1867, The Social History of Canada, History of the Canadian West, History of French Canada: 1867 to the Present, Municipal Public Administration in Canada, Canadian Public Finance, Canadian Public Administration, Canadian Government and Politics, Canada and the Global Political Economy, Introductory Physical Geography I, The Canadian North, Canadian Urban Development, The Inuit Way, Native Peoples of

Canada, Introduction to Native Studies I, Community Development, The Métis, Women and Work in Canada, The Sociology of Work and Industry, and Canadian Ethnic Studies.

Career Development

Degree Offered: Certificate

Program Web Address: www.athabascau.ca/ html/programs/u_cert/cardev.htm

Application Requirements: Please see the appropriate Web site for information about this program and its application requirements.

Program Contact: Information Centre
Athabasca University
(800) 788-9041
auinfo2@athabascau.ca

Commerce

Degree Offered: Bachelor of Commerce

Degrees Awarded: 12

Application Requirements: If you have a recognized university degree, the total number of credit hours you must earn through this program may be reduced by up to 60 credits. This depends on the coursework you completed for your first degree. You will not be admitted to this program if you have a degree in administration, business, commerce, or management.

Completion Requirements: You must successfully complete 120 hours for this degree.

Example Course Titles: Some of the course titles in this program include Introductory Financial Accounting, Cost Analysis, Administrative Principles, Writing in Organizations, Microcomputer Applications in Business (Windows), Microeconomics, Macroeconomics, Commercial Law, Statistics for Business and Economics I, Statistics for Business and Economics II, Introduction to Calculus I, English,

Strategic and Competitive Analysis, Business Policy, Management Information Systems, Overview of Corporate Finance, and Introduction to Production and Operations Management.

Communication Studies

Degree Offered: Bachelor of Professional Arts in Communication Studies

Program Background: This program allows students to apply their knowledge within a national and international context of mass media and communication. It is designed for students who have an approved two-year communications-related diploma (such as public relations, advertising, journalism, multi-media, broadcasting, library and information studies, legal assistant, and marketing) or equivalent. Students may apply for prior learning assessment credits in this program or discuss an academic assessment by the program coordinator.

Completion Requirements: You must successfully complete 39 credit hours for this degree.

Example Course Titles: Some of the course titles in this program include Communication Theory and Analysis, Communication in History, Computers and Human Experience, and Popular Culture and the Media.

Computing and Information Systems

Degree Offered: Bachelor of Science in Computing and Information Systems

Degrees Awarded: 6

Program Background: This program is designed for students who want applications-oriented skills in using computers in business, education, and other applications areas.

Completion Requirements: You must successfully complete 120 hours for this degree.

Example Course Titles: Some of the course titles in this program include Writing in Organizations, Introduction to Computing and Information Systems, Introduction to Computer Programming (Java), Data Structures (Java), Computer Organization, Data Communications, System Analysis and Design, Introduction to Database Management, Computer and Information Systems Project I, Introductory Composition, Introduction to Statistics, Introduction to Calculus I, Linear Algebra I, Discrete Mathematics, Quantitative Approaches to Decision Making, Organizational Behavior, and Professional Ethics.

Computer Information Systems

Degree Offered: Bachelor of Science in Computer Information Systems

Application Requirements: This program is designed for students who have a Canadian Information Processing Society (CIPS)-accredited applied diploma or any approved three-year applied computing diploma. It prepares students for positions in the field of computer information systems.

Completion Requirements: You must successfully complete 120 hours for this degree. You can be awarded up to 60 credits toward this 120 if you have an applied diploma. If that diploma is not a Canadian Information Processing Society diploma, you may be required to complete prerequisite work for admission into this degree program.

Example Course Titles: Some of the course titles in this program include Administrative Principles, Introductory Composition, Writing in Organizations, Finite Mathematics, Discrete Mathematics, Organizational Behavior, Critical

Thinking, Professional Ethics, and Ethics, Science, Technology, and the Environment.

Computers and Management Information Systems

Degree Offered: Certificate

Program Web Address: www.athabascau.ca/html/programs/u_cert/cmis.htm

Application Requirements: Please see the appropriate Web site for information about this program and its application requirements.

Program Contact: Information Centre
Athabasca University
(800) 788-9041
auinfo2@athabscau.ca

Computing and Information Systems

Degree Offered: Certificate

Program Web Address: www.athabascau.ca/html/programs/u_cert/info.htm

Application Requirements: Please see the appropriate Web site for information about this program and its application requirements.

Program Contact: Information Centre
Athabasca University
(800) 788-9041
auinfo2@athabascau.ca

Counseling Women

Degree Offered: Certificate

Program Web Address: www.athabascau.ca/html/programs/u_cert/counwom.htm

Application Requirements: Please see the appropriate Web site for information about this program and its application requirements.

Program Contact: Information Centre
Athabasca University
(800) 788-9041
auinfo2@athabascau.ca

Criminal Justice

Degree Offered: Bachelor of Professional Arts in Criminal Justice

Degrees Awarded: 6

Program Background: The Bachelor of Professional Arts (Criminal Justice) is designed for students who have a two-year approved diploma in criminal justice-related areas from a college or technical institute. The program provides students with two years of arts and administrative studies courses along with specialized senior level courses in criminal justice.

Completion Requirements: You must successfully complete 60 credit hours on top of the courses required to earn a two-year diploma in criminal justice.

Example Course Titles: Some of the course titles in this program include Administrative Principles, Community Policing, Victims of Crimes, Special Needs Policing, Environmental Protection and Enforcement, White Collar Crime and Investigation, Aboriginal Government and Law, Civil Liberties and Individual Rights, Administrative Law, and Canadian Legal System.

Distance Education

Degree Offered: Master of Distance Education

Program Web Address: www.athabascau.ca/html/depts/mde/mdebroch.h

Online Program Started: 1994

Students Enrolled: 400

Degrees Awarded: 11

Program Background: Students in this program use their computers to interact with the instructors and other students via e-mail, to transfer files to and from others, and to access electronic databases. The school provides students with a basic course package of various materials (such as textbooks, study guides, or audio/video tapes).

Application Requirements: You must have a Bachelor's degree from a recognized institution of higher education to enroll in the Master's program. You need to complete an application and submit it with an application fee, a current resume, and three letters of recommendation. You must apply by March 1 to enroll in the program beginning in September of the same year.

If you don't want to enroll in the degree-seeking program but you wish to take courses in this field, you may do so. Courses are filled on a first-come, first serve basis, space permitting.

Completion Requirements: You must successfully complete 42 credit hours for this degree. You can earn these credits in one of three ways: the thesis route, the project route, and the course-based route. The thesis route requires five core courses, five electives, and 12 credits of thesis work. The project route requires five core courses, five electives, and 12 credits of project work. And the course-based route requires five core courses, nine electives, and a written examination or oral defense.

You may enroll in courses on a full- or part-time basis. Full-time students are required to take a minimum of nine credits (three courses) per semester, and part-time students are required to take a minimum of six credits (two courses) per semester.

Time for Completion: You have up to seven years from your first enrollment to complete this program.

On Campus Requirements: You need to contact the school directly for information about on-campus requirements.

System Requirements These are the minimum hardware and software requirements for courses in this program: a personal computer with a Pentium processor, 32 MB RAM, 100 MB free disk space, a floppy disk drive, a CD-ROM drive, Sound Blaster (or equivalent) sound card and speakers, a mouse, 33.6 baud modem (or faster), Windows 95, Microsoft Office, and an Internet Service Provider.

While the preceding identifies the very minimum you should have, Athabasca recommends a system that meets these requirements: a personal computer with a Pentium MMX 200 or greater processor, 64 MB RAM, 4 MB of video RAM, 1 GB free disk space, an SVGA-compatible monitor, a 3.5″ floppy drive, a 24X CD-ROM drive, a mouse, 33.6 baud modem, Windows 95/98, a printer, a Zip or other backup drive, and an Internet Service Provider.

Example Course Titles: Some of the course titles in this program include Introduction to Distance Education and Training, Methods of Inquiry and Decision Making, Systems Design in Distance Education, Instructional Design and Program Evaluation in Distance Education, and Planning and Management in Distance Education and Training.

Program Contact: Master of Distance Education—Program Director
Athabasca University
1 University Drive
Athabasca, Alberta T9S 3A3
(780) 675-6179
(780) 675-6170
mde@athabascau.ca

Distance Education (Technology)

Degree Offered: Advanced Graduate Diploma in Distance Education (Technology)

Program Web Address: www.athabascau.ca/html/depts/mde/agdde.htm

Degrees Awarded: 39

Program Background: The Advanced Graduate Diploma in Distance Education (Technology) is intended for students who are interested in issues related to the use of technology in distance education and training. The program emphasizes concepts and skills required of students who are employed as instructors, teachers, trainers, decision makers, planners, managers, and administrators in distance education. It focuses on using technology to prepare, deliver, and manage instruction.

The AGDDE(T) program is a focused 18-credit, six-course program, designed to provide a solid grounding in the current principles and practices of technology use in distance education and instruction.

Application Requirements: You need to complete and submit an application with a $50 application fee, official transcripts from each college or university you've attended, three letters of recommendation, the Advanced Graduate Diploma application questionnaire, and a current resume.

You may transfer some credits toward this diploma. If you intend to submit transfer credits, you should make your intentions clear in your letter of application, and you should supply transcripts with your application.

Program Restrictions: You must apply by March 1 for consideration in the program starting in September.

Completion Requirements: You must successfully complete two courses (for six credits) each academic year.

Time for Completion: You have up to three years to complete this program.

On Campus Requirements: You are required to attend some courses on-campus.

System Requirements: You must have a personal computer with a Pentium processor running Windows 95/98/NT, a CD-ROM drive, 100 MB of free hard drive space, 32 MB RAM, a 33.6 baud modem (or faster), a 3.5" floppy drive, SoundBlaster sound card and speakers, an Internet Service Provider, and Microsoft Office.

Example Course Titles: Some of the course titles for this program include Introduction to Distance Education and Training, Systems Design in Distance Education, Instructional Design and Program Evaluation in Distance Education and Training, Introduction to Technology in Distance Education and Training, and Human Factors in Educational Technology.

Program Contact: AGDDE(T) Advisor, Centre for Distance Education
Athabasca University
1 University Drive
Athabasca, Alberta T9S 3A3
(780) 675-6179
(780) 675-6170
mde@athabascau.ca

English

Degree Offered: Bachelor of Arts in English

Program Background: Students in this program can select courses covering British, Canadian, and American literature, as well as major literary genres and historical periods.

Completion Requirements: You must successfully complete 120 credit hours for this degree.

Example Course Titles: Some of the course titles in this program include Prose Forms, Plays and Poetry, Developing Reading and Writing Skills, English for Academic Purposes, and Introductory Composition.

English Language Studies

Degree Offered: Certificate

Program Web Address: www.athabascau.ca/html/programs/u_cert/engl.htm

Application Requirements: Please see the appropriate Web site for information about this program and its application requirements.

Program Contact: Information Centre
Athabasca University
(800) 788-9041
auinfo2@athabascau.ca

French

Degree Offered: Bachelor of Arts in French

Program Background: This program emphasizes oral and written expressions in French vocabulary, grammar, and idiomatic expressions. Students learn pronunciation, oral comprehension, and reading and writing skills. Graduates should be able to handle social situations and talk about themselves, their opinions, and their experiences, as well as read short stories in French.

Completion Requirements: You must successfully complete 120 credit hours for this degree.

Example Course Titles: Some of the course titles in this program include First Year University French I, First Year University French II, and Introduction a la Littérature Canadienne-Française.

French Language Proficiency

Degree Offered: Certificate

Program Web Address: www.athabascau.ca/html/programs/u_cert/fren.htm

Application Requirements: Please see the appropriate Web site for information about this program and its application requirements.

Program Contact: Information Centre
Athabasca University
(800) 788-9041
auinfo2@athabascau.ca

General Studies

Degree Offered: Bachelor of General Studies

Degrees Awarded: 96

Program Background: This program provides a framework of individualized study within an Arts and Science or an Applied Studies designation that gives students the freedom to choose courses that meet their career or educational goals.

Completion Requirements: You must successfully complete 90 credits. This degree program is comparable to a three-year program.

On Campus Requirements: There are no residency requirements.

Example Course Titles: Some of the course titles include Global Environmental Change: The Scientific and Social Issues, Psychology as a Natural Science, Cognitive Psychology, Learning, Biological Psychology, and Experimental Psychology.

Health Administration

Degree Offered: Bachelor of Administration in Health Administration

Program Background: This program provides students with the professional knowledge base and practical skills needed in today's rapidly changing field of health administration.

Completion Requirements: You must successfully complete 90 credits for this degree.

Example Course Titles: Some of the course titles in this program include Community Health Planning, The Organization of the Canadian Health Care System, Health Policy in Canada, Introduction to Epidemiology, Introduction to Human Health, Organizational Behaviour, Professional Ethics, and Research Methods in the Social Sciences.

Health Development Administration

Degree Offered: Certificate

Program Web Address: www.athabascau.ca/html/programs/u_cert/hlth.htm

Application Requirements: Please see the appropriate Web site for information about this program and its application requirements.

Program Contact: Information Centre
Athabasca University
(800) 788-9041
auinfo2@athabascau.ca

Health Studies—Nursing

Degree Offered: Master of Health Studies (MHS), Advanced Nursing Practice

Program Web Address: www.athabascau.ca/html/depts/nursing/mhs.ht

Online Program Started: 1999

Program Background: The purpose of the Master's program is to prepare health professionals for leadership positions in the health system, and the Advanced Nursing Practice stream pertains specifically to nurses. Students are prepared to assume broader roles in providing health services to people of all ages. The program integrates theoretical and clinical preparation.

Application Requirements: To be admitted to the Master of Health Studies program, you must have a Bachelor's degree in nursing from an accredited university, two years of practice, proof of nursing registration, and proof of certification. You should submit an application with an application fee, three letters of recommendation, a current resume, and official transcripts from any college and university you've attended.

You can take the courses in this program on an independent, non-degree seeking basis if space is available.

Completion Requirements: You must successfully complete six credit hours of coursework during each academic year and maintain a minimum grade of 70 percent in all core courses. You may not interrupt your studies for more than one semester without approval from the program coordinator.

Time for Completion: You have up to six years to complete this program.

On Campus Requirements: You need to contact the program director directly for information about on-campus requirements.

System Requirements: You must have access to a personal computer with a Pentium processor running Windows 95, color monitor, CD-ROM drive, 16 MB RAM, 1 MB of free disk space, floppy disk drive, mouse, 28.8 kpbs modem, printer, various software, and an Internet Service Provider.

Example Course Titles: Some of the course titles in this program include Foundations of Advanced Nursing Practice, Advanced Nursing Practice: Children: Infants to School Age, Philosophical Foundations of Health Systems, Managing Information in Health Systems: Informatics, Advanced Nursing Practice: Women's Health: Pregnancy/Newborn, and Advanced Nursing Practice: Adolescent and Adult.

Program Contact: Centre for Nursing and Health Studies
Athabasca University
1 University Drive
Athabasca, Alberta T9S 3A3
(780) 675-6300
(780) 675-6468
mhs@athabascau.ca

History

Degree Offered: Bachelor of Arts in History

Completion Requirements: You must successfully complete 120 credit hours for this degree.

Example Course Titles: Some of the course titles in this program include Europe: Medieval to Modern, The Era of World Wars, 1900–1950, History of Canada to 1867, Canadian History: 1867 to Present, The Pacific Century, Twentieth-Century China, Western Culture I: Before the Reformation, Western Culture II: Since the Reformation, History of Popular Music I: Blues to Big Bands, 1900–1940, History of Popular Music II: Be-bop to Beatles, 1940–1970, Rome and Early Christianity I, Rome and Early Christianity II, and The Folk Music Revival I: Before 1945.

Home Health Nursing

Degree Offered: Certificate

Program Web Address: www.athabascau.ca/html/programs/u_cert/hhn.htm

Application Requirements: Please see the appropriate Web site for information about this program and its application requirements.

Program Contact: (800) 788-9041
auinfo2@athabascau.ca

Human Science

Degree Offered: Bachelor of Science in Human Science

Program Background: This program is designed for students interested in pursuing a concentrate in Human Science. It is particularly suited for students who wish to continue professional careers in health sciences and research and development.

Completion Requirements: You must successfully complete 120 hours for this degree.

Example Course Titles: Some of the course titles in this program include Principles of Biology I, Principles of Biology II, Biological Laboratories, Introductory Microbiology, Introductory Ecology, Chemical Principles I, Chemical Principles II, Introduction to Statistics, Introduction to Calculus I, Linear Algebra I, Introduction to Computing and Information Systems, and Scientific Reasoning.

Humanities

Degree Offered: Bachelor of Arts in Humanities

Completion Requirements: You must successfully complete 120 credit hours for this degree.

Example Course Titles: Some of the course titles in this program include A Survey of Western Art I, A Survey of Western Art II, A History of Drama—Part I: Early Stages, A History of Drama—Part II: Modernist Theatre, Literature of the Americas, The Medieval World I: The Early Middle Ages, The Medieval World II: The High Middle Ages, The Renaissance, The Northern Renaissance and the Reformation, Historical Foundations of Modern Science, Classical Music: An Introduction, From Socrates to Sartre, Ethics, Science, Technology, and the Environment, Introduction to World Religions, and Ancient Civilizations of the Americas.

Industrial Relations

Degree Offered: Bachelor of Administration in Industrial Relations

Program Background: This program is designed for students who want to develop the knowledge and skills necessary for a career in industrial relations and human resource management. It is also for students who want a better understanding of the industrial relations in their own workplace.

Completion Requirements: You must successfully complete 90 credit hours for this degree.

Example Course Titles: Some of the course titles in this program include Labor Unions, Rights at Work: Grievance Arbitration, Collective Bargaining, Public Sector Labor Relations, Occupational Health and Safety, Industrial Relations: A Critical Introduction, Labor Relations and the Law, Directed Study in Industrial Relations, Doing Research in Organizations, The Impact of the Canadian Charter on Labour Relations, and Introduction to Human Resource Management.

Information Systems

Degree Offered: Bachelor of Arts in Information Systems

Program Background: This program produces graduates that have the skills to process, use, and manage information systems required by business, education, and government. The courses in this major deal with both computer science and business applications.

Completion Requirements: You must successfully complete 120 credit hours for this degree.

Example Course Titles: Some of the course titles in this program include Microcomputer Applications in Business, Introduction to Computing and Information Systems, Computer Programming (Java), Computer Organization, Systems Analysis and Design, Human Factors in Computer Systems, Computer and Information Systems Projects I, Accessing Information, Management Information Systems, C/C++ for Programmers, Introduction to

Database Management, Object-Oriented Programming Using C++, Object-Oriented Design, and Artificial Intelligence and Expert Systems in PROLOG.

Information Technology Management

Degree Offered: Advanced Graduate Diploma in Information Technology Management

Program Web Address: www.athabascau.ca/mba/www42a.htm

Online Program Started: 2000

Program Background: This Advanced Graduate Diploma is for students who do not wish to pursue the Master of Business Administration in Information Technology from Athabasca University. Students must complete seven courses and a comprehensive examination. The program prepares students for their jobs and advancement in Information Technology professional positions, management roles, or general management positions.

Application Requirements: You must have a bachelor's degree or the equivalent from an accredited college or university and have completed at least three years of professional or managerial experience, or have an acceptable professional designation and at least five years of professional or managerial experience demonstrating progressive responsibility. If you don't meet either of these requirements, you may still be considered for the program if you can demonstrate to the Admissions Committee that you have substantive managerial experience (at least eight to ten years) and relevant training. You may be required to take the Graduate Management Admissions Test (GMAT).

You should submit a completed application with a letter stating why you're interested in this degree and your background experience, three letters of recommendation, and a current resume.

Program Restrictions: If you are denied admission to the program, the Admissions Committee will send you a letter with a brief explanation why and outlining what you can do to improve your chances should you apply again.

Completion Requirements: You must successfully complete seven courses and a comprehensive examination.

On Campus Requirements: You are required to attend two weekend schools and a week long summer school on campus.

System Requirements: You should have a personal computer with a Pentium 166 MHz, 32MB RAM, 1 GB of free space on the hard drive, Windows 95/98/NT 4.0, 800×600 SVGA, 28.8 or faster modem, and Lotus Notes. You should also have an Internet Service Provider that must have port 1352 enabled on their firewall in order to connect to Notes Server.

Example Course Titles: Some of the course titles in this program include Thinking About Strategy, Information Technology and Performance, Human Factors in Information Technology, Project Management for Information Technology Projects, Electronic Commerce, Systems Integration Knowledge Management, and Improving Business Performance Through the Application of Information Technology.

Program Contact: Centre for Innovative Management
301 Grandin Park Plaza
22 Sir Winston Churchill Ave.
St. Albert, Alberta T8N 1B4
(780) 459-1144
(780) 459-2093
cimoffice@athabascau.ca

Information Technology Management

Degree Offered: Master of Business Administration in Information Technology Management (MBA-ITM)

Program Web Address: www.athabascau.ca/mba/www42.htm

Program Background: This Master's program just began in September 1999 and was developed through a collaboration of Athabasca University and users and vendors in the information technology industry. The program is designed to prepare students to become managers of information technology in public and private sectors. Students learn to communicate and apply knowledge of management practices, comprehend human factors in information technology, manage information technology-based projects, understand and work with electronic commerce, and effectively integrate information technology systems in organizations.

Application Requirements: You must have a Bachelor's or first degree from an accredited college or university and have a minimum of three years of professional or managerial experience, or you must have an acceptable professional designation and have a minimum of five years of professional or managerial experience in an information technology field with progressive responsibility. You should complete and submit an application for the program. If you are not admitted, Athabasca University will provide you with an explanation outlining what steps you can take to improve your chances of being admitted in the future.

Completion Requirements: You must successfully complete one course or comprehensive examination in any 12-month period to maintain active status.

Time for Completion: Typcially, students can complete this program in two-and-a-half to three years. But you have up to six years to do so.

On Campus Requirements: You are required to attend two weekend schools (at any point during the program) and one week of summer school in residence.

System Requirements: This program uses Lotus Notes groupware as its platform. The school will provide you with a copy of Lotus Notes and Microsoft Office upon enrollment.

You should have a personal computer with a 166 MHz Pentium processor running Windows 95/98/NT, 32 MB RAM, 1 GB free hard drive space, a 256-color monitor (800×600 SVGA), a 28.8 kpbs or faster modem, an Internet Service Provider, and a printer. Your Internet Service Provider must have post 1352 enabled on their firewall in order for you to connect to the Lotus Notes server at the University.

Example Course Titles: Some of the course titles for this program include Thinking About Strategy, Strategic Marketing, Human Resource Management, Operations and Decision Making, Financial Accounting, Managerial Accounting, Information Technology and Performance, Human Factors in Information Technology, and Electronic Commerce.

Program Contact: Centre for Innovative Management
Athabasca University
301 Grandin Park Plaza
22 Sir Winston Churchill Ave.
St. Albert, Alberta T8N 1B4
(780) 459-1144
(780) 459-2093
cimoffice@athabascau.ca

Labor Relations

Degree Offered: Certificate

Program Web Address: www.athabascau.ca/

html/programs/u_cert/lbrrel.htm

Application Requirements: Please see the appropriate Web site for information about this program and its application requirements.

Program Contact: Information Centre
Athabasca University
(800) 788-9041
auinfo2@athabascau.ca

Labor Studies

Degree Offered: Certificate

Program Web Address: www.athabascau.ca/html/programs/u_cert/lbrst.htm

Application Requirements: Please see the appropriate Web site for information about this program and its application requirements.

Program Contact: Information Centre
Athabasca University
(800) 788-9041
auinfo2@athabascau.ca

Labor Studies

Degree Offered: Bachelor of Arts in Labour Studies

Completion Requirements: You must successfully complete 120 credit hours for this degree.

Example Course Titles: Some of the course titles in this program include Introduction to Labour Studies, History of Canadian Labour, Sociology of Work and Industry, Economics of Inequality and Poverty, The Literature of Work, The Social History of Canada, Pre-Industrial Origins of Labour and Socialist Thought, Labour and Socialist Thought in the Early Industrial Revolution, 1800-1850, Labour and Socialist Thought in the Later Industrial Revolution,1850-1917, The Industrial Revolution, Labour Unions, and Rights at Work: Grievance Arbitration.

Management

Degree Offered: Advanced Graduate Diploma in Management

Program Web Address: www.athabascau.ca/mba/www44.htm

Degrees Awarded: 228

Program Background: The Advanced Graduate Diploma in Management (AGDM) is designed to meet the ongoing educational needs of managers who do not wish to pursue a Master of Business Administration.

Application Requirements: You must have a Bachelor's degree or the equivalent from an accredited college or university and have completed at least three years of professional or managerial experience, or have an acceptable professional designation and at least five years of professional or managerial experience demonstrating progressive responsibility. If you don't meet either of these requirements, you may still be considered for the program if you can demonstrate to the Admissions Committee that you have substantive managerial experience (at least eight to ten years) and relevant training. You may be required to take the Graduate Management Admissions Test (GMAT).

You should submit a completed application with a letter stating why you're interested in this degree and your background experience, three letters of recommendation, and a current resume.

Program Restrictions: If you are denied admission to the program, the Admissions Committee will send you a letter with a brief explanation why and outlining what you can do to improve your chances should you apply again.

Completion Requirements: You must successfully complete one course module or comprehensive examination during any 12-month period to maintain active status.

Time for Completion: Typically, students can complete the Advanced Graduate Diploma in Management Program in 18 months. However, you have up to four years to do so.

On Campus Requirements: There are no on-campus requirements for this program.

System Requirements: You should have a personal computer with a Pentium 166 MHz, 32MB RAM, 1 GB free hard drive space, Windows 95/98/NT 4.0, 800×600 SVGA monitor, 28.8 modem or faster, and Lotus Notes. You should also have an Internet Service Provider that must have port 1352 enabled on their firewall in order to connect to Notes Server.

Example Course Titles: Some of the course titles in this program include Thinking About Strategy, Strategic Marketing, Human Resource Management Operations and Decision Making, Financial Accounting, and Managerial Accounting.

Program Contact: Center for Innovative Management
Athabasca University
301, 22 Sir Winston Churchill Ave.
St. Albert, Alberta T8N 1B4
(780) 459-1144
(780) 459-2093
cimoffice@athabascau.ca

Management

Degree Offered: Bachelor of Administration in Management

Program Background: This program in Management prepares students for positions in the major functional areas of management today.

Completion Requirements: You must successfully complete 90 credits for this degree.

Example Course Titles: Some of the course titles in this program include Cost Analysis, Business Policy, Overview of Corporate Finance, Commercial Law, Statistics for Business and Economics, International Marketing and Exporting, Marketing Strategy, The Changing Global Economy, Business, Society, and the Public Sector, and Canada and the Global Political Economy.

Management

Degree Offered: Master of Business Administration

Program Web Address: www.athabascau.ca/mba/index.html

Program Background: This program focuses on strategic management and provides students with a variety of skills in the areas of team management and decision-making. Students work with case studies, assigned tasks, and confront global challenges, integrating theory and practice.

The curriculum is structured as a sequence, building on the skills that students learn. Students learn to become effective managers, develop strategic views of organizations, and become aware of ethical issues.

Application Requirements: You must have a Bachelor's degree from an accredited college or university and at least three years of professional or managerial experience, or hold an acceptable professional designation and have at least five years of professional or managerial experience reflecting progressive responsibility. If you don't meet these requirements, you may qualify for admission into the Advanced Graduate Diploma in Management program. You have to demonstrate to the Admissions Committee that you have substantive managerial experience (at least eight years) and relevant training. Successfully completing the Advanced Graduate Diploma in Management serves as an academic credential for admission into the MBA program.

You need to complete an application and submit it with an application fee ($150), a letter of application, a current resume, a 750-word essay about your managerial experience, three letters of recommendation, and official transcripts from any institution of higher education you've attended. You should apply by June 15 to begin the program in September, October 15 to begin in January, or February 15 to begin in May.

Completion Requirements: You must successfully complete 12 courses, two comprehensive examinations, one applied projects, two theme-based weekend seminars, and one week-long summer school to earn this degree. To maintain active status in the program, you must successfully complete one course or comprehensive examination during any 12-month period.

Time for Completion: Typically, students can complete this program in two-and-a-half to three years. However, six years is the maximum that a student has to complete it.

On Campus Requirements: You are required to attend two weekend-long seminars and one week-long summer school in residence. You can complete the weekend sessions at any time during the program and the week-long session anytime after you've completed your first three courses.

System Requirements: This program (and the Advanced Graduate Diploma in Management program) is designed and delivered using Lotus Notes groupware. The school provides the software to you at the beginning of your studies, but you must have a computer that supports it.

At a minimum, you should have a personal computer with a 166 MHz Pentium processor running Windows 95/98/NT, 32 MB RAM, 1 GB of free hard drive space, a 256-color monitor (800×600 SVGA), 28.8 baud modem (or faster), a sound card and speakers, an Internet Service Provider that has a firewall, and a printer.

Example Course Titles: Some of the course titles in this program include Thinking About Strategy, Strategic Marketing, Human Resource Management, Operations and Decision Making, Financial Accounting, Managerial Accounting, Global Marketing Management, Making Sense of Major Change, The Learning Organization, and Total Quality Management in the Public Sector.

Program Contact: Centre for Innovative Management
Athabasca University
301 Grandin Park Plaza
22 Sir Winston Churchill Ave.
St. Albert, Alberta T8N 1B4
(780) 459-1144
(780) 459-2093
cimoffice@athabascau.ca

Nursing

Degree Offered: Bachelor of Nursing

Degrees Awarded: 34

Program Background: This program serves students with previous educational experiences and qualifications in nursing. These students enroll with a core of valuable knowledge and skills obtained during R.N. education and through work experience. The program is designed to build on that foundation, and to provide learning opportunities through which these competencies can be extended.

Application Requirements: You must be a graduate of an approved nursing diploma program, and have a current registration with a provincial, territorial or state nursing association, and an average of 60 percent in all previous applicable university studies accepted as transfer credit.

Completion Requirements: You must successfully complete 69 credits for this degree.

Example Course Titles: Some of the course titles in this program include Principles of Teaching and Learning for Health Professionals, Nursing Informatics, Concepts in Nursing Practice, Health Promotion: Health Assessment with Individuals, Understanding Research in Nursing, Principles of Management in Nursing Practice, Trends and Issues in Nursing, Health Promotion with Communities, Health Promotion with Families, and Senior Focus.

Organization

Degree Offered: Bachelor of Administration in Organization

Program Background: Students enrolled in this program develop a thorough understanding of the many ways individuals and groups organize tasks to effectively meet set objectives. The focus is on globalized production.

Completion Requirements: You must successfully complete 90 credit hours for this degree.

Example Course Titles: Some of the course titles in this program include Business Policy, Organization Theory, Organizational Behaviour, Introduction to Human Resource Management, Organizational Culture, The Changing Global Economy, Business, Society, and the Public Sector, and Canada and the Global Political Economy.

Psychology

Degree Offered: Bachelor of Arts in Psychology

Completion Requirements: You must successfully complete 120 credit hours for this degree.

Example Course Titles: Some of the course titles in this program include Introduction to Statistics, Psychology as a Natural Science, General Psychology, Experimental Psychology,

Research Methods in the Social Sciences, Theories of Career Development, Career Development Resources in the Changing World of Work, Creating a Working Alliance, Experiential Learning and Reflection Practice I, Experiential Learning and Reflection Practice II, The Practice of Interpersonal Communications, Introduction to Exceptional Children, Introduction to Computer-Based Instruction, Principles of Teaching and Learning for Health Professionals, Motivation and Productivity, Organizational Behaviour, Introduction to Human Resource Management, Introduction to Applied Social Psychology, Psychology of Aesthetics, Issues and Strategies in Counseling Women, and An Introduction to Learning Disabilities.

Public Administration

Degree Offered: Certificate

Program Web Address: www.athabascau.ca/html/programs/u_cert/padm.htm

Application Requirements: Please see the appropriate Web site for information about this program and its application requirements.

Program Contact: Information Centre
Athabasca University
(800) 788-9041
auinfo2@athabscau.ca

Public Administration

Degree Offered: Bachelor of Administration in Public Administration

Program Background: This program is designed for those who wish to develop skills appropriate to the public sector.

Completion Requirements: You must successfully complete 90 credit hours for this degree.

Example Course Titles: Some of the course titles in this program include Industrial Relations: A Critical Introduction, Administrative Law, Commercial Law, Municipal Public Administration in Canada, Canadian Public Finance, Canadian Public Administration, Public Policy, Introduction to Political Science I: Concepts, Structures, and Institutions, Canadian Government and Politics, and Research Methods in the Social Sciences.

Sociology

Degree Offered: Bachelor of Arts in Sociology

Program Background: This program studies society, institutions, and social relationships, as well as how interactions and changes influence and impact these relationships.

Completion Requirements: You must successfully complete 120 credit hours for this degree.

Example Course Titles: Some of the course titles in this program include The Family in World Perspective and Research Methods in the Social Sciences.

University Diploma in Arts

Degree Offered: Certificate

Program Web Address: www.athabascau.ca/html/programs/u_cert/udip

Application Requirements: Please see the appropriate Web site for information about this program and its application requirements.

Program Contact: Office of the Registrar
Athabasca University
1 University Drive
Athabasca, Alberta, Canada T9S 3A3
(800) 788-9041
auinfo2@athabascau.ca

University Diploma in Inclusive Education

Degree Offered: Certificate

Program Web Address: www.athabascau.ca/html/programs/u_cert/udip

Application Requirements: Please see the appropriate Web site for information about this program and its application requirements.

Program Contact: Office of the Registrar
Athabasca University
1 University Drive
Athabasca, Alberta, Canada T9S 3A3
(800) 788-9041
auinfo2@athabascau.ca

Women's Studies

Degree Offered: Bachelor of Arts in Women's Studies

Completion Requirements: You must successfully complete 120 credit hours for this degree.

Example Course Titles: Some of the course titles in this program include Perspectives on Women: An Introduction to Women's Studies, Anthropology of Gender, Economics of Inequality and Poverty, Women in Literature, The Women's West: Women and Canadian Frontier Settlement, Women and the Family in Urban Canada, 1880s-1940s, The History of the Family in Western Europe: From the Middle Ages to the Industrial Revolution, Women and Unions, Aboriginal Women in Canadian Contemporary Society, Introduction to Canadian Political Economy, Issues and Strategies in Counselling Women, The Family in World Perspective, and Women and Work in Canada.

ATLANTIC CAPE COMMUNITY COLLEGE

General Contact Information

5100 Black Horse Pike
Mays Landing, New Jersey 08330

Phone: (609) 343-5000

FAX: (609) 343-5122
E-mail: wall@atlantic.edu
WWW: www.atlantic.edu

Online Learning Information

5100 Black Horse Pike
Mays Landing, New Jersey 08330

Phone: (609) 343-4987
FAX: (609) 343-5122
E-mail: wall@atlantic.edu
WWW: www.atlantic.edu

Institution Background

Atlantic Cape Community College (ACCC) is an accredited community college that has an open-admission policy and offers three degrees online. Tuition and fees are $80 per credit.

Founded: 1978
Type of Institution: Public
Accreditation: Middle States Association of Colleges and Schools

Online Course Background: As of the fall 1999, ACCC had 30 course sections and three Associate's degree programs that could be completed online. The degree programs are in liberal arts, history, and business. The online courses use WebCT or First Class.

Online Course Offered: 36

Online Students Enrolled: 600

Special Programs/Partnerships: ACCC is a member of the New Jersey Virtual Community College Consortium.

Services Offered to Students: ACCC offers online registration, book ordering, access to the library, and online tutoring.

Financial Aid: Students enrolled in online courses and programs of study at ACCC may be eligible to receive financial aid through stan-

dard federal and New Jersey assistance programs.

Registration: You can register for courses via mail, phone, and the World Wide Web.

Programs
Liberal Arts

Degree Offered: Associate of Arts in Liberal Arts

Program Web Address: atlantic.edu

Online Program Started: 1996

Application Requirements: You are required to take an entrance examination for admission into this program.

Program Restrictions: You must be able to read and write English.

Completion Requirements: You must successfully complete 64 credits for this degree.

On Campus Requirements: There are no on-campus requirements.

System Requirements: You need to have a computer and an Internet Service Provider.

Example Course Titles: Some of the course titles in this program include English Communications, U.S. History, and General Psychology.

Program Contact: Mary Wall
5100 Black Horse Pike
Mays Landing, New Jersey 08330
(609) 343-4987
(609) 343-5122
wall@atlantic.edu

BAKER COLLEGE
General Contact Information

1050 West Bristol Road

Flint, Michigan 48507

Phone: (810) 766-4000
FAX: (810) 766-4049
E-mail: info@baker.edu
WWW: www.baker.edu

Online Learning Information

Baker College On-Line
1050 West Bristol Road
Flint, Michigan 48507

Phone: (800) 469-3165
FAX: (810) 766-4399
E-mail: online@baker.edu
WWW: www.baker.edu/online/main.html

Institution Background

Founded: 1888
Accreditation: North Central Association of Colleges and Schools

Programs
Business Administration

Degree Offered: Certificate

Program Web Address: www.baker.edu/catalog/OnlinePrograms/prodev.html

Application Requirements: You must complete and submit an application (which is available online), and include a short essay on your future objectives and three letters of recommendation.

You need to have experience using computers, including installing software and using a word processor. You will be required to complete a technical orientation before you can register for your first online course.

Program Restrictions: You can't take more than two online courses during any six-week period.

Completion Requirements: You must successfully complete 20 credit hours to earn this certificate.

System Requirements: You will need to have a computer with a Pentium 100 or higher processor, Windows 95 or Windows 98, a minimum of 32 MB of RAM, a 3.5 high-density floppy drive, a 14.4 modem or faster, a CD-ROM drive, word processor (Microsoft Word 97 preferred), Internet Service Provider, and Netscape Navigator 4.0 or Microsoft Internet Explorer 4.0 (or higher). Baker College strongly recommends that you have Microsoft Office 97. If you prefer, you can use a Macintosh system that addresses the preceding requirements.

Example Course Titles: Some of the course titles in this program include Compensation and Benefits, Labor and Industrial Relations, Personnel and Staff Selection, and Training and Development.

Program Contact: Center for Graduate Studies
Baker College
1050 W. Bristol Road
Flint, Michigan 48507
(800) 469-3165
(810) 766-4399
gradschl@baker.edu

Business Administration

Degree Offered: Bachelor of Business Administration

Program Web Address: www.baker.edu/catalog/OnlinePrograms/bbaaccelerated.html

Program Background: This Bachelor of Business Administration program is designed for the working professional. It combines core coursework with independent research and experiential credit to provide an accelerated contemporary business degree. As part of the program, students create an experiential credit portfolio.

Application Requirements: You must have an associate's degree or have 90 quarter credit-hours to apply to the program.

Completion Requirements: You must successfully complete 180 quarter hours for this degree.

System Requirements: You should have a personal computer with a Pentium 100 MHz processor (or higher), Windows 95/98, 32 MB of RAM (minimum), 3.5″ high density floppy drive, 14.4 modem or higher, a CD-ROM drive, Word Processor (preferably Microsoft Word 97), Internet Service Provider, and a Web browser (Netscape Navigator 4.0 or Internet Explorer 4.0 or higher). The school also strongly recommends that you have Microsoft Office 97. If you prefer, you may use a Macintosh system that is equivalent to the PC just described.

Example Course Titles: Some of the course titles in this program include Accounting for Managers, Human Behavior in Organizations, Information Systems in Management, Leadership and Management, Marketing Management, Management Strategy, Applied Economics, Methods of Research, and Organizational Communication.

Program Contact: Baker College On-Line
1050 W. Bristol Road
Flint, Michigan 48507
(800) 469-4062

Business Administration

Degree Offered: Master of Business Administration

Program Web Address: www.baker.edu/catalog/GradPrograms/mbatraditional.html

Program Background: This program combines conventional academic training with field-based learning. The curriculum covers accounting, computers, finance, communications, ethics, marketing, and management.

Program Restrictions: You cannot take more than two online courses during any six week period, and you must complete a technical orientation before registering for your first online course.

Completion Requirements: You must successfully complete 60 credit hours for this degree.

System Requirements: You should have a personal computer with a Pentium 100 MHz processor (or higher), Windows 95/98, 32 MB of RAM (minimum), 3.5″ high density floppy drive, 14.4 modem or faster, a CD-ROM drive, word processor (preferably Microsoft Word 97), Internet Service Provider, and a Web browser (Netscape Navigator 4.0 or Internet Explorer 4.0 or higher). The school also strongly recommends that you have Microsoft Office 97. If you prefer, you may use a Macintosh system that is equivalent to the PC just described.

Example Course Titles: Some of the course titles in this program include Human Resources Management, Human Behavior in the Management of Organizations, Accounting for the Contemporary Manager, Financial Environment of Business, Economic Environment of Business, Marketing Environment of Business, Management Information Systems, Research and Statistics for Managers, and Strategy in a Global Environment.

Program Contact: Baker College
Center for Graduate Studies
1050 W. Bristol Road
Flint, Michigan 48507
(800) 469-3165
(810) 766-4399

gradschl@baker.edu

Business Administration— Human Resource Management

Degree Offered: Master of Business Administration

Program Web Address: www.baker.edu/catalog/GradPrograms/hrmbaccmodels.htm

Program Background: This Master of Business Administration (MBA) program has a Human Resources Management concentration and is designed specifically for people who work within a personnel or human resources area. Students will receive exposure to issues that Human Resources personnel encounter on a daily basis.

Application Requirements: You must complete and submit an application (which is available online), and include a short essay on your future objectives and three letters of recommendation.

You need to have experience using computers, including installing software and using a word processor. You will be required to complete a technical orientation before you can register for your first online course.

Program Restrictions: You can't take more than two online courses during any six-week period.

Completion Requirements: You must successfully complete 50 credit hours for this degree.

System Requirements: You will need to have a computer with a Pentium 100 or higher processor, Windows 95 or Windows 98, a minimum of 32 MB of RAM, a 3.5″ high-density floppy drive, a 14.4 modem or faster, a CD-ROM drive, word processor (Microsoft Word 97 preferred), Internet Service Provider, and Netscape Navigator 4.0 or Microsoft Internet Explorer 4.0 (or higher). Baker College strongly recommends that you have Microsoft Office

97. If you prefer, you can use a Macintosh system that addresses the preceding requirements.

Example Course Titles: Some of the course titles include Human Resources Management, Human Behavior in the Management of Organizations, Financial Environment of Business, Marketing Environment of Business, Management Information Systems, and Strategy in a Global Environment.

Program Contact: Center for Graduate Studies
Baker College
1050 W. Bristol Road
Flint, Michigan 48507
(800) 469-3165
(810) 766-4399
gradschl@baker.edu

Computer Information Systems

Degree Offered: Certificate

Program Web Address: www.baker.edu/catalog/OnlinePrograms/prodev.html

Application Requirements: You should have some computer experience, knowing how to load software and use a word processor. You must submit an application with a short essay on your future objectives and three letters of recommendation.

Program Restrictions: You may not take more than two online courses during any six week period, and you are required to complete a technical orientation before you can register for your first online class.

Completion Requirements: You must successfully complete 20 credit hours.

System Requirements: You should have a personal computer with a Pentium 100 MHz processor (or higher), Windows 95/98, 32 MB of RAM (minimum), 3.5″ high density floppy drive, 14.4 modem or faster, a CD-ROM drive, word processor (preferably Microsoft Word 97), Internet Service Provider, and a Web browser (Netscape Navigator 4.0 or Internet Explorer 4.0 or higher). The school also strongly recommends that you have Microsoft Office 97. If you prefer, you may use a Macintosh system that is equivalent to the PC just described.

Example Course Titles: Some of the course titles in this program include Decision Support and Expert Systems, Applied Database Management Systems, The Design of Information Systems, Telecommunications and Computer Networks, and Information Resource Management.

Program Contact: Baker College
Center for Graduate Studies
1050 W. Bristol Road
Flint, Michigan 48507
(800) 469-3165
(810) 766-4399
gradschl@baker.edu

Computer Information Systems

Degree Offered: Master of Business Administration

Program Web Address: www.baker.edu/catalog/GradPrograms/cismbaccmodels.htm

Program Background: This program is designed for managers who work with and understand the Information Resources of their companies. Students are exposed to very specific Information Management issues which confront managers every day.

Application Requirements: You should have some computer experience, knowing how to load software and use a word processor. You must submit an application with a short essay on your future objectives, and three letters of recommendation.

Program Restrictions: You may not take more than two online courses during any six week period and you are required to complete a technical orientation before you can register for your first online class.

Completion Requirements: You must successfully complete 50 credit hours.

System Requirements: You should have a personal computer with a Pentium 100 MHz processor (or higher), Windows 95/98, 32 MB of RAM (minimum), 3.5″ high-density floppy drive, 14.4 modem or faster, a CD-ROM drive, word processor (preferably Microsoft Word 97), Internet Service Provider, and a Web browser (Netscape Navigator 4.0 or Internet Explorer 4.0 or higher). The school also strongly recommends that you have Microsoft Office 97. If you prefer, you may use a Macintosh system that is equivalent to the PC just described.

Example Course Titles: Some of the course titles in this program include Human Resources Management, Human Behavior in the Management of Organizations, Accounting for the Contemporary Manager, Financial Environment of Business, The Economics Environment of Business, The Marketing Environment of Business, Management Information Systems, Research and Statistics for Managers, Strategy in a Global Environment, and Decision Support and Expert Systems.

Program Contact: Baker College Center for Graduate Studies
1050 W. Bristol Road
Flint, Michigan 48507
(800) 469-3165
(810) 766-4399
gradschl@baker.edu

Economic Development

Degree Offered: Certificate

Program Web Address: www.baker.edu/catalog/OnlinePrograms/prodev.html

Application Requirements: You should have some computer experience, knowing how to load software and use a word processor. You must submit an application with a short essay on your future objectives and three letters of recommendation.

Program Restrictions: You may not take more than two online courses during any six week period and you are required to complete a technical orientation before you can register for your first online class.

Completion Requirements: You must successfully complete 20 credit hours.

System Requirements: You should have a personal computer with a Pentium 100 MHz processor (or higher), Windows 95/98, 32 MB of RAM (minimum), 3.5″ high-density floppy drive, 14.4 modem or faster, a CD-ROM drive, word processor (preferably Microsoft Word 97), Internet Service Provider, and a Web browser (Netscape Navigator 4.0 or Internet Explorer 4.0 or higher). The school also strongly recommends that you have Microsoft Office 97. If you prefer, you may use a Macintosh system that is equivalent to the PC just described.

Example Course Titles: Some of the course titles in this program include Dynamics of Leadership, Leadership Theory and Practice, Evolution of Management and Leadership Thought, Profiles in Leadership, and Team Leadership/Group Dynamics.

Program Contact: Baker College
Center for Graduate Studies
1050 W. Bristol Road
Flint, Michigan 48507
(800) 469-3165
(810) 766-4399
gradschl@baker.edu

General Business

Degree Offered: Associate of Business Administration

Program Web Address: www.baker.edu/catalog/OnlinePrograms/genbusaba.html

Program Background: This program is designed for students who want a good background of business facts and knowledge upon which to build a career in business.

Application Requirements: You must have a high school diploma or equivalent. If you don't meet this requirement, you may be admitted based on test results.

Completion Requirements: You must successfully complete 96 quarter hours.

System Requirements: You should have a personal computer with a Pentium 100 MHz processor (or higher), Windows 95/98, 32 MB of RAM (minimum), 3.5″ high-density floppy drive, 14.4 modem or faster, a CD-ROM drive, Word Processor (preferably Microsoft Word 97), Internet Service Provider, and a Web browser (Netscape Navigator 4.0 or Internet Explorer 4.0 or higher). The school also strongly recommends that you have Microsoft Office 97. If you prefer, you may use a Macintosh system that is equivalent to the PC just described.

Example Course Titles: Some of the course titles in this program include Management and Supervision, Human Resource Management, Management Seminar, Small Business Management, Principle of Marketing, Sales, Advertising, Applied Marketing, Fundamentals of Accounting, Principles of Macroeconomics, Principles of Microeconomics, Business Law, Composition, Introductory Algebra, and Business Communications.

Program Contact: Baker College
Baker College On-Line
1050 W. Bristol Road
Flint, Michigan 48507
(800) 469-4062

Health Care Management

Degree Offered: Certificate

Program Web Address: www.baker.edu/ catalog/OnlinePrograms/prodev.html

Application Requirements: You should have some computer experience, knowing how to load software and use a word processor. You must submit an application with a short essay on your future objectives and three letters of recommendation.

Program Restrictions: You may not take more than two online courses during any six week period, and you are required to complete a technical orientation before you can register for your first online class.

Completion Requirements: You must successfully complete 20 credit hours.

System Requirements: You should have a personal computer with a Pentium 100 MHz processor (or higher), Windows 95/98, 32 MB of RAM (minimum), 3.5″ high-density floppy drive, 14.4 modem or faster, a CD-ROM drive, Word Processor (preferably Microsoft Word 97), Internet Service Provider, and a Web browser (Netscape Navigator 4.0 or Internet Explorer 4.0 or higher). The school also strongly recommends that you have Microsoft Office 97. If you prefer, you may use a Macintosh system that is equivalent to the PC just described.

Example Course Titles: Some of the course titles in this program include Foundations of Health and Wellness, Quality Utilization Review, Principles and Practices of Health Care Administration, Organization and Management Of Health/Wellness Programs, and Current Topics in Health Care.

Program Contact: Baker College
Center for Graduate Studies
1050 W. Bristol Road
Flint, Michigan 48507

(800) 469-3165
(810) 766-4399
gradschl@baker.edu

Health Care Management

Degree Offered: Master of Business Administration

Program Web Address: www.baker.edu/ catalog/GradPrograms/healthcarembaccmo

Program Background: This program integrates academic training and field-based learning, with an emphasis on the allied health field. Students learn about costs, services, and quality of health care. The curriculum covers most business disciplines and is intended to help students improve their management skills.

Application Requirements: You should have some computer experience, knowing how to load software and use a word processor. You must submit an application with a short essay on your future objectives and three letters of recommendation.

Program Restrictions: You may not take more than two online courses during any six week period and you are required to complete a technical orientation before you can register for your first online class.

Completion Requirements: You must successfully complete 50 credit hours.

System Requirements: You should have a personal computer with a Pentium 100 MHz processor (or higher), Windows 95/98, 32 MB of RAM (minimum), 3.5″ high-density floppy drive, 14.4 modem or faster, a CD-ROM drive, word processor (preferably Microsoft Word 97), Internet Service Provider, and a Web browser (Netscape Navigator 4.0 or Internet Explorer 4.0 or higher). The school also strongly recommends that you have Microsoft Office 97. If you prefer, you may use a Macintosh system that is equivalent to the PC just described.

Example Course Titles: Some of the course titles in this program include Human Resources Management, Human Behavior in the Management of Organizations, Accounting for the Contemporary Manager, Financial Environment of Business, The Economics Environment of Business, The Marketing Environment of Business, Management Information Systems, Research and Statistics for Managers, Strategy in a Global Environment, Foundations of Health and Wellness, Quality Utilization Review, Principles and Practices of Health Care Administration, Organization and Management of Health/Wellness Programs, and Current Topics in Health Care.

Program Contact: Baker College
Center for Graduate Studies
1050 W. Bristol Road
Flint, Michigan 48507
(800) 469-3165
(810) 766-4399
gradschl@baker.edu

Industrial Management

Degree Offered: Certificate

Program Web Address: www.baker.edu/catalog/OnlinePrograms/prodev.html

Application Requirements: You must complete and submit an application (which is available online), and include a short essay on your future objectives and three letters of recommendation.

You need to have experience using computers, including installing software and using a word processor. You will be required to complete a technical orientation before you can register for your first online course.

Program Restrictions: You can't take more than two online courses during any six-week period.

Completion Requirements: You must successfully complete 20 credit hours for this certificate.

System Requirements: You will need to have a computer with a Pentium 100 or higher processor, Windows 95 or Windows 98, a minimum of 32 MB of RAM, a 3.5 high-density floppy drive, a 14.4 modem or faster, a CD-ROM drive, word processor (Microsoft Word 97 preferred), Internet Service Provider, and Netscape Navigator 4.0 or Microsoft Internet Explorer 4.0 (or higher). Baker College strongly recommends that you have Microsoft Office 97. If you prefer, you can use a Macintosh system that addresses the preceding requirements.

Example Course Titles: Some of the course titles in this program include Multicriteria Decision Making, Manufacturing and Quality Assurance, Management of CIM Systems, Production Control, and Production/Operations Management.

Program Contact: Center for Graduate Studies
Baker College
1050 W. Bristol Road
Flint, Michigan 48507
(800) 469-3165
(810) 766-4399
gradschl@baker.edu

Industrial Management

Degree Offered: Master of Business Administration

Program Web Address: www.baker.edu/catalog/GradPrograms/indmgtmbaccmodel

Program Background: Baker College's Industrial Management program has been designed to complement the undergraduate degrees of many of the students who are enrolled in the program and who work in manufacturing and industrial corporations in Michigan. The program has core MBA courses and manufacturing-oriented courses.

Application Requirements: You must complete and submit an application (which is available online), and include a short essay on your future objectives and three letters of recommendation.

You need to have experience using computers, including installing software and using a word processor. You will be required to complete a technical orientation before you can register for your first online course.

Program Restrictions: You can't take more than two online courses during any six-week period.

Completion Requirements: You must successfully complete 50 credit hours for this degree.

System Requirements: You will need to have a computer with a Pentium 100 or higher processor, Windows 95 or Windows 98, a minimum of 32 MB of RAM, a 3.5 high-density floppy drive, a 14.4 modem or faster, a CD-ROM drive, word processor (Microsoft Word 97 preferred), Internet Service Provider, and Netscape Navigator 4.0 or Microsoft Internet Explorer 4.0 (or higher). Baker College strongly recommends that you have Microsoft Office 97. If you prefer, you can use a Macintosh system that addresses the preceding requirements.

Example Course Titles: Some of the course titles in this program include Human Resources Management, Human Behavior in the Management of Organizations, Accounting for the Contemporary Manager, Financial Environment of Business, The Marketing Environment of Business, Management Information Systems, Research and Statistics for Managers, and Strategy in a Global Environment.

Program Contact: Center for Graduate Studies
Baker College
1050 W. Bristol Road
Flint, Michigan 48507
(800) 469-3165
(810) 766-4399

gradschl@baker.edu

Integrated Health Care

Degree Offered: Certificate

Program Web Address: www.baker.edu/ catalog/OnlinePrograms/prodev.html

Application Requirements: You must complete and submit an application (which is available online), and include a short essay on your future objectives and three letters of recommendation.

You need to have experience using computers, including installing software and using a word processor. You will be required to complete a technical orientation before you can register for your first online course.

Program Restrictions: You can't take more than two online courses during any six-week period.

Completion Requirements: You must successfully complete 32 credit hours for this degree.

System Requirements: You will need to have a computer with a Pentium 100 or higher processor, Windows 95 or Windows 98, a minimum of 32 MB of RAM, a 3.5 high-density floppy drive, a 14.4 modem or faster, a CD-ROM drive, word processor (Microsoft Word 97 preferred), Internet Service Provider, and Netscape Navigator 4.0 or Microsoft Internet Explorer 4.0 (or higher). Baker College strongly recommends that you have Microsoft Office 97. If you prefer, you can use a Macintosh system that addresses the preceding requirements.

Example Course Titles: Some of the course titles in this program include Healthier Communities, Administrative and Clinical Challenges in American Health Care, Introduction to Holistic Health Care, Psychological and Physiological Interface, Integrative Therapies, and Development and Management of Integrated Medicine Centers.

Program Contact: Center for Graduate Studies
Baker College
1050 W. Bristol Road
Flint, Michigan 48507
(800) 469-3165
(810) 766-4399
gradschl@baker.edu

Integrated Health Care

Degree Offered: Master of Business Administration

Program Web Address: www.baker.edu/ catalog/GradPrograms/integratedhealthmba

Program Background: This Master's program was designed to address the needs of entrepreneurs who want to start businesses in the health field, people who want to manage health facilities, and people who are seeking employment and promotion in the health field. While extensive coverage of the core business administration is provided, emphasis is placed on entrepreneurial and systems approaches to health.

Application Requirements: You must complete and submit an application (which is available online), and include a short essay on your future objectives and three letters of recommendation.

You need to have experience using computers, including installing software and using a word processor. You will be required to complete a technical orientation before you can register for your first online course.

Program Restrictions: You can't take more than two online courses during any six-week period.

Completion Requirements: You must successfully complete 60 credit hours for this degree.

System Requirements: You will need to have a computer with a Pentium 100 or higher processor, Windows 95 or Windows 98, a minimum of 32 MB of RAM, a 3.5 high-density floppy drive, a 14.4 modem or faster, a CD-ROM drive, word processor (Microsoft Word 97 preferred), Internet Service Provider, and Netscape Navigator 4.0 or Microsoft Internet Explorer 4.0 (or higher). Baker College strongly recommends that you have Microsoft Office 97. If you prefer, you can use a Macintosh system that addresses the preceding requirements.

Example Course Titles: Some of the course titles in this program include Human Behavior in the Management of Organizations, Economics Environment of Business, Management Information Systems, Research and Statistics for Managers, Strategy in a Global Environment, Transformational Leadership, Introduction to Holistic Health Care, and Maintaining Health in Human and Organizational Structures.

Program Contact: Center for Graduate Studies
Baker College
1050 W. Bristol Road
Flint, Michigan 48507
(800) 469-3165
(810) 766-4399
gradschl@baker.edu

International Business

Degree Offered: Certificate

Program Web Address: www.baker.edu/ catalog/OnlinePrograms/prodev.html

Application Requirements: You must complete and submit an application (which is available online), and include a short essay on your future objectives and three letters of recommendation.

You need to have experience using computers, including installing software and using word processors. You will be required to complete a technical orientation before you can register for your first online course.

Program Restrictions: You can't take more than two online courses during any six-week period.

Completion Requirements: You must successfully complete 20 credit hours for this degree.

System Requirements: You will need to have a computer with a Pentium 100 or higher processor, Windows 95 or Windows 98, a minimum of 32 MB of RAM, a 3.5 high-density floppy drive, a 14.4 modem or faster, a CD-ROM drive, word processor (Microsoft Word 97 preferred), Internet Service Provider, and Netscape Navigator 4.0 or Microsoft Internet Explorer 4.0 (or higher). Baker College strongly recommends that you have Microsoft Office 97. If you prefer, you can use a Macintosh system that addresses the preceding requirements.

Example Course Titles: Some of the course titles in this program include Multinational Business Management, Multinational Business Finance, International Trade, and Economic Development.

Program Contact: Baker College
Center for Graduate Studies
1050 W. Bristol Road
Flint, Michigan 48507
(800) 469-3165
(810) 766-4399
gradschl@baker.edu

International Business

Degree Offered: Master of Business Administration

Program Web Address: www.baker.edu/ catalog/GradPrograms/intlbusinessccmodel

Program Background: Students get an in-depth study of modern concepts, principles, analytic techniques, and problem-solving techniques in this program. Courses require students to actively participate in discussions about practical business applications, current events, case studies, and other learning activities.

Application Requirements: You must complete and submit an application (which is available online), and include a short essay on your future objectives and three letters of recommendation.

You need to have experience using computers and installing software. You will be required to complete a technical orientation before you can register for your first online course.

Program Restrictions: You can't take more than two online courses during any six-week period.

Completion Requirements: You must successfully complete 50 credit hours for this degree.

System Requirements: You will need to have a computer with a Pentium 100 or higher processor, Windows 95 or Windows 98, a minimum of 32 MB of RAM, a 3.5 high-density floppy drive, a 14.4 modem or faster, a CD-ROM drive, word processor (Microsoft Word 97 preferred), Internet Service Provider, and Netscape Navigator 4.0 or Microsoft Internet Explorer 4.0 (or higher). Baker College strongly recommends that you have Microsoft Office 97. If you prefer, you can use a Macintosh system that addresses the preceding requirements.

Example Course Titles: Some of the course titles in this program include Human Resources Management, Human Behavior in the Management of Organizations, Accounting for the Contemporary Manager, Financial Environment of Business, Management Information Systems, Research and Statistics for Managers, Strategy in a Global Environment, and Integration Portfolio.

Program Contact: Baker College
Center for Graduate Studies
1050 W. Bristol Road
Flint, Michigan 48507
(800) 469-3165
(810) 766-4399

gradschl@baker.edu

Leadership Studies

Degree Offered: Master of Business Administration

Program Web Address: www.baker.edu/catalog/GradPrograms/leadershipmbaccmo

Program Background: This program is designed for students who seek promotion to upper-level administrative and management positions. It incorporates core MBA courses, and courses focusing on specific leadership issues and theories. The goal is to prepare students with vision and problem-solving skills so they can effectively lead an organization in today's society.

Application Requirements: You must complete and submit an application (which is available online), and include a short essay on your future objectives and three letters of recommendation.

You need to have experience using computers, including installing software and using a word processor. You will be required to complete a technical orientation before you can register for your first online course.

Program Restrictions: You can't take more than two online courses during any six-week period.

Completion Requirements: You must successfully complete 50 credit hours for this degree.

System Requirements: You will need to have a computer with a Pentium 100 or higher processor, Windows 95 or Windows 98, a minimum of 32 MB of RAM, a 3.5 high-density floppy drive, a 14.4 modem or faster, a CD-ROM drive, word processor (Microsoft Word 97 preferred), Internet Service Provider, and Netscape Navigator 4.0 or Microsoft Internet Explorer 4.0 (or higher). Baker College strongly recommends that you have Microsoft Office 97. If you prefer, you can use a Macintosh system that addresses the preceding requirements.

Example Course Titles: Some course titles in this program include Human Resources Management, Graduate Seminar, Human Behavior in the Management of Organizations, Accounting for the Contemporary Manager, Financial Environment of Business, Management Information Systems, Research and Statistics for Managers, and Strategy in a Global Environment.

Program Contact: Baker College
Center for Graduate Studies
1050 W. Bristol Road
Flint, Michigan 48507
(800) 469-3165
(810) 766-4399
gradschl@baker.edu

Marketing

Degree Offered: Certificate

Program Web Address: www.baker.edu/catalog/OnlinePrograms/prodev.html

Application Requirements: You must complete and submit an application (which is available online), and include a short essay on your future objectives and three letters of recommendation.

You need to have experience using computers, including installing software and using a word processor. You will be required to complete a technical orientation before you can register for your first online course.

Program Restrictions: You can't take more than two online courses during any six-week period.

Completion Requirements: You must successfully complete 20 credit hours for this degree.

System Requirements: You will need to have a computer with a Pentium 100 or higher processor, Windows 95 or Windows 98, a minimum of 32 MB of RAM, a 3.5 high-density floppy drive, a 14.4 modem or faster, a CD-ROM drive, word processor (Microsoft Word 97 preferred), Internet Service Provider, and Netscape Navigator 4.0 or Microsoft Internet Explorer 4.0 (or higher). Baker College strongly recommends that you have Microsoft Office 97. If you prefer, you can use a Macintosh system that addresses the preceding requirements.

Example Course Titles: Some of the course titles in this program include Marketing Environment, International Marketing, Marketing Strategy, Promotional Management, and Marketing Research.

Program Contact: Baker College
Center for Graduate Studies
1050 W. Bristol Road
Flint, Michigan 48507
(800) 469-3165
(810) 766-4399
gradschl@baker.edu

Marketing

Degree Offered: Master of Business Administration

Program Web Address: www.baker.edu/catalog/GradPrograms/marketingmbaccmo

Program Background: This Baker College's Master of Business Administration degree program is designed for student who work in marketing, advertising, or public relations. Students are required to take core courses in business administration, as well as courses that expose them to current marketing issues.

Application Requirements: You must complete and submit an application (which is available online), and include a short essay on your future objectives and three letters of recommendation.

You need to have experience using computers, including installing software and using a word processor. You will be required to com-

plete a technical orientation before you can register for your first online course.

Program Restrictions: You can't take more than two online courses during any six-week period.

Completion Requirements: You must successfully complete 50 credit hours for this degree.

System Requirements: You will need to have a computer with a Pentium 100 or higher processor, Windows 95 or Windows 98, a minimum of 32 MB of RAM, a 3.5 high-density floppy drive, a 14.4 modem or faster, a CD-ROM drive, word processor (Microsoft Word 97 preferred), Internet Service Provider, and Netscape Navigator 4.0 or Microsoft Internet Explorer 4.0 (or higher). Baker College strongly recommends that you have Microsoft Office 97. If you prefer, you can use a Macintosh system that addresses the preceding requirements.

Example Course Titles: Some of the course titles in this program include Human Resources Management, Human Behavior in the Management of Organizations, Accounting for the Contemporary Manager, Financial Environment of Business, Management Information Systems, Research and Statistics for Managers, and Strategy in a Global Environment.

Program Contact: Baker College
Center for Graduate Studies
1050 W. Bristol Road
Flint, Michigan 48507
(800) 469-3165
(810) 766-4399
gradschl@baker.edu

BARTON COUNTY COMMUNITY COLLEGE

General Contact Information

245 NE 30th Road

Great Bend, Kansas 67530

Phone: (316) 792-2701 ext. 241
FAX: (316) 792-3238
WWW: www.barton.cc.ks.us

Online Learning Information

WWW: www.bartonline.org

Institution Background

Founded: 1965
Type of Institution: Public
Accreditation: North Central Association of Colleges and Schools

Programs
General Studies

Degree Offered: Associate in General Studies

Program Web Address: bartonline.org/index.real?action=Courses&subaction=Militar

Program Background: Barton County Community College's General Studies program is designed for members of the Armed Forces who are looking for long-term advancement in the military and non-active duty students who are simply interested in military history.

Completion Requirements: You must successfully complete 66 credit hours, 15 of which must be completed through Barton County Community College. And you must maintain an overall grade point average of 2.0 or higher.

Example Course Titles: Some of the course titles in this program include Technical Report Writing, Fundamentals of Speech, Introduction to Philosophy, General Psychology, Leadership and Management, Total Quality Management, American Military History, American West, Military History of the American Revolution, Military History of the Civil War, and World and Regional Geography.

Program Contact: Barton County Community College
P.O. Box 2463
Fort Riley, Kansas 66442
(785) 239-0404
militaryadmissions@bartonline.org

BELLEVUE UNIVERSITY

General Contact Information

1000 Galvin Road South
Bellevue, Nebraska 68005-3098

Phone: (402) 293-3766
FAX: (402) 293-3730
E-mail: bellevue_u@scholars.bellevue.edu
WWW: www.bellevue.edu

Online Learning Information

100 Galvin Road South
Bellevue, Nebraska 68005

Phone: (800) 756-7920
FAX: (402) 293-2020
E-mail: bellevue_u@scholars.bellevue.edu
WWW: http://www.bellevue.edu/Framesets/online/startfs.html

Institution Background

Founded: 1966
Type of Institution: Private
Accreditation: North Central Association of Colleges and Schools

Financial Aid: For more information:
Financial Aid/Veteran Services:
(402) 293-3762 or (800) 756-7920
FAX: (402) 293-2062

e-mail: finaid@scholars.bellevue.edu

Programs

Business Administration

Degree Offered: Master of Business Administration

Program Web Address: www.bellevue.edu/ Non_trad/Grad/buo_mba.htm

Program Background: Students enrolled in this program gain a broad understanding of the tools and methods necessary to effectively run a business.

Application Requirements: You must have a bachelor's degree from a regionally accredited college or university, three years of relevant work experience, a minimum grade point average of 2.5 on the last 60 credit hours of your undergraduate study, and a minimum grade point average of 3.0 on any prior graduate work. You need to submit an application with your responses to questions contained in the application packet and two letters of recommendation.

Completion Requirements: You must successfully complete 36 credit hours for this degree.

Time for Completion: Students typically complete this program within 18 months. Courses are 12-weeks long—designed to facilitate rapid progress toward completion of the degree.

Example Course Titles: Some of the course titles in this program include Quantitative Methods, Consumer Behavior, Survey of Business Processes and Functions, Survey of Accounting and Information Systems, Applied Production and Operations Management, Advanced Organizational Behavior, Marketing Strategy, Survey of Statistics and Quantitative Methods, and Survey of the Environment of Business.

Program Contact: Bellevue University (800) 756-7920

Business Information Systems

Degree Offered: Bachelor of Science

Program Web Address: www.bellevue.edu/ Non_trad/Under/buo_bis.htm

Program Background: This program develops students who are "knowledge workers" or individuals who use business and technology knowledge, intellectual capacity, computer-related skills to accomplish special tasks.

Application Requirements: You must have an Associate's degree or 60 transferable semester hours from an accredited institution of higher education, a minimum grade point average of C in all courses you want to transfer, be employed a minimum of 30 hours per week, and have three years of significant work experience relevant to the program. You need to submit an application with application fee.

Completion Requirements: You must successfully complete 127 credit hours for this degree.

Example Course Titles: Some of the course titles in this program include Career Management, Systems Thinking, Management—Project/Fiscal, Enterprise and Strategic, Programming Fundamentals, Database Concepts, Business Telecommunications, Internet Marketing, Legal and Ethical Issues, and Current Trends in Information Technology.

Program Contact: (800) 756-7920

Global Business Management

Degree Offered: Bachelor of Science

Program Web Address: www.bellevue.edu/ Non_trad/Under/buo_gbm.htm

Program Background: This program prepares students to evaluate international business opportunities, develop action plans for potential business activities, and manage multi-national activities.

Application Requirements: You must have an associate's degree or 60 transferable semester hours from an accredited institution of higher education, a minimum grade point average of C in all courses you want to transfer, be employed a minimum of 30 hours per week, and have three years of significant work experience relevant to the program. You need to submit an application with application fee.

Completion Requirements: You must successfully complete 127 credit hours.

Example Course Titles: Some of the course titles in this program include Cultural Geography, Probability and Statistics, and Marketing Research and Communication.

Program Contact: (800) 756-7920

Leadership

Degree Offered: Master of Arts

Program Web Address: www.bellevue.edu/ Non_trad/Grad/buo_mal.htm

Program Background: Bellevue University's Master of Arts in Leadership program encourages individual thought and teaches how to synthesize group contributions and assimilate practical and theoretical teachings.

Application Requirements: You need to have a bachelor's degree from a regionally accredited college or university (or the equivalent). You also need to have at least a 2.5 grade point average (on a 4.0 scale) on the last 60 credit hours of your undergraduate program or a 3.0 or higher grade point average on any prior graduate work, and three years of work experience

(or the equivalent). You must complete and submit an application, official college transcripts, responses to questions in the application packet (regarding life and work experiences), and two letters of recommendation (professional or academic). You may be required to interview with the Graduate Admissions and Standards Committee.

Completion Requirements: You must successfully complete 36 credit hours for this degree.

Example Course Titles: Some of the course titles in this program include Concepts of Leadership, Leadership in Formal Organizational Systems, Strategic Leadership Communication, Team Group Dynamics, and Organizational Change and Development Leadership.

Program Contact: (800) 756-7920

Criminal Justice Administration

Degree Offered: Bachelor of Science

Program Web Address: www.bellevue.edu/ Non_trad/Under/buo_cja.htm

Program Background: This program is designed for students who are employed in the field and who are entering management roles. The curriculum covers budgeting, strategic planning, information systems, and facilities issues.

Application Requirements: You must have an associate's degree or 60 transferable semester hours from an accredited institution of higher education, a minimum grade point average of C in all courses you want to transfer, be employed a minimum of 30 hours per week, and have three years of significant work experience relevant to the program. You need to submit an application with application fee.

Completion Requirements: You must successfully complete 127 credit hours for this degree.

Example Course Titles: Some of the course titles in this program include Overview of the Criminal Justice System, Research and Statistics, Management Principles for Criminal Justice, Ethics, Policy and Law in Criminal Justice, Criminal Justice Studies, Criminal Justice Human Resource Allocation, Facility and Material Management of Criminal Justice, Criminal Justice Agency Accounting/Finance, Information Management in Criminal Justice, Strategic and Tactical Planning Systems, Special Topics in Criminal Justice, and Special Problems in Criminal Justice.

Program Contact: (800) 756-7920

Management

Degree Offered: Bachelor of Science

Program Web Address: www.bellevue.edu/ Non_trad/Under/buo_m.htm

Program Background: This is an accelerated online program that teaches students how to successfully evaluate business opportunities.

Application Requirements: You must have an Associate's degree and three years of work experience related to management. And you need to be employed at least 30 hours per week in an environment where you can apply what you're learning. You need to complete and submit an application with an application fee. You can transfer up to 60 credit hours from an accredited college or university for courses in which you earned at least a C.

Completion Requirements: You must successfully complete 127 credit hours for this degree.

Example Course Titles: Some of the course titles for this program include Developing Management Skills, Essentials of Management, Business Information Systems, Introduction to Research, Introduction to Statistics, Organizational Behavior, and Fiscal Management.

Program Contact: (800) 756-7920

Management of Information Systems

Degree Offered: Bachelor of Science

Program Web Address: www.bellevue.edu/ Non_trad/Under/buo_mis.htm

Program Background: This program is designed for students who have completed coursework or Associate's degrees in computer programming or related areas. It focuses on issues and applications in information technology.

Application Requirements: You must have your Associate's degree. You need at least 60 semester credit hours to transfer toward this degree, and must have received a C or better in each of the courses you intend to transfer. You're also required to work at least 30 hours per week in a setting where you can apply what you're learning, and have three years of work experience that relates to your degree program. You need to complete an application and submit it with an application fee and official transcript(s).

Completion Requirements: You must successfully complete 127 credit hours to earn this degree.

Example Course Titles: Some of the course titles for this program include Management Essentials, Communication Skills for Information Systems Managers, Information Systems Planning and Management, Managerial Finance and Accounting, Operations Management and Quantitative Methods, and Operations of Markets.

Program Contact: (800) 756-7920

BEMIDJI STATE UNIVERSITY

General Contact Information

1500 Birchmont Drive NE
Bemidji, Minnesota 56601

Phone: (218) 755-2040
FAX: (218) 755-4048
E-mail: admissions@vax1.bemidji.msus.edu
WWW: http://www.bemidji.msus.edu/

Online Learning Information

Center for Extended Learning
333 Deputy Hall
1500 Birchmont Drive NE
Bemidji, Minnesota 56601-2699

Phone: (218) 755-2068
FAX: (218) 755- 2074
E-mail: cel@vax1.bemidji.msus.edu
WWW: http://cel.bemidji.msus.edu/cel/

Institution Background

Founded: 1919
Type of Institution: Public
Accreditation: North Central Association of Colleges and Schools

Financial Aid: Students enrolled in online courses are not eligible for financial aid unless they are concurrently enrolled in at least six credit hours of traditional classroom courses.

Individual Undergraduate Courses: Bemidji State University offers online undergraduate courses in the following fields: accounting, anthropology, biology, business, chemistry, criminal justice, economics, education, English, environmental studies, geography, health, history, humanities, information technology, music, nursing, physical education, philosophy, political science, psychology, science, and social work.

Programs

Criminal Justice

Degree Offered: Associate of Science

Program Web Address: cel.bemidji.msus.edu/cel/apply.html

Application Requirements: You must request application materials directly from the school.

Completion Requirements: You must successfully complete a minimum of 64 semester credits, with a minimum of 22 earned semester credits in course work from Bemidji State University.

Program Contact: Center for Extended Learning
Deputy Hall
Bemidji State University
Bemidji, Minnesota 56601-2699
(800) 475-2001 ext. 2738

Criminal Justice

Degree Offered: Bachelor of Science

Program Web Address: cel.bemidji.msus.edu/cel/apply.html

Application Requirements: You must request application materials directly from the school.

Completion Requirements: You must successfully complete a minimum of 128 semester credits for this degree. Within the 128 semester credits, you must have at least 64 semester credits from a four-year institution, as well as a minimum of 30 semester credits earned from Bemidji State University over a minimum of two semesters.

Program Contact: Center for Extended Learning
Deputy Hall
Bemidji State University
Bemidji, Minnesota 56601-2699
(800) 475-2001 ext. 2738

Liberal Studies

Degree Offered: Associate of Arts

Program Web Address: cel.bemidji.msus.edu/cel/apply.html

Application Requirements: You need to request admission materials from the External Studies Program at the Center for Extended Learning, Deputy Hall, Bemidji State University, Bemidji, Minnesota 56601-2699, (218) 755-3924 or 1-800-475-2001 extension 2738.

Completion Requirements: You must successfully complete 64 semester credits overall, 22 of which must be completed in coursework from Bemidji State University.

Program Contact: Center for Extended Learning
Deputy Hall
Bemidji State University
Bemidji, Minnesota 56601-2699
(800) 475-2001 ext. 2738

BLADEN COMMUNITY COLLEGE

General Contact Information

P.O. Box 266
Dublin, North Carolina 28332

Phone: (910) 862-2164 ext. 207
FAX: (910) 862-7424
E-mail: jkornegay@bladen.cc.nc.us
WWW: www.bcc.cc.nc.us

Online Learning Information

Director of Technology
P.O. Box 266
Dublin, North Carolina 28332

Phone: (910) 862-2164
FAX: (910) 862-7424
E-mail: dperry@encore.ncren.net
WWW: 204.211.37.12/dl/

Institution Background

Bladen Community College is part of the North Carolina Community College System and maintains an open-door policy.

Founded: 1967
Type of Institution: Public
Accreditation: Southern Association of Colleges and Schools

Online Course Background: Online courses at Bladen Community College combine telecourse and Internet technologies.

Online Course Offered: 13

Online Students Enrolled: 195

Special Programs/Partnerships: Bladen Community College has a partnership with the North Carolina Information Highway, which is an interactive video classroom. Bladen Community College is also a member of the Public Broadcasting System's Going the Distance project.

Services Offered to Students: Every student enrolled in a course through Bladen Community College is assigned an instructor for the course, and has access to the instructor via e-mail or phone. Also, online students have access to library resources.

Financial Aid: Online students may be eligible for federal student aid (including the Federal Pell Grant, Veterans benefits, and the Hope scholarship), North Carolina Community College scholarships, and/or local scholarships.

Registration: You can register for courses at Bladen Community College via the mail.

Programs

Business Administration

Degree Offered: Associate of Applied Science

Program Web Address: www.bcc.cc.nc.us

Online Program Started: 1996

Students Enrolled: 100+

Degrees Awarded: 20+

Program Background: This program leads to a two-year degree in Business Administration.

Application Requirements: You are required to take a placement exam.

Completion Requirements: You must successfully complete 71 hours for this degree.

Time for Completion: You have up to two years to complete this program.

On Campus Requirements: There are no on-campus requirements.

System Requirements: You should have a personal computer with Internet access and e-mail.

Example Course Titles: Some of the course titles in this program include Principles of Accounting I, Business Law, Principles of Management, Principles of Marketing, Survey of Economics, Principles of Accounting II, Introduction to Business, Business Math, Personal Finance, Business Finance, Business Statistics, Small Business Management, Business Application Seminar, Introduction to Computers, and Spreadsheet I.

Program Contact: Dr. Sherry Garner
P.O. Box 266
Dublin, North Carolina 28332
(910) 862-2164
(910) 862-7424
sgarner@bladen.cc.nc.us

General Studies

Degree Offered: Associate in Applied Science

Program Web Address: www.bcc.cc.nc.us

Online Program Started: 1996

Students Enrolled: 100+

Degrees Awarded: 50+

Program Background: This program prepares students to transfer to a four-year college at the junior level.

Application Requirements: You must be a high school graduate or have your GED.

Program Restrictions: You are required to take a placement exam.

Time for Completion: You have up to two years to complete this program.

On Campus Requirements: There are no on-campus requirements.

System Requirements: You should have a computer with Internet access and e-mail.

Example Course Titles: Some of the course titles in this program include College Student Success, Expository Writing, Introduction to Computers, Western Civilization, Elementary Spanish, and College Algebra.

Program Contact: Dr. Sherry Garner
PO Box 266
Dublin, North Carolina 28332
(910) 862-2164
(910) 862-7424
sgarner@bladen.cc.nc.us

BOISE STATE UNIVERSITY

General Contact Information

1910 University Drive
Boise, Idaho 83725

Phone: (800) 824-7017
FAX: (208) 385-4253
E-mail: BSUinfo@boisestate.edu
WWW: www.idbsu.edu

Online Learning Information

Distance Education and Corporate Relations
1910 University Drive
Boise, Idaho 83725

Phone: (208) 385-1709
FAX: (208) 385-3467
E-mail: jatkinso@bsu.idbsu.edu
WWW: www.boisestate.edu/conted/

Institution Background

Founded: 1932
Type of Institution: Public
Accreditation: Northwest Association of Schools and Colleges

Individual Undergraduate Courses: Boise State University offers individual courses online for the following subjects: chemistry, computers and information systems, economics, engineering, geology, history, international business, business management, marketing, nursing, and operations management.

Programs

Instructional and Performance Technology

Degree Offered: Master of Science

Program Web Address: coen.boisestate.edu/dep/ipt.htm

Program Background: This degree is intended to prepare students for careers in instructional technology, performance technology, instructional design, performance improvement, training, education and training management, human resources, organizational development, and human performance consulting.

Application Requirements: You must apply and be accepted for admission to the Graduate College and the Instructional and Performance Technology (IPT) program. Acceptance to the Graduate College does not guarantee admission into the IPT program.

The IPT department requires that you have a Bachelor's degree from an accredited institution and a minimum grade point average of 3.0 for the last two years of your undergraduate study. If your grade point average for the last two years is below a 3.0, you must submit proof of a minimum score of 50 on the Miller Analogy Test (MAT) or a minimum of 500 on the Verbal section of the Graduate Record Examination (GRE). You must submit an application to the IPT department, including a resume of your qualifications and work experience, and an essay (one to two pages) explaining why you want to pursue this degree and how it will help you.

If you're a new student, you must submit a completed application and $20 application fee to the Graduate College as well. After you've submitted your completed application, any other institutions that you've attended since high school must send official transcripts for you directly to the Graduate College at Room 141, Math/Geosciences Building, Boise State University, 1910 University Drive, Boise, Idaho 83725. If you're a returning student, you can reapply to Boise State by completing the online Graduate Admissions Application Form.

Program Restrictions:

Completion Requirements: You must successfully complete 36 credits (18 core plus 18 electives) to earn this degree.

System Requirements: You must own or have convenient access to a computer system—a personal computer with a Pentium processor running Windows 95 or higher operating system, or a Macintosh running System 7.5 or higher. The computer should have at least 250 MB free hard drive space, 32 MB RAM, a 28.8 baud or faster modem or a network connection, CD-ROM or CD/DVD-ROM drive, sound card and speakers, an Internet Service Provider, and an e-mail account. Some of the courses are delivered via Lotus Notes, and require students to have an Internet connection that can be used for replication of Lotus Notes databases. Most Internet Service Providers meet this requirement.

If you have a Pentium computer, you need to purchase Lotus Notes Desktop Client version 4.6. If you have a Macintosh system, you need to purchase Lotus Notes Desktop Client version 4.5.

You are required to complete and submit an Equipment Availability Checklist, which the IPT Systems Manager will review and verify. If you have questions about the checklist or need help, you can contact Ron Grames, the IPT Systems Manager, at 208-426-3144 or 1-800-824-7017, ext. 3144.

Example Course Titles: Some of the course titles for this program include Evaluation Methodology, Learning Theory for Instructional Designers, Introduction to Instructional and Performance Technology, Delivery Technology for Instruction, Human Performance Technology, Internet Applications for IPT Professionals, Applications of Learning Styles in IPT, and Human Factors Engineering.

Program Contact: IPT Department, ET-338
College of Engineering
Boise State University

1910 University Dr.
Boise, Idaho 83725-2070
(800) 824-7017 ext. 1312
(208) 426-1970
lburnett@boisestate.edu

BOWLING GREEN STATE UNIVERSITY

General Contact Information

110 Mcfall Center
Bowling Green, Ohio 43403

Phone: (419) 372-2086
FAX: (419) 372-6955
E-mail: admissions@bgnet.bgsu.edu
WWW: www.bgsu.edu

Institution Background

Founded: 1910
Type of Institution: Public
Accreditation: North Central Association of Colleges and Schools

Programs
Technology Management

Degree Offered: Doctor of Philosophy

Program Web Address: web.indstate.edu:80/tech/acadprog/grad/cphd/cphd.html

Program Background: This degree program is geared toward technologists and combines traditional doctoral research with an innovative delivery system, a consortium of universities, and advanced technical specialization. It is a collaborative program that is administered by the School of Technology at Indiana State University. Other schools that participate include Bowling Green State University, Central Connecticut State University, Central Missouri

State University, East Carolina University, Eastern Michigan University, North Carolina A&T State University, Texas Southern University, and University of Wisconsin-Stout.

Application Requirements: You must apply to Indiana State University for admission to this doctoral program. You should have a bachelor's degree from a regionally accredited college or university, a minimum undergraduate grade point average of 3.0 (on a 4.0 scale) and a minimum graduate grade point average of 3.5, two years of appropriate work experience, and a score of at least 500 on each section of the Graduate Record Examination. With your application, you should submit five letters of recommendation.

Completion Requirements: You must successfully complete a minimum of 90 semester hours of graduate study, with a majority of your coursework at the 600-level. Your program of study will be divided into five areas: Major Area of Specialization (24–30 semester hours), Internship (six semester hours), Research Core (27–33 semester hours), General Technology Core (12–18 semester hours), and Cognate Studies.

On Campus Requirements: You are required to complete two residencies for this program, but you have two options for fulfilling this requirement. You can complete two consecutive semesters at Indiana State University, or you can complete one semester at Indiana State University and one semester at the home university/consortium university where you're completing your specialization.

Example Course Titles: Some of the course titles in this program include Strategic Planning of Technological Processes, Internet Research Methods, Impacts of Technology, Legal Aspects of Industry, and Technological System, Assessment, and Innovation.

Program Contact: esavage@bgnet.bgsu.edu

BREVARD COMMUNITY COLLEGE

General Contact Information

1519 Clearlake Road
Cocoa, Florida 32922-9987

Phone: (407) 632-1111
FAX: (407) 633-1013
WWW: www.brevard.cc.fl.us

Online Learning Information

Admissions Department
1519 Clearlake Road
Cocoa, Florida 32922

Phone: (407) 632-1111 ext. 63703
FAX: (407) 634-3752
E-mail: kelley.m@brevard.cc.fl.us
WWW: www.brevard.cc.fl.us

Institution Background

Founded: 1960
Type of Institution: Public
Accreditation: Southern Association of Colleges and Schools

Programs

Associate in Arts

Degree Offered: Associate in Arts

Program Web Address: www.brevard.cc.fl.us/catalog/ProgramsofInstructionAADeg

Application Requirements: You need to submit an application with a $20.00 application fee, official transcripts from your high school and all colleges you've attended, and your scores on the SAT or ACT.

Completion Requirements: You must successfully complete 64 credit hours for this degree.

Example Course Titles: Some of the course titles in this program include Communications I, Communications II, Fundamentals of Speech, Math for Liberal Arts I, Math for Liberal Arts II, Botany, General Biology, Survey of Human Anatomy and Physiology, and Microbiology.

Associate in Science

Degree Offered: Associate in Science

Program Web Address: www.brevard.cc.fl.us/catalog/ASSOCIATEINSCIENCET

Program Background: This program requires two years of study and is designed for students who plan to enter employment as a technician or semi-professional, or students who are employed and plan to use their educational experiences to advance in their career.

Application Requirements: You need to submit an application with a $20.00 application fee, official transcripts from your high school and all colleges you've attended, and your scores on the SAT or ACT.

Completion Requirements: You must successfully complete 64 credit hours for this degree.

Example Course Titles: Some of the course titles in this program include Communication Fundamentals, College Algebra, Fundamentals of Mathematics, United States History I, United States Foreign Policy, Principles of Economics (Macroeconomics), Western Civilization I, Social Science, American National Government, and Introduction to Sociology.

BUCKS COUNTY COMMUNITY COLLEGE

General Contact Information

434 Swamp Road

Newtown, Pennsylvania 18940

Phone: (215) 968-8100
FAX: (215) 968-8110
WWW: www.bucks.edu

Online Learning Information

Admissions Office
Swamp Road
Newtown, Pennsylvania 18940

Phone: (215) 968-8101
E-mail: kulicke@bucks.edu
WWW: www.bucks.edu/distance/index.html

Institution Background

Founded: 1964
Type of Institution: Public
Accreditation: Middle States Association of Colleges and Schools

Individual Undergraduate Courses: Bucks County Community College offers individual online courses in the following subjects: accounting, art, biology, chemistry, communications, composition, computers, economics, education, foreign language, health, history, institutional management, humanities, integration of knowledge, law, literature, management, marketing, mathematics, music, office administration, philosophy, physics, political science, psychology, science, reading, sociology, and women's studies.

Programs

Business Administration

Degree Offered: Associate of Arts

Program Web Address: www.bucks.edu/catalog/1009.html

Program Background: This program prepares students for upper-division coursework leading to a bachelor's degree in Business Administration. The program parallels the first two years of study required by similar programs offered at four-year colleges and universities. Students select the area of concentration best suited to their interests and aptitudes.

Completion Requirements: You must successfully complete 62 credit hours for this degree.

Example Course Titles: Some of the course titles in this program include Principles of Accounting I, Principles of Accounting II, English Composition I, English Composition II, Effective Speaking, Introduction to Information System, Computer Science I, Principles of Economics: Macro, Principles of Economics: Micro, Introduction to Business, Business Law, and Principles of Management.

Program Contact: (888) BUCKS77 ext. 8052

Liberal Arts

Degree Offered: Associate of Arts

Program Web Address: www.bucks.edu/catalog/1002.html

Program Background: This program provides a strong training in written and oral expression, as well as introduces mathematics and science. It is intended for students who want a general education exploring the social and behavioral sciences, humanities, science, and mathematics.

Example Course Titles: Some of the course titles for this program include Effective Speaking, English Composition, College Level Mathematics, College Level Science, Cultural Perspectives, Philosophy, and History.

Program Contact: (888) BUCKS77 ext. 8052

Management/Marketing

Degree Offered: Associate of Arts

Program Web Address: www.bucks.edu/catalog/2015-17-54.html

Program Background: This program prepares students for entry-level jobs in management or marketing. Courses provide instruction in accounting, marketing, business law, and communication. Students can choose whether to specialize in accounting, marketing, or management, and they work closely with their academic advisors as they select their courses.

Time for Completion: You can complete this program in two years if you take classes on a full-time basis.

Example Course Titles: Some of the courses in this program include Introductory Accounting, Introduction to Information Systems, Effective Speaking, English Composition, Introduction to Business, Business Law, Principles of Marketing, Business Letter and Report Writing, Stress Management, and Cultural Perspectives.

Program Contact: (888) BUCKS77 ext. 8052

CALIFORNIA INSTITUTE OF INTEGRAL STUDIES

General Contact Information

1453 Mission Street
San Francisco, California 94103

Phone: (415) 674-5500
FAX: (415) 674-5555
E-mail: info@ciis.edu
WWW: www.ciis.edu

Online Learning Information

9 Peter Yorke Way
San Francisco, California 94109

Phone: (415) 674-5500
FAX: (415) 674-5555
WWW: www.ciis.edu/online/

Institution Background

The California Institute of Integral Studies was founded over 30 years ago. Its mission is to impart to individuals and communities worldwide an integrated insight into intellect, spirit, and wisdom.

Founded: 1968
Accreditation: Western Associations of Schools and Colleges

Individual Graduate Courses: The Institute provides individual graduate courses online in the following subjects: cultural consciousness, integral scholarship, intuition, parapsychology and consciousness, transformative learning, human sciences, research methods, and the realm of ancestors.

Registration: You can register for courses by mail.

Programs

Human and Organizational Transformation

Degree Offered: Master of Arts in Cultural Anthropology and Social Transformation

Program Web Address: www.ciis.edu/academic/degrees/HORT/index.html

Application Requirements: You must submit an application with two letters of recommen-dation. Additionally, you should submit an example of a recent scholarly writing.

On Campus Requirements: You are required to attend a week-long residency in August, and a five-day residency in San Francisco in March.

System Requirements: You should have a computer and an account with MetaNetwork.

Example Course Titles: Some of the course titles in this program include History and Theory of Organizational Development and Transformation, Managing Organizational Change, Organizational Diagnosis and Intervention, The Learning Organization, The Culture of Organizations, Conflict Resolution, and Spirit in Work.

Transformative Learning and Change

Degree Offered: Doctor of Philosophy in Humanities

Program Web Address: www.ciis.edu/academic/degrees/TLC/index.html

Program Background: This program is designed for students who want to combine innovative scholarship with a commitment to action. Students have diverse backgrounds from which they can contribute experiences—education, social action, business, the arts, psychology, and community development.

Application Requirements: You should have a Master's degree in Cultural Anthropology and Social Transformation or in a closely related field, and a minimum grade point average of 3.0. You need to complete an application and submit it with two letters of recommendation and a recent example of a scholarly writing.

Completion Requirements: You become a member of a cohort for the duration of this program. Upon completion of the course requirements, your cohort must demonstrate mastery. Additionally, you are required to present evidence of your progress toward the learning objectives as an individual.

On Campus Requirements: You are required to participate in a week-long intensive seminar in August and a five-day residency in March.

System Requirements: You must have an online account with MetaNetwork.

Example Course Titles: Some of the course titles for this program include Transformative Learning, Windows and Worldviews on the Self, Living Systems Theory and Transformative Change, Principles and Practices of Ethnographic Inquiry, Small Groups as Living Systems, Systems Analysis of Problems in a Postmodern World, and Cultural Synergy.

CALIFORNIA STATE UNIVERSITY AT NORTHRIDGE

General Contact Information

P.O. Box 1286
Northridge, California 91328

Phone: (818) 667-3700
FAX: (677) 885-3766
WWW: www.csun.edu

Online Learning Information

Distance Learning Services
18111 Nordhoff Street
Northridge, California 91330-8324

Phone: (818) 677-2355
FAX: (818) 677-2316
E-mail: sheri.kaufmann@csun.edu
WWW: www.csun.edu/exl/

Institution Background

Founded: 1958
Type of Institution: Public
Accreditation: Western Association of Schools and Colleges

Programs

Communicative Disorders

Degree Offered: Master of Science

Program Web Address: exled.csun.edu/fr-10.html

Program Background: This program focuses on Speech-Language Pathology.

Application Requirements: You must be employed by a California school district and have a Bachelor's degree in Communication Disorders. If you have a Bachelor's degree in another area, you may satisfy the degree requirement by taking 30 semester units of study in qualifying prerequisite courses. You must submit your scores from the Graduate Record Examination (GRE) or the Miller's Analogy Test (MAT), transcripts of academic work, all required University and department forms, and the University graduate fee.

System Requirements: You should have a personal computer with a 300 MHz Pentium processor running Windows 95/98/NT or a Macintosh with OS 7.x or newer, 8X CD-ROM drive (minimum), 64MB of RAM, 28.8 kbps modem or faster, and sound capabilities. You should also have a Web browser that supports Java and Javascript, RealPlayer, and QuickTime for Windows.

Example Course Titles: Some of the course titles in this program include Computer Applications in Communication Disorders, Independent Study: Leveling the Background, Interviewing and Counseling in Communication Disorders, Research in Communication Disorders, Language Disorders, Neuroanatomy and Neurophysiology of Language, Clinical Practicum, and Seminar in Affective and Cognitive Communication Disorders.

Program Contact: Department of Communication Disorders and Sciences
California State University, Northridge
(818) 677-2852
cds@csun.edu

CALIFORNIA STATE UNIVERSITY, DOMINGUEZ HILLS

General Contact Information

1000 E. Victoria Street
Carson, California 90747

Phone: (310) 243-3601
WWW: www.csudh.edu/

Online Learning Information

Division of Extended Education
1000 E. Victoria Street
Carson, California 90747

Phone: (310) 243-3741
FAX: (310) 516-3971
E-mail: eereg@dhvx20.csudh.edu
WWW: www.csudh.edu/

Institution Background

California State University, Dominguez Hills was founded in 1960 and began serving students in 1965. It is located on the site of Rancho San Pedro, the oldest Spanish Land Grant in metropolitan Los Angeles. It is one of 22 California State University campuses and offers an array of programs, including a number of certificate and credential programs in addition to bachelor's and master's degrees programs.

Founded: 1960
Type of Institution: Public
Accreditation: Western Association of Schools and Colleges

Registration: You can register for courses via mail and phone.

Programs

Business Administration

Degree Offered: Master of Business Administration

Program Web Address: www.csudh.edu/tvmba/

Program Background: All of the courses in this program are offered on PrimeOne Tele-TV, some Cable TV systems, and the Internet. Students have the ability to interact with faculty during class by telephone line, and by e-mail at other times.

Application Requirements: You must have a Bachelor's degree from an accredited college or university, be in good standing at the last institution attended, and have a minimum grade point average of 2.75 during the last 60 credit hours of your undergraduate study. You should submit an application, two official transcripts from each college or university you've attended, and your scores on the Graduate Management Admission Test. (You need a minimum GMAT score of 450 or scores at or above the 25th percentile on both the verbal and quantitative portions of the test.)

Completion Requirements: You must successfully complete 30 units for this degree.

On Campus Requirements: You are required to attend courses on campus two Saturday mornings during each 14-week trimester.

System Requirements: You should have a personal computer with Internet access. You also need access to specified television stations.

Example Course Titles: Some of the course titles in this program include Financial Management, Organizational Behavior, Advanced Marketing, Business Strategy, Management Accounting, and International Business.

Program Contact: MBA Office
California State University, Dominguez Hills
1000 East Victoria Street
Carson, California 90747
(310) 243-2162
(310) 516-4178
pputz@soma.csudh.edu

Humanities

Degree Offered: Master of Arts

Program Web Address: www.csudh.edu/hux/index.html

Students Enrolled: 600

Program Background: The external degree program in the Humanities was formed in 1974 by faculty of the then-California State College, Dominguez Hills (now a California State University). Initially, it offered both undergraduate and graduate degrees. Eventually, the undergraduate degree program was dropped due to low enrollment. The graduate program continues to grow today, serving students worldwide.

Application Requirements: You must have a Bachelor's degree (in Arts or Science) from a regionally accredited institution and a grade point average of 3.0 during your last 60 semester units or 90 quarter units of undergraduate study. Lower-division work completed after you've obtained your bachelor's degree does not count in the 3.0 grade point average requirement.

Program Restrictions: The Program Coordinator may grant provisional or probationary admittance to the program to students who had a grade point average below 3.0 but above 2.5 during their last 60 semester/90 quarter units of undergraduate study.

Completion Requirements: You must successfully complete 30 units. The Program Coordinator has the discretion to accept up to 9 semester units of transfer credit for graduate work completed at another institution. You must maintain an overall grade point average of 3.0 or higher. And you must receive a passing grade on the Master of Arts in Humanities—Advancement to Candidacy Examination.

Time for Completion: You have up to five years to complete this program.

System Requirements: You need to have a computer and Internet connection.

Example Course Titles: Some of the course titles in this program include Defining the Humanities: History, The Rational Perspective, The Non-Western World, World Religious Perspective, Key Individuals—Art: Frank Lloyd Wright, and Key Periods and Movements—Literature: Female Coming of Age in World.

Program Contact: Humanities External Degree Program
California State University, Dominguez Hills
1000 East Victoria Street—SAC2-2126
Carson, California 90747
(310) 243-3743
(310) 516-4399
HUXOnline@dhvx20.csudh.edu

Negotiation and Conflict Management

Degree Offered: Master of Arts in Behavioral Science

Program Web Address: www.csudh.edu/dominguezonline/beh.htm

Program Background: Working professionals can earn a Master's degree in two years through this program. Students learn skills that they can apply in almost any work environment.

Application Requirements: You must have a Bachelor's degree from an accredited college or university with a minimum grade point average of 3.0 during your last 60 units of undergraduate work. If you don't meet the grade point average requirement, you may be admitted on a conditional basis in which you can complete two classes to prove your potential in the program.

Completion Requirements: You must successfully complete eight ten-week courses for this degree.

Example Course Titles: Some of the course titles in this program include Applied Behavioral Science, Community Conflict, and Theories of Conflict.

Program Contact: Mediated and Distance Learning Office
(310) 243-3741

Nursing

Degree Offered: Bachelor of Science

Program Web Address: www.e-education. com/collegeconnection/univs/csubsn.html

Program Background: This is a bachelor's degree completion program that gives students an individualized approach to nursing education. It is designed for students who are self-directed and employed professionals. It prepares registered nurses as generalists in professional nursing practice, equipping them to serve as leaders, managers, and resource persons in a variety of health care settings.

This program is accredited by the National League for Nursing, approved by the Western Association of Schools and Colleges, and is a member of the American Association of Colleges of Nursing (AACN), National League for Nursing (NLN), and Western Institute of Nursing (WIN).

Application Requirements: You must have at least 56 semester credit hours that will transfer to California State University, Dominguez Hills, a minimum grade point average of 2.0, and a current license or interim permit as a Registered Nurse in the United States. You need to complete an application and submit it with an application fee and official transcripts from all colleges or universities you've attended.

Completion Requirements: You must successfully complete a total of 124 semester units, with 40 of them being from upper-division courses. Also, you must complete all courses with a grade of C or better.

System Requirements: You need to have a television and videotape player and a personal computer with a 100 MHz Pentium processor (or faster), 16 MB RAM, a 28.8 kbps modem (or faster), Internet access (including e-mail capabilities), and Netscape 3.01 or Microsoft Internet Explorer 4.0 or higher.

Example Course Titles: Some of the course titles in this program include Technology for the Information Age, Human Diversity and Health Care, Expanding Professional Nursing Horizons, Life Cycle, Culture and Health, Biochemistry, Professional Relationships in Nursing Practice, Health Assessment, and Leadership in Nursing Practice.

Program Contact: California State University, Dominguez Hills
(877) GO-HILLS
eereg@dhvx20.csudh.edu

Production and Inventory Control

Degree Offered: Certificate

Program Web Address: www.csudh.edu/

lapicsonline/

Program Background: This certificate is given in cooperation with the Los Angeles Chapter of APICS (a Society for Resource Management). The program is designed for students who want a broad education in the principles of production and inventory control. The program is open to those already in this field and those who are interested in a career in production and inventory control.

Completion Requirements: You must complete five out of seven courses and achieve a minimum grade point average of 2.3 for this certificate.

Example Course Titles: Some of the course titles include Introduction to Supply Chain Management, Inventory Management, Material and Capacity Requirements Planning, Just-in-Time/Total Quality Management, and Manufacturing Management Systems and Technology.

Program Contact: California State University, Dominguez Hills
Division of Extended Education
1000 East Victoria Street
Carson, California 90747
(310) 516-3741
(310) 516-3971
ajhall@gateway.net

Purchasing

Degree Offered: Certificate

Program Web Address: www.csudh.edu/purchasingonline/

Program Background: This program is designed for students who want a broad education in the principles of procurement management. It provides students with a comprehensive introduction to the field of purchasing and helps them prepare for certification examinations.

Completion Requirements: You must successfully complete four courses and maintain an overall grade point average of at least 2.3.

Example Course Titles: Some of the course titles in this program include Purchasing Fundamentals, Cost/Price Analysis and Negotiation, Public Sector Procurement, and Advanced Purchasing Concepts.

Program Contact: California State University, Dominguez Hills
Division of Extended Education
1000 East Victoria Street
Carson, California 90747
(310) 516-3741
(310) 516-3971
ajhall@gateway.net

Quality Assurance

Degree Offered: Master of Science

Program Web Address: www.csudh.edu/msqa/msqahome.htm

Online Program Started: 1995

Program Background: Students in this program learn technical and administrative foundations of quality assurance, as well as skills training in the current practices and methods requirement for implementing and improving operational performance and customer satisfaction. Students work in all areas of management in manufacturing, service, government, and health care organizations.

Application Requirements: You must have a Bachelor's degree in a technical field from an accredited college or university. If your Bachelor's degree is in a non-technical field, you can seek approval to enroll from the Quality Assurance Academic Program Committee. You also need to have background experience that includes preparation in college-level mathematics and computer concepts and a minimum grade point average of 2.5 (on a 4.0 scale) during your last 60 semester units of undergraduate study.

Completion Requirements: You must successfully complete 33 units of approved graduate coursework with a minimum grade point average of 3.0, complete a culminating project, and satisfy the graduate writing competency.

On Campus Requirements: There are no on-campus requirements for this program.

System Requirements: You should have a computer and Internet access. Any platform of computer will work provided it has sufficient RAM and an operating system that can run a graphical browser such as Netscape or Microsoft Internet Explorer.

Example Course Titles: Some of the course titles in this program include Advanced Probability and Statistics, Quality Function Management and TQM, Statistical Quality Control and Sampling, Advanced Experimental Design, Human Factors in Quality Assurance, and Measurement and Testing Techniques.

Program Contact: MSQA-Internet Program Director
(310) 243-3355
msqa@dhvx20.csudh.edu

CAPELLA UNIVERSITY

General Contact Information

330 Second Avenue South, Suite 550
Minneapolis, Minnesota 55401

Phone: (888) CAPELLA
FAX: (612) 339-8022
WWW: www.CapellaUniversity.edu

Online Learning Information

330 Second Avenue South, Suite 550
Minneapolis, Minnesota 55401

Phone: (888) CAPELLA
FAX: (612) 339-8022
WWW: www.CapellaUniversity.edu

Institution Background

Accreditation: North Central Association of Colleges and Schools

Financial Aid: Online students at Capella University may be eligible for a variety of assistance programs, including monthly tuition payment plans, employer reimbursement programs, Veterans' benefits, and student loans. For more information about financial aid, contact an Admissions Counselor or the Financial Aid Office at 1-800-227-3552 or info@capella.edu.

Programs
Addiction Psychology

Degree Offered: Certificate

Program Web Address: www.CapellaUniversity.com/10/102a.htm

Program Background: This program is designed to address the needs of individuals who are working in the field of addiction psychology and want to enhance their understanding of effective treatments through certificate courses.

Completion Requirements: You must successfully complete 20 quarter credits for this certificate.

On Campus Requirements: There are no on-campus requirements for this program.

System Requirements: You need to have a personal computer with a minimum processor speed of 486DX (Pentium or equivalent recommended) or the Macintosh equivalent, a 28.8K modem (or faster), enough RAM (memory) to support your operating system (for example, a minimum of 16MB for Windows 95), a video card (800 × 600 pixel screen resolution and a minimum of 16-bit colors), CD-ROM drive, and sound card. The school recommends the following software: Windows 95 or higher for an operating system (or the Macintosh equivalent), a Web browser (must be Netscape Navigator 3.0, Microsoft Internet Explorer 3.0, or America Online 3.0 or higher) with Java and JavaScript options enabled, a word processor (Microsoft Word 6.0 or higher recommended), and e-mail software.

Example Course Titles: Some of the course titles in this program include Psychopharmacology, Principles of Psychopathology, Substance Abuse Therapies, and Compulsive Disorders and the Disturbance of the Self.

Program Contact: School of Psychology
Capella University
330 Second Avenue South, Suite 550
Minneapolis, Minnesota 55401
(888) CAPELLA

Addiction Psychology

Degree Offered: Master of Science

Program Web Address: www. CapellaUniversity.com/10/102a.htm

Application Requirements: You should have a Bachelor's degree or the foreign equivalent from a regionally accredited college or university, or from an internationally recognized institution, and a minimum undergraduate grade point average of 2.7 (on a 4.0 scale).

Completion Requirements: You must successfully complete 60 quarter credits for this degree. In addition to the required courses, you have an option to complete a comprehensive examination or research project. You can choose between an integrative project and a more conventional thesis as a means of completing the research project. You can tailor your degree program through your selection of elective courses.

On Campus Requirements: There are no on-campus requirements for this program.

System Requirements: You need to have a personal computer with a minimum processor speed of 486DX (Pentium or equivalent recommended) or the Macintosh equivalent, a 28.8K modem (or higher), enough RAM (memory) to support your operating system (for example, a minimum of 16MB for Windows 95), a video card (800 $\times$ 600 pixel screen resolution and a minimum of 16-bit colors), CD-ROM drive, and sound card. The school recommends the following software: Windows 95 or higher for an operating system (or the Macintosh equivalent), a Web browser (must be Netscape Navigator 3.0, Microsoft Internet Explorer 3.0, or America Online 3.0 or higher) with Java and JavaScript options enabled, a word processor (Microsoft Word 6.0 or higher recommended), and e-mail software.

Example Course Titles: Some of the course titles in this program include History and Systems of Psychology, Advanced Biological Psychology, Adolescent Psychology, Adult Psychology, Geriatric Psychology, Psychology of Learning, Cognitive Psychology, Tests and Measurements, Inferential Statistics, Qualitative Analysis, Methods of Clinical Inquiry, and Substance Abuse Therapies.

Program Contact: School of Psychology
Capella University
330 Second Avenue South, Suite 550
Minneapolis, Minnesota 55401
(888) CAPELLA

Addiction Psychology

Degree Offered: Doctor of Philosophy

Program Web Address: www. CapellaUniversity.com/10/102a.htm

Application Requirements: You must have a master's degree or the foreign equivalent from a regionally accredited college or university, or an internationally recognized institution, and a minimum grade point average of 3.0 (on a 4.0 scale).

Completion Requirements: You must successfully complete 120 quarter credits for this degree.

On Campus Requirements: You are required to attend a series of brief residencies. Please contact the school directly for additional information about on-campus requirements.

System Requirements: You need to have a personal computer with a minimum processor speed of 486DX (Pentium or equivalent recommended) or the Macintosh equivalent, a 28.8K modem (or higher), enough RAM (memory) to support your operating system (for example, a minimum of 16MB for Windows 95), a video card (800 × 600 pixel screen resolution and a minimum of 16-bit colors), CD-ROM drive, and sound card. The school recommends the following software: Windows 95 or higher for an operating system (or the Macintosh equivalent), a Web browser (must be Netscape Navigator 3.0, Microsoft Internet Explorer 3.0, or America Online 3.0 or higher) with Java and JavaScript options enabled, a word processor (Microsoft Word 6.0 or higher recommended), and e-mail software.

Example Course Titles: Some of the course titles in this program include History and Systems of Psychology, Advanced Biological Psychology, Adolescent Psychology, Adult Psychology, Geriatric Psychology, Psychology of Learning, Cognitive Psychology, Social Psychology, and Group Psychology.

Program Contact: School of Psychology
Capella University
330 Second Avenue South, Suite 550
Minneapolis, Minnesota 55401
(888) CAPELLA

Adult Education

Degree Offered: Certificate

Program Web Address: www. CapellaUniversity.com/8/82b.htm

Program Background: This program is designed for students who work with adult learners in academic and business settings. Students build a foundation for developing programming for adults.

Completion Requirements: You must successfully complete 16 quarter credits for this certificate.

On Campus Requirements: Residency is required for some courses. Please contact the school directly for more information.

System Requirements: You need to have a personal computer with a minimum processor speed of 486DX (Pentium or equivalent recommended) or the Macintosh equivalent, a 28.8K modem (or higher), enough RAM (memory) to support your operating system (for example, a minimum of 16MB for Windows 95), a video card (800 × 600 pixel screen resolution and a minimum of 16-bit colors), CD-ROM drive, and sound card. The school recommends the following software: Windows 95 or higher for an operating system (or the Macintosh equivalent), a Web browser (must be Netscape Navigator 3.0, Microsoft Internet Explorer 3.0, or America Online 3.0 or higher) with Java and JavaScript options enabled, a word processor (Microsoft Word 6.0 or higher recommended), and e-mail software.

Example Course Titles: Some of the course titles in this program include Intellectual Development and Learning Styles Across the Lifespan, Theory and Methods of Educating Adults, The Collaborative Nature of Adult Education, Teaching and Learning with Diverse

Populations, and Critical Thinking in Adult Education.

Program Contact: School of Education and Professional Development
Capella University
330 Second Avenue South, Suite 550
Minneapolis, Minnesota 55401
(888) CAPELLA

Adult Education

Degree Offered: Master of Science

Program Web Address: www. CapellaUniversity.com/8/82b.htm

Program Background: This Master of Science degree program provides an overview of adult education for professionals working in diverse adult education settings. Students gain the knowledge and experience they need to provide leadership in developing, implementing, and managing effective educational programs.

Application Requirements: You must have a Bachelor's degree or the foreign equivalent from a regionally accredited college or university, or internationally recognized institution, and have a minimum undergraduate grade point average of 2.7 (on a 4.0 scale).

Completion Requirements: You must successfully complete 48 quarter credits for this degree.

On Campus Requirements: Residency is required for some courses. Please contact the school directly for more information.

System Requirements: You need to have a personal computer with a minimum processor speed of 486DX (Pentium or equivalent recommended) or the Macintosh equivalent, a 28.8K modem (or higher), enough RAM (memory) to support your operating system (for example, a minimum of 16MB for Windows 95), a video card (800 × 600 pixel screen resolution and a minimum of 16-bit colors), CD-ROM drive, and sound card. The school recommends the following software: Windows 95 or higher for an operating system (or the Macintosh equivalent), a Web browser (must be Netscape Navigator 3.0, Microsoft Internet Explorer 3.0, or America Online 3.0 or higher) with Java and JavaScript options enabled, a word processor (Microsoft Word 6.0 or higher recommended), and e-mail software.

Example Course Titles: Some of the course titles in this program include Survey of Research in Societal and Cultural Change, Evaluating the Effectiveness of the Educational Process, The Future of Educational Institutions: Topics and Trends, Survey of Research Methodology, and Intellectual Development and Learning Styles Across the Lifespan.

Program Contact: School of Education and Professional Development
Capella University
330 Second Avenue South, Suite 550
Minneapolis, Minnesota 55401
(888) CAPELLA

Adult Education

Degree Offered: Doctor of Philosophy

Program Web Address: www. CapellaUniversity.com/prgms/ed/phd/adult_ed.htm

Program Background: This program is designed for professionals who are interested in working in adult-oriented programs in education, corporate training, military, and health-related educational settings. Students deepen their knowledge through courses and research related to administering adult education programs, philosophies of adult education, characteristics of adult learners, training, facilitating adult education, and integrating various technologies to support teaching and learning.

Application Requirements: You must have a Master's degree or the foreign equivalent from a regionally accredited college or university, or internationally recognized institution, and have a minimum undergraduate grade point average of 3.0 (on a 4.0 scale).

Completion Requirements: You must successfully complete 48 quarter credits for this degree.

On Campus Requirements: Residency is required for some courses. Please contact the school directly for more information.

System Requirements: You need to have a personal computer with a minimum processor speed of 486DX (Pentium or equivalent recommended) or the Macintosh equivalent, a 28.8K modem (or higher), enough RAM (memory) to support your operating system (for example, a minimum of 16MB for Windows 95), a video card (800 × 600 pixel screen resolution and a minimum of 16-bit colors), CD-ROM drive, and sound card. The school recommends the following software: Windows 95 or higher for an operating system (or the Macintosh equivalent), a Web browser (must be Netscape Navigator 3.0, Microsoft Internet Explorer 3.0, or America Online 3.0 or higher) with Java and JavaScript options enabled, a word processor (Microsoft Word 6.0 or higher recommended), and e-mail software.

Example Course Titles: Some of the course titles in this program include Survey of Research in Societal and Cultural Change, Survey of Research in Human Development and Behavior, Survey of Research in Organizational and Group Dynamics, A Historical Perspective and Philosophy of Adult Education, The Governance of Educational Institutions, and Evaluating the Effectiveness of the Educational Process.

Program Contact: School of Education and Professional Development
Capella University
330 Second Avenue South, Suite 550
Minneapolis, Minnesota 55401
(888) CAPELLA

Business Administration

Degree Offered: Master of Business Administration

Program Web Address: www.CapellaUniversity.com/7/72c.htm

Program Background: This program prepares students to be leaders. Building on their individual professional experiences, the courses help students develop knowledge that the students can put to use immediately. Because the program is offered online, students can access their courses any time of the day, from anywhere in the world.

Application Requirements: You must have a Bachelor's degree from an accredited institution, and two to three years of business related experience. You should submit an application with the application fee, official transcripts of the highest degree you've earned, a resume, and an academic goal statement.

Completion Requirements: You must successfully complete 52 credits made up of nine required core courses and four elective courses. Students in the Master of Business Administration (MBA) program may waive a maximum of 16 credits (four courses) from their required courses on the basis of transferable coursework.

System Requirements: You should have a personal computer with a 166 MHz (or higher) Pentium processor, 64MB RAM, 12x CD-ROM, 56K Baud Modem or ISDN Connection, Windows 95/98, a Web browser (Netscape Navigator 3.0 or later or Microsoft Internet Explorer 3.0 or later), and e-mail capability.

Example Course Titles: Some of the course titles in this program include The Manager as Leader, Applied Managerial Accounting, Managerial Finance, Managing the Marketing Process, Operations Management, Leading the Organization: Structure, Culture and Change, Applied Quantitative Analysis, Information Technology Management, and Strategic Management.

Program Contact: School of Business
Capella University
330 Second Avenue South, Suite 550
Minneapolis, Minnesota 55401
(888) CAPELLA

Clinical Psychology

Degree Offered: Certificate

Program Web Address: www. CapellaUniversity.com/10/102b.htm

Program Background: Students enrolled in this certificate program can specialize in Clinical Supervision, Geriatric Care, Forensic Psychology, or Psycho-Neurological Testing. Most of the students in this program are currently work in the field and expect to enhance their understanding of effective treatments through certificate courses.

Application Requirements: To be admitted to the Clinical Supervision or Geriatric Care specialties, you must have at least a Bachelor's degree. For admission to the Forensic Psychology or Psycho-Neurological Testing specialties, you must have a graduate degree.

Completion Requirements: You must successfully complete 20 quarter credits for this certificate.

System Requirements: You need to have a personal computer with a minimum processor speed of 486DX (Pentium or equivalent recommended) or the Macintosh equivalent, a 28.8K modem (or faster), enough RAM (mem-

ory) to support your operating system (for example, a minimum of 16MB for Windows 95), a video card (800 × 600 pixel screen resolution and a minimum of 16-bit colors), CD-ROM drive, and sound card. The school recommends the following software: Windows 95 or higher for an operating system (or the Macintosh equivalent), a Web browser (must be Netscape Navigator 3.0, Microsoft Internet Explorer 3.0, or America Online 3.0 or higher) with Java and JavaScript options enabled, a word processor (Microsoft Word 6.0 or higher recommended), and e-mail software.

Example Course Titles: Some of the course titles in this program include Ethics and Standards of Professional Practice, Strategies of Clinical Supervision, Issues and Challenges of Supervision, Practicum in Supervision, Bereavement and Loss Therapy, Principles of Health Psychology, Geriatric Psychology, Research in the Aging Process, Psychology and the Law, Techniques of Forensic Practice, Current Issues and Trends in Forensic Practice, Learning Disabilities in the Classroom, Advanced Psychopathology, Advanced Psychological Testing, and Psycho-Neurological Assessments.

Program Contact: School of Psychology
Capella University
330 Second Avenue South, Suite 550
Minneapolis, Minnesota 55401
(888) CAPELLA

Clinical Psychology

Degree Offered: Master of Science

Program Web Address: www. CapellaUniversity.com/10/102b.htm

Program Background: Students enrolled in this program can tailor their degree through the selection of electives. Additionally, students select whether to complete a comprehensive examination or research project.

Application Requirements: You must have a Bachelor's degree (or its foreign equivalent) from a regionally accredited or internationally recognized institution, a minimum undergraduate grade point average of 2.7 (on a 4.0 scale) or its equivalent from an international institution.

Completion Requirements: You must successfully complete 60 quarter credits.

On Campus Requirements: You are required to attend a one week residency during a summer session for this master's degree.

System Requirements: You need to have a personal computer with a minimum processor speed of 486DX (Pentium or equivalent recommended) or the Macintosh equivalent, a 28.8K modem (or faster), enough RAM (memory) to support your operating system (for example, a minimum of 16MB for Windows 95), a video card (800 × 600 pixel screen resolution and a minimum of 16-bit colors), CD-ROM drive, and sound card. The school recommends the following software: Windows 95 or higher for an operating system (or the Macintosh equivalent), a Web browser (must be Netscape Navigator 3.0, Microsoft Internet Explorer 3.0, or America Online 3.0 or higher) with Java and JavaScript options enabled, a word processor (Microsoft Word 6.0 or higher recommended), and e-mail software.

Example Course Titles: Some of the course titles in this program include Child Psychology, Adolescent Psychology, Adult Psychology, Geriatric Psychology, Tests and Measurements, Methods of Clinical Inquiry, Research Methods, Clinical Interventions, Principles of Psychopathology, Psychological Testing, and Ethics and Standards of Professional Practice.

Program Contact: School of Psychology
Capella University
330 Second Avenue South, Suite 550
Minneapolis, Minnesota 55401

(888) CAPELLA

Clinical Psychology

Degree Offered: Doctor of Philosophy

Program Web Address: www. CapellaUniversity.com/10/102b.htm

Program Background: This program is distinguished by flexibility in the choice of core and specialty courses available to students, as well as the additional opportunity to customize the specialization through the selection of elective courses from psychology or other disciplines.

Application Requirements: You must have a Master's degree (or its foreign equivalent) from a regionally accredited or internationally recognized institution, and a minimum graduate grade point average of 3.0 (on a 4.0 scale) or its equivalent from an international institution.

Completion Requirements: You must successfully complete 120 quarter credits for this degree.

On Campus Requirements: You are required to attend some short residencies for this degree. You should contact the school directly for additional information.

System Requirements: You need to have a personal computer with a minimum processor speed of 486DX (Pentium or equivalent recommended) or the Macintosh equivalent, a 28.8K modem (or faster), enough RAM (memory) to support your operating system (for example, a minimum of 16MB for Windows 95), a video card (800 × 600 pixel screen resolution and a minimum of 16-bit colors), CD-ROM drive, and sound card. The school recommends the following software: Windows 95 or higher for an operating system (or the Macintosh equivalent), a Web browser (must be Netscape Navigator 3.0, Microsoft Internet Explorer 3.0, or America Online 3.0 or higher) with Java and JavaScript options enabled, a word processor

(Microsoft Word 6.0 or higher recommended), and e-mail software.

Example Course Titles: Some of the course titles in this program include History and Systems of Psychology, Advanced Biological Psychology, Child Psychology, Adolescent Psychology, Adult Psychology, Geriatric Psychology, Cognitive Psychology, Social Psychology, Tests and Measurements, Inferential Statistics, Qualitative Analysis, Research Methods, Methods of Clinical Inquiry, Advanced Psychopathology, Theories of Psychotherapy, Research in Psychotherapy, Advanced Psychological Testing, and Ethics and Standards of Professional Practice.

Program Contact: School of Psychology
Capella University
330 Second Avenue South, Suite 550
Minneapolis, Minnesota 55401
(888) CAPELLA

Communication Technology

Degree Offered: Master of Science

Program Web Address: www. CapellaUniversity.com/7/72b.htm

Program Background: This program is designed for professionals seeking to broaden their technical and managerial base. Students learn about the rapidly developing technology, new applications, and increasing demand for services.

Application Requirements: You must have a Bachelor's degree (or its foreign equivalent) from a regionally accredited or internationally recognized institution, and a minimum undergraduate grade point average of 2.7 (on a 4.0 scale) or its equivalent from an international institution.

Completion Requirements: You must successfully complete 48 quarter credits for this degree. If you have previous graduate coursework

with a grade of B or better from a regionally accredited school, you may transfer up to 12 applicable quarter credits toward this degree.

System Requirements: You should have a personal computer with a 166 MHz Pentium Processor, 64MB RAM, 12x CD-ROM, 56K Baud Modem or ISDN Connection, Windows 95 or 98, Web browser (Netscape Navigator 3.0 or later, or Microsoft Internet Explorer 3.0 or later), and e-mail capability.

Example Course Titles: Some of the course titles in this program include Accounting and Financial Management, Strategic Planning, Quantitative Analysis, Survey of Research Methodology, Information Systems Management, Integrative Project, Introduction to Digital Transmission, Network Technology (for Communications Technology, and Systems Development Life Cycle.

Program Contact: School of Business
Capella University
330 Second Avenue South, Suite 550
Minneapolis, Minnesota 55401
(888) CAPELLA

Communication Technology

Degree Offered: Doctor of Philosophy

Program Web Address: www. CapellaUniversity.com/7/72b.htm

Program Background: This program leads to a scholar-practitioner degree, awarded for a student's demonstrated knowledge and evidence of independent scholarship. Students build upon their established professional background and demonstrate knowledge of the intellectual and theoretical foundations of technology.

Application Requirements: You must have a Master's degree (or its foreign equivalent) from a regionally accredited or internationally recognized institution and minimum graduate grade point average of 3.0 (on a 4.0 scale) or its equivalent from an international institution.

Completion Requirements: You must successfully complete advanced level courses, a comprehensive, a dissertation, and residency requirements for this degree. If you have a Master's degree from a regionally accredited or internationally recognized institution, you may transfer up to 48 applicable quarter credits of course work with a grade of B or better toward this degree.

System Requirements: You need to have a personal computer with a minimum processor speed of 486DX (Pentium or equivalent recommended) or the Macintosh equivalent, a 28.8K modem (or faster), enough RAM (memory) to support your operating system (for example, a minimum of 16MB for Windows 95), a video card (800 × 600 pixel screen resolution and a minimum of 16-bit colors), CD-ROM drive, and sound card. The school recommends the following software: Windows 95 or higher for an operating system (or the Macintosh equivalent), a Web browser (must be Netscape Navigator 3.0, Microsoft Internet Explorer 3.0, or America Online 3.0 or higher) with Java and JavaScript options enabled, a word processor (Microsoft Word 6.0 or higher recommended), and e-mail software.

Example Course Titles: Some of the course titles in this program include Survey of Research in Organizational and Group Dynamics, Survey of Research in Societal and Cultural Change, Survey of Research in Human Development and Behavior, Advanced Study in Research Methods, Management and Organizational Behavior, Accounting and Financial Management, Strategic Planning, Information Systems Management, Introduction to Digital Transmission, and Network Technology.

Program Contact: School of Business
Capella University
330 Second Avenue South, Suite 550

Minneapolis, Minnesota 55401
(888) CAPELLA

Communications Technology Management

Degree Offered: Certificate

Program Web Address: www. CapellaUniversity.com/7/72d.htm

Program Background: This program instructs students in the rapidly developing technology, new applications, and increasing demand for services. It is intended to familiarize students with the nature of one of the most important and fastest-growing industries in the world.

Completion Requirements: You must successfully complete 20 quarter credits for this certificate.

System Requirements: You need to have a personal computer with a minimum processor speed of 486DX (Pentium or equivalent recommended) or the Macintosh equivalent, a 28.8K modem (or faster), enough RAM (memory) to support your operating system (for example, a minimum of 16MB for Windows 95), a video card (800 × 600 pixel screen resolution and a minimum of 16-bit colors), CD-ROM drive, and sound card. The school recommends the following software: Windows 95 or higher for an operating system (or the Macintosh equivalent), a Web browser (must be Netscape Navigator 3.0, Microsoft Internet Explorer 3.0, or America Online 3.0 or higher) with Java and JavaScript options enabled, a word processor (Microsoft Word 6.0 or higher recommended), and e-mail software.

Example Course Titles: Some of the course titles in this program include Introduction of Digital Transmission, Network Technology, Telephony, Telecommunications Applications, Planning and Design, Network Management, Java and JavaScript, Industry Structure, Roles and Change, Regulatory Issues, Environmental /Societal Issues in Telecommunications, and Intranet and E-Commerce.

Program Contact: School of Business
Capella University
330 Second Avenue South, Suite 550
Minneapolis, Minnesota 55401
(888) CAPELLA

Distance Education

Degree Offered: Certificate

Program Web Address: www. CapellaUniversity.com/8/82c.htm

Program Background: This certificate program benefits students who are working in academic and business settings and who are initiating distance education programming. The certificate provides a foundation for professionals in this rapidly expanding field.

Completion Requirements: You must successfully complete 16 quarter credits.

System Requirements: You need to have a personal computer with a minimum processor speed of 486DX (Pentium or equivalent recommended) or the Macintosh equivalent, a 28.8K modem (or faster), enough RAM (memory) to support your operating system (for example, a minimum of 16MB for Windows 95), a video card (800 × 600 pixel screen resolution and a minimum of 16-bit colors), CD-ROM drive, and sound card. The school recommends the following software: Windows 95 or higher for an operating system (or the Macintosh equivalent), a Web browser (must be Netscape Navigator 3.0, Microsoft Internet Explorer 3.0, or America Online 3.0 or higher) with Java and JavaScript options enabled, a word processor (Microsoft Word 6.0 or higher recommended), and e-mail software.

Example Course Titles: Some of the course titles in this program include Introduction to Multimedia and Web-Based Instruction, Advanced Techniques in Instructional Design, Developing Effective Online Assessment, Overview of Distance Education, Instructional Design for Distance Education, and Ethics and Social Responsibility in Distance Education.

Program Contact: School of Education and Professional Development
Capella University
330 Second Avenue South, Suite 550
Minneapolis, Minnesota 55401
(888) CAPELLA

Distance Education

Degree Offered: Master of Science

Program Web Address: www. CapellaUniversity.com/8/82c.htm

Program Background: This program is designed for a diverse group of professionals working in education or running businesses.

Application Requirements: You must have a Bachelor's degree (or its foreign equivalent) from a regionally accredited or internationally recognized institution, and a minimum undergraduate grade point average of 2.7 (on a 4.0 scale) or its equivalent from an international institution.

Completion Requirements: You must successfully complete 48 quarter credits.

System Requirements: You need to have a personal computer with a minimum processor speed of 486DX (Pentium or equivalent recommended) or the Macintosh equivalent, a 28.8K modem (or faster), enough RAM (memory) to support your operating system (for example, a minimum of 16MB for Windows 95), a video card (800 × 600 pixel screen resolution and a minimum of 16-bit colors), CD-ROM drive, and sound card. The school recommends the following software: Windows 95 or higher for an operating system (or the Macintosh equivalent), a Web browser (must be Netscape Navigator 3.0, Microsoft Internet Explorer 3.0, or America Online 3.0 or higher) with Java and JavaScript options enabled, a word processor (Microsoft Word 6.0 or higher recommended), and e-mail software.

Example Course Titles: Some of the course titles in this program include Survey of Research in Societal and Cultural Change, Evaluating the Effectiveness of the Educational Process, The Future of Educational Institutions: Topics and Trends, Survey of Research Methodology, Integrative Project, Introduction to Multimedia and Web-Based Instruction, Advanced Techniques in Instructional Design, Developing Effective Online Assessment, Overview of Distance Education, Instructional Design for Distance Education, and Ethics and Social Responsibility in Distance Education.

Program Contact: School of Education and Professional Development
Capella University
330 Second Avenue South, Suite 550
Minneapolis, Minnesota 55401
(888) CAPELLA

E-Business

Degree Offered: MBA Certificate

Program Web Address: www. CapellaUniversity.com/7/72d.htm

Program Background: Students enrolled in this program learn about electronic technologies that are forcing business environments and practices to evolve. It prepares managers to plan, develop, and manage e-business, including online commerce and community.

Completion Requirements: You must successfully complete 16 quarter credits.

System Requirements: You need to have a personal computer with a minimum processor speed of 486DX (Pentium or equivalent rec-

ommended) or the Macintosh equivalent, a 28.8K modem (or faster), enough RAM (memory) to support your operating system (for example, a minimum of 16MB for Windows 95), a video card (800 × 600 pixel screen resolution and a minimum of 16-bit colors), CD-ROM drive, and sound card. The school recommends the following software: Windows 95 or higher for an operating system (or the Macintosh equivalent), a Web browser (must be Netscape Navigator 3.0, Microsoft Internet Explorer 3.0, or America Online 3.0 or higher) with Java and JavaScript options enabled, a word processor (Microsoft Word 6.0 or higher recommended), and e-mail software.

Example Course Titles: Some of the course titles in this program include Introduction to E-Business, E-Business: Business Development for the Web, E-Business: Managing in the Technical Environment, E-Business: Technical Infrastructure, E-Business: Marketing, and Customers and Virtual Community.

Program Contact: School of Business
Capella University
330 Second Avenue South, Suite 550
Minneapolis, Minnesota 55401
(888) CAPELLA

Educational Administration

Degree Offered: Certificate

Program Web Address: www. CapellaUniversity.com/8/82d.htm

Program Background: The certificate program is designed for students who want to prepare or renew their competency in educational administration. It focuses on leadership in a variety of organizations where educational administrative skills are a prerequisite to organization performance outcomes.

Completion Requirements: You must successfully complete 16 quarter credits.

On Campus Requirements: You are required to fulfill residencies for this program. Please contact the school for additional information.

System Requirements: You need to have a personal computer with a minimum processor speed of 486DX (Pentium or equivalent recommended) or the Macintosh equivalent, a 28.8K modem (or faster), enough RAM (memory) to support your operating system (for example, a minimum of 16MB for Windows 95), a video card (800 × 600 pixel screen resolution and a minimum of 16-bit colors), CD-ROM drive, and sound card. The school recommends the following software: Windows 95 or higher for an operating system (or the Macintosh equivalent), a Web browser (must be Netscape Navigator 3.0, Microsoft Internet Explorer 3.0, or America Online 3.0 or higher) with Java and JavaScript options enabled, a word processor (Microsoft Word 6.0 or higher recommended), and e-mail software.

Example Course Titles: Some of the course titles in this program include Principles of Educational Administration, The Funding of Educational Institutions, The Java and JavaScript, Education and the Law, Supervisory Principles, Innovative Leadership, Politics of Higher Education, and Personnel Administration.

Program Contact: School of Education and Professional Development
Capella University
330 Second Avenue South, Suite 550
Minneapolis, Minnesota, 55401
(888) CAPELLA

Educational Administration

Degree Offered: Doctor of Philosophy

Program Web Address: www. CapellaUniversity.com/8/82b.htm

Program Background: This program prepares students for leadership roles in higher education in a variety of work settings. The curriculum focuses on understanding the interconnectedness of the society, the organization, and the unique dimensions of higher and adult continuing education organizations. It integrates theory and practice, and strives to help students develop an awareness of their own roles and abilities related to organizations and emerging societal issues.

Application Requirements: You must have a Master's degree (or its foreign equivalent) from a regionally accredited or internationally recognized institution, and a minimum graduate grade point average of 3.0 (on a 4.0 scale) or its equivalent from an international institution.

Completion Requirements: You must successfully complete 120 quarter credits.

On Campus Requirements: There are residency requirements for this programs.

System Requirements: You need to have a personal computer with a minimum processor speed of 486DX (Pentium or equivalent recommended) or the Macintosh equivalent, a 28.8K modem (or faster), enough RAM (memory) to support your operating system (for example, a minimum of 16MB for Windows 95), a video card (800 × 600 pixel screen resolution and a minimum of 16-bit colors), CD-ROM drive, and sound card. The school recommends the following software: Windows 95 or higher for an operating system (or the Macintosh equivalent), a Web browser (must be Netscape Navigator 3.0, Microsoft Internet Explorer 3.0, or America Online 3.0 or higher) with Java and JavaScript options enabled, a word processor (Microsoft Word 6.0 or higher recommended), and e-mail software.

Example Course Titles: Some of the course titles in this program include Survey of Research in Societal and Cultural Change, Survey of Research in Human Development and Behavior, Survey of Research in Organizational and

Group Dynamics, The Governance of Educational Institutions, Funding and Managing Education Enterprises, Higher Education Administration, The History of Higher Education, Advanced Study in Research Methods, The Funding of Educational Institutions, Education and the Law, The Politics of Higher Education, Personnel Administration, and Leadership in Higher Education.

Program Contact: School of Education and Professional Development
Capella University
330 Second Avenue South, Suite 550
Minneapolis, Minnesota 55401
(888) CAPELLA

Educational Administration

Degree Offered: Master of Science

Program Web Address: www. CapellaUniversity.com/8/82b.htm

Program Background: This program prepares professionals to assume leadership positions in a variety of organizational environments, including schools, human services agencies, military units and religious organizations.

Application Requirements: You must have a Bachelor's degree (or its foreign equivalent) from a regionally accredited or internationally recognized institution, and a minimum undergraduate grade point average of 2.7 (on a 4.0 scale) or its equivalent from an international institution.

Completion Requirements: You must successfully complete 48 quarter credits

On Campus Requirements: This program has residency requirements. Please contact the school directly for additional information.

System Requirements: You need to have a personal computer with a minimum processor speed of 486DX (Pentium or equivalent recommended) or the Macintosh equivalent, a 28.8K modem (or faster), enough RAM (memory) to support your operating system (for example, a minimum of 16MB for Windows 95), a video card (800 × 600 pixel screen resolution and a minimum of 16-bit colors), CD-ROM drive, and sound card. The school recommends the following software: Windows 95 or higher for an operating system (or the Macintosh equivalent), a Web browser (must be Netscape Navigator 3.0, Microsoft Internet Explorer 3.0, or America Online 3.0 or higher) with Java and JavaScript options enabled, a word processor (Microsoft Word 6.0 or higher recommended), and e-mail software.

Example Course Titles: Some of the course titles in this program include Survey of Research in Societal and Cultural Change, Evaluating the Effectiveness of the Educational Process, The Future of Educational Institutions: Topics and Trends, Survey of Research Methodology, Integrative Project, Principles of Educational Administration, The Funding of Educational Institutions, Education and the Law, Supervisory Principles, and Innovative Leadership.

Program Contact: School of Education and Professional Development
Capella University
330 Second Avenue South, Suite 550
Minneapolis, Minnesota 55401
(888) CAPELLA

Educational Psychology

Degree Offered: Certificate

Program Web Address: www. CapellaUniversity.com/10/102c.htm

Program Background: This program is designed for graduates of the Master of Science degree in educational psychology with a school psychology emphasis or others who have similar educational backgrounds.

Completion Requirements: You must successfully complete 29 quarter credits.

System Requirements: You need to have a personal computer with a minimum processor speed of 486DX (Pentium or equivalent recommended) or the Macintosh equivalent, a 28.8K modem (or faster), enough RAM (memory) to support your operating system (for example, a minimum of 16MB for Windows 95), a video card (800 × 600 pixel screen resolution and a minimum of 16-bit colors), CD-ROM drive, and sound card. The school recommends the following software: Windows 95 or higher for an operating system (or the Macintosh equivalent), a Web browser (must be Netscape Navigator 3.0, Microsoft Internet Explorer 3.0, or America Online 3.0 or higher) with Java and JavaScript options enabled, a word processor (Microsoft Word 6.0 or higher recommended), and e-mail software.

Example Course Titles: Some of the course titles in this program include Ethics and Standards of Professional Practice, Principles of School Psychology, Internship in School Psychology, and Principles of Learning and Instructional Design.

Program Contact: School of Psychology
Capella University
330 Second Avenue South, Suite 550
Minneapolis, Minnesota 55401
(888) CAPELLA

Educational Psychology

Degree Offered: Master of Science

Program Web Address: www. CapellaUniversity.com/10/102c.htm

Program Background: Students in this program can specialize in Academic Psychology, Developmental Psychology, or School Psychology. Additionally, students can tailor their degree program through the selection of elective courses.

Application Requirements: You must have a Bachelor's degree (or its foreign equivalent) from a regionally accredited or internationally recognized institution and a minimum undergraduate grade point average of 2.7 (on a 4.0 scale) or its equivalent from an international institution.

Completion Requirements: You must successfully complete 60 quarter credits.

System Requirements: You need to have a personal computer with a minimum processor speed of 486DX (Pentium or equivalent recommended) or the Macintosh equivalent, a 28.8K modem (or faster), enough RAM (memory) to support your operating system (for example, a minimum of 16MB for Windows 95), a video card (800 × 600 pixel screen resolution and a minimum of 16-bit colors), CD-ROM drive, and sound card. The school recommends the following software: Windows 95 or higher for an operating system (or the Macintosh equivalent), a Web browser (must be Netscape Navigator 3.0, Microsoft Internet Explorer 3.0, or America Online 3.0 or higher) with Java and JavaScript options enabled, a word processor (Microsoft Word 6.0 or higher recommended), and e-mail software.

Example Course Titles: Some of the course titles in this program include Lifespan Development, Adult Psychology, Psychology of Learning, Cognitive Psychology, Tests and Measurements, Methods of Clinical Inquiry, Research Methods, Teaching Psychology, Computer-Mediated Instruction, and Adult Learner in the Classroom.

Program Contact: School of Psychology
Capella University
330 Second Avenue South, Suite 550
Minneapolis, Minnesota 55401
(888) CAPELLA

Educational Psychology

Degree Offered: Doctor of Philosophy

Program Web Address: www. CapellaUniversity.com/10/102c.htm

Program Background: Students in this program can choose an area of emphasis from Academic Psychology, Developmental Psychology, and School Psychology. Additionally, students may tailor their degree program through the selection of elective courses from Psychology or other disciplines.

Application Requirements: You must have a Master's degree (or its foreign equivalent) from a regionally accredited or internationally recognized institution, and a minimum graduate grade point average of 3.0 (on a 4.0 scale) or its equivalent from an international institution.

Completion Requirements: You must successfully complete 120-124 quarter credits.

On Campus Requirements: This program has a series of brief residencies that you are required to attend. You should contact the school directly for additional information.

System Requirements: You need to have a personal computer with a minimum processor speed of 486DX (Pentium or equivalent recommended) or the Macintosh equivalent, a 28.8K modem (or faster), enough RAM (memory) to support your operating system (for example, a minimum of 16MB for Windows 95), a video card (800 × 600 pixel screen resolution and a minimum of 16-bit colors), CD-ROM drive, and sound card. The school recommends the following software: Windows 95 or higher for an operating system (or the Macintosh equivalent), a Web browser (must be Netscape Navigator 3.0, Microsoft Internet Explorer 3.0, or America Online 3.0 or higher) with Java and JavaScript options enabled, a word processor (Microsoft Word 6.0 or higher recommended), and e-mail software.

Example Course Titles: Some of the course titles in this program include Lifespan Developmentor, Adolescent Psychology, Adult Psychology, Psychology of Learning, Cognitive Psychology, Tests and Measurements, Inferential Statistics, Qualitative Analysis, Methods of Clinical Inquiry, Research Methods, Teaching Psychology, Computer-Mediated Instruction, Adult Learner in the Classroom, Mentoring Psychological Research, and Career and Life Planning.

Program Contact: School of Psychology
Capella University
330 Second Avenue South, Suite 550
Minneapolis, Minnesota 55401
(888) CAPELLA

General Management

Degree Offered: Certificate

Program Web Address: www. CapellaUniversity.com/7/72d.htm

Program Background: This program is designed to give students a broad managerial education. The courses cover the major components of management in any type organization.

Completion Requirements: You must successfully complete five required courses.

System Requirements: You need to have a personal computer with a minimum processor speed of 486DX (Pentium or equivalent recommended) or the Macintosh equivalent, a 28.8K modem (or faster), enough RAM (memory) to support your operating system (for example, a minimum of 16MB for Windows 95), a video card (800 × 600 pixel screen resolution and a minimum of 16-bit colors), CD-ROM drive, and sound card. The school recommends the following software: Windows 95 or higher for an operating system (or the Macintosh equivalent), a Web browser (must be Netscape Navigator 3.0, Microsoft Internet Explorer 3.0, or America Online 3.0 or higher) with Java and JavaScript options enabled, a word processor (Microsoft Word 6.0 or higher recommended), and e-mail software.

Example Course Titles: Some of the course titles in this program include Management and Organizational Behavior, Marketing Strategy and Practice, Accounting and Financial Management, Strategic Planning, and Information Systems Management.

Program Contact: School of Business
Capella University
330 Second Avenue South, Suite 550
Minneapolis, Minnesota 55401
(888) CAPELLA

Health Care Administration

Degree Offered: Certificate

Program Web Address: www. CapellaUniversity.com/9/92c.htm

Program Background: This program is designed for students currently work in technical or scientific positions in the field, who wish to enhance their education and advance their careers by obtaining the certificate.

Completion Requirements: You must successfully complete 16 quarter credits

System Requirements: You need to have a personal computer with a minimum processor speed of 486DX (Pentium or equivalent recommended) or the Macintosh equivalent, a 28.8K modem (or faster), enough RAM (memory) to support your operating system (for example, a minimum of 16MB for Windows 95), a video card (800 × 600 pixel screen resolution and a minimum of 16-bit colors), CD-ROM drive, and sound card. The school recommends the following software: Windows 95 or higher for an operating system (or the Macintosh equivalent), a Web browser (must be Netscape Navigator 3.0, Microsoft Internet Explorer 3.0, or America Online 3.0 or higher) with Java and JavaScript options enabled, a word processor (Microsoft Word 6.0 or higher recommended), and e-mail software.

Example Course Titles: Some of the course titles in this program include Families, Systems, and Healthcare, Contexts and Models of Health, Health in the Workplace, and Managed Care and the Health Services Industry.

Program Contact: School of Human Services
Capella University
330 Second Avenue South, Suite 550
Minneapolis, Minnesota 55401
(888) CAPELLA

Health Care Administration

Degree Offered: Master of Science

Program Web Address: www. CapellaUniversity.com/9/92c.htm

Program Background: This program is designed for students who are professionals practicing in the field of health care service delivery. These include nurses, nurse practitioners and physician's assistants, who wish to advance their careers by obtaining additional education and a Master's degree.

Application Requirements: You must have a Bachelor's degree (or its foreign equivalent) from a regionally accredited or internationally recognized institution, and minimum undergraduate grade point average of 2.7 (on a 4.0 scale) or its equivalent from an international institution.

Completion Requirements: You must successfully complete 48 quarter credits.

System Requirements: You need to have a personal computer with a minimum processor speed of 486DX (Pentium or equivalent recommended) or the Macintosh equivalent, a 28.8K modem (or faster), enough RAM (memory) to support your operating system (for example, a minimum of 16MB for Windows 95), a video card (800 × 600 pixel screen resolution and a minimum of 16-bit colors), CD-ROM drive, and sound card. The school recommends the following software: Windows 95 or higher for an operating system (or the Macintosh equivalent), a Web browser (must be Netscape Navigator 3.0, Microsoft Internet Explorer 3.0, or America Online 3.0 or higher) with Java and JavaScript options enabled, a word processor (Microsoft Word 6.0 or higher recommended), and e-mail software.

Example Course Titles: Some of the course titles in this program include Survey of Research in Human Development, Survey of Research in Societal and Cultural Change, Survey of Research Methodology, Social Systems, Scope of Human Services, Integrative Project, Families, Systems, and Healthcare, Contexts and Models of Health, Health in the Workplace, Managed Care and the Health Services Industry, Health Care Counseling, Health Advocacy in the Community, Mind/Body Healing Practices, Health Care Communication: Providers and Receivers, Role/Function of Boards and CEO's, Accounting and Financial Management, Strategic Planning Power and Politics in Organizations, Human Resources Management, and Leadership Tools for Successful Project Management.

Program Contact: School of Human Services
Capella University
330 Second Avenue South, Suite 550
Minneapolis, Minnesota 55401
(888) CAPELLA

Health Care Administration

Degree Offered: Doctor of Philosophy

Program Web Address: www. CapellaUniversity.com/9/92c.htm

Program Background: This program is designed for students who have a Master's degree in health care or a related field such as business or public administration, or are licensed health care professionals who wish to advance their careers to administrative or supervisory levels.

Application Requirements: You must have a Master's degree (or its foreign equivalent) from a regionally accredited or internationally recognized institution, and a minimum graduate grade point average of 3.0 (on a 4.0 scale) or its equivalent from an international institution.

Completion Requirements: You must successfully complete 120 quarter credits.

On Campus Requirements: There are residency requirements for this program. You should contact the school directly for information about them.

System Requirements: You need to have a personal computer with a minimum processor speed of 486DX (Pentium or equivalent recommended) or the Macintosh equivalent, a 28.8K modem (or faster), enough RAM (memory) to support your operating system (for example, a minimum of 16MB for Windows 95), a video card (800 × 600 pixel screen resolution and a minimum of 16-bit colors), CD-ROM drive, and sound card. The school recommends the following software: Windows 95 or higher for an operating system (or the Macintosh equivalent), a Web browser (must be Netscape Navigator 3.0, Microsoft Internet Explorer 3.0, or America Online 3.0 or higher) with Java and JavaScript options enabled, a word processor (Microsoft Word 6.0 or higher recommended), and e-mail software.

Example Course Titles: Some of the course titles in this program include Survey of Research in Human Development, Survey of Research in Organizational and Group Dynamics, Survey of Research in Societal and Cultural Chang, Proseminar, Social Systems, Scope of Human Services, Families, Systems and Healthcare, Contexts and Models of Health, Health in the Workplace, Managed Care and Health Services, and Advanced Research Methodology.

Program Contact: School of Human Services

Capella University
330 Second Avenue South, Suite 550
Minneapolis, Minnesota 55401
(888) CAPELLA

Health Psychology

Degree Offered: Master of Science

Program Web Address: www.
CapellaUniversity.com/10/102d.htm

Application Requirements: You must have a Bachelor's degree (or its foreign equivalent) from a regionally accredited or internationally recognized institution, and minimum undergraduate grade point average of 2.7 (on a 4.0 scale) or its equivalent from an international institution.

Completion Requirements: You must successfully complete 60 quarter credits.

System Requirements: You need to have a personal computer with a minimum processor speed of 486DX (Pentium or equivalent recommended) or the Macintosh equivalent, a 28.8K modem (or faster), enough RAM (memory) to support your operating system (for example, a minimum of 16MB for Windows 95), a video card (800 × 600 pixel screen resolution and a minimum of 16-bit colors), CD-ROM drive, and sound card. The school recommends the following software: Windows 95 or higher for an operating system (or the Macintosh equivalent), a Web browser (must be Netscape Navigator 3.0, Microsoft Internet Explorer 3.0, or America Online 3.0 or higher) with Java and JavaScript options enabled, a word processor (Microsoft Word 6.0 or higher recommended), and e-mail software.

Example Course Titles: Some of the course titles in this program include Biological Basis of Behavior, Psychology of Learning, Cognitive Psychology, Tests and Measurements, Methods

of Clinical Inquiry, Research Method, Principles of Health Psychology, Environmental Health and Behavior, and Health Care Delivery.

Program Contact: School of Psychology
Capella University
330 Second Avenue South, Suite 550
Minneapolis, Minnesota 55401
(888) CAPELLA

Health Psychology

Degree Offered: Doctor of Philosophy

Program Web Address: www.
CapellaUniversity.com/10/102d.htm

Application Requirements: You must have a Master's degree (or its foreign equivalent) from a regionally accredited or internationally recognized institution, and minimum graduate grade point average of 3.0 (on a 4.0 scale) or its equivalent from an international institution.

Completion Requirements: You must successfully complete 120 quarter credits.

On Campus Requirements: There are several brief residencies you are required to attend. You should contact the school directly for additional information.

System Requirements: You need to have a personal computer with a minimum processor speed of 486DX (Pentium or equivalent recommended) or the Macintosh equivalent, a 28.8K modem (or faster), enough RAM (memory) to support your operating system (for example, a minimum of 16MB for Windows 95), a video card (800 × 600 pixel screen resolution and a minimum of 16-bit colors), CD-ROM drive, and sound card. The school recommends the following software: Windows 95 or higher for an operating system (or the Macintosh equivalent), a Web browser (must be Netscape Navigator 3.0, Microsoft Internet Explorer 3.0, or America Online 3.0 or higher) with Java and JavaScript options enabled, a word processor (Microsoft Word 6.0 or higher recommended), and e-mail software.

Example Course Titles: Some of the course titles in this program include Life Span Development, Child Psychology, Adolescent Psychology, Adult Psychology, Geriatric Psychology, Psychology of Learning, Cognitive Psychology, Social Psychology, Group Psychology, Multicultural Perspectives in Human Behavior, Tests and Measurements, Inferential Statistics, Qualitative Analyses, Methods of Clinical Inquiry, Research Methods, Principles of Health Psychology, Environmental Health and Behavior, Health Care Delivery, Community Psychology, Innovative Health Care Practices, Coping with Chronic Physical Illness, and Cognitive-Affective Basis of Physical Illness.

Program Contact: School of Psychology
Capella University
330 Second Avenue South, Suite 550
Minneapolis, Minnesota 55401
(888) CAPELLA

Human Services

Degree Offered: Master of Science

Program Web Address: www. CapellaUniversity.com/9/92a.htm

Program Background: This Master's program is the most popular in Capella's School of Human Services because of its flexibility and relevance to the professional goals of most of the students who enroll in it. It has a student-centered curriculum, featuring fewer required foundation and core courses yet maintaining a certain number of research courses.

Application Requirements: For admission in the Master of Science program, you must have a Bachelor's degree (or equivalent) from a re-

gionally accredited or internationally recognized institution, and an undergraduate grade point average of at least 2.7 (on a 4.0 scale) or its equivalent from an international institution.

Completion Requirements: You must successfully complete 48 quarter credits.

System Requirements: You need to have a personal computer with a minimum processor speed of 486DX (Pentium or equivalent recommended) or the Macintosh equivalent, a 28.8K modem (or faster), enough RAM (memory) to support your operating system (for example, a minimum of 16MB for Windows 95), a video card (800 × 600 pixel screen resolution and a minimum of 16-bit colors), CD-ROM drive, and sound card. The school recommends the following software: Windows 95 or higher for an operating system (or the Macintosh equivalent), a Web browser (must be Netscape Navigator 3.0, Microsoft Internet Explorer 3.0, or America Online 3.0 or higher) with Java and JavaScript options enabled, a word processor (Microsoft Word 6.0 or higher recommended), and e-mail software.

Example Course Titles: Some of the course titles in this program include a Survey of Research in Human Development, Proseminar, Social Systems, Scope of Human Services, and Survey of Research Methodology.

Program Contact: School of Human Services
Capella University
330 Second Avenue South, Suite 550
Minneapolis, Minnesota 55401
(888) CAPELLA

Human Services

Degree Offered: Doctor of Philosophy

Program Web Address: www. CapellaUniversity.com/9/92a.htm

Program Background: This Doctoral program is the most popular in Capella's School of Human Services because of its flexibility and relevance to the professional goals of most of the students who enroll in it. It has a student-centered curriculum, featuring fewer required foundation and core courses yet maintaining a certain number of research courses.

Application Requirements: You must have a Master's degree (or its foreign equivalent) from a regionally accredited or internationally recognized institution and a graduate-school grade point average of at least 3.0 (on a 4.0 scale) or its equivalent from an international institution.

Completion Requirements: You must successfully complete 120 quarter credits to earn this doctoral degree.

On Campus Requirements: Please contact the School of Human Services for information about residency requirements.

System Requirements: You need to have a personal computer with a minimum processor speed of 486DX (Pentium or equivalent recommended) or the Macintosh equivalent, a 28.8K modem (or faster), enough RAM (memory) to support your operating system (for example, a minimum of 16MB for Windows 95), a video card (800 × 600 pixel screen resolution and a minimum of 16-bit colors), CD-ROM drive, and sound card. The school recommends the following software: Windows 95 or higher for an operating system (or the Macintosh equivalent), a Web browser (must be Netscape Navigator 3.0, Microsoft Internet Explorer 3.0, or America Online 3.0 or higher) with Java and JavaScript options enabled, a word processor (Microsoft Word 6.0 or higher recommended), and e-mail software.

Example Course Titles: Some of the course titles include Survey of Research in Human Development, Survey of Research in Organizational and Group Dynamics, Survey of Research in Societal and Cultural Change, Proseminar, Social Systems, Scope of Human Services, and Advanced Research Methodology.

Program Contact: School of Human Services
Capella University
330 Second Avenue South, Suite 550
Minneapolis, Minnesota 55401
(888) CAPELLA

Information Technology

Degree Offered: Business Administration Certificate

Program Web Address: www. CapellaUniversity.com/7/72d.htm

Program Background: Capella University's Certificate in Information Technology is designed to prepare students as managers to plan, develop, and manage technology systems. The courses encourage students to apply what they are learning in their companies or organizations.

Completion Requirements: You must successfully complete 16 quarter credits.

System Requirements: You need to have a personal computer with a minimum processor speed of 486DX (Pentium or equivalent recommended) or the Macintosh equivalent, a 28.8K modem (or faster), enough RAM (memory) to support your operating system (for example, a minimum of 16MB for Windows 95), a video card (800 × 600 pixel screen resolution and a minimum of 16-bit colors), CD-ROM drive, and sound card. The school recommends the following software: Windows 95 or higher for an operating system (or the Macintosh equivalent), a Web browser (must be Netscape Navigator 3.0, Microsoft Internet Explorer 3.0, or America Online 3.0 or higher) with Java and

JavaScript options enabled, a word processor (Microsoft Word 6.0 or higher recommended), and e-mail software.

Example Course Titles: Some of the course titles for this program include Technology Management, Information Systems Strategy, Managing Network and Information Systems, Managing in the Technical Environment, and Technical Infrastructure.

Program Contact: School of Business
Capella University
330 Second Avenue South, Suite 550
Minneapolis, Minnesota 55401
(888) CAPELLA

Instructional Design

Degree Offered: Certificate

Program Web Address: www. CapellaUniversity.com/7/72d.htm

Program Background: This certificate program is designed to address the growing need for qualified instructional designers. Not only is it intended to train people for a career in the instructional technology field, but it is also intended to benefit those already in the field. Courses emphasize design over implementation.

Completion Requirements: You must successfully complete 16 quarter credits for this certificate.

System Requirements: You need to have a personal computer with a minimum processor speed of 486DX (Pentium or equivalent recommended) or the Macintosh equivalent, a 28.8K modem (or faster), enough RAM (memory) to support your operating system (for example, a minimum of 16MB for Windows 95), a video card (800 × 600 pixel screen resolution and a minimum of 16-bit colors), CD-ROM drive, and sound card. The school recommends the following software: Windows 95 or higher

for an operating system (or the Macintosh equivalent), a Web browser (must be Netscape Navigator 3.0, Microsoft Internet Explorer 3.0, or America Online 3.0 or higher) with Java and JavaScript options enabled, a word processor (Microsoft Word 6.0 or higher recommended), and e-mail software.

Example Course Titles: Some of the course titles in this program include Introduction to Multimedia and Web-Based Instruction, Advanced Techniques in Instructional Design, Interface Design, Instructional Design, Developing Effective Assessment, Project Management for Multimedia Development, and Authorware Fundamentals.

Program Contact: School of Business
Capella University
330 Second Avenue South, Suite 550
Minneapolis, Minnesota 55401
(888) CAPELLA

Instructional Design

Degree Offered: Certificate

Program Web Address: www. CapellaUniversity.com/8/82e.htm

Program Background: This certificate program is intended to benefit professionals who are already working in the field of instructional design, as well as people who want to enter the field. The courses emphasize design over implementation. Students who earn this certificate and want to pursue their Master's or doctorate through Capella University may apply all of the credits (up to 16 quarter credits) from this certificate toward their graduate degree.

Completion Requirements: You must complete 16 quarter credits for this certificate.

On Campus Requirements: You need to contact Capella University directly for information about on-campus requirements.

System Requirements: You need to have a personal computer with a minimum processor speed of 486DX (Pentium or equivalent recommended) or the Macintosh equivalent, a 28.8K modem (or faster), enough RAM (memory) to support your operating system (for example, a minimum of 16MB for Windows 95), a video card (800 × 600 pixel screen resolution and a minimum of 16-bit colors), CD-ROM drive, and sound card. The school recommends the following software: Windows 95 or higher for an operating system (or the Macintosh equivalent), a Web browser (must be Netscape Navigator 3.0, Microsoft Internet Explorer 3.0, or America Online 3.0 or higher) with Java and JavaScript options enabled, a word processor (Microsoft Word 6.0 or higher recommended), and e-mail software.

Example Course Titles: Some of the course titles in this program include Introduction to Multimedia and Web-Based Instruction, Advanced Techniques in Instructional Design, Interface Design, Instructional Design, Developing Effective Assessment, Project Management for Multimedia Development, and Authorware Fundamentals.

Program Contact: School of Education and Professional Development
Capella University
330 Second Avenue South, Suite 550
Minneapolis, Minnesota 55401
(888) CAPELLA

Instructional Design

Degree Offered: Master of Science

Program Web Address: www.CapellaUniversity.com/8/82b.htm

Program Background: This Master of Science program has a specialization in Instructional Design and is geared toward professionals who are already working in business, training, and education.

Application Requirements: You must have a bachelor's degree from a regionally accredited institution or the foreign equivalent from an internationally recognized institution. Also you must have a minimum undergraduate grade point average of 2.7 (on a 4.0 scale).

Completion Requirements: You must successfully complete 48 quarter credits for this degree.

On Campus Requirements: You need to contact Capella University directly for information about on-campus requirements.

System Requirements: You need to have a personal computer with a minimum processor speed of 486DX (Pentium or equivalent recommended) or the Macintosh equivalent, a 28.8K modem (or faster), enough RAM (memory) to support your operating system (for example, a minimum of 16MB for Windows 95), a video card (800 × 600 pixel screen resolution and a minimum of 16-bit colors), CD-ROM drive, and sound card. The school recommends the following software: Windows 95 or higher for an operating system (or the Macintosh equivalent), a Web browser (must be Netscape Navigator 3.0, Microsoft Internet Explorer 3.0, or America Online 3.0 or higher) with Java and JavaScript options enabled, a word processor (Microsoft Word 6.0 or higher recommended), and e-mail software.

Example Course Titles: Some of the course titles in this program include Survey of Research in Societal and Cultural Change, Evaluating the Effectiveness of the Educational Process, The Future of Educational Institutes: Topics and Trends, Survey of Research Methodology, Advanced Techniques in Instructional Design, Developing Effective Online Assessment, and Authorware Fundamentals.

Program Contact: School of Education and Professional Development
Capella University

330 Second Avenue South, Suite 550
Minneapolis, Minnesota 55401
(888) CAPELLA

Instructional Design

Degree Offered: Doctor of Philosophy

Program Web Address: www.
CapellaUniversity.com/8/82b.htm

Program Background: Capella University's Doctor of Philosophy (PhD) with a specialization in Instructional Design is intended for professionals in the instructional technology field who are interested in leadership roles.

Application Requirements: You must have a Master's degree from a regionally accredited institution or its foreign equivalent from an internationally recognized institution. Also you must have a minimum grade point average of 3.0 (on a 4.0 scale).

Completion Requirements: You must successfully complete 120 quarter credits for this degree.

On Campus Requirements: You need to contact Capella University directly for information about on-campus requirements.

System Requirements: You must have Internet access and an e-mail address. And you need to have a personal computer with a minimum processor speed of 486DX (Pentium or equivalent recommended) or the Macintosh equivalent, a 28.8K modem (or faster), enough RAM (memory) to support your operating system (for example, a minimum of 16MB for Windows 95), a video card (800 × 600 pixel screen resolution and a minimum of 16-bit colors), CD-ROM drive, and sound card. The school recommends the following software: Windows 95 or higher for an operating system (or the Macintosh equivalent), a Web browser (must be Netscape Navigator 3.0, Microsoft Internet Explorer 3.0, or America Online 3.0 or higher)

with Java and JavaScript options enabled, a word processor (Microsoft Word 6.0 or higher recommended), and e-mail software.

Example Course Titles: Some of the course titles for this program include Survey of Research in Societal and Cultural Change, Survey of Research in Human Development and Behavior, Evaluating the Effectiveness of the Education Process, The Future of Educational Institutions: Topics and Trends, Theoretical Basis of Instructional Design, Ethics and Social Responsibility in Distance Education, and Advanced Study in Research Methods.

Program Contact: School of Education and Professional Development
Capella University
330 Second Avenue South, Suite 550
Minneapolis, Minnesota 55401
(888) CAPELLA

Leadership

Degree Offered: Business Administration Certificate

Program Web Address: www.
CapellaUniversity.com/7/72d.htm

Program Background: This certificate program prepares students to become leaders who are capable of critical thought and problem solving. It focuses on the study of ethics, team building, and managing change.

Completion Requirements: You must successfully complete 16 quarter credits.

System Requirements: You need to have a personal computer with a minimum processor speed of 486DX (Pentium or equivalent recommended) or the Macintosh equivalent, a 28.8K modem (or faster), enough RAM (memory) to support your operating system (for example, a minimum of 16MB for Windows 95), a video card (800 × 600 pixel screen resolution and a minimum of 16-bit colors), CD-ROM drive, and sound card. The school recommends the following software: Windows 95 or higher for an operating system (or the Macintosh equivalent), a Web browser (must be Netscape Navigator 3.0, Microsoft Internet Explorer 3.0, or America Online 3.0 or higher) with Java and JavaScript options enabled, a word processor (Microsoft Word 6.0 or higher recommended), and e-mail software.

Example Course Titles: Some of the course titles in this program include Leading the Organization: Structure, Culture and Change, Management Ethics and Values, Leadership and Change Management, The Self-Directed Leader, and Applied Leadership.

Program Contact: School of Business
Capella University
330 Second Avenue South, Suite 550
Minneapolis, Minnesota 55401
(888) CAPELLA

Marriage and Family Services

Degree Offered: Certificate

Program Web Address: www.
CapellaUniversity.com/9/92d.htm

Program Background: Most of the students enrolled in this program are pursuing a degree in another division of the University and want to broaden their knowledge. Students who have completed courses similar to the ones in this program elsewhere can tailor their program of study by replacing the courses with the approval of the dean. This certificate does not substitute for a license to practice in any state or province.

Application Requirements: You must have your Bachelor's degree or a graduate degree.

Completion Requirements: You must successfully complete 16 quarter credits for this certificate.

Time for Completion: You can complete the coursework for this certificate in two to four quarters, depending on whether you enroll on a full- or part-time basis.

On Campus Requirements: This program has no on-campus requirements.

System Requirements: You need to have a personal computer with a minimum processor speed of 486DX (Pentium or equivalent recommended) or the Macintosh equivalent, a 28.8K modem (or faster), enough RAM (memory) to support your operating system (for example, a minimum of 16MB for Windows 95), a video card (800 $\times$ 600 pixel screen resolution and a minimum of 16-bit colors), CD-ROM drive, and sound card. The school recommends the following software: Windows 95 or higher for an operating system (or the Macintosh equivalent), a Web browser (must be Netscape Navigator 3.0, Microsoft Internet Explorer 3.0, or America Online 3.0 or higher) with Java and JavaScript options enabled, a word processor (Microsoft Word 6.0 or higher recommended), and e-mail software.

Example Course Titles: Some of the course titles in this program include Marriage and Family Systems, Marriage and Marital Therapy, Methods of Family Research, and Family Therapy: Theories and Methods.

Program Contact: School of Human Services
Capella University
330 Second Avenue South, Suite 550
Minneapolis, Minnesota 55401
(888) CAPELLA

Marriage and Family Services

Degree Offered: Master of Science

Program Web Address: www.
CapellaUniversity.com/9/92d.htm

Program Background: This program is designed for professionals in marital and family therapy who wish to advance in their careers, and for people who are working in an unrelated field and want to change careers.

Application Requirements: For admission in the Master of Science program, you must have a Bachelor's degree (or equivalent) from a regionally accredited or internationally recognized institution, and an undergraduate grade point average of at least 2.7 (on a 4.0 scale) or its equivalent from an international institution.

Completion Requirements: You must successfully complete 48 quarter credits.

On Campus Requirements: You need to contact the school directly for information about on-campus requirements.

System Requirements: You need to have a personal computer with a minimum processor speed of 486DX (Pentium or equivalent recommended) or the Macintosh equivalent, a 28.8K modem (or faster), enough RAM (memory) to support your operating system (for example, a minimum of 16MB for Windows 95), a video card (800 × 600 pixel screen resolution and a minimum of 16-bit colors), CD-ROM drive, and sound card. The school recommends the following software: Windows 95 or higher for an operating system (or the Macintosh equivalent), a Web browser (must be Netscape Navigator 3.0, Microsoft Internet Explorer 3.0, or America Online 3.0 or higher) with Java and JavaScript options enabled, a word processor (Microsoft Word 6.0 or higher recommended), and e-mail software.

Example Course Titles: Some of the course titles for this program include Survey of Research in Human Development, Survey of Research Methodology, Social Systems, Scope of Human Services, Marriage and Family Systems, Methods of Family Research, Family

Therapy: Theories and Methods, Aging and Death, and Child and Adolescent Counseling.

Program Contact: School of Human Services
Capella University
330 Second Avenue South, Suite 550
Minneapolis, Minnesota 55401
(888) CAPELLA

Marriage and Family Services

Degree Offered: Doctor of Philosophy

Program Web Address: www. CapellaUniversity.com/9/92d.htm

Program Background: Most of the students enrolled in this program have their Master's degrees in professional counseling or another field related to marriage and family therapy.

Application Requirements: You must have a Master's degree (or its foreign equivalent) from a regionally accredited or internationally recognized institution and a graduate-school grade point average of at least 3.0 (on a 4.0 scale) or its equivalent from an international institution.

Completion Requirements: You must successfully complete 120 quarter hours for this degree.

On Campus Requirements: You need to contact the school directly for information about on-campus requirements.

System Requirements: You need to have a personal computer with a minimum processor speed of 486DX (Pentium or equivalent recommended) or the Macintosh equivalent, a 28.8K modem (or faster), enough RAM (memory) to support your operating system (for example, a minimum of 16MB for Windows 95), a video card (800 × 600 pixel screen resolution and a minimum of 16-bit colors), CD-ROM drive, and sound card. The school recommends the following software: Windows 95 or higher for an operating system (or the Macintosh equivalent), a Web browser (must be Netscape Navigator 3.0, Microsoft Internet Explorer 3.0, or America Online 3.0 or higher) with Java and JavaScript options enabled, a word processor (Microsoft Word 6.0 or higher recommended), and e-mail software.

Example Course Titles: Some of the course titles for this program include Survey of Research in Human Development, Survey of Research Methodology, Social Systems, Scope of Human Services, Marriage and Family Systems, Methods of Family Research, Family Therapy: Theories and Methods, Aging and Death, and Child and Adolescent Counseling.

Program Contact: School of Human Services
Capella University
330 Second Avenue South, Suite 550
Minneapolis, Minnesota 55401
(888) CAPELLA

Organization and Management

Degree Offered: Master of Science

Program Web Address: www. CapellaUniversity.com/7/72a.htm

Program Background: Capella University's Master of Science program is designed for management professionals who want additional knowledge and skills to advance in their careers. The program encourages students to incorporate their work experiences and corporate training in their degree programs.

Application Requirements: For admission in the Master of Science program, you must have a Bachelor's degree (or equivalent) from a regionally accredited or internationally recognized institution, and an undergraduate grade point average of at least 2.7 (on a 4.0 scale) or its equivalent from an international institution.

Completion Requirements: You must successfully complete 48 quarter credits for this degree.

If you received at least a B on any previous graduate coursework at a regionally accredited college or university, you may transfer up to 12 quarter credits towards this Master's degree.

Time for Completion: The minimum completion time for this degree is one year, and the maximum is three years. Typically, students fulfill all requirements within 18 months to 3 years, depending on the number of courses the students are able to take during a quarter.

System Requirements: You need to have a personal computer with a minimum processor speed of 486DX (Pentium or equivalent recommended) or the Macintosh equivalent, a 28.8K modem (or faster), enough RAM (memory) to support your operating system (for example, a minimum of 16MB for Windows 95), a video card (800 × 600 pixel screen resolution and a minimum of 16-bit colors), CD-ROM drive, and sound card. The school recommends the following software: Windows 95 or higher for an operating system (or the Macintosh equivalent), a Web browser (must be Netscape Navigator 3.0, Microsoft Internet Explorer 3.0, or America Online 3.0 or higher) with Java and JavaScript options enabled, a word processor (Microsoft Word 6.0 or higher recommended), and e-mail software.

Example Course Titles: Some of the course titles for this program include Management and Organizational Behavior, Marketing Strategy and Practice, Accounting and Financial Management, Strategic Planning, Information Systems Management, Quantitative Analysis, and Integrative Project.

Program Contact: School of Business

Capella University
330 Second Avenue South, Suite 550
Minneapolis, Minnesota 55401
(888) CAPELLA

Organization and Management

Degree Offered: Doctor of Philosophy

Program Web Address: www.
CapellaUniversity.com/7/72a.htm

Program Background: Students in this doctoral program build upon their own professional experiences. The program integrates theory and practice, and teaches students to relate their work to the foundations of management.

Application Requirements: You must have a Master's degree from a regionally accredited college or university, or the international equivalent. You must also have a minimum grade point average of 3.0 (on a 4.0 scale).

Completion Requirements: You must successfully complete 64 credit hours for this degree.

On Campus Requirements: You are required to attend an orientation session and three 2.5-day seminars in residence.

System Requirements: You need to have a personal computer with a minimum processor speed of 486DX (Pentium or equivalent recommended) or the Macintosh equivalent, a 28.8K modem (or faster), enough RAM (memory) to support your operating system (for example, a minimum of 16MB for Windows 95), a video card (800 × 600 pixel screen resolution and a minimum of 16-bit colors), CD-ROM drive, and sound card. The school recommends the following software: Windows 95 or higher for an operating system (or the Macintosh equivalent), a Web browser (must be Netscape Navigator 3.0, Microsoft Internet Explorer 3.0, or America Online 3.0 or higher) with Java and JavaScript options enabled, a word processor (Microsoft Word 6.0 or higher recommended), and e-mail software.

Example Course Titles: Some of the course titles for this program include Management and Organizational Behavior, Marketing Strategy and Practice, Accounting and Financial Management, Strategic Planning, Quantitative Analysis, Information Systems Management, and Advanced Study in Research Methods.

Program Contact: School of Business
Capella University
330 Second Avenue South, Suite 550
Minneapolis, Minnesota 55401
(888) CAPELLA

Organizational Psychology

Degree Offered: Certificate

Program Web Address: www.
CapellaUniversity.com/10/102e.htm

Program Background: This program is designed to enhance students' understanding of organizations and their management skills.

Application Requirements: You must have a bachelor's or graduate degree in order to enroll in this program.

Completion Requirements: You must successfully complete 20 quarter credits for this certificate.

Time for Completion: Students can typically complete the coursework for this certificate in two to three quarters.

On Campus Requirements: There are no on-campus requirements for this certificate.

System Requirements: You need to have a personal computer with a minimum processor speed of 486DX (Pentium or equivalent recommended) or the Macintosh equivalent, a 28.8K modem (or faster), enough RAM (memory) to support your operating system (for example, a minimum of 16MB for Windows 95), a video card (800 × 600 pixel screen resolution and a minimum of 16-bit colors), CD-ROM drive, and sound card. The school recommends the following software: Windows 95 or higher for an operating system (or the Macintosh equivalent), a Web browser (must be Netscape Navigator 3.0, Microsoft Internet Explorer 3.0, or America Online 3.0 or higher) with Java and JavaScript options enabled, a word processor (Microsoft Word 6.0 or higher recommended), and e-mail software.

Example Course Titles: Some of the course titles in this program include Psychotherapy Research, Ethics and Standards of Professional Practice, Health Care Delivery, and Managing Psychological Services.

Program Contact: School of Psychology
Capella University
330 Second Avenue South, Suite 550
Minneapolis, Minnesota 55401
(888) CAPELLA

Organizational Psychology

Degree Offered: Master of Science

Program Web Address: www. CapellaUniversity.com/10/102e.htm

Application Requirements: You must have a bachelor's degree from a regionally accredited college or university or an internationally recognized institution, and an undergraduate grade point average of at least 2.7 (on a 4.0 scale).

Completion Requirements: You must successfully complete 60 quarter credits for this degree. In addition to required courses, you have the option of completing either a comprehensive examination or a research project (an integrative project or a thesis). You also have the opportunity to tailor your coursework through your electives.

Time for Completion: Students typically complete this program in six quarters (18 months).

On Campus Requirements: There are no on-campus requirements.

System Requirements: You need to have a personal computer with a minimum processor speed of 486DX (Pentium or equivalent recommended) or the Macintosh equivalent, a 28.8K modem (or faster), enough RAM (memory) to support your operating system (for example, a minimum of 16MB for Windows 95), a video card (800 × 600 pixel screen resolution and a minimum of 16-bit colors), CD-ROM drive, and sound card. The school recommends the following software: Windows 95 or higher for an operating system (or the Macintosh equivalent), a Web browser (must be Netscape Navigator 3.0, Microsoft Internet Explorer 3.0, or America Online 3.0 or higher) with Java and JavaScript options enabled, a word processor (Microsoft Word 6.0 or higher recommended), and e-mail software.

Example Course Titles: Some of the course titles in this program include Lifespan Development, Adult Psychology, Psychology of Learning, Cognitive Psychology, Methods of Clinical Inquiry, Research Methods, Principles of Organizational Psychology, Psychology of Leadership, and Personnel Psychology.

Program Contact: School of Psychology
Capella University
330 Second Avenue South, Suite 550
Minneapolis, Minnesota 55401
(888) CAPELLA

Organizational Psychology

Degree Offered: Doctor of Philosophy

Program Web Address: www. CapellaUniversity.com/10/102e.htm

Program Background: This program is flexible in terms of the student's choice of core and specialty courses. Students also have the opportunity to customize their experience through their selection of electives from psychology and other disciplines.

Application Requirements: You must have a Master's degree (or the foreign equivalent) from a regionally accredited college or university, or an internationally recognized institution, and a minimum graduate grade point average of 3.0 (on a 4.0 scale).

Completion Requirements: You must successfully complete 120 quarter credits.

Time for Completion: Typically, students complete all program requirements in 12 quarters (three years).

On Campus Requirements: You are required to attend a series of brief on-campus residencies.

System Requirements: You need to have a personal computer with a minimum processor speed of 486DX (Pentium or equivalent recommended) or the Macintosh equivalent, a 28.8K modem (or faster), enough RAM (memory) to support your operating system (for example, a minimum of 16MB for Windows 95), a video card (800 × 600 pixel screen resolution and a minimum of 16-bit colors), CD-ROM drive, and sound card. The school recommends the following software: Windows 95 or higher for an operating system (or the Macintosh equivalent), a Web browser (must be Netscape Navigator 3.0, Microsoft Internet Explorer 3.0, or America Online 3.0 or higher) with Java and JavaScript options enabled, a word processor (Microsoft Word 6.0 or higher recommended), and e-mail software.

Example Course Titles: Some of the course titles in this program include Biological Bases of Behavior, Adult Psychology, Psychology of Learning, Social Psychology, Tests and Measurements, Methods of Clinical Inquiry, Principles of Organizational Psychology, Psy-

chology of Leadership, Personnel Psychology, and Performance Enhancement and Motivation.

Program Contact: School of Psychology
Capella University
330 Second Avenue South, Suite 550
Minneapolis, Minnesota 55401
(888) CAPELLA

Professional Counseling

Degree Offered: Certificate

Program Web Address: www.
CapellaUniversity.com/9/92b.htm

Program Background: This certificate program is designed for students who want to broaden their scope of knowledge in professional counseling. The resulting certificate is not intended to be a professional license to practice counseling in any state or province.

Application Requirements: You must have a Bachelor's or graduate degree.

Completion Requirements: You must successfully complete 16 quarter credits (four courses).

On Campus Requirements: You need to contact the school directly for information about on-campus requirements.

System Requirements: You need to have a personal computer with a minimum processor speed of 486DX (Pentium or equivalent recommended) or the Macintosh equivalent, a 28.8K modem (or faster), enough RAM (memory) to support your operating system (for example, a minimum of 16MB for Windows 95), a video card (800 × 600 pixel screen resolution and a minimum of 16-bit colors), CD-ROM drive, and sound card. The school recommends the following software: Windows 95 or higher for an operating system (or the Macintosh equivalent), a Web browser (must be Netscape Navigator 3.0, Microsoft Internet Explorer 3.0, or America Online 3.0 or higher) with Java and

JavaScript options enabled, a word processor (Microsoft Word 6.0 or higher recommended), and e-mail software.

Example Course Titles: Some of the course titles in this program include Theories of Personality, Professional and Scientific Ethics, Mental Health Counseling, and Psychopathology: Assessment and Treatment.

Program Contact: School of Human Services
Capella University
330 Second Avenue South, Suite 550
Minneapolis, Minnesota 55401
(888) CAPELLA

Professional Counseling

Degree Offered: Master of Science

Program Web Address: www.
CapellaUniversity.com/9/92b.htm

Program Background: This program is designed for students who are professionals in counseling careers and who want to advance in their careers by getting additional education, as well as for people who are practicing in another field, but wish to become professional counselors.

Application Requirements: You must have a Bachelor's degree or the foreign equivalent from a regionally accredited college or university or an internationally recognized institution, and a minimum undergraduate grade point average of 2.7 (on a 4.0 scale).

Completion Requirements: You must successfully complete 48 quarter credits for this degree.

On Campus Requirements: You need to contact the school directly for information about on-campus requirements.

System Requirements: You need to have a personal computer with a minimum processor speed of 486DX (Pentium or equivalent rec-

ommended) or the Macintosh equivalent, a 28.8K modem (or faster), enough RAM (memory) to support your operating system (for example, a minimum of 16MB for Windows 95), a video card (800 × 600 pixel screen resolution and a minimum of 16-bit colors), CD-ROM drive, and sound card. The school recommends the following software: Windows 95 or higher for an operating system (or the Macintosh equivalent), a Web browser (must be Netscape Navigator 3.0, Microsoft Internet Explorer 3.0, or America Online 3.0 or higher) with Java and JavaScript options enabled, a word processor (Microsoft Word 6.0 or higher recommended), and e-mail software.

Example Course Titles: Some of the course titles in this program include Survey of Research in Human Development, Survey of Research in Societal and Cultural Change, Survey of Research Methodology, Social Systems, Scope of Human Services, Integrative Project, Theories of Personality, Professional and Scientific Ethics, Mental Health Counseling, and Psychopathology: Assessment and Treatment.

Program Contact: School of Human Services
Capella University
330 Second Avenue South, Suite 550
Minneapolis, Minnesota 55401
(888) CAPELLA

Professional Counseling

Degree Offered: Doctor of Philosophy

Program Web Address: www.
CapellaUniversity.com/9/92b.htm

Program Background: This program is designed for students who have a Master's degree in counseling and are licensed in one of eight areas of professional counseling—mental health, career, college, school, addiction, rehabilitation, gerontology, or sports. Students prepare to teach, research in their field, administer treatment programs, supervise clinicians, or pursue private practice.

Application Requirements: You must have a Master's degree or the foreign equivalent from a regionally accredited college or university or an internationally recognized institution, and a minimum graduate grade point average of 3.0 (on a 4.0 scale).

Completion Requirements: You must successfully complete 120 quarter credits for this degree.

On Campus Requirements: You need to contact the school directly for information about on-campus requirements.

System Requirements: You need to have a personal computer with a minimum processor speed of 486DX (Pentium or equivalent recommended) or the Macintosh equivalent, a 28.8K modem (or faster), enough RAM (memory) to support your operating system (for example, a minimum of 16MB for Windows 95), a video card (800 × 600 pixel screen resolution and a minimum of 16-bit colors), CD-ROM drive, and sound card. The school recommends the following software: Windows 95 or higher for an operating system (or the Macintosh equivalent), a Web browser (must be Netscape Navigator 3.0, Microsoft Internet Explorer 3.0, or America Online 3.0 or higher) with Java and JavaScript options enabled, a word processor (Microsoft Word 6.0 or higher recommended), and e-mail software.

Example Course Titles: Some of the course titles in this program include Survey of Research in Human Development, Survey of Research in Organizational and Group Dynamics, Survey of Research in Societal and Cultural Change, Theories of Personality, Professional and Scientific Ethics, Social Systems, Scope of Human Services, Mental Health Counseling, Psychology: Assessment and Treatment, and Advanced Research Methodology.

Program Contact: School of Human Services
Capella University
330 Second Avenue South, Suite 550
Minneapolis, Minnesota 55401
(888) CAPELLA

Social and Community Services

Degree Offered: Certificate

Program Web Address: www. CapellaUniversity.com/9/92e.htm

Program Background: Most of the students who enroll in this program are pursuing degrees in other areas, and want to broaden their professional scope by getting this certificate as well.

Application Requirements: You must have at least a Bachelor's degree in order to pursue this certificate.

Completion Requirements: You must successfully complete 16 quarter credits for this certificate.

On Campus Requirements: There are no on-campus requirements.

System Requirements: You need to have a personal computer with a minimum processor speed of 486DX (Pentium or equivalent recommended) or the Macintosh equivalent, a 28.8K modem (or faster), enough RAM (memory) to support your operating system (for example, a minimum of 16MB for Windows 95), a video card (800 × 600 pixel screen resolution and a minimum of 16-bit colors), CD-ROM drive, and sound card. The school recommends the following software: Windows 95 or higher for an operating system (or the Macintosh equivalent), a Web browser (must be Netscape Navigator 3.0, Microsoft Internet Explorer 3.0, or America Online 3.0 or higher) with Java and JavaScript options enabled, a word processor (Microsoft Word 6.0 or higher recommended), and e-mail software.

Example Course Titles: Some of the course titles in this program include Philosophy of Social Work, Utilization of Community Resources, Applied/Clinical Sociology, and Role of Transportation in Human Services.

Program Contact: School of Human Services
Capella University
330 Second Avenue South, Suite 550
Minneapolis, Minnesota 55401
(888) CAPELLA

Social and Community Services

Degree Offered: Master of Science

Program Web Address: www. CapellaUniversity.com/9/92e.htm

Program Background: This program is designed for students who are working in the field of social and community services and who wish to advance in their careers by obtaining additional education. It is also appropriate for those who are employed in unrelated fields who wish to change professions.

Application Requirements: You must have a Bachelor's degree or its foreign equivalent from a regionally accredited college or university, or an internationally recognized institution, and a minimum grade point average of 2.7 (on a 4.0 scale).

Completion Requirements: You must successfully complete 48 quarter credits for this degree.

System Requirements: You need to have a personal computer with a minimum processor speed of 486DX (Pentium or equivalent recommended) or the Macintosh equivalent, a 28.8K modem (or faster), enough RAM (memory) to support your operating system (for example, a minimum of 16MB for Windows 95), a video card (800 × 600 pixel screen resolution and a minimum of 16-bit colors), CD-ROM drive, and sound card. The school recommends the following software: Windows 95 or higher for an operating system (or the Macintosh equivalent), a Web browser (must be Netscape Navigator 3.0, Microsoft Internet Explorer 3.0, or America Online 3.0 or higher) with Java and JavaScript options enabled, a word processor (Microsoft Word 6.0 or higher recommended), and e-mail software.

Example Course Titles: Some of the course titles in this program include Survey of Research in Human Development, Survey of Research in Societal and Cultural Change, Survey of Research Methodology, Social Systems, Scope of Human Services, and Philosophy of Social Work.

Program Contact: School of Human Services
Capella University
330 Second Avenue South, Suite 550
Minneapolis, Minnesota 55401
(888) CAPELLA

Social and Community Services

Degree Offered: Doctor of Philosophy

Program Web Address: www. CapellaUniversity.com/9/92e.htm

Program Background: This program is designed for students who have a Master's degree in sociology, psychology, or a related field, and may be licensed clinical social workers, psychologists, or professional counselors. It prepares the students to advance their careers to administration or supervisory levels in the field.

Application Requirements: You must have a Master's degree or the foreign equivalent from a regionally accredited college or university, or from an internationally recognized institution, and a minimum grade point average of 3.0 (on a 4.0 scale).

Completion Requirements: You must successfully complete 120 quarter credits for this degree.

On Campus Requirements: You should contact the school directly for information about on-campus requirements.

System Requirements: You need to have a personal computer with a minimum processor speed of 486DX (Pentium or equivalent recommended) or the Macintosh equivalent, a 28.8K modem (or faster), enough RAM (memory) to support your operating system (for example, a minimum of 16MB for Windows 95), a video card (800 × 600 pixel screen resolution and a minimum of 16-bit colors), CD-ROM drive, and sound card. The school recommends the following software: Windows 95 or higher for an operating system (or the Macintosh equivalent), a Web browser (must be Netscape Navigator 3.0, Microsoft Internet Explorer 3.0, or America Online 3.0 or higher) with Java and JavaScript options enabled, a word processor (Microsoft Word 6.0 or higher recommended), and e-mail software.

Example Course Titles: Some of the course titles in this program include Survey of Research in Human Development, Survey of Research in Organizational and Group Dynamics, Survey of Research in Societal and Cultural Change, Social Systems, Scope of Human Services, Philosophy of Social Work, and Utilization of Community Resources.

Program Contact: School of Human Services
Capella University
330 Second Avenue South, Suite 550
Minneapolis, Minnesota 55401
(888) CAPELLA

Sport Psychology

Degree Offered: Certificate

Program Web Address: www. CapellaUniversity.com/10/102f.htm

Program Background: This program is designed to help people currently working in the field of sport psychology enhance their under-standing of applying psychological principles to their work with amateur and professional athletes.

Application Requirements: You must have a Bachelor's or graduate degree to apply to this program.

Completion Requirements: You are required to successfully complete 20 quarter credits.

On Campus Requirements: There are no on-campus requirements for this program.

System Requirements: You need to have a personal computer with a minimum processor speed of 486DX (Pentium or equivalent recommended) or the Macintosh equivalent, a 28.8K modem (or faster), enough RAM (memory) to support your operating system (for example, a minimum of 16MB for Windows 95), a video card (800 × 600 pixel screen resolution and a minimum of 16-bit colors), CD-ROM drive, and sound card. The school recommends the following software: Windows 95 or higher for an operating system (or the Macintosh equivalent), a Web browser (must be Netscape Navigator 3.0, Microsoft Internet Explorer 3.0, or America Online 3.0 or higher) with Java and JavaScript options enabled, a word processor (Microsoft Word 6.0 or higher recommended), and e-mail software.

Example Course Titles: Some of the course titles in this program include Principles of Sports Psychology, Performance Enhancement in Sport, Applied Sport Psychology, and Exercise Psychology.

Program Contact: School of Psychology
Capella University
330 Second Avenue South, Suite 550
Minneapolis, Minnesota 55401
(888) CAPELLA

Sport Psychology

Degree Offered: Master of Science

Program Web Address: www. CapellaUniversity.com/10/102f.htm

Application Requirements: You must have a Bachelor's degree or foreign equivalent from a regionally accredited college or university or an internationally recognized institution, and a minimum undergraduate grade point average of 2.7 (on a 4.0 scale).

Completion Requirements: You must successfully complete 60 quarter credits for this degree.

System Requirements: You need to have a personal computer with a minimum processor speed of 486DX (Pentium or equivalent recommended) or the Macintosh equivalent, a 28.8K modem (or faster), enough RAM (memory) to support your operating system (for example, a minimum of 16MB for Windows 95), a video card (800 × 600 pixel screen resolution and a minimum of 16-bit colors), CD-ROM drive, and sound card. The school recommends the following software: Windows 95 or higher for an operating system (or the Macintosh equivalent), a Web browser (must be Netscape Navigator 3.0, Microsoft Internet Explorer 3.0, or America Online 3.0 or higher) with Java and JavaScript options enabled, a word processor (Microsoft Word 6.0 or higher recommended), and e-mail software.

Example Course Titles: Some of the course titles for this program include Biological Basis of Behavior, Psychology of Learning, Cognitive Psychology, Tests and Measurements, Methods of Clinical Inquiry, Research Methods, Principles of Sport Psychology, Performance Enhancement in Sport, and Applied Sport Psychology.

Program Contact: School of Psychology
Capella University
330 Second Avenue South, Suite 550
Minneapolis, Minnesota 55401
(888) CAPELLA

Sport Psychology

Degree Offered: Doctor of Philosophy

Program Web Address: www. CapellaUniversity.com/10/102f.htm

Program Background: Students in this program can customize the content of their program through elective courses in psychology or related disciplines.

Application Requirements: You must have a Master's degree or its foreign equivalent from a regionally accredited college or university or an internationally recognized institution, and have a minimum graduate grade point average of 3.0 (on a 4.0 scale).

Completion Requirements: You must successfully complete 120 quarter credits for this degree.

On Campus Requirements: You are required to attend a series of brief residencies. Please contact the school for additional information.

System Requirements: You need to have a personal computer with a minimum processor speed of 486DX (Pentium or equivalent recommended) or the Macintosh equivalent, a 28.8K modem (or faster), enough RAM (memory) to support your operating system (for example, a minimum of 16MB for Windows 95), a video card (800 × 600 pixel screen resolution and a minimum of 16-bit colors), CD-ROM drive, and sound card. The school recommends the following software: Windows 95 or higher for an operating system (or the Macintosh equivalent), a Web browser (must be Netscape Navigator 3.0, Microsoft Internet Explorer 3.0, or America Online 3.0 or higher) with Java and JavaScript options enabled, a word processor (Microsoft Word 6.0 or higher recommended), and e-mail software.

Example Course Titles: Some of the course titles in this program include Life Span Development, Adolescent Psychology, Adult

Psychology, Psychology of Learning, Cognitive Psychology, Social Psychology, Group Psychology, Multicultural Perspectives in Human Behavior, and Tests and Measurements.

Program Contact: School of Psychology
Capella University
330 Second Avenue South, Suite 550
Minneapolis, Minnesota 55401
(888) CAPELLA

Teaching/Training Online

Degree Offered: Certificate

Program Web Address: www.CapellaUniversity.com/8/teach_traincert.htm

Program Background: This certificate program is designed for professionals already working in education or corporate training, as well as those who want to enter these fields. Students learn strategies and tactics for teaching with online tools such as bulletin boards, search engines, and Web pages. They also learn practical strategies for developing online learning communities.

Students who decide to pursue their Master's or doctoral degree through Capella after earning the Certificate in Teaching/Training Online may apply all credits earned for the certificate toward the applicable graduate degree (up to 16 quarter credits) upon admission to the graduate program.

Completion Requirements: You must successfully complete 16 quarter credits for this certificate.

System Requirements: You need to have a personal computer with a minimum processor speed of 486DX (Pentium or equivalent recommended) or the Macintosh equivalent, a 28.8K modem (or faster), enough RAM (memory) to support your operating system (for example, a minimum of 16MB for Windows 95), a video card (800 × 600 pixel screen resolution and a minimum of 16-bit colors), CD-ROM

drive, and sound card. The school recommends the following software: Windows 95 or higher for an operating system (or the Macintosh equivalent), a Web browser (must be Netscape Navigator 3.0, Microsoft Internet Explorer 3.0, or America Online 3.0 or higher) with Java and JavaScript options enabled, a word processor (Microsoft Word 6.0 or higher recommended), and e-mail software.

Example Course Titles: Some of the course titles in this program include Critical Skills for Facilitating Online Learning, Tools and Techniques for Online Learning, Strategies for Building Online Learning Communities, and Practical Applications for Online Teaching and Training.

Program Contact: School of Education and Professional Development
Capella University
330 Second Avenue South, Suite 550
Minneapolis, Minnesota 55401
(888) CAPELLA

Training and Development

Degree Offered: Certificate

Program Web Address: www.CapellaUniversity.com/7/72d.htm

Program Background: This certificate program is designed for students who already work in training and development in corporations and other organizations, and those who wish to pursue a career in this field. It focuses on training systems and the activities that make these systems effective. Students gain a thorough understanding of all aspects of designing and implementing effective training programs.

Completion Requirements: You must successfully complete 20 quarter credits for this certificate.

System Requirements: You need to have a personal computer with a minimum processor speed of 486DX (Pentium or equivalent recommended) or the Macintosh equivalent, a 28.8K modem (or faster), enough RAM (memory) to support your operating system (for example, a minimum of 16MB for Windows 95), a video card (800 × 600 pixel screen resolution and a minimum of 16-bit colors), CD-ROM drive, and sound card. The school recommends the following software: Windows 95 or higher for an operating system (or the Macintosh equivalent), a Web browser (must be Netscape Navigator 3.0, Microsoft Internet Explorer 3.0, or America Online 3.0 or higher) with Java and JavaScript options enabled, a word processor (Microsoft Word 6.0 or higher recommended), and e-mail software.

Example Course Titles: Some of the course titles in this program include Introduction to Training Systems, Training Needs Assessment, Evaluation Methodologies, Instructional Design, and Instructional Delivery Systems.

Program Contact: School of Business
Capella University
330 Second Avenue South, Suite 550
Minneapolis, Minnesota 55401
(888) CAPELLA

Training and Development

Degree Offered: Master of Science

Program Web Address: www. CapellaUniversity.com/8/82f.htm

Program Background: The Master of Science with specialization in training and development is geared to students who wish to supplement their graduate degree and professional practice with a strong foundation of theory and practice.

Application Requirements: You must have a Bachelor's degree or its foreign equivalent from a regionally accredited college or university or an internationally recognized institution, and a minimum undergraduate grade point average of 2.7 (on a 4.0 scale).

Completion Requirements: You must successfully complete 48 quarter credits for this degree.

On Campus Requirements: You need to contact the school directly for information about on-campus requirements.

System Requirements: You need to have a personal computer with a minimum processor speed of 486DX (Pentium or equivalent recommended) or the Macintosh equivalent, a 28.8K modem (or faster), enough RAM (memory) to support your operating system (for example, a minimum of 16MB for Windows 95), a video card (800 × 600 pixel screen resolution and a minimum of 16-bit colors), CD-ROM drive, and sound card. The school recommends the following software: Windows 95 or higher for an operating system (or the Macintosh equivalent), a Web browser (must be Netscape Navigator 3.0, Microsoft Internet Explorer 3.0, or America Online 3.0 or higher) with Java and JavaScript options enabled, a word processor (Microsoft Word 6.0 or higher recommended), and e-mail software.

Example Course Titles: Some of the course titles in this program include Survey of Research in Societal and Cultural Change, Evaluating the Effectiveness of the Educational Process, The Future of Educational Institutes: Topics and Trends, Survey of Research Methodology, Integrative Project, Introduction to Training Systems, Training Needs Assessment, Evaluation Methodologies, Instructional Design, and Instructional Delivery Systems.

Program Contact: School of Education and Professional Development
Capella University
330 Second Avenue South, Suite 550
Minneapolis, Minnesota 55401
(888) CAPELLA

CENTRAL MAINE TECHNICAL COLLEGE

General Contact Information

1250 Turner Street
Auburn, Maine 04210

Phone: (207) 784-2385
FAX: (207) 777-7353
E-mail: admissions@cmtc.mtcs.tec.me.us
WWW: www.cmtc.net

Institution Background

Founded: 1964
Type of Institution: Public
Accreditation: New England Association of Schools and Colleges

Programs

Occupational Health and Safety

Degree Offered: Certificate

Program Web Address: www.cmtc.net/ohs/ohs.html

Online Program Started: 1998

Program Background: This Associate's program prepares students to work independently or as part of a team to make their workplaces safer and healthier. Students learn how to identify potential job-related hazards, as well as how to address them.

This program gives students the choice to earn either a certificate or an Associate's degree. Students who earn the Associate's degree may transfer directly into the University of South Maine's Bachelor's degree program in Industrial Technology.

Completion Requirements: You must successfully complete 30 credit hours for this certificate.

On Campus Requirements: You are required to attend a one-week residency for the Industrial Hygiene Lab. You may fulfill this requirement with an internship or portfolio.

Example Course Titles: Some of the course titles for this program include Basic Principles of Occupational Health, Worksite Evaluation, Emergency Planning and Response, Legal Rights and Responsibilities for OHS, and Basic Principles of Safety Engineering.

Program Contact: Central Maine Technical College
1250 Turner St.
Auburn, Maine 04210
(207) 755-5406

Occupational Health and Safety

Degree Offered: Associate Degree in Applied Science

Program Web Address: www.cmtc.net/ohs/ohs.html

Online Program Started: 1998

Program Background: This Associate's program prepares students to work independently or as part of a team to make their workplaces safer and healthier. Students learn how to identify potential job-related hazards, as well as how to address them.

This program gives students the choice to earn either a certificate or an Associate's degree. Students who earn the Associate's degree may transfer directly into the University of South Maine's Bachelor's degree program in Industrial Technology.

Completion Requirements: You must successfully complete 66 credit hours for the Associate in Applied Science Degree.

On Campus Requirements: You are required to attend a one-week residency for the Industrial Hygiene Lab. You may fulfill this requirement with an internship or portfolio.

Example Course Titles: Some of the course titles for this program include Basic Principles of Occupational Health, Worksite Evaluation, Emergency Planning and Response, Legal Rights and Responsibilities for OHS, and Basic Principles of Safety Engineering.

Program Contact: Central Maine Technical College
1250 Turner St.
Auburn, Maine 04210
(207) 755-5406

CENTRAL MISSOURI STATE UNIVERSITY

General Contact Information

403 Humphreys
Warrensburg, Missouri 64093

Phone: (660) 543-8480
FAX: (660) 543-8333
E-mail: extcamp@cmsuvmb.cmsu.edu
WWW: www.cmsu.edu/extcamp

Online Learning Information

Coordinator of Distance Learning
403 Humphreys
Warrensburg, Missouri 64093

Phone: (660) 543-8480
FAX: (660) 543-8333
E-mail: criswell@cmsu1.cmsu.edu
WWW: www.cmsu.edu/extcamp

Institution Background

Central Missouri State University is a comprehensive university that offers around 150 areas of study to some 12,000 students. It has a wide range of academic programs, excellent faculty, and a commitment to service and excellence. Central has been given a statewide mission in professional technology to meet the educational needs of Missouri.

Founded: 1871
Type of Institution: Public
Accreditation: North Central Association of Colleges and Schools

Online Course Background: Central Missouri State University provides a variety of online courses, ranging from a basic "Introduction to the Internet Via the Internet" course to Ph.D. programs in Technology Management. Some of the online courses may require on-campus visits for tests, labs, and so forth.

Online Course Offered: 21

Online Students Enrolled: 398

Special Programs/Partnerships: Central Missouri State University is a founding member of the Western Missouri Educational Technology Consortium (WeMET), which is the largest educational cooperative in the state. It is also an active member of the Missouri Distance Learning Association (MODLA) and a charter member of the Missouri On-line and Research Educational Network (MOREnet).

Services Offered to Students: Students taking online courses have access to a toll-free enrollment number, library services, the bookstore, e-mail accounts, academic advising, and financial aid. Students can also get extended campus identification cards if they wish to visit the main campus to use any university facilities.

Financial Aid: Online students may be eligible for financial aid and should contact the Office of Financial Aid and Veteran Services directly. The number is (660) 543-4040.

Individual Undergraduate Courses: Central Missouri State University offers courses that vary by semester. You should visit their Web site to see a full listing of online courses.

Individual Graduate Courses: Central Missouri State University offers courses that vary by semester. You should visit their Web site to see a full listing of online courses.

Registration: You can register for courses via mail, phone, e-mail, or the World Wide Web.

Programs

Technology Management

Degree Offered: Doctor of Philosophy in Technology Management

Program Web Address: www.indstate.edu/tech/

Online Program Started: 1998

Students Enrolled: 45

Program Background: This program, which is offered through a consortium of nine schools, is designed for students who have knowledge about scientific and engineering developments, economic and political organizations worldwide, and who are sensitive to ethical and moral issues surrounding technology.

Application Requirements: You must apply to Indiana State University's School of Graduate Studies, the institution from which you want your degree, or via the Web at www.indstate.edu/grad/applications.html.

You must have a Bachelor's degree from an accredited college or university with a minimum undergraduate grade point average of 3.0 (on a 4.0 scale) or a minimum graduate grade point average of 3.5. You also need to complete the Graduate Records Examination (GRE) with a score of 500 in each of the sections. Also, you should submit five letters of recommendation, validation of your occupational experience, and a personal statement of your goals.

Completion Requirements: You must successfully complete 90 graduate credit hours, a dissertation, and an internship.

Time for Completion: You have up to seven years to complete this program.

On Campus Requirements: You are required to spend two semesters on-campus. You can fulfill this requirement by attending at Indiana State University in Terra Haute, Indiana, or by spending one semester at your home school (one of the nine cooperating in this program) and one semester at Indiana State University.

Example Course Titles: Some of the course titles in this program include Current Issues in Manufacturing, Ethics and Professional Issues of the Construction Process, and Legal Aspects of Industry.

Program Contact: Debbie Bassore
Extended Campus, HUM 403
Central Missouri State University
Warrensburg, Missouri 64093
(660) 543-8480
(660) 543-8333
extcamp@cmsuvmb.cmsu.edu

CERRO COSO COMMUNITY COLLEGE

General Contact Information

3000 College Heights Blvd.
Ridgecrest, California 93555

Phone: (760) 384-6100
FAX: (760) 375-4775
E-mail: jboard@cc.cc.ca.us
WWW: www.cc.cc.ca.us

Institution Background

Founded: 1973
Type of Institution: Public

Accreditation: Western Association of Schools and Colleges

Programs

Administration of Justice

Degree Offered: Associate of Science

Program Web Address: www.cc.cc.ca.us/cconline/programs/AdministrationOfJustic

Program Background: This program prepares students for careers in the criminal justice field. This course of study offers a broad base of knowledge, which is designed to provide the foundation for the pursuit of advanced studies in criminal justice.

Completion Requirements: You must successfully complete 21 units for this degree.

Example Course Titles: Some of the course titles in this program include Introduction to Administration of Justice, Concepts of Criminal Law, Principles and Procedures of the Justice System, Legal Aspects of Evidence, Community Relations, Principles of Investigation, Principles of Investigation, and California Vehicle Code.

Program Contact: Matt Hightower
Cerro Coso Community College
3000 College Heights Blvd
Ridgecrest, California 93555
(888) 537-6932
(760) 934-6019
mhightow@cc.cc.ca.us

Business Administration

Degree Offered: Associate of Science

Program Web Address: www.cc.cc.ca.us/cconline/programs/BusinessAdministration

Program Background: This program is designed to develop skills that students can use for immediate employment in an increasingly challenging business environment. Students get a broad preparation for a career in business.

Completion Requirements: You must successfully complete 26 units for this degree.

Example Course Titles: Some of the course titles in this program include Principles of Accounting I, Business Law I, Human Relations in Business, Business Correspondence, Introduction to Business, Introduction to Computers, Beginning Word Processing, Beginning Spreadsheets, Beginning Database, Presentation Software, Introduction to the Internet, Principles of Economics I, Introduction to Economics, and Introduction to Work Experience.

Program Contact: Matt Hightower
Cerro Coso Community College
College Heights Blvd
Ridgecrest, California 93555
(888) 537-6932
(760) 934-6019
mhightow@cc.cc.ca.us

Business General

Degree Offered: Associate of Arts

Program Web Address: www.cc.cc.ca.us/cconline/programs/BusinessGeneral.htm

Program Background: This program prepares students to transfer at the junior level to colleges and universities offering Bachelor's degrees in business.

Completion Requirements: You must successfully complete 21 units for this degree.

Example Course Titles: Some of the course titles in this program include Principles of Accounting, Principles of Economics, Elementary Probability and Statistics, and Introduction to Computers.

Program Contact: Matt Hightower
Cerro Coso Community College

3000 College Heights Blvd
Ridgecrest, California 93555
(888) 537-6932
(760) 934-6019
mhightow@cc.cc.ca.us

Business Management

Degree Offered: Associate of Arts

Program Web Address: www.cc.cc.ca.us/
cconline/programs/BusinessManagement.html

Program Background: The Business Management program is designed to provide students with key management skills in a technological business environment, as well as a foundation to transfer to a four-year college.

Completion Requirements: You must successfully complete 27 units for this degree.

Example Course Titles: Some of the course titles in this program include Principles of Accounting, Business Law, Human Relations in Business, Principles of Management and Organization, Human Resource Management, Business Correspondence, Introduction to Business, Introduction to Computers, Principles of Economics, Introduction to Telecommunications, Beginning Word Processing, Beginning Spreadsheets, and Beginning Database.

Program Contact: Matt Hightower
Cerro Coso Community College
3000 College Heights Blvd
Ridgecrest, California 93555
(888) 537-6932
(760) 934-6019
mhightow@cc.cc.ca.us

Comparative Literature

Degree Offered: Associate of Arts

Program Web Address: www.cc.cc.ca.us/
cconline/programs/ComparativeLiterature

Program Background: This program focuses on identifying universal themes and comparing the treatment of those themes across cultures. It is primarily a transfer oriented program that prepares students for further study in comparative literature, philosophy, history and other focused areas in the Humanities.

Completion Requirements: You must successfully complete 18 units for this degree.

Example Course Titles: Some of the course titles in this program include Critical Thinking Through Literature, World Literature, Intermediate French, Intermediate Latin, Intermediate Spanish, Survey of Latin America Literature, Introduction to Types of Literature, British Literature, American Literature, Introduction to Shakespeare, and Women's Literature.

Program Contact: Matt Hightower
Cerro Coso Community College
3000 College Heights Blvd
Ridgecrest, California 93555
(888) 537-6932
(760) 934-6019
3mhightow@cc.cc.ca.us

Computer Information Systems

Degree Offered: Associate of Science

Program Web Address: www.cc.cc.ca.us/
cconline/programs/ComputerInformationS

Program Background: This program is designed to help students develop skills that they can use for immediate employment in an increasingly challenging business environment, as well as provide students with the foundation to transfer to a four year institution to continue studies in Computer Information Systems, Management Information Systems, or other comparable course of study.

Example Course Titles: Some of the course titles in this program include Principles of Accounting, Introduction to Business, Introduction to Computers, Introduction to Structured Programming with Visual Basic, C++ Programming Language, and Introduction to Telecommunications.

Program Contact: Matt Hightower
Cerro Coso Community College
3000 College Heights Blvd
Ridgecrest, California 93555
(888) 537-6932
(760) 934-6019
mhightow@cc.cc.ca.us

Economics

Degree Offered: Associate of Science

Program Web Address: www.cc.cc.ca.us/cconline/programs/Economics.htm

Program Background: The Economics program is designed to prepare students with skills and knowledge of both macro and micro economic theory, as related to the modern business environment.

Completion Requirements: You must successfully complete 22 units for this degree.

Example Course Titles: Some of the course titles in this program include Principles of Accounting, Introduction to Computers, Principles of Economics, Basic Functions and Calculus for Business, Elementary Probability and Statistics, American Government, and Beginning Spreadsheets.

Program Contact: Matt Hightower
Cerro Coso Community College
3000 College Heights Blvd
Ridgecrest, California 93555
(888) 537-6932
(760) 934-6019
mhightow@cc.cc.ca.us

English

Degree Offered: Associate of Arts

Program Web Address: www.cc.cc.ca.us/cconline/programs/English.htm

Program Background: This program prepares students for careers in teaching, writing, editing, journalism, business, insurance, communications, film and video work, public relations, and the professions (law, politics, and medicine). The degree will transfer as fulfilling the undergraduate requirements for most four-year colleges and universities.

Completion Requirements: You must successfully complete 30 units for this degree.

Example Course Titles: Some of the course titles in this program include Exploratory Composition, Critical Thinking Through Literature, Critical Reasoning and Composition, Introduction to Literature, World Literature, Survey of British Literature, and Survey of American Literature.

Program Contact: Matt Hightower
Cerro Coso Community College
College Heights Blvd
Ridgecrest, California 93555
(888) 537-6932
(760) 934-6019
mhightow@cc.cc.ca.us

History

Degree Offered: Associate of Arts

Program Web Address: www.cc.cc.ca.us/cconline/programs/History.htm

Program Background: This program is designed for students who want an understanding of the American political, economic, and social past. It serves as preparation for transfer into a Bachelor's degree program.

Completion Requirements: You must successfully complete 18 units.

Example Course Titles: Some of the course titles in this program include History of Western Civilization, History of the United States, History of Western Art, The City in Western Civilization, History of the Americans, History of Mexico, History of the American West, History of California, and History of Arab-Islamic Culture.

Program Contact: Matt Hightower
Cerro Coso Community College
3000 College Heights Blvd
Ridgecrest, California 93555
(888) 537-6932
(760) 934-6019
mhightow@cc.cc.ca.us

Liberal Arts

Degree Offered: Associate of Arts

Program Web Address: www.cc.cc.ca.us/
cconline/programs/LiberalArtsGeneralStu

Program Background: Cerro Coso Community College designs its programs on the philosophy that a given curriculum should consist of courses that are meaningful to particular students and appropriate for their life goals. Therefore, the College tries to provide maximum flexibility in combining courses from broader concentrations to create a program culminating with the awarding of this Associate's degree.

Completion Requirements: You must successfully complete 60 units for this degree.

Program Contact: Matt Hightower
Cerro Coso Community College
3000 College Heights Blvd
Ridgecrest, California 93555
(888) 537-6932
(760) 934-6019
mhightow@cc.cc.ca.us

Literature

Degree Offered: Associate of Arts

Program Web Address: www.cc.cc.ca.us/
cconline/programs/Humanities.htm

Completion Requirements: You must successfully complete 18 units.

Example Course Titles: Some of the course titles in this program include History of Western Art, Basic Drawing, Introduction to Art, Fundamentals of Acting, Critical Thinking Through Literature, and Multi-Ethnic American Literature.

Program Contact: Matt Hightower
Cerro Coso Community College
3000 College Heights Blvd.
Ridgecrest, California 293555
(888) 537-6932
(760) 934-6019
mhightow@cc.cc.ca.us

Social Sciences

Degree Offered: Associate of Arts

Program Web Address: www.cc.cc.ca.us/
cconline/programs/SocialSciences.htm

Completion Requirements: You must successfully complete 18 units for this degree.

Example Course Titles: Some of the courses in this program include Physical Anthropology, Cultural Geography, Introduction to Sociology, American Government, and General Psychology.

Program Contact: Matt Hightower
Cerro Coso Community College
3000 College Heights Blvd
Ridgecrest, California 93555
(888) 537-6932
(760) 934-6019
mhightow@cc.cc.ca.us

CHAMPLAIN COLLEGE

General Contact Information

163 South Willard Street, Box 670
Burlington, Vermont 05402-0670

Phone: (802) 860-2727
FAX: (802) 860-2772
E-mail: admission@champlain.edu
WWW: www.champlain.edu

Online Learning Information

Continuing Education Division
163 South Willard Street
Burlington, Vermont 05402

Phone: (802) 860-2777
FAX: (802) 860-2774
E-mail: ced@champlain.edu
WWW: www.champlain.edu

Institution Background

Founded: 1878
Type of Institution: Private
Accreditation: New England Association of Schools and Colleges

Programs

Accounting

Degree Offered: Certificate

Program Web Address: www.champlain.edu/OLDE/account.htm

Program Background: Champlain College's accounting program prepares students for careers in public or private organizations by giving them a thorough knowledge of accounting practices, as well as mathematics and computer skills relevant to the field. The program integrates theory and hands-on practice.

Completion Requirements: You must successfully complete five courses for this certificate.

Example Course Titles: Some of the course titles in this program include Financial Accounting, Managerial Accounting, Intermediate Accounting I, Cost Accounting I, and Federal Taxes I.

Program Contact: Champlain College Online
163 South Willard Street
Burlington, Vermont 05402-0670
(888) 545-3459
online@champlain

Accounting

Degree Offered: Associate

Program Web Address: www.champlain.edu/OLDE/account.htm

Program Background: This program prepares students for rewarding and challenging careers in public, private, and governmental accounting. Students gain a thorough knowledge of accounting, and learn mathematics and computer skills that are relevant to their future work. The program integrates theory and hands-on practice.

Completion Requirements: You must successfully complete 60 credits for this degree.

Example Course Titles: Some of the course titles in this program include Financial Accounting, Computer Applications—Word Processing, Computer Applications—Spreadsheets, English Composition, Business Management, College Algebra, Managerial Accounting, Interpersonal Communication, Mathematics in Accounting and Finance, and Introduction to Statistics.

Program Contact: Champlain College Online
163 South Willard Street
Burlington, Vermont 05402-0670
(888) 545-3459
online@champlain.edu

Business

Degree Offered: Certificate

Program Web Address: www.champlain.edu/OLDE/business.htm

Program Background: This degree is designed for students who have not yet decided in which area of business to specialize or for those who wish to individualize their programs. Students take a core of practical business courses and electives that make it possible for students to design their own areas of specialization, such as accounting, marketing or management.

Completion Requirements: You must successfully complete seven courses.

Example Course Titles: Some of the course titles in this program include Financial Accounting, Computer Applications, Business Law I, Business Management, Human Resource Management, and Marketing.

Program Contact: Champlain College Online
163 South Willard Street
Burlington, Vermont 05402-0670
(888) 545-3459
online@champlain.edu

Business

Degree Offered: Associate

Program Web Address: www.champlain.edu/OLDE/business.htm

Program Background: This degree is designed for students who have not yet decided in which area of business to specialize or for those who wish to individualize their programs. Students take a core of practical business courses and electives that make it possible for students to design their own areas of specialization, such as accounting, marketing or management.

Completion Requirements: You must successfully complete 60 credits.

Example Course Titles: Some of the course titles in this program include Financial Accounting, Computer Applications—Word Processing, Computer Applications—Spreadsheets, Computer Applications—Database Management, English Composition, Introduction to Business Administration, Marketing, Managerial Accounting, Business Management, and Small Business Management.

Program Contact: Champlain College Online
163 South Willard Street
Burlington, Vermont 05402-0670
(888) 545-3459
online@champlain.edu

Computer Information Systems

Degree Offered: Bachelor

Program Web Address: www.champlain.edu/CLnD/cismjr.htm

Program Background: Students in this program develop skills and knowledge in computer networks, computer programming, telecommunications, and Web site development. Students choose to study a specialty in-depth, then add coursework from three other areas during their last two years of undergraduate study.

Completion Requirements: You must successfully complete 120 credits for this degree.

Example Course Titles: Some of the course titles in this program include Themes for Writing, Major Themes in Western Civilization, Introduction to Statistics, Introduction to Sociology, Introduction to Psychology, Microeconomics, Major Themes in Western Civilization, Algebra and Trigonometry, and Modern American Social History.

Program Contact: Champlain College Online
163 South Willard Street

Burlington, Vermont 05402-0670
(888) 545-3459
online@champlain.edu

Computer Programming

Degree Offered: Certificate

Program Web Address: www.champlain.edu/
OLDE/compprog.htm

Program Background: This program trains students in business programming for the personal computer.

Completion Requirements: You must successfully complete 23 credits.

Example Course Titles: Some of the course titles in this program include Computer Applications-Word Processing, Computer Applications-Spreadsheets, Computer Applications-Database Management, Programming Logic, Advanced Computer Applications-Word Processing, Advanced Computer Applications-Spreadsheets, Advanced Computer Applications-Database Management, Systems Analysis and Design for Business, Introduction to Programming in C, and Object-Oriented Programming in C++.

Program Contact: Champlain College Online
163 South Willard Street
Burlington, Vermont 05402-0670
(888) 545-3459
online@champlain.edu

Computer Programming

Degree Offered: Associate

Program Web Address: www.champlain.edu/
OLDE/compprog.htm

Program Background: This program trains students in business programming for the personal computer.

Completion Requirements: You must successfully complete 60 credits.

Example Course Titles: Some of the course titles in this program include Financial Accounting, Computer Applications—Word Processing, Computer Applications—Spreadsheets, Computer Applications—Database Management, Introduction to Programming Logic, English Composition, College Algebra, Managerial Accounting, Systems Analysis and Design for Business, Introduction to Programming in C/C++, Business Management, Mathematics in Accounting and Finance, Relational Database, Object-Oriented Programming Using C++, Interpersonal Communication, Advanced Computer Applications—Word Processing, Advanced Computer Applications—Spreadsheets, and Advanced Computer Applications—Database Management.

Program Contact: Champlain College Online
163 South Willard Street
Burlington, Vermont 05402-0670
(888) 545-3459
online@champlain.edu

Hotel-Restaurant Management

Degree Offered: Certificate

Program Web Address: www.champlain.edu/
OLDE/hrm.htm

Program Background: This program provides students with skills they need for a successful career in hospitality management.

Completion Requirements: You must successfully complete 16 credits.

Example Course Titles: Some of the course titles in this program include Hospitality and Travel Industry, Food Fundamentals/Lab, Hospitality Services, Hospitality Supervision and Management, Food and Beverage Cost Control, and Hotel-Restaurant Management—Front Office Operations.

Program Contact: Champlain College Online
Title163 South Willard Street
Burlington, Vermont 05402-0670
Hospitality and Travel Industry
(888) 545-3459
online@champlain.edu

Hospitality Supervision and Management

Degree Offered: Associate

Program Web Address: www.champlain.edu/OLDE/hrm.htm

Program Background: This program allows you to choose from Food and Beverage of Front Office Operations.

Completion Requirements: You must successfully complete 60 credits.

Example Course Titles: Some of the course titles in this program include Financial Accounting, English Composition, Hospitality and Travel Industry, Food Fundamentals/Food Lab, Hospitality Services/Services Lab, Computer Applications—Word Processing, Computer Applications—Spreadsheets, Managerial Accounting, Marketing, Interpersonal Communication, Food and Beverage Cost Control, and Front Office Operations.

Program Contact: Champlain College Online
163 South Willard Street
Burlington, Vermont 05402-0670
(888) 545-3459
online@champlain.edu

Management

Degree Offered: Certificate

Program Web Address: www.champlain.edu/OLDE/mngmnt.htm

Program Background: This certificate is designed for students who want a career in business or non-profit management. Students learn about goal setting, planning and control, legal issues, marketing, human resources, finance, and computer applications.

Completion Requirements: You must successfully complete 22 credit hours for this certificate.

Example Course Titles: Some of the course titles for this program include Financial Accounting, Business Law, Business Management, Human Resource Management, and Financial Management.

Program Contact: Champlain College Online
163 South Willard Street
Burlington, Vermont 05402-0670
(888) 545-3459
online@champlain.edu

Management

Degree Offered: Associate

Program Web Address: www.champlain.edu/OLDE/mngmnt.htm

Program Background: This Management Associate's degree is designed for students who want a career in business or non-profit management. Students have courses that cover goal setting, planning and control, legal issues, marketing, human resource management, analysis and interpretation of financial statements, computer applications and strategy formulation.

Completion Requirements: You must successfully complete 60 credit hours for this degree.

Example Course Titles: Some of the course titles for this program include Financial Accounting, English Composition, Introduction to Business Administration, Marketing, Introduction to Sociology, Managerial Accounting,

Computer Applications—Database Management, and College Algebra.

Program Contact: Champlain College Online
163 South Willard Street
Burlington, Vermont 05402-0670
(888) 545-3459
online@champlain.edu

Professional Studies

Degree Offered: Bachelor

Program Web Address: www.champlain.edu/CLnD/cismjr.htm

Program Background: This program is designed for students who have an Associate's degree and want to complete their Bachelor's degree. Students gain a broader understanding of the global economy and strengthen their communication and problem-solving skills. The curriculum depends upon the student's individual background and goals.

Completion Requirements: You must successfully complete 120 credit hours, 60 of which may be transferred into the program from your Associate's degree program.

Example Course Titles: Some of the course titles in this program include Interpersonal Communication, Themes for Writing, American History I: (1492-1865), American History II: (1865 to Present), Major Themes in Western Civilization I, College Algebra, and Philosophy.

Program Contact: Champlain College Online
163 South Willard Street
Burlington, Vermont 05402-0670
(888) 545-3459
online@champlain.edu

Telecommunications

Degree Offered: Certificate

Program Web Address: www.champlain.edu/OLDE/telecom.htm

Program Background: This program trains students for jobs in one of the fastest growing areas of industry—telecommunications. Students learn skills necessary to work with high-tech voice and data communications systems.

Completion Requirements: You must successfully complete 23 credit hours for this certificate.

Example Course Titles: Some of the course titles in this program include Introduction to Data Communications, Operating Systems, Basic Telephony and Switching Systems, Protocols Laboratory, Contemporary Network Architectures, Fast Packet Technologies, and Integrated Services Networks.

Program Contact: Champlain College Online
Champlain College
163 South Willard Street
Burlington, Vermont 05402-0670
(888) 545-3459
online@champlain.edu

Telecommunications

Degree Offered: Associate

Program Web Address: www.champlain.edu/OLDE/telecom.htm

Program Background: This program trains students for jobs in one of the fastest growing areas of industry—telecommunications. Students learn skills necessary to work with high-tech voice and data communications systems.

Completion Requirements: You must successfully compete 60 credit hours for this degree.

Example Course Titles: Some of the course titles in this program include Computer Applications—Word Processing, Computer Applications—DOS, Advanced Computer Applications—DOS, Interpersonal Communication, English Composition, College Algebra, Basic Telephony and Switching Systems, and Introduction to Data Communication.

Program Contact: Champlain College Online
Champlain College
163 South Willard Street
Burlington, Vermont 05402-0670
(888) 545-3459
online@champlain.edu

Web Site Development and Management

Degree Offered: Associate

Program Web Address: www.champlain.edu/
CLnD/webdev.htm

Program Background: This program trains students for careers in Web site development and management. Students are immersed in computer and Web technology from the start of the program, and learn everything from system architecture to electronic-commerce, while gaining hands-on expertise.

Completion Requirements: You must successfully complete 60 credits for this degree.

Example Course Titles: Some of the course titles in this program include Computer Applications—Word Processing, Computer Applications—Multimedia, Computer Applications—Navigating the Internet, and Introduction to Web Page Development.

Program Contact: Champlain College Online
163 South Willard Street
Burlington, Vermont 05402-0670
(888) 545-3459
online@champlain.edu

CHEMEKETA COMMUNITY COLLEGE

General Contact Information

Box 14007
Salem, Oregon 97309

Phone: (503) 399-5006
FAX: (503) 399-3918
E-mail: broc@chemek.cc.or.us
WWW: www.chemek.cc.or.us

Institution Background

Founded: 1962
Type of Institution: Public
Accreditation: Northwest Association of Schools and Colleges

Programs

Associate of Arts

Degree Offered: Associate of Arts

Program Web Address: www.chemek.cc.or.us/
academics/degrees/degree_grids/aa_

Program Background: This program encompasses the core curriculum of a liberal arts education, including coursework in the areas of communications, humanities, social sciences, mathematics, sciences, computer science, and physical education or health. Students are also encouraged to explore a broad range of subjects through elective coursework.

Completion Requirements: You are required to successfully complete 90 credit hours for this degree.

Program Contact: Chemeketa Online
4000 Lancaster Dr. NE
Salem, Oregon 97309-7070
(503) 399-7873
(503) 399-6992
ccc@bbs.chemek.cc.or.us

Associate of General Studies

Degree Offered: Associate of General Studies

Program Web Address: www.chemek.cc.or.us/
academics/degrees/degree_grids/ags

Program Background: This program addresses the needs of students who are not seeking an Oregon Associate of Arts transfer degree or the specific program requirements of an Associate of Applied Science degree. Students can combine a broad core of basic courses with a program of study that may be tailored to their academic or professional goals. This program can enhance your employment, fulfill the requirements of a specific four-year college program, or meet the special expectations of agency-sponsored students.

Completion Requirements: You must successfully complete 90 credit hours for this degree.

Program Contact: Chemeketa Online
4000 Lancaster Dr. NE
Salem, Oregon, 97309-7070
(503) 399-7873
(503) 399-6992
ccc@bbs.chemek.cc.or.us

Fire Protection Technology

Degree Offered: Associate of Applied Science

Program Web Address: www. chemek.cc.or.us/academics/areas/ fire_protection/fire

Program Background: This program trains students for careers in fire protection.

Application Requirements: You are required to take an assessment test and you may need to complete some prerequisite courses.

Completion Requirements: You must successfully complete 100 required credit hours.

Example Course Titles: Some of the course titles in this program include Introduction to Microcomputer Applications, Introduction to Fire Protection, Fundamentals of Fire Prevention, Intermediate Algebra, College Algebra, English Composition-Exposition, Building Construction for Fire Suppression, Fire Codes and Ordinances, and Fire Prevention Inspection.

Program Contact: Chemeketa Online
Chemeketa Community College
4000 Lancaster Dr. NE
Salem, Oregon 97309-7070
(503) 399-7873
(503) 399-6992
ccc@bbs.chemek.cc.or.us

Hospitality and Tourism Management

Degree Offered: Associate of Applied Science

Program Web Address: www.chemek.cc.or.us/ academics/areas/hospitality/degree/in

Program Background: This program focuses on management of today's exciting hospitality industry.

Application Requirements: You must take the college's assessment test to determine your admission status.

Completion Requirements: You must successfully complete 96 credit hours.

Example Course Titles: Some of the course titles in this program include Introduction to the Hospitality Industry, Introduction to the Travel and Tourism Industry, English Composition-Exposition, Introduction to Computer Science, Hotel, Restaurant and Travel Law, Introduction to the Food and Beverage Industry, General Psychology-Biological Emphasis, Introduction to Lodging Industry, Sanitation and Safety for Managers, and Elementary Algebra.

Program Contact: Chemeketa Online
Chemeketa Community College
4000 Lancaster Dr. NE
Salem, Oregon 97309-7070
(503) 399-7873
(503) 399-6992
ccc@bbs.chemek.cc.or.us

CHRISTOPHER NEWPORT UNIVERSITY

General Contact Information

1 University Place
Newport News, Virginia 23606

Phone: (757) 594-7015
FAX: (757) 594-7333
E-mail: admit@cnu.edu
WWW: www.cnu.edu

Online Learning Information

1 University Place
Newport News, Virginia 23606

Phone: (757) 594-7607
FAX: (757) 594-7481
E-mail: online@cnu.edu
WWW: www.cnu.edu

Institution Background

Founded: 1960
Type of Institution: Public
Accreditation: Southern Association of Colleges and Schools

Online Course Offered: 49

Online Students Enrolled: 768

Individual Undergraduate Courses: Christopher Newport University offers online undergraduate courses in business, economics, English, government, history, mathematics, philosophy, religious studies, sociology, and Spanish.

Programs

Governmental Administration

Degree Offered: Bachelor of Science

Program Background: This degree program provides students with the analytical, political, and quantitative skills needed for understanding and solving public problems that require technical knowledge and political insight.

CITY UNIVERSITY

General Contact Information

919 Southwest Grady Way
Renton, Washington 98055

Phone: (425) 637-1010
FAX: (425) 277-2437
E-mail: info@cityu.edu
WWW: www.cityu.edu

Online Learning Information

Distance Learning Advisor
919 Southwest Grady Way, 2nd Floor
Renton, Washington 98055

Phone: (800) 426-5596
FAX: (425) 277-2437
E-mail: info@cityu.edu
WWW: www.cityu.edu

Institution Background

City University is a private, nonprofit institution of higher education that was founded over 20 years ago to serve working adults who want to further their educations. Its mission is to make education available to all who desire it.

Founded: 1973
Type of Institution: Private
Accreditation: Northwest Association of Schools and Colleges

Financial Aid: Students enrolled in online courses may be eligible for institutional scholarships or employer tuition reimbursement programs. City University does not administer any federal financial aid programs currently.

Individual Undergraduate Courses: City University offers online undergraduate courses in the following subject areas: accounting, business and marketing, communications, computer programming, critical thinking, English, information systems, law, organization and administration, philosophy, science and technology, self-expression, sociology, and statistics.

Registration: You can register for courses via mail and e-mail.

Programs

Accounting

Degree Offered: Certificate

Program Web Address: www.wcc-eun.com/ city/certificates.html#anchor36584505

Program Background: This program is designed for students who are preparing for the Certified Public Accounting examination.

Application Requirements: You must submit your completed application and pay the one time $75 application fee before you register for courses. You may register for up to two courses at the same time you apply. Along with your application, you must include transcripts from any colleges/universities you've attended in the past, and a copy of your DD-214 if you've completed military courses. All application documents should be sent to the City University Registrar, 335 116th Avenue, Bellevue WA 98004.

Completion Requirements: You must successfully complete 45 credits for this certificate.

Example Course Titles: Some of the course titles in this program include Intermediate Accounting I, Intermediate Accounting II, Intermediate Accounting III, Cost Accounting, Advanced Accounting, Auditing, Federal Income Taxation I, Federal Income Taxation II, and Business Law and Ethics for Accountants.

Program Contact: Distance Learning Advisor
919 Southwest Grady Way, 2nd Floor
Renton, Washington 98055
(800) 426-5596
(425) 277-2437
info@cityu.edu

Accounting

Degree Offered: Bachelor of Science

Program Web Address: www.wcc-eun.com/ city/bs.html#anchor1542148

Program Background: This program provides students with an understanding of the importance and application of accounting in the management of a company and the analysis of its business decisions. It also prepares students for the Certified Public Accountant examination.

Application Requirements: You must submit your completed application and pay the one time $75 application fee before you register for courses. You may register for up to two courses at the same time you apply. Along with your application, you must include transcripts from any colleges/universities you've attended in the past, and a copy of your DD-214 if you've completed military courses. All application documents should be sent to the City University Registrar, 335 116th Avenue, Bellevue WA 98004.

Completion Requirements: You must successfully complete 180 credits for this degree.

Example Course Titles: Some of the course titles in this program include Approaches to Critical Thinking, Efficient and Effective Self-Expression, Business, Government and Society, Financing Organizations, Effective Organizational Communications, International Business, Information Systems, Intermediate Accounting, Cost Accounting, Auditing, Federal Income Taxation, and Business Law and Ethics for Accountants.

Program Contact: Distance Learning Advisor
919 Southwest Grady Way, 2nd Floor
Renton, Washington 98055
(800) 426-5596
(425) 277-2437
info@cityu.edu

Business Administration

Degree Offered: Bachelor of Science

Program Web Address: www.wcc-eun.com/
city/bs.html#anchor1552555

Program Background: This degree program provides students who are employed in or aspiring to managerial positions with the tools they need to be effective leaders within their organizations. The program reviews the classic business disciplines of accounting, finance, marketing, economics, law, quantitative methods, and personnel administration. Students strengthen skills in communication and decision-making, and learn about the central importance of behavioral factors within business.

Application Requirements: You must submit your completed application and pay the one time $75 application fee before you register for courses. You may register for up to two courses at the same time you apply. Along with your application, you must include transcripts from any colleges/universities you've attended in the past, and a copy of your DD-214 if you've completed military courses. All application documents should be sent to the City University Registrar, 335 116th Avenue, Bellevue WA 98004.

Completion Requirements: You must successfully complete 180 credit hours for this degree.

Example Course Titles: Some of the course titles in this program include Approaches to Critical Thinking, Efficient and Effective Self-Expression, Interpreting Statistics and Data, Science, Technology and Community Values, Contemporary Social, Political and Cultural Controversies, Uses and Abuses of Ethics, Understanding and Influencing Consumer Behavior, Decision Modeling and Analysis, Interpretation of Financial Accounting, Financing Organizations, Legal Issues in the Workplace, The Effective Organization, Business, Government and Society, Effective Organizational Communications, International Business, Operations Management, Global Economics, and Information Systems.

Program Contact: Distance Learning Advisor
919 Southwest Grady Way, 2nd Floor
Renton, Washington 98055
(800) 426-5596
(425) 277-2437
info@cityu.edu

C++ Programming

Degree Offered: Certificate

Program Web Address: www.wcc-eun.com/
city/certificates.html#anchor36588004

Program Background: Students gain a thorough understanding of C++ programming, as well as the ability to interact with other professionals in the field.

Application Requirements: You must submit your completed application and pay the one time $75 application fee before you register for courses. You may register for up to two courses at the same time you apply. Along with your application, you must include transcripts from any colleges/universities you've attended in the past, and a copy of your DD-214 if you've completed military courses. All application documents should be sent to the City University Registrar, 335 116th Avenue, Bellevue WA 98004.

Completion Requirements: You must successfully complete 45 credits for this degree.

Example Course Titles: Some of the course titles in this program include Introduction to Visual Basic, System Development in Visual Basic, Program Design in "C", Object Oriented Programming using C++, Data Structures, Local Area Networks, Programming Language Survey, Systems Analysis/Object-Oriented Design, and Advanced Windows Application Development.

Program Contact: Distance Learning Advisor
919 Southwest Grady Way, 2nd Floor
Renton, Washington 98055
(800) 426-5596
(425) 277-2437
info@cityu.edu

Commerce

Degree Offered: Bachelor of Arts

Program Web Address: www.wcc-eun.com/city/ba.html#anchor1625901

Program Background: This program is designed to help students become better managers, identify and meet client needs, and communicate more effectively.

Application Requirements: You must submit your completed application and pay the one time $75 application fee before you register for courses. You may register for up to two courses at the same time you apply. Along with your application, you must include transcripts from any colleges/universities you've attended in the past, and a copy of your DD-214 if you've completed military courses. All application documents should be sent to the City University Registrar, 335 116th Avenue, Bellevue WA 98004.

Completion Requirements: You must successfully complete 180 credits for this degree.

Example Course Titles: Some of the course titles in this program include Approaches to Critical Thinking, Efficient and Effective Self-Expression, Interpreting Statistics and Data, Science, Technology and Community Values,

Contemporary Social, Political and Cultural Controversies, Uses and Abuses of Ethics, Understanding and Influencing Consumer Behavior, Legal Issues in the Workplace, The Effective Organization, Business, Government and Society, Effective Organizational Communication, Information Systems, Marketing Research, Consumer Behavior, International Marketing, Services Marketing, Advertising, and Marketing Strategy.

Program Contact: Distance Learning Advisor
919 Southwest Grady Way, 2nd Floor
Renton, Washington 98055
(800) 426-5596
(425) 277-2437
info@cityu.edu

Computer Information Systems

Degree Offered: Bachelor of Science

Program Web Address: www.wcc-eun.com/city/bs.html#anchor1555547

Program Background: This program prepares students for careers in computer information systems. Students are exposed to programming, computer-aided software engineering, the management of computer information systems, database management, and systems analysis.

Application Requirements: You must submit your completed application and pay the one time $75 application fee before you register for courses. You may register for up to two courses at the same time you apply. Along with your application, you must include transcripts from any colleges/universities you've attended in the past, and a copy of your DD-214 if you've completed military courses. All application documents should be sent to the City University Registrar, 335 116th Avenue, Bellevue WA 98004.

Completion Requirements: You must successfully complete 180 credits for this degree.

Example Course Titles: Some of the course titles in this program include Introduction to Visual Basic, Principles of Information Processing, Approaches to Critical Thinking, Efficient and Effective Self-Expression, Interpreting Statistics and Data, Science, Technology and Community Values, Contemporary Social, Political and Cultural Controversies, Uses and Abuses of Ethics, Decision Modeling and Analysis, Interpretation of Financial Accounting, Financing Organizations, and The Effective Organization.

Program Contact: Distance Learning Advisor
919 Southwest Grady Way, 2nd Floor
Renton, Washington 98055
(800) 426-5596
(425) 277-2437
info@cityu.edu

General Studies

Degree Offered: Bachelor of Arts

Program Web Address: www.wcc-eun.com/city/ba.html#anchor1636062

Application Requirements: You must submit your completed application and pay the one time $75 application fee before you register for courses. You may register for up to two courses at the same time you apply. Along with your application, you must include transcripts from any colleges/universities you've attended in the past, and a copy of your DD-214 if you've completed military courses. All application documents should be sent to the City University Registrar, 335 116th Avenue, Bellevue WA 98004.

Completion Requirements: You must successfully complete 180 credits.

Example Course Titles: Some of the course titles in this program include Approaches to Critical Thinking, Efficient and Effective Self-

Expression, Interpreting Statistics and Data, Science, Technology and Community Values, Contemporary Social, Political and Cultural Controversies, and Uses and Abuses of Ethics.

Program Contact: Distance Learning Advisor
919 Southwest Grady Way, 2nd Floor
Renton, Washington 98055
(800) 426-5596
(425) 277-2437
info@cityu.edu

General Studies

Degree Offered: Bachelor of Science

Program Web Address: www.wcc-eun.com/city/bs.html#anchor1562051

Program Background: Students in this program get an individually designed degree that serves their needs and interests.

Application Requirements: You must submit your completed application and pay the one time $75 application fee before you register for courses. You may register for up to two courses at the same time you apply. Along with your application, you must include transcripts from any colleges/universities you've attended in the past, and a copy of your DD-214 if you've completed military courses. All application documents should be sent to the City University Registrar, 335 116th Avenue, Bellevue WA 98004.

Completion Requirements: You must successfully complete 180 credits.

Program Contact: Distance Learning Advisor
919 Southwest Grady Way, 2nd Floor
Renton, Washington 98055
(800) 426-5596
(425) 277-2437
info@cityu.edu

Humanities

Degree Offered: Bachelor of Arts

Program Web Address: www.wcc-eun.com/ city/ba.html#anchor1640123

Program Background: City University's Bachelor's program with an emphasis in Humanities can lead students to have a greater appreciation of the historical and contemporary significance of creative expression, and build a framework for applying it to one's life experience.

Application Requirements: You must submit your completed application and pay the one time $75 application fee before you register for courses. You may register for up to two courses at the same time you apply. Along with your application, you must include transcripts from any colleges/universities you've attended in the past, and a copy of your DD-214 if you've completed military courses. All application documents should be sent to the City University Registrar, 335 116th Avenue, Bellevue WA 98004.

Completion Requirements: You must have a total of 180 credits to receive this degree. If you choose the Humanities Emphasis, you'll be required to complete 60 credits of upper-division core and arts competencies, plus 30 credits from one of the humanities concentrations.

Example Course Titles: Some of the course titles for this program include Approaches to Critical Thinking, Efficient and Effective Self-Expression, Interpreting Statistics and Data, Uses and Abuses of Ethics, Journalistic Writing, Communication and Public Relations, Electoral Politics and the Mass Media, The Philosophy of Cultures and Nations, and Philosophical Understanding of Corporations.

Program Contact: Distance Learning Advisor
City University
919 Southwest Grady Way, 2nd Floor
Renton, Washington 98055
(800) 426-5596
(425) 277-2437
info@cityu.edu

Internetworking

Degree Offered: Certificate

Program Web Address: www.wcc-eun.com/ city/certificates.html#anchor397320

Program Background: This certificate program prepares students for the ever-changing field of information technology. Students gain a working knowledge of Internet principles, the World Wide Web, and programming Web pages.

Application Requirements: You must complete and submit an application with a $75 application fee, transcripts from any colleges or universities you've attended, and scores for any standardized tests that you've taken. If you've had courses in the military that you want City University to consider for credit, you also need to submit a copy of your DD-214. You can register for up to two courses when you apply.

Completion Requirements: You must successfully complete 45 credit hours for this certificate.

Example Course Titles: Some of the course titles in this program include Principles of Information Processing, Introduction to Internet and Web Publishing, Advanced Internet Publishing and Web Design, Local Area Networks, Network Operating Systems Survey, Java Programming, Internet Client/Servers, Research and Business Applications, and Data Communications.

Program Contact: Distance Learning Advisor
919 Southwest Grady Way, 2nd Floor
Renton, Washington 98055
(800) 426-5596
(425) 277-2437

info@cityu.edu

Management

Degree Offered: Bachelor of Science

Program Web Address: www.wcc-eun.com/city/bs.html#anchor1591783

Program Background: This concentration provides students with a broad knowledge of management theories and practices.

Application Requirements: You must submit your completed application and pay the one time $75 application fee before you register for courses. You may register for up to two courses at the same time you apply. Along with your application, you must include transcripts from any colleges/universities you've attended in the past, and a copy of your DD-214 if you've completed military courses. All application documents should be sent to the City University Registrar, 335 116th Avenue, Bellevue WA 98004.

Completion Requirements: You must successfully complete 180 credit hours for this degree.

Example Course Titles: Some of the course titles for this program include Approaches to Critical Thinking, Efficient and Effective Self-Expression, Interpreting Statistics and Data, Uses and Abuses of Ethics, Decision Modeling and Analysis, Financing Organizations, and Legal Issues in the Workplace.

Program Contact: Distance Learning Advisor
919 Southwest Grady Way, 2nd Floor
Renton, Washington 98055
(800) 426-5596
(425) 277-2437
info@cityu.edu

Marketing

Degree Offered: Bachelor of Science

Program Web Address: www.wcc-eun.com/city/bs.html#anchor1594516

Program Background: This program is designed for students who manage others in a field that requires them to have technical skills. It provides an overview of business administration and focuses on marketing.

Application Requirements: You must submit your completed application and pay the one time $75 application fee before you register for courses. You may register for up to two courses at the same time you apply. Along with your application, you must include transcripts from any colleges/universities you've attended in the past, and a copy of your DD-214 if you've completed military courses. All application documents should be sent to the City University Registrar, 335 116th Avenue, Bellevue WA 98004.

Completion Requirements: You must successfully complete 180 credit hours for this degree.

Example Course Titles: Some of the course titles in this program include Approaches to Critical Thinking, Efficient and Effective Self-Expression, Interpreting Statistics and Data, Uses and Abuses of Ethics, Understanding and Influencing Consumer Behavior, Decision Modeling and Analysis, Financing Organizations, and Legal Issues in the Workplace.

Program Contact: Distance Learning Advisor
919 Southwest Grady Way, 2nd Floor
Renton, Washington 98055
(800) 426-5596
(425) 277-2437
info@cityu.edu

Network/Telecommunications

Degree Offered: Certificate

Program Web Address: www.wcc-eun.com/city/certificates.html#anchor396823

Program Background: Students interested in this program must get permission from a City

University senior faculty member to apply. The program focuses on design, programming, implementation, and management of telecommunications networks.

Application Requirements: You must complete and submit an application with a $75 application fee, transcripts from any colleges or universities you've attended, and scores for any standardized tests that you've taken. If you've had courses in the military that you want City University to consider for credit, you also need to submit a copy of your DD-214. You can register for up to two courses when you apply.

Completion Requirements: You must successfully complete 45 credit hours to earn this certificate.

Example Course Titles: Some of the course titles in this program include Introduction to the Internet and Web Publishing, Local Area Networks, Network Operating Systems Survey, LAN Implementation, Network Design, Network Management, Enterprise Networking, and Data Communications.

Program Contact: Distance Learning Advisor
919 Southwest Grady Way, 2nd Floor
Renton, Washington 98055
(800) 426-5596
(425) 277-2437
info@cityu.edu

Paralegal Studies

Degree Offered: Certificate

Program Web Address: www.wcc-eun.com/city/certificates.html#anchor1751898

Program Background: City University's Paralegal Studies certificate program is a series of courses delivered via the World Wide Web. They prepare students for work as a law office secretary, legal assistant, or paralegal in a law office, government office, or private business. While the program is designed for students who already have a degree in a related field, it is open to students without degrees too.

Students take seven out of the nine paralegal courses offered—four are required. All are lower-division courses.

Application Requirements: You must complete and submit an application with a $75 application fee, transcripts from any colleges or universities you've attended, and scores for any standardized tests that you've taken. If you've had courses in the military that you want City University to consider for credit, you also need to submit a copy of your DD-214. You can register for up to two courses when you apply.

Completion Requirements: You must successfully complete 45 credit hours.

Example Course Titles: The course titles for this program are Personal Injury Litigation and Torts, Civil Procedure, Business Organizations, Legal Writing and Research, Probate Law, Family Law, Bankruptcy Law, Criminal Law, and Real Estate Law.

Program Contact: Distance Learning Advisor
919 Southwest Grady Way, 2nd Floor
Renton, Washington 98055
(800) 426-5596
(425) 277-2437
info@cityu.edu

Quantitative Studies

Degree Offered: Bachelor of Arts

Program Web Address: www.wcc-eun.com/city/ba.html#anchor1643363

Program Background: This program deepens student understanding of quantitative concepts and forces that affect nearly every aspect of society.

Application Requirements: You must complete and submit an application with a $75 application fee, transcripts from any colleges or universities you've attended, and scores for any standardized tests that you've taken. If you've had courses in the military that you want City University to consider for credit, you also need to submit a copy of your DD-214. You can register for up to two courses when you apply.

Completion Requirements: You must successfully complete 180 credits for this degree.

Example Course Titles: Some of the course titles in this program include Approaches to Critical Thinking, Efficient and Effective Self-Expression, Interpreting Statistics and Data, Uses and Abuses of Ethics, Advanced Environmental Science, Astronomy, and Oceanography.

Program Contact: Distance Learning Advisor
919 Southwest Grady Way, 2nd Floor
Renton, Washington 98055
(800) 426-5596
(425) 277-2437
info@cityu.edu

Social Science

Degree Offered: Bachelor of Arts

Program Web Address: www.wcc-eun.com/city/ba.html#anchor1649603

Program Background: This program provides students with knowledge and understanding of internal and external systems, how people relate to them, and which tools will allow people to work more effectively within them.

Application Requirements: You must complete and submit an application with a $75 application fee, transcripts from any colleges or universities you've attended, and scores for any standardized tests that you've taken. If you've had courses in the military that you want City University to consider for credit, you also need to submit a copy of your DD-214. You can register for up to two courses when you apply.

Completion Requirements: You must successfully complete 180 credit hours for this degree.

Example Course Titles: Some of the course titles for this program include Approaches to Critical Thinking, Efficient and Effective Self-Expression, Interpreting Statistics and Data, International Relations, International Economic Problems, Contemporary Environmental Issues, and International Law.

Program Contact: Distance Learning Advisor
City University
919 Southwest Grady Way, 2nd Floor
Renton, Washington 98055
(800) 426-5596
(425) 277-2437
info@cityu.edu

CLAYTON COLLEGE AND STATE UNIVERSITY

General Contact Information

5900 North Lee Street
Morrow, Georgia 30260

Phone: (770) 961-3500
FAX: (770) 961-3700
E-mail: ccsu-info@ce.clayton.edu
WWW: www.clayton.edu

Online Learning Information

Academic Director of Distance Learning
5900 North Lee Street
Morrow, Georgia 30260-0285

Phone: (770) 961-3634
FAX: (770) 961-3630
E-mail: carpenter@gg.clayton.edu
WWW: www.clayton.edu

Institution Background

Founded: 1969
Type of Institution: Public
Accreditation: Southern Association of Colleges and Schools

Programs

Integrative Studies

Degree Offered: Associate of Arts/Associate of Science

Program Web Address: distancelearning. clayton.edu/online_degrees/aaas.html

Program Background: Students in this program create their own curriculum of courses and experiences that meet their individual career needs. Developing their own academic programs requires careful planning on the part of the students, so students should clarify their career or learning goals as they begin creating their curriculums. Having students design their own curriculums sets this program apart from many traditional Bachelor's programs which focus on preparing students for advanced work in an academic discipline.

Completion Requirements: You must successfully complete 60 hours for this degree.

Example Course Titles: Some of the course titles in this program include English Composition I, Mathematics, College Alegebra, Critical Thinking, Thinking Across the Curriculum, Communications Software Applications, Computing with Spreadsheets, Ethics in Contemporary Perspective, The Arts and Society, and Music Appreciation.

Program Contact: Clayton College and State University
5900 N. Lee Street
Morrow, Georgia 30260
(770) 961-3500
(770) 961-3752
ccsu-info@mail.clayton.edu

Integrative Studies

Degree Offered: Bachelor of Arts/Bachelor of Science

Program Web Address: distancelearning. clayton.edu/online_degrees/aaas.html

Program Background: Students in this program create their own curriculum of courses and experiences that meet their individual career needs. Developing their own academic programs requires careful planning on the part of the students, so students should clarify their career or learning goals as they begin creating their curriculums. Having students design their own curriculums sets this program apart from many traditional bachelor's programs which focus on preparing students for advanced work in an academic discipline.

Completion Requirements: You must successfully complete 120 hours for this degree.

Program Contact: Clayton College and State University
5900 N. Lee Street
Morrow, Georgia 30260
(770) 961-3500
(770) 961-3752
ccsu-info@mail.clayton.edu

CLEVELAND STATE UNIVERSITY

General Contact Information

1860 East 22nd Street
Cleveland, Ohio 44114-4435

Phone: (216) 687-5322
FAX: (216) 687-9290
E-mail: j.crocker@csuohio.edu
WWW: www.csuohio.edu

Online Learning Information

Off-Campus Academic Programs
Rhodes Tower, Room 1209
1860 East 22nd Street
Cleveland, Ohio 44115

Phone: (216) 687-3588
FAX: (216) 687-9290
E-mail: j.f.gage@csuohio.edu
WWW: www.csuohio.edu

Institution Background

Cleveland State University is a public, urban university that serves over 16,000 students annually. Its mission is to provide higher education opportunities primarily to residents of northeastern Ohio. The University offers 65 Bachelor's degree programs, 31 Master's degree programs, two advanced law degrees, and six doctoral programs.

Founded: 1964
Type of Institution: Public
Accreditation: North Central Association of Colleges and Schools

Online Course Background: Currently, Cleveland State University offers online programs in health sciences, and individual courses in education, e-commerce, and urban studies.

Online Courses Offered: 2

Online Students Enrolled: 25

Services Offered to Students: Students enrolled in online courses have access to the University library through the World Wide Web, and free delivery of journal articles via fax or U.S. Mail. They also have advisors available via the Web, fax, or phone.

Financial Aid: Students taking courses online are eligible to apply for financial aid to see if they meet the criteria to receive assistance through the federal aid programs, state-supported programs, and other scholarships.

Registration: You may register for courses via mail.

Programs
Health Sciences

Degree Offered: Master of Science in Health Sciences

Program Web Address: www.csuohio.edu/mshealth

Online Program Started: 1999

Program Background: This is a post-professional degree designed to prepare students for leadership roles in the rapidly changing health care environment. It is intended for health care professionals who want to enhance their career options and achieve increased excellence in the provision of patient services.

Application Requirements: You must have a Bachelor's degree. You need to submit an application, official undergraduate transcripts, your scores on the Graduate Record Examination (GRE), and three letters of recommendation.

Completion Requirements: You must successfully complete 36 semester credit hours (11 courses and a capstone research project).

Time for Completion: You have up to six years to complete this program.

On Campus Requirements: You are required to attend one ten-day intensive seminar.

Example Course Titles: Some of the course titles in this program include Issues in Health Sciences, Leadership Roles, Research and Analysis, Culture and Health Care, Health Care in a Changing Environment, Evolving Technologies, Outcomes Assessment, and Seminar in Health Sciences Professions.

Program Contact: Dr. Bette Bonder
Department of Health Sciences
Cleveland State University

Cleveland, Ohio 44115
(216) 687-3567
(216) 687-9316
healthsci@csuohio.edu

COLLEGE OF ST. SCHOLASTICA

General Contact Information

1200 Kenwood Avenue
Duluth, Minnesota 55811-4199

Phone: (218) 723-6046
FAX: (218) 723-6394
E-mail: admissions@css1.css.edu
WWW: www.css.edu

Online Learning Information

1200 Kenwood Avenue
Duluth, Minnesota 55811

Phone: (218) 723-6046
FAX: (218) 723-5991
E-mail: admiss@css.edu
WWW: www.css.edu

Institution Background

Founded: 1912
Type of Institution: Private
Accreditation: North Central Association of Colleges and Schools

Programs

Behavioral Arts and Sciences

Degree Offered: Bachelor of Arts

Program Background: This program provides students with a broad education with a special focus in one academic area. This major tends to be more liberal arts in nature. It stresses critical thinking, writing, and communication.

Completion Requirements: You must successfully complete 192 credits for this degree—48 of them must be from the College of St. Scholastica in-residence, and the other 64 must be in courses numbered 300 or above.

Education

Degree Offered: Master of Education

Program Web Address: www.css.edu/medl/

Application Requirements: You should have two years of professional experience in an educational setting and an undergraduate grade point average of 2.8. You should submit an application for admission, official transcripts, two letters of recommendation (one from a supervisor), and an essay.

Completion Requirements: You must successfully complete 18 credits.

On Campus Requirements: You are required to fulfill two weekend seminars on campus.

Example Course Titles: Some of the course titles in this program include The Highly Effective Teacher, Teaching in the Diverse Classroom, Assessing Student Learning, Introduction to Classroom Action Research, Conducting Classroom Action Research, Colloquium: Reflective Practice, Motivation in Today's Learners, Strategies for Teaching Thinking, Conflict Resolution, Integrating Curricula, Learning is Inquiry, Topics: The Internet in the Classroom, Strategies for Creating Inclusive Classrooms, Topics: Teacher-Parent Relationships, and Topics: Teaching the American Indian Student.

Program Contact: The College of St. Scholastica
Master of Education Department

1200 Kenwood Ave
Duluth, Minnesota 55811
(800) 888-8796
dgorder@css.edu

Management

Degree Offered: Bachelor of Arts

Program Web Address: www.css.edu

Program Background: This program prepares students to manage effectively in any business, government, or other environment. Students develop skills to help them communicate, analyze and solve problems, and apply knowledge practically. The program emphasizes a broad education and liberal learning in combination with practical business skills. Faculty who instruct the courses are experienced management professionals and full-time teachers.

Completion Requirements: You must successfully complete 128 credit hours and maintain a minimum grade point average of 2.0 for this degree. Also you must complete a core of liberal arts courses and a core of management courses.

Example Course Titles: Some of the course titles for this program include Composition, Interpersonal Communication, Computers in Business, Marketing Principles, Macroeconomics, Financial Management, Human Resource Management, Policies and Strategies, and Management Communication: Written.

Program Contact: College of St. Scholastica
1200 Kenwood Avenue
Duluth, Minnesota 55811
(218) 723-6046
(218) 723-5991
admiss@css.edu

COLORADO COMMUNITY COLLEGE ONLINE

General Contact Information

9075 East Lowry Blvd.
Denver, Colorado 80220

Phone: (800) 801-5040
FAX: (303) 365-8803
E-mail: sb_mike@cccs.cccoes.edu
WWW: www.ccconline.org

Programs

Accounting

Degree Offered: Associate of Applied Science

Program Web Address: www.ccconline.org/catalog/Acct.cfm

Online Program Started: 2000

Program Background: This program is designed to prepare students for immediate employment in a full-time skilled or paraprofessional occupation in accounting. Although most of the college credits that students earn with this A.A.S. program are accepted for transfer by four-year colleges and universities, this degree itself is not specifically designed to facilitate transfer. Students who anticipate transferring should check the requirements of the respective institution carefully.

Completion Requirements: You must successfully complete a minimum of 60 semester credits for this degree.

Example Course Titles: Some of the course titles in this program include Accounting Principles, Intermediate Financial Accounting, Accounting Information Systems and e-Business, Introduction to Business, Business Communications and Report Writing, Legal

Environment of Business, Spreadsheets Applications, and Principles of Management.

Agriculture Business

Degree Offered: Associate of Applied Science

Program Web Address: www.ccconline.org/catalog/AgBus.cfm

Online Program Started: 2000

Program Background: This program is designed to prepare students for immediate employment in a full-time skilled or paraprofessional occupation in agricultural business.

Application Requirements: You need to review the course and program offerings, then apply to the appropriate partner or college that offers that program. If you select a program that is offered by a group of the partner colleges, you need to choose a college from among the partners.

Completion Requirements: You must successfully complete 63 credit hours for this degree.

Example Course Titles: Some of the course titles in this program include Animal Science, Agricultural Economics, Farm and Ranch Management, Agri-Business Marketing, Agri-Business Management, Equine Management, Beef Cattle Management, and Feeds and Feeding.

Business

Degree Offered: Associate of Applied Science

Program Web Address: www.ccconline.org/catalog/Bus.cfm

Program Background: Students enrolled in this program prepare for immediate employment in a full-time skilled and/or paraprofessional occupation in business.

Application Requirements: Look over the listing of available courses and programs, and decide which certificate or degree program you are interested in pursuing. If you are interested in a certificate or degree program that is offered by a specific partner college, you will need to choose that college as your college of record. If you are interested in a certificate or degree program that is offered by a group of our partner colleges, you will need to choose your college from among that group of colleges.

Completion Requirements: You must successfully complete a minimum of 60 semester credits for this degree.

Example Course Titles: Some of the course titles in this program include Principles of Accounting I, Principles of Accounting II, Introduction to Business, Legal Environment of Business, Business Communication and Report Writing, Business Statistics, Small Business Management, Principles Of Management, Principles Of Marketing, Human Resource Management, Principles of Sales, Introduction to Microcomputer Applications, and Introduction to Spread Sheets.

Computer Networking

Degree Offered: Associate of Applied Science

Program Web Address: www.ccconline.org/catalog/Net.cfm

Online Program Started: 2000

Completion Requirements: You must successfully complete 60 credit hours.

Example Course Titles: Some of the course titles in this program include Introduction to Computers, Introduction to Computer Networking, Introduction to Networking, Local Area Networks and Internetworking, Local Area Networks and Internetworking, Wide Area Networks, Wide Area Networks, Processes and Protocols, Network Architectures and TCP/IP, Internet Technologies, TCP/IP and Network Architectures, System Analysis and Design, Network Design and Installation, Network Analysis and Design, Introduction to Web Authoring Tools—HTML, and Web Page Design and Layout—Front Page.

Construction Technology

Degree Offered: Associate of Applied Science

Program Web Address: www.ccconline.org/catalog/Constr.html

Program Background: This program is designed to allow students having served an apprenticeship program through the National Joint apprenticeship (NJATC) to earn an associate's degree. Students can combine trade skills with academic skills.

Completion Requirements: You must successfully complete 61 credit hours.

Program Contact: Red Rocks Community College
Academic Advisor
Electrical Programs
(303) 914-6242
greg.morey@rrcc.cccoes.edu

Emergency Management and Planning

Degree Offered: Associate of Applied Science

Program Web Address: www.ccconline.org/catalog/EMP.cfm

Program Background: This program provides students with the skills necessary to pursue full-time employment in emergency management and planning.

Completion Requirements: You must successfully complete 60 semester credits of approved coursework.

Example Course Titles: Some of the course titles in this program include Technical Writing, English Composition, Statistics, General Psychology, Introduction to Sociology, Geographical Information Systems, Introduction to Environmental Science, Hazardous Materials Awareness and Operations, Instructional Methodology, Principles of Supervision, Principles of Management, Interpersonal Communications, Mass Casualty, Public Policy in Emergency Management, and Radiological Fundamentals.

Emergency Management and Planning

Degree Offered: Certificate

Program Web Address: www.ccconline.org/catalog/EMP.cfm

Completion Requirements: You must successfully complete 30 semester credits of approved coursework for this certificate.

Example Course Titles: Some of the course titles in this program include Principles of Emergency Management, Emergency Planning, Exercise Design and Evaluation, Emergency Operations Center and Communications, Incident Command System, Leadership and Influence, Decision Making and Problem Solving, Effective Communications, Developing Volunteer Resources, and Public Information Officer.

General Education

Degree Offered: Associate of Arts

Program Web Address: www.ccconline.org/catalog/arts.cfm

Program Background: This degree is for students who want to pursue education for personal enrichment or to transfer into a four-year college. Students get a foundation in communication, social science, and arts or humanities.

Completion Requirements: You must successfully complete 60 hours.

Occupational Safety

Degree Offered: Certificate

Program Web Address: www.ccconline.org/catalog/Osha.cfm

Program Background: The Occupational Safety and Health Technology program provides occupational safety training to students who are already working in the field, and those who wish to pursue careers in this field. The courses provide students with knowledge and training based on the American Society of Safety Engineers and Board of Certified Safety Professionals standards.

Completion Requirements: You must successfully complete 44 credit hours for this certificate.

Example Course Titles: Some of the course titles for this program include Accident Prevention, Economics: Managing Task Stress, Industrial Hygiene, Case Study Evaluation, and Safety Training Methods.

Occupational Safety

Degree Offered: Associate of Applied Science

Program Web Address: www.ccconline.org/catalog/Osha.cfm

Program Background: The Occupational Safety and Health Technology program provides occupational safety training to students who are already working in the field, and those who wish to pursue careers in this field. The courses provide students with knowledge and training based on the American Society of Safety Engineers and Board of Certified Safety Professionals standards.

Completion Requirements: You must successfully complete 69 credit hours for this degree.

Example Course Titles: Some of the course titles in this program include Technical Writing, Speech, Introduction to Chemistry, General Psychology, Fire Protection and Analysis, General Industry Standards, Construction Standards, Safety Program Planning, and Hazardous Materials.

Public Administration

Degree Offered: Associate of Arts

Program Web Address: www.ccconline.org/catalog/PubAdmin.cfm

Program Background: Students in this program are pursuing an Associate's degree in Public Administration for career enrichment or to prepare for employment in government, law, education, the arts, or social sciences. The program provides a broad foundation in communications, social science, arts, or humanities.

Application Requirements: You must determine exactly which program you wish to be admitted to and identify the school through which you will enroll. After you've determined these two things, you can complete an application online.

Completion Requirements: You must successfully complete 60 credit hours.

Example Course Titles: Some of the course titles in this program include Human Resource Management, Introduction to Microcomputer Applications, Principles of Management, State and Local Government, Introduction to Public Finance, and Community Development and Planning.

COLORADO STATE UNIVERSITY

General Contact Information

Spruce Hall
Fort Collins, Colorado 80523-0015

Phone: (970) 491-6909
FAX: (970) 491-7799
E-mail: admissions@colostate.edu
WWW: www.colostate.edu

Online Learning Information

Division of Educational Outreach
Spruce Hall
Fort Collins, Colorado 80523-1040

Phone: (970) 491-5288
FAX: (970) 491-7885
E-mail: info@learn.colostate.edu
WWW: www.colostate.edu

Institution Background

Founded: 1870
Type of Institution: Public
Accreditation: North Central Association of Colleges and Schools

Programs

Agriculture

Degree Offered: Master of Agriculture

Program Web Address: www.csun.colostate.edu/depts/agric.html

Program Background: The Master of Agriculture is a professional degree administered by the College of Agricultural Sciences in cooperation with several departments, both within and outside the college. Interdisciplinary in nature, this program provides maximum flexibility in curriculum design. It provides students with a broader area of study than the more research-oriented, traditional Master of Science degree. Plans of study are individually designed to meet students' professional needs and specific goals.

Application Requirements: You should have a Bachelor's degree and minimum undergraduate grade point average of 3.0. You need to submit an application, letters of recommendation, statement or evidence of professional experience and leadership potential, and your scores on the Graduate Record Examination (GRE) and Test of English as a Foreign Language (TOEFL), if appropriate.

Completion Requirements: You select which plan to pursue—Plan A requires applied research and a formal thesis, and Plan B requires more coursework and a scholarly paper rather than a thesis.

System Requirements: You should have a personal computer with a 100 MHz 486 processor (Pentium processors are preferred and may be required for classes in Computer Science), 16 MB RAM (minimum), a 28.8 kbps modem, color SVGA monitor, 8 MB available hard drive space, a Web browser (Netscape 3.0, Microsoft Internet Explorer 3.0, or AOL 4.0). WebTV devices are not capable of carrying out the functions of online study, so they are not acceptable.

Program Contact: Associate Dean
College of Agricultural Sciences
121 Shepardson, Colorado State University
Fort Collins, Colorado 80523
(970) 491-6274

Bioresource and Agricultural Engineering and Chemical Engineering

Degree Offered: Master of Science

Program Web Address: www.csun.colostate.edu/depts/biore.html

Program Background: There are two separate graduate programs administered through the Department of Chemical and Bioresource Engineering: Bioresource and Agricultural Engineering, and Chemical Engineering.

The Bioresource and Agricultural Engineering degree program includes these areas of study: irrigation and drainage, groundwater hydrology, power and machinery, food engineering, and environmental engineering. And the Chemical Engineering program emphasizes biotechnology, food processing, advanced materials, and environmental engineering. The two programs are highly complementary, resulting in an overall program of unusual breadth and depth.

These programs are intended to develop the students ability to conduct research, and to develop proficiency in a specialized area of chemical or bioresource and agricultural engineering. The Masters degree is an appropriate step toward a Ph.D. degree or a means to train engineers capable of applied research and technical leadership in industry or government. It is an excellent way for qualified students to gain a deeper insight into a specific subject, and to expand the general engineering knowledge obtained during undergraduate education.

Completion Requirements: You must successfully complete at least 30 to 32 semester credits in coursework and research approved for graduate credit by students advisory committee.

Program Contact: Chair, Bioresource and Agricultural Adviser
Department of Chemical and Bioresource Engineering
Colorado State University
Fort Collins, Colorado 80523
(970) 491-5253

Business Administration

Degree Offered: Master of Business Administration

Program Web Address: www.csun.colostate. edu/depts/mba.html

Program Background: This program is designed to provide potential or practicing managers the opportunity to develop and sharpen their professional skills. The curriculum focuses on the broad function of business operations with specific emphasis on team building, information technology, and globalization.

Application Requirements: You are required to take the Graduate Management Admissions Test (GMAT). Your application will not be considered until your GMAT scores have been received. Scores that are more than five years old will not be accepted. Few candidates are admitted with a GMAT score below 550. You may request a waiver of the GMAT if you have at least eight years of full-time work experience and cumulative collegiate grade point average of at least 3.0 (on a 4.0 scale).

Completion Requirements: You must successfully complete 36 credits for this degree. You are not required to complete a thesis, project, or final examination.

Time for Completion: You may complete this program on a two-year or four-year plan. The two-year plan requires you to take two courses concurrently. The four-year plan requires you to take only one course at a time. Both plans require you to take courses during the summer.

Example Course Titles: Some of the course titles in this program include Accounting Systems, Management, Leadership, and Team Dynamics, Strategic Management for Competitive Advantage, Managerial Communication Strategies, Information Technology Infrastructure, Strategic Uses of Information Technology, Statistics and Economics for the World Market, Financial Principles and Practice, Financial Markets and Investments, Enterprise Electronic Business Strategies, Manufacturing and Service, Marketing Management, Social and Regulatory

Issues in Business, and Analysis of Dynamic Enterprises.

Program Contact: Distance Education and Media
College of Business
Colorado State University
Fort Collins, Colorado 80523
(800) 491-4MBA ext. 6

Civil Engineering

Degree Offered: Master of Science

Program Web Address: www.csun.colostate.edu/depts/civeng.html

Program Background: Students enrolled in this program will complete courses in environmental engineering, hydraulics and wind engineering, structural and geotechnical engineering, water resources, hydrologic and environmental sciences, and water resources planning and management. The program integrates study and research.

Application Requirements: You must have a Bachelor's degree in engineering to apply to this program. If you don't have an engineering background, but have a degree in science or a related field, you may apply and might be admitted with some prerequisite work.

Program Contact: Student Adviser
Department of Civil Engineering
Colorado State University
Fort Collins, Colorado 80523
(970) 491-5844

Computer Science

Degree Offered: Bachelor of Science

Program Web Address: www.csun.colostate.edu/depts/comsci.html

Program Background: This is intended to be a second Bachelor's program. Students in this program can specialize in systems architecture, artificial intelligence, formal methods, graphics, languages and compilers, networks and distributed computing, computer vision, operating systems, parallel processing and functional languages, or software engineering.

Application Requirements: You should have a Bachelor's degree in a technical subject (such as mathematics, physics, or engineering).

Program Contact: Advisor
Computer Science Department
Colorado State University
Fort Collins, Colorado 80523
(970) 491-7137

Computer Science

Degree Offered: Master of Science

Program Web Address: www.csun.colostate.edu/depts/comsci.html

Program Background: Students in this program can specialize in systems architecture, artificial intelligence, formal methods, graphics, languages and compilers, networks and distributed computing, computer vision, operating systems, parallel processing and functional languages, or software engineering.

Application Requirements: You must have a solid background in computer science, including having completed some undergraduate preparatory courses.

Program Contact: Advisor
Computer Science Department
Colorado State University
Fort Collins, Colorado 80523
(970) 491-7137

Electrical Engineering

Degree Offered: Master of Electrical Engineering

Program Web Address: www.csun.colostate.edu/depts/eleceng.html

Program Background: This degree is designed for students who want an education beyond that afforded through a Bachelor's program, but who are not interested in pursuing a traditional research oriented Master's degree. This degree is based entirely on coursework and offers considerable flexibility for designing a program of study consisting of courses in electrical engineering in addition to credits in other areas such as business or computer science.

Application Requirements: You must have a Bachelor's degree and a minimum undergraduate grade point average of 3.0.

Completion Requirements: You must successfully complete 30 semester credits of coursework.

Program Contact: Graduate Coordinator
Electrical Engineering Department
Colorado State University
Fort Collins, Colorado 80523
(970) 491-6706

Electrical Engineering

Degree Offered: Master of Science

Program Web Address: www.csun.colostate.edu/depts/eleceng.html

Application Requirements: You must have Bachelor's degree and a minimum undergraduate grade point average of 3.0.

Completion Requirements: You must successfully complete 30 semester credits and a thesis under Plan A, or 32 semester credits and no thesis under Plan B.

Program Contact: Graduate Coordinator
Electrical Engineering Department
Colorado State University
Fort Collins, Colorado 80523

(970) 491-6706

Electrical Engineering

Degree Offered: Doctor of Philosophy

Program Web Address: www.csun.colostate.edu/depts/eleceng.html

Application Requirements: You must have a Master's degree and a graduate grade point average of at least 3.5. Additionally, you are required to take the Graduate Record Examination and submit your scores. You must have a 1100 combined on the verbal and quantitative sections to be admitted to this program.

Completion Requirements: You must successfully complete a minimum of 42 credits.

Program Contact: Graduate Coordinator
Electrical Engineering Department
Colorado State University
Fort Collins, Colorado 80523
(970) 491-6706

Engineering Management

Degree Offered: Master of Science in Mechanical Engineering

Program Web Address: www.csun.colostate.edu/depts/engmang.html

Application Requirements: You must submit an application and supporting documents, include your test scores on the Graduate Record Examination (GRE) general test. You should have a quantitative score of about 700, an analytical score above 650, and a verbal score above 500.

Completion Requirements: You must successfully complete 30 credits.

Example Course Titles: Some of the course titles in this program include Management, Leadership, and Team Dynamics, Strategic

Management for Competitive Advantage, Managerial Communication Strategies, Manufacturing and Service, Social and Regulatory Issues in Business, Systems Engineering and Optimization, Linear Programming and Network Flows, Manufacturing Simulation, Manufacturing Quality Design and Control, Quality Control, Reliability Engineering, and Introduction to Probability Theory.

Program Contact: Advisor
Mechanical Engineering Department
Colorado State University
Fort Collins, Colorado 80523
(970) 491-5597

Environmental Engineering Program

Degree Offered: Master of Science

Program Web Address: www.csun.colostate. edu/depts/enveng.html

Program Background: This program is designed to provide basic knowledge to practice environmental engineering, to provide a perspective on the breadth of environmental engineering problem areas, and to introduce students to the environmental engineering profession.

Application Requirements: You must have a Bachelor's degree in engineering, or equivalent course work.

Program Contact: Advisor
Bioresource and Agricultural Engineering
Colorado State University
Fort Collins, Colorado 80523
(970) 491-6308

Human Resource Development

Degree Offered: Masters of Education in Education and Human Resource Studies

Program Web Address: www.csun.colostate.

edu/depts/hrdev.html

Program Background: This program prepares students for roles and responsibilities in management and operations of business, government, industry, medical, military, social service, and nonprofit organizations.

Example Course Titles: Some of the course titles in this program include Introduction to Research Methods, Philosophy/Organization of Workforce Education, Management, Leadership, and Team Dynamics, Strategic Management for Competitive Advantage, Career and Employment Concepts, Human Resource Development, Consultation and Analysis of Organizations, and Adult Teaching and Learning.

Program Contact: Human Resource Development
School of Education
Education Building
Fort Collins, Colorado 80523
(970) 491-6317

Industrial Engineering Program

Degree Offered: Master of Science in Mechanical Engineering

Program Web Address: www.csun.colostate. edu/depts/indeng.html

Program Background: Students enrolled in the Master of Science program can specialize in industrial engineering, which emphasizes application of operations research, engineering economy, quality control, reliability, and computer methods to the problems of manufacturing, government, and service industries.

Completion Requirements: Students will discuss the specialization they wish to pursue with their advisors and work closely with their advisors to determine their program of study. Students are required to write a thesis as part of the Master's program.

Example Course Titles: Some of the course titles in this program include Linear Programming and Network Flows, Manufacturing Simulation, Manufacturing Quality Design and Control, Industrial and Systems Engineering, Reliability Engineering, and Fundamentals of Robot Mechanics and Controls.

Program Contact: Coordinator
Mechanical Engineering Department
Colorado State University
Fort Collins, Colorado 80523
(970) 491-5859

Mechanical Engineering

Degree Offered: Master of Science

Program Web Address: www.csun.colostate.edu/depts/mecheng.html

Program Background: Colorado State University's graduate program in mechanical engineering focuses on the fields of energy and the environment, computer-aided design and manufacturing, manufacturing and industrial engineering, mechanics and materials, biomedical/biomaterial engineering, space propulsion, and engineering management.

Program Contact: Mechanical Engineering Department
Colorado State University
Fort Collins, Colorado 80523
(970) 491-5597

Mechanical Engineering

Degree Offered: Doctor of Philosophy

Program Web Address: www.csun.colostate.edu/depts/mecheng.html

Program Background: Colorado State University's graduate program in mechanical engineering focuses on the fields of energy and the environment, computer-aided design and man-ufacturing, manufacturing and industrial engineering, mechanics and materials, biomedical/biomaterial engineering, space propulsion, and engineering management.

Program Contact: Mechanical Engineering Department
Colorado State University
Fort Collins, Colorado 80523
(970) 491-5597

Statistics

Degree Offered: Master of Science

Program Web Address: www.csun.colostate.edu/depts/stat.html

Program Background: The field of statistics holds many opportunities for people who like interpreting the world in quantitative ways. Students in Colorado State University's Master's program develop methods to explain quantitative patterns in social, physical, and natural sciences, as well as business and industry.

Application Requirements: While your undergraduate major does not have to be in a certain area for you to be eligible to apply for this program, you do need some prerequisite work in mathematics and statistics. Colorado State University recommends that applicants have at least three semesters of calculus and six credits from upper-division statistics courses. They also recommend that you have experience with at least one computer programming language.

Completion Requirements: You must successfully complete a sequence of courses and a Master's project.

Time for Completion: The typical pace for this program is one course per semester. The department schedules courses and directs you to ensure that you meet the requirements within five years.

Example Course Titles: Some of the course titles in this program include Statistical Science, Introduction to Probability Theory, Mathematical Statistics, Data Analysis and Regression, Practicum in Consulting Techniques, Design and Linear Modeling I, Stochastic Processes I, Analysis of Time Series I, Theory of Sampling Techniques, and Design and Linear Modeling II.

Program Contact: Program Assistant
Department of Statistics
Colorado State University
Fort Collins, Colorado 80523
(970) 491-5269

COLUMBUS STATE UNIVERSITY

General Contact Information

4225 University Avenue
Columbus, Georgia 31907-5645

Phone: (706) 568-2035
FAX: (706) 568-2462
WWW: www.colstate.edu

Online Learning Information

Distance Learning Coordinator
4225 University Avenue
Columbus, Georgia 31907

Phone: (706) 569-3455
FAX: (706) 568-2459
E-mail: daniels_timothy@colstate.edu
WWW: www.colstate.edu

Institution Background

Founded: 1958
Type of Institution: Public
Accreditation: Southern Association of Colleges and Schools

Programs

Computer Science

Degree Offered: Master

Program Web Address: cs.colstate.edu/online.htm

Program Background: This program is designed for computer software professionals. It emphasizes distributed client-server software design, development, and deployment using the most important industry technologies.

Application Requirements: You must have a Bachelor's degree from an accredited college or university with a major in computer science, applied computer science, computer information science/systems, computer engineering, or other closely related fields. You must also have a minimum undergraduate cumulative grade point average of 2.75, and score a minimum of 800 on the aptitude section of the GRE.

Completion Requirements: You must successfully complete 36 semester hours (24 hours of required courses and 12 hours in electives).

System Requirements: You should have a personal computer with a Pentium processor, Windows NT, 128 MB memory, a CD-ROM drive, and Internet access.

Example Course Titles: Some of the course titles in this program include Object-Oriented Development with Components, Client-Server Database Systems, Web Site Development and Technologies, Distributed Enterprise Software Design and Development, Enterprise Web Application Development, Software Architecture and Development, and Networking Essentials.

Program Contact: Department of Computer Science, 110 FOB
Columbus State University
4225 University Ave.
Columbus, Georgia 31907
(706) 568-2410

(706) 565-3529
brewer_connie@colstate.edu

COMMUNITY COLLEGE OF AURORA

General Contact Information

16000 East Centre Tech Parkway
Aurora, Colorado 80011

Phone: (303) 361-7391
FAX: (303) 360-4761
WWW: www.cca.cccoes.edu

Institution Background

Founded: 1983
Type of Institution: Public
Accreditation: North Central Association of Colleges and Schools

Programs:

Associate of Applied Science

Degree Offered: Associate of Applied Science

Program Web Address: www.cca.cccoes.edu/distance/_distance.html

Example Course Titles: Some of the course titles in this program include Advanced COBOL Programming, Advanced Visual Basic, Advanced Windows 95, Advertising and Promotion, Beginning German, Business Communication and Report Writing, Business Law I, English Composition I, Ethics, Human Nutrition, Human Resources Management I, Introduction to Astronomy, Introduction to Criminal Justice, Managerial Finance, Personal Selling, and Principles of Microeconomics.

Program Contact: Learning Resource Center
Community College of Aurora
16000 East Centre Tech Parkway
Aurora, Colorado 80011

(303) 361-7391
Lisa.CheneySteen@cca.cccoes.edu

COMMUNITY COLLEGE OF DENVER

General Contact Information

P.O. Box 173363
Denver, Colorado 80217

Phone: (303) 556-2600
FAX: (303) 556-8555

Institution Background

Founded: 1970
Type of Institution: Public
Accreditation: North Central Association of Colleges and Schools

Programs

Gerontology

Degree Offered: Certificate

Program Web Address: www.ccconline.org/catalog/GNT.cfm

Program Background: This program is designed for students who want to work full-time in gerontology-related fields. Students gain an understanding of the process of aging. The program is beneficial to professionals in nursing, dentistry, physical and occupational therapy, accounting, real estate, human services and social work.

Completion Requirements: You must successfully complete 30 credit hours.

Example Course Titles: Some of the course titles in this program include Introduction to Gerontology, Practicum in Gerontology, Physiological Aspects of Aging, Psychology of Aging, Social Aspects of Aging, Aging in a Diverse Society, Overview of Programs and Services to the Aged, Nutrition and Aging, Nutrition, Death and Dying, and Leadership Development.

Program Contact: Community College of Denver
Gerontology Program Coordinator
(303) 556-3891
cd_karentm@cccs.cccoes.edu

Gerontology

Degree Offered: Associate of Applied Science

Program Web Address: www.ccconline.org/catalog/GNT.cfm

Program Background: This program is designed for students who want to work full-time in gerontology-related fields. Students gain an understanding of the process of aging. The program is beneficial to professionals in nursing, dentistry, physical and occupational therapy, accounting, real estate, human services and social work.

Completion Requirements: You must successfully complete 60 credit hours.

Example Course Titles: Some of the course titles in this program include Introduction to Gerontology, Practicum in Gerontology, Physiological Aspects of Aging, Psychology of Aging, Social Aspects of Aging, Aging in a Diverse Society, Overview of Programs and Services to the Aged, Nutrition and Aging, Nutrition, Death and Dying, and Leadership Development.

Program Contact: Community College of Denver
Gerontology Program Coordinator
(303) 556-3891
cd_karentm@cccs.cccoes.edu

CONNECTICUT STATE UNIVERSITY SYSTEM

Online Learning Information
WWW: onlinecsu.ctstateu.edu

Programs
Library Science

Degree Offered: Master of Library Science

Program Web Address: onlinecsu.ctstateu.edu/index.real?action=degreeinfo

Program Background: Library science, information science, and instructional technology are all integrated in this degree program that prepares students for careers in libraries and information science areas. The American Library Association accredits this program, and the school media specialist concentration is approved by the Connecticut State Board of Education.

Application Requirements: You need to have a minimum undergraduate grade point average of no less than 2.7 (on a 4.0 scale) overall or a minimum of 3.0 during your last two years as an undergraduate. You should also have basic computer skills and knowledge that can be acquired through a college-level computer literacy course. This includes knowing how to use a word processor, e-mail, and a Web browser, as well as a basic understanding of hardware, software, and telecommunications capabilities.

You must complete and submit an application (by July 1 for fall admission, November 1 for spring admission, or April 1 for summer admission) with a $40 application fee. Your application must include two copies of official transcripts from any college and university you've attended, two letters of recommendation, a statement (250-500 words) explaining your interest in the program and your career goals, and your scores on the Graduate Record Examination (GRE). You should have a minimum score of at least 400 in each of the GRE categories and a minimum of 1000 on two out of the three sections if you are a native-English speaker. If you have an advanced degree from a regionally accredited college or university, you may request a waiver of the GRE requirement. You will also be required to interview for admittance to the program.

If English is not your native or primary language, you must take the GRE and the Test of English as a Foreign Language (TOEFL) examination. You should have a minimum score of 400 on the mathematics category of the GRE and a minimum score of 550 on the TOEFL, and a combined minimum of 1000 points on the GRE mathematics category and the TOEFL.

Completion Requirements: You must successfully complete 36 credit hours for this program.

Example Course Titles: Some of the course titles for this program include Introduction to Information Science and Technology, Foundations of Librarianship, Reference and Information Resources and Services, Information Analysis and Organization, and Evaluation and Research.

Program Contact: mls@onlinecsu.ctstateu.edu

CROWN COLLEGE

General Contact Information

6425 County 30
St. Bonifacius, Minnesota 55375

Phone: (612) 446-4100
FAX: (612) 446-4149

E-mail: info@gw.crown.edu
WWW: www.crown.edu

Online Learning Information

WWW: crownonline.org

Institution Background

Founded: 1916
Type of Institution: Private
Accreditation: North Central Association of Colleges and Schools; Accrediting Association of Bible Colleges

Programs
Christian Ministry

Degree Offered: Bachelor of Arts

Program Web Address: crownonline.org

Online Program Started: 1999

Application Requirements: You must be at least 25 years old and have completed approximately two years of college with a minimum grade point average of 2.0 (on a 4.0 scale). You should complete an application and submit it with an application fee and original transcripts from any college or university you've attended.

Program Contact: Crown College
6425 County 30
St. Bonifacius, Minnesota 55375
(612) 446-4100
(612) 446-4149

Church Leadership

Degree Offered: Master of Arts

Program Web Address: crownonline.org

Online Program Started: 2000

Program Background: 2000.

Program Contact: Crown College
6425 County 30
St. Bonifacius, Minnesota 55375
(612) 446-4100
(612) 446-4149

DALLAS BAPTIST UNIVERSITY

General Contact Information

3000 Montain Creek Parkway
Dallas, Texas 75211

Phone: (214) 333-5360
FAX: (214) 333-5447
E-mail: admiss@dbu.edu
WWW: www.dbu.edu

Online Learning Information

E-mail: online@dbuonline.org
WWW: www.dbuonline.org

Institution Background

Founded: 1965
Type of Institution: Private
Accreditation: Southern Association of Colleges and Schools

Programs:

Business Administration

Degree Offered: Bachelor of Arts and Sciences

Program Web Address: dalbapt.redirect.
ecollege.com/D2index.real?area=173&
subarea=182

Online Program Started: 1998

Completion Requirements: You must successfully complete a minimum of 126 semester hours for this degree.

Example Course Titles: Some of the course titles in this program include Principles of Financial Accounting, Principles of Managerial Accounting, Principles of Macroeconomics, Principles of Microeconomics, Corporate Financial Management, Principles of Management, Managerial Statistics, Business and Public Law, and Strategy and Problems in Management.

Program Contact: Dallas Baptist University
(800) 460-8188
online@dbuonline.org

Business Administration

Degree Offered: Master of Business Administration

Program Web Address: dalbapt.redirect.
ecollege.com/D2index.real?area=173&
subarea=182

Online Program Started: 1999

Program Background: This program covers concepts and theories for understanding and resolving human problems in organizational settings.

Completion Requirements: You must successfully complete 36 hours for this degree.

Example Course Titles: Some of the course titles in this program includue Leadership in Management, Business Ethics, Managerial Accounting, Management Information Systems, International Management, Organizational Behavior, Human Resources Management, Operations and Quality Management, Financial Accounting, and Orientation to American Business Techniques and Culture.

Program Contact: Dallas Baptist University
(800) 460-8188
anonline@dbuonline.org

DAVID N. MYERS COLLEGE

General Contact Information

112 Prospect Avenue East
Cleveland, Ohio 44115

Phone: (216) 696-9000
FAX: (216) 696-6430
E-mail: tpayton@dnmyers.edu
WWW: www.dnmyers.edu

Online Learning Information

Assistant Director of Admissions
112 Prospect Avenue
Cleveland, Ohio 44115

Phone: (216) 696-9000
FAX: (216) 696-6430
E-mail: admissions@dnmyers.edu
WWW: www.dnmyers.edu

Institution Background

David N. Myers College is a private school that specializes in business education. Many of the College's courses are taught by professionals in their fields with a hands-on approach.

Founded: 1848
Type of Institution: Private
Accreditation: North Central Association of Colleges and Schools

Online Course Background: Myers College Options On-Line (COOL) began in 1995 and has grown every year since. COOL offers courses for-credit towards the Bachelor's de-gree in a distance format utilizing the Web, electronic conferences, and e-mail.

Online Course Offered: 28

Online Students Enrolled: 64

Special Programs/Partnerships: Myers College is a member of the Association of Independent Colleges and Universities of Ohio.

Services Offered to Students: Students enrolled in online courses are afforded all college aca-demic services.

Financial Aid: Students enrolled in online courses are eligible to apply for federal and state grants, institutional scholarships and grants, and student loans.

Registration: You can register for courses via mail, phone, e-mail, and the World Wide Web.

Programs
Business Administration

Degree Offered: Bachelor of Science in Busi-ness Administration

Program Web Address: www.dnmyers.edu/cool

Online Program Started: 1995

Students Enrolled: 46

Program Background: Students are assigned accounts on the Myers College systems, and are placed in a class with peers who study together.

Application Requirements: You should be mo-tivated for independent work, including taking responsibility for communicating regularly with the instructor and completing assign-ments on time.

Completion Requirements: You must dem-onstrate reasonable progress toward your de-gree.

On Campus Requirements: There are no on-campus requirements for this degree.

System Requirements: You should have a personal computer, full Internet access, Microsoft Office, and a Netscape Web browser.

Program Contact: Dr. Donna Trivison
112 Prospect Ave. E.
Cleveland, Ohio 44115
(216) 523-3850
(216) 696-6430
dtrivison@dnmyers.edu

DUKE UNIVERSITY

General Contact Information

2138 Campus Drive
Durham, North Carolina 27708

Phone: (919) 684-3214
FAX: (919) 681-8941
E-mail: askduke@admiss.duke.edu
WWW: www.fuqua.duke.edu

Online Learning Information

Box 90127
Durham, North Carolina 27708

Phone: (919) 660-7802
FAX: (919) 660-8044
E-mail: veraldi@mail.duke.edu
WWW: www.fuqua.duke.edu

Institution Background

Founded: 1838
Type of Institution: Private
Accreditation: Southern Association of Colleges and Schools

Financial Aid: Students enrolled in the Duke Master's of Business Administration, Global Executive Program are not eligible for institutional scholarships or grants. However, they are eligible to apply for federal student loans by completing a Free Application for Federal Student Aid (FAFSA) by March 1.

Programs

Business Administration

Degree Offered: Master of Business Administration

Program Web Address: www.fuqua.duke. edu/admin/gemba/index.html

Program Background: The Master of Business Administration—Global Executive program is a 19-month program in which students convene at sites in North America, Europe, Asia, and South America. Between residential sessions, courses are delivered online. Students learn how to use information technology, as well as develop an understanding of how this technology can and should be used to manage global organizations.

Application Requirements: Admission to this program is selective. You must have a minimum of ten years professional experience, and international managerial responsibilities within your company. You also need to have a Bachelor's degree from an accredited four-year college or university, achievement in quantitative areas, and a knowledge of current information technologies. You must be proficient in written and spoken English. If you are an international student whose native language is not English, you must take the Test of English as a Foreign Language (TOEFL).

Completion Requirements: You must successfully complete the entire program for this degree. This includes five terms with three courses per term, 11 weeks of residential education on four continents, and 50 weeks of online learning.

Time for Completion: You will complete this program in 19 months.

On Campus Requirements: You are required to spend a total of 11 weeks in residential classes at various program sites around the world.

Example Course Titles: Some of the course titles in this program include Managerial Effectiveness for the Global Executive I, International Financial Statement Analysis, Decision Models, Global Managerial Economics, Managerial Effectiveness for the Global Executive II, Interpersonal and Group Relationships in the Global Organization, Statistical Models, Marketing in a Global Environment, Global Economic Environment of the Firm, Financial Management in a Global Economy, Cost Management and Control in Global Organizations, Global Operations Management, Strategy Design and Implementation, Corporate Restructuring, and Global Business Simulation.

DURHAM TECHNICAL COMMUNITY COLLEGE

General Contact Information

1637 Lawson Street
Durham, North Carolina 27703

Phone: (919) 686-3333
FAX: (919) 686-3669
WWW: www.dtcc.cc.nc.us

Online Learning Information

WWW: open.dtcc.cc.nc.us

Institution Background

Founded: 1958
Type of Institution: Public
Accreditation: Southern Association of Colleges and Schools

Programs
Basic Opticianry Option

Degree Offered: Certificate

Program Web Address: open.dtcc.cc.nc.us/opticianry/oph-pos.htm

Program Background: This program is designed to complement and enhance the opticianry apprentice program in North Carolina. This program meets the requirements of the N.C. Board of Opticians for the formal training portion of the apprenticeship experience. The courses include basic optical theory, basic optical dispensing, ophthalmic laboratory concepts, anatomy of the eye, and fitting techniques for rigid and soft contact lenses.

Application Requirements: You must be a high school graduate or have your GED. You should be working in the optical field in an optical shop, or in an Optometry or Ophthalmology practice.

Completion Requirements: You must successfully complete 15 hours for this certificate.

Example Course Titles: Some of the course titles in this program include Math for Opticians, Ophthalmic Laboratory Concepts, Anatomy and Physiology of the Eye, Dispensing I, Optical Theory I, and Special Topics/Contact Lenses.

Program Contact: Durham Technical Community College
1637 Lawson Street
Durham, North Carolina 27703

EAST CAROLINA UNIVERSITY

General Contact Information

106 Whichard Building
Greenville, North Carolina 27858

Phone: (252) 328-6640
FAX: (252) 328-6945
WWW: www.dcs.ecu.edu

Online Learning Information

Distance Learning
Erwin Building
Greenville, North Carolina 27858

Phone: (800) 398-9275
FAX: (919) 328-4350
E-mail: byrdj@mail.ecu.edu
WWW: www.dcs.ecu.edu

Institution Background

The East Carolina University (ECU) Global Campus has a long tradition of serving adult learners. Since the 1930s, ECU has used contemporary technology to deliver courses to students. Many of the students who enroll in ECU's Global Campus are working adults with careers and families. Internet-based courses enable these students to complete their educational goals around their other commitments.

Founded: 1907
Type of Institution: Public
Accreditation: Southern Association of Colleges and Schools

Individual Graduate Courses: East Carolina University offers online graduate courses in communication, computer science, education, health and nutrition, library and information studies, music, nursing, and public safety.

Programs
Industrial Technology

Degree Offered: Bachelor of Science

Program Web Address: www.dcs.ecu.edu/extension/bsit.htm

Online Program Started: 1995

Application Requirements: To apply to this program, you must have successfully completed 63 transferable semester hours of the required 126 with a C average or higher from a qualified Associate of Science degree program. (Only courses with a grade of C or higher will transfer.) The other 63 semester hours of the required 126 must be completed at an accredited four-year college or university. Thirty of the semester hours must be completed at East Carolina University, and you must complete 12 semester hours of writing intensive courses.

On Campus Requirements: None

Example Course Titles: Some of the course titles of this program include Quality Assurance, Manufacturing Processes, Technical Writing, Computer Systems for Industrial Environments, Systems Design, and Industrial Supervision.

Program Contact: Division of Continuing Studies
East Carolina University
Erwin Building
Greenville, North Carolina 27858
(800) 398-9275
(252) 328-0613
byrdj@mail.ecu.edu

Industrial Technology

Degree Offered: Master of Science

Program Web Address: www.sit.ecu.edu/SITOnline/

Online Program Started: 1994

Program Background: East Carolina University's School of Industry and Technology has been delivering instruction using a variety of technology systems since 1994. The School currently focuses on delivery of classes via the Internet for students both on and off campus. Courses use the the World Wide Web, e-mail, mailing lists (also called listservs), newsgroups, Internet relay chat, and video conferencing.

The Industrial Technology program has three areas of concentration including Manufacturing, Digital Communications Technology, and Occupational Safety and Environmental Planning and Development.

Application Requirements: You must be accepted to East Carolina University's Graduate School and submit the School of Industry and Technology's Admission Information Form. Also you need to take the MAT or GRE and have the scores sent to the University.

Completion Requirements: You must successfully complete 30 credits to earn this degree.

System Requirements: You must have a personal computer with a 300 MHz Pentium class processor, 64 MB of RAM, a 56K modem, Windows 95/98/NT, a microphone, and a SoundBlaster compatible sound card (full duplex with speakers and microphone). Some courses may have additional hardware requirements.

Example Course Titles: Some of the course titles in this program include Statistical Process Control, Research in Industrial Technology, Technology Assessment and Forecasting, Project Management, Digital Control of Manufacturing, Networking Technology for Industry, Managing Technological Change, Ergonomics, Fire Protection and Prevention, and Systems Safety Analysis.

Program Contact: East Carolina University
Office of Graduate Studies
School of Industry and Technology

Rawl 121
Greenville, North Carolina 27858-4353
(252) 328-6704

Instructional Technology

Degree Offered: Master of Arts Education

Program Web Address: soe.eastnet.ecu.edu/lset/ma-it.htm

Program Background: East Carolina's Department of Broadcasting, Librarianship, and Educational Technology offers this Master of Arts Education (MAEd) in Instructional Technology. In this program, students learn to design and develop computer-based instructional materials for use in education, business, and government.

Application Requirements: You must apply to East Carolina University's Graduate School and the program department. You must have a Bachelor's degree from a regionally accredited institution, and a satisfactory grade point average as an undergraduate.

The Graduate School requires you to submit a completed application, transcripts from each institution of higher education you've attended, and your scores on the General Record Examination (GRE) or the Miller Analogy Test (MAT). The Graduate School uses a formula including your test scores and grade point average so acceptable scores for admission into the program vary. If you have an overall grade point average of 3.0 or higher or you hold a master's or doctorate from a regionally accredited institution, East Carolina will waive the requirement for you to submit test scores.

The Department of Broadcasting, Librarianship, and Educational Technology requires a completed application and three letters of recommendation that you should have your references send directly to the program director, Dr. Constance A. Mellon.

Completion Requirements: You must successfully complete 36 hours of graduate credit, which is equivalent to 12 three-hour courses.

System Requirements: You must have a personal computer with at least a 486-class processor, 8 MB of RAM, a 28.8 (or faster) modem, and Windows 95/NT/3.1, or a Macintosh with a MAC 68030 processor, 8 MB of RAM, and a 28.8 (or faster) modem.

Example Course Titles: Some of the course titles in this program include Technology in Education, Principles of Instructional Design, Authoring Systems for Instructional Product Development, Multimedia Instructional Product Development, Development of Video Instruction, Virtual Reality: Principles and Applications, and Introduction to Distance Learning.

Program Contact: Dr. Constance A. Mellon
Director of Graduate Studies
East Carolina University
116 Joyner East
Greenville, North Carolina 27858
(252) 328-4338
(252) 328-4368
lsmellon@eastnet.ecu.edu

Technology Management

Degree Offered: Doctor of Philosophy

Program Web Address: web.indstate.edu:80/tech/acadprog/grad/cphd/cphd.html

Program Background: This degree program is geared toward technologists, and combines traditional doctoral research with an innovative delivery system, a consortium of universities, and advanced technical specialization. It is a collaborative program that is administered by the School of Technology at Indiana State Uni-

versity. Other schools that participate include Bowling Green State University, Central Connecticut State University, Central Missouri State University, East Carolina University, Eastern Michigan University, North Carolina A&T State University, Texas Southern University, and University of Wisconsin-Stout.

Application Requirements: You must apply to Indiana State University for admission to this doctoral program. You should have a Bachelor's degree from a regionally accredited college or university, a minimum undergraduate grade point average of 3.0 (on a 4.0 scale) and a minimum graduate grade point average of 3.5, two years of appropriate work experience, and a score of at least 500 on each section of the Graduate Record Examination. With your application, you should submit five letters of recommendation.

Completion Requirements: You must successfully complete a minimum of 90 semester hours of graduate study, with a majority of your coursework at the 600-level. Your program of study will be divided into five areas: Major Area of Specialization (24-30 semester hours), Internship (six semester hours), Research Core (27-33 semester hours), General Technology Core (12-18 semester hours), and Cognate Studies.

On Campus Requirements: You are required to complete two residencies for this program, but you have two options for fulfilling this requirement. You can complete two consecutive semesters at Indiana State University, or you can complete one semester at Indiana State University and one semester at the home university/consortium university where you're completing your specialization.

Example Course Titles: Some of the course titles in this program include Strategic Planning of Technological Processes, Internet Research Methods, Impacts of Technology, Legal Aspects of Industry, and Technological System, Assessment, and Innovation.

Program Contact: duvallj@mail.ecu.edu

EASTERN MENNONITE UNIVERSITY

General Contact Information

1200 Park Road
Harrisonburg, Virginia 22802-2462

Phone: (540) 432-4257
E-mail: yoderda@emu.edu
WWW: www.emu.edu

Online Learning Information

1200 Park Road
Harrisonburg, Virginia 22802-2462

Phone: (540) 432-4257
FAX: (540) 432-4444
E-mail: yoderda@emu.edu
WWW: www.emu.edu

Institution Background

Eastern Mennonite Seminary is the graduate division of Eastern Mennonite University and a graduate theological school of the Mennonite Church. Its mission is to prepare people for Christian ministry, and to this end it offers a variety of acadmic programs designed to equip individuals for various ministries.

Founded: 1917
Type of Institution: Private
Accreditation: Southern Association of Colleges and Schools and Association of Theological Schools

Online Course Background: Eastern Mennonite Seminary began offering its first distance learning course in January 1997.

Online Course Offered: 2

Online Students Enrolled: 16

Services Offered to Students: Students enrolled in online courses have access to the University's library and research services.

Financial Aid: Students enrolled full-time (minimum of 9 credit hours) may be eligible for financial aid.

Registration: You may register for courses via mail.

Programs

Theological Studies

Degree Offered: Certificate in Theological Studies

Online Program Started: 1997

Students Enrolled: 16

Program Background: Students in this program devote at least eight hours a week to a 13 week course. This includes reading time, homework, online interaction with other students and with the professor, and time for reflection and evaluation.

Application Requirements: You must have an undergraduate degree from an accredited institution.

Completion Requirements: You must successfully complete eight courses for this certificate.

Time for Completion: There is no time limit in which you must complete this program.

On Campus Requirements: There are no on-campus requirements.

System Requirements: You need a computer with Internet access, and an e-mail account.

Example Course Titles: Some of the course titles in this program include Old Testament: Text in Context, Church in Mission, New Testament: Text in Context, and Mennonite History.

Program Contact: Don Yoder
Eastern Mennonite University
Harrisonburg, Virginia 22802
(540) 432-4257

EASTERN MICHIGAN UNIVERSITY

General Contact Information

400 Pierce Hall
Ypsilanti, Michigan 48197

Phone: (734) 487-3060
FAX: (734) 487-1484
E-mail: undergraduate.admissions@emich.edu
WWW: www.emich.edu

Online Learning Information

Distance Education Coordinator
327 Goodison Hall
Ypsilanti, Michigan 48197

Phone: (734) 487-1081
FAX: (734) 487-6695
E-mail: distance.education@emich.edu
WWW: www.emich.edu

Institution Background

Founded: 1849
Type of Institution: Public
Accreditation: North Central Association of Colleges and Schools

Programs

Technology Management

Degree Offered: Doctor of Philosophy

Program Web Address: web.indstate.edu:80/tech/acadprog/grad/cphd/cphd.html

Program Background: This degree program is geared toward technologists and combines traditional doctoral research with an innovative delivery system, a consortium of universities, and advanced technical specialization. It is a collaborative program that is administered by the School of Technology at Indiana State University. Other schools that participate include Bowling Green State University, Central Connecticut State University, Central Missouri State University, East Carolina University, Eastern Michigan University, North Carolina A&T State University, Texas Southern University, and University of Wisconsin-Stout.

Application Requirements: You must apply to Indiana State University for admission to this doctoral program. You should have a Bachelor's degree from a regionally accredited college or university, a minimum undergraduate grade point average of 3.0 (on a 4.0 scale) and a minimum graduate grade point average of 3.5, two years of appropriate work experience, and a score of at least 500 on each section of the Graduate Record Examination. With your application, you should submit five letters of recommendation.

Completion Requirements: You must successfully complete a minimum of 90 semester hours of graduate study, with a majority of your coursework at the 600-level. Your program of study will be divided into five areas: Major Area of Specialization (24-30 semester hours), Internship (six semester hours), Research Core (27-33 semester hours), General Technology Core (12-18 semester hours), and Cognate Studies.

On Campus Requirements: You are required to complete two residencies for this program, but you have two options for fulfilling this requirement. You can complete two consecutive semesters at Indiana State University, or you can complete one semester at Indiana State University and one semester at the home university/consortium university where you're completing your specialization.

Example Course Titles: Some of the course titles in this program include Strategic Planning of Technological Processes, Internet Research Methods, Impacts of Technology, Legal Aspects of Industry, and Technological System, Assessment, and Innovation.

Program Contact: be_mcdole@online. emich.edu

EASTERN OREGON UNIVERSITY

General Contact Information

1410 L Avenue
La Grande, Oregon 97850-2899

Phone: (541) 962-3393
FAX: (541) 962-3418
E-mail: admissions@eou.edu
WWW: www.eou.edu

Online Learning Information

Zabel Hall #232
1410 L Avenue
La Grande, Oregon 97850-2899

Phone: (541) 962-3378
FAX: (541) 962-3627
E-mail: jhart@eou.edu
WWW: www.eou.edu

Institution Background

Founded: 1929
Type of Institution: Public
Accreditation: Northwest Association of Schools and Colleges

Programs

Business/Economics

Degree Offered: Bachelor of Arts/Bachelor of Science

Program Web Address: www.eosc.osshe.edu/ jhart/regbus.html

Program Background: This program allows students to choose from three specializations: accounting, economics, or business administration. Students must complete a lower and upper division common core of classes and required skill courses.

Program Contact: Eastern Oregon University Division of Extended Programs
1410 "L" Avenue
La Grande, Oregon 97850
(541) 962-3378
(541) 962-3627

Liberal Studies

Degree Offered: Bachelor of Arts/Bachelor of Science

Program Web Address: www.eosc.osshe.edu/ jhart/ls.html

Program Background: This degree program is designed to address the needs of students who cannot attend traditional courses at Eastern Oregon University, but wish to pursue a college degree. The program offers several options for degree completion as each individual program is tailored to a student's career goals and background knowledge. Students work closely with advisors in developing the individualized plans.

Within the overall program, students can choose to complete a pre-approved program, combine courses from two minors, or create an individualized degree plan. Currently, Eastern Oregon University offers online minors in Anthropology/Sociology, Business, Crop Science, Economics, Geography and Regional Planning, Office Administration, Philosophy, Physical Education/Health, Political Science, and Psychology. Students also have the option of combining one minor from Eastern Oregon with a minor from another accredited institution to create the coursework they need to complete this degree.

Application Requirements: You should request an informational packet from Eastern Oregon University using the Web form or sending an e-mail to dep@eou.edu. This packet will help you determine if Eastern Oregon's program is for you. If you find that it is, you need to attend a Degree Orientation Session (for those living in Oregon) or purchase an Orientation Videotape ($10).

After you decide which distance learning degree is best for you (BA/BS in: Liberal Studies; Business/Economics; Philosophy, Politics, and Economics; Physical Education and Health), you need to apply for admission. Do this by completing and submitting an application and $50 application fee. (The application comes in the information packet or can be downloaded at www.eou.edu/admissions.) Upon admission, you need to participate in the On-Line Degree Planning Workshop, which costs $65, to plan your program of study and understand all requirements. You are then assigned an advisor.

Program Contact: Eastern Oregon University Division of Extended Programs

1410 L Avenue
La Grande, Oregon 97850
(541) 962-3378
(541) 962-3627

Nursing

Degree Offered: Bachelor of Arts/Bachelor of Science

Program Web Address: www.eosc.osshe.edu/jhart/nurs.html

Program Background: This is a cooperative program between Eastern Oregon University and Oregon Health Science University School of Nursing. It enables students to earn a Bachelor's degree in Nursing and prepare for licensure as a registered nurse in La Grande, Enterprise, Baker City, John Day, Burns, and Lakeview. The courses are delivered via individualized study, ED-NET, videotape, and other non-traditional methods.

Application Requirements: There are prerequisite classes that you must complete before you can enroll in courses in this program. These prerequisites are offered in Pendleton, Enterprise, La Grande, Baker City, Ontario, John Day, Burns, and Lakeview. Students in some areas are required to attend an off-site class together to view video lectures.

You must have an active Oregon license as a registered nurse, and pass the NLN Mobility II examinations.

Program Restrictions: This program is available only to students who live in Oregon.

Completion Requirements: You must complete any course during the term in which it is offered.

System Requirements: You should have access to a computer and modem, and have knowledge of word processing, using the Internet, and using the CLASS system. You will need to pay a fee and get a password to access CLASS.

Please contact Lory Stout at (541) 962-3803 for information about accessing CLASS.

Program Contact: Eastern Oregon University School of Education and Business Programs
1410 "L" Avenue
La Grande, Oregon 97850
(541) 962-3644
(541) 962-3627

Office Administration

Degree Offered: Associate of Science

Program Web Address: www.eosc.osshe.edu/jhart/oadm.html

Program Background: This program prepares students for work as clerical staff or office administrators. It's available only to students who live in certain parts of Oregon because some of the courses are delivered using methods other than online. Students can specialize in executive, medical, legal, and computer office technology.

Students in this program may transfer coursework from it directly into Eastern Oregon University's Bachelor's degree programs in business and economics, liberal studies, or the teacher education program.

Application Requirements: You must be at least a junior in high school to enroll in this program.

Completion Requirements: You must successfully complete 96 quarter hours of approved coursework, maintain a minimum grade point average of 2.0, and receive a C or higher on all courses within your core of required courses.

System Requirements: You should have a personal computer and modem.

Program Contact: Eastern Oregon University Division of Extended Programs
1410 "L" Avenue
La Grande, Oregon 97850
(541) 962-3378

(541) 962-3627

Philosophy, Politics, and Economics

Degree Offered: Bachelor of Arts/Bachelor of Science

Program Web Address: www.eosc.osshe.edu/jhart/ppe.html

Program Background: This program integrates broad academic areas in the humanities and the social and behavioral sciences. Philosophy, political science, and economics form a foundation for exploring social problems and policy, as well as for critically analyzing social policy.

Program Contact: Eastern Oregon University Division of Extended Programs
1410 "L" Avenue
La Grande, Oregon 97850
(541) 962-3378
(541) 962-3627

Physical Education and Health

Degree Offered: Bachelor of Science

Program Web Address: www.eou.edu/jhart/peh.html

Program Background: This program prepares students physically, emotionally, socially, spiritually, and intellectually so that they can attain optimal health and promote physical education. Students pursuing this degree online can obtain a minor in Health.

Completion Requirements: You must successfully complete 30 hours of core courses and 30 hours in Health.

Program Contact: Eastern Oregon University Division of Extended Programs
1410 "L" Avenue
La Grande, Oregon 97850
(541) 962-3378

(541) 962-3627

Teacher Education

Degree Offered: Masters of Teacher Education

Program Web Address: redtail.eou.edu/sebp/MTE/MTE_Home.htm

Program Background: This is a graduate preparation program leading to Oregon basic licensure in elementary or secondary education.

Application Requirements: You must have a bachelor's degree and a minimum grade point average of 3.0 on your upper-division undergraduate work and graduate coursework. You also should have a passing score on all sections of an approved test of basic skills: The California Basic Education Skills Test (C-BEST) or the Pre-Professional Skill Test (PPST), a passing score on the Praxis Test, and successful experience teaching and working with children. In addition to an application, you have to submit two letters of recommendation.

Program Contact: Eastern Oregon University Division of Extended Programs
1410 L Avenue
La Grande, Oregon 97850
(541) 962-3378
(541) 962-3627

EMBRY-RIDDLE AERONAUTICAL UNIVERSITY

General Contact Information

600 South Clyde Morris Boulevard
Daytona Beach, Florida 32114-3900

Phone: (800) 359-3728
FAX: (904) 226-7627
E-mail: indstudy@cts.db.erau.edu
WWW: www.ec.erau.edu/cdl/index.htm

Online Learning Information

Center for Distance Learning
600 South Clyde Morris Boulevard
Daytona Beach, Florida 32114-3900

Phone: (904) 226-6398
FAX: (904) 226-7627
E-mail: pettitt@cts.db.erau.edu
WWW: www.ec.erau.edu/cdl/index.htm

Institution Background

Embry-Riddle Aeronautical University is a non-sectarian, non-profit, coeducational university with a history dating back to the early days of aviation. The University serves culturally diverse students pursuing careers in aviation and aerospace. The University's purpose is to provide a comprehensive education preparing graduates for productive careers supporting the needs of aviation, aerospace engineering, and related fields.

Founded: 1926
Type of Institution: Private
Accreditation: Southern Association of Colleges and Schools

Online Course Background: The Embry-Riddle Center for Distance Learning is an integral part of the Extended Campus. It was established in 1980 with the goal of extending the opportunity for a higher education to those who live in areas where it is not feasible for Embry-Riddle to establish resident learning centers.

Online Course Offered: 75

Online Students Enrolled: 5,000

Services Offered to Students: Students enrolled in online courses through Embry-Riddle have access to research assistance from the Hunt Library and inter-library loan. Reference librarians communicate with students via e-mail, phone, fax, or mail. Students also have access to: magazine, newspaper, and newsletter articles through the World Wide Web; aviation and aerospace research citations through the Aerospace Database; and selected Web sites through the University's Internet Research Tools.

Financial Aid: Students accepted for admission into a degree program are eligible for student loans.

Registration: You may register for courses via mail, phone, e-mail, and the World Wide Web.

Programs

Aeronautical Science

Degree Offered: Master of Aeronautical Science

Program Web Address: www.ec.erau.edu/cdl/index.htm

Online Program Started: 1993

Students Enrolled: 822

Degrees Awarded: over 300

Program Background: This program prepares students for upper-level management positions by giving them the analytical skills they need to make informed decisions and set realistic goals.

Application Requirements: You must have a Bachelor's degree from a regionally accredited college or university or the international equivalent. You must have a minimum undergraduate grade point average of 2.50 (on a 4.0 scale).

Completion Requirements: You must successfully complete 36 semester credit hours of coursework and maintain a grade point average of 3.0 or higher to earn this degree.

Time for Completion: You must complete all of the requirements for this degree within seven years of starting.

On Campus Requirements: There are no on-campus requirements.

System Requirements: You should have a personal computer with a minimum processor speed of 486 MHz. You need to have a word processor and spreadsheet program on your computer.

Example Course Titles: Some of the course titles for this program include Global Information Management, Seminar in Labor Relations, Airport Management, The Air Transportation System, Aircraft and Spacecraft Development, Human Factors in the Aviation/Aerospace Industry, Reasearch Methods and Statistics, Industrial Safety Management, Airport Operations Safety, and Integrated Logistical Support.

Program Contact: Jim Gallogly
Embry-Riddle Aeronautical University
600 S. Clyde Morris Blvd.
Daytona Beach, Florida 32114-3900
(800) 866-6271
(904) 226-7627
galloglj@cts.db.erau.edu

Aviation Business Administration

Degree Offered: Associate of Science in Aviation Business Administration

Program Web Address: www.ec.erau.edu/cdl/index.htm

Online Program Started: 1997

Students Enrolled: 300

Degrees Awarded: 100

Program Background: The Aviation Business Administration program is designed for students who want a strong business foundation with emphasis on aviation applications. It has courses in general education, introduction to business, and some aviation business applications.

Application Requirements: You must submit an application with a $30 application fee ($50 for international students). You also need to submit evidence of your military occupational specialty training or three years of work experience, official transcripts from the high school you graduated from or proof of your GED, and official transcripts from each college or university you've attended, and your official scores on any CLEP or DANTES tests. If you have professional training or experience that you want to count as credit toward advanced standing, you must submit an original, notarized, or properly authenticated third-part documentation of your training or experience. Upon admission to the program, you have up to one year to matriculate.

Completion Requirements: You must successfully complete 60 credit hours for this degree. While in the program, you must maintain continuing status by taking at least one course in any two year period.

On Campus Requirements: There are no on-campus requirements.

System Requirements: You should have a personal computer with a 486 processor or faster, and a modem. Your computer should also have a word processor and spreadsheet program.

Example Course Titles: Some of the course titles in this program include Communications Theory and Skills, Mathematics, Computer Science, Physical and Life Sciences, Humanities, and Social Science.

Program Contact: Linda Dammer
Center for Distance Learning
600 S. Clyde Morris Blvd.
Daytona Beach, Florida 32114-3900
(800) 359-3728
(904) 226-7627
dammerl@cts.db.erau.edu

Management of Technical Operations

Degree Offered: Bachelor of Science in Management of Technical Operations

Program Web Address: www.ec.erau.edu/cdl/index.htm

Online Program Started: 1997

Students Enrolled: 400

Degrees Awarded: 100

Program Background: This program is designed for students who possess some technical expertise either through previous coursework, licensing, or experience. It is a flexible yet solid business program.

Application Requirements: You should have a minimum of 15 semester hours that you earned in an area of technical operations or through CLEP, DANTES, or military or industrial education programs that are recognized by the American Council on Education. Additionally, you may receive credit for aviation-related licenses. You shouldn't have more than five years of supervisory experience in a mid-level position.

You must submit an application with a $30 application fee ($50 for international students). You also need to submit evidence of your military occupational specialty training or three years of work experience, official transcripts from the high school you graduated from or proof of your GED, and official transcripts from each college or university you've attended, and your official scores on any CLEP or DANTES tests. If you have professional training or experience that you want to count as credit toward advanced standing, you must submit an original, notarized, or properly authenticated third-part documentation of your training or experience. Upon admission to the program, you have up to one year to matriculate.

Completion Requirements: You must successfully complete 120 credit hours for this degree.

Time for Completion: You must enroll in at least one course during any two year period in order to maintain active status in the program.

On Campus Requirements: There are no on-campus requirements.

System Requirements: You should have a personal computer with a 486 processor (or faster), a modem, and software including a word processor and spreadsheet program.

Example Course Titles: Some of the course titles in this program include Humanities/Social Sciences, Computer Science/Mathematics, Economics/Management, Physical Science, Communications Theory and Skills, Aviation Safety, Corporate and Business Aviation, Airport Management, and Management of Air Cargo.

Program Contact: Linda Dammer
Center for Distance Learning
600 S. Clyde Morris Blvd.
Daytona Beach, Florida 32114-3900
(800) 359-3728
(904) 226-7627
dammerl@cts.db.erau.edu

Professional Aeronautics

Degree Offered: Associate of Science/Bachelor of Science in Professional Aeronautics

Program Web Address: www.ec.erau.edu/cdl/index.htm

Online Program Started: 1985

Students Enrolled: 3,500

Degrees Awarded: 3,000

Program Background: This program is designed for students who have already established and progressed in an aviation career. The curriculum builds on knowledge and skills that students acquire through training and experience in their work. Students prepare for career growth and increased responsibility by completing courses in aeronautical science, management, computer science, economics, communications, humanities, social science, mathematics, and physical science.

Application Requirements: You must submit an application with a $30 application fee ($50 for international students). You also need to submit evidence of your military occupational specialty training or three years of work experience, official transcripts from the high school you graduated from or proof of your GED, and official transcripts from each college or university you've attended, and your official scores on any CLEP or DANTES tests. If you have professional training or experience that you want to count as credit toward advanced standing, you must submit an original, notarized, or properly authenticated third-part documentation of your training or experience. Upon admission to the program, you have up to one year to matriculate.

Program Restrictions: You must be able to document that you have a verifiable level of competence in an aviation occupation for admission to this program.

Completion Requirements: You must successfully complete 120 credit hours for this degree. While in the program, you must maintain continuing status by taking at least one course in any two year period.

On Campus Requirements: There are no on-campus requirements for this program.

System Requirements: You should have a personal computer with a 486 processor or faster, and a modem. Your computer should also have a word processor and spreadsheet program.

Example Course Titles: Some of the course titles in this program include Humanities/Social Sciences, Computer Science/Mathematics, Economics/Management, Physical Science, Communications Theory and Skills. Course titles include but are not limited to: Aviation Legislation, Flight Physiology, Aviation Insurance, and General Aviation Marketing.

Program Contact: Linda Dammer
Center for Distance Learning
600 S. Clyde Morris Blvd.
Daytona Beach, Florida 32114-3900
(800) 359-3728
(904) 226-7627
dammerl@cts.db.erau.edu

EMPORIA STATE UNIVERSITY

General Contact Information

1200 Commercial
Emporia, Kansas 66801-5087

Phone: (316) 341-5465
FAX: (316) 341-5037
WWW: www.empria.edu

Online Learning Information

Lifelong Learning
1200 Commercial Street
Emporia, Kansas 66801-5087

Phone: (316) 341-5385

FAX: (316) 341-5744
E-mail: conted@emporia.edu
WWW: www.empria.edu

Institution Background

Founded: 1863
Type of Institution: Public
Accreditation: North Central Association of Colleges and Schools

Financial Aid: Students enrolled in at least six credit hours of an online degree program through Emporia State University are eligible to apply for financial aid by completing the Free Application for Federal Student Aid (FAFSA). Students who are enrolled for less than six credit hours should contact the Financial Aid Office to see if there is any type of assistance for which they may be eligible.

Programs

Business Education

Degree Offered: Master of Science

Program Web Address: www.emporia.edu/business/bemasters.htm

Program Background: This program prepares students to supervise business and computer departments in middle schools, senior high schools, technical schools, and community colleges, as well as to teach business and computer courses at a variety of grade levels. It also trains students to coordinate computer usage, and provide technical support in schools.

Application Requirements: You should have a minimum grade point average of 2.7 during your last 60 credit hours of undergraduate study, and at least 15 undergraduate credit hours in computer information systems, accounting, finance, management, and/or marketing. You also need a minimum score of 1000 on the Graduate Record Examination (GRE).

Completion Requirements: You must successfully complete 35 credit hours for this degree.

Time for Completion: You have up to seven years to complete this program.

Example Course Titles: Some of the course titles in this program include Business and Computer Curriculum Development, Technology Tools for Education/Business, Emerging Issues in Computer and Business Education, Research in Business/Computer Education, Instructional Technology Selection and Facilities Design, Methods of Teaching Computer Studies, Designing Computer Presentations, Electronic Communications (LANs and the Internet), PC Troubleshooting, DOS for Teachers (LAN commands), and Windows for Teachers.

Program Contact: Division of Business Education and General Business
Emporia State University, Campus Box 4023
Emporia, Kansas 66801
(316) 341-5345

Health, Physical Education and Recreation

Degree Offered: Master of Science

Program Web Address: www.emporia.edu/hper/masters/masters.htm

Application Requirements: You must have an undergraduate degree in health, physical education, or recreation, and a minimum undergraduate grade point average of 2.75 (on a 4.0 scale). You need to submit an application, transcripts from each school you've attended, three letters of recommendation, and a letter of intent.

Completion Requirements: You must successfully complete 34 credit hours and a thesis, or 35 credit hours without a thesis.

System Requirements: You should have a Pentium computer with a 33.6 baud modem, a current Web browser (Netscape Communicator or Microsoft Internet Explorer), and Microsoft Office 97.

Example Course Titles: Some of the course titles in this program include Ethics in Health, Sport, and Movement Sciences, Applied Psychology of Health, Sport and Movement Science, Advanced Exercise Physiology, Issues and Trends in Health, Sport and Movement Science, Design and Assessment in Health, Sport and Movement Science, and Advanced Technology in HPER.

Program Contact: Health, Physical Education, Recreation
Emporia State University
Emporia, Kansas 66801
(316) 341-5399

Integrated Studies

Degree Offered: Bachelor of Integrated Studies

Program Web Address: www.emporia.edu/lifelong/bis/index.htm

Program Background: Emporia State University's online Bachelor of Integrated Studies Degree Completion Program provides students returning to finish their degrees with a quality multidisciplinary program of study. The program focuses on fulfilling traditional university requirements while meeting students' specific goals. Academic coursework is required in communication, information literacy, problem solving and decision making, and community leadership.

Application Requirements: You can print a copy of Emporia State's registration form from its Web site. You must submit a completed form and submit it with your tuition payment by the enrollment deadline that is specific for the semester in which you wish to enroll in the program. You can phone in your registration information and pay with a credit card at (316) 341-5385. You can fax your registration form and pay with a credit card at (316) 341-5744. Or you can mail your registration form with payment.

If you pay with a check, make it payable to Emporia State University. You can pay with any of the following credit cards: Visa, MasterCard, or Discover. If you are receiving financial aid or a third party is paying for your tuition, you must include a copy of your award letter or a letter of verification with your registration form. If you wish to pay your tuition in installments, a copy of your Tuition and Fee Installment Agreement must accompany your registration form.

Completion Requirements: You must complete at least 124 semester hours to earn this degree. You must earn at least 60 semester hours at an accredited, four-year college or university and a total of 75 hours at Emporia State University. Also, you must submit a portfolio and successfully complete a capstone course, as well as successfully pass the university's competency examination.

On Campus Requirements: There are no on-campus requirements.

System Requirements: You need to have a computer with Microsoft Internet Explorer 3.0 (or higher) or Netscape Navigator 3.0 (or higher) and Windows 95, or a Macintosh system 7. Your computer needs to have at least 16 MB of RAM, a 28.8 baud (or faster) modem, and a CD-ROM drive.

Example Course Titles: Some of the course titles in this program include Business and Society, Online Seminar, Information Literacy: Skills for Lifelong Learning, Introduction to Geospatial Analysis, Business Writing, Ice Age Environments, Applied Computer Concepts, Music Fundamentals for Non-Musicians, Ethics in the Modern World, and Social Psychology.

Program Contact: Office of Lifelong Learning-Box 4052

Emporia State University
1200 Commercial
Emporia, Kansas 66801
(316) 341-5385

Library Science

Degree Offered: Master of Library Science

Program Web Address: slim.emporia.edu/ program/distance/distance.htm

Program Background: Although Emporia State University offers an increasing number of the courses for this program online, the majority of the program is still classroom based. Faculty and students use e-mail, mailing lists, and Web pages to communicate with each other and collaborate.

On Campus Requirements: Rather than having students come to Emporia State University, the school goes to the students to deliver the courses in this program. Emporia recruits a group of students in a particular area, then faculty travel to the class about once a month to teach the courses on the weekend. Students attend courses about 12 to 14 weekends per year. Emporia delivers classes for eight semesters (including summers), and at the end of the eighth semester the group of students graduates.

Program Contact: School of Library and Information Management
Emporia State University
1200 Commercial Campus Box 4025
Emporia, Kansas 66801
(800) 552-4770
(316) 341-5233

ENDICOTT COLLEGE

General Contact Information

376 Hale Street
Beverly, Massachusetts 01919

Phone: (800) 325-1114
E-mail: admissio@endicott.edu
WWW: www.endicott.edu

Institution Background

Founded: 1939
Type of Institution: Private
Accreditation: New England Association of Schools and Colleges

Programs

Communications

Degree Offered: Bachelor of Science

Program Web Address: www.endicott.edu/ production/academic/ec-online/eprogram

Program Background: This program prepares students for entry into the field of communications by integrating communication skills and practices with a professional concentration of the students' choice. Areas of concentration include media, advertising, and public relations.

Application Requirements: You must complete a course which includes evaluating transfer credits you may have from accredited colleges and universities, and evaluating your professional work experience for proficiency credits. If you are an international student, you must also take the Test of English as a Foreign Language (TOEFL) and score at least a 500.

Completion Requirements: You must successfully complete 128 credits for this degree.

Example Course Titles: Some of the course titles in this program include Electronic Media Production, Introduction to Mass Communications, Writing for the Media, Video/Film Concepts, and Telecommunications.

Program Contact: Endicott College
376 Hale Street

Beverly, Massachusetts 01919
(800) 325-1114
econline@endicott.edu

Psychology

Degree Offered: Bachelor of Science

Program Web Address: www.endicott.edu/ production/academic/ec-online/eprogram

Program Background: This program offers students a broad background in liberal arts and sciences, as well as teaches them valuable research skills and gives them field experience. Students study how human behavior changes over time (from infancy to old age), and they learn how to critically evaluate research and develop their own research techniques.

Application Requirements: You must complete the ACA 100 course, which includes evaluating your transfer credits from other accredited colleges and university, and evaluating your work experience for proficiency credits. If you're an international student, you must score at least a 500 on the Test of English as a Foreign Language (TOEFL).

Completion Requirements: You must successfully complete 128 credit hours for this degree.

Program Contact: Endicott College
376 Hale Street
Beverly, Massachusetts 01919
(800) 325-1114
econline@endicott.edu

FAYETTEVILLE TECHNICAL COMMUNITY COLLEGE

General Contact Information

2201 Hull Road
P.O. Box 35236
Fayetteville, North Carolina 28303

Phone: (910) 678-8473
FAX: (910) 484-6600
WWW: www.faytech.cc.nc.us

Online Learning Information

Dean of Business
P.O. Box 35236
Fayetteville, North Carolina 28303

Phone: (910) 678-8466
FAX: (910) 678-8215
E-mail: ervinb@ftccmail.faytech.cc.nc.us
WWW: www.faytech.cc.nc.us

Institution Background

Founded: 1961
Type of Institution: Public
Accreditation: Southern Association of Colleges and Schools

Individual Undergraduate Courses: Fayetteville Technical Community College offers online undergraduate courses in accounting, art, business, computers, criminal justice, economics, education, English, funeral service, history, mathematics, marketing, networking, political science, psychology, religious studies, sociology, and Spanish.

Programs

Business Administration

Degree Offered: Associate of Applied Science

Program Web Address: nemesis.faytech. cc.nc.us/busproj/business.htm

Program Background: This program is designed to introduce students to the various aspects of the free enterprise system. Students get a fundamental knowledge of business functions, processes, and an understanding of business organizations in today's global economy. The courses cover accounting, business law, economics, management, and marketing. And students develop skills applying these concepts by studying computer applications, communication, team building, and decision making.

Application Requirements: You must be a high school graduate or have a state equivalency certificate or General Education Development (GED) certificate. You should submit an application with your high school transcripts or GED scores, official transcripts from any college or university you've attended, and your SAT scores. You may be required to take placement tests.

Completion Requirements: You must successfully complete 76 semester hours for this degree.

Example Course Titles: Some of the course titles in this program include Success and Study Skills, Introduction to Business, Business Law I, Basic PC Literacy, Expository Writing, and Mathematical Models.

Program Contact: Fayetteville Technical Community College
P.O. Box 35236
Fayetteville, North Carolina 28303
(910) 678-8425

FIELDING INSTITUTE

General Contact Information

2112 Santa Barbara Street
Santa Barbara, California 93105

Phone: (800) 340-1099
FAX: (805) 687-9793
E-mail: admissions@fielding.edu
WWW: www.fielding.edu

Online Learning Information

Enrollment Management Services
2112 Santa Barbara Street
Santa Barbara, California 93105

Phone: (805) 687-1099
FAX: (805) 687-9793
E-mail: sawilliams@fielding.edu
WWW: www.fielding.edu

Institution Background

The Fielding Institute was founded on the principles of adult learning and distance learning. It offers opportunities for mid-career adults to pursue graduate degrees and professional continuing education programs while maintaining commitments to family, work, and community. Electronic communication combined with occasional in-person events at various locations helps form an active, widespread geographical learning community.

Founded: 1974
Type of Institution: Private
Accreditation: Western Association of Schools and Colleges; the Ph.D. program in clinical psychology is accredited by the American Psychological Association.

Services Offered to Students: Students enrolled in online courses have access to a librarian who will assist them with research and training in using online databases.

Financial Aid: Online students may be eligible for student loans and/or the Fielding Diversity Scholarship.

Programs
Clinical Psychology

Degree Offered: Doctor of Philosophy

Students Enrolled: 350

Program Background: This program is designed for a geographically dispersed cohort of students who are professionals in clinical psychology. Students develop intervention and research skills, and can tailor their education to their specific goals.

Application Requirements: You must have a Bachelor's degree from an accredited college or university, as well as have academic and professional experience in the field.

Program Restrictions: You must reside within the continental United States.

Completion Requirements: You must successfully complete 13 acadmenic area components, clinical training (practicum and internship), and a dissertation for this degree.

Time for Completion: Generally, students can complete this degree within five or six years.

On Campus Requirements: There may be some on-campus requirements for this program. You need to contact the school directly for information.

System Requirements: You should have a computer with Internet access, and a Web browser.

Educational Leadership and Change

Degree Offered: Doctor of Education

Online Program Started: 1997

Students Enrolled: 220

Program Background: This program is designed for students who want to affect change within educational systems.

Application Requirements: You must have a Bachelor's degree from an accredited institution.

Completion Requirements: You must successfully complete eight curriculum areas and a dissertation.

Time for Completion: You have up to three or four years to complete this program.

System Requirements: You need a computer and access to the World Wide Web.

Example Course Titles: Some of the course titles in this program include Action Research, Systems Thinking, Leadership and Management, Education and Law, and Public Policy for Education.

Human and Organization Development

Degree Offered: Doctor of Philosophy

Online Program Started: 1979

Students Enrolled: 400

Application Requirements: You must have a Bachelor's degree from an accredited school, and be a mid-career professional.

Completion Requirements: You must successfully complete eight curriculum areas and a dissertation.

Time for Completion: You have up to four or five years to complete this program.

On Campus Requirements: There are some on-campus requirements for this program. Please contact the school directly for additional informatin.

System Requirements: You need a computer with access to the Internet and e-mail capabilities.

Example Course Titles: Some of the course titles in this program include Inquiry and Research, Organizational Theories, Social Change, and Human Development and Consciousness.

Organizational Design and Effectiveness

Degree Offered: Master of Art

Online Program Started: 1997

Students Enrolled: 80

Program Background: This program is designed for professionals who wish to learn how to manage networked and virtual organizations.

Application Requirements: You must have a Bachelor's degree from an accredited institution.

Completion Requirements: You are required to successfully complete three core courses (each with four content areas) and a Master's thesis or project.

Time for Completion: You have 20 months to complete this program.

System Requirements: You should have a computer with Internet access and e-mail capabilities.

Example Course Titles: The course titles for this program include Human Development and Leadership, Group Process, and Organizational Structures and Sociocultural Systems.

FLORENCE-DARLINGTON TECHNICAL COLLEGE

General Contact Information

P.O. Box 100548
Florence, South Carolina 29501

Phone: (800) 228-5745
E-mail: kirvenp@flo.tec.sc.us
WWW: www.flo.tec.sc.us

Online Learning Information

P.O. Box 100548
Florence, South Carolina 29501

Phone: (843) 661-8133
FAX: (843) 661-8217
E-mail: whitea@fdtc.flo.tec.sc.us
WWW: www.flo.tec.sc.us

Institution Background

Founded: 1964
Type of Institution: Public
Accreditation: Southern Association of Colleges and Schools

Individual Undergraduate Courses: Florence-Darlington Technical College offers online courses in business, computer technology, criminal justice, English, French, health studies, history, marketing, mathematics, music, physical science, political science, psychology, Spanish, and speech communication.

Programs

Liberal Arts

Degree Offered: Associate in Arts

Program Web Address: www.flo.tec.sc.us/online_college_web_fall_1999/associate_

Online Program Started: 1998

Application Requirements: To be eligible for this program, you must be a high school graduate or have your GED. Also you must have an RSAT score of 830 (430 Verbal/400 Math), an SAT score of 700 (350 Verbal/350 Math), or CPT scores of Reading—85; Sentence Skills—88; Math—75; and Algebra—90.

You must complete and submit an application, $15 application fee, your test scores, and high school and/or college transcripts.

Completion Requirements: You must successfully complete at least 62 credit hours for this degree.

Example Course Titles: Some of the course titles for this program include Microcomputer Applications, English Composition , Public Speaking, and General Psychology.

Program Contact: Florence-Darlington Technical College
P.O. Box 100548
Florence, South Carolina 29501
(843) 661-8133
(843) 661-8217
whitea@fdtc.flo.tec.sc.us

FLORIDA INSTITUTE OF TECHNOLOGY

General Contact Information

150 West University Blvd.
Melbourne, Florida 32901

Phone: (407) 674-8030
FAX: (407) 723-9468
E-mail: admissions@fit.edu
WWW: www.fit.edu

Institution Background

Founded: 1958
Type of Institution: Private
Accreditation: Southern Association of Colleges and Schools

Programs

Business Administration

Degree Offered: Master of Business Administration

Program Web Address: www.segs.fit.edu/

srec/html/programs.html

Program Background: This program is designed to meet the needs of students who are just starting out in business, as well as those who are looking for career advancement. It gives students the skills they need to be adaptable performers in current positions, and the competencies for long term career development. Students develop the techniques for effective team leadership, and learn how to apply integrity, social responsibility, and a high degree of professionalism in every day operations.

Application Requirements: You must have a Bachelor's degree, but it doesn't have to be in business administration.

Completion Requirements: You must successfully complete 36 credit hours for this degree.

Example Course Titles: Some of the course titles for this program include Managerial Accounting, Corporate Finance, Intermediate Managerial, Organizational Behavior, Information Systems, Policy and Strategy for Business, Marketing, Advanced Analytical Methods for Management, and Economics for Business.

Program Contact: Florida Institute of Technology
School of Extended Graduate Studies
1501 Robert J. Conlan Blvd., Suite 140
Palm Bay, Florida 32905
(407) 674-8880
(407) 951-7694
rmarshal@fit.edu

Management

Degree Offered: Master of Science

Program Web Address: www.segs.fit.edu/srec/html/programs.html

Program Background: This Master of Science in Management program prepares students for changes in their current positions and long term career development. It develops leadership skills and techniques including integrity, social responsibility, and professionalism.

Application Requirements: You must have a Bachelor's degree, but it doesn't have to be in business administration. If you do have an undergraduate business degree or courses in business, you may be able to waive some program requirements. If your undergraduate major is outside the area of business, you may be required to meet some prerequisites. Additionally, you may be required to take the GRE or GMAT.

Completion Requirements: You must successfully complete 33 credit hours of graduate coursework plus other course requirements for this degree.

Example Course Titles: Some of the course titles in this program include Corporate Finance, Introductory Managerial Statistics, Information Systems, Organizational Planning and Development, Program Management, Marketing, Personnel Management and Industrial Relations, and Basic Economics.

Program Contact: Florida Institute of Technology
School of Extended Graduate Studies
1501 Robert J. Conlan Blvd., Suite 140
Palm Bay, Florida 32905
(407) 674-8880
(407) 951-7694
rmarshal@fit.edu

FLORIDA STATE UNIVERSITY

General Contact Information

Tallahassee, Florida 32306

Phone: (850) 644-6200
FAX: (850) 644-0197
E-mail: admissions@admissions.fsu.edu
WWW: www.idl.fsu.edu

Online Learning Information

Learning Systems Institute
4600C University Center
Tallahassee, Florida 32306

Phone: (850) 644-1604
FAX: (850) 644-5803
E-mail: dl@lsi.fsu.edu
WWW: www.idl.fsu.edu

Institution Background

Founded: 1857
Type of Institution: Public
Accreditation: Southern Association of Colleges and Schools

Programs

Computer and Information Science

Degree Offered: Bachelor of Science

Program Web Address: connected2.fsu.edu/2+2/student/cs.htm

Online Program Started: 1999

Program Background: This program is designed for students preparing for careers as software professionals, or who are preparing for graduate work in computer science. There are two tracks within the program, and both overlap significantly. The curricula for both majors take a systems view of computing, emphasizing the interdependence of design, object orientation, and distributed systems and networks, from basic software through systems design to software engineering.

Application Requirements: You must have an Associate of Arts degree and meet program prerequisites. You need to apply by completing and submitting both a State University System admission application and a 2+2 Program supplemental application. Both forms may be completed online. There is a $20.00 application fee.

Completion Requirements: You must successfully complete 60 hours of coursework.

Example Course Titles: Some of the course titles in this program include Introduction to Computer Science, Object-Oriented Programming, Object-Oriented Analysis and Design, Mathematics for Computer Science, Computer Organization, Operating Systems and Concurrent Programming, Distributed Systems and Networks, Probability and Statistics, Data Structures, Algorithms, Programming, Complexity and Analysis of Data, Formal Methods in Software Engineering, and Software Engineering Principles and Practice.

Program Contact: Chris Lacher, Lead Faculty
Computer Science Department
Florida State University
Tallahassee, Florida 32306
(850) 644-9386
clacher@lsi.fsu.edu

Criminal Justice Administration

Degree Offered: Master

Program Web Address: www.criminology.fsu.edu/dlstudents.htm

Online Program Started: 1999

Application Requirements: You must have a score of at least 1000 (combined verbal and quantitative sections) on the Graduate Record Examination, and a minimum grade point average of 3.0 (on a 4.0 scale) during the last two years of undergraduate study. You should also have at least two years of professional experience in a criminal justice related field, and you must write an essay describing your reasons for seeking a professional degree via distance learning.

Completion Requirements: You must successfully complete 36 hours of graduate credit.

System Requirements: You should have a Pentium-II 233MHz or Pentium-II Celeron 300MHz with 128K Cache, 32MB RAM, 6GB Hard Drive, 24x CD-ROM, Accelerated video card with 2MB RAM, Sound Blaster compatible sound card with speakers, 56kbps V.90 modem, Windows 98, and Netscape Navigator 4.08 or Internet Explorer 4.01 or higher. Or you may choose to use a Macintosh system, in which case you should have a PowerPC G3 266MHz, 32MB RAM, 6GB Hard Drive, 24x CD-ROM, Accelerated video card with 2MB RAM, 56kbps V.90 modem, MacOS 8, and Netscape Navigator 4.08 or Internet Explorer 4.01 or higher.

Example Course Titles: Some of the course titles in this program include Survey Criminological Theories, Science, Evidence and the Law, Computer Technology for Criminal Justice, Survey of Criminal Justice Studies, Criminal Law, Procedures and Rights, Crime Prevention, Race, Ethnicity, Crime and Social Justice, Research in Criminal Justice, Criminal Justice Administration, Risk Management in Criminal Justice, Neighborhood Problem Solving, Police and Society, Program Development and Grant Writing, and Ecology of Crime.

Program Contact: School of Criminology
Florida State University
Tallahassee, Florida 32306
(850) 644-4746
cgreek@mailer.fsu.edu

Information Studies

Degree Offered: Bachelor of Science

Program Web Address: connected2.fsu.edu/ 2+2/student/is.htm

Online Program Started: 1999

Program Background: Students in Florida State University's Information Studies program learn to efficiently manage the multiple information and communication technologies that society depends on. Courses instruct students in tools and technologies, disseminating information, ways in which information is structured and organized, fundamental principles of access to information, and models of effective interactions. Students learn the skills to facilitate user interactions with information and communications products, services, and organizations.

This program is especially effective in developing a cutting edge career for those who enjoy using computers, have good communications skills, enjoy searching for answers, and enjoy working with people.

Application Requirements: You must have your Associate of Arts degree or higher and have successfully completed all program prerequisites. To enter the upper-division major, you must have your Associate of Arts degree or you must have completed all of your liberal studies coursework and a total of 52 credit hours. For more information about the prerequisites and required coursework, please contact the school directly.

Completion Requirements: You must successfully complete a total of 60 upper-division (3000- and 4000-level) credit hours to earn this degree. Of these 60 credit hours, 36 must be in your major. Eighteen of the 36 major credit hours must be in the core courses. And students are encouraged to pursue internship opportunities for up to six credit hours.

Example Course Titles: Some of the course titles in this program include New Communication Technology and Contemporary Society, Group Dynamics and Leadership, Information

Needs and Preferences, Technical and Professional Communication, Managing Networks and Telecommunication, Desktop Multimedia, Foundations of Organizational Communication, Interface Design for Information Specialists, and Communication and Information Policy.

Program Contact:
Todd Wagar, Undergraduate Advisor
Computer Science Department
Florida State University
Tallahassee, Florida 32306
(850) 644-5775
wagar@lis.fsu.edu

Library and Information Studies

Degree Offered: Master of Science

Program Web Address: www.fsu.edu/lis/

Program Background: Many of the Library and Information Studies courses are delivered via distributed education, including online. Florida State designs its course schedules so that students who are employed full-time and/or have families can participate in the program and earn a Master's degree in just two years.

Application Requirements: You must have a Bachelor's degree from an approved college or university. Also you must have a 3.0 grade point average (on a 4.0 scale) during the last two years of the baccalaureate program or during a Master's degree program at an accredited institution of higher education, or you must have a minimum score of 1000 on the combined verbal/quantitative parts of the Graduate Record Examination (GRE). All students must submit transcripts for past collegiate work and GRE scores. International students must present proof of a minimum Test of English as a Foreign Language (TOEFL) score of 550 in addition to the other requirements.

Program Contact: School of Information Studies
Florida State University
Tallahassee, Florida 32306
(850) 644-5775
(850) 644-9763
maatta@lis.fsu.edu

Library Studies

Degree Offered: Master of Science

Program Web Address: www.fsu.edu/~lis/

Program Background: This Master's program is designed for students who are full-time employees and/or have families can complete their degree in two years. Many of the courses are delivered online so that students can earn this degree using their computer at home or work.

Application Requirements: You must have a Bachelor's degree from an approved college or university. You need to complete and submit an application with evidence of a minimum grade point average of 3.0 (on a 4.0 scale) during your last two years of undergraduate study or during your graduate study at another institution. Additionally, you must have a minimum score of 1000 on the combined verbal and quantitative portions of the Graduate Record Examination (GRE) and submit proof of your scores. If you are an international student, you must have a minimum score of 550 on the Test of English as a Foreign Language (TOEFL) and submit proof of your scores.

Program Contact: School of Information Studies
Florida State University
Tallahassee, Florida 32306
(850) 644-5775
(850) 644-9763
maatta@lis.fsu.edu

Mathematics Education

Degree Offered: Master of Science

Program Web Address: www.fsu.edu/CandI/ADMIT/MathDade.html

Program Background: This program is designed for elementary and middle-school teachers in Dade County public schools, and focuses on the nature of learning mathematics.

Application Requirements: You must have a score of 1000 on the verbal and quantitative portions of the General Records Examination (GRE). If you do not have a score of at least 1000, you must have taken the GRE and have a minimum grade point average of 3.0 during the last two years of your undergraduate study.

You need to complete an application and submit it with copies of your GRE scores, three letters of recommendation, and official transcripts from each college or university you've attended.

Program Restrictions: You need to be a teacher in a Dade County public school to participate in this program.

Completion Requirements: You must successfully complete 33 semester hours and a comprehensive examination to earn this degree. The courses extend over seven semesters.

On Campus Requirements: You are required to attend three summer semesters in Miami.

Example Course Titles: Some of the course titles in this program include Number Systems, Calculus with Analytic Geometry, Mathematics Learning and Teaching, School Mathematics Curriculum, Elements of Geometry, Ethnomathematics, Using History in the Teaching of Mathematics, and Seminar on Research in Mathematics Education.

Program Contact: College of Education
Florida State University
Tallahassee, Florida 32306

(850) 644-6553
(850) 644-1880

Nursing

Degree Offered: Bachelor of Science in Nursing

Program Web Address: www.fsu.edu/distance/nursing.html

Program Background: This program is designed for registered nurses who want to advance in their careers and need additional education to do so. Prior learning and experience are central to the curriculum.

Application Requirements: You must have an Associate of Arts degree from a Florida community college, and have your license as a registered nurse (or be eligible to take the NCLEX examination). You need to be located near the St. Petersburg Junior College, which is the campus that technologically supports this distance learning program.

Completion Requirements: Typically, students can complete this program in three years of part-time study.

Example Course Titles: Some of the course titles in this program include Nursing: Role and Scope, Dynamics of Aging, Introduction to Research, Advanced Health Assessment, Nursing Concepts, Leadership in Nursing, Community Health Nursing, and Multicultural Factors and Health.

Program Contact: Brenda Arosemena
Academic Coordinator, School of Nursing
Florida State University
Tallahassee, Florida 32306
(850) 644-5107
baroseme@mailer.fsu.edu

Open and Distance Learning

Degree Offered: Master of Instructional Systems

Program Web Address: idl.fsu.edu/odl/ Visitor/default.html

Application Requirements: You must complete an application and submit it to the Office of Graduate Studies with official transcripts from each college or university you've attended, and official test results from the Graduate Record Examination (GRE). If you're an international student, you must also submit official copies of your scores on the Test of English as a Foreign Language (TOEFL).

Completion Requirements: You must successfully complete 36 credit hours for this degree.

System Requirements: You need to have access to a computer capable of running Netscape Communicator 4.0 or higher, or Microsoft Internet Explorer 4.0 or higher. Your computer should also have a CD-ROM drive, and you need to have an Internet connection with an e-mail account.

Example Course Titles: Some of the course titles for this program include Introduction to Distance Learning, Introduction to Instructional Systems, Collaborative Learning Online, Theories of Learning and Cognition, Development of Multimedia Instruction, and Analysis and Application of Webbased Delivery Systems.

Program Contact: Department of Educational Research
Florida State University
Tallahassee, Florida 32306
(850) 644-4592
mmckee@ODDL.fsu.edu

Science Education

Degree Offered: Master of Science

Program Web Address: www.fsu.edu/CandI/ADMIT/ScienceDade.html

Program Background: This Master's program is limited to Dade County public school teachers.

Application Requirements: You must have a score of 1000 on the verbal and quantitative portions of the General Records Examination (GRE). If you do not have a score of at least 1000, you must have taken the GRE and have a minimum grade point average of 3.0 during the last two years of your undergraduate study.

You need to complete an application and submit it with copies of your GRE scores, three letters of recommendation, and official transcripts from each college or university you've attended.

Program Restrictions: This program is available only to Dade County public school teachers.

Completion Requirements: You must successfully complete 33 semester hours and comprehensive examinations.

On Campus Requirements: You are required to attend three summer semesters in Miami.

Example Course Titles: Some of the course titles for this program include Florida Ecosystems, Teaching and Learning Science, Research Methods in Science Education, Physics Teaching, Earth/Space Science, and Research Methods in Science Education.

Program Contact: College of Education
Florida State University
Tallahassee, Florida 32306
(850) 644-6553
(850) 644-1880

Speech Language Pathology

Degree Offered: Master of Science

Program Web Address: www.fsu.edu/commdis/ms.html

Online Program Started: 1999

Program Background: This program is offered in conjunction with the University of West Florida, and is accredited by the Council on Academic Accreditation of the American Speech-Language-Hearing Association. The program's goal is to educate speech-language pathologists so that they function optimally in a variety of clinical and school settings and, if desired, to enable them to pursue the doctoral degree. Students learn through classroom instruction, research, and individualized clinical practicum under the close supervision of certified faculty and staff. Students are encouraged to collaborate with faculty on research and clinical program development.

Application Requirements: You must have a Bachelor's degree in communication disorders. You need to submit applications to the University and to the department offering this program. You can find an application on the University's Web site. In addition to your application, you must submit two letters of recommendation, copies of your Graduate Record Examination scores, and transcripts from each college or university you've attended.

To be admitted to the University, you must have a minimum undergraduate grade point average of 3.0 or a score of 1000 on the combined verbal and mathematics sections of the Graduate Record Examination.

Program Contact: Department of Communication Disorders
Florida State University
Tallahassee, Florida 32306
(850) 644-2253
pwinne@mailer.fsu.edu

FULLER THEOLOGICAL SEMINARY

General Contact Information

135 North Oakland Avenue

Pasadena, California 91182

Phone: (800) 235-2222
FAX: (626) 584-5313
WWW: www.fuller.edu

Online Learning Information

E-mail: idl@fuller.edu
WWW: www.fulleronline.org

Institution Background

Founded: 1947
Type of Institution: Private
Accreditation: Western Association of Schools and Colleges

Programs
Christian Studies

Degree Offered: Certificate

Program Web Address: fulleronline.org/D2index.real?area=195&subarea=208

Program Background: Students in this program can focus their course of study to match their interests and goals.

Completion Requirements: You must successfully complete six course for this certificate.

Program Contact: Distance Learning Office
Fuller Theological Seminary
135 North Oakland Ave
Pasadena, California 91182
(800) 999-9578 ext. 5266
Idl-info@dept.fuller.edu

GEORGE FOX UNIVERSITY

General Contact Information

414 North Meridian

Newberg, Oregon 97132

Phone: (503) 538-8383
FAX: (503) 538-7234
E-mail: admissions@georgefox.edu
WWW: www.georgefox.edu

Online Learning Information

WWW: georgefoxonline.org

Institution Background

Founded: 1891
Type of Institution: Private
Accreditation: Northwest Association of Schools and Colleges

Programs

Management and Organizational Leadership

Degree Offered: Bachelor of Arts

Program Web Address: georgefoxonline.org/ D2index.real?area=401

Program Background: This Management and Organizational Leadership program addresses the needs of adult, working students who want to complete their Bachelor's degree in a manner that is convenient yet challenging. It is designed to be completed in 18 months, and to provide students a curriculum, including basic concepts, that the student can build upon in their future experiences. Students enter the program in cohorts, which enables them to cooperate and share professional and personal experiences along the degree path, developing a valuable support system.

Application Requirements: You must have at least 62 semester credit hours or 93 quarter credit hours to transfer into the program from an accredited institution and an overall grade point average of 2.0 or higher. You can earn up to 30 semester hours by completing and submitting for review a life-experience portfolio.

You should have at least five years of professional experience.

Program Restrictions: This program incorporates various course delivery methods, including online courses and tradition, classroom courses.

System Requirements: You should have a personal computer with a 90 MHz Pentium processor and Windows 95/98/NT or a Macintosh OS 8.1 or higher with at least a 605 PowerPC processor, 32 MB of RAM, a 28.8 kbps modem (or higher), a sound card, speakers, RealPlayer software, an Internet Service Provider (ISP), an e-mail account, and a Java-capable Web browser.

Example Course Titles: Some of the course titles for this program include Dynamics of Group and Organizational Behavior, Effective Writing, Organizational Theory and Analysis, Organizational Communication, Introduction to Survey Research Methods, Survey Research Methods, and Principles of Management and Supervision.

Program Contact: George Fox University
414 North Meridian St. #6098
Newberg, Oregon 97132-2697
(888) 888-0178
(503) 554-3834
conted@georgefoxonline.org

GOLDEN GATE UNIVERSITY

General Contact Information

536 Mission Street
San Francisco, California 94105-2968

Phone: (415) 442-7800
FAX: (415) 442-7807

E-mail: infor@ggu.edu
WWW: cybercampus.ggu.edu

Online Learning Information

536 Mission Street
San Francisco, California 94105

Phone: (415) 442-7060
FAX: (415) 896-2394
E-mail: cybercampus@ggu.edu
WWW: cybercampus.ggu.edu

Institution Background

Founded: 1853
Type of Institution: Private
Accreditation: Western Association of Schools and Colleges

Programs

Accounting

Degree Offered: Master of Accountancy

Program Web Address: cybercampus.ggu.edu/maaccounting.html

Program Background: Golden Gate University's Accounting program provides instruction in theories and practices, as well as gives students a broad-based education. In addition to taking a core set of courses, students can choose courses from other business and technology disciplines. Students graduate with a rich understanding of contemporary accounting practices and theories, and how to apply them.

Application Requirements: You must have a Bachelor's degree from a regionally accredited college or university, or from a recognized foreign institution.

Completion Requirement: You are required to successfully complete 30 to 51 units, depending on the number of prerequisite courses you completed previously. You also must maintain a minimum grade point average of 3.0 in all courses that you take from Golden Gate University.

Example Course Titles: Some of the course titles in this program include Financial Accounting, Intermediate Accounting I, Intermediate Accounting II, Intermediate Accounting III, Cost Accounting, Federal Income Tax I, and Business Law.

Program Contact: Department of Accountancy
Golden Gate University
536 Mission Street
San Francisco, California 94105
(415) 442-6500

Business Administration

Degree Offered: Master of Business Administration

Program Web Address: cybercampus.ggu.edu/mba.html

Program Background: This program is one of the largest in the nation. The curriculum consists of four foundation courses (12 units), eight core courses (24 units), and four concentration courses (12 units). Students who have completed equivalent courses with a grade of B or better at a regionally accredited school may waive the foundation courses.

Application Requirements: You must have a Bachelor's degree from a regionally accredited college or university or a recognized foreign institution. You also must complete the GMAT examination. If you have a Master's or higher degree, or achieved a cumulative minimum grade point average of 3.5 in your undergraduate studies, then the GMAT requirement may be waived. If you have a professional license or designation earned by passing a nationally recognized examination (for example, the Certified Public Accountancy exam), you may petition the Dean for an exemption of the GMAT requirement.

Completion Requirements: You must successfully complete 48 units for this degree.

Example Course Titles: Some of the course titles in this program include Accounting for Managers, Economics for Managers, Finance for Managers, Statistics and Quantitative Analysis for Managers, Managerial Information Systems, Financial Management, Managerial Communication and Analysis, International Business Management, Management Theory and Applications, Business Policy and Strategy, Marketing Management, and Operations Management.

Program Contact: School of Business
Golden Gate University
536 Mission Street
San Francisco, California 94105
(415) 442-6500
biz@ggu.edu

Finance

Degree Offered: Master of Science

Program Web Address: cybercampus.ggu.edu/msfinance.html

Program Background: This is a specialized degree, designed to give students a deeper and richer understanding of finance and a strong set of analytical skills.

Application Requirements: You must have a Bachelor's degree from a regionally accredited institution or from a recognized foreign institution, demonstrated capability to study at the graduate level, and the quantitative, writing, and computing skills needed for graduate study.

Completion Requirements: You must successfully complete 51 units.

Example Course Titles: Some of the course titles in this program include Accounting for Managers, Financial Analysis for Managers, Computer Technology for Managers, Economics for Managers, Calculus, Statistical Analysis for Managers, Financial Management, Investments, and Financial Markets and Institutions.

Program Contact: Department of Finance and Economics
Golden Gate University
536 Mission Street
San Francisco, California 94105
(415) 442-6585
cybercampus@ggu.edu

Health Care Administration

Degree Offered: Master of Healthcare Administration

Program Web Address: cybercampus.ggu.edu/mha.html

Program Background: The lectures in this program form step-by-step modules on the Web, with separate conference space for student and instruction interaction. The program is geared toward qualified healthcare managers.

Application Requirements: You must have a Bachelor's degree from a regionally accredited institution or from a recognized foreign institution. You must also demonstrate the capacity for graduate study, and possess the skills necessary to succeed in advanced studies.

Completion Requirements: You must successfully complete 36 graduate units.

Example Course Titles: Some of the course titles in this program include Health Services Organization and Administration, Healthcare Policy and Economics, Managed Care Concepts, Legal and Ethical Aspects of Healthcare, Financial Management of Healthcare Organizations, Strategic Planning and Healthcare Marketing, Design and Management of Healthcare Information Systems, and Long-Term Care Systems and Social Policy.

Program Contact: Program Chair, Master of Health Care Administration
Golden Gate University
536 Mission Street
San Francisco, California 94105
(415) 442-7888
tfogarty@ggu.edu

Marketing and Public Relations

Degree Offered: Master of Science

Program Web Address: cybercampus.ggu.edu/msmarketing.html

Program Background: This degree program integrates theory and practice to prepare students for success in the field of marketing. The courses are taught by leading professors and practitioners. Students work closely with their advisors to develop a program of study that meets their objectives.

Application Requirements: You must have a Bachelor's degree from a regionally accredited college or university in the United States or from a recognized foreign institution. You must also demonstrate capacity for graduate study, and skills in writing and computing.

Completion Requirements: You must successfully complete 45 units for this degree, 33 of which will be in the Marketing Advanced Program.

Example Course Titles: Some of the course titles in this program include Marketing Research, Consumer Behavior, Business-to-Business Marketing, Sales Management, New Product Decisions, Marketing Strategy and Planning, Advertising Strategy, and Legal Aspects of Marketing.

Program Contact: Department of Marketing and Public Relations
Golden Gate University

536 Mission Street
San Francisco, California 94105
(415) 442-6521
cybercampus@ggu.edu

Public Administration

Degree Offered: Bachelor of Public Administration

Program Web Address: cybercampus.ggu.edu/bpa.html

Program Background: This online program is designed for students who want a broad understanding and overview of public management in American government and institutions. Students are introduced to relevant skills they will need to secure employment in the public sector. The program focuses on institutional relationships in government using an interdisciplinary approach.

Application Requirements: The online Bachelor of Public Administration program is set up as a degree completion program so admission to it is contingent upon your demonstration that you've met lower-division course requirements. You must submit official transcripts from any undergraduate programs you've attended. College-level credits earned from regionally accredited colleges or universities are usually acceptable.

Completion Requirements: You must successfully complete 39 units through this program for the Bachelor's of Public Administration degree.

Example Course Titles: Some of the course titles in this program include Public Administration and Public Affairs, Organizational Behavior and Administrative Communication, Management Policies in Public Administration, Policy Making and Analysis, Administrative Issues in Intergovernmental Relations, Public Budgeting Techniques and Processes, and Public Personnel and Supervisory Practice.

Program Contact: CyberCampus
Golden Gate University
536 Mission Street
San Francisco, California 94105
(888) 874-CYBER
cybercampus@ggu.edu

Public Administration

Degree Offered: Master of Public Administration

Program Web Address: cybercampus.ggu.edu/empa.html

Program Background: This Executive Master of Public Administration is offered entirely online. Students enrolled in it are interested in gaining a thorough understanding of the processes and practices of management in the public sector. The program is designed for administrators who already have knowledge and skills in certain areas, but who need broader knowledge of other areas, such as finance, human resources, and labor-management relations, in order to qualify for advancement.

The Executive program differs from traditional Master of Public Administration programs because it assumes that students have already developed competence in specific areas. Rather than focusing on such training, it emphasizes in-depth exposure to the many facets of middle and upper level management in all public organizations.

Application Requirements: You must have a Bachelor's degree from a regionally accredited college or university, demonstrate academic and professional capability to study at the graduate level, and possess the skills needed to succeed.

Completion Requirements: You are required to successfully complete 36 semester hours in nine classes.

Example Course Titles: Some of the course titles for this program include Research Methods and Analysis, Policy Analysis and Program Evaluation, Organization Analysis and Development, Public Enterprise Management and Public Sector Business Relations, Budgeting and Financial Management, Public Service and The Law, Personnel Management and Labor Relations, and Graduate Research Project in Public Management.

Program Contact: CyberCampus
Golden Gate University
536 Mission Street
San Francisco, California 94105
(888) 874-CYBER
cybercampus@ggu.edu

Taxation

Degree Offered: Master of Science

Program Web Address: cybercampus.ggu.edu/mstax.html

Program Background: Students can earn a fully accredited graduate degree in taxation online through Golden Gate's program. The lectures are delivered as step-by-step modules on the World Wide Web and each topic has a separate conference area where students and the instructor can interact and discuss the subject matter. Students can ask questions as they arise and contribute to the discussions anytime, then check back later to see responses.

Application Requirements: You must have a Bachelor's degree from a regionally accredited college or university or from a recognized foreign institution. Also you must demonstrate academic and professional capability to study at the graduate level, and possess the quantitative, writing, and computing skills needed to succeed in this program.

Completion Requirements: You must successfully complete 41 units for this degree.

Example Course Titles: Some of the course titles in this program include Introductory Financial Accounting, Advanced Federal Income Taxation, Federal Tax Procedure, Federal Income Taxation of Partners and Partnership, Tax Research and Decision Making, Tax Characterization, and Tax Timing.

Program Contact: School of Taxation
Golden Gate University
536 Mission Street
San Francisco, California 94105
(415) 442-7882
cybercampus@ggu.edu

Telecommunications Management

Degree Offered: Master of Science

Program Web Address: cybercampus.ggu.edu/mstelecomm.html

Program Background: This program is designed for the working professional who needs to learn about advancements in telecommunications technology and management. The program focuses on three forces that shape the future of business and society—telecommunications, information, and globalization. Students learn how to lead in the ever-changing world of real-time global communications, internetworking, the Internet and World Wide Web, electronic commerce, and mobile and wireless communications.

Application Requirements: You must have a Bachelor's degree from a regionally accredited college or university or a recognized foreign institution, demonstrate the capability for graduate study, and possess the skills necessary to succeed in this program.

Completion Requirements: You must successfully complete 42 units for this degree.

Example Course Titles: Some of the course titles for this program include Accounting For

Managers, Financial Analysis For Managers, Statistical Analysis For Managers, Decision Science For Managers, Management of Telecommunications, Strategic Telecommunications, and The Futures of Telecommunications.

Program Contact: Telecommunications Department
Golden Gate University
536 Mission Street
San Francisco, California 94105
(415) 442-6543
(415) 442-7049
colson@ggu.edu

GOUCHER COLLEGE

General Contact Information

1021 Dulaney Valley Road
Baltimore, Maryland 21204

Phone: (800) 697-4646
FAX: (410) 337-6085
E-mail: center@goucher.edu
WWW: www.goucher.edu

Online Learning Information

1021 Dulaney Valley Road
Baltimore, Maryland 21204

Phone: (410) 337-6200
FAX: (410) 337-6085
E-mail: center@goucher.edu
WWW: www.goucher.edu

Institution Background

Goucher College was one of the first in the United States to offer online courses as part of an undergraduate curriculum, and to require computer literacy of all graduates.

Founded: 1885
Type of Institution: Private

Accreditation: Middle States Association of Colleges and Schools

Online Course Background: Goucher College offers three limited residency master's degree programs and one teacher's certificate program with specialization in technology leadership.

Online Course Offered: 14

Online Students Enrolled: 100

Services Offered to Students: Students enrolled in online courses at Goucher College can access the library on the World Wide Web. They also have access to a technology coordinator/facilitator for each course.

Financial Aid: Students enrolled in online courses may be eligible for student loans.

Registration: You can register for courses by mail and phone.

Programs

Technology for Teachers

Degree Offered: Certificate of Specialization in Education Technology

Program Web Address: gouchercenter.edu/

Online Program Started: 1998

Students Enrolled: 40

Degrees Awarded: 2

Program Background: This program focuses on using technology in the field of teaching. Students in the program get hands-on, practical experience in creating effective technological-based lessons. Students enrolled in the program are encouraged to take courses on campus during the Summer Teacher's Institute or during the year at cooperating schools. Online courses meet in forums and chat rooms and assignments are posted online.

Application Requirements: You must have a Bachelor's degree from an accredited four-year college.

Completion Requirements: You must successfully complete five three-credit courses for a total of 15 credit hours.

Time for Completion: You have up to three years to complete this program.

On Campus Requirements: You are required to attend an orientation for the first class of all online courses.

System Requirements: You should have a personal computer with a Pentium processor or a PowerMac, 32 MB RAM, an Internet Service Provider, an e-mail account, and a current Java enabled Web browser.

Example Course Titles: Some of the course titles for this program include Basic Internet Skills for Teachers, Effective Use of Computer Technology in Your Classroom, and Technology Integration.

Program Contact: Carole Redline
Goucher College
1021 Dulaney Valley Road
Baltimore, Maryland 21204
(410) 323-6200
(410) 337-6085
credline@goucher.edu

HARVARD UNIVERSITY

General Contact Information

Byerly Hall, 8 Garden Street
Cambridge, Massachusetts 02138

Phone: (617) 495-1551
FAX: (617) 495-8821
E-mail: college@fas.harvard.edu
WWW: www.harvard.edu

Online Learning Information

Director of Academic Computing
51 Brattle Street
Cambridge, Massachusetts 02138

Phone: (617) 495-9096
FAX: (617) 495-9176
WWW: distanceed.dce.harvard.edu

Institution Background

Founded: 1636
Type of Institution: Private
Accreditation: New England Association of Schools and Colleges

Programs

Applied Sciences

Degree Offered: Certificate in Applied Sciences

Program Web Address: www.dce.harvard.edu/extension/1999-00/programs/certific

Completion Requirements: You must successfully complete eight courses in order to receive your certificate.

System Requirements: At a minimum, you must have a computer with a reliable 56kbps dial-in access link, although a cable modem, xDSL or T1 access is recommended. Harvard does not provide dial-in access to students.

The Harvard Extension School recommends the following in terms of a personal computer: a Pentium I or II processor, Windows 98 or Windows NT 4.0, 64 MB or more of RAM, support for 256 colors and a resolution of 1024 by 768.

Example Course Titles: Some of the course titles in this program include Introduction to Computer Science I, Introduction to Computer Science II, Networks and Data Communications, and Management, Finance, and Control.

Program Contact: Harvard Extension School
CAS Office
51 Brattle Street
Cambridge, Massachusetts 02138-3722
(617) 495-4024

Computer Science

Degree Offered: Certificate in Applied Sciences

Program Web Address: www.dce.harvard.edu/extension/1999-00/programs/certific

Completion Requirements: You must successfully complete eight courses.

System Requirements: You should have a computer with a reliable 56 kbps modem and dial-in access link to view the lectures.

Example Course Titles: Some of the course titles in this program include Introduction to Computer Science and Data Structures.

Program Contact: Harvard Extension School
CAS Office
51 Brattle Street
Cambridge, Massachusetts 02138-3722
(617) 495-4024

Information Technology

Degree Offered: Master of Liberal Arts

Program Web Address: www.dce.harvard.edu/extension/1999-00/programs/alm/it/d

Program Background: The Master of Liberal Arts (ALM) in Information Technology is one of two ALM tracts at Harvard. The requirements for each of the two tracts differ, and the Information Technology degree requires a software project.

Application Requirements: To be admitted to the ALM Program in Information Technology (IT), you must have a Bachelor's degree from a regionally accredited college or university, or the international equivalent which will be reviewed by the IT office. If you have a graduate degree, you can only earn the ALM if your existing degree is in a field other than information technology.

Also you must successfully complete three courses (12 units) in information technology through Harvard Extension School or Harvard Summer School. To successfully complete a course, you must earn a grade of B or higher. The 12 units will count toward the overall 40 units you must have for the ALM in Information Technology.

You must demonstrate your proficiency in English if you are not a native-English speaker. If your native language is not English, and you have not completed a four-year Bachelor's degree in an English-language curriculum, you must earn a 250 on the computer-based Test of English as a Foreign Language (TOEFL), or a 600 on the paper-based TOEFL and a 5 on the Test of Written English (TWE). All scores must be sent to the IT office.

If you have questions about the ALM in Information Technology, you should call Dr. Leitner at (617) 495-9414. Also, you are invited to attend one of the orientations held at the beginning of each term (mid-September and late-January typically).

Completion Requirements: You must complete ten IT units, five required courses, four elective courses, and an original software project under the supervision of a Harvard faculty member. And you must maintain a 3.0 grade point average in all IT courses.

Time for Completion: You have up to five years to complete this degree program.

System Requirements: At a minimum, you must have a computer with a reliable 56kbps dial-in access link, although a cable modem, xDSL or T1 access is recommended. Harvard does not provide dial-in access to students.

The Harvard Extension School recommends the following in terms of a personal computer: a Pentium I or II processor, Windows 98 or Windows NT 4.0, 64 MB or more of RAM, support for 256 colors and a resolution of 1024 by 768.

Example Course Titles: Some of the course titles in this program include Algorithms and Data Structures, Theory of Computation and Its Applications, Communication Systems and Technology, Java for Distributed Computing, UNIX Systems Programming, Web Programming in Perl, Digital Libraries and the Internet, Developing Windows Applications, Artificial Intelligence, and Computer Architecture.

Program Contact: Harvard Extension School
51 Brattle Street
Cambridge, Massachusetts 02138-3722
(617) 495-4024

Liberal Arts

Degree Offered: Master of Liberal Arts

Program Web Address: www.dce.harvard.edu/extension/1999-00/programs/alm/ls/d

Program Background: The standard Master of Liberal Arts (ALM) is one of two ALM tracts at Harvard. The requirements for each of the two tracts differ, and the standard degree requires a thesis at the end of the program. The thesis enables students to demonstrate what they've learned and how to apply the methods of their given discipline. It is a research-based requirement for all fields except for literature and creative writing, which has a creative thesis project instead.

Application Requirements: To be admitted to the ALM Program, you must have a Bachelor's degree from a regionally accredited college or university, or the international equivalent. If you have a graduate degree, you can only earn the ALM if your existing degree is in another field.

Also you must successfully complete three courses (12 units) in information technology through Harvard Extension School or Harvard Summer School. To successfully complete a course, you must earn a grade of B or higher. The 12 units will count toward the overall 40 units you must have for the ALM. One of the three courses must be a proseminar in the student's concentration field. Additionally, students enrolled in the literature and creative writing concentration must take at least one creative writing course. All students working on preliminary courses need to make their own arrangements for access to various libraries, or they can buy a special borrower's card from Widener Library.

You must demonstrate your proficiency in English if you are not a native-English speaker. If your native language is not English, and you have not completed a four-year bachelor's degree in an English-language curriculum, you must earn a 250 on the computer-based Test of English as a Foreign Language (TOEFL), or a 600 on the paper-based TOEFL and a 5 on the Test of Written English (TWE).

All students enrolling in the ALM program are invited to attend one of the orientation meetings held at the beginning of each term (generally in mid-September and late-January).

Completion Requirements: You must complete ten graduate-credit courses (40 units), each with a grade of B- or higher and an overall grade point average of B.

System Requirements: At a minimum, you must have a computer with a reliable 56kbps dial-in access link, although a cable modem, xDSL or T1 access is recommended. Harvard does not provide dial-in access to students.

The Harvard Extension School recommends the following in terms of a personal computer: a Pentium I or II processor, Windows 98 or Windows NT 4.0, 64 MB or more of RAM, support for 256 colors and a resolution of 1024 by 768.

Program Contact: Harvard Extension School

51 Brattle Street
Cambridge, Massachusetts 02138-3722
(617) 495-4024

Software Engineering

Degree Offered: Certificate in Applied Sciences

Program Web Address: www.dce.harvard.edu/ extension/1999-00/programs/certific

Completion Requirements: You must successfully complete eight courses for this certificate.

System Requirements: You must have reliable 56 kbps dial-up Internet access to view the lectures.

Example Course Titles: Some of the courses in this program include Introduction to Computer Science I and II, Data Structures, and Software Methodology.

Program Contact: Harvard Extension School
CAS Office
51 Brattle Street
Cambridge, Massachusetts 02138-3722
(617) 495-4024

Technical Writing and Multimedia

Degree Offered: Certificate in Applied Sciences

Program Web Address: www.dce.harvard.edu/ extension/1999-00/programs/certific

Completion Requirements: You must successfully complete eight courses for this certificate.

System Requirements: You should have a personal computer with a Pentium processor, Windows 98/NT, 64 MB of RAM, and support for 256-colors and a resolution of 1024x768. You must have reliable 56 kbps dial-up Internet access to view the lectures.

Example Course Titles: Two of the course titles in this program are Introduction to Computer Science I and II.

Program Contact: Harvard Extension School
CAS Office
51 Brattle Street
Cambridge, Massachusetts 02138-3722
(617) 495-4024

HOPE INTERNATIONAL UNIVERSITY

General Contact Information

2500 East Nutwood Avenue
Fullerton, California 92831

Phone: (714) 879-3901
FAX: (714) 879-1041
E-mail: uadmissions@hiu.edu
WWW: www.hiu.edu

Online Learning Information

WWW: hopeonline.edu

Institution Background

Founded: 1928
Type of Institution: Private
Accreditation: Western Association of Schools and Colleges

Programs

Christian Ministry

Degree Offered: Bachelor of Science

Program Web Address: hopeonline.edu/D2index.real?area=5

Online Program Started: 2000

Program Background: This program prepares students for leadership in ministry. The courses focus on how to read and study the Bible, New and Old Testament books, group and organizational communication, cultural diversity, preaching/teaching, worship, evangelism and discipleship, ethics, equipping servant leaders, and resources for church ministry. A field practicum experience is required.

Application Requirements: You must have at least 45 semester units from an accredited college, and preferably be 25 years or older. You need to have a minimum grade point average of 2.0 (on a 4.0 scale) on all prior academic work. You should complete an application and submit it with a personal statement, a $30 application fee, verification of your high school diploma or equivalent, official transcripts from each college you've attended, a personal reference, and a signature verification form.

Completion Requirements: You must successfully complete 124 semester units of credit, fulfill all curricular requirements, maintain a minimum grade point average of C (2.0), and make financial payment to receive this degree.

System Requirements: You should have a personal computer with a 90 MHz Pentium processor running Windows 95/98/NT or a Macintosh with a PowerPC processor or MacOs 8.1, 32 MB of RAM, a 28.8 kbps modem, speakers, Internet Service Provider, e-mail account, and Java capable browser.

Example Course Titles: Some of the course titles in this program include Group and Organizational Behavior, Introduction to Biblical Studies, Methodology for Biblical Studies, Advanced Interpersonal Communication, Preaching/Teaching I, Gospels, A Foundation for Ethics, Worship, Evangelism and Discipleship, Old Testament Literature, Ministering in a Culturally Diverse World, Equipping for Servant Leadership, New Testament Letters, Biblical Theology, and Resources for Church Ministry.

Program Contact: Hope International University
2500 E Nutwood Ave
Fullerton, California 92831
(714) 879-3903 ext. 2244
(714) 526-0231
jwilson@hiu.edu

Human Development

Degree Offered: Bachelor of Science

Program Web Address: hopeonline.edu/ D2index.real?area=5

Program Background: This program is for students interested in the social sciences, teaching, counseling, or other helping professions. Courses include the study of individuals and group interaction, developmental, learning, and counseling theories, abnormal psychology, cultural diversity, research methods, ethics and strategies for service and servant leadership based on a Christian Biblical foundation.

Application Requirements: You must have at least 45 semester units from an accredited college, and preferably be 25 years or older. You need to have a minimum grade point average of 2.0 (on a 4.0 scale) on all prior academic work. You should complete an application and submit it with a personal statement, a $30 application fee, verification of your high school diploma or equivalent, official transcripts from each college you've attended, a personal reference, and a signature verification form.

Completion Requirements: You must successfully complete no fewer than 124 semester units of credit, fulfill all curricular requirements, and maintain a minimum grade point average of C (2.0).

System Requirements: You should have a personal computer with a 90 MHz Pentium processor running Windows 95/98/NT or a Macintosh with a PowerPC processor or MacOs 8.1, 32 MB of RAM, a 28.8 kbps modem, speakers, Internet Service Provider, e-mail account, and Java capable browser.

Example Course Titles: Some of the course titles in this program include Group and Organizational Behavior, Writing and Research Skills, Introduction to Biblical Literature, Organizational Communication, Principles of Management and Supervision, Applied Quantitative Methods for Management, A Foundation for Ethics, Managerial Economics, Marketing in a Global Economy, Servant Leadership, Human Resource Management, Managerial Accounting, Business Strategy, and Strategies for Service.

Program Contact: Hope International University
2500 E Nutwood Ave
Fullerton, California 92831
(714) 879-3903 ext. 2244
(714) 526-0231
jwilson@hiu.edu

Organizational Management

Degree Offered: Bachelor of Science

Program Web Address: hopeonline.edu/ D2index.real?area=5

Program Background: This bachelor's program is designed for students who want to improve their communication, management, and leadership skills. Courses are in the areas of communication, human resource management and supervision, business strategy, economics, marketing, accounting, ethics, and strategies for service.

Application Requirements: You should be at least 25 years old and you must have completed a minimum of 45 semester units at an accredited college or university, and have a minimum grade point average of 2.0 (on a 4.0 scale). You need to complete an application and submit it with a personal statement, an application fee of $30, official transcripts from your high school or equivalency, official transcripts from all colleges or universities you've attended, and a completed personal reference form.

Completion Requirements: You must successfully complete a minimum of 124 semester units of credit, as well as fulfill all requirements for the program.

System Requirements: You should have a personal computer with a 90 MHz Pentium processor (or faster) or a Macintosh running OS 8.1, 32 MB RAM, a 28.8 kbps modem (or faster), a sound card and speakers, a Java-capable Web browser, an Internet Service Provider, an e-mail account, and Internet RealPlayer.

Example Course Titles: Some of the course titles in this program include Group and Organizational Behavior, Writing and Research Skills, Prenatal through Early Childhood Development, Mid-Childhood and Adolescent Development, Introduction to Biblical Literature, Statistics for the Social Sciences, and A Foundation for Ethics.

Program Contact: Hope International University
2500 E Nutwood Ave
Fullerton, California 92831
(714) 879-3903 ext. 2244
(714) 526-0231
jwilson@hiu.edu

INDIAN RIVER COMMUNITY COLLEGE

General Contact Information

3209 Virginia Avenue
Fort Pierce, Florida 34981

Phone: (561) 462-4740

FAX: (561) 462-4599
WWW: www.ircc.cc.fl.us

Institution Background

Founded: 1960
Type of Institution: Public
Accreditation: Southern Association of Colleges and Schools

Individual Undergraduate Courses: Indian River Community College offers online courses in American history, computer sciences, chemistry, education, economics, English, history, humanities, library and information sciences, mathematics, political science, psychology, Spanish, statistics, and sociology.

Programs

Library Technical Assistant

Degree Offered: Associate of Science

Program Web Address: www.ircc.cc.fl.us/learnres/libsrv/libresrc/lta.html

Program Background: This Instructional Services Technology Program is designed to address the needs of the evolving field of library operations. Students learn how to assist professional librarians as a Library Technical Assistant by receiving instruction in principles, systems, processes and procedures of library operations. They learn about library resources and services, as well as how to acquire, catalog, store, and display resources. The program emphasizes high-technology resources.

Completion Requirements: You must successfully complete 48 semester hours of library, computer, and specialized courses and 15 semester hours of general education courses.

Time for Completion: You can complete this program in two years.

Example Course Titles: Some of the course titles in this program include Introduction to Computer Usage, Electronic Access to Health Sciences Resources, Introduction to Electronic Access to Information, Electronic Access to Educational Resources, Electronic Access to Business Resources, Electronic Access to Legal Resources, Introduction to Internet Research, and Media Technologies for Information Services.

Program Contact: pprofeta@ircc.cc.fl.us

INDIANA STATE UNIVERSITY

General Contact Information

Tirey Hall
Terre Haute, Indiana 47809

Phone: (812) 237-2121
FAX: (812) 237-8023
E-mail: admleah@amber.indstate.edu
WWW: web.indstate.edu

Online Learning Information

Director of Distance Education
Erickson Hall, Room 217
Terre Haute, Indiana 47809

Phone: (812) 237-3181
FAX: (812) 237-3495
E-mail: tvshawk@ruby.indstate.edu

Institution Background

Founded: 1865
Type of Institution: Public
Accreditation: North Central Association of Colleges and Schools

Individual Undergraduate Courses: Indiana State University offers online courses in aviation, business, criminal justice, economics, education, electronics, English, educational psychology, geography, health, industrial mechanics and technology, insurance, instructional technology, life sciences, nursing, psychology, and recreation and sports management.

Programs

Human Resource Development

Degree Offered: Master of Science

Program Web Address: web.indstate.edu/distance/hrd.html

Program Background: This program prepares students for careers in human resource development in higher education, industry, government, and other agencies. Students choose a specialization to reflect their current area of employment, previous work experience, or particular area of interest. Additionally, students get on-the-job training by completing an internship, which can be completed while maintaining current employment, but requires affiliation with industry or appropriate organizations.

Completion Requirements: You must successfully complete 33–36 hours.

On Campus Requirements: There are no on-campus requirements.

Example Course Titles: Some of the course titles in this program include International and Cross Cultural Training, Occupation Internship, Systematic Design of Technical Training Curriculum, Leadership of Human Resources in Education and Training, Rationale and Evaluation of Occupational Programs, and Research Methods in ITE.

Program Contact: Chairperson
Industrial Technology Education
(800) 468-5236
tchgilb@ruby.indstate.edu

Public Administration

Degree Offered: Certificate

Program Web Address: web.indstate.edu/distance/publicadmin.html

Program Background: This is a professional development program designed for public administrators and non-profit agency managers.

Application Requirements: You must have a Bachelor's degree in any field from an accredited college or university. If you are an international student, you must also have a score of 550 on the Test of English as a Foreign Language (TOEFL).

Completion Requirements: You must successfully complete 12 semester hours for this certificate.

On Campus Requirements: There are no on-campus requirements.

Example Course Titles: Some of the course titles in this program include Proseminar in Public Administration, Organizational Behavior in Public Agencies, Public Personnel Administration, and Budgeting in Governmental Agencies.

Program Contact:
Director, Public Administration Program
(800) 444-GRAD
psmohad@scifac.indstate.edu

Student Affairs

Degree Offered: Master of Arts/Master of Science

Program Web Address: web.indstate.edu/distance/studentaffairsadmin.html

Program Background: This program prepares student for work in a variety of student affairs offices in colleges and universities. The curriculum includes significant supervised practice and blends a variety of learning experiences. The program is designed for student affairs professionals who work full-time.

Completion Requirements: You must successfully complete 48 semester hours for this degree.

Time for Completion: Students taking this program online can typically fulfill all of the requirements within three years.

On Campus Requirements: Three of the courses in this degree program must be taken in traditional classrooms. They are Group Dynamics, Techniques of Counseling, and Multi-Cultural Counseling.

Example Course Titles: Some of the course titles in this program include Adult Development, Career Development, Introduction to College Student Personnel Work, Administration in Student Affairs, and Collegiate Environments: Theory, Assessment, and Application.

Program Contact: Chairperson
Department of Counseling
(800) 444-GRAD
willbarratt@indstate.edu

Technology Management

Degree Offered: Doctor of Philosophy

Program Web Address: web.indstate.edu:80/tech/acadprog/grad/cphd/cphd.html

Program Background: This degree program is geared toward technologists and combines traditional doctoral research with an innovative delivery system, a consortium of universities, and advanced technical specialization. It is a collaborative program that is administered by the School of Technology at Indiana State University. Other schools that participate include Bowling Green State University, Central Connecticut State University, Central Missouri State University, East Carolina University, Eastern Michigan University, North Carolina A&T State University, Texas Southern University, and University of Wisconsin-Stout.

Application Requirements: You must apply to Indiana State University for admission to this doctoral program. You should have a Bachelor's degree from a regionally accredited college or university, a minimum undergraduate grade point average of 3.0 (on a 4.0 scale) and a minimum graduate grade point average of 3.5, two years of appropriate work experience, and a score of at least 500 on each section of the Graduate Record Examination. With your application, you should submit five letters of recommendation.

Completion Requirements: You must successfully complete a minimum of 90 semester hours of graduate study, with a majority of your coursework at the 600-level. Your program of study will be divided into five areas: Major Area of Specialization (24-30 semester hours), Internship (six semester hours), Research Core (27-33 semester hours), General Technology Core (12-18 semester hours), and Cognate Studies.

On Campus Requirements: You are required to complete two residencies for this program, but you have two options for fulfilling this requirement. You can complete two consecutive semesters at Indiana State University, or you can complete one semester at Indiana State University and one semester at the home university/consortium university where you're completing your specialization.

Example Course Titles: Some of the course titles in this program include Strategic Planning of Technological Processes, Internet Research Methods, Impacts of Technology, Legal Aspects of Industry, and Technological System, Assessment, and Innovation.

Program Contact: School of Technology Indiana State University

INDIANA UNIVERSITY

General Contact Information

Owen Hall, Room 002
790 E. Kirkwood Ave.
Bloomington, Indiana 47405

Phone: (800) 334-1011 (toll free);
(812) 855-2292 (local)
FAX: (812) 855-8680
E-mail: bulletin@indiana.edu
WWW: www.extend.indiana.edu

Online Learning Information

School of Continuing Studies
Owen Hall, Room 001
790 E. Kirkwood Ave.
Bloomington, Indiana 47405

Phone: (800) 334-1011
FAX: (812) 855-8680
E-mail: bulletin@indiana.edu
WWW: www.extend.indiana.edu

Institution Background

Indiana University has been recognized by Forbes magazine and Yahoo! Internet Life as one of the top 20 most "wired" universities in the country. The IU School of Continuing Studies' distance learning courses have won more national awards than courses from any other institution.

Founded: 1820
Type of Institution: Public
Accreditation: North Central Association of Colleges and Schools

Online Course Background: The School of Continuing Studies plans to convert all of its courses to online formats within the next five years.

Online Course Offered: 4

Online Students Enrolled: 40

Services Offered to Students: Students enrolled in online courses receive one-on-one advising and university e-mail accounts. They may order books online and have access to library resources.

Financial Aid: Students enrolled in online courses may apply for student loans.

Individual Undergraduate Courses: Students may enroll in any of Indiana University's 260-level distance education courses without being enrolled in our General Studies Degree Program.

Individual Graduate Courses: Students may enroll in any of Indiana University's adult education courses without being enrolled in the Master of Science in Adult Education program.

Registration: You may register for courses via mail and phone.

Programs

Language Education

Degree Offered: Master of Science

Program Web Address: education.indiana.edu/disted/masters.html

Program Background: This Master's program is primarily for K-12 teachers who instruct in English, English as a Second Language/Foreign Language, foreign languages, and reading. It focuses on improving instruction through an understanding of language and the literacy process, integrating formal and informal assessment and instruction, and applying research to practice. It prepares students for leadership positions in the language field. And students have the opportunity to work directly with children, youth, and adults in the courses.

Application Requirements: You must complete and submit an application, $40 application fee, sealed envelopes containing three letters of recommendation, a personal goal statement, and official transcripts from each college or university you've attended. You may be asked to submit scholarly writing samples.

Completion Requirements: You must successfully complete at least 36 credit hours for this degree.

Example Course Titles: Some of the course titles for this program include Methods of Teaching Language, Teaching with the Internet Across the Curriculum, Instructional Issues in Language Learning, Critical Reading and Reasoning in the Content Areas, Reading and Learning Skills Development at Post-Secondary Level, Advanced Study in the Teaching of Reading in Junior High and Secondary Schools, and The Online Classroom.

Program Contact: Distance Education
Wendell W. Wright Education Building
Room 4105
Bloomington, Indiana 47405
(800) 605-8255
jshedd@indiana.edu

INTERNATIONAL SCHOOL OF INFORMATION MANAGEMENT UNIVERSITY

General Contact Information

501 South Cherry Street, Suite 350
Denver, Colorado 80246

WWW: www.isimu.edu

Online Learning Information

501 South Cherry Street, Suite 350
Denver, Colorado 80246

Phone: (303) 333-4224
FAX: (303) 336-1144
E-mail: admissions@isimu.edu

Institution Background

The International School of Information Management (ISIM) University was founded in 1987 and was the outgrowth of the International Academy (founded in the 1960s) and its Information Institute (founded in 1982). Its mission is to provide a structured educational program using information technology.

Founded: 1987
Accreditation: Distance Education and Training Council

Online Course Background: ISIM uses Top-Class, a proprietary software for virtual classrooms, to deliver courses to students. It allows online students to communicate with each other and the instructors.

Financial Aid: Although ISIM does not participate in Federal financial aid programs, it does offer private financial assistance through the Education Credit Corporation (ECC). You should contact ECC directly (1-800-477-4977) for information and application procedures.

Registration: You can register for courses using the World Wide Web.

Programs

Business Administration

Degree Offered: Master of Business Administration

Program Web Address: www.isimu.edu/grad/mba.htm

Program Background: This program focuses on success-building skills such as leadership, management, decision making, team dynamics, and communication. The curriculum provides a comprehensive overview of essential business concepts, and students develop an understanding of business fundamentals by applying principles, skills, and strategies to real situations.

Application Requirements: You must have a Bachelor's degree or 20 or more years of professional experience. You need to complete an application and submit it with a $75 application fee, current resume, copies of college transcripts, a goals statement, and three letters of recommendation.

Completion Requirements: You must successfully complete 36 credits for this degree.

Example Course Titles: Some of the course titles in this program include Management Theory, Accounting, Quantitative Analysis, Marketing Management, Managerial Economics, Finance, Business Ethics, Strategic Management, Strategies for Change, Information Systems in Business, and Organizational Behavior.

Program Contact: ISIM University
Admissions Office
501 South Cherry St.
Denver, Colorado 80246
(800) 441-4746
admissions@isimu.edu

Information Management

Degree Offered: Master of Science

Program Web Address: www.isimu.edu/grad/msim.htm

Program Background: The Master's program in Information Management bridges theory and practical application. Its core courses will help you build a foundation of knowledge and skills, enabling you to make informed decisions and to become an effective leader in your field. And the curriculum has two elective tracks, allowing you to concentrate your studies in management or technology.

Application Requirements: You must compete an application for admission and submit it along with a statement of your goals, copies of all of your college transcripts, a current resume, $75 application fee, and three letters of recommendation.

Completion Requirements: You must successfully complete 36 credits to earn this degree—eight core courses for three credits each, three elective courses for three credits each, and a final project worth three credits. Also you must pass two proctored examinations.

Example Course Titles: Some of the course titles in this program include Managing in an Age of Information, Technology Change, Management of Information Systems, and Business Ethics.

Program Contact: Admissions Office
ISIM University
501 South Cherry St.
Denver, Colorado 80246
(800) 441-4746
admissions@isimu.edu

Project Management

Degree Offered: Certificate

Program Web Address: www.isimu.edu/about/certregistration.htm

Program Background: This program provides students with the practical tools and skills to successfully manage a project from the planning stage to final completion and evaluation. Each student is required to produce a project plan, and students are encouraged to use projects they are currently working on in their

professional experience. The Project Management Certificate program was developed with a focus on the Project Management Institute's competencies as listed in the Project Management Book of Knowledge (PMBOK).

Completion Requirements: You must successfully complete the three courses in this program for the certificate.

Example Course Titles: The courses for this program are Project Management Essentials, Project Management Organization Framework, and Project Management Integration Framework with Project.

Program Contact: Project Management Program
International School of Information Management
501 South Cherry St.
Denver, Colorado 80246
(800) 441-4746
admissions@isimu.edu

IOWA STATE UNIVERSITY

General Contact Information

102 Scheman
Ames, Iowa 50011-1112

Phone: (800) 262-0015
FAX: (515) 294-6146
E-mail: lspicer@iastate.edu
WWW: www.lifelearner.iastate.edu

Online Learning Information

102 Scheman
Ames, Iowa 50011-1112

Phone: (515) 294-1327
FAX: (515) 294-6146
E-mail: lspicer@iastate.edu
WWW: www.lifelearner.iastate.edu

Institution Background

Iowa State University is a land-grant institution that serves students and the society through interrelated programs of instruction, research, and extension. It is one of only 62 major research universities in the United States and Canada named to the prestigious Association of American Universities.

Founded: 1858
Type of Institution: Public
Accreditation: North Central Association of Colleges and Schools

Online Course Background: Iowa State offers freshman-level courses in biology and zoology, undergraduate courses in agriculture (including microbiology), and graduate-level agronomy couses online.

Online Course Offered: 19

Online Students Enrolled: 253

Financial Aid: Students enrolled in online courses at Iowa State are eligible to apply for the same financial aid programs as students on-campus.

Individual Undergraduate Courses: Iowa State offers online courses in agricultural systems technology, biology, economics, engineering, entomology, food science and human nutrition, genetics, microbiology, and zoology.

Individual Graduate Courses: Iowa State offers online courses in food science and human nutrition, genetics, and microbiology.

Registration: You may register for online courses via mail, phone, and the World Wide Web.

Programs

Agronomy

Degree Offered: Master of Science

Program Web Address: masters.
agron.iastate.edu/

Online Program Started: 1998

Students Enrolled: 20

Program Background: This program focuses on problem-solving rather than research, and it emphasizes practical skills in crop management, soil and water management, and integrated pest management. It's intended for working professionals.

Application Requirements: You must have a Bachelor's degree from an accredited college or university and a minimum undergraduate grade point average of 2.8 (on a 4.0 scale). You must have completed basic agriculture courses.

Program Restrictions: You must live in the United States or Canada to enroll in this program. And you must maintain satisfactory progress within the time allotted for each course.

Completion Requirements: You must successfully complete 30 credit hours for this degree—12 courses plus you must complete and defend a creative component.

Time for Completion: You have up to five years to complete this program.

On Campus Requirements: You are required to attend a one three-day workshop on-campus.

System Requirements: At a minimum, you need to have a personal computer with a 150 MHz or faster processor running Windows 95 /98/NT that is video, audio, and graphics capable. Your system should also have 32 MB RAM, an 8X CD-ROM drive, Microsoft Office 97, and an Internet Service Provider.

Example Course Titles: Some of the course titles in this program include Crop Growth and Development, Climate and Crop Growth, Crop Improvement, and Crop Management and Ecology.

Program Contact: Dan Dobill
G443 Agronomy Hall
Iowa State University
Ames, Iowa 50011-1010
(800) 747-4478
msagron@iastate.edu

IVY TECH STATE COLLEGE—WABASH VALLEY

General Contact Information

7999 U.S. Highway 41, South
Terre Haute, Indiana 47802

Phone: (812) 299-1121
FAX: (812) 299-8770
E-mail: darney@ivy.tec.in.us
WWW: ivytech7.cc.in.us

Online Learning Information

7999 U.S. Highway 41, South
Terre Haute, Indiana 47802

Phone: (812) 299-1121
FAX: (812) 299-5723
E-mail: ncottrel@ivy.tec.in.us
WWW: ivytech7.cc.in.us

Institution Background

Ivy Tech is a state college dedicated to providing access to Associate-degree programs, continuing education, and workforce development.

Founded: 1963
Type of Institution: Public
Accreditation: North Central Association of Colleges and Schools

Online Course Background: Ivy Tech's online courses are delivered using conventional Web-based materials, and they follow the same syllabus and requirements as on-campus offerings. Ivy Tech at Terre Haute was one of the first institutions accredited by the North Central Association specifically for online distance learning.

Online Course Offered: 90

Online Students Enrolled: 1025

Services Offered to Students: Students enrolled in online courses have access to all library resources, including research databases.

Financial Aid: Online students are elgible to apply for all typical Federal financial aid programs.

Registration: You can register for courses using mail, phone, e-mail, and the World Wide Web.

Programs

Accounting

Degree Offered: Associate of Applied Science

Program Web Address: ivytech7.cc.in.us

Online Program Started: 1997

Students Enrolled: 126

Program Background: This program allows students to pursue either a technical certificate or an Associate in Applied Science degree. Students learn basic accounting principles and how to apply them, as well as skills including maintaining journals and ledgers, processing banking transactions, billing, preparing payroll, maintaining inventory records, preparing financial statements, and analyzing managerial reports. A large portion of the hands-on application in classes revolves around state-of-the-art computer software.

Application Requirements: You need to complete an application and submit it with official high school transcripts or proof of your GED. You are required to participate in assessment testing by the college.

Completion Requirements: You must successfully complete 60 credit hours for the Associate's degree.

On Campus Requirements: There are no on-campus requirements for this program.

System Requirements: You should have a personal computer with a 486DX processor (or faster) or a Macintosh 68040 or PowerPC. Your computer should have a CD-ROM drive, a 28.8 kbps modem (or faster), and an Internet Service Provider. You also need an e-mail account and word processor software. Some classes have additional computer and software requirements.

Example Course Titles: Some of the course titles in this program include College Life/Success Seminar, Introduction to Business, Introduction to Microcomputers, English Composition, Intermediate Algebra, Accounting Principles, Payroll Accounting, Fundamentals of Public Speaking, Advanced Spreadsheets, Principles of Microeconomics, Integrated Accounting Software, Microcomputer Operating Systems, and Managerial Finance.

Program Contact: Deanna King
7999 US Hwy 41 South
Terre Haute, Indiana 47802
(812) 299-1121
(812) 299-5723
dking@ivy.tec.in.us

Business Administration

Degree Offered: Associate of Applied Science

Program Web Address: ivytech7.cc.in.us

Online Program Started: 1997

Students Enrolled: 138

Program Background: This program is designed for students who want to start their own business, as well as those who want to advance their careers in an existing business. Students can choose to specialize in Management, Marketing, Total Quality Management, Banking and Financial Management, Health Care Management, or Restaurant Management.

Application Requirements: You need to submit an application with your high school transcripts or evidence of your GED. You are required to take assessment testing, and you may be required to complete prerequisite work before you are admitted to this program.

Completion Requirements: You must successfully complete 60 credit hours for this degree.

On Campus Requirements: There are no on-campus requirements.

System Requirements: You should have a personal computer with a 486DX processor (or faster) or Macintosh 68040 or Power PC, a CD-ROM drive, a 28.8 baud modem (or faster), Internet access, and an e-mail address. Your computer should also have a word processor (Microsoft Word is preferred). Some courses have additional system and software requirements.

Example Course Titles: Some of the course titles in this program include College Life/Success Seminar, English Composition, Fundamentals of Public Speaking, Intermediate Algebra, Introduction to Business, Principles of Marketing, Accounting Principles I, Introduction to Microcomputers, Principles of Management, Business Law, Human Resources Management, Managerial Finance, Business Development, Principles of Selling, Logistics/Purchasing Control, and Business Communications.

Program Contact: Janet Trout
7999 US Hwy 41 South

Terre Haute, Indiana 47802
(812) 299-1121
(812) 299-5723
jtrout@ivy.tec.in.us

Design Technology

Degree Offered: Associate of Applied Science

Program Web Address: ivytech7.cc.in.us

Online Program Started: 1997

Students Enrolled: 63

Program Background: Students learn the skills necessary to have successful professional experience working in architectural or mechanical drafting, or computer-aided drafting. Students learn various CAD packages common in industry.

Application Requirements: You must submit a completed application for admissions and proof (transcripts) of a high school diploma or GED results. You are required to participate in assessment testing by the college, and you must complete specific program requirements.

Completion Requirements: You must successfully complete 64 credit hours.

System Requirements: You should have a personal computer with a 486DX or faster processor or a Macintosh 68040 or PowerPC, an Internet connection (28.8 Modem or faster recommended), and an e-mail account.

Example Course Titles: Some of the course titles in this program include College Life/Success Seminar, CAD Fundamentals, English Composition, Intermediate Algebra, Algebra/Trigonometry, Technical Graphics, Computer Fundamentals for Technology, Fundamentals of Public Speaking, Construction Materials and Specifications, Architectural CAD, Descriptive Geometry, Advanced CAD, Geometry-Trigonometry, Facilities Design and Layout, Residential Drafting, Structural Detailing, Statics, Physics, Commercial Structures, CAD Mapping, and Strength of Materials.

On Campus Requirements: There are no on-campus requirements.

Program Contact: Mike Stolfe
7999 US Hwy 41 South
Terre Haute, Indiana 47802
(812) 299-1121
(812) 299-5723
mstolfe@ivy.tec.in.us

JOHN WOOD COMMUNITY COLLEGE

General Contact Information

150 South 48th Street
Quincy, Illinois 62301

Phone: (217) 224-6500
FAX: (217) 224-4208
E-mail: mcnett@jwcc.edu
WWW: www.jwcc.edu

Online Learning Information

150 South 48th Street
Quincy, Illinois 62301

Phone: (217) 224-6500
FAX: (217) 224-4339
E-mail: mcnett@jwcc.edu
WWW: www.jwcc.edu

Institution Background

John Wood Community College features individualized learning and self-paced instruction. It is nationally recognized for participating in open learning programs, including online education.

Founded: 1974

Type of Institution: Public

Accreditation: North Central Association of Colleges and Schools

Online Course Background: John Wood Community College's first online courses, in military science, were developed and delivered by faculty from Western Illinois University in the ROTC program. John Wood Community College began offering online courses developed by its own faculty in January 2000.

Online Course Offered: 1

Online Students Enrolled: 2

Special Programs/Partnerships: John Wood Community College is a member of the Western Illinois Educational Consortium (WIEC).

Services Offered to Students: Students enrolled in online courses at John Wood Community College have limited use of the campus library, and access to books through interlibrary loan.

Financial Aid: Students are eligible to apply for federal and state aid programs, private scholarships, and more.

Programs

Military Science

Degree Offered: courses only

Program Web Address: www.jwcc.edu

Online Program Started: 1998

Students Enrolled: 2

Program Background: Students can enroll in two introductory military science courses to learn about the roles that officers play in to-day's army. Completing these two courses makes students eligible to continue to the advanced military science course.

Time for Completion: You have up to 30 weeks to complete each course.

System Requirements: You should have a computer and access to the Internet.

Example Course Titles: The two course titles are Introduction to Military Science and Intermediate Military Science.

Program Contact: Scott Johnson
John Wood Community College
150 S. 48th Street
Quincy, Illinois 62301
(217) 224-6500
(217) 224-4208
johnsons@jwcc.edu

JONES INTERNATIONAL UNIVERSITY

General Contact Information

P.O. Box 6512
Englewood, Colorado 80155-6512

Phone: (800) 811-JONES
WWW: www.jonesinternational.edu

Online Learning Information

P.O. Box 6512
Englewood, Colorado 80155-6512

Phone: (303) 784-8045
FAX: (303) 784-8547
E-mail: durban@international.edu
WWW: www.jonesinternational.edu

Institution Background

Founded: 1995

Accreditation: North Central Association of Colleges and Schools

Financial Aid: Students enrolled in online courses at Jones International University are eligible to apply for student loans.

Programs

Bachelor of Arts

Degree Offered: Bachelor of Arts

Program Web Address: www. jonesinternational.edu/academics/degrees/ba.html

Program Background: This program allows students to complete the last 60 semester credit hours of a 120 credit hour Bachelor's degree program.

Application Requirements: You should have an Associate's degree or equivalent from an accredited college or university, or have earned at least 60 semester credit hours from an accredited college or university. You must have satisfied the general education requirements for this Bachelor's degree, and have a cumulative minimum grade point average of 2.5. You should complete an application packet and submit it to Jones International University.

Completion Requirements: You must successfully complete 120 credit hours total for this degree. Of the 120, 60 credit hours are required for admission to this program. You must then complete 48 credit hours from the Interdisciplinary and Core Curriculum courses, and 12 credit hours by specializing in one subject area (Communication Management Specialization or Applied Telecommunications Specialization). You must take at least 10 courses (or 30 credit hours) at Jones International University. And you must maintain a minimum cumulative grade point average of 2.0, and pay a graduation fee prior to your final course.

Time for Completion: You have up to seven years to complete this degree.

System Requirements: You should have a personal computer with a Web Browser (Netscape 3.0 or higher), RealAudio or RealPlayer, Shockwave for Authorware, and Microsoft Video.

Example Course Titles: Some of the course titles in this program include Integrated Humanities: Knowledge of the Self, Integrated Science and Math, Integrated Social Science: Global Interdependence, Integrated Business Communication and English, Public Speaking, Organizational Communications, Human Communication, Fundamentals of Business Writing, Oral and Written Business Communications, New Communications Technologies, Ethical Issues in Information Technology, Organizational Assessment/Evaluation, Public Relations, International Communication, History of Media, Team Communication, and Telecom Applications 1.

Program Contact: Jones International University
9697 East Mineral Avenue
Englewood, Colorado 80112
(303) 784-8045
(303) 784-8547
info@international.edu

Business Communication

Degree Offered: Master of Arts

Program Web Address: www. jonesinternational.edu/academics/degrees/ma.html

Application Requirements: You must have a Bachelor's degree from a regionally accredited college or university, and have undergraduate coursework in public speaking and business writing. If you didn't have undergraduate courses in these areas, you may fulfill this requirement through Jones International University prior to entering the degree program.

You must complete an application and submit it with copies of official transcripts from any institution of higher education that you've attended.

Completion Requirements: You must successfully complete 35 credit hours for this degree. This includes graduate level courses, a Capstone course, and a demonstration of your knowledge and abilities.

System Requirements: You should have a personal computer with a Web browser (Netscape 3.0 or higher recommended) that is Java enabled. You also need RealAudio or RealPlayer, Shockwave for Authorware, and Microsoft Video.

Example Course Titles: Some of the course titles for this program include Research Methods for Graduate Studies, Essentials for Developing a Web-Based Course, Planning and Designing a Web-Based Course, New Instructional Strategies: Teaching and Learning Online, Fundamentals of Teaching and Learning Online, and Understanding the Human Communication Process.

Program Contact: Jones International University
9697 East Mineral Avenue
Englewood, Colorado 80112
(303) 784-8045
(303) 784-8547
info@international.edu

Global Communication

Degree Offered: Certificate

Program Web Address: www. jonesinternational.edu/academics/certificates/global.html

Completion Requirements: You must successfully complete three courses.

System Requirements: You need a computer with a Web browser (Netscape version 3.0 or higher), RealAudio or RealPlayer, Shockwave for Authorware, and Microsoft Video.

Example Course Titles: Some of the course titles in this program include Integrated Social Science: Global Interdependence, International Communication, Using the Internet, Cyber Marketing—Competitive Advantages Using the Internet, Marketing Electronically, and Understanding the Human Communication Process.

Program Contact: Jones International University
9697 East Mineral Avenue
Englewood, Colorado 80112
(303) 784-8045
(303) 784-8547
info@international.edu

Leadership and Communication Skills for Managers and Executives

Degree Offered: Certificate

Program Web Address: www. jonesinternational.edu/academics/certificates/leadershi

Program Background: This program helps students discover the potential impact the Internet can have on organizations. It focuses on designing strategies that students can use to improve team communication and performance. Within the program, students can earn one of four certificates.

Completion Requirements: You must successfully complete two to four courses for this certificate.

System Requirements: You must have a computer with Netscape 3.0 or higher, RealAudio or RealPlayer (link provided for plug-in), Java capabilities, Shockwave for Authorware (link provided for plug-in), and Microsoft Video.

Example Course Titles: Some of the course titles in this program include Public Speaking, Fundamentals of Business Writing, Oral and Written Business Communication, Human Resource Management for Changing Environments, Organizational Assessment and Evaluation, and Negotiation and Conflict Management.

Program Contact: Jones International University
9697 East Mineral Avenue
Englewood, Colorado 80112
(303) 784-8045
(303) 784-8547
info@international.edu

New Communication Technologies

Degree Offered: Certificate

Program Web Address: www.
jonesinternational.edu/academics/certificates/
newtech

Program Background: Students enrolled in this certificate program learn to analyze advanced communication technologies and explore the implications of media convergence. Within the program, three certificates are actually offered: Applied Fundamentals for Telecommunications in Business; Telecommunications Applications for Managers; and New Business Solutions Through Communications Technology.

Completion Requirements: You must successfully complete three courses for this certificate.

System Requirements: You must have a computer with Netscape 3.0 or higher, RealAudio

or RealPlayer (link provided for plug-in), Java capabilities, Shockwave for Authorware (link provided for plug-in), and Microsoft Video.

Example Course Titles: Some of the course titles in this program include Telecommunications Applications, Using the Internet, and Telecommunications Applications for Managers.

Program Contact: Jones International University
9697 East Mineral Avenue
Englewood, Colorado 80112
(303) 784-8045
(303) 784-8547
info@international.edu

Public Relations and Marketing

Degree Offered: Certificate

Program Web Address: www.
jonesinternational.edu/academics/certificates/
marketing

Program Background: This program exposes students to tools and new technologies in the field of public relations. Students learn to use these tools, which include telecommunications technologies for marketing and public relations.

Within the program, there are actually four certificates that a student can choose to pursue: Public Relations Fundamentals for the New Media Merger; Advanced Public Relations for the Wired World; Marketing Fundamentals in Today's Electronic Business Environment; and Cyber Marketing—Competitive Advantages Using the Internet.

Completion Requirements: You must successfully complete three courses for this certificate.

System Requirements: You should have a personal computer with a Web browser (Netscape 3.0 or higher), RealAudio or RealPlayer, Shockwave for Authorware, and Microsoft Video.

Example Course Titles: Some of the course titles in this program include Fundamentals of Business Writing, Public Relations, Using the Internet, Public Relations, Using the Internet in Business, and Perfecting the Presentation.

Program Contact: Jones International University
9697 East Mineral Avenue
Englewood, Colorado 80112
(303) 784-8045
(303) 784-8547
info@international.edu

Using the Internet in Education

Degree Offered: Certificate

Program Web Address: www.jonesinternational.edu/academics/certificates/education

Program Background: This program is designed to help innovative educators at all levels build their telecommunications skills so they can enhance learning environments and broaden their own career opportunities. Students in this program discuss the Internet and its uses as a resource and alternative instructional delivery system. They learn how to create and use Internet-based materials.

Two certificates are offered through this program: Using the Internet in K-12 Education and Using the Internet in Higher Education.

Completion Requirements: You must successfully complete two or three courses.

System Requirements: You should have a personal computer with a Web browser (Netscape 3.0 or higher), RealAudio or RealPlayer, Shockwave for Authorware, and Microsoft Video.

Example Course Titles: Some of the course titles for this program include Essentials for Developing a Web-Based Course, Planning and Designing a Web-Based Course, and New Instructional Strategies: Teaching and Learning Online.

Program Contact: Jones International University
9697 East Mineral Avenue
Englewood, Colorado 80112
(303) 784-8045
(303) 784-8547
info@international.edu

LAKESHORE TECHNICAL COLLEGE

General Contact Information

1290 North Avenue
Cleveland, Wisconsin 53015-9761

Phone: (800) 443-2129
E-mail: enroll@ltc.tec.wi.us
WWW: www.ltc.tec.wi.us

Online Learning Information

1290 North Avenue
Cleveland, Wisconsin 53015-1414

Phone: (800) 443-2129
FAX: (920) 693-3561
E-mail: jamal@ltc.tec.wi.us
WWW: www.ltc.tec.wi.us

Institution Background

Type of Institution: Public
Accreditation: North Central Association of Colleges and Schools

Programs

Health Physics

Degree Offered: Associate of Science

Program Web Address: www.tcbi.com/ltc

Online Program Started: 1997

Students Enrolled: 7

Degrees Awarded: 4

Program Background: This program prepares students for work in the radiation safety field. Students can focus their studies on nuclear power plants, hospitals, universities, research labs, Department of Energy sites, governmental agencies, or environmental restoration.

Completion Requirements: You must successfully complete 64-67 credits.

Time for Completion: You have up to five years to complete this program.

On Campus Requirements: There are no on-campus requirements.

System Requirements: You should have a computer with Internet access and a CD-ROM drive.

Example Course Titles: Some of the course titles in this program include Nuclear Sources and Systems, Radiation Biology, Radiation Physics, Introduction to Nuclear Technology and Regulations, Applied Health Physics, Radiation Shielding, Radiochemistry, Radiological Emergencies, Radioactive Waste Disposal and Management, and Advanced Instrumentation and Calibration.

Program Contact: Douglas Gossen Ph.D.
1290 North Ave.
Cleveland, Wisconsin 53015
(920) 693-1221
(920) 693-3564
dogo@ltc.tec.wi.us

LANSING COMMUNITY COLLEGE

General Contact Information

422 North Washington Square

Lansing, Michigan 48901-7210

Phone: (517) 483-1200
FAX: (517) 483-9668
WWW: vcollege.lansing.cc.mi.us

Online Learning Information

Director of Distance Learning
8270 RCH, Box 40010
Lansing, Michigan 48901-7210

Phone: (517) 483-9940
FAX: (512) 483-9750
E-mail: kmilton@lansing.cc.mi.us
WWW: vcollege.lansing.cc.mi.us

Institution Background

Founded: 1957
Type of Institution: Public
Accreditation: North Central Association of Colleges and Schools

Individual Undergraduate Courses: Lansing Community College offers online courses in accounting, astronomy, business, computer applications, chemistry, computer information systems, criminal justice, economics, electrical engineering, legal studies, management, mathematics, philosophy, political science, psychology, speech communication, and writing.

Programs

Business

Degree Offered: Associate

Program Web Address: vcollege. lansing.cc.mi.us/index.html

Application Requirements: You should complete the online application and submit it online or via fax or mail, or call the school at (517) 483-1200 or 1-800-644-4LCC to request an application form.

System Requirements: You should have a personal computer with a 486 processor (or faster) or a Macintosh 040, a 14.4 kbps modem, 16 MB RAM, 100 MB free hard disk space, a Web browser, a CD-ROM drive, and a sound card.

Program Contact: LCC Advising Center
Lansing Community College
P.O. Box 40010
Lansing, Michigan 48901-7210
(517) 483-1904

LEE UNIVERSITY

General Contact Information

1120 North Ocoee Street
Cleveland, Tennessee 37311

Phone: (423) 614-8500
FAX: (423) 614-8533
WWW: www.leeuniversity.edu

Online Learning Information

WWW: leeonline.org

Institution Background

Founded: 1918
Type of Institution: Private
Accreditation: Southern Association of Colleges and Schools

Programs

Christian Ministry

Degree Offered: Bachelor of Arts

Program Web Address: leeonline.org/D2index.real?area=245&subarea=254

Program Background: Students enrolled in this program can specialize in Bible, Christian Education, Pastoral Ministries, Theology, or Urban Ministries. The program is designed to prepare students for Christian ministry in the contemporary world.

Application Requirements: You should have your high school diploma or GED. You can take up to 90 credits online. You need to submit an application, official transcripts from each college or university you've attended, and high school transcripts or proof of your GED.

Completion Requirements: You must successfully complete 130 hours for this degree.

System Requirements: You should have a personal computer with a 90 MHz Pentium processor running Windows 95/98/NT or a Macintosh with OS 8.1 or a PowerPC processor, 32 MB of RAM, 28.8 kbps modem, Sound Card, Speakers, and RealPlayer.

Example Course Titles: Some of the course titles in this program include Personal Evangelism, The Christian Family, Ministry of Worship, Methods of Bible Study, Spiritual Formation and Discipleship, Synoptic Gospels, Pentateuch, Romans and Galatians, Christian Ethics, Person and Work of the Holy Spirit, Old Testament Survey, New Testament Survey, 1 and 2 Corinthians, Christian Thought, Church of God History and Polity, History of Christianity, Old Testament Theology, History of Christian Doctrine, and Systematic Theology.

Program Contact: Lee University
Department of External Studies
100 Eighth Street, NE
Cleveland, Tennessee 37311
(800) 256-5916
(423) 614-8377

LEWIS-CLARK STATE COLLEGE

General Contact Information

500 Eighth Avenue

Lewiston, Idaho 83501-2698

Phone: (208) 799-2076
WWW: www.lcsc.edu/cip/

Online Learning Information

500 Eighth Avenue
Lewiston, Idaho 83501

Phone: (208) 799-2239
FAX: (208) 799-2444
E-mail: kmartin@lcsc.edu
WWW: www.lcsc.edu/cip/

Institution Background

The Lewis-Clark State College offers distance learning courses via videotape, videoconferencing, interactive television, audiotape, and print, as well as computer-based courses using software, CD-ROM, computer conferencing, the Internet, and e-mail. Students may meet with instructors virtually or in-person.

Founded: 1893
Type of Institution: Public
Accreditation: Northwest Association of Schools and Colleges

Online Course Background: Since 1995, Lewis-Clark State College has offered credit courses online to address the needs of students with time and geographic constraints. Although most courses don't have structured class meeting times, they do have deadlines for course assignments and examinations. All online course offerings follow the same academic calendar dates and registration procedures as on-campus classes.

Online Course Offered: 104

Online Students Enrolled: 690

Services Offered to Students: Students enrolled in online courses have access to library services, academic advising, tutoring, and the bookstore.

Financial Aid: Online students are eligible to apply for all types of financial aid administered by Lewis-Clark.

Registration: You can register for courses via mail.

Programs
Interdisciplinary Studies

Degree Offered: Bachelor of Science (Interdisciplinary Studies)

Program Web Address: www.lcsc.edu/bsis. htm

Online Program Started: 1995

Students Enrolled: 23

Program Background: This is an interdisciplinary degree combining business and communication studies.

Completion Requirements: You must successfully complete 128 credits for this degree.

On Campus Requirements: You are required to take three weekend courses on-campus. You may take them simultaneously during one week in the summer.

System Requirements: You should have a personal computer with Internet access, e-mail, and a word processor.

Example Course Titles: Some of the course titles in this program include Introduction to Business, Principles of Accounting, Micro/Macroeconomics, Statistics, Financial Management, Business and Society, Principles of Marketing, Foundations of Management Theory, Small Business & Entrepreneurial Management, Interpersonal Communications, Small Group Communications, Public Speaking Organizational Communication, Persuasion, Professional Communication, Intercultural Communication, and Communication Theory.

Program Contact: Kathy L. Martin
500 8th Avenue
Lewiston, Idaho 83501
(208) 799-2076
(208) 799-2444
kmartin@lcsc.edu

Liberal Arts

Degree Offered: Associate of Arts in Liberal Arts

Program Web Address: www.lcsc.edu/cip

Online Program Started: 1995

Completion Requirements: You must successfully complete 64 credits for this degree.

Time for Completion: It takes most students about two years to complete this degree.

System Requirements: You need to have a computer and an Internet connection.

Program Contact: Kathy L. Martin
500 8th Avenue
Lewiston, Idaho 83501
(208) 799-2076
(208) 799-2444
kmartin@lcsc.edu

MARYLHURST UNIVERSITY

General Contact Information

17600 Pacific Highway, P.O. Box 261
Marylhurst, Oregon 97036

Phone: (800) 634-9982
FAX: (503) 636-9526
E-mail: learning@marylhurst.edu
WWW: www.marylhurst.edu

Online Learning Information

17600 Pacific Highway, P.O. Box 261
Marylhurst, Oregon 97036

Phone: (503) 699-6316
FAX: (503) 636-9526
E-mail: kpaul@marylhurst.edu
WWW: www.marylhurst.edu

Institution Background

Marylhurst University is a private institution of higher education, which is dedicated to making innovative education accessible to self-directed students of any age. Marylhurst offers coursework leading to bachelor's and master's degrees, and to other goals such as career transition, professional development, and personal enrichment.

Founded: 1893
Type of Institution: Private
Accreditation: Northwest Association of Schools and Colleges

Online Course Background: Regionally reconized as a pioneer in Web-based education, Marylhurst University piloted its first online course in 1996. It now offers almost two hundred online courses annually, as well as providing a BA/BS Degree Completion Program and an MBA program entirely online.

Online Course Offered: 35

Online Students Enrolled: 195

Special Programs/Partnerships: Marylhurst University is a member of Western Governors University.

Services Offered to Students: Students enrolled in online courses may access all necessary materials and services available to students on campus. Remote access to library services, online registration, academic advising, financial aid information, and other services are available through either the general website, password-protected sites, e-mail, or telephone.

Financial Aid: Online students are eligible to apply for financial aid.

Individual Undergraduate Courses: Online students may enroll in courses without formal admission, with the exception of graduate courses and the BA/BS Degree Completion Program.

Programs

Management/Organizational Communication

Degree Offered: Bachelor of Science in Management

Program Web Address: www.marylhurst.edu/online/programs/babsonline.html

Online Program Started: 1998

Students Enrolled: 12

Program Background: This program is designed for students who already have 90 hours of college credit, and want the flexibility to complete their degree on the Internet. The selective admission process ensures a cohort of peers, as well as the benefits of small, intimate classes, personalized attention, and academic excellence. The competency-based core curriculum helps students demonstrate and document the tangible skills they will acquire through the program.

Application Requirements: You should have an approved Associate's degree or equivalent (90 credits), minimum grade point average of 3.0, and two years of full-time employment. You need to complete and submit an application with a $50 application fee, two letters of recommendation, a personal goals statement, current resume, official transcripts from each

college or university you've attended, and proof of your high school completion.

Time for Completion: You must successfully complete six terms for this degree.

On Campus Requirements: There are no on-campus requirements.

System Requirements: You should have a personal computer with a 486 (or faster) processor, Windows 95, communications software, a 28.8 baud modem (or faster), and an Internet Service Provider (ISP).

Example Course Titles: Some of the course titles in this program include Effective Listening, Basic Statistics, Interpersonal Communication, Small Group Communication, Marketing, Public Presentations, Project Management, Human Resources/Introduction to Supervision, Intercultural Communication, Team Building, Applied Statistics, Business and Professional Speaking, Conflict Management, Business Finance, and Ethics and Leadership.

Program Contact: Mark Jenkins
P.O. Box 261
Marylhurst, Oregon 97036
(503) 699-6315
(503) 636-9526
mjenkins@marylhurst.edu

MCGILL UNIVERSITY

General Contact Information

3700 McTavish Street
Montreal, Quebec H3A 1Y2 Canada

Phone: (514) 398-3457
FAX: (514) 398-2182
E-mail: distance@education.mcgill.ca
WWW: www.education.mcgill.ca/distance

Online Learning Information

3700 McTavish Street
Montreal, Quebec H3A 1Y2 Canada

Phone: (514) 398-3457
FAX: (514) 398-2182
E-mail: distance@education.mcgill.ca
WWW: www.education.mcgill.ca/distance

Institution Background

McGill University is one of Canada's top ten research universities and consistently receives high ratings in the annual Maclean Magazine report on Canadian universities.

Founded: 1821
Type of Institution: Public
Accreditation: Province of Quebec Ministry of Education

Online Course Background: McGill offers undergraduate-level, three-credit professional development courses for teachers anywhere, and two certificate programs online.

Online Course Offered: 51

Online Students Enrolled: 450

Financial Aid: Students enrolled in online courses at McGill are not eligible for financial aid.

Registration: You can register for courses via mail.

Programs

Educational Technology

Degree Offered: Certificate in Educational Technology

Program Web Address: www.education.mcgill.ca/distance

Online Program Started: 1986

Students Enrolled: 275

Degrees Awarded: 22

Program Background: This program is designed for experienced teachers.

Application Requirements: You must have an undergraduate degree to be admitted to this program.

Program Restrictions: This program is restricted only to teachers and those in related occupations (such as school board technicians).

Completion Requirements: You must successfully complete 30 credits for this certificate.

Time for Completion: You have up to five years to complete this program.

On Campus Requirements: There are no on-campus requirements.

System Requirements: You should have a personal computer running Windows or a Macintosh equivalent.

Example Course Titles: Some of the course titles in this program include Desktop Publishing, Internet Resources/Designing School Web Sites, and Educational Software/Logo/Instruct Programming.

Program Contact: Peter Burpee
McGill University
3700 McTavish Street
Montreal, Quebec H3A 1Y2
(514) 398-3457
(514) 398-2182
distance@education.mcgill.ca

MICHIGAN STATE UNIVERSITY

General Contact Information

250 Administration Building
East Lansing, Michigan 48824

Phone: (517) 355-8332
FAX: (517) 353-1647
E-mail: admis@msu.edu
WWW: www.msu.edu/unit/outreach

Online Learning Information

Evening and Off-Campus Programs
51 Kellogg Center
East Lansing, Michigan 48824

Phone: (517) 353-0791
FAX: (517) 432-1327
E-mail: spurginm@pilot.msu.edu
WWW: www.msu.edu/unit/outreach

Institution Background

Michigan State University is one of only 62 members of the Association of American Universities and a member of the Big Ten conference. As provided in the Constitution of the State of Michigan, Michigan State University is under the general supervision of its Board of Trustees.

The University established six principles to guide Michigan State into the next century. They are to improve access to quality education and expert knowledge, achieve more active learning, generate new knowledge and scholarship across the mission, promote problem solving to address society's needs, advance diversity within the community, and make people matter.

Founded: 1855
Type of Institution: Public
Accreditation: North Central Association of Colleges and Schools

Services Offered to Students: Students enrolled in online courses have access to the library, writing center, bookstore, and other resources of the University.

Financial Aid: Students enrolled in online courses are eligible to apply for all financial aid

administered by Michigan State. Additionally, all online courses, regardless of where they are taken, are eligible for in-state tuition rates.

The Virtual University Beam Physics Tuition Fellowship is awarded on a competitive basis; for more information, contact vubeam@nscl.msu.edu. Teaching or Research Assistantships during any period of residency at MSU are awarded on a competitive basis.

Registration: You can register for courses via mail and World Wide Web.

Programs

Beam Physics

Degree Offered: Masters of Science

Program Web Address: vubeam.nscl.msu.edu/

Program Background: Virtual University, the Department of Physics and Astronomy, and the NSCL at Michigan State University along with the U.S. Particle Accelerator School offer this suite of courses and an online degree program in Beam Physics. Courses are broadcast live via Internet/ISDN or are interactive and self-paced. They cover an introduction to beam physics as well as various advanced topics.

Application Requirements: You need to submit an application, a current resume/vitae, letter of intent, three letters of recommendation, and transcripts from each institution of higher education you've attended. All applications materials should be sent directly to Prof. Martin Berz, Department of Physics and Astronomy, Michigan State University, East Lansing, MI 48824.

Completion Requirements: You must successfully complete a total of 30 credits, of which up to 9 can be transferred from accredited universities and at least 16 of which must be at the graduate level. You are also required to pass a departmental qualifying exam at the Master's or Ph.D. level, respectively. If you're pursuing the Ph.D., you also have to complete a dissertation under the guidance of a mutually selected mentor and/or Michigan State University.

System Requirements: You should have a personal computer with a Pentium processor running Windows 95/98/NT or a Macintosh with OS 7.5 or higher, 16 MB RAM, a 28.8 or faster kbps modem or direct connection to the Internet, Web browser (Netscape 4.0 or higher, or Microsoft Internet Explorer 4.0 or higher). Some courses may have additional system or software requirements.

Example Course Titles: Some of the course titles in this program include Introduction to Beam Physics, Nonlinear Dynamics, Particle Accelerators of the World, US Particle Accelerator School, and Seminar in Beam Physics Research.

Program Contact: Department of Physics and Astronomy
Michigan State University
East Lansing, Michigan 48824
(517) 353-5286
(517) 353-4500
vubeam@nscl.msu.edu

Beam Physics

Degree Offered: Doctor of Philosophy

Program Web Address: vubeam.nscl.msu.edu/

Program Background: Virtual University, the Department of Physics and Astronomy, and the NSCL at Michigan State University along with the U.S. Particle Accelerator School offer this suite of courses and an online degree program in Beam Physics. Courses are broadcast live via Internet/ISDN or are interactive and self-paced. They cover an introduction to beam physics as well as various advanced topics.

Application Requirements: You need to submit an application, a current resume/vitae, letter of intent, three letters of recommendation, and transcripts from each institution of higher education you've attended. All applications materials should be sent directly to Prof. Martin Berz, Department of Physics and Astronomy, Michigan State University, East Lansing, MI 48824.

Completion Requirements: You must successfully complete a total of 30 credits, of which up to 9 can be transferred from accredited universities and at least 16 of which must be at the graduate level. You are also required to pass a departmental qualifying exam at the Master's or Ph.D. level, respectively. If you're pursuing the Ph.D., you also have to complete a dissertation under the guidance of a mutually selected mentor and/or Michigan State University.

System Requirements: You should have a personal computer with a Pentium processor running Windows 95/98/NT or a Macintosh with OS 7.5 or higher, 16 MB RAM, a 28.8 or faster kbps modem or direct connection to the Internet, Web browser (Netscape 4.0 or higher, or Microsoft Internet Explorer 4.0 or higher). Some courses may have additional system or software requirements.

Example Course Titles: Some of the course titles in this program include Introduction to Beam Physics, Nonlinear Dynamics, Particle Accelerators of the World, US Particle Accelerator School, and Seminar in Beam Physics Research.

Program Contact: Department of Physics and Astronomy
Michigan State University
East Lansing, Michigan 48824

(517) 353-5286
(517) 353-4500
vubeam@nscl.msu.edu

Computer Aided Design

Degree Offered: Certificate

Program Web Address: www.vu.msu.edu/
preview/hed490/index.html

Program Background: Students enrolled in
this program learn to use Computer Aid Design (CAD) as a design tool, and gain an understanding of Computer Aided Design
principles and strategies.

Application Requirements: To enroll contact
MSU Virtual University, or contact Melissa Del
Rio at (517) 353-0791.

Completion Requirements: You must successfully complete all required courses.

System Requirements: You should have a personal computer with a Pentium processor running Windows 95/98/NT or a Macintosh with
OS 7.5 or higher, 16MB or more of RAM (32
MB recommended), 28.8 or faster modem
(56K recommended) or direct connection to
the Internet, and a Web browser (Netscape 4.0
or higher, or Microsoft Internet Explorer 4.0 or
higher).

Example Course Titles: One of the course titles
in this program is Computer-Aided Design
Technologies.

Program Contact: Human Environment and
Design
Michigan State University
204 Human Ecology
East Lansing, Michigan 48824
(517) 353-3054
vredevoo@msu.edu

Criminal Justice

Degree Offered: Masters of Science

Program Web Address: www.vu.msu.edu/
info/cj_ma/

Application Requirements: You must have a
Bachelor's degree from an accredited institution, a minimum undergraduate grade point
average of 3.2, scores on the Graduate Record
Examination (GRE) at the 50th percentile or
higher, and evidence of personal traits and
characteristics considered important for successful scholarly performance. You should also
have at least 12 credits of undergraduate
coursework in political science, economics, sociology, psychology, anthropology, history, social work or any combination of such courses.

On Campus Requirements: You are required
to attend a two-day orientation at the beginning of the program.

System Requirements: You need a computer
with Internet access.

Example Course Titles: Some of the course titles in this program include Proseminar in
Criminal Justice, Design and Analysis in Criminal Justice Research, Criminal Justice Management Seminar, Seminar in Management Topics,
Security Management, Security Administration,
Independent Study, Internship/Practicum, Policy Analysis Under Conditions of Change, and
Organizational Behavior and People Management.

Program Contact: Michigan State University
East Lansing, Michigan 48824
(877) GO-TO-MSU
msumidmi@msu.edu

Facility Management

Degree Offered: Master's Level Certificate

Program Web Address: vu.msu.edu/info/
hed_cert/

Program Background: This program is designed to train professionals in facility management in areas including real estate, workplace safety, security, and accessibility, communication systems, cost/productivity ratios, planning and design, construction, business services, and code compliance.

Application Requirements: You should have a Bachelor's degree. If you do not, you may be eligible to participate in this program if you have significant work experience in facility management.

Completion Requirements: You must successfully complete four courses.

System Requirements: You need a personal computer with a Pentium processor, 16MB or more of RAM (32 MB recommended), 28.8 or faster modem (56K recommended) or direct connection to the Internet, Web browser (Netscape 4.0 or higher, or Microsoft Internet Explorer 4.0 or higher), and Windows 95/98/NT. You should also have Microsoft Office 97 or higher (including Word, Excel, Powerpoint, and Binder) and virus protection software. Or you need the Macintosh equivalent to the system described.

Example Course Titles: Some of the course titles in this program include Facility Management: Theory and Principles, Information Management for Facility Professionals, Organizational Effectiveness, and Facility Real Estate and Building Economics.

Program Contact: Enrollment Coordinator
MSU Outreach Instructional Programs
51 Kellogg Center
East Lansing, Michigan 48824
(877) GO-TO-MSU
msumidmi@msu.edu

MINNESOTA WEST COMMUNITY AND TECHNICAL COLLEGE

General Contact Information

1450 Collegeway Drive
Worthington, Minnesota 56187

Phone: (507) 372-2685
FAX: (507) 372-3454
E-mail: siverson@wr.mnwest.mnsw.edu
WWW: www.mnwest.mnscu.edu

Online Learning Information

1450 Collegeway
Worthington, Minnesota 56187-3099

Phone: (507) 372-3400
FAX: (507) 372-5801
E-mail: dgraber@wr.mnwest.mnscu.edu
WWW: www.mnwest.mnscu.edu

Institution Background

Minnesota West is known for its faculty of academic and technical instructors who are comfortable with new and innovative delivery technologies. Minnesota West views the Web as a mechanism for bringing people together and raising learning standards.

Founded: 1936
Type of Institution: Public
Accreditation: North Central Association of Colleges and Schools

Online Course Background: Minnesota West started with five campuses scattered over a 300-mile circumfrence, which were ideally sutuated to initiate and perfect distance learning. The school began using the Internet to enhance interactive television courses, but now uses the Web as a primary delivery platform to students of all ages.

Online Course Offered: 7

Online Students Enrolled: 119

Special Programs/Partnerships: Minnesota West has several noteworthy partnerships including collaborate distance learning projects with out-of-state professors, and software producers and distributors.

Services Offered to Students: Students enrolled in Minnesota West's online courses have access to the PALS Library system online. Online students also have free extended, hours direct phone support to their academic advisor, the financial aid office, registrar, distance learning office, and librarian.

Financial Aid: Students enrolled in online courses are eligible to apply for the same financial aid programs as traditional, on-campus students.

Individual Undergraduate Courses: Minnesota West offers online courses in accounting.

Programs

Minnesota West offers an online program of study in accounting.

MONTANA STATE UNIVERSITY-BOZEMAN

General Contact Information

108 Montana Hall
Bozeman, Montana 59717

Phone: (406) 994-4145
FAX: (406) 994-4733
E-mail: grad@montana.edu
WWW: btc.montana.edu

Online Learning Information

Burns Telecommunications Center, EPS 128
Bozeman, Montana 59717

Phone: (406) 994-6550
FAX: (406) 994-7856
E-mail: kboyce@montana.edu
WWW: btc.montana.edu

Institution Background

Montana State University-Bozeman was Montana's first state-supported institution of higher education and a land-grant college.

Founded: 1893
Type of Institution: Public
Accreditation: Northwest Association of Schools and Colleges

Online Course Background: Montana State University (MSU) began its online courses when it received a grant from the National Science Foundation in 1992 to deliver math and science courses to K-12 in-service teachers. Since then, MSU has begun offering some online graduate degree programs.

Online Course Offered: 20

Online Students Enrolled: 300

Special Programs/Partnerships: Montana State University is part of the National Science Foundation's National Teacher Enhancement Network.

Services Offered to Students: Students enrolled in online courses have access to the MSU Library on-line proxy server and technical assistance from Burns Telecommunication Center.

Financial Aid: Students may be eligible to apply for financial aid. For more information, please contact MSU Financial Aid Services at (406) 994-2845.

Registration: You can register for courses via mail, phone, e-mail, and the World Wide Web.

Programs

Mathematics Education

Degree Offered: Master of Science

Program Web Address: www.montana.edu

Online Program Started: 1997

Students Enrolled: 20

Degrees Awarded: 10

Program Background: Montana State University-Bozeman began offering courses in this mathematics program, which has been popular among students for 15 years, online in 1997. It is designed for middle school, high school, and junior college mathematics teachers. The courses are usually taught by tenured or tenure-track faculty.

Students can complete one-half to two-thirds of this program online, while the remainder of the program must be completed on-campus during summer sessions.

Application Requirements: You must have your Bachelor's degree in mathematics or a related field, and have a minimum undergraduate grade point average of 3.0 (on a 4.0 scale). You should also have teaching experience at the 5th through 14th grade levels.

Completion Requirements: You must successfully complete 30 semester hours of coursework and a final examination or Capstone project.

Time for Completion: You have up to six years to complete this program.

On Campus Requirements: You must spend at least six weeks on campus while completing this program.

System Requirements: You should have access to the Internet.

Example Course Titles: Some of the course titles in this program include The Language of Mathematics: An Advanced Perspective, Advanced Mathematical Modeling for Teachers, Statistics for Teachers, Applications of Statistics in Mathematics Classrooms, Problem Solving in the Middle Grades, Linear Algebra for Teachers, and Analysis For Teachers.

Program Contact: Dr. Maurice Burke
Department of Mathematical Sciences
Montana State University—Bozeman
Bozeman, Montana 59717-2400
(406) 994-3601
(406) 994-1789
burke@math.montana.edu

Science Education

Degree Offered: Master of Science in Science Education

Program Web Address: btc.montana.edu/nten/sciedmasters.shtml

Online Program Started: 1997

Students Enrolled: 50

Degrees Awarded: 23

Program Background: This program is designed for middle-school and high-school teachers of science, and is sponsored by the Montana State University—Bozeman colleges of Agriculture, Letters and Science, Graduate Studies, and Education, Health, and Human Development. Students can take about two-thirds of the courses and credits online, and typically can complete the degree within two or three years. The courses are divided into core courses and interdisciplinary combinations of science courses. Faculty committees made up of three people advise students and plans of study are tailored to take into account the student's background, interests, and career goals.

Application Requirements: You must have a Bachelor's degree in science, science education, or a related field, and a minimum undergraduate grade point average of 3.0 (on a 4.0 scale). You also need to be certified to teach science in grades 6 through 12, have two years of teaching experience, and submit your scores on the General Records Examination (GRE).

Completion Requirements: The program begins with a six-week summer session that you are required to attend on-campus, and ends with a two-week symposium (also on-campus). You can take the remaining courses online.

You must successfully complete 30 credit hours to earn this degree. You'll earn 15 of these credit hours in core courses, and 15 in science from two or more content areas. One of the core courses you must successfully complete is a Capstone project.

Time for Completion: While most students complete this program in two years, you have up to six years to fulfill all of the requirements for this degree.

On Campus Requirements: You are required to attend a six-week summer session when you begin this program and a two-week summer session to present your Captsone project at the end of the program. Both sessions are held on-campus.

System Requirements: You should have a personal computer running Windows 3.1 or higher, or a Macintosh running OS 7.1 or higher. You also need an Internet Service Provider. Some of the courses have other specific system requirements.

Example Course Titles: Some of the course titles in this program include Cell and Molecular Biology, Infection and Immunity, Agricultural and Medical Biotechnology, Terrestrial Ecology of Plains and Prairies, Life in Streams and Ponds, Biology of Riparian Zones and Wetlands, Critical Concepts in Chemistry, and Quantum Principles.

Program Contact: Dr. Carol Thoresen, Coordinator
Montana State University Bozeman
401 Linfield Hall
Bozeman, Montana 59717
(406) 994-1741
(406) 994-3733
thoresen@montana.edu

MONTGOMERY COUNTY COMMUNITY COLLEGE

General Contact Information

340 DeKalb Pike
Blue Bell, Pennsylvania 19422

Phone: (215) 641-6550
WWW: www.mc3.edu

Online Learning Information

340 DeKalb Pike, P.O. Box 400
Blue Bell, Pennsylvania 19422

Phone: (215) 641-6430
FAX: (215) 619-7161
E-mail: bgottfri@admin.mc3.edu
WWW: www.mc3.edu

Institution Background

Montgomery County Community College offers degrees in a variety of areas and an array of programs and services geared toward ensuring the success of its students.

Founded: 1964
Type of Institution: Public
Accreditation: Middle States Association of Colleges and Schools

Online Course Background: Montgomery County Community College's online courses are highly interactive and asynchronous discussion is an important component of all regular online courses.

Online Course Offered: 24

Online Students Enrolled: 385

Special Programs/Partnerships: Montgomery County Community College has a partnership with Temple University in business and accounting degrees. Also it is part of the Pennsylvania Virtual Community College.

Services Offered to Students: Online students have access to the school's library, tutoring center, counseling, advising, financial aid, bookstore, and business office.

Financial Aid: Students may be eligible for federal financial aid programs administered by Montgomery County Community College.

Registration: You may register for courses via mail and phone.

Programs

Accounting

Degree Offered: Associate of Science in Accounting

Program Web Address: www.mc3.edu

Online Program Started: 1999

Students Enrolled: 20

Program Background: This program is designed for students who wish to transfer to a four-year institution to complete a Bachelor's degree in accounting.

Application Requirements: Montgomery County Community College has open admissions for this program.

Completion Requirements: You must successfully complete 60 credits in a prescribed curriculum for this degree.

Time for Completion: There are no time restrictions on completion of this program.

On Campus Requirements: There are no on-campus requirements.

System Requirements: You should have a personal computer with a Pentium processor, access to the Internet, and a Web browser.

Example Course Titles: Some of the course titles in this program include Accounting I and II, Introduction to Business, Western Civilization, and English Composition.

Program Contact: Dr. Brad Gottfried
Montgomery County Community College
340 DeKalb Pike
Blue Bell, Pennsylvania 19422
(215) 641-6430
(215) 619-7161
bgottfried@mc3.edu

Business Administration

Degree Offered: Associate of Science in Business Administration

Program Web Address: www.mc3.edu

Online Program Started: 1999

Students Enrolled: 3

Program Background: This program is designed for students who wish to transfer to a four-year institution to complete a Bachelor's degree in business administration.

Application Requirements: This program has open admissions.

Completion Requirements: You must successfully complete 60 credits in prescribed courses.

On Campus Requirements: There are no on-campus requirements.

System Requirements: You should have a personal computer with a Pentium processor, access to the Internet, and a Web browser.

Example Course Titles: Some of the course titles in this program include Economics, Statistics, English Composition, Western Civilization, and Introduction to Business.

Program Contact: Dr. Brad Gottfried
Montgomery County Community College
340 DeKalb Pike
Blue Bell, Pennsylvania 19422
(215) 641-6430
(215) 619-7161
bgottfried@mc3.edu

General Studies

Degree Offered: Associate of General Studies

Program Web Address: www.mc3.edu

Online Program Started: 1998

Students Enrolled: 80

Program Background: This program is geared toward students who want a general degree that can be used in various fields and areas.

Application Requirements: Montgomery County Community College has open admissions to anyone who wants to pursue an education.

Completion Requirements: You must successfully complete 60 credits.

On Campus Requirements: There are no on-campus requirements.

System Requirements: You should have a Pentium computer, Internet access, and a Web browser.

Example Course Titles: Some of the course titles in this program include English Composition, General Psychology, and Western Civilization.

Program Contact: Dr. Brad Gottfried
340 DeKalb Pike
Blue Bell, Pennsylvania 19422
(215) 641-6430

(215) 619-7161
bgottfried@mc3.edu

NEW JERSEY INSTITUTE OF TECHNOLOGY

General Contact Information

Phone: (973) 596-3060
FAX: (973) 596-3203
E-mail: dl@adm.nijt.edu
WWW: www.njit.edu/dl

Online Learning Information

GITC Building, Suite 5600
University Heights
Newark, New Jersey 07102

Phone: (973) 596-3177
FAX: (973) 596-3203
E-mail: dl@njit.edu
WWW: www.njit.edu/dl

Institution Background

The New Jersey Institute of Technology has been recognized by Yahoo! Internet Life as America's Most Wired Public University. It serves as a national model for incorporating technologies into the educational process.

Founded: 1881
Type of Institution: Public
Accreditation: Middle States Association for Colleges and Schools, Commision on Higher Education. Also, AACSB, CSAC/CSAB, EAC of ABET, NAAB, NLNAC, TAC of ABET.

Online Course Background: New Jersey Institute of Technology offers two Bachelor's and two master's degree programs online.

Online Course Offered: about 100

Financial Aid: Students enrolled in online courses may be eligible for financial aid and should contact the Financial Aid office at (973) 596-3479.

Individual Graduate Courses: New Jersey Institute of Technology offers online courses in Web development.

Registration: You can register for courses via mail and the World Wide Web.

Programs

Computer Science

Degree Offered: Bachelor of Arts or Master of Science

Program Web Address: www.njit.edu/dl

Application Requirements: You should have a background in computer science and mathematics equivalents.

Example Course Titles: Some of the course titles in this program include Computer Architecture, Operating System Design, Data Management System Design, Data Structures and Algorithms, Computer Programming Languages, Artificial Intelligence, and Knowledge Based Systems.

Program Contact: Division of CPE
University Heights
Newark, New Jersey 07102
(973) 596-3060
(973) 596-3203
dl@njit.edu

Information Systems

Degree Offered: Bachelor of Arts or Master of Science

Program Web Address: www.njit.edu/dl

Program Background: This degree program allows you to specialize in one of the following areas: Interdisciplinary Information Systems, Management Information Systems, Electronic Enterprise Design, Multimedia Communication, Biomedical Information, Interdisciplinary Information Systems, Evaluation Methods and Tools, or Data Analysis and Modeling Tools.

Application Requirements: You should have a degree in one of the following areas in order to be sufficiently prepared for this program: information systems, computer science, computer engineering, or related fields of study that helped you develop strong computer skills.

Completion Requirements: You must successfully complete 36 credits—nine credits in core courses, three credits in other required courses, six credits in an area of specialization, and 18 credits in electives.

Example Course Titles: Some of the course titles in this program include Organizational Behavior, Quantitative Methods in Marketing, Communication Theory, Software Design and Production Methodology, Information System Principles, Object-Oriented Programming, Data Structures and Algorithms, Computer Networks, and Systems Simulation.

Program Contact: Division of CPE
University Heights
Newark, New Jersey 07102
(973) 596-3060
(973) 596-3203
dl@njit.edu

NEW SCHOOL FOR SOCIAL RESEARCH

General Contact Information

66 West 12th Street

New York, New York 10011

Phone: (212) 229-5630
FAX: (212) 989-3887
WWW: www.dialnsa.edu

Online Learning Information

66 West 12th Street
New York, New York 10011

Phone: (212) 229-5630
FAX: (212) 989-3887
E-mail: admissions@dialnsa.edu
WWW: www.dialnsa.edu

Institution Background

Founded: 1919
Accreditation: Middle States Association of Schools and Colleges

Programs

General Studies

Degree Offered: Bachelor of Arts

Program Web Address: www.dialnsa.edu/degcert3a.htm

Program Background: This program is geared toward adult students who want to complete their Bachelor's degree, but have responsibilities that prevent them from attending traditional classes. Students set their own pace of studying full- or part-time.

Application Requirements: You need to have 60 semester credits toward a Bachelor's degree from an accredited college or university to apply for this program at the New School for Social Research.

Program Contact: (212) 229-5630
admissions@dialnsa.edu

English Language Teaching

Degree Offered: Certificate

Program Web Address: www.dialnsa.edu/degcert3e.htm

Program Background: This program stresses communicative, student-centered learning and has a very practical orientation. Students are introduced to a wide variety of methods and techniques that are readily applicable to classroom teaching, and they study the theories underlying those methods.

Program Contact: admissions@dialnsa.edu

Group Practice Management

Degree Offered: Certificate

Program Web Address: www.dialnsa.edu/degcert3f.htm

Program Background: Students in this certificate program gain dynamic cutting-edge knowledge and management skills for the field of medical practice. Students increase their administration, financial, communication, and planning skills.

Program Contact: (212) 229-5462
admissions@dialnsa.edu

Media Management

Degree Offered: Certificate

Program Web Address: www.dialnsa.edu/degcert3c.htm

Program Background: Students in the Media Management Certificate program prepare for top media management jobs and responsibilities. The program integrates business and technology in media. Students can transfer the credits earned in this certificate program toward the Master's program.

On Campus Requirements: You are required to attend two-day sessions on-site in October, December, February, and April.

Program Contact: (212) 229-8903
admissions@dialnsa.edu

Media Studies

Degree Offered: Master of Arts

Program Web Address: www.dialnsa.edu/degcert3b.htm

Online Program Started: 1999

Program Background: The Master of Arts in Media Studies program integrates theoretical and practical knowledge in the field of communication technology and business. Students develop skills that are relevant to work in film, broadcasting, public relations, advertising, and digital media, as well as teaching and information sciences.

Program Contact: (212) 229-8903
admissions@dialnsa.edu

World Wide Web Page Design

Degree Offered: Certificate

Program Web Address: www.dialnsa.edu/degcert3d.htm

Program Background: This certificate is awarded to non-credit students who successfully complete a structured program in Web page design and construction.

Time for Completion: This program can generally be completed in one year.

Program Contact: (212) 229-5876
admissions@dialnsa.edu

NEW YORK INSTITUTE OF TECHNOLOGY

General Contact Information

211 Carleton Avenue
P.O. Box 9029
Central Islip, New York 11722-9029

Phone: (800) 222-NYIT
FAX: (516) 348-0299
E-mail: stan@nyit.edu
WWW: www.nyit.edu/olc

Online Learning Information

Admissions and Recruitment
On-Line Campus
P.O. Box 9029
Central Slip, New York 11722-9029

Phone: (800) 222-NYIT
FAX: (516) 348-1107
E-mail: olc@iris.nyit.edu
WWW: www.nyit.edu/olc

Institution Background

The New York Institute of Technology was founded in 1955, and is a nonsectarian and nonprofit institution of higher learning that provides a variety of programs leading to degrees at all levels from Associate's to doctoral.

Founded: 1955
Type of Institution: Proprietary
Accreditation: Middle States Association of Schools and Colleges

Online Course Background: The On-Line Campus of New York Institute of Technology (OLC/NYIT) has an innovative degree program which allows students to acquire a four-year degree entirely through Web-based computer conferencing with no campus residency required. It's a convenient and flexible alternative for people who can't attend a traditional campus because of job schedule, geography, personal commitments, or other limitations.

Online Course Offered: 110

Online Students Enrolled: 1023

Services Offered to Students: Students enrolled in online courses have access to tutoring and the New York Institute of Technology Learning Center, which provides free individual and group tutorial assistance. The Institute's library system includes a number of general, computer, and specialty library facilities at each of the school's campuses. And students can purchase textbooks online.

Financial Aid: Online students may be eligible for federal financial aid, including student loans.

Individual Undergraduate Courses: Any subject may be taken as long as the prerequisites are met.

Individual Graduate Courses: Graduate courses in Instructional Technology, Business and Engineering are available online. These courses are part of a degree program that can be completed on campus.

Registration: You can register for courses via mail.

Programs

Behavioral Science

Degree Offered: Bachelor of Science in Behavioral Sciences

Program Web Address: www.nyit.edu/olc/bsbs.html

Students Enrolled: 31

Degrees Awarded: 1

Program Background: This program prepares students for clinical, social educational, industrial or law enforcement careers.

Application Requirements: You must have your high school diploma or equivalent. You need to submit an application with a $50 application fee, copies of your standardized test scores (SAT or ACT), high school transcripts, and official transcripts from any college you've attended. If you are an international student, you must also submit a transcript evaluation.

Completion Requirements: You must successfully complete 128 credits for this degree.

On Campus Requirements: There are no on-campus requirements.

System Requirements: You need a personal computer with a 28.8 kbps modem, an Internet Service Provider, e-mail account (available from the school), a Web browser (Netscape Navigator 3.02 or higher, or Microsoft Internet Explorer 4.0 or better), a printer, and a VGA monitor. The school also strongly recommends that your computer have an audio system.

Example Course Titles: Some of the course titles in this program include Measurement Concepts, Theories of Personality, Introductory Research Methods, Organizational Psychology, Communication and Interviewing Techniques, Social Stratification, Juvenile Delinquency, Political Sociology, Physiological Basis of Behavior, and Ethics and Social Philosophy.

Program Contact: Dr. Esther Rister
New York Institute of Technology
P.O. Box 8000
Old Westbury, New York 11568
(516) 686-7505
(516) 626-6946
erister@nyit.edu

Business Administration

Degree Offered: Bachelor of Science in Business Administration

Program Web Address: www.nyit.edu/olc/bsba.html

Students Enrolled: 23

Degrees Awarded: 3

Program Background: The Business Administration degree combines core courses in business, economics, and humanities with specialized courses in management. It is intended to give students the analytical skills they need, and a firm grasp of underlying ethical issues that will enable students to be effective leaders in business.

Application Requirements: You must have a high school diploma or equivalency. You should submit an application with a $50 application fee, copies of your standardized test scores (SAT or ACT), high school transcripts, and official transcripts from any college or university you have attended. If you are an international student, you also need to submit a transcript evaluation.

Completion Requirements: You must successfully complete a total of 120 credit hours for this degree.

On Campus Requirements: There are no on-campus requirements.

System Requirements: You need a personal computer with a 28.8 kbps modem, an Internet service provider, e-mail account (available from the school), a Web browser (Netscape Navigator 3.02 or higher, or Microsoft Internet Explorer 4.0 or better), a printer, and a VGA monitor. The school also strongly recommends that your computer have an audio system.

Example Course Titles: Some of the course titles in this program include Principles of Economics I and II, Money and Banking, Managerial Accounting, Business Law I and II, Corporation Finance, Statistical Sampling Theory, Introduction to Management Information Systems, Business Organization and Adminis-

tration, Organizational Behavior, Production and Operations Management, and Business Policy Seminar.

Program Contact: Dean J.C. Spender
New York Institute of Technology
P.O. Box 8000
Old Westbury, New York 11568
(516) 686-7423
(516) 484-8328
spender@nyit.edu

Hospitality Management

Degree Offered: Bachelor of Professional Studies (BPS)

Program Background: Students in this program gain relevant insight and education in the hospitality instustry. The program is designed for students who wish to enter or advance in the industry. The coursework covers management, personnel, labor relations, accounting, and computer applications.

Application Requirements: You must have your high school diploma or equivalency, and take a standardized test (SAT or ACT). You need to submit an application with a $50 fee, high school transcripts, and official copies of your college transcripts.

Completion Requirements: You must successfully complete 120–122 credits.

System Requirements: You need a computer with e-mail access, a 28.8 modem, an Internet Service Provider, and a Web browser (Netscape Navigator 3.02 or higher, or Microfot Internet Explorer 4.0 or higher.

Example Course Titles: Some of the course titles in this program include Hospitality Management, Managerial Accounting, Financial Management for the Hospitality Industry, Hospitality Industry Marketing, Labor-

Management Relations, Law for the Hospitality Industry, Convention and Meeting Planning, Facilities Maintenance, Menu and Design and Planning, Software Applications for Hotel Management, Facilities Layout and Design, Principles of Beverage Management, Personnel Management for the Hospitality Industry, Italian Cuisine: A Survey of the Regional Specialities, Transportation, and Travel and Tourism.

Program Contact: Prof. James Turely
New York Institute of Technology
P.O. Box 9029
Central Islip, New York 11722
(516) 348-3064
(516) 348-3247
jturley@nyit.edu

Interdisciplinary Studies

Degree Offered: Bachelor of Arts (BA); Bachelor of Science (BS); Bachelor of Professional Studies

Program Web Address: www.nyit.edu/olc/is.html

Students Enrolled: 19

Degrees Awarded: 4

Program Background: This program focuses on the importance and applicability of interdisciplinary knowledge, and gives students various perspectives on the world which help them better prepare for work or graduate study.

Although all students are required to take the same core courses, the individual degree plans are different. The Bachelor of Arts requires over 90 credits in liberal arts courses, the Bachelor of Science requires 60-89 credits in liberal arts courses, and the Bachelor of Professional Studies requires 30-59 credit hours in liberal arts courses. Students in any of the degree plans can apply prior learning credit, and can transfer up to 90 credit hours toward this degree.

Application Requirements: You must have your high school diploma or equivalent. You need to submit a completed application, $50 application fee, copies of your SAT or ACT test scores, copies of you high school transcripts, and copies of any college transcripts. If you are a foreign student, you need to submit a transcript evaluation as well.

Completion Requirements: You must successfully complete 120 credit hours—39 credit hours of courses in the common core, 42 credits from electives, and a three credit hour Capstone Seminar.

On Campus Requirements: There are no on-campus requirements.

System Requirements: You need a computer with a 28.8 baud modem, an Internet Service Provider, a Web browser that supports attachments (such as Netscape Navigator 3.02 or higher or Microsoft Internet Explorer 4.0 or higher), a printer, and a VGA monitor. You also need an e-mail account, which is available from the school if you don't have one through other means.

Example Course Titles: Some of the course titles for this program include Capstone Seminar, The Art of Poetry, and Technical Writing.

Program Contact: Prof. Maggie Lehmann
New York Institute of Technology
P.O. Box 9029
Central Islip, New York 11722-9029
(800) 222-NYIT
(516) 348-3056
MLehmann@acl.nyit.edu

NEW YORK UNIVERSITY

General Contact Information

330 Shimkin Hall, 50 West 4th Street
New York, New York 10003

Phone: (212) 998-7060
FAX: (212) 995-4134
WWW: www.scps.nyu.edu

Online Learning Information

Center for Career, Education and Life Planning
330 Shimkin Hall, 50 West 4th Street
New York, New York 10003

Phone: (212) 998-7060
FAX: (212) 995-4134
E-mail: spcs.advise@nyu.edu
WWW: www.scps.nyu.edu

Institution Background

Founded: 1831
Type of Institution: Private
Accreditation: Middle States Association of Schools and Colleges

Individual Undergraduate Courses: New York University offers online courses in American literature, architecture, biochemistry, biology, business, chemistry, communication, computer programming, economics, education, English, finance, health, history, humanities, journalism, law, mathematics, media studies, music, natural science, nursing, nutrition and food studies, philosophy, physical therapy, political science, religious studies, sociology, and vocational development.

Programs

Customer Service Management for the Hospitality and Tourism Industries

Degree Offered: Certificate

Program Web Address: www.scps.nyu.edu/dyncon/hosp/degr_adva.html

Program Background: This certificate program provides students with management skills in customer service. Courses cover tourism and hospitality, and focus on good customer service relations.

Application Requirements: You must have a Bachelor's degree from an accredited undergraduate institution.

Completion Requirements: You must successfully complete four courses (three credits each).

Example Course Titles: Some of the course titles in this program include Advertising and Public Relations Campaigns, Technology for Marketing Travel, International Tourism Marketing and Sales, Database Marketing in Tourism, Destination Marketing, Destination Management, Management of Non-profit Organizations, and Sports and Events Tourism.

Program Contact: Hospitality, Tourism, and Travel Administration
48 Cooper Square, Room 103
New York, New York 10003
(212) 998-9100
(212) 995-3656
scps.hospitality@nyu.edu

Direct Marketing Communications

Degree Offered: Master of Science

Program Web Address: www.scps.nyu.edu/dyncon/dirm/mast.html

Application Requirements: You must have a Bachelor's degree from an accredited undergraduate institution. You need to submit an application, transcripts from every college you've attended, your scores on the GMAT or GRE or other standard graduate admissions test, TOEFL scores (for international students), a personal essay, and letters of recommendation.

Program Contact: Center for Direct Marketing
NYU Midtown Center
11 West 42nd Street, Room 401
New York, New York 10036
(212) 790-3221
(212) 995-3656
scps.dirmktng@nyu.edu

Hospitality and Industry Studies

Degree Offered: Master of Science

Program Web Address: www.scps.nyu.edu/
dyncon/hosp/degr_ms_i.html

Program Background: This program emphasizes the areas of knowledge needed for effective decision making by hotel entrepreneurs,
investors, financial analysts, directors of operations, directors of customer service, revenue
managers, and general managers who wish to
advance or change the direction of their careers.

Application Requirements: You must have a
Bachelor's degree from an accredited undergraduate institution.

Completion Requirements: You must successfully complete 39 points of graduate academic
credit with an average of B or better.

Program Contact: Hospitality, Tourism, and
Travel Administration
48 Cooper Square, Room 103
New York, New York 10003
(212) 998-9100
(212) 995-3656
scps.hospitality@nyu.edu

Information Technology

Degree Offered: Certificate

Program Web Address: www.scps.nyu.edu/
dyncon/inft/degr_prog_adva.html

Program Background: New York University's
Information Technologies Institute offers this
graduate program through which you can earn
an Advanced Professional Certificate (APC) in
Information Technology. The program is intended for non-technical students who need to
analyze and develop information systems for
their jobs.

Some of the courses in this program may
be used to satisfy course requirements in the
Master of Science in Management and Systems
degree program, also offered by the Information Technologies Institute.

Application Requirements: You must have a
Bachelor's degree or higher from an accredited
college or university, and good writing skills.
Admission is based on a review of your academic credentials and professional experience.
You are required to submit a completed application along with a personal statement, copies
of your college transcripts, and a $20 applica-
tion fee.

Program Restrictions: Transfer credits from
other schools are not accepted for this program.

Completion Requirements: You must complete 16 credit hours of coursework for this certificate.

Time for Completion: You have two years to
complete the requirements for the certificate.

System Requirements: You must have a Pentium PC with Windows 95, 98 or NT, the latest
version of Netscape Navigator or Internet Explorer Web browser, a 28.8 K or faster modem,
and an Internet Service Provider.

Example Course Titles: Some of the course titles in this program include Information Technology, Database Management, Network
Administration, Electronic Commerce, Systems
Auditing, Information Security, Network Analysis and Design, and Client/Server Systems.

Program Contact: Office of Admissions
New York University
School of Continuing and Professional Studies
50 West 4th Street, Room 231
New York, New York 10012

Information Technology

Degree Offered: Master of Science

Program Web Address: www.scps.nyu.edu/ dyncon/inft/degr_prog_adva.html

Program Background: This graduate program through New York University's Information Technologies Institute leads to a Master of Science in Management and Systems.

Application Requirements: You must have a Bachelor's degree or higher from an accredited college or university, and good writing skills. Admission is based on a review of your academic credentials and professional experience. You are required to submit a completed application along with a personal statement, copies of your college transcripts, and an application fee.

Completion Requirements: You must complete 40 credits of coursework for this degree. Some of the courses in the Advanced Professional Certificate in Information Technology program will fulfill requirements for this degree program. If you transfer the full 16 credits from the certificate program, you are required to complete a minimum of 24 credits of coursework in the Master's program.

System Requirements: You must have a Pentium PC with Windows 95, 98 or NT, the latest version of Netscape Navigator or Internet Explorer Web browser, a 28.8 K or faster modem, and an Internet Service Provider.

Program Contact: Office of Admissions
New York University
School of Continuing and Professional Studies
50 West 4th Street, Room 231

New York, New York 10012

Management and Systems

Degree Offered: Master of Science

Program Web Address: www.scps.nyu.edu/ dyncon/inft/degr_prog_mast.html

Application Requirements: You must have a Bachelor's degree from an accredited undergraduate institution, but it need not be in any particular field of concentration. Your undergraduate transcripts, scores on the Graduate Management Admissions Test (GMAT), personal statement, personal and work experience, and letters of recommendation will all be considered for admissions. If you're an international student, you are also required to submit your scores on the Test of English as a Foreign Language (TOEFL). Typically, successful candidates for admission score a 570 or higher on the TOEFL.

You need to complete the self-managed application and submit it to New York University's Office of Admissions. All of the supporting documents except your test scores should accompany your application in the same envelope. Your test scores should be sent directly to New York University from the Educational Testing Service. Official copies of your transcripts and your letters of recommendation should each be in a sealed envelope within your application packet.

To get a copy of the application materials, e-mail the Master of Science in Management and Systems program at scps.virtual@nyu.edu. Submit your completed application to the Office of Admissions, NYU School of Continuing and Professional Studies, 50 West 4th Street, Room 231, New York, NY 10012-1165.

Completion Requirements: You must successfully complete 36 credits of graduate education for this degree. You will select your courses from a set of required core courses and a group of electives, and you'll have a final Master's project.

Time for Completion: Typically, students complete this program within two to three years of part-time study.

On Campus Requirements: There are no on-campus requirements as all the coursework for this degree is conducted from your home or work via personal computer.

System Requirements: You must have a Pentium personal computer with Windows 95/98/NT, the latest version of Netscape Navigator or Microsoft Internet Explorer Web browser, and a 28.8 kbaud (or faster) modem. You are responsible for getting your own account with an Internet Service Provider, and the charges related to your Internet connection are not included in course tuition and fees.

Example Course Titles: Some of the course titles for this program include Quantitative Methods, Economic Analysis, Organizational Behavior, Financial Management, Marketing, Information Technology, Database Management, Network Administration, Electronic Commerce, Systems Auditing, Information Security, and Network Analysis and Design.

Program Contact: Master of Science in Management and Systems
NYU School of Continuing and Professional Studies
7 East 12th Street, 11th Floor
New York, New York 10003
(212) 995-3656
scps.virtual@nyu.edu

Management Training

Degree Offered: Certificate

Program Web Address: www.nyuonline.com/

Online Program Started: 2000

NORTH CAROLINA A&T STATE UNIVERSITY

General Contact Information

1601 East Market Street
Greensboro, North Carolina 27411

Phone: (336) 334-7946
FAX: (336) 334-7013
E-mail: uadmit@ncat.edu
WWW: www.ncat.edu

Institution Background

Founded: 1891
Type of Institution: Public
Accreditation: Southern Association of Colleges and Schools

Programs
Technology Management

Degree Offered: Doctor of Philosophy

Program Web Address: web.indstate.edu:80/tech/acadprog/grad/cphd/cphd.html

Program Background: This degree program is geared toward technologists and combines traditional doctoral research with an innovative delivery system, a consortium of universities, and advanced technical specialization. It is a collaborative program that is administered by the School of Technology at Indiana State University. Other schools that participate include Bowling Green State University, Central Connecticut State University, Central Missouri State University, East Carolina University, Eastern Michigan University, North Carolina A&T State University, Texas Southern University, and University of Wisconsin-Stout.

Application Requirements: You must apply to Indiana State University for admission to this doctoral program. You should have a Bachelor's degree from a regionally accredited college or university, a minimum undergraduate grade point average of 3.0 (on a 4.0 scale) and a minimum graduate grade point average of 3.5, two years of appropriate work experience, and a score of at least 500 on each section of the Graduate Record Examination. With your application, you should submit five letters of recommendation.

Completion Requirements: You must successfully complete a minimum of 90 semester hours of graduate study, with a majority of your coursework at the 600-level. Your program of study will be divided into five areas: Major Area of Specialization (24-30 semester hours), Internship (six semester hours), Research Core (27-33 semester hours), General Technology Core (12-18 semester hours), and Cognate Studies.

On Campus Requirements: You are required to complete two residencies for this program, but you have two options for fulfilling this requirement. You can complete two consecutive semesters at Indiana State University, or you can complete one semester at Indiana State University and one semester at the home university/consortium university where you're completing your specialization.

Example Course Titles: Some of the course titles in this program include Strategic Planning of Technological Processes, Internet Research Methods, Impacts of Technology, Legal Aspects of Industry, and Technological System, Assessment, and Innovation.

Program Contact: trived@aurora.ncat.edu

NORTHWESTERN COLLEGE

General Contact Information

1441 North Cable Road

Lima, Ohio 45805

E-mail: info@nc.edu
WWW: www.nc.edu

Online Learning Information

1441 North Cable Road
Lima, Ohio 45805

Phone: (419) 227-3141
FAX: (419) 229-6926
E-mail: info@nc.edu

Institution Background

Founded: 1920
Type of Institution: Private
Accreditation: North Central Association of Colleges and Schools

Programs

Accounting

Degree Offered: Associate

Program Web Address: www2.nc.edu/dl/accountg.html

Program Background: This program trains students in preparing financial reports, statements, cost procedures, and audit and finance for business firms. The sequence of major course offerings starts summer and fall quarters.

Completion Requirements: You must successfully complete 108 credit hours for this degree.

Example Course Titles: Some of the course titles in this program include Personal Taxes, Accounting, Payroll Accounting, Governmental Accounting, Contract Law, Introduction to Business, Written Communications, Introduction to Microcomputing, Relational Databases on Microcomputers, Interpersonal Communications, English Composition, and Advanced Composition.

Program Contact: Distance Learning Division
Northwestern College
1141 N. Cable Road
Lima, Ohio 45805
(419) 227-3141
info@nc.edu

Accounting

Degree Offered: Bachelor

Program Web Address: www2.nc.edu/dl/ac.html

Program Background: This program extends from the Associate's degree program in Accounting, and it trains students in preparing financial reports, statements, cost procedures, and audit and finance for business firms. The sequence of major course offerings starts summer and fall quarters.

Completion Requirements: You must successfully complete the Associate's degree requirements (108 credit hours) plus an additional 90 credit hours.

Example Course Titles: Some of the course titles in this program include Business Taxes, Cost Accounting II, Accounting Information Systems, Advanced Accounting I, Managerial Accounting, Auditing, Advanced Accounting II, Business Policy and Strategies, Business Law, Organizational Behavior, Management Issues, Data Processing Elective, and Ethics.

Program Contact: Distance Learning Division
Northwestern College
1141 N. Cable Road
Lima, Ohio 45805
(419) 227-3141
info@nc.edu

Administrative Assistant

Degree Offered: Associate

Program Web Address: www2.nc.edu/dl/adminast.html

Program Background: This Associate's degree program provides training in all phases of the office career. Students learn how to use document processing equipment, and business courses give the students a broad background. The sequence of major course offerings starts summer and fall quarters.

Completion Requirements: You must successfully complete 108 hours for this program.

Example Course Titles: Some of the course titles in this program include Administrative Block I, Administrative Block II, Contract Law, Introduction to Business, Written Communications, Introduction to Microcomputing, Introduction to Business Presentations and Publications, Spreadsheet Applications, and Principles of Management.

Program Contact: Distance Learning Division
Northwestern College
1141 N. Cable Road
Lima, Ohio 45805
(419) 227-3141
info@nc.edu

Agribusiness Marketing/ Management Technology

Degree Offered: Associate

Program Web Address: www2.nc.edu/dl/agmarman.html

Program Background: This program prepares students who are entering the agribusiness marketing environment, whether its in wholesale, retail, or production. Students learn the skills to operate a family farm, manage a retail agri-business supply firm, sell agricultural equipment and products, and to fill other agriculture-related positions. The sequence of major course offerings starts fall quarter.

Completion Requirements: You must successfully complete 108 hours for this degree.

Example Course Titles: Some of the course titles in this program include Payroll Accounting, Introduction to Agribusiness, Agribusiness Terminology and Measurements, Farm Management and Financial Records, Economics and Agribusiness, Agribusiness Non-Farm Management, Agricultural Marketing, Personal/Agribusiness Finances and Credit, Agronomy, Animal Sciences, Contract Law, and Introduction to Microcomputing.

Program Contact: Distance Learning Division
Northwestern College
1141 N. Cable Road
Lima, Ohio 45805
(419) 227-3141
info@nc.edu

Automotive Management

Degree Offered: Associate

Program Web Address: www2.nc.edu/dl/automan.html

Program Background: This program prepares students for positions in automotive aftermarket environments, with an emphasis on management skills.

Completion Requirements: You must successfully complete 108 hours for this degree.

Example Course Titles: Some of the course titles in this program include Accounting I, Accounting II, Professional Selling, Contract Law, International Business, Written Communications, Introduction to Microcomputing, Computers and Society, Spreadsheet Applications, Principles of Management, Computer-Assisted Management, Introduction to the Automotive Industry, and Parts and Service Management.

Program Contact: Distance Learning Division
Northwestern College
1141 N. Cable Road
Lima, Ohio 45805
(419) 227-3141
info@nc.edu

Business Administration

Degree Offered: Associate

Program Web Address: www2.nc.edu/dl/busadmin.html

Completion Requirements: You must successfully complete 108 hours for this degree.

Example Course Titles: Some of the course titles in this program include Accounting I, Accounting II, Personal Taxes, Professional Selling, Contract Law, Introduction to Business, International Business I, Written Communications, Introduction to Microcomputing, Computers and Society, Introduction to Business Presentations and Publications, Spreadsheet Applications, Principles of Management, Small Business Management, Retail Management, Human Resources Management, Business Math, Advertising, Marketing I, Interviewing and Employment Skills, and Beginning Keyboarding.

Program Contact: Distance Learning Division
Northwestern College
1141 N. Cable Road
Lima, Ohio 45805
(419) 227-3141
info@nc.edu

Business Administration

Degree Offered: Bachelor

Program Web Address: www2.nc.edu/dl/ba.html

Program Background: This program trains students for a wide range of entry-level positions in the service, banking and manufacturing industries, as well as in small businesses.

Completion Requirements: You must successfully complete 90 credit hours for this degree.

Example Course Titles: Some of the course titles in this program include Business Policy and Strategies, Business Law, Seminar in Business, Practicum in Business, Introduction to Information Systems, Corporate Finance, Current Topics in Management, Organizational Behavior, Human Resources Management II, Information Management, Entrepreneurship, Strategic Management, and International Marketing.

Program Contact: Distance Learning Division
Northwestern College
1141 N. Cable Road
Lima, Ohio 45805
(419) 227-3141
info@nc.edu

Computer Technology

Degree Offered: Associate

Program Web Address: www2.nc.edu/dl/comptech.html

Program Background: This program focuses on hands-on experience on the microcomputer and minicomputer. Students learn to use many kinds of software that were developed for business applications.

Completion Requirements: You must successfully complete 108 hours.

Example Course Titles: Some of the course titles in this program include Accounting, Payroll Accounting, Introduction to Business, Written Communications, Introduction to Microcomputing, Document Processing with Microcomputers, Programming Microcomputers Using BASIC, Relational Databases on the Microcomputer, Introduction to Computer-Based Systems, COBOL, Relational Database Pro-

gramming, Microcomputer Operating Systems, Programming in C, Spreadsheet Applications, Advanced Spreadsheet Applications, Advanced Data Processing Concepts, Business Math, and Computer Math and Logic.

Program Contact: Distance Learning Division
Northwestern College
1141 N. Cable Road
Lima, Ohio 45805
(419) 227-3141
info@nc.edu

Health Care Management

Degree Offered: Bachelor

Program Web Address: www2.nc.edu/dl/hc.html

Application Requirements: This is a completion program so students must have an Associate's degree in the health or medical field, or a related field. Students enter the program with status as juniors, and must complete coursework for an additionally two years to earn the degree.

Completion Requirements: You must successfully complete 90 credit hours.

Program Contact: Distance Learning Division
Northwestern College
1141 N. Cable Road
Lima, Ohio 45805
(419) 227-3141
info@nc.edu

Legal Assisting

Degree Offered: Associate

Program Web Address: www2.nc.edu/dl/legalast.html

Program Background: This program trains paralegals to aid the legal community. Students gain general background knowledge as well through business courses that the program offers. The sequence of major courses begins in the fall quarter.

Completion Requirements: You must successfully complete 108 credit hours for this degree.

Example Course Titles: Some of the course titles for this program include Accounting, Personal Taxes, Introduction to Business, Business Law, Written Communications, Introduction to Microcomputing, Introduction to the Legal System, Litigation, Probate Administration, and Legal Research.

Program Contact: Distance Learning Division
Northwestern College
1141 N. Cable Road
Lima, Ohio 45805
(419) 227-3141
info@nc.edu

Legal Secretarial

Degree Offered: Associate

Program Web Address: www2.nc.edu/dl/lsnoteop.html

Program Background: This program is designed to prepare students for a career as a legal secretary. Courses focus on general secretarial skills, using computers, and business. Students may choose to participate in the professional practice option that gives practical experience.

Completion Requirements: You must successfully complete 108 credit hours for this degree.

Example Course Titles: Some of the course titles in this program include Contract Law, Introduction to Business, Written Communications, Introduction to Microcomputing, Computers and Society, Introduction to Business Presentations and Publications, Spreadsheet Applications, Notehand Theory, Notehand Dictation, and Notehand Transcription.

Program Contact: Distance Learning Division

Northwestern College
1141 N. Cable Road
Lima, Ohio 45805
(419) 227-3141
info@nc.edu

Marketing

Degree Offered: Associate

Program Web Address: www2.nc.edu/dl/marktg.html

Program Background: This Associate's degree program prepares students for marketing positions in retail, wholesale, or manufacturing fields.

Completion Requirements: You must successfully complete 108 credit hours for this degree.

Example Course Titles: Some of the course titles for this program include Personal Taxes, Professional Selling, Contract Law, Introduction to Business, Written Communications, Computers and Society, Principles of Management, and Human Resources Management.

Program Contact: Distance Learning Division
Northwestern College
1141 N. Cable Road
Lima, Ohio 45805
(419) 227-3141
info@nc.edu

Medical Secretarial

Degree Offered: Associate

Program Web Address: www2.nc.edu/dl/msnoteop.html

Program Background: This program prepares students for jobs in the medical secretarial field. Students learn to use computers and notehand. Students can also get on-the-job experience, and a general understanding of business practices.

Completion Requirements: You must successfully complete 108 credit hours for this degree.

Example Course Titles: Some of the course titles in this program include Contract Law, Introduction to Business, Computers and Society, Principles of Management, Medical Terminology, Notehand Theory, Notehand Dictation, Interviewing and Employment Skills, Word Processing, Basic English, Psychology, and Interpersonal Communications.

Program Contact: Distance Learning Division
Northwestern College
1141 N. Cable Road
Lima, Ohio 45805
(419) 227-3141
info@nc.edu

Medical Technology

Degree Offered: Associate

Program Web Address: www2.nc.edu/dl/medastec.html

Completion Requirements: You must successfully complete 108 credit hours for this degree.

Example Course Titles: Some of the course titles in this program include Contract Law, Introduction to Business, Written Communications, Introduction to Microcomputing, Computers and Society, Business Math, Medical Terminology, Anatomy and Physiology, and Records Management.

Program Contact: Distance Learning Division
Northwestern College
1141 N. Cable Road
Lima, Ohio 45805
(419) 227-3141
info@nc.edu

Pharmacy Assistant Technology

Degree Offered: Associate

Program Web Address: www2.nc.edu/dl/pharmtec.html

Program Background: This program trains students to serve as pharmacy technicians who assist registered pharmacists in their duties. Students admitted to the program must have proof of their immunizations on file with Northwestern College. The sequence of major courses begins in the fall quarter and some have prerequisites.

Completion Requirements: You must successfully complete 108 credit hours.

Example Course Titles: Some of the course titles in this program include Introduction to Microcomputing, Principles of Management, Medical Terminology, Pharmacy Experience, Dosage/Measurements, Pharmacy Practice, and Pathophysiology, Pharmacology, and Therapeutics.

Program Contact: Distance Learning Division
Northwestern College
1141 N. Cable Road
Lima, Ohio 45805
(419) 227-3141
info@nc.edu

Travel Management

Degree Offered: Associate

Program Web Address: www2.nc.edu/dl/travlmgt.html

Program Background: This program prepares graduates for careers in the travel industry. A Caribbean cruise is an integral part of this curriculum. The sequence of major courses begins fall quarter.

Completion Requirements: You must successfully complete 108 hours for this degree.

Example Course Titles: Some of the course titles in this program include Professional Selling, Contract Law, Introduction to Business, Written Communications, Introduction to Microcomputing, Computerized Reservations, Computers and Society, Spreadsheet Applications, and Principles of Management.

Program Contact: Distance Learning Division Northwestern College
1141 N. Cable Road
Lima, Ohio 45805
(419) 227-3141
info@nc.edu

Word Processing Administrative Support

Degree Offered: Associate

Program Web Address: www2.nc.edu/dl/wordpros.html

Program Background: This program prepares students for positions as administrative assistants in document processing. Students learn about document processing concepts and management theories, as well as receiving extensive computer training.

Completion Requirements: You must successfully complete 108 hours for this degree.

Example Course Titles: Some of the course titles for this program include Contract Law, Introduction to Business, Written Communications, Introduction to Microcomputing, Programming Microcomputers Using BASIC, Computers and Society, and Introduction to Business Presentations and Publications.

Program Contact: Distance Learning Division Northwestern College
1141 N. Cable Road
Lima, Ohio 45805
(419) 227-3141
info@nc.edu

NORWICH UNIVERSITY

General Contact Information

65 South Main Street

Northfield, Vermont 05663

Phone: (802) 485-2002
FAX: (802) 485-2032
E-mail: nuadm@norwich.edu
WWW: www.norwich.edu

Institution Background

Founded: 1819
Type of Institution: Private
Accreditation: New England Association of Schools and Colleges

Financial Aid: Students enrolled in online courses may be eligible for federal financial aid and those from Vermont may be eligible for all forms of federal financial aid that are available for attendance at New College. You should contact the Financial Aid office at 1-800-336-6794, extension 2.

Programs

Humanities and Social Sciences

Degree Offered: Master of Arts

Program Web Address: www.norwich.edu/vermontcollege/gradolpage.html

Program Background: Norwich University's graduate program allows adults with families and careers to earn a Master of Arts degree with concentrations in the Humanities and Social Sciences. Students design their own program of study under the guidance of experienced faculty advisors. These individualized studies build on academic, work, and life experiences.

The Graduate Program is designed to meet the unique needs of non-traditional students, and flexible scheduling allows students to maintain work and family responsibilities without compromising the quality of education. Depending on the number of credits that a student is seeking, degrees can be completed in as few as 18 months.

The Online Option of the Graduate Program replaces regional or weekend meetings with collaborative work conducted online in an asynchronous format. The range of possible study areas is the same for Online Option students as it is for students in other Graduate Program options, with the exception of preparing for a professional license (such as counseling psychology studies).

Application Requirements: You should apply for admission in advance of the date on which you would like to enroll. The Admissions Committee reviews applications monthly. You must have earned a Bachelor's degree from a regionally accredited U.S. institution, or a Bachelor's degree from a school in an English-speaking country outside the United States. You must submit your transcript for evaluation and approval by Norwich University's registrar. If you have a Bachelor's degree from a college in a non-English speaking country, your transcript must be evaluated and approved by the Educational Credential Evaluators, Inc. in Milwaukee, Wisconsin. You may be required to take the Test of English as a Foreign Language (TOEFL) examination to demonstrate competency in English.

In addition to submitting your transcript(s), you should submit any other proof of your academic achievements and/or relevant post-graduate experience that would indicate your potential for success in this program. You should include evidence of your ability to organize a program integrating theory and practice, such as a preliminary study plan, and of your knowledge of community resources. You also must submit letters of recommendation from people who know you both academically and professionally.

For more information about application requirements and procedures, please contact an Admissions Counselor through email (vcad-mis@norwich.edu) or by phone (1-800-336-6794). The school will supply sample study proposals and discuss them with you in detail to help you better understand the requirements for admissions.

Program Restrictions: You must demonstrate competency in English and may be asked to take a TOEFL examination.

Completion Requirements: You must complete 36 credit hours and complete a substantial scholarly paper, not unlike the thesis in most graduate programs. Typically, students produce the scholarly paper during the final six months of their studies. This document demonstrates the student's knowledge of the scholarly literature and professional practice in his/her field of study.

On Campus Requirements: Students enrolled in the Online Option in the Graduate Program are required to attend one five-day colloquium on the Montpelier, Vermont campus in the month of their enrollment. There are only two enrollment dates each year for students in the Online Option: April and October.

Program Contact: Graduate Admissions
Vermont College of Norwich University
Montpelier, Vermont 05602
(800) 336-6794
(802) 828-8855
jamesg@norwich.edu

Liberal Studies

Degree Offered: Bachelor of Arts

Program Web Address: www.norwich.edu/newcollege/

Online Program Started: 1997

Program Background: This degree program prepares students for many entry-level jobs and/or for graduate and professional studies. Students enrolled in the program design their own individualized plan for their area of concentration and all students attend traditional liberal arts seminars. Areas of concentration, include American Studies, Anthropology, Art History, Cultural Studies, English, Environmental Studies, Film and Culture, Gender Studies, History, Literature and Writing, Multimedia Studies, Philosophy, Playwriting and the Theatre, Political Science, Psychology, Religion, and Sociology.

Application Requirements: You must have a high school diploma or GED and you need to attend a Learning Assessment Seminar, which is held in Vermont and online, to see if this is the program and school for you. If you decide to apply, you need to submit proof of your high school diploma or GED, transcripts for any college or university you've attended, copies of your SAT or ACT scores (recommended but not required), and evidence of your potential as a student in this program. This includes writing samples that show you can write clearly and effectively, as well as think critically.

You can transfer credit from regionally accredited colleges and universities that you've attended in the past for courses in which you earned a C− or higher.

Completion Requirements: You must successfully complete 120 credit hours overall. You must earn at least 60 of the 120 through Norwich. You must attend each residency and its activities while enrolled at Norwich, as well as enroll full-time (12 to 15 credits per semester).

On Campus Requirements: You're required to begin each semester with a two-week residency on campus in Vermont during which you'll attend lectures, film screenings, and other activities. This enables you to build connections with other students and the faculty that you can foster electronically throughout the rest of the semester. The spring semester ends with a five-day residency in June during which students make presentations to their study groups.

Program Contact: (800) 336-6794

mjason@norwich.edu

Social Sciences

Degree Offered: Master of Arts

Program Web Address: www.norwich.edu/ vermontcollege/gradolpage.html

Program Background: This program allows adults with families and careers to pursue a master's degree without disrupting their entire way of life. Students design their own program of study under the guidance of faculty advisors. The individualized study plans build on academic, work, and life experiences, as well as goals and interests.

Application Requirements: You must have a Bachelor's degree from a regionally accredited college or university or from a school in an English-speaking country outside the United States. If you're an international student whose native language is not English, you may be asked to take the Test of English as a Foreign Language (TOEFL).

You need to submit an application, official transcripts from any college or university you've attended, evidence of your academic achievements, evidence of your ability to organize a susbstantial, credible program of graduate study, and three letters or recommendation.

Completion Requirements: You must successfully complete 36 credit hours and a final document.

On Campus Requirements: You are required to attend one five-day colloquium on-campus in Montpelier, Vermont during the month of your initial enrollment (April or October).

Program Contact: Graduate Admissions Vermont College of Norwich University Montpelier, Vermont 05602 (800) 336-6794 (802) 828-8855 jamesg@norwich.edu

NOVA SOUTHEASTERN UNIVERSITY

General Contact Information

3100 SW 9th Avenue
Fort Lauderdale, Florida 33315

Phone: (800) 986-2247 ext. 2000
FAX: (954) 262-3915
E-mail: scisinfo@scis.nova.edu
WWW: www.scis.nova.edu

Online Learning Information

3100 Southwest Ninth Avenue
Fort Lauderdale, Florida 33315

Phone: (800) 986-2247 ext. 2000
FAX: (954) 262-3872
E-mail: scisinfo@scis.nova.edu

Institution Background

Founded: 1964
Type of Institution: Private
Accreditation: Southern Association of Colleges and Schools

Programs

Computer Information Systems

Degree Offered: Master of Science, Doctor of Philosophy

Program Web Address: www.scis.nova.edu

Program Background: The graduate program in computer information systems focuses on technological foundations, including the areas of database systems, human-computer interaction, data and computer communications, computer security, computer graphics, software engineering, and object-orientation. The program blends theory and practice into a learning experience that enables students to develop skills that are applicable to complex real-world problems.

Application Requirements: You must have an appropriate degree from an accredited institution. You need to submit an application with a fee, official transcripts from any college you've attended, three letters of recommendation, a comprehensive portfolio or GRE score, proof of your proficiency in English language, and a 500 word essay.

Program Restrictions: This program is restricted to students with majors in computer science, information systems, engineering, mathematics, or physics. Applicants must have knowledge of data structures and algorithms, assembly language and computer architecture, and structured programming in a modern high-level language.

Completion Requirements: You must successfully complete 36 credit hours for the Master's degree or 64 credit hours for the doctoral degree. Any prerequisite credit hours are in addition to degree program credit hours.

Time for Completion: You have up to five years to complete the Master's program, or seven years to complete the doctoral program.

On Campus Requirements: There are no on-campus requirements for the Master's program. Students in the doctoral program are required to attend four cluster sessions per year. These sessions are held quarterly over an extended weekend at the university during the first two years of the program. Cluster sessions are held in September, December, March, and June.

System Requirements: You should have a personal computer with a modem and Internet access.

Example Course Titles: Some of the course titles in this program include Survey of Programming Languages, Operating Systems Concepts, Information Systems, Computer Graphics, Database Systems, Software Engineering, Data Communications Networks, Object-Oriented Applications, Client-Server Computing, Artificial Intelligence and Expert Systems, Decision Support Systems, Human-Computer Interaction, Data Communications and Computer Networking, Database Systems, Artificial Intelligence and Expert Systems, Software Engineering, Multimedia Systems, and Client-Server Computing.

Program Contact: Admissions Office
NSU School of Computer and Information
Sciences
P.O. Box 290600
Ft. Lauderdale, Florida 33329-0600
(800) 986-2247
(954) 262-3915
scisinfo@scis.nova.edu

Computer Science

Degree Offered: Master of Science, Doctor of Philosophy

Program Web Address: www.scis.nova.edu

Program Background: This program is designed to give students a thorough knowledge of the computer science field and a foundation for future professional growth. The program integrates theory and practice into a learning experience that develops skills applicable to complex real-world problems.

Application Requirements: You should have an appropriate degree from an accredited institution. You need to submit an application and fee, official transcripts for any college courses you've taken, three letters of recommendation, a comprehensive portfolio or GRE score, proof of your proficiency in English language, and a 500 word essay.

Program Restrictions: This program is designed for students with majors in computer science, engineering, mathematics, or physics, and who have completed courses in data structures and algorithms, assembly language, computer architecture, structured programming in a high-level language, system software compilers or operating systems), calculus (differential and integral calculus), and discrete mathematics.

Completion Requirements: You must successfully complete 36 credit hours for the Master's degree and 64 credit hours for the doctoral degree.

Time for Completion: You have up to five years to complete the Master's degree, or seven years to complete a doctorate.

On Campus Requirements: There are no on-campus requirements for the Master's program. Doctoral students are required to attend four cluster sessions per year, which are held quarterly over an extended weekend at the university during the first two years of their programs. Cluster sessions are held in September, December, March, and June.

System Requirements: You should have a computer with a modem and an Internet Service Provider.

Example Course Titles: Some of the course titles in this program include—Programming Languages, Design and Analysis of Algorithms, Compiler Design Theory, Operating Systems Theory and Design, Data Communications Networks, Database Management Systems, Client-Server Computing, Artificial Intelligence, Software Engineering, Theory and Principles of Programming, Operating Systems, Data Communications and Computer Networking, Database Management Systems, Artificial Intelligence, Software Engineering, Computer Graphics, Human-Computer Interaction, and Knowledge Discovery in Databases.

Program Contact: Admissions Office
NSU School of Computer and Information
Sciences
P.O. Box 290600
Ft. Lauderdale, Florida 33329-0600
(800) 986-2247
(954) 262-3915
scisinfo@scis.nova.edu

Computing Technology in Education

Degree Offered: Master of Science, Doctor of Education, Doctor of Philosophy

Program Web Address: www.scis.nova.edu

Program Background: This program leads to advanced graduate degrees in computing technology in education, and is designed to meet the needs of professionals such as teachers, educational administrators, and trainers working in either the public or private sector. The program integrates theory and practice, and helps students develop skills that are applicable to complex real-world problems.

Application Requirements: You should have an appropriate degree from an accredited institution. You need to submit an application and fee, official transcripts for any college courses you've taken, three letters of recommendation, a comprehensive portfolio or GRE score, proof of your proficiency in English language, and a 500 word essay.

Program Restrictions: This program is restricted to students with majors in education, training and learning, instructional design, information systems, or educational leadership, and who have extensive experience with computer applications and the Internet.

Completion Requirements: You must successfully complete 36 credit hours for the Master's degree or 64 credit hours for the doctoral degree. Any prerequisite credit hours are in addition to degree program credit hours.

Time for Completion: You have up to five years to complete the Master's degree, or seven years to complete a doctorate.

On Campus Requirements: There are no on-campus requirements for the Master's program. Doctoral students are required to attend four cluster sessions per year, which are held quarterly over an extended weekend at the university during the first two years of their programs. Cluster sessions are held in September, December, March, and June.

System Requirements: You should have a computer with a modem and an Internet Service Provider.

Program Contact: Admissions Office
NSU School of Computer and Information
Sciences
PO Box 290600
Ft. Lauderdale, Florida 33329-0600
(800) 986-2247
(954) 262-3915
scisinfo@scis.nova.edu

OHIO UNIVERSITY

General Contact Information

120 Chubb Hall
Athens, Ohio 45701-2979

E-mail: uadmiss1@ohiou.edu
WWW: www.ohiou.edu

Online Learning Information

302 Tupper Hall
Athens, Ohio 45701

Phone: (800) 444-2910
FAX: (740) 593-2901
E-mail: indstudy@ouvaxa.cats.ohiou.edu

Institution Background

Founded: 1804
Type of Institution: Public
Accreditation: North Central Association of Colleges and Schools

Programs

Associate of Arts

Degree Offered: Associate of Arts

Program Web Address: www.ohiou.edu/ adultlearning/PROSPECTIVE/degrees.htm

Program Background: The Associate of Arts is a general studies degree and is an excellent stepping stone towards the Bachelor's degree.

Application Requirements: You need to submit an application, which you can get out of the External Student Program brochure. The program has a rolling admission, meaning you can start any time throughout the year. Along with your application, you need to submit official transcripts from each institution you have previously attended.

Program Contact: External Student Program
Tupper Hall 301
Ohio University
Athens, Ohio 45701
(800) 444-2420
(740) 593-0452
external.student@ohio.edu

Associate of Individualized Studies

Degree Offered: Associate of Individualized Studies

Program Web Address: www.ohiou.edu/ adultlearning/PROSPECTIVE/degrees.htm

Program Background: This program allows students to design their own program of study to meet particular goals.

Application Requirements: You need to submit an application, which you can get out of the External Student Program brochure. The program has a rolling admission, meaning you can start any time throughout the year. Along with your application, you need to submit official transcripts from each institution you have previously attended.

Program Contact: External Student Program
Tupper Hall 301
Ohio University
Athens, Ohio 45701
(800) 444-2420
(740) 593-0452
external.student@ohio.edu

Associate of Science

Degree Offered: Associate of Science

Program Web Address: www.ohiou.edu/ adultlearning/PROSPECTIVE/degrees.htm

Program Background: This is a general studies degree that emphasizes the sciences. It is designed to prepare students for studies toward a Bachelor's degree. Students can complete all of the general education requirements toward a Bachelor's while still completing quite a few electives in a variety of areas.

Application Requirements: You need to submit an application, which you can get out of the External Student Program brochure. The program has a rolling admission, meaning you can start any time throughout the year. Along with your application, you need to submit official transcripts from each institution you have previously attended.

Program Contact: External Student Program
Tupper Hall 301
Ohio University

Athens, Ohio 45701
(800) 444-2420
(740) 593-0452
external.student@ohio.edu

Specialized Studies

Degree Offered: Bachelor of Specialized Studies

Program Web Address: www.ohiou.edu/ adultlearning/PROSPECTIVE/degrees.htm

Program Background: This program gives students the opportunity to design an area of concentration that is equivalent to an established major. Students also can combine available courses to create a unique field of study.

Program Restrictions: The degree cannot duplicate an established major program at Ohio University. Additionally, this program is not well suited for a scientific, technical, or professional education degree. Areas like education and accounting have a variety of state licensing or professional certification requirements that cannot be met through this program. Areas like engineering and computer science require many technical courses that are not available through the program.

Program Contact: External Student Program
Tupper Hall 301
Ohio University
Athens, Ohio 45701
(800) 444-2420
(740) 593-0452
external.student@ohio.edu

OKLAHOMA STATE UNIVERSITY

General Contact Information

470 Student Union
Stillwater, Oklahoma 74078

Phone: (405) 744-6700
FAX: (405) 744-7793
E-mail: ext-dl@okstate.edu
WWW: distancelearning.okstate.edu

Online Learning Information

470 Student Union
Stillwater, Oklahoma 74078

Phone: (405) 744-6390
FAX: (405) 744-7793
E-mail: ics-inf@okway.okstate.edu

Institution Background

Oklahoma State University has distance learning programs that allow qualified adult students to earn their degrees entirely off-campus from anywhere in the world.

Founded: 1890
Type of Institution: Public
Accreditation: North Central Association of Colleges and Schools

Online Course Background: Online courses by Oklahoma State University are typically delivered asynchronously using Lotus LearningSpace for text-based courses and RealPlayer for video streamed courses. Some courses utilize CD-ROM with online supplements.

Online Course Offered: 25

Online Students Enrolled: 400

Special Programs/Partnerships: Oklahoma State University is a partner in the National Technological University, the A*DEC (agricultural) consortium and the Association for Media-based Continuing Education for Engineers. Also, Oklahoma State University cooperates with a number of international groups to deliver distance education.

Services Offered to Students: Students enrolled in online courses have access to all necessary student services needed to complete course and degree requirements.

Financial Aid: Online students may be eligible for the same financial aid programs as full-time, traditional students. Students enrolled only part-time students may receive company or organization tuition assistance.

Programs

Engineering and Technology Management

Degree Offered: Master of Science in Engineering and Technology Management

Program Web Address: www2.okstate.edu/msetm/home.html

Online Program Started: 1998

Students Enrolled: 50

Program Background: The Master of Science in Engineering and Technology Management is a multi-disciplinary degree integrating engineering, business, and computer science. All of the students in the program are working professionals taking courses from a distance.

On Campus Requirements: There are no on-campus requirements.

Example Course Titles: Some of the course titles in this program include Technology Strategy Development, Project Management, Change Management, Quality Control, Cost Control and Financial Accounting, Global Marketing and Manufacturing, and New Product Planning and Development.

Program Contact: Dr. Ken Case
322 Engineering North
Stillwater, Oklahoma 74078
(405) 744-6055
(405) 744-6187
iem-etm@okstate.edu

Telecommunications Management

Degree Offered: Master of Science in Telecommunications Management

Program Web Address: www.mstm.okstate.edu

Online Program Started: 1997

Students Enrolled: 180

Degrees Awarded: 20

Program Background: This program is designed for working professionals in telecommunications fields. It integrates coursework in business, engineering, and computer science.

On Campus Requirements: You are required to attend one week of laboratory experiences on campus.

Example Course Titles: Some of the course titles for this program include Telecommunications Systems, International Telecommunications, Network Design and Management, Industry Overview and Telecommunications Applications, and Telecommunications Analysis, Planning, and Design.

Program Contact: Ms. Cathy Shuffield
102 Gundersen
Stillwater, Oklahoma 74078
(405) 744-9000
(405) 744-7474
mstm-osu@okstate.edu

PENNSYLVANIA STATE UNIVERSITY, UNIVERSITY PARK CAMPUS

General Contact Information

201 Shields Building, Box 3000
University Park, Pennsylvania 16802

Phone: (814) 865-5471
FAX: (814) 863-7590
E-mail: admissions@psu.edu
WWW: www.outreach.psu.edu

Online Learning Information

Department of Distance Education
207 Mitchell Building
University Park, Pennsylvania 16802

Phone: (800) 252-3592
FAX: (814) 865-3290
E-mail: psude@cde.psu.edu

Institution Background

Founded: 1855
Type of Institution: Public
Accreditation: Middle States Association of Colleges and Schools

Individual Graduate Courses: Pennsylvania State University offers online courses in architecture and engineering.

Programs

Adult Education

Degree Offered: Master of Education

Program Web Address: www.worldcampus. psu.edu/pub/adm/facts/adted_facts.shtm

Program Background: This degree program focuses on how to help adults build on their existing knowledge to allow them to continue to learn in a purposeful way. This learning may take place individually, in groups, or in community settings.

Application Requirements: You should complete and submit an application to the Graduate School. Along with your application, you need to include an application fee of $40, your scores on the Graduate Record Examination (GRE) or Miller Analogies Test (MAT), two of-ficial transcripts from each school you've attended, a statement of purpose outlining your objectives, three letters of recommendation, and writing samples. If you're an international student, you must also submit your test scores on the Test of English as a Foreign Language (TOEFL). You must have at least a 550 on the paper test or a 213 on the computer-based test for admission.

Completion Requirements: You must successfully complete 33 credit hours for this degree.

System Requirements: You should have a personal computer with 100 MHz (or faster) or a Macintosh 8.1, Windows 95/98/NT, 32 MB RAM, 100 MB free disk space, Netscape 4.0 (or higher) or Microsoft Internet Explorer 4.0 or higher (Java and Javascript must be enabled), a 28.8 kbps modem, CD-ROM drive, sound card, and printer.

Example Course Titles: Some of the course titles in this program include Introduction to Adult Education, Research and Evaluation in Adult Education, Introduction to Distance Education, The Teaching of Adults, Program Planning in Adult Education, Historical and Social Issues in Adult Education, and Professional Seminar: Research and Adult Education.

Program Contact: World Campus
The Pennsylvania State University
207 Mitchell Building
University Park, Pennsylvania 16802-3601
(800) 252-3592
(814) 865-3290
psuwd@psu.edu

Basic Supervisory Leadership

Degree Offered: Certificate

Program Web Address: www.worldcampus. psu.edu/pub/programs/mdev/index.shtm

Program Background: This Basic Supervisory Leadership Certificate program is designed for busy professionals who need to develop or fine-tune their leadership skills. Its goal is to teach communication, project management, and leadership techniques needed to succeed in the workplace.

Completion Requirements: You must successfully complete six courses for the certificate.

Example Course Titles: Some of the course titles in this program include Supervisory Roles, Responsibilities, and Relationships, Performance Management, and Solving Problems and Managing Priorities.

Program Contact: World Campus
The Pennsylvania State University
207 Mitchell Building
University Park, Pennsylvania 16802-3601
(800) 252-3592
(814) 865-3290
psuwd@psu.edu

Chemical Dependency Counselor

Degree Offered: Certificate

Program Web Address: www.worldcampus.psu.edu/pub/adm/facts/chemdep_facts.s

Program Background: This program places a strong emphasis on applying knowledge to problems and practices in the fields of chemical dependency treatment, intervention, and prevention. It is designed for counselors. This program leads to a Penn State Certificate and may be a step toward professional certification, licensing, or further academic study.

Completion Requirements: You must successfully complete 18 credits for this certificate.

System Requirements: You should have a personal computer with a 100 MHz processor with Windows 95/98/NT or a Macintosh System 8.1, 32 MB of RAM, 100 MB free disk space, a Web browser (Netscape 4.0 or higher, or Mi-crosoft Internet Explorer 4.0 or higher) with Java and Javascript enabled, a 28.8 kbps or higher speed modem, a printer, a CD-ROM drive, a sound card and speakers, and a 14″ Monitor (800 x 600 resolution). You also need access to a video tape player.

Example Course Titles: Some of the course titles in this program include Foundations of Chemical Dependency Counseling, Foundations of Guidance and Counseling Processes, Interpersonal Relationships and AOD Dependency, Chemical Dependency: Youth at Risk, Dual Disorders, and Trends and Issues.

Program Contact: World Campus
The Pennsylvania State University
207 Mitchell Building
University Park, Pennsylvania 16802-3601
(800) 252-3592
(814) 865-3290
psuwd@psu.edu

Customer Relationship Management

Degree Offered: Certificate

Program Web Address: www.worldcampus.psu.edu/pub/programs/cusrel/index.shtm

Program Background: This program is designed for today's busy professionals who need to initiate and maintain contact with important clients. Students learn communication and decision-making skills.

Completion Requirements: You must successfully complete 11 credits.

Example Course Titles: Some of the course titles in this program include The Role of Customer Service in the Context of Business, Contemporary American Marketing, Customer Contact, Effective Speech, Introduction to Business Information, and Microcomputer Application in Business Statistics.

Program Contact: World Campus
The Pennsylvania State University
207 Mitchell Building
University Park, Pennsylvania 16802-3601
(800) 252-3592
(814) 865-3290
psuwd@psu.edu

Dietary Manager

Degree Offered: Certificate

Program Web Address: www.hrrm.psu.edu/
dpde/dm.htm

Program Background: Students in this program gain training to become dietary managers. The program is approved by the Dietary Managers Association. Students learn skills to supervise food service personnel, oversee food and kitchen resources, manage food production and service, implement nutrition care plans, utilize a computer to manage food service resources, and be a vital member of the dietetic health care team.

Application Requirements: You must have a high school diploma or equivalent, be employed in an approved hospital or nursing home at least 15 hours a week, have access to a computer for some classes, and work under the supervision of a registered dietitian (called your proctor).

Completion Requirements: You must successfully complete 15 to 18 credits.

Example Course Titles: Some of the course titles in this program include Introduction to Dietary Management, Human Resource Management in Food Service, Operations, Principles of Quantity Food Production, Management and Analysis of Quantity Food Production, and Diet Therapy and Nutrition Care in Disease.

Program Contact: World Campus
The Pennsylvania State University

207 Mitchell Building
University Park, Pennsylvania 16802-3601
(800) 252-3592
(814) 865-3290
dpde@psu.edu

Dietetic Technician

Degree Offered: Associate

Program Web Address: www.hrrm.psu.edu/
dpde/dtmore.htm

Program Background: This program prepares students for careers in dietetics. Students gain knowledge and skills in nutrition screening and assessment, providing nutrition care to individuals and groups, counseling clients and families on specific diets as well as educating clients about a healthy diet, monitoring quality of food and nutrition products and services, managing food production, distribution, and service functions, implementing an effective food sanitation program, utilizing a computer in dietetic operations, and effective team building.

Application Requirements: You must have a high school diploma, including two units of high school math, four units of high school English, and two units of science; or your GED, plus two units of high school math. You also need to be employed at least 15 hours per week in a food service facility. And you need a proctor/mentor who has a Bachelor's degree in dietetics, and at least three years of work experience.

If you've taken a college aptitude test, you can submit your scores to Pennsylvania State for consideration. If you've earned 18 or more credit hours at other accredited colleges or universities, you don't need to submit your test scores. Rather, you should have official transcripts forwarded to Pennsylvania State University.

Completion Requirements: You must successfully complete 67 credits.

Example Course Titles: Some of the course titles in this program include Sanitation Practices in Food Service Operations, Food Services Management: Theory and Practice, Field Experience in Community Dietetics, Human Resource Management in Food Service Operations, Principles of Quantity Food Production, Management and Analysis of Quantity Food Production, Professional Staff Field Experience, Rhetoric and Composition, Nutrition Component of the Food Service System, Introductory Principles of Introductory Sociology, and Psychology.

Program Contact: World Campus
The Pennsylvania State University
207 Mitchell Building
University Park, Pennsylvania 16802-3601
(800) 252-3592
(814) 865-3290
dpde@psu.edu

Dietetics and Aging

Degree Offered: Certificate

Program Web Address: www.hrrm.psu.edu/dpde/da.htm

Program Background: This program is designed for students who work with the elderly in community or institutional settings. Students take courses that help them understand the process of aging and develop the nutrition care competencies they need to handle the growing elderly population. Topics include: basic nutrition, quantity food production, food and nutrition needs of the elderly, physiological, social, and psychological aspects of aging, food safety and sanitation, and communication.

Application Requirements: You must be a high school graduate or have your GED.

Completion Requirements: You must successfully complete 21 credits.

Example Course Titles: Some of the course titles in this program include Nutrition Component of the Food Service System, Introduction to the Biology of Aging, Nutrition Care of the Elderly, Rhetoric and Composition, Sanitation Practices in Food Service Operations, and Principles of Quantity Food Production.

Program Contact: World Campus
The Pennsylvania State University
207 Mitchell Building
University Park, Pennsylvania 16802-3601
(800) 252-3592
(814) 865-3290
dpde@psu.edu

Educational Technology Integration

Degree Offered: Certificate

Program Web Address: www.worldcampus.psu.edu/pub/programs/edtech/index.shtml

Program Background: This program is designed for teachers and trainers who need to integrate technology into their curricula. Students develop the freedom and flexibility to apply their new-found technology skills to the classroom or training environment.

Application Requirements: You must have completed 60 credits of undergraduate coursework.

Completion Requirements: You must successfully complete 18 credits for this certificate.

Example Course Titles: Some of the course titles in this program include Introduction to Instructional Technologies for Educators, Computers as Learning Tools, Using the Internet in the Classroom, Video and Hypermedia in the Classroom, Designing Computer Networks for Education, and Coordinating Technology Use in Education.

Program Contact: World Campus
The Pennsylvania State University
207 Mitchell Building
University Park, Pennsylvania 16802-3601
(800) 252-3592
(814) 865-3290
psuwd@psu.edu

Geographic Information Systems

Degree Offered: Certificate

Program Web Address: www.worldcampus. psu.edu/pub/programs/gis/index.shtml

Program Background: Students in this program learn how to identify where customers and resources are located, how products and services can be delivered most efficiently, and where new facilities should be built. They develop the necessary skills to collect, manage, and analyze geographic data.

Application Requirements: You don't have to meet any prerequisites for this program.

Completion Requirements: You must successfully complete four courses.

Example Course Titles: Some of the course titles in this program include The Nature of Geographic Information, Elements of GIS, and GIS in Practice: Environmental Applications.

Program Contact: World Campus
The Pennsylvania State University
207 Mitchell Building
University Park, Pennsylvania 16802-3601
(800) 252-3592
(814) 865-3290
psuwd@psu.edu

Hotel, Restaurant, and Institutional Management

Degree Offered: Associate

Program Web Address: www.worldcampus.

psu.edu/pub/programs/2hrim_index.shtml

Program Background: This degree provides advancement opportunities for students who work in commercial food service, hotel facilities, or other hospitality positions.

Application Requirements: You should work at least 15 hours per week in a commercial food service, institutional food service, hotel, or other hospitality-related facility.

Completion Requirements: You must successfully complete 66-68 credits.

Example Course Titles: Some of the course titles in this program include Food Safety and Sanitation, Rhetoric and Composition, Effective Business Writing, Introduction to Management in the Hospitality Industry, Quantity Food Production Analysis, Hospitality Administration Seminar, Analysis of Field Experience, Restaurant Management, Hotel, Restaurant, and Institutional Purchasing and Cost Control, Hospitality Facilities Management, Hotel Management, Survey of Management Hotel and Restaurant Marketing and Merchandising, and Contemporary American Marketing.

Program Contact: World Campus
The Pennsylvania State University
207 Mitchell Building
University Park, Pennsylvania 16802-3601
(800) 252-3592
(814) 865-3290
psuwd@psu.edu

Logistics and Supply Chain Management

Degree Offered: Certificate

Program Web Address: www.worldcampus. psu.edu/pub/programs/blog/index.shtml

Program Background: This program prepares students for a career or advancement in the field of logistics and supply management. It addresses global sourcing and distribution, managing the flow of materials and information, and preparing for an advanced degree.

An academic college of the University approves each of the courses and helps define the course's objectives. And each course has to meet certain University standards that guarantee its quality and academic integrity. While some courses have prerequisites, the program is flexible and students choose a study plan that fits their needs.

Application Requirements: You should have completed college-level mathematics and English courses. You must be proficient in English. If you are an international student who has not received a Bachelor's or Master's degree from an institution in which instruction is in English, you should take the Test of English as a Foreign Language (TOEFL).

Completion Requirements: You must successfully complete four courses for this certificate.

Example Course Titles: Some of the course titles for this program include Business Logistics Management, Transportation Supply and Infrastructure, Procurement and Contract Logistics, Purchasing Management, Logistics Analysis, and Independent Research Project.

Program Contact: World Campus
The Pennsylvania State University
207 Mitchell Building
University Park, Pennsylvania 16802-3601
(800) 252-3592
(814) 865-3290
psuwd@psu.edu

Noise Control Engineering

Degree Offered: Certificate

Program Web Address: www.worldcampus. psu.edu/pub/programs/nce/index.shtml

Program Background: Students in this program learn about the needs for noise control and the skills to control product, workplace, and environmental noise levels. The program focuses on acoustics, building on Pennsylvania State's experience and reputation as the educational leader in acoustics and related fields for more than 30 years.

Application Requirements: You must have a Bachelor's degree from an accredited college or university to enroll in these courses for credit. If you don't have your Bachelor's degree, but you have completed at least 60 college-level credit hours, you may petition to enroll in the courses.

Completion Requirements: You must successfully complete three courses with a B or better for this certificate.

Example Course Titles: The course titles in this program are Noise and Vibration Control I, II, and III.

Program Contact: World Campus
The Pennsylvania State University
207 Mitchell Building
University Park, Pennsylvania 16802-3601
(800) 252-3592
(814) 865-3290
psuwd@psu.edu

School Food Service

Degree Offered: Associate

Program Web Address: www.hrrm.psu.edu/ dpde/sfs.htm

Program Background: This Associate's degree program in Dietetic Food Systems Management prepares students for careers in school food service. Students learn to implement dietary guidelines, direct the preparation of health cuisines, establish standards for food quality and safety, respond to diverse customer needs, market products and services, and become technologically competent.

Application Requirements: You must have a high school diploma, including two units of high school math, four units of high school English, and two units of science; or your GED, plus two units of high school math. You also need to be employed at least 15 hours per week in a food service facility. And you need a proctor/mentor who has a Bachelor's degree in dietetics, nutrition, hotel or restaurant management, or a related field, and at least three years of work experience.

If you've taken a college aptitude test, you can submit your scores to Pennsylvania State for consideration. If you've earned 18 or more credit hours at other accredited colleges or universities, you don't need to submit your test scores. Rather, you should have official transcripts forwarded to Pennsylvania State University.

Completion Requirements: You must successfully complete 67 credit hours for this degree.

Example Course Titles: Some of the course titles for this program include Sanitation Practices in Food Service Operations, Food Services Management: Theory and Practice, Field Experience in Community Dietetics, Human Resource Management in Food Service Operations, and Principles of Quantity Food Production.

Program Contact: World Campus
The Pennsylvania State University
207 Mitchell Building
University Park, Pennsylvania 16802-3601
(800) 252-3592
(814) 865-3290
dpde@psu.edu

Webmaster

Degree Offered: Certificate

Program Web Address: www.worldcampus. psu.edu/pub/programs/turfgrass/index.s

Program Background: This program teaches students the skills to become a Webmaster. Students develop foundation-level skills in Web-based communications, while learning to create, design, and maintain Web sites.

Completion Requirements: You must successfully complete 12 courses for this certificate.

Time for Completion: You have up to nine months to complete all coursework.

Example Course Titles: Some of the course titles in this program include Overview of Internet Technology, HTML Level 1, HTML Level 2, JavaScripting Level 1, Legal and Ethical Issues, Visual and Graphic Design, Multimedia and the Web, Web Server Administration, and Security Issues and Basics.

Program Contact: World Campus
The Pennsylvania State University
207 Mitchell Building
University Park, Pennsylvania 16802-3601
(800) 252-3592
(814) 865-3290
psuwd@psu.edu

Turfgrass Management

Degree Offered: Certificate

Program Web Address: www.worldcampus. psu.edu/pub/programs/turfgrass/index.s

Program Background: This program is designed to keep professionals in turfgrass management up-to-date on technological advancements and practical applications. Students get a blend of basic and applied knowledge, business management, and practice in problem solving.

Completion Requirements: You must successfully complete 15 to 16 credit hours for this certificate.

Example Course Titles: Some of the course titles in this program include Turfgrass Pesticides, Turfgrass Pest Management, and Turfgrass Weed Control.

Program Contact: World Campus
The Pennsylvania State University
207 Mitchell Building
University Park, Pennsylvania 16802-3601
(800) 252-3592
(814) 865-3290
psuwd@psu.edu

PURDUE UNIVERSITY

General Contact Information

1586 Stewart Center, Room 116
West Lafayette, Indiana 47907-1586

Phone: (765) 496-3338
FAX: (765) 496-6384
E-mail: jburrous@purdue.edu
WWW: www.purdue.edu/distance

Online Learning Information

1586 Stewart Center, Room 116
West Lafayette, Indiana 47907-1586

Phone: (800) 830-0269
FAX: (765) 496-2484
E-mail: jltowler@cea.purdue.edu

Institution Background

Founded: 1869
Type of Institution: Public
Accreditation: North Central Association of Colleges and Schools

Individual Undergraduate Courses: Purdue University has online courses in veterinary technology.

Individual Graduate Courses: Purdue University has online courses in statistics.

Programs

Educational Administration

Degree Offered: Doctor of Philosophy

Program Web Address: distance.soe.purdue.edu/

Program Background: This program develops leaders for the schools of Indiana and the nation. Students can specialize in educational administration at both K-12 and higher education levels, or in educational foundations.

Application Requirements: You must have a Master's degree in educational administration. You should earn Indiana superintendent licensure in the program.

Completion Requirements: You must successfully complete a minimum of 60 semester hours, preliminary examinations, and a dissertation.

Time for Completion: You have up to three years to complete this program.

On Campus Requirements: You are expected to attend all cohort classes on campus.

Example Course Titles: Some of the course titles in this program include Educational Policy and Decision Making, The Social and Cultural Context of Educational Administration, Analytical Techniques in Educational Management, Administration of Educational Systems, Learning Environments, and Transformative Leadership.

Program Contact: Department of Educational Studies
Purdue University
1446 Liberal Arts and Education Building, Room 5133
West Lafayette, Indiana 47907-1446
(765) 494-7299
(765) 496-1228

Food and Agricultural Business

Degree Offered: Master of Business Administration

Program Web Address: www.emba-agbus. purdue.edu/

Program Background: Students in this program learn about the globalization of markets, explosion of new technology, fragmenting demands of consumers, rapidly evolving role of governments, and intense competitive pressures that combine to create today's food and agribusiness marketplace. They learn to work within the marketplace and develop the skills to be effective leaders.

Application Requirements: Admission is determined based on your scores on the Graduate Management Admissions Test, your previous academic record, your work experience, and your employer's recommendations. You must have a Bachelor's degree with an undergraduate grade point average of at least 3.0 (on a 4.0 scale).

Completion Requirements: You must successfully complete 48 credits.

On Campus Requirements: You are required to attend a one-week orientation and four two-week residencies over two years.

System Requirements: You need a laptop with multimedia capabilities. It should run Windows 95/98/NT. The school will provide additional requirements when you are admitted.

Example Course Titles: Some of the course titles in this program include Food and Agribusiness, Market Environment, Economics for Food and Agribusiness Managers, Applied Quantitative, Methods for Decision Making, Human Resource Management, Organizational Behavior, The Food System Policy, Trade, and Regulatory Environment, Financial and Managerial Accounting, Marketing Management, Strategic Food and Agribusiness Management, and Risk Analysis and Management.

Program Contact: Executive MBA in Food and Agricultural Business
Purdue University
1145 Krannert Building
West Lafayette, Indiana 47907
(765) 494-4262
(765) 496-1224

REGIS UNIVERSITY
General Contact Information

3333 Regis Boulevard
Denver, Colorado 80221

E-mail: regisadm@regis.edu
WWW: www.regis.edu

Online Learning Information

Distance Learning
7600 East Orchard Road, Suite 100N
Englewood, Colorado 80111

Phone: (303) 458-4383
FAX: (303) 694-1554
WWW: www.regis.edu

Institution Background

Founded: 1877
Type of Institution: Private
Accreditation: North Central Association of Colleges and Schools

Programs
Business Administration

Degree Offered: Bachelor of Science

Program Web Address: www.regis.edu/rdl/degree.htm

Completion Requirements: You must successfully complete 128 credit hours for this degree.

System Requirements: You should have a personal computer with a Pentium processor, 16 MB RAM, CD-ROM, sound card and speakers, color monitor (256-color), 28.8 modem, Microsoft Word 6.0 or higher (all courses), Netscape 4.0 (or higher) Web browser, and Adobe Acrobat Reader (free download). Some courses may require additional software.

Example Course Titles: Some of the course titles in this program include English Composition, Principles of Accounting, Marketing, Management, Business Law, Intro to Business Research, Principles of Macroeconomics, Principles of Microeconomics, Introduction to Statistics, Business Finance, Management of Human Resources, Managing Technology for Business Strategies, and Ethical Decision Making in Business.

Program Contact: Regis University
Denver, Colorado 80221
(800) 967-3237
mualc@regis.edu

Business Administration

Degree Offered: Master of Business Administration

Program Web Address: www.mbaregis.com/

Program Background: This graduate program offers students multiple, flexible learning formats that can be easily customized to fit their individual educational needs and lifestyles.

Application Requirements: You should submit an application including transcripts reflecting your undergraduate and graduate (if applicable) grade point averages, your test scores on the Graduate Management Admissions Test (GMAT) score, a resume or personal statement of your professional experiences, and two let-

ters of recommendation. Additionally, you will be required to interview with a faculty member.

Completion Requirements: You must successfully complete 30 credit hours for this degree.

Example Course Titles: Some of the course titles in this program include The Economics of Management, The Ethical and Legal Environment of Business, Financial Decision Making, Marketing Management, Issues in International Business, Production and Operations Management, Managing Change, Managerial Leadership, Innovation and Enterprise, and Strategies in a Global Environment.

Program Contact: External MBA Program
Regis University
3333 Regis Blvd, L-16
Denver, Colorado 80221-1099
(800) 404-7355
(303) 694-1554
mba@mbaregis.com

Computer Information Systems

Degree Offered: Master of Science

Program Web Address: www.regis.edu/spsmscis/default.htm

Program Background: This program integrates management and technological challenges of computer information systems. The curriculum is designed to provide a solid foundation in computer hardware and software, systems design, communications, and project/team management skills for the rapidly changing computer environment.

Completion Requirements: You must successfully complete 12 courses (36 credit hours) for this degree.

System Requirements: You should have a personal computer with a Pentium processor, a 28.8 baud modem, Internet access, and e-mail account. You should use a Web browser such as Netscape 4.X or Microsoft Internet Explorer 4.X or better. You should also have Microsoft Office 97 in order to properly view the presentations and download Word and Excel documents.

Example Course Titles: Some of the course titles in this program include Systems Analysis and Design for Database Applications, Survey of Programming Logic with Java, Object-Oriented Control and Data Structures with Java, Computer Systems Architecture, Human-Computer Interaction, UNIX Concepts, Systems Integration in a Networked Enterprise, Advanced UNIX Concepts, Presentation of Technical Materials, C Programming, and Object-Oriented Programming (C++).

Program Contact: Graduate Programs
Regis University
3333 Regis Blvd, L-16
Denver, Colorado 80221-1099
(800) 677-9270
(303) 964-5538
admarg@regis.edu

Database Technologies

Degree Offered: Certificate

Program Web Address: www.regis.edu/spsmscis/default.htm

Program Background: This program is designed for students with data processing experience, who wish to develop specific skills and knowledge in database management systems.

Completion Requirements: You must successfully complete a minimum of 12 semester hours of credit for this certificate.

Example Course Titles: Some of the course titles in this program include Client Server Application Development with Oracle, Database Administration, Database Application Devel-

opment using PowerBuilder, CASE Technologies, Performance and Tuning, RAD and Prototyping, and Advanced Database Technologies.

Program Contact: Graduate Programs
Regis University
3333 Regis Blvd, L-16
Denver, Colorado 80221-1099
(800) 677-9270
(303) 964-5538
admarg@regis.edu

Management of Technology

Degree Offered: Certificate

Program Web Address: www.regis.edu/spsmscis/default.htm

Program Background: This certificate program is geared toward students who have data processing experience and want to enhance their knowledge and skills in applied computer technology.

Application Requirements: You must meet the requirements for the Master of Science in Computer Information Systems degree program, as well as have specific skills for this certificate program.

Completion Requirements: You must successfully complete at least 12 semester hours for this certificate.

Example Course Titles: Some of the course titles in this program include Managing Technology for Business Strategies, Systems Analysis and Design Prerequisites, Database Concepts, Local Area Networks, Network Management, and Business Issues in Multimedia.

Program Contact: Graduate Programs
Regis University
3333 Regis Blvd, L-16
Denver, Colorado 80221-1099

(800) 677-9270
(303) 964-5538
admarg@regis.edu

Multimedia Technologies

Degree Offered: Certificate

Program Web Address: www.regis.edu/spsmscis/default.htm

Program Background: This certificate program is intended for students who have data processing experience, and who want new and specific skills and knowledge in multimedia design and development. Students get hands-on experience through their assignments using MacroMedia Director, Adobe Photoshop, and Adobe Premier.

Application Requirements: You must meet the requirements for admission to the Master of Science in Computer Information Systems degree program and meet the prerequisite skills and knowledge for this program.

Completion Requirements: You must successfully complete a minimum of 12 semester hours for this degree.

Example Course Titles: Some of the course titles in this program include Introduction to Multimedia Technologies, Multimedia Authoring with Director, Digital Video Post Production for Multimedia, Business Issues in Multimedia, and Asset Acquisition and Development for Multimedia.

Program Contact: Graduate Programs
Regis University
3333 Regis Blvd, L-16
Denver, Colorado 80221-1099
(800) 677-9270
(303) 964-5538
admarg@regis.edu

Networking Technologies

Degree Offered: Certificate

Program Web Address: www.regis.edu/spsmscis/default.htm

Program Background: This certificate program is intended for students who have data processing experience, and who want to develop skills in network technologies and systems.

Application Requirements: You must meet the requirements for the Master of Science in Computer Information Systems degree program, as well as some prerequisites for the certificate.

Completion Requirements: You must successfully complete 12 semester hours for this certificate.

Example Course Titles: Some of the course titles in this program include Local Area Networks, Wide Area Networks, Systems Integration in a Networked Enterprise, Network Management, and Internet: Concepts and Topics.

Program Contact: Graduate Programs
Regis University
3333 Regis Blvd, L-16
Denver, Colorado 80221-1099
(800) 677-9270
(303) 964-5538
admarg@regis.edu

Non-profit Management

Degree Offered: Master of Non-profit Management

Program Web Address: www.regis.edu/spsmnm/default.htm

Program Background: This program integrates concepts, theories, and applications to help students improve their leadership skills and management capabilities within nonprofit environments.

Completion Requirements: You must successfully complete 36 credit hours for this degree. Additionally, you are required to complete a professional project in which you create, develop, improve, or evaluate a product or program. One of the requirements of the professional project is a thesis.

System Requirements: You should have a computer and Internet access, e-mail capabilities, a Web browser, and InterRelay Chat capabilities.

Example Course Titles: Some of the course titles for this program include Communication Skills for Non-profit Organization Leaders, Legal and Governmental Issues, Non-profit Organizational Politics, Advocacy and The Third Sector, Organizational Change and Program Development, Non-profit Enterprise, and Marketing and Public Relations for Non-profit Organizations.

Program Contact: Graduate Programs
Regis University
3333 Regis Blvd, L-16
Denver, Colorado 80221-1099
(800) 677-9270
(303) 964-5538
admarg@regis.edu

Object-Oriented Technologies

Degree Offered: Certificate

Program Web Address: www.regis.edu/ spsmscis/default.htm

Program Background: This certificate program is designed for students who have data processing experience, and who want to develop new skills in object-oriented techniques and technologies.

Application Requirements: You must meet the requirements for admission in the University's Master of Science in Computer Information Systems degree program, and the specific prerequisites for this certificate.

Completion Requirements: You must successfully complete 12 semester hours for this certificate.

Example Course Titles: Some of the course titles in this program include Object-Oriented Analysis and Design, Object-Oriented Programming, Software Testing, and Java Programming.

Program Contact: Graduate Programs
Regis University
3333 Regis Blvd, L-16
Denver, Colorado 80221-1099
(800) 677-9270
(303) 964-5538
admarg@regis.edu

ROCHESTER INSTITUTE OF TECHNOLOGY

General Contact Information

58 Lomb Memorial Drive
Rochester, New York 14623-5604

Phone: (716) 475-2229
FAX: (716) 475-7164
E-mail: opes@rit.edu
WWW: www.distancelearning.rit.edu

Online Learning Information

Part-Time and Graduate Enrollment Services
Bausch and Lomb Center
58 Lomb Memorial Drive
Rochester, New York 14623

Phone: (800) CALLRIT

FAX: (716) 475-7164
E-mail: opes@rit.edu

Institution Background

Rochester Institute of Technology is committed to offering the highest quality in online programs and degrees to students across the United States and internationally. The faculty who teach the distance learning courses also teach traditional campus-based courses.

Founded: 1829
Type of Institution: Private
Accreditation: Middle States Association of Colleges and Schools

Online Course Background: Rochester Institute of Technology's distance learning program is a recognized leader in this field and has been offering full degrees to students since 1991. The school offers over 200 online courses, seven Master's degrees, three undergraduate degrees, and 16 professional certificates.

Online Course Offered: 85

Online Students Enrolled: 1300

Services Offered to Students: Students enrolled in online courses have full electronic access to the library, and can order materials online from the bookstore.

Financial Aid: Students enrolled in distance learning programs at Rochester Institute of Technology may be eligible for financial aid.

Individual Undergraduate Courses: Rochester Institute of Technology offers online courses in liberal arts, digitial imaging, and digital photography.

Registration: You can register for courses via mail, phone, and the World Wide Web.

Programs

Applied Arts and Science

Degree Offered: Bachelor of Science

Program Web Address: distancelearning. rit.edu/BSAppliedArts.html

Program Background: This program allows you to design a college education that fits your specific needs. It begins with what you already know and what you've learned. Your previous college credits, professional certifications or licenses, military training, college level learning can be reviewed, and where possible, credited toward your degree. You can choose up to three concentrations for your degree, and use the courses available in the distance-learning format to complete the upper-level requirements or combine them with on-campus courses at Rochester Institute of Technology or other colleges (with approval).

Application Requirements: You must have some prior college experience or an associate's degree to participate in the online courses. You can transfer credit for coursework that you've completed at regionally accredited institutions of higher education. Simply submit official transcripts reflecting this work, and your advisor will evaluate it to see what will transfer.

Completion Requirements: You are required to complete at least 45 quarter hours of credit from Rochester Institute of Technology for your degree. You will work closely with your advisor to plan your program and select areas of concentration.

Example Course Titles: Some of the course titles in this program include Introduction to Programming, Programming Design and Validation, Computer Concepts and Software Systems, Data Communications and Computer Networks, Applied Database Management, Networking Technologies, Earth Science For

The Emergency Manager, Manmade Hazards, and Emergency Management Laws and Regulations.

Program Contact: College of Applied Science and Technology
Center for Multidisciplinary Studies
(716) 475-2078

Applied Statistics

Degree Offered: Master of Science

Program Web Address: distancelearning. rit.edu/MsAppliedStats.html

Program Background: This degree program is designed to provide instruction in state-of-the-art statistical thinking and methods. The online courses have the same objectives, rigorous workload, tuition and academic credit as on-campus courses. Each course features videotapes that are professionally prepared for distance learners, not simply videos of recent lectures that were captured on tape. Each course also includes weekly or biweekly live chat sessions, using an electronic medium that allows students and instructor to interact. There is no distinction made between students who take courses in a distance-learning format and those who take courses on campus. Because distance learning courses are designed for the motivated professional who is not able to attend on-campus classes, we recommend enrollment to those over 25 years of age with at least three years of professional employment.

Application Requirements: You must have a Bachelor's degree from an accredited college or university with acceptable mathematics credits, including university-level calculus through multiple integration, and acceptable probability and statistics college credits. Applicants who fail to meet these requirements will be required to complete these prerequisites prior to matriculation in the graduate program.

You should submit an application with transcripts of all previous undergraduate and graduate work, and two letters of recommendation. If you're an international student whose native language is not English, you must have a TOEFL score of at least 550.

Completion Requirements: You must successfully complete 24 credits in 800-level courses, attain an overall grade point average of 3.0, and take an oral examination during your last quarter of the program.

Time for Completion: You have up to seven years to complete the requirements for this degree.

Example Course Titles: Some of the course titles in this program include Design of Experiments II, Theory of Statistics I, Statistical Process Control, Statistical Acceptance Control, Quality Management, Quality Engineering, Interpretation of Data, Reliability Statistics I, Empirical Modeling, and Quality Engineering by Design.

Program Contact: Joseph Voelkel
(716) 475-2231
jgvcqa@rit.edu

Cross-Disciplinary Professional Studies

Degree Offered: Master of Science

Program Web Address: distancelearning. rit.edu/MsCrossDStudies.html

Program Background: This program is specifically designed to enable experienced professionals to fashion a customized plan of graduate study tailored to their educational or career objectives. Students may concentrate on Applied Statistics, Environmental, Health and Safety Management, Health Systems Administration Information Technology, Microelectronics Manufacturing Engineering, Software

Development and Management, Career and Human Resource Development, or Business Management and Marketing.

Application Requirements: You must have a Bachelor's degree from a regionally accredited college or university, three to five years full time work experience, and an undergraduate cumulative grade point average of 3.0 or better.

Completion Requirements: You must successfully complete 48 quarter credit hours for this degree.

Example Course Titles: Some of the course titles in this program include Environmental, Health and Safety Management, Environmental, Health and Safety Systems Design and Performance Management, Integrating Environmental Health and Safety into Business Management, Statistical Process Control, Statistical Acceptance Control, Quality Management, Quality Engineering Integrated Health Systems, Health Systems Administration, Information Systems for Health Systems, and Computer Programming and Problem Solving.

Program Contact: Lawerenc Bell
(716) 475-5872
lwbcad@rit.edu

Electrical/Mechanical Engineering Technology

Degree Offered: Bachelor of Science

Program Web Address: distancelearning. rit.edu/BSEM.html

Program Background: This program is designed for students who have an Associate degree or the equivalent in electrical technology, mechanical technology, or a related field. Students complete core coursework in electrical, mechanical, and manufacturing engineering technology.

Application Requirements: You must submit transcripts for evaluation. You are required to earn 45 credits through the Rochester Institute of Technology. You should have a background in Mathematics through Introductory Calculus, Physics, English/Social Studies/Humanities, or Computer Programming.

Completion Requirements: You must successfully complete 193 credits.

On Campus Requirements: You are required to complete five on-site labs over a four to five year timeframe.

Example Course Titles: Some of the course titles in this program include Production and Operations Management II, Robust Design, Product Design, Data Communication and Computer Networks, Voice Communications, Switching Technologies, Networking Technology, Introduction to Telecommunications Policy, Network Management, Calculus for Technologists, Metallurgy and Materials Testing, Solutions of Engineering Problems, Electrical Principles of Design, Pneumatics and Hydraulics, Computer Programming, Applied Mechanics, Machines and Transformers, Applied Mechanics, Applied Microprocessors, Effective Technical Communications, Mechanical Engineering Technology Lab, Fundamentals of Chemistry, Introduction to Chemistry of Materials, Engineering Economics, Controls for Industrial Automation, Elementary Statistics Materials Technology, Data Communications and Computer Networks, and Elementary Statistics.

Program Contact: James Scudder
E/MET Program
(716) 475-2055
jscudder@firstclass.rit.edu

Environmental Health and Safety Management

Degree Offered: Master of Science

Program Web Address: www.rit.edu/ 804www/common/scripts/info.cgi?programs

Program Background: This program is designed to give students a solid grounding in technical and managerial aspects of leading practices in environmental, health and safety management.

Application Requirements: You must have a Bachelor's degree from an accredited college or university with acceptable mathematics credits, including university-level calculus through multiple integration, and acceptable probability and statistics college credits. Applicants who fail to meet these requirements will be required to complete these prerequisites prior to matriculation in the graduate program.

You should submit an application with transcripts of all previous undergraduate and graduate work, and two letters of recommendation. If you're an international student whose native language is not English, you must have a TOEFL score of at least 550.

Completion Requirements: You must successfully complete a minimum of 48 quarter credit hours and a graduate thesis or graduate project for the Master's degree. You must also maintain a program cumulative grade point average of at least 3.0.

Example Course Titles: Some of the course titles in this program include Environmental, Health and Safety Management, Organizational Behavior and Leadership, EHS Management Systems Design and Performance Measurement, Integrating EHS into Business Management, and Environmental, Health and Safety Auditing.

Program Contact: John Morelli
Environmental Management
(716) 475-7213
jxmctp@rit.edu

Environmental Management and Technology

Degree Offered: Bachelor of Science

Program Web Address: distancelearning.rit.edu/BSEnvTech.html

Program Background: This program teaches students how to design and implement systems for managing air emissions, wastewater effluents, and solid and hazardous wastes. Students develop skills to manage environmental projects, and gain knowledge about staying in compliance with environmental regulations. The overall objective is to prepare our students to become effective environmental project managers with access to a broad range of resources, and the most current knowledge in the field.

Application Requirements: You must have at least three years of high school mathematics, including trigonometry, and high school chemistry is preferred. You may be able to transfer some credits if you have completed coursework at another institution. If you have an Associate's degree, your courses probably fulfill many of the general education requirements from the first two years of this program. Depending on your situation, you may be admitted with junior standing.

Completion Requirements: You must successfully complete 190 credits for this degree.

Example Course Titles: Some of the course titles in this program include Chemistry Principles, Introduction to Organic Chemistry, General Biology, Field Biology/Ecology, Physics, Introduction to Computers and Programming, Technical Math, Data Analysis I, Geology for Environmental Management, Hydrology for Environmental Management, Monitoring and Measuring for Environmental, Management, Financial Accounting, Environmental Regulatory Law Technical Writing, Introduction to Work Organizations, Principles of Environmental Management, Solid and Hazardous Waste Management, Industrial Wastewater Management, Air Emissions Management, Corporate Environmental Management, Environmental Permitting, Occupational Health, and Occupational Safety.

Program Contact: John Morelli
Environmental Management and Technology
(716) 475-7213
j_morelli@cast-fc.rit.edu

Health Systems Administration

Degree Offered: Master of Science

Program Web Address: www.rit.edu/ hsawww/intro-exec.htm

Application Requirements: You must have a Bachelor's degree from a regionally accredited college or university, three to five years full time work experience, and an undergraduate cumulative grade point average of 3.0 or better. If you are an international student, you must have a minimum score of 600 on the Test of English as a Foreign Language (TOEFL).

Completion Requirements: You must successfully complete 57 quarter credit hours of study. You may transfer up to 12 hours of credit from another school as well as receive credit by exam or experience.

Example Course Titles: Some of the course titles in this program include Statistical Concepts, Integrated Health Systems, Health Systems Quality, Preventive Epidemiology, Information Systems for Health Administrators, Health Systems Policy and Law, Health Systems Administration, Health Systems Economics and Finance, Health Systems Issues, and Health Systems Planning.

Program Contact: Health Systems Administration
31 Lomb Memorial Drive

Rochester, New York 14623-5603
(716) 475-7359
wwwcad@rit.edu

Information Technology

Degree Offered: Master of Science

Program Web Address: distancelearning. rit.edu/Msinformationtech.html

Program Background: Recognizing that the future of society will include a mixture of computers, media, and communication technologies, Rochester Institute of Technology's Master of Science in Information Technology degree focuses on teaching students to learn how to use all three types of evolving technologies. Its intent is to help students effectively communicate and compute interactively using new media technology.

Application Requirements: You must have a Bachelor's degree or equivalent from an accredited institution and a minimum grade point average of 3.0 (on a 4.0 scale). If your undergraduate grade point average was less than 3.0, you may be required to submit copies of your Graduate Record Examination test scores. You need to submit a completed application, two professional recommendations, and copies of your college transcripts.

If you're an international student, Rochester Institute of Technology recommends that you take the General Record Examination. Contact the Graduate Program coordinator for additional information. If English is not your first or primary language, you must take the Test of English as a Foreign Language (TOEFL) exam, and receive a score of 550 or higher. Students who score lower than 550 may be admitted conditionally to the program at Rochester Institute of Technology's discretion.

Completion Requirements: You must earn 48 credit hours of graduate study for this degree.

The curriculum has a core set of courses with a choice of concentrations and electives.

Example Course Titles: Some of the course titles for this program include Theories of Interactive Computing, Fundamentals of Tele-communications Technology, Telecommunications Technology, Telecommunications Management, Software Development and Management, and Information Technology Strategy.

Program Contact: Rayno Niemi
(716) 475-2202
rdn@it.rit.edu

Software Development and Management

Degree Offered: Master of Science

Program Web Address: distancelearning. rit.edu/Msinformationtech.html

Program Background: This program is designed to help students establish and use sound methodologies in the production of computer software.

Application Requirements: You must have a Bachelor's degree or equivalent from an accredited institution and a minimum grade point average of 3.0 (on a 4.0 scale). If your undergraduate grade point average was less than 3.0, you may be required to submit copies of your Graduate Record Examination test scores. You need to submit a completed application, two professional recommendations, and copies of your college transcripts.

If you're an international student, Rochester Institute of Technology recommends that you take the General Record Examination. Contact the Graduate Program coordinator for additional information. If English is not your first or primary language, you must take the Test of English as a Foreign Language (TOEFL) exam, and receive a score of 550 or higher. Students who score lower than 550 may be ad-

mitted conditionally to the program at Rochester Institute of Technology's discretion.

Completion Requirements: You must successfully complete 48 quarter credit hours for this degree.

Example Course Titles: Some of the course titles for this program include Software Design and Implementation, Data Modeling and Design, Reusable Software Design, Systems and Software Engineering, Specification and Design of Information Systems, Specification and Design of Embedded Systems, Software Project Management, and Software Project Planning.

Program Contact: Rayno Niemi
(716) 475-2202
rdn@it.rit.edu

ROGERS STATE UNIVERSITY

General Contact Information

1701 W. Will Rogers Blvd.
Claremore, Oklahoma 74017

Phone: (918) 343-7777
FAX: (918) 343-7595
E-mail: info@rsu.edu
WWW: www.rsu.edu

Online Learning Information

1701 W. Will Rogers Blvd.
Claremore, Oklahoma 74017

Phone: (918) 343-7777
FAX: (918) 343-7595
E-mail: info@rsu.edu

Institution Background

Rogers State University has a variety of options to address the educational needs of students attending college for the first time, enrolling in classes while still in high school, transferring from another college or university, or returning to college as an adult.

Founded: 1909
Type of Institution: Public
Accreditation: North Central Association of Colleges and Schools

Online Course Background: Rogers State University has been a national pioneer in distance education since its inception in 1992. Rogers State combines the best in distance learning delivery with the hometown atmosphere of learning that students have grown to enjoy on our campuses.

Financial Aid: Students enrolled in online courses may be eligible for financial aid in the form of grants, scholarships, and loans from federal, state, institutional, and private sources.

Registration: You can register for courses via the World Wide Web.

Programs

Business Administration

Degree Offered: Associate of Arts

Program Web Address: www.ruonline.edu/index.real?action=academic&subaction=degree&subsubaction=BusinessAdmin

Application Requirements: You must provide proof of your high school graduation or GED certificate to enroll in any course.

System Requirements: You should have a personal computer with a 90 MHz Pentium processor (or faster) running Windows 95/98/NT or a Macintosh with OS 7.5.1 (or newer) and PowerPC processor, 16 MB of RAM or more, 28.8 kbps modem or faster, sound card, and speakers.

Example Course Titles: Some of the course titles in this program include Accounting, Principles of Economics, Principles of Manage-

ment, Marketing, Microcomputer Applications, Business Law, Personal Finance, Business Finance Principles, Principles of Collective Bargaining, Office Machines (Calculators), Consumer Issues in American Society, Keyboarding, Introduction to Business, Intermediate Accounting, and Business Statistics.

Program Contact: Attn: Online Advisor
RSU Admissions
1701 W Will Rogers Blvd
Claremore, Oklahoma 74017
(918) 343-7548
(918) 343-7595

Computer Science

Degree Offered: Associate of Science

Program Web Address: www.ruonline.edu/index.real?action=academic&subaction=degree&subsubaction=Compsci

Application Requirements: You must have your high school diploma or equivalent (GED certificate). You need to submit an application and proof of high school graduation or GED certificate.

System Requirements: You should have a personal computer with a 90 MHz Pentium or faster processor running Windows 95/98/NT or a Macintosh with OS 7.5.1 or later and a PowerPC, 16 MB of RAM, 28.8 kbps modem, Sound Card, and Speakers.

Program Contact: Attn: Online Advisor
RSU Admissions
1701 W Will Rogers Blvd
Claremore, Oklahoma 74017
(918) 343-7548
(918) 343-7595

Liberal Arts

Degree Offered: Associate of Arts

Program Web Address: www.ruonline.edu/index.real?action=academic&subaction=degree&subsubaction=Liberalart

Application Requirements: You must be at least 18 years old and be a high school graduate or have your GED certificate to be eligible to take courses through Rogers State. If you're 18 to 20 years old, you can apply for admission by completing an application and submitting it with an official high school transcript or your GED transcript/certificate, and your ACT, ACT COMPASS, or SAT test scores dated within the past five years. If you're 21 or older, you can apply by completing and submitting an application with an official high school transcript or your GED transcript/certificate, and your ACT or SAT test scores.

If you're a student transferring to Rogers State University, you need to complete and submit an application, an official high school transcript or your GED transcript/certificate (only if you're transferring less than 24 credit hours), official transcripts from each college you've attended, and your ACT or SAT test scores (if you're 18 to 20 years old).

If you're currently in high school and wish to pursue this degree, you must complete an application and submit it with your current high school transcript, your ACT scores, and a concurrent approval form that an administrator from your high school must complete.

If you're an international student, you must complete an application and submit it with an official high school transcript (translated to English if necessary), your TOEFL scores (you must have a score of 500 or greater on the standard test or a score of 173 on the electronic TOEFL), and your ACT COMPASS scores (if you live within 60 miles of any Rogers State campus).

Rogers State University admits students in two kind of status: full admission and Special Student Status. Students who receive full admission are degree-seeking and eligible for financial aid. Students awarded Special Student Status can earn up to nine credit hours or take three classes, but may be required to submit proof of prerequisite work or certain standardized test scores, and are not eligible for financial aid.

Completion Requirements: You must successfully complete 60 credit hours for this degree.

System Requirements: You need a personal computer with a 90 MHz Pentium processor and Windows 95/98/NT or a Macintosh with OS 7.5.1 or higher, at least 16 MB of RAM, 28.8 kbps modem (or faster), and a Sound Card and Speakers.

Example Course Titles: Some of the course titles for this program include Speech Communication, Interpersonal Communication, Creative Writing, Technical Writing, Art Appreciation, Music Appreciation, American History to 1865, American Federal Government, College Algebra, and Mathematics for Critical Thinking.

Program Contact: Attn: Online Advisor
Rogers State University Admissions
1701 W. Will Rogers Blvd.
Claremore, Oklahoma 74017
(918) 343-7548
(918) 343-7595

RUTGERS UNIVERSITY

General Contact Information

406 Penn Street
Camden, New Jersey 08102
E-mail: admissions@asb-ugadm.rutgers.edu
WWW: ce1766.rutgers.edu

Online Learning Information

Continuous Education and Outreach
83 Somerset Street, Old Queens
New Brunswick, New Jersey 08903

Phone: (908) 932-5935

FAX: (908) 932-9225
E-mail: caprio@andomeda.rutgers.edu

Institution Background

Rutgers, the State University of New Jersey, has over 48,000 students on campuses in Camden, Newark, and New Brunswick, and is one of the major state university systems in the nation. It was chartered in 1766 as Queen's College, the eighth institution of higher education founded in the colonies, and opened its doors in New Brunswick in 1771 with one instructor, one sophomore, and a handful of first-year students. During this early period, the college developed as a classical liberal arts institution, and in 1825, the name of the college was changed to Rutgers to honor a former trustee and revolutionary war veteran, Colonel Henry Rutgers. Rutgers College became the land-grant school of New Jersey in 1864 and established the Rutgers Scientific School with departments of agriculture, engineering, and chemistry.

Founded: 1766
Type of Institution: Public
Accreditation: Middle States Association of Colleges and Schools

Registration: You can register for courses via mail.

Programs

Communication Management

Degree Offered: Certificate

Program Web Address: www.scils.rutgers.edu/de/index.html

Online Program Started: 1995

Program Background: This program focuses on establishing quality processes for analyzing, planning, and establishing organizational policy, communication, and information campaigns.

Completion Requirements: You must successfully complete four three-credit courses selected from offerings in organizational communication.

System Requirements: You should have a computer, modem, and Internet access.

Example Course Titles: Some of the course titles in this program include Organizational Decision Making, Organizational Cultures, Organizational Publics and Communication Campaigns, Organizational Communication and Quality Assessment, Organizational Quality and Communication Improvement, and Public Relations Management.

Program Contact: Karen Novick
Professional Development, SCILS
4 Huntington Street
New Brunswick, New Jersey 08903
(732) 932-7500

SALT LAKE COMMUNITY COLLEGE

General Contact Information

4600 South Redwood Road
P.O. Box 30808
Salt Lake City, Utah 84120-0808

Phone: (801) 957-3912
FAX: (801) 957-3848
E-mail: headda@slcc.edu
WWW: www.slcc.edu; ecampus.slcc.edu

Online Learning Information

4600 South Redwood Road
Salt Lake City, Utah 84130

Phone: (801) 957-4064

FAX: (801) 957-4890
E-mail: schaefsh@slcc.edu
WWW: www.slcc.edu; ecampus.slcc.edu

Institution Background

Founded: 1949
Type of Institution: Public
Accreditation: Northwest Association of Schools and Colleges

Online Course Background: Salt Lake Community College has two complete degrees that students can attain from a distance—an associate's degree in general studies and an associate's degree in business.

Online Course Offered: 36

Online Students Enrolled: 974

Special Programs/Partnerships: Salt Lake Community College is a participating partner with the Utah Electronic Community College (www.utah-ecc.org). Non-credit distance courses are offered in partnership with Education2Go.

Services Offered to Students: Students enrolled in online courses have access to online admissions, registration, advising, and the library. And they can purchase books and materials online.

Financial Aid: Online students may be eligible for all of the financial aid programs that Salt Lake Community College administers.

Registration: You can register for courses via phone, e-mail, and the World Wide Web.

Programs

Business

Degree Offered: Associate of Science

Program Web Address: ecampus.slcc.edu

Online Program Started: 1995

Program Background: The program is designed as a transfer degree to four-year institutions for students seeking a degree in business or other related fields.

Application Requirements: You must successfully complete the CPT, ACT, or SAT entrance examination.

Completion Requirements: You must successfully complete 64 or 65 credit hours for this degree.

Time for Completion: There are no time constraints on your completion of this program.

On Campus Requirements: There are no on-campus requirements.

System Requirements: You should have access to a personal computer with at least a Pentium 100 MHz processor, 15 MB available hard drive space, and Internet modem connection of 28.8 kbps.

Example Course Titles: Some of the courses in this program include Introduction to Writing, Technical Writing, College Algebra, American Civilization, Fitness for Life, Elements of Effective Communication, Introduction to Biology, Introduction to the Humanities, Introduction to Sociology, Financial Accounting, Managerial Accounting, Business and Society, Business Communication, Calculus for Business, Microeconomics, Macroeconomics, Legal Environment of Business, and Business Statistics I and II.

Program Contact: Shanna Schaefermeyer
Salt Lake Community College
P.O. Box 30808
Salt Lake City, Utah 84130-0808
(801) 957-4064
(801) 957-4609
schaefsh@slcc.edu

General Studies

Degree Offered: Associate of Science

Program Web Address: ecampus.slcc.edu

Online Program Started: 1995

Program Background: This program is designed for students who want to earn general education requirements for transfer to a four-year school to complete a Bachelor's degree.

Application Requirements: You must take an entrance exam or the SAT or ACT.

Completion Requirements: You must successfully complete 12-13 credits in core skill areas, three to seven credits in institutional requirements, 18 credits in distribution areas, and 30 additional general studies or vocational/technical electives.

On Campus Requirements: There are no on-campus requirements.

System Requirements: You need to have a Pentium computer with a modem, 15 MB hard drive space, and Web browser.

Example Course Titles: Some of the course titles in this program include Introduction to Biology, Elements of Effective Communication, American Civilization, College Algebra, Elementary Physics, Fitness for Life, Conceptual Astronomy, Business and Society, Business Communications, Business Calculus, Principles of Microeconomics, Organizational Communication, Introduction to Writing, Technical Writing, Introduction to the Humanities, and Introduction to Sociology.

Program Contact: Shanna Schaefermeyer
Salt Lake Community College
P.O. Box 30808
Salt Lake City, Utah 84130-0808
(801) 957-4064
(801) 957-4609
schaefsh@slcc.edu

SALVE REGINA UNIVERSITY

General Contact Information

100 Ochre Point Avenue
Newport, Rhode Island 02840

Phone: (401) 847-6650
E-mail: sruadmis@salve.edu
WWW: www.salve.edu

Online Learning Information

100 Ochre Point Avenue
Newport, Rhode Island 02840

Phone: (800) 637-0002
FAX: (401) 849-0702
E-mail: mistol@salve.edu
WWW: www.salve.edu

Institution Background

Salve Regina University was first chartered in the state of Rhode Island in 1934. It was established as an independent university in the Catholic tradition of education, which acknowledged the critical importance of higher education for women and men. The University presently serves 2200 men and women in 38 states and 10 foreign countries, and has more than 10,000 alumni.

Founded: 1934
Type of Institution: Private
Accreditation: New England Association of Schools and Colleges

Financial Aid: Students enrolled in online courses may be eligible for student loans and Veterans benefits.

Registration: You can register for courses via mail.

Programs

Human Development

Degree Offered: Master of Arts

Program Web Address: www.wcc-eun.com/salve/requirements.html#anchor658338

Program Background: This program provides students with the opportunity to integrate theory and practice. They learn about fulfilling themselves spiritually, emotionally, and intellectually.

Application Requirements: You must complete and submit an application with a $25 application fee. You also need to submit official transcripts from all institutions you've attended, two letters of recommendation, and your scores on the Miller Analogy Test (MAT), Graduate Records Examination (GRE), or General Management Aptitude Test (GMAT). If you're a foreign student, you must provide a copy of your TOEFL scores and a certificate of financial ability.

Time for Completion: You have up to five years to complete this program.

On Campus Requirements: You are required to fulfill a residency requirement. You can do this by attending a five-day summer institute which is scheduled through the last weekend in June, by on-campus attendance during a semester, or by special arrangement.

Example Course Titles: Some of the course titles in this program include Developmental Psychology—Infancy through Adolescence, Developmental Psychology—Adulthood to Aging, Psychology of Personality, Ethical Perspectives on Global Issues, and Great Writers.

Program Contact: Leona Mistro

Director
100 Ochre Point Avenue
Newport, Rhode Island 02840
(800) 637-0002
(401) 849-0702
mistol@salve.edu

International Relations

Degree Offered: Master of Arts

Program Web Address: www.wcc-eun.com/salve/index.html#anchor556763

Application Requirements: You must complete and submit an application with a $25 application fee. You also need to submit official transcripts from all institutions you've attended, two letters of recommendation, and your scores on the Miller Analogy Test (MAT), Graduate Records Examination (GRE), or General Management Aptitude Test (GMAT). If you're a foreign student, you must provide a copy of your TOEFL scores, and a certificate of financial ability.

Completion Requirements: You must successfully complete 36 credits to earn this degree.

On Campus Requirements: You must fulfill a residency requirement by attending a five-day summer institute (through the last weekend in June), attending on-campus during a semester, or by special arrangement.

Example Course Titles: Some of the course titles for this program include Ethical Perspectives on Global Issues, Foundations of International Relations, International Law, Russia and Eastern European Politics, Africa's Global Perspectives, and North America and the New World.

Program Contact: Leona Mistro
Director
100 Ochre Point Avenue

Newport, Rhode Island 02840
(800) 637-0002
(401) 849-0702
mistol@salve.edu

SETON HALL UNIVERSITY

General Contact Information

400 South Orange Avenue
South Orange, New Jersey 07079-2689
WWW: www.setonworldwide.net

Online Learning Information

400 South Orange Avenue
South Orange, New Jersey 07079

Phone: (888) SETONWW
FAX: (973) 761-9758
E-mail: setonworldwide@shu.edu
WWW: www.setonworldwide.net

Institution Background

Founded: 1856
Type of Institution: Private
Accreditation: Middle States Association of Colleges and Schools

Programs

Counseling

Degree Offered: Master of Arts

Program Web Address: www.setonworldwide.net/index.real?action=GraduateDegre

Program Background: This program prepares students to serve as counselors, playing a vital role as catalysts and facilitators for change and growth in the capacity to think, feel, and act in constructive, holistic ways. Courses cover ethics, values, spirituality and religion, technology, and cultural variables, and encourage students to develop critical thinking skills.

Application Requirements: You must have a Bachelor's degree or the equivalent. You are required to take a standardized test—the GRE or MAT, and TOEFL (as appropriate)—and must submit your scores on these tests within the past five years. If you have a Master's degree or higher, this requirement may be waived.

Completion Requirements: You must successfully complete 48 credits.

On Campus Requirements: A residency is required.

Example Course Titles: Some of the course titles in this program include Counseling Theory, Counseling Skills, Psychology of Human Development, Career Development and Information, Community Agencies, Cross Cultural Psychology, Problems and Techniques in Counseling, Group Counseling, Seminar: Ethical and Legal Issues in Professional Psychology, Statistical Theory and Computer Applications, Tests and Measurement, Seminar in Research Methodology, Group Dynamics, and Internship in Counseling.

Program Contact: MA Counseling Admissions Committee
Kozlowski Hall, Room 522
Seton WorldWide
Seton Hall University
South Orange, New Jersey 07079
(888) SETON-WW
(973) 761-9234
setonworldwide@shu.edu

Education

Degree Offered: Master of Arts

Program Web Address: www. setonworldwide.net/index.real?action= GraduateDegrees&subaction= Education

Program Background: This program provides students with an extensive preparation in educational administration, covering a myriad of academics, skills and techniques. It focuses on four central pillars: academic rigor, practical application, technology, and ethical standards.

Application Requirements: You must have a Bachelor's degree from an accredited college or university, and a minimum undergraduate grade point average of 3.0. You need to submit an application with transcripts from each college you've attended, graduate-level test scores, and three letters of recommendation. You should have a minimum of five years of education-related experience.

Completion Requirements: You must successfully complete 36 semester hours of coursework.

On Campus Requirements: You are required to attend three weekend sessions on campus.

Example Course Titles: Some of the course titles in this program include Microcomputers for Administrators, Supervision of Instruction and Evaluation, Organization and Administration of Education, Leadership Dynamics: Analysis of Supervisory Behavior, Curriculum Development and Evaluation, Curriculum: Design and Engineering, Ethical Foundations of Professional Helping Relationships, School Law, Leadership and Management Assessment, Finance in Administration, Directed Research in Administration and Supervision, Culminating Research Seminar, and Administrative Internship.

Program Contact: MA Education Admissions Committee
Kozlowski Hall, Room 522
Seton WorldWide
Seton Hall University

South Orange, New Jersey 07079
(888) SETON-WW
(973) 761-9234
setonworldwide@shu.edu

Education/Catholic School Leadership

Degree Offered: Master of Arts in Education

Program Web Address: www. setonworldwide.net/index.real?action= GraduateDegrees&subaction= EducationCatholic

Program Background: Students in this degree program learn how to become effective leaders in a Catholic school. The program emphasizes the mission of the school and the formation of Catholic educators. Courses draw upon both the secular field of educational leadership as well as the Catholic educational and spiritual tradition, with attention to contemporary issues in the life of the Catholic Church and schools.

Application Requirements: You must have a Bachelor's degree from an accredited college or university, a minimum undergraduate grade point average of 3.0, and five years education-related experience. You need to submit an application, three letters of recommendation, a letter of intent explaining your reasons for applying to the program, a current resume, and your test scores (within last three years) from the Miller Analogies Test (MAT) or the Graduate record Examination (GRE).

Completion Requirements: You must successfully complete 36 semester hours of coursework.

On Campus Requirements: You are required to participate in three weekend residencies.

Example Course Titles: Some of the course titles in this program include Catholic Education—Yesterday, Today and Tomorrow,

Microcomputers for Administrators, Supervision of Instruction and Evaluation, Organization and Administration of Education, Directed Research in Administration, Principal as Spiritual Leadership, Curriculum Development and Evaluation, Leadership and Management Assessment, School Law, Finance in Administration, Catholic Identity, Ethos and Culture, Culminating Research Seminar, and Administrative Internship.

Program Contact: MA Education Admissions Committee
Kozlowski Hall, Room 522
Seton WorldWide
Seton Hall University
South Orange, New Jersey 07079
(888) SETON-WW
(973) 761-9234
setonworldwide@shu.edu

Healthcare Administration

Degree Offered: Master of Healthcare Administration

Program Web Address: www.
setonworldwide.net/index.real?action=
GraduateDegrees&subaction=
HealthcareAdmin

Program Background: This program provides students with a comprehensive understanding of the healthcare environment and the enhanced management skills that serve their organization through the application of real-world strategies.

Application Requirements: You must have a Bachelor's degree from an accredited college or university.

Completion Requirements: You must successfully complete 39 credits.

Time for Completion: You have up to 20 months to complete this program with your cohort.

On Campus Requirements: You are required to attend three weekend sessions.

Example Course Titles: Some of the course titles in this program include Introduction to the Healthcare System, Healthcare Management, Financial Management and Control, Healthcare Financial Management and Accounting, Healthcare Economics, Managerial Decision-Making, Strategic Planning and Marketing, Ethics in Healthcare: Clinical, Legal, Policy, and Professions, and Research Methods and Statistical Analysis.

Program Contact: MA Education Admissions Committee
Kozlowski Hall, Room 522
Seton WorldWide
Seton Hall University
South Orange, New Jersey 07079
(888) SETON-WW
(973) 761-9234
setonworldwide@shu.edu

Law Enforcement Leadership

Degree Offered: Master of Arts in Education

Program Web Address: www.
setonworldwide.net/index.real?action=
GraduateDegrees&subaction=LawEnforcement

Program Background: This program focuses on private and public security, and policing settings. It is intended for students who are law enforcement professionals in international, federal, state, and local agencies. This degree is designed to enhance and develop the leadership potential of all students.

Application Requirements: You must have a Bachelor's degree from an accredited college or university.

Completion Requirements: You must successfully complete 36 semester hours of coursework.

On Campus Requirements: You are required to participate in three weekend sessions on campus.

Example Course Titles: Some of the course titles in this program include Microcomputers for Administrators, Leadership Dynamics: Analysis of Supervisory Behavior, Directed Research in Administration, Organizational Structures and Processes in Administration, Adult Learning for Human Resources Development Personnel, Performance Improvement Strategies, Personnel Administration, Current Legal Issues of Public Policies at Local, State and Federal Level, Policy Analysis in Administration, Public Relations in Administration, Ethical Foundations of Professional Helping Relationships, and Psychological Issues and Implications: Community Policing Programs.

Program Contact: MA Education Admissions Committee
Kozlowski Hall, Room 522
Seton WorldWide
Seton Hall University
South Orange, New Jersey 07079
(888) SETON-WW
(973) 761-9234
setonworldwide@shu.edu

Strategic Communication and Leadership

Degree Offered: Master of Arts

Program Web Address: www. setonworldwide.net/index. real?action=GraduateDegre

Program Background: Students in this program learn the communication skills necessary for achievement in today's business world. The program has an interactive curriculum that allows for significant discussion about strategies and solutions to current issues in effective leadership and executive communication. The program provides an opportunity to network and study with colleagues and experts in specialized disciplines, with the flexibility of online course delivery.

Application Requirements: You need to have a Bachelor's degree from an accredited college or university. You should submit an application, transcripts from each college or university you've attended, a current resume, and two letters of recommendation. You should also have significant experience in a corporate, military, governmental, association, or nonprofit organization, and be ready for a new executive position.

Completion Requirements: You must successfully complete 36 credit hours through five 12-week modules.

Example Course Titles: Some of the course titles in this program include Building the Business: Transforming Corporate Culture, Delivering the Message: Credibility, Clarity and Confidence, Working Together: The Opportunities of Diversity and Globalization, and Developing Strategies for Success: Shaping Organizational Goals and Policy.

Program Contact: MA Education Admissions Committee
Kozlowski Hall, Room 522
Seton WorldWide
Seton Hall University
South Orange, New Jersey 07079
(888) SETON-WW
(973) 761-9234
setonworldwide@shu.edu

Work-Life Ministry

Degree Offered: Certificate

Program Web Address: www. setonworldwide.net/index. real?action=GraduateDegre

Program Background: This program is intended to prepare students to serve as Catholic lay-ministers who can assist others in faith convictions, spiritual insights, and work conflicts.

Application Requirements: You should have a Bachelor's degree from an accredited college or university, and submit three letters of recommendation, a current resume, and your scores on the Miller Analogies Test (MAT) or the Graduate Record Examination (GRE).

Completion Requirements: You must successfully complete 15 credits for this certificate.

Example Course Titles: Some of the course titles in this program include Introduction to Work-Life Ministry, Theology of Work, Catholic Social Teaching, and Christian Decision-Making.

Program Contact: Work-Life Ministry Admissions Committee
Presidents Hall, 3rd Floor
Seton WorldWide
Seton Hall University
South Orange, New Jersey 07079
(888) SETON-WW
(973) 761-9234
setonworldwide@shu.edu

SOUTHWEST MISSOURI STATE UNIVERSITY

General Contact Information

901 South National
Springfield, Missouri 65804-0094

Phone: (417) 836-5000
E-mail: smsuinfo@vma.smsu.edu
WWW: www.smsu.edu

Online Learning Information

901 South National
Springfield, Missouri 65804

Phone: (417) 836-4128

FAX: (417) 836-6016
E-mail: dianagarland@mail.smsu.edu
WWW: www.smsu.edu

Institution Background

Founded: 1906
Type of Institution: Public
Accreditation: North Central Association of Colleges and Schools

Programs
Administrative Studies

Degree Offered: Master of Science

Program Web Address: www.smsu.edu/contrib/com/msas/index.htm

Program Background: This program is cross-disciplinary and focuses on enhancing administrative abilities, particularly in the areas of Applied Communication, Community Analysis, and Environmental Management. It is designed to meet the needs of students who are established in careers, and are seeking professional growth and advancement within their vocations.

Application Requirements: You must have your Bachelor's degree in any field from a regionally accredited college or university, and a minimum grade point average of 2.75 (on a 4.0 scale) during the last 60 hours of your undergraduate study. All students are screened by the Program Director and Program Advisory Committee for the program. You need to submit a completed application with evidence of three years of work experience, a current resume, your scores on the Graduate Record Examination (GRE) or Graduate Management Aptitude Test (GMAT), and transcripts from each school you've attended.

Completion Requirements: You must successfully complete 36 hours for this degree.

System Requirements: You should have a personal computer with a Pentium processor, 8 MB RAM, a 28.8 kbps modem, sound card and speakers, 65,000-color video display card, Windows 95, Internet access, and a Web browser. You may also need a printer.

Example Course Titles: Some of the course titles for this program include Financial Accounting Concepts for Managers, Financial Management for State and Local Government, Concepts and Analysis of Communication, Management Information Systems, Administrative Law, Personnel Selection, and Placement and Classification.

Program Contact: MSAS Program Director
Communication and Mass Media
SMSU 901 South National Avenue
Springfield, Missouri 65804
(417) 836-5218
jsb806f@mail.smsu.edu

Computer Information Systems

Degree Offered: Master of Science

Program Web Address: www. cis.masters.smsu.edu/Default.htm

Program Background: This program was developed to meet the educational needs of working Information Systems personnel. It combines solid instruction and rich content exposure with a flexible format, and was carefully designed to deliver the additional perspectives and management skills that students say they need in order to advance in their careers.

Application Requirements: You must have three years of documented professional information systems work experience, a Bachelor's degree, and a grade point average of at least 2.75 for the last 60 hours of academic work. You should also have an acceptable score on the Graduate Management Admissions Test (GMAT).

Completion Requirements: You must successfully complete 36 hours for this degree. A thesis paper is not required.

System Requirements: You need a personal computer with a Pentium processor, 8 MB RAM, 28.8 kbps modem, Internet access, a Java-enabled Web browser (such as Microsoft Internet Explorer 4.01 or better), a sound card and speakers, RealNetwork's RealPlayer software, and Windows 95/98. Or you can use a Macintosh system that is equivalent to the personal computer just described.

Example Course Titles: Some of the course titles in this program include Information Systems Planning, Staffing the Information System Function, Network Planning and Administration, Information System Project Management, Comparative System Development Methodologies, Management of End-User Computing, Information System Management, Data Modeling and Database Administration, Information System Resource Acquisition, Organizational Transformation, System Development Programming Operations, and Operating Systems.

Program Contact: Master of Science in CIS Program
CIS Department, 359 Glass Hall
SMSU 901 South National Avenue
Springfield, Missouri 65804
(417) 836-4131
(417) 836-6907
mscis@mail.smsu.edu

ST. PETERSBURG JUNIOR COLLEGE

General Contact Information

Box 13489
St. Petersburg, Florida 33733

WWW: tech.spjc.cc.fl.us

Online Learning Information

P.O. Box 13489
St. Petersburg, Florida 33733

Phone: (813) 545-6563
FAX: (813) 545-6543
E-mail: womerl@mail.spjc.cc.fl.us
WWW: tech.spjc.cc.fl.us

Institution Background

Founded: 1927
Type of Institution: Public

Accreditation: Southern Association of Colleges and Schools

Programs

Veterinary Technology

Degree Offered: Associate in Science

Program Web Address: hec.spjc.cc.fl.us/chip/vtde/vtde1.html

Online Program Started: 1994

Students Enrolled: 140

Program Background: This program serves veterinary hospital employees who wish to earn an Associate's degree to qualify to sit for state certification or licensure examination. Students and instructors communicate primarily through America Online, and the program has an access-controlled area inside a subscription area called Veterinary Information Network. Each course meets in a real-time text chat session once per week for the semester.

Application Requirements: You must have a minimum grade point average of 2.0, have completed most or all of the general education courses, work for a veterinarian, and have computer skills.

You need to submit an application to the college with a $25 application fee and official transcripts from any college or university you've attended.

Completion Requirements: You must successfully complete 73 credits—22 general education and support course credits and 51 veterinary technology course credits.

System Requirements: You need access to a computer and 28.8 kbps (or faster) modem during evening hours Monday through Thursday, 7 to 10 p.m. (Eastern time) and at other unscheduled times for homework. The computer should run the current Windows or Macintosh version of America Online software.

Example Course Titles: Some of the course titles for this program include Canine Organs, Cat Disection, Clinical Practice 1, Animal Physiology, Online Book of Parrots, Care and Handling of Ferrets, Care of Iguanas, Rabbit Care, and Animal Lab Procedures 1.

STATE UNIVERSITY OF NEW YORK EMPIRE STATE COLLEGE

General Contact Information

2 Union Avenue
Saratoga Springs, New York 12866

WWW: www.esc.edu

Online Learning Information

3 Union Avenue
Saratoga Springs, New York 12866

Phone: (518) 587-2100 ext. 300
FAX: (518) 587-2660
E-mail: cdl@scscva.esc.edu
WWW: www.esc.edu

Institution Background

Founded: 1971
Type of Institution: Public
Accreditation: Middle States Association of Colleges and Schools

Programs

Business

Degree Offered: Associate of Science

Program Web Address: sln1.esc.edu/ ESConline/online1.nsf/wholeshortlinks2/ Online

Program Background: Students learn about work environments and internal functioning of organizations so that they can better perform as professionals. Additionally, they gain an understanding of the impact of domestic, political, social, ethical, international, technological, economic and environmental issues. And they learn to think critically and analyze situations in a variety of different contexts.

Application Requirements: You should contact the school directly for information about applying to this program.

Completion Requirements: You must successfully complete 64 credits for this degree.

Example Course Titles: Some of the course titles in this program include Management Principles, Marketing Principles, Introductory Accounting, Economics—Macro, Economics—Micro, Legal Environment of Business, Educational Planning, College Writing, and Communication for Professionals.

Program Contact: Center for Distance Learning
SUNY Empire State College
3 Union Avenue
Saratoga Springs, New York 12866-4391
(800) 847-3000 ext. 300

(518) 587-2660
cdl@sln.esc.edu

Business Administration

Degree Offered: Bachelor of Professional Studies

Program Web Address: sln1.esc.edu/ ESConline/online1.nsf/wholeshortlinks2/ Online

Application Requirements: You need to contact the school directly to get an application for admission.

Completion Requirements: You must successfully complete 128 credits for this degree.

Example Course Titles: Some of the course titles in this program include Management Principles, Marketing Principles, Introductory Accounting, Economics—Macro, Economics—Micro, Legal Environment of Business, International Business, Corporate Finance, Organizational Behavior, Human Resource Management, Diversity in the Workplace, Operations Management, Management Information Systems, Business Ethics, Business Policy, Educational Planning, College Writing, and Communication for Professionals.

Program Contact: Center for Distance Learning
SUNY Empire State College
3 Union Avenue
Saratoga Springs, New York 12866-4391
(800) 847-3000 ext. 300
(518) 587-2660
cdl@sln.esc.edu

Business Administration

Degree Offered: Bachelor of Science

Program Web Address: sln1.esc.edu/ ESConline/online1.nsf/wholeshortlinks2/ Online

Application Requirements: You need to contact the school directly to get an application for admission.

Completion Requirements: You must successfully complete 128 credits for this degree.

Example Course Titles: Some of the course titles in this program include Management Principles, Marketing Principles, Introductory Accounting, Economics—Macro, Economics—Micro, Legal Environment of Business, International Business, Corporate Finance, Organizational Behavior, Human Resource Management, Diversity in the Workplace, Operations Management, Management Information Systems, Business Ethics, Business Policy, Educational Planning, College Writing, and Communication for Professionals.

Program Contact: Center for Distance Learning
SUNY Empire State College
3 Union Avenue
Saratoga Springs, New York 12866-4391
(800) 847-3000 ext. 300
(518) 587-2660
cdl@sln.esc.edu

Business Management

Degree Offered: Bachelor of Professional Studies

Program Web Address: sln1.esc.edu/
ESConline/online1.nsf/wholeshortlinks2/
Online

Application Requirements: You need to contact the school directly to get an application for admission.

Completion Requirements: You must successfully complete 128 credits for this degree.

Example Course Titles: Some of the course titles in this program include Management Principles, Marketing Principles, Introductory Accounting, Economics—Macro, Econom-

ics—Micro, Legal Environment of Business, International Business, Corporate Finance, Organizational Behavior, Human Resource Management, Diversity in the Workplace, Operations Management, Management Information Systems, Business Ethics, Business Policy, Educational Planning, College Writing, and Communication for Professionals.

Program Contact: Center for Distance Learning
SUNY Empire State College
3 Union Avenue
Saratoga Springs, New York 12866-4391
(800) 847-3000 ext. 300
(518) 587-2660
cdl@sln.esc.edu

Business Management

Degree Offered: Bachelor of Science

Program Web Address: sln1.esc.edu/
ESConline/online1.nsf/wholeshortlinks2/
Online

Application Requirements: You need to contact the school directly to get an application for admission.

Completion Requirements: You must successfully complete 128 credits for this degree.

Example Course Titles: Some of the course titles in this program include Management Principles, Marketing Principles, Introductory Accounting, Economics—Macro, Economics—Micro, Legal Environment of Business, International Business, Corporate Finance, Organizational Behavior, Human Resource Management, Diversity in the Workplace, Operations Management, Management Information Systems, Business Ethics, Business Policy, Educational Planning, College Writing, and Communication for Professionals.

Program Contact: Center for Distance Learning

SUNY Empire State College
3 Union Avenue
Saratoga Springs, New York 12866-4391
(800) 847-3000 ext. 300
(518) 587-2660
cdl@sln.esc.edu

Health Services Management

Degree Offered: Bachelor of Science

Program Web Address: sln1.esc.edu/ESConline/online1.nsf/wholeshortlinks2/Online

Application Requirements: You need to contact the school directly to get an application for admission.

Completion Requirements: You must successfully complete 128 credits.

Example Course Titles: Some of the course titles in this program include Management Principles, Marketing Principles, Introductory Accounting, Economics—Macro, Economics—Micro, Organizational Behavior, and Diversity in the Workplace.

Program Contact: Center for Distance Learning
SUNY Empire State College
3 Union Avenue
Saratoga Springs, New York 12866-4391
(800) 847-3000 ext. 300
(518) 587-2660
cdl@sln.esc.edu

Health Services Management

Degree Offered: Bachelor of Professional Studies

Program Web Address: sln1.esc.edu/ESConline/online1.nsf/wholeshortlinks2/Online

Application Requirements: You need to contact the school directly to get an application for admission.

Completion Requirements: You must successfully complete 128 credits.

Example Course Titles: Some of the course titles in this program include Management Principles, Marketing Principles, Introductory Accounting, Economics—Macro, Economics—Micro, Organizational Behavior, and Diversity in the Workplace.

Program Contact: Center for Distance Learning
SUNY Empire State College
3 Union Avenue
Saratoga Springs, New York 12866-4391
(800) 847-3000 ext. 300
(518) 587-2660
cdl@sln.esc.edu

Marketing

Degree Offered: Bachelor of Professional Studies

Program Web Address: sln1.esc.edu/ESConline/online1.nsf/wholeshortlinks2/Online

Application Requirements: You need to complete and submit an application, which you can get from the Center for Distance Learning by e-mailing them at cdl@sln.esc.edu. You can enter the program as a degree-seeking student (in which case you'll be assigned an advisor) or as a non-degree student who simply wants to take one or more courses.

Completion Requirements: You must successfully complete 128 credits for this degree.

Example Course Titles: Some of the course titles for this program include Management Principles, Marketing Principles, Introductory Accounting, Economics, Legal Environment of Business, and Diversity in the Workplace.

Program Contact: Center for Distance Learning
SUNY Empire State College
3 Union Avenue
Saratoga Springs, New York 12866-4391
(800) 847-3000 ext. 300
(518) 587-2660
cdl@sln.esc.edu

STRAYER UNIVERSITY

General Contact Information

WWW: www.strayer.edu

Online Learning Information

8382-F Terminal Road
Lorton, Virginia 22079

Phone: (703) 339-1850
FAX: (703) 339-1852
WWW: www.strayer.edu

Institution Background

Strayer University was founded in Washington, D.C in 1892, and has over 100 years of experience educating working adults. There are more than 10,000 students currently enrolled at Strayer and the majority of them work full-time.

Founded: 1892
Type of Institution: Proprietary
Accreditation: Middle States Association of Colleges and Schools

Programs
Accounting

Degree Offered: Associate

Program Web Address: www.strayer.edu/online/fprog.htm

Application Requirements: You must be a high school graduate or equivalent. You are required to take placement tests to determine the appropriate level at which you should start in mathematics and English. If you have transfer credits in mathematics or English, or you have SAT scores of 400 or higher, then you are waived from placement testing.

System Requirements: You should have a computer with at least a 300 MHz processor (Pentium II equivilant or higher), 64 MB RAM, 4 GB hard drive, 2 MB of video memory, CD-ROM drive, 56K modem, speakers, Windows 98, and Microsoft Office 97 Professional Edition (or higher version).

Program Contact: jct@strayer.edu

Accounting

Degree Offered: Bachelor

Program Web Address: www.strayer.edu/online/fprog.htm

Application Requirements: You must be a high school graduate or equivalent. You are required to take placement tests to determine the appropriate level at which you should start in mathematics and English. If you have transfer credits in mathematics or English, or you have SAT scores of 400 or higher, then you are waived from placement testing.

System Requirements: You should have a computer with at least a 300 MHz processor (Pentium II equivilant or higher), 64 MB RAM, 4 GB hard drive, 2 MB of video memory, CD-ROM drive, 56K modem, speakers, Windows 98, and Microsoft Office 97 Professional Edition (or higher version).

Program Contact: jct@strayer.edu

Business Administration

Degree Offered: Associate

Program Web Address: www.strayer.edu/

online/fprog.htm

Application Requirements: You must be a high school graduate or equivalent. You are required to take placement tests to determine the appropriate level at which you should start in mathematics and English. If you have transfer credits in mathematics or English, or you have SAT scores of 400 or higher, then you are waived from placement testing.

System Requirements: You should have a computer with at least a 300 MHz processor (Pentium II equivilant or higher), 64 MB RAM, 4 GB hard drive, 2 MB of video memory, CD-ROM drive, 56K modem, speakers, Windows 98, and Microsoft Office 97 Professional Edition (or higher version).

Program Contact: jct@strayer.edu

Business Administration

Degree Offered: Bachelor

Program Web Address: www.strayer.edu/online/fprog.htm

Application Requirements: You must be a high school graduate or equivalent. You are required to take placement tests to determine the appropriate level at which you should start in mathematics and English. If you have transfer credits in mathematics or English, or you have SAT scores of 400 or higher, then you are waived from placement testing.

System Requirements: You should have a computer with at least a 300 MHz processor (Pentium II equivilant or higher), 64 MB RAM, 4 GB hard drive, 2 MB of video memory, CD-ROM drive, 56K modem, speakers, Windows 98, and Microsoft Office 97 Professional Edition (or higher version).

Program Contact: jct@strayer.edu

Business Administration

Degree Offered: Master

Program Web Address: www.strayer.edu/online/fprog.htm

Application Requirements: You must have a Bachelor's degree from an accredited college or university. If your proposed graduate major is totally unrelated to your undergraduate degree field, you may be required to complete some undergraduate prerequisites for your graduate program. You must also demonstrate satisfactory performance in one of the following: a minimum Graduate Management Admissions Test (GMAT) score of 450, a minimum cumulative score of 1,000 on the Graduate Records Examination (GRE), a cumulative grade point average of 2.75 (on a 4.0 scale) during the last 60 semester hours or 90 quarter hours of your undergraduate study, or evidence of your potential as a graduate student (for example, three or more years of professional experience).

System Requirements: You need a computer with a 300 MHz (Pentium II or higher) processor, 64 MB RAM, 4 GB hard drive, 12.1″ SVGA TFT Display (laptop) or larger (desktop), 1.44 floppy drive, an Integrated Windows 95 compatible keyboard, 2 MB of video memory, a 24X CD-ROM (laptop) or 40X (desktop), a 56 K PCMCIA Fax modem, 10/100 Ethernet (laptop only), and Integrated microphone and stereo speakers. In terms of software, you'll need Windows 98 and Microsoft Office 97 Professional Edition (or higher version).

Program Contact: jct@strayer.edu

Computer Information Systems

Degree Offered: Associate

Program Web Address: www.strayer.edu/online/fprog.htm

Application Requirements: You must have your high school diploma or the equivalent. You are required to take placement tests to determine the appropriate level for courses in English and mathematics. If you have transfer credits in English or mathematics, or you scored above a 400 on the SAT, then you are waived from placement testing.

System Requirements: You need a computer with a 300 MHz (Pentium II or higher) processor, 64 MB RAM, 4 GB hard drive, 12.1″ SVGA TFT Display (laptop) or larger (desktop), 1.44 floppy drive, an Integrated Windows 95 compatible keyboard, 2 MB of video memory, a 24X CD-ROM (laptop) or 40X (desktop), a 56 K PCMCIA Fax modem, 10/100 Ethernet (laptop only), and Integrated microphone and stereo speakers. In terms of software, you'll need Windows 98 and Microsoft Office 97 Professional Edition (or higher version).

Program Contact: jct@strayer.edu

Computer Information Systems

Degree Offered: Bachelor

Program Web Address: www.strayer.edu/online/fprog.htm

Application Requirements: You must have your high school diploma or the equivalent. You are required to take placement tests to determine the appropriate level for courses in English and mathematics. If you have transfer credits in English or mathematics, or you scored above a 400 on the SAT, then you are waived from placement testing.

System Requirements: You need a computer with a 300 MHz (Pentium II or higher) processor, 64 MB RAM, 4 GB hard drive, 12.1″ SVGA TFT Display (laptop) or larger (desktop), 1.44 floppy drive, an Integrated Windows 95 compatible keyboard, 2 MB of video memory, a 24X CD-ROM (laptop) or 40X (desk-

top), a 56 K PCMCIA Fax modem, 10/100 Ethernet (laptop only), and Integrated microphone and stereo speakers. In terms of software, you'll need Windows 98 and Microsoft Office 97 Professional Edition (or higher version).

Program Contact: jct@strayer.edu

Computer Networking

Degree Offered: Bachelor

Program Web Address: www.strayer.edu/online/fprog.htm

Application Requirements: You must have your high school diploma or the equivalent. You are required to take placement tests to determine the appropriate level for courses in English and mathematics. If you have transfer credits in English or mathematics, or you scored above a 400 on the SAT, then you are waived from placement testing.

System Requirements: You need a computer with a 300 MHz (Pentium II or higher) processor, 64 MB RAM, 4 GB hard drive, 12.1″ SVGA TFT Display (laptop) or larger (desktop), 1.44 floppy drive, an Integrated Windows 95 compatible keyboard, 2 MB of video memory, a 24X CD-ROM (laptop) or 40X (desktop), a 56 K PCMCIA Fax modem, 10/100 Ethernet (laptop only), and Integrated microphone and stereo speakers. In terms of software, you'll need Windows 98 and Microsoft Office 97 Professional Edition (or higher version).

Program Contact: jct@strayer.edu

Economics

Degree Offered: Associate

Program Web Address: www.strayer.edu/online/fprog.htm

Application Requirements: You must have your high school diploma or the equivalent. You are required to take placement tests to determine the appropriate level for courses in English and mathematics. If you have transfer credits in English or mathematics, or you scored above a 400 on the SAT, then you are waived from placement testing.

System Requirements: You need a computer with a 300 MHz (Pentium II or higher) processor, 64 MB RAM, 4 GB hard drive, 12.1″ SVGA TFT Display (laptop) or larger (desktop), 1.44 floppy drive, an Integrated Windows 95 compatible keyboard, 2 MB of video memory, a 24X CD-ROM (laptop) or 40X (desktop), a 56 K PCMCIA Fax modem, 10/100 Ethernet (laptop only), and Integrated microphone and stereo speakers. In terms of software, you'll need Windows 98 and Microsoft Office 97 Professional Edition (or higher version).

Program Contact: jct@strayer.edu

Economics

Degree Offered: Bachelor

Program Web Address: www.strayer.edu/ online/fprog.htm

Application Requirements: You must have your high school diploma or the equivalent. You are required to take placement tests to determine the appropriate level for courses in English and mathematics. If you have transfer credits in English or mathematics, or you scored above a 400 on the SAT, then you are waived from placement testing.

System Requirements: You need a computer with a 300 MHz (Pentium II or higher) processor, 64 MB RAM, 4 GB hard drive, 12.1″ SVGA TFT Display (laptop) or larger (desktop), 1.44 floppy drive, an Integrated Windows 95 compatible keyboard, 2 MB of video memory, a 24X CD-ROM (laptop) or 40X (desk-

top), a 56 K PCMCIA Fax modem, 10/100 Ethernet (laptop only), and Integrated microphone and stereo speakers. In terms of software, you'll need Windows 98 and Microsoft Office 97 Professional Edition (or higher version).

Program Contact: jct@strayer.edu

General Studies

Degree Offered: Associate

Program Web Address: www.strayer.edu/ online/fprog.htm

Application Requirements: You must be a high school graduate or equivalent. You are required to take placement tests to determine the appropriate level at which you should start in mathematics and English. If you have transfer credits in mathematics or English, or you have SAT scores of 400 or higher, then you are waived from placement testing.

System Requirements: You should have a computer with at least a 300 MHz processor (Pentium II equivilant or higher), 64 MB RAM, 4 GB hard drive, 2 MB of video memory, CD-ROM drive, 56K modem, speakers, Windows 98, and Microsoft Office 97 Professional Edition (or higher version).

Program Contact: jct@strayer.edu

General Studies

Degree Offered: Bachelor

Program Web Address: www.strayer.edu/ online/fprog.htm

Application Requirements: You must have a high school diploma or equivalent, and you will have to take placement tests to determine the course levels you need to begin with in English and mathematics. If you have transfer credits in English or mathematics, or your SAT scores in these areas are 400 or higher, then

Strayer will waive the requirement for you to take these placement exams.

System Requirements: You need a computer with a 300 MHz (Pentium II or higher) processor, 64 MB RAM, 4 GB hard drive, 12.1″ SVGA TFT Display (laptop) or larger (desktop), 1.44 floppy drive, an Integrated Windows 95 compatible keyboard, 2 MB of video memory, a 24X CD-ROM (laptop) or 40X (desktop), a 56 K PCMCIA Fax modem, 10/100 Ethernet (laptop only), and Integrated microphone and stereo speakers. In terms of software, you'll need Windows 98 and Microsoft Office 97 Professional Edition (or higher version).

Program Contact: jct@strayer.edu

General Studies

Degree Offered: Master

Program Web Address: www.strayer.edu/online/fprog.htm

Application Requirements: You must have a Bachelor's degree from an accredited college or university. If your proposed graduate major is totally unrelated to your undergraduate degree field, you may be required to complete some undergraduate prerequisites for your graduate program. You must also demonstrate satisfactory performance in one of the following: a minimum Graduate Management Admissions Test (GMAT) score of 450, a minimum cumulative score of 1,000 on the Graduate Records Examination (GRE), a cumulative grade point average of 2.75 (on a 4.0 scale) during the last 60 semester hours or 90 quarter hours of your undergraduate study, or evidence of your potential as a graduate student (for example, three or more years of professional experience).

System Requirements: You need a computer with a 300 MHz (Pentium II or higher) processor, 64 MB RAM, 4 GB hard drive, 12.1″ SVGA TFT Display (laptop) or larger (desktop), 1.44 floppy drive, an Integrated Windows 95 compatible keyboard, 2 MB of video memory, a 24X CD-ROM (laptop) or 40X (desktop), a 56 K PCMCIA Fax modem, 10/100 Ethernet (laptop only), and Integrated microphone and stereo speakers. In terms of software, you'll need Windows 98 and Microsoft Office 97 Professional Edition (or higher version).

Program Contact: jct@strayer.edu

Marketing

Degree Offered: Associate

Program Web Address: www.strayer.edu/online/fprog.htm

Application Requirements: You must have a high school diploma or equivalent, and you will have to take placement tests to determine the course levels you need to begin with in English and mathematics. If you have transfer credits in English or mathematics, or your SAT scores in these areas are 400 or higher, then Strayer will waive the requirement for you to take these placement exams.

System Requirements: You need a computer with a 300 MHz (Pentium II or higher) processor, 64 MB RAM, 4 GB hard drive, 12.1″ SVGA TFT Display (laptop) or larger (desktop), 1.44 floppy drive, an Integrated Windows 95 compatible keyboard, 2 MB of video memory, a 24X CD-ROM (laptop) or 40X (desktop), a 56 K PCMCIA Fax modem, 10/100 Ethernet (laptop only), and Integrated microphone and stereo speakers. In terms of software, you'll need Windows 98 and Microsoft Office 97 Professional Edition (or higher version).

Program Contact: jct@strayer.edu

Professional Accounting

Degree Offered: Master

Program Web Address: www.strayer.edu/online/fprog.htm

Application Requirements: You must have a Bachelor's degree from an accredited college or university, and meet one of these testing requirements: have a minimum score of 450 of the Graduate Management Admission Test, or a minimum cumulative score of 1000 on the General Record Examination. You should also have a minimum cumulative grade point average of 2.75 (on a 4.0 scale) during the last 60 semester hours or 90 quarter hours of your undergraduate study. You should also show potential for graduate school and have at least three years of professional or business experience.

System Requirements: You should have a personal computer with 300 MHz Pentium II processor, 4 GB hard drive, 3.5″ floppy drive, 40X CD-ROM drive (24X if you have a laptop), 56K PCMCIA fax card, sound card and speakers, Windows 98, Microsoft Office 97 Professional Edition.

Program Contact: jct@strayer.edu

SUFFOLK UNIVERSITY

General Contact Information

8 Ashburton Pl.
Boston, Massachusetts 02108

Phone: (617) 573-8000
WWW: www.suffolk.edu

Institution Background

Founded: 1906
Type of Institution: Private

Accreditation: New England Association of Schools and Colleges

Financial Aid: Students enrolled in the online MBA courses may be eligible for student loans and employer-sponsored tuition assistance.

Programs
Business Adminsitration

Degree Offered: Master of Business Administration

Program Web Address: www.sawyer.suffolk.edu/grad/embaonline.htm

Online Program Started: 1999

Program Background: This program enables students to earn the same accredited degree that full-time, part-time, and Executive students on campus earn. It is an interactive, rigorous, and challenging program that prepares students for the rapidly expanding global marketplace, and the highly specialized challenges students will face.

Completion Requirements: You must successfully complete 11 to 16 courses, or 34 to 51 credits for this degree. The curriculum includes two required courses, five core courses, and nine electives.

System Requirements: You should have access to the Internet and a moderate level of experience working on the World Wide Web. The school recommends that you have a personal computer with a Pentium processor, a 28.8 baud modem, Microsoft Windows 95, and Microsoft Office 97 Professional.

Example Course Titles: Some of the course titles in this program include Basic Statistics, Tomorrow's Manager, Strategic Management, Behavior in the Workplace and Marketplace, Accounting Information and Customer Value,

Managing in the Global Legal and Economic Environment, Managing Operations and Information Technology, and Financial Management and Economic Value.

Program Contact: Director eMBA—Online MBA
Suffolk University, Sawyer School of Management
8 Ashburton Place
Boston, Massachusetts 02108-2770
(617) 573-8372
suffolkemba@suffolk.edu

TEXAS SOUTHERN UNIVERSITY

General Contact Information

3100 Cleburne Street
Houston, Texas 77004

Phone: (713) 313-7420
FAX: (713) 313-4317

Institution Background

Founded: 1947
Type of Institution: Public
Accreditation: Southern Association of Colleges and Schools

Programs

Technology Management

Degree Offered: Doctor of Philosophy

Program Web Address: web.indstate.edu:80/tech/acadprog/grad/cphd/cphd.html

Program Background: This degree program is geared toward technologists and combines traditional doctoral research with an innovative delivery system, a consortium of universities, and advanced technical specialization. It is a collaborative program that is administered by the School of Technology at Indiana State University. Other schools that participate include Bowling Green State University, Central Connecticut State University, Central Missouri State University, East Carolina University, Eastern Michigan University, North Carolina A&T State University, Texas Southern University, and University of Wisconsin-Stout.

Application Requirements: You must apply to Indiana State University for admission to this doctoral program. You should have a Bachelor's degree from a regionally accredited college or university, a minimum undergraduate grade point average of 3.0 (on a 4.0 scale) and a minimum graduate grade point average of 3.5, two years of appropriate work experience, and a score of at least 500 on each section of the Graduate Record Examination. With your application, you should submit five letters of recommendation.

Completion Requirements: You must successfully complete a minimum of 90 semester hours of graduate study, with a majority of your coursework at the 600-level. Your program of study will be divided into five areas: Major Area of Specialization (24-30 semester hours), Internship (six semester hours), Research Core (27-33 semester hours), General Technology Core (12-18 semester hours), and Cognate Studies.

On Campus Requirements: You are required to complete two residencies for this program, but you have two options for fulfilling this requirement. You can complete two consecutive semesters at Indiana State University, or you can complete one semester at Indiana State University and one semester at the home university/consortium university where you're completing your specialization.

Example Course Titles: Some of the course titles in this program include Strategic Planning of Technological Processes, Internet Research Methods, Impacts of Technology, Legal Aspects of Industry, and Technological System, Assessment, and Innovation.

Program Contact: jonathan@student.tsu.edu

THOMAS EDISON STATE COLLEGE

General Contact Information

101 West State Street
Trenton, New Jersey 08608-1176

E-mail: admissions@call.tesc.edu
WWW: www.tesc.edu

Online Learning Information

101 West State Street
Tenton, New Jersey 08608

Phone: (609) 984-1150
FAX: (609) 984-8447
E-mail: info@tesc.edu
WWW: www.tesc.edu

Institution Background

Thomas Edison State College is a national leader in distance education, enabling adult learners to complete degrees wherever they live and work. Students earn credit for college-level knowledge acquired outside the classroom (such as knowledge gained on the job or through volunteer activities). There are no residency requirements.

Founded: 1972
Type of Institution: Public
Accreditation: Middle States Association of Colleges and Schools

Individual Undergraduate Courses: Thomas Edison offers online courses in American cin-

ema, ethics, nonprofit management, environmental change, business communications, computers, marketing, photography, marriage and the family, microeconomics, management, and social psychology.

Programs

Management

Degree Offered: Master of Science

Program Web Address: www.tesc.edu/ degree_programs/masters.html

Program Background: Integrating management theory and practice in diverse organizations, educational institutions, and nonprofit agencies is the focus of Thomas Edison State College's Master of Science in Management degree program. It helps students develop analytical skills that will aid them in solving problems and making management decisions. The program is designed to serve adults who are employed and have had professional experience in a management field, especially those who are not being served by conventional or traditional programs of study.

Application Requirements: You must have your Bachelor's degree from an accredited college or universiy, and relevant work experience and career goals. The admissions committee recommends that you have at least five years of supervisory experience or managerial experience. Additionally, you must have skills in writing and presenting, be proficient in computer use, and have knowledge of accounting, business policy, finance, management principles, marketing, organizational behavior, and quantitative methods. If you need to do so, you can demonstrate your abilities in these areas through independent study courses.

Program Restrictions: You can transfer only up to six semester hours of graduate credit that you've earned at another institution.

Completion Requirements: You must successfully complete at least 36 credit hours through the computer-based courses. You'll be assigned a faculty mentor for each course.

On Campus Requirements: You're required to attend a weekend orientation and a weekend session at the end of the program in residence. Each in-residence session is held in New Jersey or in a city and state central to the students admitted to the program. You are responsible for paying your own travel and lodging expenses for these sessions.

System Requirements: You should have a computer with access to the Internet, e-mail, and a Web browser such as Netscape 4.x or higher or Microsoft Internet Explorer 4.x. or higher.

Example Course Titles: Some of the course titles for this program include Organizational Theory and Behavior, Human Resources Management, Economic Issues in Organizations, Accounting and Finance for Managers, Organizational Research, Organizational Management and Leadership, Marketing Management, Ethics for Managers, and Contemporary Topics in Leadership.

Program Contact: Associate Dean
Master of Science in Management
Thomas Edison State College
101 W. State Street
Trenton, New Jersey 08608
info@tesc.edu

TROY STATE UNIVERSITY-FLORIDA REGION

General Contact Information

81 Beal Pkwy, Suite 2A
PO Box 2829
Fort Walton Beach, Florida 32549-2829

Phone: (850) 301-2150
FAX: (850) 301-2179
E-mail: distlearn@tsufl.edu
WWW: www.tsufl.edu/distancelearning

Online Learning Information

81 Beal Parkway SE
Fort Walton Beach, Florida 32549

Phone: (850) 301-2150
FAX: (850) 301-2179
E-mail: distlearn@tsufl.edu
WWW: www.tsufl.edu/distancelearning

Institution Background

Troy State University, Florida Region, is the largest extension campus within the Troy State University system. Traditionally, it was charged with a military focus to cater to active duty personnel. But Troy State has shifted its focus to better serve the civilian community and metropolitan areas as part of its five-year strategic plan.

Founded: 1983
Type of Institution: Public
Accreditation: Southern Association of Colleges and Schools

Online Course Background: All of Troy State University's courses are Web-based with varied support modalities and can be delivered to any location designated by the student.

Online Course Offered: 45

Online Students Enrolled: 285

Services Offered to Students: Troy State University, Florida Region, offers all distance learning students full online Library access, which includes extensive searchable databases (many with full-text articles).

Financial Aid: Students enrolled in online courses may be eligible for standard federal financial aid, teaching assistantships, Veterans benefits, and DANTES education assistance. Non-U.S. citizens are not eligible for financial aid.

Individual Undergraduate Courses: Troy State University offers credit for some military experience and completed course work.

Registration: You can register for courses via mail, phone, e-mail, and the World Wide Web.

Programs

Business Administration

Degree Offered: Associate of Science

Program Web Address: 205.160.74.35/ distancelearning/programs/asba.htm

Completion Requirements: You must successfully complete 92 hours for this degree.

Example Course Titles: Some of the course titles in this program include Business Statistics, Principles of Macroeconomics, Principles of Microeconomics, Principles of Accounting, Principles of Management and Organization Behavior, Principles of Marketing, and Legal Environment.

Program Contact: distlearn@tsufl.edu

General Education

Degree Offered: Associate of Science

Program Web Address: 205.160.74.35/ operations/Handbook/Hdk_61.htm

Completion Requirements: You must successfully complete 92 hours.

Example Course Titles: Some of the course titles in this program include Orientation, Composition, and Mathematics for General Studies.

Program Contact: distlearn@tsufl.edu

International Relations

Degree Offered: Master of Science

Program Web Address: 205.160.74.35/ distancelearning/programs/msir.htm

Program Background: Students have two options in the Master of Science in International Relations (MSIR) program—one requires ten courses and a comprehensive examination, while the other requires 12 courses and an Exit Portfolio, but no comprehensive examination. Students have to choose which option to pursue and a concentration upon entering the program. Students who wish to change their option and concentration have to submit a written request and explanation, which the chair of the department reviews and decides whether to approve.

There are seven concentrations for students to choose from: International Affairs, National Security Affairs, International Political Economics, International Organizational Management, International Public Administration, Regional Affairs, International Students (ten-course option only), and Civil/Psychological Affairs (12-course option only).

At a minimum, the Exit Portfolio (required for the 12-course option) will include all of your papers (corrected and updated) from the core courses, all other papers and projects, and an up-to-date resume. Students present the portfolio to the chair of the department during an exit interview that take place during a student's last semester, and the chair will award the portfolio a grade of pass or fail.

Completion Requirements: You must successfully complete ten or 12 courses, depending on which option you're pursuing.

Example Course Titles: Some of the course titles in this program include Survey of International Relations, Research Methods in International Relations, International Economics Military History of the United States, U.S. Diplomatic History, National Security Policy, Comparative Government, Government and Politics of Developing Nations, International Law, and Theory and Ideology of International Relations.

Program Contact: distlearn@tsufl.edu

Public Administration

Degree Offered: Master of Public Administration

Program Web Address: spectrum.troyst.edu/cmi-mpa/

Program Background: This online degree program consists of seven core courses and three electives, plus comprehensive examinations. Students have the option of taking a 12-course track that does not require comprehensive examinations, but that does require a final practicum course.

Completion Requirements: You must successfully complete ten to 12 courses for this degree.

Example Course Titles: Some of the course titles in this program include Research Methods, Public Administration, Organization Theory, Public Policy, Public Personnel, Program Evaluation, Public Admininstration Law, and Public Budgeting.

Program Contact: distlearn@tsufl.edu

Resource Management

Degree Offered: Bachelor of Applied Science

Program Web Address: 205.160.74.35/operations/Handbook/Hdk_83.htm

Program Background: This program is designed to give participants technical competence and experience, along with managerial, social, and communication skills that will bet-

ter prepare them for changing conditions on the job, in their community, and on larger scales.

Completion Requirements: You must successfully complete 193 credit hours.

Example Course Titles: Some of the course titles for this program include Legal Environment, Business Information, Business Statistics, Principles of Macro Economics, Principles of Accounting, Managerial Finance, and Principles of Marketing.

Program Contact: distlearn@tsufl.edu

ULSTER COUNTY COMMUNITY COLLEGE

General Contact Information

Stone Ridge, New York 12484

Phone: (914) 687-5018
FAX: (914) 687-5083
E-mail: weathers@sunyulster.edu
WWW: www.ulster.cc.ny.us

Online Learning Information

Cottekill Road
Stone Ridge, New York 12484

Phone: (914) 687-5081
FAX: (914) 687-5083
E-mail: makowsp@sunyulster.edu
WWW: www.ulster.cc.ny.us

Institution Background

Ulster County Community College is a comprehensive, two-year college sponsored by the county of Ulster and opreated under the State University of New York. Its curricula and course offerings are registered with the New

York State Department of Education, Office of Higher Education and the Professions.

Founded: 1962
Type of Institution: Public
Accreditation: Middle States Association of Colleges and Schools

Online Course Background: Ulster County Community College is a participating member of the SUNY Learning Network, which is made up of more than 40 college and university campuses offering hundreds of online courses. The SUNY Learning Network began offering online courses in 1995. Ulster currently offers an Associate in Science in Individual Studies through the SUNY Learning Network.

Online Course Offered: 375

Online Students Enrolled: 4400

Services Offered to Students: Library access is available to online students. Professional staff members serve as student success managers for first year students.

Financial Aid: Students enrolled in online courses may be eligible for federal financial aid, tuition assistance, aid for part-time study, and Veterans benefits.

Registration: You can register for courses via mail, phone, and the World Wide Web.

Programs
Liberal Arts and Science

Degree Offered: Associate in Science

Program Web Address: www.sunyulster.edu

Online Program Started: 1999

Program Background: Ulster County Community College's multi-purpose liberal arts and sciences program enables students to plan a sequence of courses according to their individual needs and interests.

Students must complete at least six credits in courses through Ulster County Community College and a total of 30 credits through the State University of New York (SUNY) Learning Network. Students can also transfer up to 30 credits.

Application Requirements: You can receive a free application by mail.

Time for Completion: You have an unlimited amount of time to complete the program.

System Requirements: To participate in the program, you must have access to the World Wide Web and use Netscape Navigator 3.0 or higher or Internet Explorer 4.0 as your Web browser. Also a working knowledge of the Internet is necessary.

Program Contact: Susan Weatherly
SUNY at Ulster
Stone Ridge, New York 12440-8004
(800) 443-5331 ext. 5081
weathers@sunyulster.edu

UNION INSTITUTE
General Contact Information

440 East McMillan Street
Cincinnati, Ohio 45206-1925

Phone: (800) 486-3116
FAX: (513) 861-3218
E-mail: admissions@tui.edu
WWW: www.tui.edu

Online Learning Information

440 East McMillan Street
Cincinnati, Ohio 45206

Phone: (513) 861-6400

FAX: (513) 861-9026
E-mail: tmott@tui.edu
WWW: www.tui.edu

Institution Background

The Union Institute was founded for and continues to serve the educational needs of working adult learners. Individually designed courses set the Institute apart from other institutions offering only a set curriculum.

Founded: 1964
Type of Institution: Private
Accreditation: North Central Association of Colleges and Schools

Online Course Background: The Union Institute's Center for Distance Learning offers a wide range of courses using computer and other electronic-based technologies. And its degree programs/courses are individually designed for the students.

Online Course Offered: 80

Online Students Enrolled: 49

Services Offered to Students: The Union Institute provides access to extensive online research services via Internet access to its home page, as well as providing research assistance.

Financial Aid: Online students may be eligible for federal and state financial aid.

Registration: You can register for courses via mail and e-mail.

Programs

The Union Institute offers online programs of study in liberal arts and sciences.

UNITED STATES SPORTS ACADEMY

General Contact Information

WWW: www.sport.ussa.edu

Online Learning Information

One Academy Drive
Daphne, Alabama 36526

Phone: (800) 223-2668
FAX: (334) 621-2527
E-mail: academy@ussa-sport.ussa.edu
WWW: www.sport.ussa.edu

Institution Background

Founded: 1972
Type of Institution: Private
Accreditation: Southern Association of Colleges and Schools

Programs

Sport Coaching

Degree Offered: Master of Sport Science

Program Web Address: www.sport.ussa.edu/programs/sportsch.htm

Program Background: This program is designed to prepare students for leadership in coaching sports.

Application Requirements: You should have a background in sports, such as being a player or a coach, or an undergraduate major in health, physical education, recreation, or sports training.

You need to submit an application with a $50 application fee, official copies of all college transcripts, three letters of recommendation, copies of any aptitude tests you've taken in the past five years (Graduate Record Examination, Miller Analogies Test, or Graduate Management Aptitude Test), a written statement, and a current resume.

If you're an international student, you need to submit a $125 application fee, your scores on the Test of English as a Foreign Language (TOEFL), an evaluation of foreign educational credentials by an Academy approved evaluator, and a Certificate of Eligibility (form I-20) if you plan to study in the United States.

Completion Requirements: You must successfully complete 33 credit hours for this degree.

Example Course Titles: Some of the course titles in this program include Sport Administration and Finance, Sport Marketing, Professional Writing and Research Methods, Contemporary Issues in Sport, Seminar in Sports Medicine, Advanced Assessment, Treatment Procedures, and Sport Coaching Methodology.

Sport Management

Degree Offered: Master of Sport Science

Program Web Address: www.sport.ussa.edu/programs/sportman.htm

Program Background: This program is designed to prepare students for careers and leadership opportunities in sport and recreational management. Students prepare for the demands involved in the operation of sports programs at various levels.

Application Requirements: You need to submit an application with a $50 application fee, official copies of all college transcripts, three letters of recommendation, copies of any aptitude tests you've taken in the past five years (Graduate Record Examination, Miller Analogies Test, or Graduate Management Aptitude

Test), a written statement, and a current resume.

If you're an international student, you need to submit a $125 application fee, your scores on the Test of English as a Foreign Language (TOEFL), an evaluation of foreign educational credentials by an Academy approved evaluator, and a Certificate of Eligibility (form I-20) if you plan to study in the United States.

Completion Requirements: You must successfully complete 33 credit hours for this degree.

Example Course Titles: Some of the course titles in this program include Sport Marketing, Professional Writing and Research Methods, Contemporary Issues in Sport, Seminar in Sports Medicine, Advanced Assessment, Treatment Procedures, Sport Coaching Methodology, and Sport Conditioning.

Sports Medicine

Degree Offered: Master of Sport Science

Program Web Address: www.sport.ussa.edu/PROGRAMS/MEDOPTNS.HTM

Program Background: This program is designed to prepare students for opportunities including athletic training at high school, collegiate, clinical and professional levels. Students gain the knowledge needed for preventing, managing, evaluating, and rehabilitating athletic injuries.

Application Requirements: This program is appropriate for students with undergraduate majors in biology, health, physical education, nursing, physical therapy, or athletic training. You need to complete and submit an application with all supporting documentation.

Completion Requirements: You must successfully complete 33 credit hours, maintain a 3.0 grade point average, have no outstanding balances or monies owed to the institution, successfully complete a Master's comprehensive examination, and participate in a mentoring program.

Example Course Titles: Some of the course titles for this program include Professional Writing and Research, Sport Marketing, Sport Administration and Finance, and Contemporary Issues in Sport.

UNIVERSITY OF CALIFORNIA, DAVIS—UNIVERSITY EXTENSION

General Contact Information

1333 Research Park Drive
Davis, California 95616

Phone: (530) 757-8777
FAX: (530) 754-5094
E-mail: universityextension@unexmail.ucdavis.edu
WWW: www.universityextension.ucdavis.edu

Online Learning Information

1333 Research Park Drive
Davis, California 95616

Phone: (916) 327-1894
FAX: (530) 754-5104
E-mail: smcgloughlin@unexmail.ucdavis.edu
WWW: www.universityextension.ucdavis.edu

Institution Background

University Extension at the University of California, Davis, is the premier provider of professional and continuing education offering over 4,000 courses to almost 83,000 students annually. University Extension offers 21 certificate programs and three professional sequence awards, with class schedules and formats to accommodate busy working professionals.

Founded: 1960
Type of Institution: Public
Accreditation: Western Association of Schools and Colleges

Online Course Background: Students can see the classes before registering at University Extension via the virtual campus Web site. University Extension offers courses explicitly designed for the Web, rather than classroom courses converted for online use.

Online Course Offered: 4

Online Students Enrolled: 172

Services Offered to Students: Each University Extension student has access to the University of California, Davis, main library. Also each student may utilize the state-of-the-art computer lab and multimedia lab.

Financial Aid: Students who are enrolled in online courses as part of a certificate program may be eligible for student loans.

Registration: You can register for courses via mail, phone, e-mail, and World Wide Web.

Programs
Computer Programming

Degree Offered: Certificate in Computer Programming

Program Web Address: www.universityextension.ucdavis.edu

Online Program Started: 1999

Students Enrolled: 45

Degrees Awarded: 16

Program Background: This program teaches students about database design and development, and systems analysis. Students develop analytical skills and learn how to structure solid programs, develop C programming skills, and explore object technology with the choices of several languages.

Completion Requirements: You must successfully complete 30 units of coursework (including 18 units of required coursework and 12 units of elective).

Time for Completion: You should be able to complete this program within one or two years.

On Campus Requirements: Currently, only one of the required courses is available online. You will have to attend the remainder of the courses on-campus.

System Requirements: You should have a multimedia-capable personal computer, a current email account, and Internet access. You also need a Web browser and Visual Basic 6 software.

Example Course Titles: Some of the course titles in this program include Visual Basic 6: Introduction, C Language Projects, and Object-Oriented Requirements Analysis and Design.

Program Contact: University Extension
University of California, Davis
1333 Research Park Drive
Davis, California 95833
(800) 752-0881
(530) 757-8558
universityextension@ucdavis.edu

Web Page Creation

University Extension, University of California—Davis

Degree Offered: Web Page Creation Professional Sequence Award

Program Web Address: www.universityextension.ucdavis.edu

Online Program Started: 1999

Students Enrolled: 20

Degrees Awarded: 6

Program Background: This program teaches students about the technical architecture behind the Internet, what makes a Web page work, and how to create well-designed, functional Web pages. Students learn basic HTML coding.

Application Requirements: You must demonstrate proficiency using a Web browser.

Completion Requirements: You are required to complete 10 units of coursework for this certificate.

Time for Completion: Typically, most students complete this program within a year.

On Campus Requirements: Only one course is currently taught online. The remaining courses are taught in a traditional classroom.

System Requirements: You should have a multimedia-capable personal computer, an e-mail account, and Internet access.

You should also have a text editor (such as Wordpad or Notepad) and an HTML editor is recommended.

Example Course Titles: A couple of the courses in this program are Internet Architecture and Services, and Web Site Functional Design.

Program Contact: University Extension
University of Califoria, Davis
1333 Research Park Drive
Davis, Califonia 95833
(800) 752-0881
(530) 757-8558
universityextension@ucdavis.edu

Web Site Development

Degree Offered: Certificate in Web Site Development

Program Web Address: www.universityextension.ucdavis.edu

Online Program Started: 1999

Students Enrolled: 35

Degrees Awarded: 11

Program Background: This program teaches students how a Web page works, how to manage multiple Web pages, and how to implement Web sites on the Internet. Students become technically skilled with database applications on the Internet, as well as learn programming and scripting.

Application Requirements: You must be proficient with an Internet browser, and have technical skills in programming and database design.

Completion Requirements: You must successfully complete 23 units of coursework (including 17 units of required coursework and six units of electives).

Time for Completion: You should be able to complete this program in one or two years.

On Campus Requirements: Currently, only two of the required courses in this program are taught online. You must attend the remainder on-campus.

System Requirements: You should have a multimedia-capable personal computer, a current email account, and Internet access. You also need a Web browser and a text editor (such as Wordpad or Notepad). An HTML editor is recommended.

Example Course Titles: Some of the course titles in this program include Web Page Creation and Authoring, Web Page Scripting, and Internet Architecture and Services.

Program Contact: University Extension
University of California, Davis
1333 Research Park Drive

Davis, California 95616
(800) 752-0881
(530) 757-8558
universityextension@ucdavis.edu

UNIVERSITY OF BALTIMORE

General Contact Information

1420 North Charles Street
Baltimore, Maryland 21201

Phone: (410) 837-4777
FAX: (410) 837-4793
E-mail: admissions@ubmail.ubalt.edu
WWW: www.ubalt.edu

Online Learning Information

WWW: www.ubonline.edu

Institution Background

Founded: 1925
Type of Institution: Public
Accreditation: Middle States Association of Schools and Colleges

Programs

Business Administration

Degree Offered: Master of Business Administration

Program Web Address: www.ubonline.edu/webmbahome.nsf

Online Program Started: 1999

Program Background: The University of Baltimore's Merrick School of Business has created this WebMBA in Information-Leveraged Management that will allow you to learn anywhere, at any time.

Application Requirements: You must have an undergraduate degree in any field of study. You need to submit a completed application, two reference letters, Graduate Management Admission Test (GMAT) test scores, official transcripts from all colleges and universities you have attended, a letter of intent, and the name of at least one individual willing to serve as a proctor for timed examinations and some of the webMBA courses.

Completion Requirements: You must successfully complete the 16 courses comprising 48 semester hour credits. You may take two courses per quarter.

System Requirements: You should have a personal computer, an Internet connection through an Internet Service Provider (ISP), a 28.8 modem or faster, a Web Browser (Netscape 3.02 or better, or Microsoft Internet Explorer 4.0 or better), an e-mail account that supports attachments, a printer, VGA monitor, sound card, and Microsoft Office 97 Suite. You may also need access to a fax machine on occasion.

Example Course Titles: Some of the course titles in this program include Leveraged Marketing, Financial Accounting, Leveraging Economic Principles, Financial Management, Managing People in Organizations, Product and Service Operations, Accounting For Managerial, Organization Creation and Growth, Information Systems and Technology, Applied Management Science, Global/Domestic Business Environment, Strategic Innovation and Renewal, Global e-Commerce, Electronic Investment Solutions, and Information Based Management Solutions.

Program Contact: Merrick School of Business
University of Baltimore
1420 North Charles Street

Baltimore, Maryland 21201
(410) 837-4953
rfrederick@ubmail.ubalt.edu

UNIVERSITY OF BRIDGEPORT

General Contact Information

126 Park Avenue, Wahlstrom Library
Bridgeport, Connecticut 06601

Phone: (203) 576-4561
E-mail: admit@bridgeport.edu
WWW: www.bridgeport.edu

Online Learning Information

126 Park Avenue
Bridgeport, Connecticut 06601
E-mail: gmichael@cse.bridgeport.edu
WWW: www.bridgeport.edu

Institution Background

At the core of the University of Bridgeport's online courses is the individual guidance provided by the instructors, and the interactive electronic environment that allows a greater degree of class discussion and participation. The University's online instructors are practicing professionals, or University faculty who are experienced educators.

Founded: 1927
Type of Institution: Private
Accreditation: The University of Bridgeport's Human Nutrition Program is licensed and accredited by the Connecticut Board of Governors for Higher Education and the Commission on Institutions of Higher Education, New England.

Online Course Background: The University of Bridgeport offers a Master's degree (online) in

Human Nutrition, which is focused on the role of human nutrition in both health and disease.

Online Course Offered: 12

Online Students Enrolled: 125

Services Offered to Students: The University's online campus offers academic programs, library resources, and student services that are available 24 hours a day.

Financial Aid: Students enrolled in online courses may be eligible for federal student loans.

Registration: You can register for courses via mail, phone, e-mail, and the World Wide Web.

Programs

Human Nutrition

Degree Offered: Master of Science in Human Nutrition

Program Web Address: www.bridgeport.edu/disted.html

Students Enrolled: 125

Degrees Awarded: 11

Program Background: This program teaches students the science of nutrition, focusing on human nutrition in both health and disease.

Application Requirements: You should have a Bachelor's degree from an accredited college or university and an above-average academic record (a grade point average of 3.0 or higher). Also, you should have successfully completed these prerequisite courses: Introductory Biochemistry, and Human Anatomy and Physiology.

Completion Requirements: You must successfully complete 31 credits and pass a compre-

hensive examination (which takes place on-campus) to earn this degree.

Time for Completion: You have up to five years to complete this program.

On Campus Requirements: You are required to visit campus to take a comprehensive examination after you've completed the core curriculum.

System Requirements: You should have access to a personal computer with a 486 or faster processor running Windows 3.1 or higher or the Macintosh equivalent, 16 MB RAM, 20 MB of free hard drive space, a 3.5" floppy disk, a 33.6 kpbs modem, and a CD-ROM drive.

Example Course Titles: Some of the course titles in this program include Pathophysiologic Basis of Metabolic Diseases, Biochemistry of Nutrition, Vitamin and Mineral Metabolism, Clinical Biochemistry, Assessment of Nutritional Status, Nutritional Therapies, Developmental Nutrition, Research in Nutrition, and Biostatistics.

Program Contact: Michael Giampaoli
University of Bridgeport
303 University Avenue
Bridgeport, Connecticut 06601
(203) 576-5861
(203) 576-4852
ubonline@bridgeport.edu

UNIVERSITY OF CALIFORNIA EXTENSION

General Contact Information

110 Sproul Hall
Berkeley, California 94720-5800

E-mail: ouars@uclink.berkely.edu
WWW: www.berkeley.edu/

Online Learning Information

2000 Center Street, Suite 400
Berkeley, California 94704

E-mail: askcmil@uclink4.berkeley.edu
WWW: www.berkeley.edu/

Institution Background

Founded: 1868
Type of Institution: Public
Accreditation: Western Association of Schools and Colleges

Financial Aid: Generally, students enrolled in UC Extension courses are not eligible for financial aid.

Programs

Business Administration

Degree Offered: Certificate

Program Web Address: learn.berkeley.edu/catalog/html/body_bacert.html

Program Background: This program offers comprehensive coverage of the fundamentals of managing a business. Students develop an understanding of both the finances and organizational structure of businesses and the competitive environment in which they operate.

Application Requirements: You can enroll for courses online using a secure server and your credit card. To find courses in which you want to enroll, you should look over the school's online course catalog. You can order textbooks online too.

System Requirements: You should have a personal computer running Windows 3.1/95/NT or a Macintosh with OS 7.1 or higher. Your computer needs to have 16 MB RAM, 25 MB of free hard drive space, a 14.4 or faster modem, and an Internet Service Provider.

Example Course Titles: Some of the course titles in this program include Essentials of Marketing, Management Accounting for Non-Accountants, Basic Corporate Finance, The Economics of Marketing and Finance, Management of Human Resources, Organization and Management, and Topics in Business Administration.

Program Contact: Center for Media and Independent Learning
UC Extension Online
2000 Center Street, Suite 400
Berkeley, California 94704
(510) 642-4124
(510) 643-9271
nsc@unx.berkeley.edu

Computer Information Systems

Degree Offered: Certificate

Program Web Address: learn.berkeley.edu/catalog/html/body_ciscert.html

Program Background: This program trains students in systems analysis and design, database management, data communications, UNIX, and C programming.

Application Requirements: You can enroll for courses online using a secure server and your credit card. To find courses in which you want to enroll, you should look over the school's online course catalog. You can order textbooks online too.

System Requirements: You should have a personal computer running Windows 3.1/95/NT or a Macintosh with OS 7.1 or higher. Your computer needs to have 16 MB RAM, 25 MB of free hard drive space, a 14.4 or faster modem, and an Internet Service Provider.

Example Course Titles: Some of the course titles in this program include C Language Programming, Concepts of Database Management Systems, Using the UNIX Operating System, Systems Analysis and Design: An Overview, Systems Analysis and Design: Applying Structured Techniques, and Fundamentals of Data Communications.

Program Contact: Center for Media and Independent Learning
UC Extension Online
2000 Center Street, Suite 400
Berkeley, California 94704
(510) 642-4124
(510) 643-9271
nsc@unx.berkeley.edu

Hazardous Materials Management

Degree Offered: Certificate

Program Web Address: learn.berkeley.edu/catalog/html/body_hazcert.html

Program Background: This program covers foundations, principles, regulations, and technologies in the field of hazardous materials management.

Application Requirements: You can enroll for courses online using a secure server and your credit card. To find courses in which you want to enroll, you should look over the school's online course catalog. You can order textbooks online too.

System Requirements: You should have a personal computer running Windows 3.1/95/NT or a Macintosh with OS 7.1 or higher. Your computer needs to have 16 MB RAM, 25 MB of free hard drive space, a 14.4 or faster modem, and an Internet Service Provider.

Example Course Titles: Some of the course titles in this program include Principles of Haz-

ardous Materials Management, Environmental Behavior of Pollutants, Technologies for Treatment, Disposal, and Remediation of Hazardous Wastes, Pollution Prevention and Waste Minimization, Environmental Regulatory Framework, Toxicology and Risk Assessment for Environmental Decision Making, Hazardous Materials Emergency Management, and Environmental Auditing and Assessment.

Program Contact: Center for Media and Independent Learning
UC Extension Online
2000 Center Street, Suite 400
Berkeley, California 94704
(510) 642-4124
(510) 643-9271
nsc@unx.berkeley.edu

Marketing

Degree Offered: Certificate

Program Web Address: learn.berkeley.edu/catalog/html/body_markcert.html

Program Background: This program addresses the needs of students who are new to marketing, currently working in a marketing field and are interested in advancement, or currently working in marketing and interested in a broader understanding of the field. It covers new technologies and changes in company philosophies and marketing strategies.

Application Requirements: You can enroll for courses online using a secure server and your credit card. To find courses in which you want to enroll, you should look over the school's online course catalog. You can order textbooks online too.

System Requirements: You should have a personal computer running Windows 3.1/95/NT or a Macintosh with OS 7.1 or higher. Your computer needs to have 16 MB RAM, 25 MB of free hard drive space, a 14.4 or faster modem, and an Internet Service Provider.

Example Course Titles: Some of the course titles for this program include Essentials of Marketing, Marketing Research: Concepts and Techniques, Integrated Marketing Communications, Consumer Buying Behavior, International Marketing, and Strategic Marketing.

Program Contact: Center for Media and Independent Learning
UC Extension Online
2000 Center Street, Suite 400
Berkeley, California 94704
(510) 642-4124
(510) 643-9271
nsc@unx.berkeley.edu

Project Management

Degree Offered: Certificate

Program Web Address: learn.berkeley.edu/catalog/html/body_pmcert.html

Application Requirements: You can enroll for courses online using a secure server and your credit card. To find courses in which you want to enroll, you should look over the school's online course catalog. You can order textbooks online too.

Completion Requirements: You are required to successfully complete six courses—five are required and one is an elective.

System Requirements: You should have a personal computer with Windows 3.1/95/NT or a Macintosh with OS 7.1 or higher, 16 MB RAM, 25 MB hard disk space, 14.4 kbps modem (or faster), an Internet Service Provider, and Netscape 4.0 or higher. Other software may be required on a course-by-course basis.

Example Course Titles: Some of the course titles in this program include Project Risk Man-

agement, Human Factors and Team Dynamics for Quality Management, Project Management, Quality Management, and Project Planning and Control.

Program Contact: Center for Media and Independent Learning
UC Extension Online
2000 Center Street, Suite 400
Berkeley, California 94704
(510) 642-4124
(510) 643-9271
nsc@unx.berkeley.edu

UNIVERSITY OF CALIFORNIA, LOS ANGELES

General Contact Information

405 Hilgard Avenue
Los Angeles, California 90024

WWW: www.ucla.edu

Online Learning Information

10995 LeConte Avenue, Suite 639
Los Angeles, California 90024-2883

E-mail: kmcguire@unex.ucla.edu
WWW: www.ucla.edu

Institution Background

Founded: 1919
Type of Institution: Public
Accreditation: Western Association of Schools and Colleges

Individual Undergraduate Courses: UCLA offers online courses in accounting, business, computer and information systems, computer programming, education, history, human resources, leadership and human relations, marketing, mathematics, political science, public relations, Web development, and writing.

Programs

College Counseling

Degree Offered: Certificate

Program Web Address: www.OnlineLearning.net/CourseCatalog/Programs.html

Program Background: This program is designed to provide students the knowledge and skills needed to more effectively counsel other students regarding their postsecondary options. The curriculum is geared toward college counselors in a high school setting, high school counselors, junior high and middle school counselors, teachers who want to be better informed about the postsecondary options available for their students, individuals who are interested in developing an independent college counseling practice, and college admissions professionals.

Application Requirements: You must have a Bachelor's degree or equivalent.

Completion Requirements: You must successfully complete 17 quarter units of required courses with a grade of B- or better, and a six-unit practicum (consisting of 65 hours of supervised fieldwork).

Example Course Titles: Some of the course titles in this program include Counseling the College-Bound Student, The College Admissions Process, Financial Aid Fundamentals, Testing/Career Assessment, Using the Internet for College/Career Counseling, Special Issues In College Counseling, and Practicum In College Counseling.

Program Contact: UCLA Extension
Certificate Program Unit
P.O. Box 24901

Los Angeles, California 90024-0901
(310) 206-1654
ydelacru@unex.ucla.edu

Cross-Cultural Language and Academic Development

Degree Offered: Certificate

Program Web Address: www.OnlineLearning.net/CourseCatalog/Programs.html

Program Background: This Cross-Cultural Language and Academic Development (CLAD) certificate is offered by the State of California, not UCLA Extension. The CLAD coursework is directed toward two major groups: Credentialed teachers who are seeking to update the competencies covered by the Language Development Specialist (LDS) or the English as a Second Language (ESL) supplementary authorization. These courses may meet other state and district requirements for professional development or continuing education units for educators.

Application Requirements: You must have a California teaching credential or permit.

Completion Requirements: You must successfully complete all five courses on a credit basis.

Example Course Titles: Some of the course titles in this program include Methodologies for Teaching Academic Content in and through English: Specially Designed Academic Instruction in English (SDAIE) and English Language Development, Applied Methods in Teaching English Language Development, Cultural Diversity in the Classroom, Language Development and Acquisition, and Language Structure and Usage.

Program Contact: UCLA Extension
Certificate Program Unit
P.O. Box 24901
Los Angeles, California 90024-0901
(310) 206-1654

ydelacru@unex.ucla.edu

General Business Studies

Degree Offered: Certificate (Award)

Program Web Address: www.OnlineLearning. net/CourseCatalog/Programs.html

Program Background: Students can update their skills to remain at the leading edge of their profession through this program. Students may design their own programs of study selecting from a wide range of courses in various areas.

Completion Requirements: You must successfully complete nine courses.

Example Course Titles: Some of the course titles in this program include Accounting for Non-Accountants, Basic Managerial Finance, Business Economics, Creating Readable Documents, Cutting-Edge Documentation: An Online Tutorial, Design, Implementation, and Administration of Employee Compensation Programs, Developing a Business Plan, Doing Business in Latin America, E-Commerce for Businesses on the Internet, Effective Business Management, Elements of Human Resources Management, Employee Relations and Legal Aspects of Human Resources Management, Entrepreneurship and New Venture, Financial Analysis in Personal Financial Planning , Financing for Entrepreneurs: Exploring the Options, Financing the Entrepreneurial Venture, Hotel Front Office Management, Human Resources Development, Information Design, Intermediate Accounting Theory, and Practice Inernational Human Resources Management.

Program Contact: UCLA Extension
Certificate Program Unit
P.O. Box 24901
Los Angeles, California 90024-0901
(310) 206-1654
ydelacru@unex.ucla.edu

Online Teaching Program

Degree Offered: Certificate

Program Web Address: www.OnlineLearning. net/CourseCatalog/Programs.html

Program Background: This program prepares teachers for virtual classrooms, and teaches them how to effectively use technology in the delivery of education. It emphasizes theory and practice, particularly in computer-based learning.

Completion Requirements: You must successfully complete five core courses plus one elective for this certificate.

Example Course Titles: Some of the course titles in this program include Introduction to Online Technologies, Teaching and Learning Models for Online Courses, Developing Curriculum for Online Programs, Internet and Online Teaching Tools, Practicum in Online Teaching, and Facilitative Tools for Online Teaching.

Program Contact: UCLA Extension
Certificate Program Unit
P.O. Box 24901
Los Angeles, California 90024-0901
(310) 206-1654
ydelacru@unex.ucla.edu

Personal Financial Planning

Degree Offered: Professional Designation

Program Web Address: www.OnlineLearning. net/CourseCatalog/Programs.html

Program Background: This program is designed for personal financial counselors who want training on the methods for accumulating, preserving, and disposing of other individuals' wealth, as well as people who are interested in a career in this field. It is built on the experience of bankers, brokers, trust officers, lawyers, certified public accountants, and investment advisors.

This Professional Designation in Personal Financial Planning satisfies the Certified Financial Planner Board of Standards' educational requirements for students wishing to pursue the Certified Financial Planner designation.

Application Requirements: You are required to submit an application and successfully complete the Survey of Financial Analysis in Personal Financial Planning and the Survey of Personal Financial Planning with a C or better.

Completion Requirements: You must successfully complete eight courses for this designation.

Example Course Titles: Some of the course titles in this program include Financial Analysis in Personal Financial Planning, Investments in Personal Financial Planning: General Principles and Methods, and Survey of Personal Financial Planning.

Program Contact: UCLA Extension
Certificate Program Unit
P.O. Box 24901
Los Angeles, California 90024-0901
(310) 206-1654
ydelacru@unex.ucla.edu

Teaching English as a Foreign Language

Degree Offered: Certificate

Program Web Address: www.OnlineLearning. net/CourseCatalog/Programs.html

Program Background: This program was designed for students who wish to teach English outside of the United States and non-native English speakers who wish to teach English in their native language. All of the courses emphasize practical applications of English as a Second Language (ESL) teaching techniques.

Completion Requirements: To receive a verification that you've completed the Teaching English as a Foreign Language program, you must complete all six courses for-credit and with a grade of B- or better. Also, you have to submit a non-refundable $50 application fee.

Example Course Titles: Some of the course titles in this program include American Culture through Music, Materials Design for English as a Second or Foreign Language, Reading for ESL, Teaching English to Children, The Sociology of Language, Writing for ESL, American Culture, and Applied Methods in Teaching English Language Development.

Program Contact: UCLA Extension
Certificate Program Unit
P.O. Box 24901
Los Angeles, California 90024-0901
(310) 206-5883
tesol@unex.ucla.edu

Teaching English as a Foreign Language

Degree Offered: Certificate

Program Web Address: www.OnlineLearning. net/CourseCatalog/Programs.html

Program Background: This program is designed to prepare students specializing in the field of Teaching English to Speakers of Other Languages (TESOL). The program is directed toward current teachers who need to update their methodologies, credentialed teachers who are pursuing the Cross-Cultural Language and Academic Development (CLAD) certificate from the State of California's Commission on Teacher Credentialing, and individuals who want to teach English abroad.

Application Requirements: You need to have a Bachelor's degree or equivalent. If you're an international student, you must have a minimum score of 600 on the Test of English as a Foreign Language (TOEFL).

Completion Requirements: You must successfully complete 28 quarter units, including a sequence of required core courses with a grade of B- or better.

Example Course Titles: Some of the course titles in this program include American Culture, American Culture through Music, Materials Design for English as a Second or Foreign Language, Reading for ESL, Teaching English Abroad: English as a Foreign Language, Teaching English to Children, and The Sociology of Language.

Program Contact: UCLA Extension
Certificate Program Unit
P.O. Box 24901
Los Angeles, California 90024-0901
(310) 206-5883
tesol@unex.ucla.edu

UNIVERSITY OF CENTRAL FLORIDA

General Contact Information

4000 Central Florida, Box 160111
Orlando, Florida 32816

E-mail: admissio@pegasus.cc.ucf.edu
WWW: pegasus.cc.ucf.edu

Online Learning Information

Center for Distributed Learning
12424 Research Parkway, Suite 264
Orlando, Florida 32826-3269

E-mail: distrib@mail.ucf.edu
WWW: pegasus.cc.ucf.edu

Institution Background

Founded: 1963
Type of Institution: Public
Accreditation: Southern Association of Colleges and Schools

Programs

Liberal Studies

Degree Offered: Bachelor of Arts/Bachelor of Science

Program Web Address: www.cas.ucf.edu/liberal_studies/

Program Background: Students can pursue interdisciplinary studies through two tracks in this program—the Liberal Arts track and the General Studies track. Students enrolled in the Liberal Arts track have an individualized, nontraditional study plan and receive a Bachelor of Arts upon graduation. Students enrolled in the General Studies track have a university-wide program that leads to a Bachelor of Arts or a Bachelor of Science in Liberal Studies, depending on the majority of courses that a student selects.

Completion Requirements: You must have 45 semester hours in required courses for this program and maintain a minimum grade point average of 2.5. Additionally, you must fulfill requirements in ethics, critical thinking, a foreign language, and other areas.

Program Contact: College of Arts and Sciences
Undergraduate Studies
Orlando, Florida 32816
(407) 823-0218
lbrodie@pegasus.cc.ucf.edu

Nursing

Degree Offered: Bachelor of Science

Program Web Address: www.cohpa.ucf.edu/

nursing/index.cfm?page=undergraduate

Program Background: This is a full Web-based curriculum for registered nurses and Bachelor of Science in Nursing students. Students learn health information, as well as how to use new technology through the course delivery. They gain new skills including using e-mail, word processors, and the Internet.

Application Requirements: You must have a current license as a registered nurse in Florida, an Associate's degree from a Florida community college, and an overall grade point average of 2.5 or higher. Also, you need to be admitted to the University.

Completion Requirements: You must successfully complete 121 semester credit hours with at least a 2.5 grade point average. Typically, students enrolled in this program can complete coursework and clinical practica in five semester or 18 months.

System Requirements: You should have a personal computer with a 166 MHz Pentium processor, 16 MB RAM (minimum), a 500 MB hard drive (or larger), a 15″ monitor, a 28.8 kbps modem (or faster), and Windows 95.

Example Course Titles: Some of the course titles in this program include Transitional Concepts in Nursing, Health Assessment with Lab, Nursing Research, Leadership and Management Principles, Clinical Practice in the Community, Directed Nursing Practice, and Health Care Issues, Policy, and Economics.

Program Contact: RN-BSN Program Coordinator
College of Health and Public Affairs
Health & Public Affairs Building, Room 365
Orlando, Florida 32816-2200
(407) 823-0170
(407) 823-5821
lindah@pegasus.cc.ucf.edu

Training and Development

Degree Offered: Bachelor of Science

Program Web Address: reach.ucf.edu/voced/

Program Background: This program is designed for students pursuing careers in vocational education and industry or business training. It focuses on intellectual growth using research-based teaching techniques, scholarly learning, laboratory-field experience, and leadership development.

System Requirements: You need to have a computer with a Pentium processor running Windows 95/NT, or a 60 MHz 603 Macintosh with OS 7.05 of higher, a 28.8 kbps modem, and an Internet Service Provider. Your computer also needs a graphical Web Browser such as Netscape Communicator, and an e-mail client program capable of handling MIME file attachments.

Program Contact: Program in Vocational Education and Industry Training
Department of Instructional Programs
College of Education
University of Central Florida
Orlando, Florida 32816-1250
(407) 823-2815
lhudson@pegasus.cc.ucf.edu

UNIVERSITY OF COLORADO AT DENVER

General Contact Information

P.O. Box 173364, Campus Box 198
Denver, Colorado 80217-3364

Phone: (303) 556-6505
FAX: (303) 556-6530
E-mail: inquiry@cuonline.edu
WWW: cuonline.edu

Online Learning Information

P.O. Box 173364, Campus Box 198
Denver, Colorado 80217-3364

E-mail: inquiry@cuonline.edu
WWW: cuonline.edu

Institution Background

The University of Colorado at Denver is one of four institutions in the University of Colorado system, and the only public university in the Denver metropolitan area.

Founded: 1965
Type of Institution: Public
Accreditation: North Central Association of Colleges and Schools

Online Course Background: CU Online is the virtual campus of the University of Colorado at Denver, with six collegiate and professional development programs offering more than 125 courses via the Internet. CU Online offers core curriculum and elective courses in a variety of disciplines, all the same high-quality courses taught at the University of Colorado at Denver campus.

Online Course Offered: 70

Online Students Enrolled: 1100

Special Programs/Partnerships: Students who are affiliated with the Western Governor's University can register for CU Online courses through the WGU.

Services Offered to Students: CU Online offers a vast range of student services. Students can search catalogs, register for courses, order text books and other course materials, and apply for financial aid, all online. In addition students have access to the Auraria library, career services, advising, and technical support.

Financial Aid: Degree-seeking students may be eligible for financial aid. They can contact the financial aid office for more information by phone at (303) 556-2886 or by email at financial-aid@carbon.cudenver.edu.

Registration: You can register for courses via the World Wide Web.

Programs

Engineering—Geographic Information Systems

Degree Offered: Master of Engineering— Geographic Information Systems (MEng-GIS)

Program Web Address: cuonline.edu

Online Program Started: 1998

Students Enrolled: 7

Program Background: This program focuses on developing and applying Geographic Information Systems technologies. It enables students to develop computer systems for capturing, analyzing, and displaying spatial and related attribute information which is used in designing engineered facilities and other practices.

Application Requirements: You must have a Bachelor's degree in engineering or a closely-related field from an accredited college or university, and an undergraduate grade point average of 3.0 or higher. You need to complete an application and submit it with two copies of official transcripts from any college or university you've attended, and letters of recommendation from four people (two former instructors and two professional associates).

If your undergraduate grade point average was less than 3.0 but greater than 2.75, you will be required to take the Graduate Records Examination (GRE). After the review committee receives and reviews your test scores, you may receive a provisional admission.

Completion Requirements: You must successfully complete 30 semester hours of graduate credit, three of which are awarded upon your completion of an advanced applications project. You may complete up to nine semester hours of coursework via videotape.

Time for Completion: You have five years from the time you start the program to finish it.

On Campus Requirements: There are no on-campus requirements. All coursework is online.

System Requirements: You need to have a personal computer running Windows or a Macintosh equivalent, a 14.4 kbps or faster modem, a sound card and speakers, an Internet Service Provider, a Web browser, and an e-mail account.

Example Course Titles: Some of the course titles for this program include Introduction to Geographic Information Systems, Database Development, Management and Policies, and Database Systems.

Program Contact: Lynn Johnson
University of Colorado at Denver
Campus Box 113
P.O. Box 173364
Denver, Colorado 80217-3364
(303) 556-4907
(303) 556-2368
ljohnson@carbon.cudenver.edu

UNIVERSITY OF FLORIDA

General Contact Information

201 Criser Hall
Gainesville, Florida 32611-4000

Phone: (352) 392-1365
WWW: www.ufl.edu

Online Learning Information

1012 Turlington Hall
Gainesville, Florida 32611-7345

E-mail: smlegg@nersp.nerdc.ufl.edu
WWW: www.ufl.edu

Institution Background

Founded: 1853
Type of Institution: Public
Accreditation: Southern Association of Colleges and Schools; AACSB (for business programs)

Programs
Audiology

Degree Offered: Doctor of Audiology (Au.D.)

Program Web Address: www.intelicus.com or via www.ufl.edu

Online Program Started: 1998

Students Enrolled: 239

Program Background: This program combines the professional experience of the College of Health Professions with the academic excellence of the College of Liberal Arts and Sciences. It produces educated professionals who, upon graduation, are able to function and work independently in a comprehensive audiologic practice.

Application Requirements: You must have a Master's degree in Audiology from an accredited institution, a current state license, and meet the minimum requirements of the University of Florida's Graduate School (including a minimum Graduate Record Examination score of 1000 and a minimum undergraduate grade point average of 3.0).

You need to submit an application, letters of recommendation, transcripts from each college you've attended, and your scores on the Graduate Record Examination.

Completion Requirements: You must successfully pass a qualifying examination upon completion of all courses.

Time for Completion: Most students can complete this program in five semesters by enrolling on a full-time basis, and in up to three years enrolling on a part-time basis.

On Campus Requirements: There are no on-campus requirements for this program.

System Requirements: You should have a computer with a 200 MHz Pentium processor, 32 MB RAM, 1GB free hard drive space, SVGA 256 Color Monitor, 1.44 MB floppy drive, a 10X CD-ROM drive, 28.8 kbps modem, Windows 95 or greater, Microsoft Office 97, Internet access, e-mail address, and a Web browser (preferably Netscape 4.0 or higher or Microsoft Internet Explorer 5.0 or higher).

Example Course Titles: Some of the course titles in this program include Applied Electrophysiology, Cochlear Implants and Assistive Technology, Principles of Amplification, Occupational and Environmental Hearing-Conservation, Balance Disorders: Evaluation and Treatment, Audiologic Rehabilitation, Counseling, and Business and Professional Issues in Hearing Healthcare.

Program Contact: Janet M. Caffee, Director
Au.D. Distance Learning Program
UF Dept Communicative Disorders
PO Box 100174
Gainesville, Florida 32610-0174
(352) 392-3253
(352) 392-6045
jcaffee@hp.ufl.edu

Electrical Engineering

Degree Offered: Bachelor of Science in Electrical Engineering

Program Web Address: www.fcd.ufl.edu

Online Program Started: 2000

Program Background: This is a degree completion program in which students can earn the required and elective courses for the third and fourth years of the Bachelor of Science in Electrical Engineering program.

Application Requirements: You should have completed the first two years of a four-year degree program.

Completion Requirements: You must maintain satisfactory performance in all courses.

Time for Completion: This program typically takes students two to four years to complete.

On Campus Requirements: You may be required to take laboratories at the University of Florida or at other approved facilities.

System Requirements: You should have a computer with a 200 MHz Pentium processor, 32 MB RAM, 1GB free hard drive space, SVGA 256 Color Monitor, 1.44 MB floppy drive, a 10X CD-ROM drive, 28.8 kbps modem, Windows 95 or greater, Microsoft Office 97, Internet access, e-mail address, and a Web browser (preferably Netscape 4.0 or higher or Microsoft Internet Explorer 5.0 or higher).

Example Course Titles: Some of the course titles in this program include Circuits I, Circuits II, Signals and Systems, Linear Control Systems, Electromagnetic Fields, Introduction to DSP, Solid State Electronics, and Electronic Circuits.

Program Contact: Haniph Latchman
EB 463 ECE Dept.
Gainesville, Florida 32611
(352) 392-4950
(352) 392-0044
latchman@list.ufl.edu

Electrical Engineering

Degree Offered: Master of Science in Electrical Engineering

Program Web Address: www.list.ufl.edu/online

Online Program Started: 1998

Students Enrolled: 10

Program Background: This online Master's program is essentially the same as the University of Florida's traditional Master's program in Electrical Engineering. All of the online courses are streams of audio and video from the traditional classes. Students use electronic means to communicate with each other and the instructors.

Application Requirements: You must have a Bachelor's degree in an appropriate field and a score of at least 1000 on the quantitative and verbal sections of the Graduate Records Examination (GRE). For more information about admissions requirements, please see www.ece.ufl.edu.

Completion Requirements: You must successfully complete all coursework with a minimum grade point average of 3.0, and complete a thesis.

Time for Completion: Most students can complete this program in two to four years.

On Campus Requirements: You are required to visit the campus to defend your thesis. All other course assignments can be done online, and examinations can be proctored off-site.

System Requirements: You should have a personal computer with a 200 MHz or faster processor, 32 MB RAM, 1 GB of free hard drive space, an SVGA 256-color monitor, a 3.5″ floppy drive, a 10X CD-ROM drive, a 28.8 kbps modem, Internet access, and e-mail capabilities. Your system should also have Windows 95/98/NT, Microsoft Office 97, a Web browser (such as Netscape or Microsoft Internet Explorer), and RealPlayer. Some courses may require additional software.

Program Contact: Haniph Latchman
EB 463 ECE Dept
University of Florida
Gainesville, Florida 32611

(352) 392-4950
(352) 392-0044
latchman@list.ufl.edu

Business Administration

Degree Offered: Master of Business Administration

Program Web Address: www.floridamba.ufl.edu

Online Program Started: 1999

Students Enrolled: 27

Application Requirements: You must have a Bachelor's degree or the international equivalent and at least two years of full-time experience. You need to submit an application with official transcripts from each school you've attended, two letters of recommendation, essays, and your test scores on the GMAT (preferred) or GRE. You are also required to attend a personal interview.

Completion Requirements: You must successfully complete all courses of the 48-credit program with a minimum grade point average of 3.0.

Time for Completion: Typically, students can complete this program in 33 months.

On Campus Requirements: You are required to attend nine weekend seminars over the course of the 33-month program.

System Requirements: You need a notebook computer. You can find specific information about the system that is required at www.floridamba.ufl.edu.

Example Course Titles: Some of the course titles in this program include Economics of Business Decisions, Effective Writing, Operations Management, Problems and Methods in Marketing Management, Financial and Managerial Accounting, Management Statistics, Legal Environment of Business, International Business,

Business Policy, Organizational Behavior, Financial Management, and Entrepreneurship.

Program Contact: Tara Carew
134 Bryan Hall
PO Box 117152
Gainesville, Florida 32611-7152
(352) 392-7992
(352) 392-8791
floridamba@notes.cba.ufl.edu

UNIVERSITY OF HOUSTON

General Contact Information

4800 Calhoun Street
Houston, Texas 77204

E-mail: admissions@uh.edu
WWW: www.uh.edu/academics/de

Online Learning Information

4242 South Mason Road
Katy, Texas 77450

E-mail: deadvisor@uh.edu
WWW: www.uh.edu/academics/de

Institution Background

Founded: 1927
Type of Institution: Public
Accreditation: Southern Association of Colleges and Schools

Programs

Hotel and Restaurant Management

Degree Offered: Bachelor of Science

Program Web Address: www.uh.edu/uhdistance/hrmBS.html

Program Background: Students in this program learn broad information skills, flexibility in abstract problem-solving, and in-depth studies of accounting, computer science, economics, law, mathematics, and psychology.

Application Requirements: You need to submit your SAT or ACT test scores, and a high school transcript.

Completion Requirements: You must successfully complete a minimum of 132 credit hours (36 advanced).

On Campus Requirements: You must complete the last 30 hours in residence.

Example Course Titles: Some of the course titles in this program include Food and Beverage Service, Decision Support Systems for the Hospitality Industry, Introduction to the Hospitality Industry, Safety and Sanitation in the Hospitality Industry, Hospitality Practicum, Food Production in the Hospitality Industry, Facilities Management, Systems of Accounts in the Hospitality Industry, Supervision and Leadership in the Hotel, Restaurant and Hospitality Industry, Lodging Management, Hospitality Industry Law, and Hospitality Marketing.

Program Contact: (713) 743-2446
BSHRM@uh.edu

UNIVERSITY OF ILLINOIS AT CHICAGO

General Contact Information

Office of Continuing Education and Public Service (MC 165)
322 S. Green Street, Suite 202
Chicago, Illinois 60607

Phone: (312) 996-2470
FAX: (312) 996-8026
E-mail: JustineM@uic.edu
WWW: www.uic.edu

Online Learning Information

Office of Continuing Education and Public Service (MC 165)
322 S. Green Street, Suite 202
Chicago, Illinois 60607

Phone: (312) 996-2470
FAX: (312) 996-8026
E-mail: JustineM@uic.edu
WWW: www.uic.edu

Institution Background

The University of Illinois at Chicago (UIC) is the largest university in the Chicago area and one of the 88 leading research universities in the nation. It is one of only four universities with a full complement of six health sciences colleges.

Founded: 1946
Type of Institution: Public
Accreditation: North Central Association of Colleges and Schools (NCA); UIC also holds appropriate accreditations for all of its professional programs.

Online Course Background: UIC's online programs are a part of the University of Illinois Online, which is a university-wide initiative providing leadership, coordination, and financial support in the areas of Internet-based education and public service. The primary goal of this initiative is to offer new online learning opportunities, especially complete degree and certificate programs, to place-bound and time-restricted citizens. U of I Online has supported the development of 29 new online programs (including one professional degree, ten complete Master's degrees, a baccalaureate completion program, and 12 certificate programs), 19 of which are already enrolling students. You can access more information about online courses, program and public service activities from U of I Online at www.online.uillinois.edu.

Special Programs/Partnerships: UIC is a member of the University of Illinois Online (U of I Online) and the Illinois Virtual Campus (IVC).

Services Offered to Students: Online students have access all services that are necessary for effective learning, including library and computing resources.

Financial Aid: Financial aid is available to qualified students in an eligible program.

Registration: You can register for courses via mail.

Programs

Engineering

Degree Offered: Master of Engineering

Program Web Address: www.uic.edu/eng/meng/

Online Program Started: 1999

Application Requirements: You must have a Bachelor's degree or equivalent in an appropriate field of engineering or in a closely related field (such as computer science, mathematics, or physics) from a recognized institution of higher learning. You must also have a cumulative grade point average of at least 4.0 (on a 5.0) during the last 60 semester hours (90 quarter hours) of undergraduate study. If you do not meet these admissions qualifications, but you have significant professional experience in engineering, you may petition for special consideration.

Completion Requirements: You must successfully complete a minimum of 35 semester credit hours with a grade point average of at least a B for this degree.

On Campus Requirements: There are no on-campus requirements.

System Requirements: You should have a personal computer with at least a 33.6Kbs Internet connection, color monitor with 800 × 600 resolution, 16-bit sound card and speakers, double-speed CD Rom drive, Microsoft Internet Explorer 4.01 or higher or Netscape 4.01 or higher, RealPlayer, QuickTime, Flash/Shockwave, and Adobe Acrobat Reader 4.

Example Course Titles: Some of the course titles in this program include Fundamentals and Design of Microelectronics Processing, Quasistatic Electric and Magnetic Fields in MEMS, Microdevices and Micromachining Technology, and Electromagnetic Field Theory.

Program Contact: Carolyn Williams
College of Engineering MEng Program
851 South Morgan Street
Chicago, Illinois 60607-7043
(312) 996-9806
(312) 996-8664
meng@uic.edu

Health Professions Education

Degree Offered: Master of Health Professions Education

Program Web Address: www.mhpe-online.org

Online Program Started: 1999

Students Enrolled: 27

Program Background: This program is designed for health professionals who are working in educational leadership positions or individuals who are interested in having such a position and need training. The diversity of the students enrolled (including doctors, nurses, dentists, pharmacists, and allied health professionals) gives this program a broad base of experiences to learn from. Students participate in weekly activities and discussions throughout their courses, and are required to complete a group or individual project for each course.

Application Requirements: You must have a Bachelor's degree or an advanced professional degree in a health professions discipline, and a minimum grade point average of 3.75 (on a 5.0 scale). Along with a completed application, you need to submit official transcripts from each college or university you've attended, a written statement of your goals, and three letters of recommendation. If you are an international student whose native language is not English, you are also required to have a score of 550 on the TOEFL examination. Also, international students are required to submit a financial statement from a sponsoring institution.

Completion Requirements: You must successfully complete 32 credit hours. The courses are organized in three components: core courses, electives, and a thesis or project.

Time for Completion: You have up to five years to complete this degree program.

On Campus Requirements: You are required to attend a five-day conference on the University of Illinois at Chicago campus each July while enrolled in the program.

System Requirements: You need to have a personal computer with a Pentium or PowerPC processor running Windows 95 or higher, or a Macintosh running OS 7.0 or higher. Your computer should have 32 MB RAM, a 14.4 baud modem (or faster), an Internet Service Provider or setup to direct dial in to the University's network, a Web browser, e-mail software, and Acrobat Reader.

Example Course Titles: Some of the course titles in this program include Issues in Health Professions Education, Curriculum and Evaluation in Health Care Education, Leadership and Organization in Health Care Education, Ambulatory Care Education, Clinical Ethics, Instructional Methods, Research Design and Grant Writing, and Writing for Scientific Publication.

Program Contact: Janet Settle
Medical Education
UIC College of Medicine
808 S. Wood St. (MC 591)
Chicago, Illinois 60612-7309
(312) 996-4666
(312) 413-2048
JSettle@uic.edu

Health Information Management

Degree Offered: Health Information Management Certificate

Program Web Address: www.sbhis.uic.edu/ GradBk98-99/him_main.htm

Online Program Started: 1998

Program Background: This program is designed for health care professionals who have their Master's degrees, but seek an advanced understanding of the use of computers in the application and management of health care. Students learn how to create, implement, operate, and control health information systems.

Application Requirements: You must have a Master's degree. If you have a Master of Business Administration degree, it must be one that was granted by the University of Illinois at Chicago or by another school that is accredited by the American Assembly of Collegiate Schools of Business. You must satisfy several prerequisite courses through coursework or professional experience. You need to submit an application with official transcripts from each college you've attended, and you are required to interview with a faculty member.

Completion Requirements: You must successfully complete six courses with a B or better.

On Campus Requirements: You are required to attend some classes on-campus. You need to contact the school directly for additional information.

System Requirements: You need to have a personal computer with a Pentium or PowerPC processor running Windows 95 or higher, or a Macintosh running OS 7.0 or higher. Your computer should have 32 MB RAM, a 14.4 baud modem (or faster), an Internet Service Provider or setup to direct dial in to the University's network, a Web browser, e-mail software, and Acrobat Reader.

Example Course Titles: Some of the course titles in this program include Health Care Data, Health Care Information Systems, Management of Health Care Communication Systems, Health Information Systems Analysis and Design, Applications in Health Information Management, and Topics in Health Information Management.

Program Contact: School of Biomedical and Health Information Sciences
UIC College of Health and Human Development Sciences
1919 W. Taylor St.
Room 811 AHPB (MC 520)
Chicago, Illinois 60612-7249
(312) 996-6317
(312) 413-0205
GradBHI@uic.edu

Nursing

Degree Offered: Post-Master's Certificate in Advanced Nursing

Online Program Started: 1999

Program Background: This program is designed for students who have their Master's degree in nursing and who want to become a nurse practitioner or nurse-midwife. The nurse practitioner specialty is subdivided further into options preparing the family nurse practitioner (FNP), occupational health nurse practitioner (OHNP), pediatric nurse practitioner (PNP), women's health care nurse practitioner

(WHCNP), and acute care nurse practitioner (ACNP).

The core courses for this program are offered fully or partially online.

Application Requirements: You must be licensed to practice as a professional nurse in at least one jurisdiction, and have your Master's degree in nursing from a CCNE or NLNAC accredited program. You need to complete an application and submit it with official transcripts from each college or university you've attended and three letters of recommendation. After your application packet is received, you will be required to interview with a faculty member.

On Campus Requirements: Certain courses in each specialty are offered only on campus. Additionally, you are required to complete a clinical practicum in person.

System Requirements: You should have a personal computer with a Pentium with MMX processor (Pentium II with MMX preferred), 16 MB RAM, 1 GB hard drive with 200 MB free disk space, a 33.6 kbps modem, a 4X CD-ROM drive, SoundBlaster 16-bit sound card with speakers, 15″ SVGA 800x600 monitor with 1 MB Video RAM, 3.5″ floppy drive, Windows 95 or higher, a Web browser, e-mail software, and an office suite (such as Microsoft Office 97).

Example Course Titles: Some of the course titles in this program include Primary Care Nursing of Acute and Chronic Disorders, Issues of Advanced Practice in Nursing, Physiologic Basis of Nursing Practice Across the Lifespan, and Health, Environment, and Systems.

Program Contact: Leah Beckwith
UIC College of Nursing Administration
845 S. Damen Ave. (MC 802)
Chicago, Illinois 60612
(312) 996-3566

(312) 996-8066
LeahB@uic.edu

Pharmacy

Degree Offered: Doctor of Pharmacy

Program Web Address: www.uic.edu/pharmacy/offices/cco/cco.html

Online Program Started: 1998

Program Background: The Pathway to the Doctor of Pharmacy is a professional program for licensed pharmacists who have a Bachelor's degree in pharmacy from a college or university that is accredited by the Americal Council on Pharmaceutical Education, and who wish to earn a doctorate. Students who want to take courses through this program, but not pursue a doctoral degree, may do so. The program's goal is to deliver a core of unique courses and expertise in contemporary pharmacy practice.

Application Requirements: You must have a Bachelor's degree in pharmacy from an American Council on Pharmaceutical Education-accredited institution and a valid license.

You need to complete an application and submit it with a personal statement, a notarized photocopy of your valid pharmacy license, official transcripts from any college or university you've attended, and three letters of recommendation (two from colleagues or college instructors and one from your supervisor or employer).

Completion Requirements: You must successfully complete 24 semester hours of didactic coursework, and 20 semester hours of clinical clerkship, for a total of 44 semester hours.

Time for Completion: You have up to four academic years to complete the requirements for this degree. If you demonstrate good academic standing, you may petition for an additional year to complete your degree.

On Campus Requirements: You must take three out of the five clerkship courses in Chicago.

System Requirements: You should have a personal computer with a Pentium with MMX processor (Pentium II with MMX preferred), 16 MB RAM, 1 GB hard drive with 200 MB free disk space, a 33.6 kbps modem, a 4X CD-ROM drive, SoundBlaster 16-bit sound card with speakers, 15″ SVGA 800x600 monitor with 1 MB Video RAM, 3.5″ floppy drive, Windows 95 or higher, a Web browser, e-mail software, and an office suite (such as Microsoft Office 97).

Example Course Titles: Some of the course titles in this program include Pharmacoeconomics, Advances in Pharmacy, Biotechnology for Pharmacists, Pathophysiology, Clinical Pharmacokinetics, and Drug Information and Statistics.

Program Contact: Cathy Ami
Academic Affairs
UIC College of Pharmacy
833 S. Wood St., Suite 184 (MC 874)
Chicago, Illinois 60612
(312) 996-3997
(312) 413-0497
Ami@uic.edu

School Nurse

Degree Offered: Certificate

Online Program Started: 1999

Program Background: This is a post-baccalaureate program in which students can take two courses that are specific to nursing in schools.

Application Requirements: You must have a Bachelor's degree from an institution recognized by the Illinois State Board of Education prior to or simultaneous with completion of the internship, be licensed as a registered pro-

fessional nurse in Illinois, and have a cumulative grade point average of 4.0 (on a 5.0 scale). If your Bachelor's degree is in a field other than nursing, you are required to meet three prerequisite courses.

System Requirements: You should have a personal computer with a Pentium with MMX processor (Pentium II with MMX preferred), 16 MB RAM, 1 GB hard drive with 200 MB free disk space, a 33.6 kbps modem, a 4X CD-ROM drive, SoundBlaster 16-bit sound card with speakers, 15″ SVGA 800x600 monitor with 1 MB Video RAM, 3.5″ floppy drive, Windows 95 or higher, a Web browser, e-mail software, and an office suite (such as Microsoft Office 97).

Example Course Titles: The two courses in this program are School Nursing—Principles and Trends, and Clinical Methods for School Nursing.

Program Contact: Leah Beckwith
UIC College of Nursing Administration
845 S. Damen Ave. (MC 802
Chicago, Illinois 60612
(312) 996-3566
(312) 996-8066
LeahB@uic.edu

UNIVERSITY OF ILLINOIS AT SPRINGFIELD

General Contact Information

P.O. Box 19243
Springfield, Illinois 62794-9243

Phone: (217) 206-6600
WWW: www.uis.edu

Online Learning Information

Library 180
Springfield, Illinois 62794-9243

E-mail: dale.larry@uis.edu
WWW: www.uis.edu

Institution Background

The University of Illinois at Springfield (UIS) plays a broad role in serving the central Illinois region. A junior-senior and graduate-level campus that also serves lower-level students through cooperation with two-year colleges, UIS offers two online degree programs and two online certificate programs. Located in Springfield, the state capital, UIS has a special mission in public affairs and emphasizes the integration of liberal arts and professional studies in its curricula. Over the years, UIS has evolved into a comprehensive institution stressing excellent teaching, professional development, and practical experience.

Founded: 1969
Type of Institution: Public
Accreditation: North Central Association of Colleges and Schools

Online Course Background: Most online classes at UIS take advantage of a variety of asynchronous learning technologies including Web-based discussion forums, online lecture notes, streaming audio, and computer-graded quizzes. Students may also be assigned readings from textbooks or other published materials. All courses involve extensive student-student and student-instructor interaction, primarily the Web-based conferencing system.

Online Course Offered: 13

Online Students Enrolled: 203

Special Programs/Partnerships: UIS is a member of the University of Illinois Online and the Illinois Virtual Campus.

Services Offered to Students: Online students at UIS have online access to the bookstore, access to select library services including library catalog, online information resources, and article databases, as well as interlibrary loan.

Individual Undergraduate Courses: UIS has online courses in liberal studies, accounting, applied study, biology, chemistry, communication, computer science, English, history, legal studies, management, philosophy, psychology, and women's studies.

Individual Graduate Courses: UIS has online courses in management information systems, computer science, human development counseling, human services, and legal studies.

Registration: You can register for courses via phone.

Programs

Career Specialist Studies

Degree Offered: Certificate

Program Web Address: www.uis.edu/cles/workforce.html

Online Program Started: 1997

Students Enrolled: 20

Program Background: This program is designed to address the ongoing educational needs of workforce development professionals, guidance counselors, and other educators working with the education-to-careers initiative. The curriculum allows students to pursue an interdisciplinary course of study. Students gain an important understanding of concepts and master skills.

Completion Requirements: You must successfully complete four courses (12 semester hours) for this certificate.

Time for Completion: You have up to one year to complete this program.

On Campus Requirements: There are no on-campus requirements.

System Requirements: You should have a personal computer with at least a 486 processor, color monitor, 16 MB RAM, 28.8 baud modem, an Internet provider, access to a printer, and e-mail.

Example Course Titles: Some of the course titles in this program include Interpersonal Communication Skills, Career Case Management, Occupational Test Application, Interpretation, and Analysis, and Using Labor Market and Career Information.

Program Contact: Carol Esarey
UIS Center for Legal Studies
University of Illinois at Springfield
P.O. Box 19243
Springfield, Illinois 62794-9243
(217) 206-6097
(217) 206-7397
esarey.carol@uis.edu

Employment Specialist Studies

Degree Offered: Certificate

Program Web Address: www.uis.edu/cles/workforce.html

Online Program Started: 1997

Students Enrolled: 22

Program Background: This program is tailored around the skills and knowledge that are essential for students to who are working directly with the employer community. The goals and learning objectives were designed to conform to the standards benchmarked by the National Association of Workforce Development Professionals.

Completion Requirements: You must successfully complete three courses for a total of 10 credit hours.

Time for Completion: You have up to one year to complete these courses.

On Campus Requirements: There are no on-campus requirements.

System Requirements: You should have a personal computer with at least a 486 processor, a color monitor and capability of showing graphics, 16 B RAM, 28.8 baud modem, an Internet provider, access to a printer, and e-mail.

Example Course Titles: Some of the course titles in this program include Job Search Methods, Employer Relations Skills, and Effective Marketing and Public Relations Communication Skills.

Program Contact: Carol Esarey
UIS Center for Legal Studies
University of Illinois at Springfield
PO Box 19243
Springfield, Illinois 62794-9243
(217) 206-6097
(217) 206-7397
esarey.carol@uis.edu

Liberal Studies

Degree Offered: Bachelor of Arts in Liberal Studies

Program Web Address: lis.uis.edu/

Online Program Started: 1999

Program Background: Students in the University of Illinois at Springfield's Liberal Studies program design degree programs to address their own interests and educational goals. The Liberal Studies major is intended to give students a deeper understanding of values, meanings, concerns, choices, and commitments that serve as the foundations of their quality of life. Students choose coursework from a variety of disciplines that enable them to explore many themes that are universal to the human experience. These themes include understanding the present in a historical context, achieving a meaningful identity, and connecting with others through language, arts, and work.

Application Requirements: You must have at least 45 credit hours at the lower-division level of college, a minimum grade point average of 2.0 (on a 4.0 scale) from an accredited college or university, and completed three semester hours of English composition. You need to complete and submit an application to the program and have an entrance interview with Liberal Studies faculty or program staff. If you hold an Associate's degree from a regionally accredited community college, then you meet the general education requirements for the University of Illinois at Springfield.

Completion Requirements: You must successfully complete 60 semester hours, including 38 hours in a broad topical area and 12 hours in two of these types of courses: Liberal Studies Colloquia, Public Affairs Colloquia, or Applied Study Experiential Learning Term.

System Requirements: You need to have a personal computer with a Pentium 90 MHz or faster processor and Windows 95/98/NT or the Macintosh equivalent. Your computer should have at least 32 MB of RAM, 28.8 kbps (or faster) modem, sound card, and speakers.

Example Course Titles: Some of the course titles in this program include Self-Directed Learning, Plants and Society, Chemistry of Everyday Life, Perspective on Human Nature, and Contemporary Issues in Women's Lives.

Program Contact: Holly McCracken
Liberal Studies
University of Illinois at Springfield
P.O. Box 19243
Springfield, Illinois 62794-9243
(800) 323-9243
(217) 206-6217
lis@uis.edu

Management Information System

Degree Offered: Master of Science in Management Information Systems

Program Web Address: misonline.uis.edu

Online Program Started: 1997

Students Enrolled: 50

Program Background: The Management Information Systems program provides students a balance between technical skills and knowledge of business functions and processes. Students are actively involved in all courses, whether they are delivered online or traditionally. Additionally, students gain practical experience by applying concepts they are learning to organizational issues through case studies, projects, and group exercises.

Application Requirements: You must apply to both the University of Illinois at Springfield and the Department of Management Information Systems. To apply to the University, you must have a Bachelor's degree from a regionally accredited institution, and have a minimum undergraduate grade point average of 2.5 (on a 4.0 scale).

To apply to the Department, in addition to the University requirements, you must have completed the equivalent of two semesters of accounting, one semester of production/operations management, one semester of statistics, and one semester of college algebra or mathematics. Also, you must demonstrate competency in a structured programming language through you coursework or practical experience. You must submit your scores on the Graduate Management Aptitude Test (GMAT) or the Graduate Record Exam (GRE).

Completion Requirements: You must successfully complete 44 credit hours of coursework for this degree. One of the required courses is a Graduate Project and Seminar or Thesis and Seminar. The nature of your project will depend upon your career goals and discussions with your advisor.

Time for Completion: You have six consecutive years to complete your coursework toward this degree. This six years does not include any time you've spent at other institutions for which you will transfer credit toward your Master's degree.

On Campus Requirements: You are required to visit the campus once or twice a semester.

System Requirements: You need to have a personal computer with a Pentium 100 MHz processor (or better), at least 32 MB RAM, and access to the Internet for at least five hours per week per course.

Example Course Titles: Some of the course titles in this program include Technical Foundations of Information Systems, Management Information Systems, Managerial Decision Support Systems, Strategic Decision Support Systems, Management of Database Systems, Systems Analysis and Design, Competitive Information Systems, Expert Systems, Telecommunications, and Electronic Commerce.

Program Contact: Dr. Rassule Hadidi, Professor and Chair
Department of Management Information Systems
University of Illinois at Springfield
Springfield, Illinois 62794-9243
(217) 206-6067
(217) 206-7543
hadidi.rassule@uis.edu

UNIVERSITY OF ILLINOIS AT URBANA-CHAMPAIGN

General Contact Information

302 East John Street
Champaign, Illinois 61820

Phone: (217) 333-3061
FAX: (217) 244-8481
E-mail: inforequest@talon.outreach.uiuc.edu
WWW: www.outreach.uiuc.edu

Online Learning Information

302 East John Street, Suite 1405
Champaign, Illinois 61820

Phone: (217) 333-3061
FAX: (217) 244-8481
E-mail: morriss@ntx1.cso.uiuc.edu
WWW: www.outreach.uiuc.edu

Institution Background

The University of Illinois at Urbana-Champaign (UIUC) is a public, non-denominational, four-year institution with a strong research orientation. Quality is as important to the UIUC in distance education formats as it is in other off-campus and on-campus instructional delivery formats. Thus, some courses and programs require certain requisite knowledge prior to admission or course enrollment.

Founded: 1867
Type of Institution: Public
Accreditation: North Central Association of Colleges and Schools

Online Course Background: Some of the UIUC's online Master's degree programs may be completed without ever setting foot on campus; others require at least one short-term (a week or two) campus visit periodically during the program. Online courses may include synchronous chat opportunities conducted online; other courses are self-paced and completely asynchronous. Courses are offered through respective academic departments. Typically, faculty are full-time although approved adjuncts may be used at times.

Online Course Offered: 65

Online Students Enrolled: 649

Special Programs/Partnerships: The campus has distance learning partnerships with University of Illinois Online, Illinois Virtual Campus, and the Common Market of Courses and Institutes. University of Illinois Online encompasses the online programming initiatives of the University's three campuses in Chicago, Springfield, and Urbana-Champaign. Illinois Virtual Campus is an online catalog listing distance learning courses and programs from Illinois colleges and universities both public and private. The Common Market of Courses and Institutes is a online programming initiative among the Big Ten institutions and the University of Chicago. Students at these institutions can enroll in selected online courses being offered from member institutions.

Services Offered to Students: Services available to distance learning students include: advising, toll-free telephone numbers, online help desk, computer accounts, library services, bookstore functions, financial aid, and other student resources.

Financial Aid: Non-need based aid is available to off-campus learners who fulfill the following criteria: admitted to a University of Illinois degree program and enrolled in 1 1/2 units during Fall and Spring semesters and 3/4 unit during Summer sessions.

Registration: You can register for courses via mail and the World Wide Web.

Programs

Computer Science

Degree Offered: Master of Computer Science

Program Web Address: cs.uiuc.edu/imcs

Online Program Started: 1997

Students Enrolled: 50

Degrees Awarded: 15

Program Background: This is an Internet-delivered version of the University's regular Master of Computer Science program. Students can participate on either a full- or part-time basis.

Application Requirements: You can apply to the Master's program before or after you enroll in courses, but enrollment in the courses does not guarantee that you'll be admitted to the degree-seeking program. To apply, you need to complete an application and submit it to the University's Graduate College. With it, you must include a statement of purpose, an application fee, three letters of recommendation, your scores on the General Records Examination (GRE), and official transcripts from each college or university that you've attended.

Completion Requirements: You must successfully complete nine units of coursework. You are not required to complete a thesis for this degree.

Time for Completion: The maximum amount of time allowed to complete this program is five years. However, most full-time students complete it in four semesters and part-time students complete it in six semesters.

On Campus Requirements: There are no on-campus requirements.

System Requirements: You should have a personal computer with a 166MHz Pentium processor (or faster), Windows 95/98/NT, a 56K modem, an Internet Service Provider, a color monitor with 800 × 600 resolution, a 16-bit sound card and speakers, and 2X CD-Drive (or faster). Your computer also needs to have Microsoft Internet Explorer 4.01 (or higher) or Netscape 4.01 (or higher), Microsoft Media Player, Microsoft PowerPoint (included with Office Professional or you can download the free PowerPoint player if you do not have PowerPoint), Adobe Acrobat Reader, Microsoft NetMeeting (video conference card is optional), and e-mail software (Netscape and Internet Explorer each provide options for free e-mail applications). Some courses may require additional software.

Example Course Titles: Some of the course titles in this program include Multimedia Systems, Operating System Design, Computer Networks and Distributed Systems, Computer System Organization, Advanced Operating Systems, and Special Topics in Computer Science.

Program Contact: Professor Mehdi Harandi
Department of Computer Science
University of Illinois at Urbana-Champaign
2270 DCL, 1304 W. Springfield
Urbana, Illinois 61801
(217) 333-6952
(217) 244-6073
academic@cs.uiuc.edu

Curriculum, Technology, and Education Reform

Degree Offered: Master of Education

Program Web Address: cter.ed.uiuc.edu

Online Program Started: 1998

Students Enrolled: 55

Program Background: This program is designed for practicing pre-college teachers and administrators with a focus on Curriculum, Technology, and Education Reform (CTER).

The eight online courses that make up this program give teachers and school administrators a way to earn a coherent, high-quality Master's degree without leaving their local communities.

Application Requirements: You must sumbit an application to the Graduate College with a $40 application fee, official transcripts from any college or university you've attended, and three letters of recommendation.

Completion Requirements: You must successfully complete eight units of coursework.

System Requirements: You should have an elementary knowledge of a microcomputer operating system and basic knowledge of software tools, including word processing, spreadsheet, databases, electronic mail, and Internet browsers. You need a personal computer with a 486 processor running Windows 95 or higher or Macintosh 68040, 24 MB RAM memory, modem with a speed of 28.8 or higher or a direct network connection, Internet provider for home access (must have prior to start of program), SLIP, PPP, or other TCP/IP connectivity, Web browser (Netscape 4.0, Internet Explorer 3.0 or higher), and e-mail software (Eudora recommended).

Example Course Titles: Some of the course titles in this program include Computer-Assisted Instruction, Issues and Developments in Education: Technology and Educational Reform, Problems and Trends in Specialized Fields: Curriculum and Technology, Seminar for Advanced Students in Education: Evaluation of Instructional Technologies, Social Foundations of Education, Computer Uses in Education, Issues and Developments in Educational Psychology: Learning and Emotional Adjustment in the Schools, and Legal Basis of School Administration.

Program Contact: Jim Levin
Department of Educational Psychology
210 Education Building

1310 South Sixth Street
Champaign, Illinois 61820
(217) 244-0537
(217) 244-7620
j-levin@uiuc.edu

Electrical Engineering

Degree Offered: Master of Science in Electrical Engineering

Program Web Address: www.engr.uiuc.edu/OCEE/degreeprog/index.htm

Online Program Started: 1999

Program Background: This program was developed for engineers who wish to pursue the degree through off-campus study.

Application Requirements: You must have a Bachelor's degree from an accredited institution that has requirements equivalent to those of the University of Illinois, and a minimum grade point average of 3.0 (on a 4.0 scale) for the last 60 credit hours of your undergraduate study. If you are an international applicant, you must receive a score of 620 or higher on the Test of English as a Foreign Language (TOEFL), and you're required to submit copies of your scores.

You need to complete and submit an application with an application fee, two copies of official transcripts from each college and university you've attended, three letters of recommendation, your scores on the Graduate Record Examination (GRE), and an essay.

Completion Requirements: You must successfully complete eight units of credit and a thesis.

System Requirements: You must have a personal computer with a 133 MHz processor running Windows 95/98/NT, 32 MB of RAM, a 56K modem, color monitor with 800 × 600 resolution and 256 color resolution, 16-bit sound card and speakers, and a reliable Internet service provider. You should also have Micro-soft Internet Explorer 5, Microsoft Windows Media Player, Microsoft PowerPoint or you can download the free PowerPoint player (2.7 MB file), Adobe Acrobat Reader 3.01, and an e-mail software package.

Example Course Titles: Some of the course titles in this program include Communications and Power Electronics.

Program Contact: Linda Krute
Continuing Engineering Education
257 Engineering Sciences Bldg.
1101 W. Springfield
Urbana, Illinois 61801
(217) 333-6634
(217) 333-0015
L-krute@uiuc.edu

French

Degree Offered: Certificate

Program Web Address: www.outreach.uiuc.edu/french/

Online Program Started: 1999

Students Enrolled: 25

Program Background: This program gives students linguistic skills in French including knowledge of the contrasts between French and English, skills to translate, and cultural background information.

Application Requirements: You must have a Bachelor's degree in French or equivalent training.

Completion Requirements: You must successfully complete five courses.

System Requirements: You should have a computer with Internet access and Netscape 4.0 or higher.

Example Course Titles: Some of the course titles in this program include Techniques in Translation, Commercial and Economic French, and Scientific and Technical French.

Program Contact: Douglas Kibbee
Dept. of French
2090 FLB, 707 South Mathews Ave.
Urbana, Illinois 61801
(217) 333-2020
(217) 244-2223
dkibbee@uiuc.edu

Human Resource Education

Degree Offered: Master of Education

Program Web Address: www.outreach.uiuc.edu/hre/

Online Program Started: 1998

Students Enrolled: 19

Program Background: This program is designed for students currently working in or interested in working in human resource development in the private or public sectors. It focuses on employee training and development, organization development, and the use of information and technology to improve individual and organizational performance.

Application Requirements: You must have a Bachelor's degree and a minimum undergraduate grade point average of 3.0 (on a 4.0 scale). You must sumbit an application to the Graduate College with a $40 application fee, official transcripts from any college or university you've attended, and two letters of recommendation.

Completion Requirements: You must successfully complete eight units of coursework.

System Requirements: You should have a basic knowledge of software tools including word processing, spreadsheet, databases, e-mail, and Web browsers. Additionally you should have access to a computer.

Example Course Titles: Some of the course titles in this program include Issues and Developments in Educational Policy, Studies: Foundations of Work and Work Education Course, Adult Learning and Development, Instructional Design for Business and Technical Setting, Instructional Technologies for Education and Training, Training Programs in Business and Industry, Evaluation of Education and Training Program, Strategic Planning for Human Resource Development, and Applying Quality Processes in Educational Leadership.

Program Contact: Department of Human Resource Education
345 Education Building
1310 South Sixth
Champaign, Illinois 61801
(217) 333-0807
(217) 244-5632
lirle@staff.uiuc.edu

Library and Information Science

Degree Offered: Master of Science in Library and Information Sciences

Program Web Address: alexia.lis.uiuc.edu/gslis/leep3/index.html

Online Program Started: 1996

Students Enrolled: 123

Degrees Awarded: 53

Program Background: Students can complete this American Library Association-accredited degree that combines limited on-campus instruction with Internet instruction and independent learning. Students complete the majority of coursework at a site of their choice—home or work, typically. Graduates of the program are prepared to hold entry-level jobs as librarians and information scientists.

The program focuses on instruction in organizing and using electronic information. Its objectives are to teach students how to anticipate social and technological changes (as well as promote change), foster critical thinking, encourage high standards of practice, conduct, and responsibility. Courses are delivered via the World Wide Web although students still can hear instructors delivering lectures, view slides and other graphics, and chat with the instructor and other students.

Application Requirements: You must have a Bachelor's degree from an accredited institution that has requirements equivalent to those of the University of Illinois and a minimum grade point average of 3.0 (on a 4.0 scale) for the last 60 credit hours of your undergraduate study. If you are an international applicant, you must receive a score of 620 or higher on the Test of English as a Foreign Language (TOEFL), and you're required to submit copies of your scores.

You need to complete and submit an application with an application fee, two copies of official transcripts from each college and university you've attended, three letters of recommendation, your scores on the Graduate Record Examination (GRE), and an essay. If you have questions about the admissions process, contact the School of Library and Information Sciences at (217) 333-7197.

Completion Requirements: You must successfully complete ten units of coursework for this degree.

On Campus Requirements: Your enrollment begins with a 12-day on-campus course worth one-half of a unit and several non-credit technology workshops. This course is conducted during the summer. Additionally, each of the courses in the program requires one brief on-campus session. The School recommends you group the on-campus sessions together so you only have to travel to campus once during the semester.

System Requirements: You should have basic computer literacy to participate in this program. And you need to have access to a computer at home or work. The computer you use needs to support discussions on an electronic bulletin board, interactive Web browsing, chat, e-mail, desktop sharing, audio files, and sharing documents. The School has a full-time technology coordinator and some graduate assistants who provide technical support.

Example Course Titles: Some of the course titles in this program include Library Materials for Children, Using Networked Information Systems, and Reference Sources and Services.

Program Contact: Graduate School of Library and Information Science
University of Illinois at Urbana-Champaign
501 E. Daniel Street
Champaign, Illinois 61820
(217) 333-3280
(217) 244-3302
leep@alexia.lis.uiuc.edu

Mathematics

Degree Offered: for-credit courses

Program Web Address: netmath.math.uiuc.edu/home.html

Students Enrolled: 200

Program Background: The NetMath program is a joint project among the University of Illinois at Urbana-Champaign, Ohio State University, University of Pittsburgh, University of Iowa, and Harvard. It focuses on using the World Wide Web to deliver globally accessible and interactive educational services teaching mathematics through mentoring and technology. High school students, university students, home-schooled students, and adult learners may take courses through NetMath for credit from the University of Illinois. Using computers running Mathematica, students learn calculus and problem-solving skills. The electronic lessons are divided into three sections: basics, tutorials, and give it a try.

Application Requirements: If you're a high school student, you can enroll in Calculus I if you have an ACT score of at least 26 in math and a minimum grade point average of B+ in your mathematics courses. You can enroll in other courses if you meet the prerequisites for those courses.

If you're an adult learner or college student, you must complete course prerequisites.

Time for Completion: You have between one and two semesters to complete a course.

System Requirements: You should have a personal computer with a Pentium processor running Windows 95 or a Power Macintosh. Your system should have at least 32 MB RAM, Internet access with an e-mail account, Mathematica software, Netscape 3.0 or higher, and Timbuktu Pro.

Example Course Titles: Some of the course titles in NetMath include Calculus and Analytic Geometry I and II, Symbolic Computation Lab, Introductory Matrix Theory, Calculus of Several Variables, Advanced Calculus, Differential Equations and Orthogonal Functions, and Linear Transformations and Matrices.

Program Contact: Debra Woods
Department of Mathematics
273 Altgeld Hall
1409 W. Green
Urbana, Illinois 61801
(217) 265-0439
(217) 333-9576
d-woods2@uiuc.edu

Mathmatics Education

Degree Offered: for-credit courses

Program Web Address: mtl.math.uiuc.edu/

Online Program Started: 1997

Program Background: Math Teacher Link is an Internet-based professional development program for high-school and lower-division college mathematics teachers. Teachers can earn graduate credit while taking course modules (short, single-topic courses) at home or their own school. Course modules focus on using technology in instruction.

Application Requirements: You do not have to be admitted to the University of Illinois at Urbana-Champaign's Graduate College unless you want to earn an advanced degree. You can earn graduate credit through Math Teacher Link prior to enrolling in a graduate degree program, and transfer those credits toward your degree requirements.

On Campus Requirements: There are no on-campus requirements.

System Requirements: You should have a personal computer running Windows 95/NT or higher or a Macintosh with OS 7.5 or higher, an Internet connection, Netscape 3.0 or higher, and decompression software. Some of the course modules have additional system requirements.

Example Course Titles: Some of the course titles in Math Teacher Link include Calculus and Mathematica for Mathematics Teachers, Dynamic Geometry With Geometer's SketchPad, Discrete Dynamical Systems for Mathematics Teachers, Computers and Connections, Using Internet Resources for High School Mathematics Instruction, and Using Mathematica in High School Mathematics.

Program Contact: Anthony L. Peressini

Mathematics Department
University of Illinois at Urbana-Champaign
273 Altgeld Hall
1409 W. Green Street
Urbana, Illinois 61801
(217) 333-6336
(217) 333-9576
peressin@uiuc.edu

Theoretical and Applied Mechanics

Degree Offered: Master of Science in Theoretical and Applied Mechanics

Program Web Address: www.engr.uiuc.edu/OCEE/degreeprog/

Online Program Started: 1999

Program Background: This program was designed for engineers who wish to pursue a Master of Science degree through off-campus study. Students can complete this entire degree online. The online degree program is exactly the same as its on-campus counterpart.

Application Requirements: You must have Bachelor's degree from an institution equivalent to the University of Illinois, a minimum undergraduate grade point average of 3.0 (on a 4.0 scale), and be adequately prepared for graduate study. The Department of Electrical and Computer Engineering must recommend you for admission to the Graduate College. The Department requires that you take the Graduate Record Examination (GRE), and if you're an international student, the Test of English as a Foreign Language (TOEFL).

Completion Requirements: You must successfully complete nine units of graduate course work, or eight units of coursework and two units of thesis, for this degree. You are also required to maintain a minimum grade point average of 3.0 while pursuing this degree.

System Requirements: You must have access to a personal computer with a 133 MHz processor running Windows 95/98/NT, 32 MB RAM, a 56K modem, color monitor with 800×600 resolution and 256 colors, 16-bit sound card and speakers, and a reliable Internet Service Provider. The software requirements are Microsoft Internet Explorer 5, Microsoft Windows Media Player, Microsoft PowerPoint, Adobe Acrobat Reader 3.01, and an e-mail software package.

Example Course Titles: Some of the course titles in this program include Solid Mechanics, Communications I, Power Electronics, Reliability Engineering, Valuation and Planning of New Products, Properties and Selection of Engineering Materials, and Genetic Algorithms in Search, Optimization, and Machine Learning.

Program Contact: Linda Krute
Continuing Engineering Education
University of Illinois at Urbana-Champaign
257 Engineering Science Bldg.
1101 W. Springfield
Urbana, Illinois 61801
(217) 333-6634
(217) 333-0015
L-krute@uiuc.edu

UNIVERSITY OF MAINE AT FORT KENT

General Contact Information
25 Pleasant Street
Fort Kent, Maine 04743

Phone: (800) TRY-UMFK
E-mail: umfkadm@maine.maine.edu
WWW: www.umfk.maine.edu

Online Learning Information

25 Pleasant Street
Fort Kent, Maine 04743

E-mail: goudreau@maine.maine.edu
WWW: www.umfk.maine.edu

Institution Background

The University of Maine at Fort Kent prides itself on personalized attention for each student. This philosophy is carried through in the online courses.

Founded: 1876
Type of Institution: Public
Accreditation: New England Association of Schools and Colleges; National League for Nursing

Online Course Offered: 15

Online Students Enrolled: 100

Services Offered to Students: Some students enrolled in online courses have access to library services.

Financial Aid: Students enrolled in online courses may be eligible for the same financial aid as on-campus students.

Registration: You can register for courses via mail, phone, e-mail, and the World Wide Web.

Programs

Nursing

Degree Offered: Bachelor of Science in Nursing

Program Web Address: www.umfk.maine.edu

Online Program Started: 1997

Students Enrolled: 35

Degrees Awarded: 7

Program Background: This is a very individualized program so it's best to contact the school directly for information.

Time for Completion: There are no limits on the amount of time you can take to complete this program. On average, students complete the requirements within three years.

On Campus Requirements: There are no on-campus requirements.

System Requirements: You need a computer that can support chat programs and Internet access.

Example Course Titles: Some of the course titles in this program include Nursing Transition, Community Health, Nursing Research, and Total Health Assessment.

Program Contact: Kelly A. Goudreau
Division of Nursing
25 Pleasant Street
Fort Kent, Maine 04743
(800) TRY-UMFK
(207) 834-7577
goudreau@maine.edu

UNIVERSITY OF MAINE AT MACHIAS

General Contact Information

9 O'Brien Avenue
Machias, Maine 04654

Phone: (207) 255-1374
FAX: (207) 255-1376
E-mail: bcook@acad.umm.maine.edu
WWW: www.umm.maine.edu/BEX

Online Learning Information

BEX Program
9 O'Brien Avenue
Machias, Maine 04654-1397

E-mail: jlehman@acad.umm.maine.edu
WWW: www.umm.maine.edu/BEX

Institution Background

The University of Maine at Machias takes pride in taking a personal approach to your education.

Founded: 1909
Type of Institution: Public
Accreditation: New England Association of Schools and Colleges

Online Course Offered: 8

Online Students Enrolled: 250

Special Programs/Partnerships: The BEX program is supported by the Tri-Campus Consortium which is composed of the University of Maine at Fort Kent, University of Maine at Machias, and the University of Maine at Presque Isle.

Services Offered to Students: All library services are available to matriculated students in the BEX program.

Financial Aid: Students enrolled in online courses may be eligible for federal financial aid.

Individual Undergraduate Courses: The BEX program has online courses in psychology, sociology, and philosophy.

Registration: You can register for courses via the phone and e-mail.

Programs

Behavioral Science

Degree Offered: Bachelor of Arts

Program Web Address: www.umm.maine.edu/BEX

Online Program Started: 1996

Students Enrolled: 50

Degrees Awarded: 1

Program Background: This program focuses on the ideals of access and integrity.

Application Requirements: You must have already earned 45 to 60 credit hours before applying to this program. To apply, you need to submit an application, $25 application fee, and official transcripts from each college you've attended.

Completion Requirements: You must successfully complete a total of 120 credit hours for this degree.

On Campus Requirements: There are no on-campus requirements.

System Requirements: You should have access to a personal computer with a 486 or Pentium processor running Windows 3.1/95 or a Macintosh 68040 or PowerPC, 16 MB RAM, a 28.8 baud modem, and a printer.

Example Course Titles: Some of the course titles in this program include Behavioral Science in the Information Age, Psychological Models, Sociocultural Models, Research Methods, and Ethical Dimensions.

Program Contact: Bonnie Cook
BEX Program Assistant
9 O'Brien Ave.
Machias, Maine 04654
(207) 255-1374

(207) 255-1376
bcook@acad.umm.maine.edu

UNIVERSITY OF MARYLAND—UNIVERSITY COLLEGE

General Contact Information

University Boulevard at Adelphi Road
College Park, Maryland 20742-1672

Phone: (301) 985-7000
FAX: (301) 985-7236
E-mail: umucinfo@nova.umuc.edu
WWW: www.umuc.edu/distance

Online Learning Information

University Boulevard at Adelphi Road
College Park, Maryland 20742-1636

E-mail: distance@nova.umuc.edu
WWW: www.umuc.edu/distance

Institution Background

The University of Maryland University College (UMUC) is a complete public university designed for the adult learner. UMUC operates the largest and most sophisticated virtual university in the world. During the 1998–1999 academic year, UMUC counted more than 21,000 online enrollments around the world, and they expect that number to double this year.

Founded: 1947
Type of Institution: Public
Accreditation: Middle States Association of Colleges and Schools

Online Course Background: UMUC's experience in distance education spans more than a quarter century. Its programs connect you to your faculty, coursemates, and advisors through today's communication technology, including online computer conferencing, and e-mail.

Online Course Offered: 161

Online Students Enrolled: 4801

Special Programs/Partnerships: UMUC is a member of MarylandOnline, a consortium of Maryland community colleges and universities offering online programs. It also has partnerships with the U.S. General Services Administration, UMUC and three other instituions offer graduate program to develop Chief Information Officers for the government. The school also has partnerships with the Southern Regional Education Board and the U.S. Navy.

Services Offered to Students: UMUC delivers student services directly to the student. Admissions, registration, academic counseling, financial aid, library services, and career resources are all available at a distance.

Financial Aid: Students enrolled in online courses may be eligible for finanicial aid from the federal government, the state of Maryland, employers, and other scholarships.

Programs

Accounting

Degree Offered: Bachelor of Arts or Bachelor of Science

Program Web Address: www.umuc.edu

Program Background: Students enrolled in this program learn how to measure the economic activities of organizations, turn the information into reports, and communicate findings to decision makers within the organizations.

Application Requirements: You should have your high school diploma or equivalent to apply to the University of Maryland, University College. You can apply and enroll in courses by mail, fax, or on the Web. If you have a Bachelor's degree from a regionally accredited college or university in the United States, you can be admitted to the program immediately, and you can register for courses when you submit your application.

Completion Requirements: You must successfully complete a minimum of 120 semester credit hours for this degree.

On Campus Requirements: There are no on-campus requirements.

System Requirements: You need to have a personal computer with a 486 processor (or faster), 16 MB RAM, a VGA or better monitor, a modem, and a mouse. You also need an Internet Service Provider, Windows 3.01/95/98, and Netscape 4.0. Some courses have additional software requirements.

Example Course Titles: Some of the course titles in this program include Principles of Accounting, Intermediate Accounting, Cost Accounting, Income Tax Accounting, Fund Accounting, Ethics and Professionalism in Accounting, and Advanced Tax Accounting.

Program Contact: Dr. Mary Ellen Hrutka
University of Maryland, University College
University Blvd. at Adelphi Rd.
College Park, Maryland 20742
(800) 283-6832
umucinfo@nova.umuc.edu

Behavioral and Social Sciences

Degree Offered: Bachelor of Arts/Bachelor of Science

Program Web Address: www.umuc.edu/prog/ugp/soc-para/behs.html

Program Background: This program in behavioral and social sciences studies individuals and society from a variety of perspectives. Behavioral and social sciences explores human development, the workings of social institutions, and patterns of behavior that characterize social life. Students prepare for the workplace through the development of research and analytical skills, understanding of social organizations, knowledge of the human life cycle, and awareness of factors defining cultural diversity.

Example Course Titles: Some of the course titles in this program include Discovering Psychology, Introduction to Behavioral and Social Sciences, Introduction to Research Methods and Statistics, Social Psychology, The Adult Years: Continuity and Change, Issues in Criminal Justice, Stress and the Social System, and Exploring the Future.

Business Administration

Degree Offered: Master of Business Administration

Program Web Address: www.umuc.edu

Program Background: The goal of this program is to integrate theory and practice addressing the needs of working professionals from a variety of backgrounds. It covers a wide range of current topics and themes.

Program Contact: University of Maryland—University College
University Blvd. at Adelphi Rd.
College Park, Maryland 20742
(800) 283-6832

Business and Management

Degree Offered: Bachelor of Arts/Bachelor of Science

Program Web Address: www.umuc.edu/prog/ugp/business/bmgt.html

Program Background: This program is intended to deal with complexities in the business environment and the individual organization. It covers policies, procedures, planning, budgeting, organization staffing, controlling and researching knowledge and skills. Students enrolled in it cultivate analytical skills, problem-solving ability, and critical thinking that will enable them to serve as effective managers.

System Requirements: You need to have a personal computer with a 486 processor (or faster), 16 MB RAM, a VGA or better monitor, a modem, and a mouse. You also need an Internet Service Provider, Windows 3.01/95/98, and Netscape 4.0. Some courses have additional software requirements.

Example Course Titles: Some of the course titles in this program include Introduction to Business Management, Business Statistics, Business Finance, Labor Relations, Business Law, Organizational Behavior, and Employment Law for Business.

Communication Studies

Degree Offered: Bachelor of Arts/Bachelor of Science

Program Web Address: www.umuc.edu/prog/ugp/comm/comm.html

Program Background: This program integrates theory and practice in information development, journalism, and professional communication. It emphasizes applications that are appropriate to government, business, industry, and mass media. And students develop appropriate investigative techniques as well as develop and refine written and oral skills that they will need for professional communication in workplace and public environments.

Example Course Titles: Some of the course titles in this program include Writing for Managers, Technical Writing, Business Writing, Seminar in Workplace Communication, and Writing for the Computer Industry.

Computer and Information Science

Degree Offered: Bachelor of Arts/Bachelor of Science

Program Web Address: www.umuc.edu/prog/ugp/cmis/welcome.html

Program Background: Students enrolled in this program study the development and implementation of effective solutions to practical problems using computer-based systems.

Example Course Titles: Some of the course titles in this program include Data Structures and Abstraction, Relational Databases, Software Engineering Principles and Techniques, Data Communications, Computer Networking, Software Design and Development, and Software Verification and Validation.

English

Degree Offered: Bachelor of Arts

Program Web Address: www.umuc.edu/prog/ugp/comm/english.html

Program Background: Students enrolled in this program study the nature and significance of literature through various approaches to literary works.

Example Course Titles: Some of the course titles in this program include Introduction to Writing, Critical Approaches to Literature, and Critical Analysis in Reading and Writing.

Humanities

Program Background: The University of Maryland—University College's humanities program focuses on human thought and culture, including philosophy, the arts, literature, language and religion. It provides a broad perspecitve on human behavior, morality, and spitituality, and focuses on the social cultural and aesthetic values of history, politics, religion, and philosophy.

Example Course Titles: Some of the courses available from the University of Maryland include America in Perspective, Cosmos, Modern Moral Choices, Business and Professional Ethics, The Religious Quest, Myth and Culture, and Legacies: A History of Women and the Family in America to 1870.

Program Contact: Individual Studies
University of Maryland—University College

Technology and Management

Degree Offered: Bachelor of Art or Bachelor of Science.

Program Web Address: www.umuc.edu

Program Background: This is an interdisciplinary program that studies how executives manage people and technology to make their companies more productive, competitive, and profitable. The program is geared toward managers who are seeking up-to-date knowledge, professional advancement, and leadership positions in private business, government, nonprofit organizations, and the military.

Application Requirements: You must have a high school diploma or the equivalent, and you can apply via mail, fax, or on the Web. If you already have a Bachelor's degree from a regionally accredited college or university, you are immediately admissible and you can register for courses when you submit your application.

Completion Requirements: You must successfully complete 120 semester credit hours for this degree.

On Campus Requirements: There are no on-campus requirements for this program.

Example Course Titles: Some of the course titles in this program include Introduction to Computer-Based Systems, Finance for the Nonfinancial Executive, Human Resource Management, Systems Performance, and International Management in the Global Economy.

Program Contact: Dr. Mary Ellen Hrutka
University of Maryland, University College
University Blvd. at Adelphi Rd.
College Park, Maryland 20742
(800) 283-6832
umucinfo@nova.umuc.edu

UNIVERSITY OF MASSACHUSETTS-LOWELL

General Contact Information

One University Avenue
Lowell, Massachusetts 01854

Phone: (978) 934-2588
FAX: (978) 934-3087
E-mail: cybered@uml.edu
WWW: www.uml.edu/DCE

Online Learning Information

One University Avenue
Lowell, Massachusetts 01854-2881

E-mail: cybered@cs.uml.edu
WWW: www.uml.edu/DCE

Institution Background

The University of Massachusetts Lowell specializes in science and technology. It offers more than 100 different degree programs in the Colleges of Arts and Sciences, Education, Engineering, Health Profession and Management. The Division of Continuing Studies and Corporate Education (CSCE), which includes evening and summer schools of the university, is one of the largest programs of its kind in New England.

Founded: 1894
Type of Institution: Public
Accreditation: New England Association of Schools and Colleges

Online Course Background: The University of Massachusetts Lowell started its online program in 1996. It is now one of the largest online degree programs in New England. The CyberEd Program offers accredited undergraduate courses, degrees, and certificates to students from around the world.

Online Course Offered: 35

Online Students Enrolled: 700

Special Programs/Partnerships: The University of Massachusetts Lowell offers a Data Telecommunications Certificate in collaboration with Nortel; an Online Plastics Technology Certificate in collaboration with NYPRO; a range of off-campus programs in collaboration with regional employers; and is currently involved in a technology development partnership with IntraLearn Software.

Services Offered to Students: The Division of Continuing Education has developed a series of online tutorials as an introduction to both the CyberEd program and to the software used in the program. Students are able to order books online from the bookstore as well as having access to searchable databases from the library online. Telephone and e-mail technical support are available to students requiring more than an online tutorial can provide. Advising services are available online, by phone, and in person. Seven days a week technical support is available by phone, email or online.

Financial Aid: Students enrolled in online programs may be eligible for financial aid includ-

ing the Hoff Scholarship, Hoff Merit Scholarship, Merrimack Valley Branch of American Association of University Women (AAUW), and Alpha Sigma Lambda Scholarship (ASL). Students interested in more information of these scholarships should contact Enrollment Services at (978) 934-2588.

Registration: You can register for courses via mail, phone, and e-mail.

Programs
Information Systems

Degree Offered: Associate of Science in Information Systems

Program Web Address: cybered.uml.edu

Program Background: This program teaches students the skills that are vital for success in today's information age. Students can focus their studies on such specialized areas as UNIX, Information Technology, Multimedia Applications, Website Design and Development, or Data/Telecommunications.

Application Requirements: You must have your high school diploma or equivalency certificate (GED), as evidenced by your transcripts. The program operates on a rolling admissions basis and your application is reviewed when it is complete.

You need to submit an application, official transcripts and course descriptions from any college or university you've attended, and your high school transcripts or copy of your GED certificate.

Program Restrictions: If you have not yet completed 18 credit hours in your degree program, you may be admitted on a provisional basis.

Completion Requirements: You must successfully complete at least nine semester credits of regular coursework in your major department and at least 24 semester credits through the University of Massachusetts Lowell.

On Campus Requirements: You may be required to attend some experimental learning sessions on-campus. You may be able to fulfill this requirement at a local institution, and transfer them into the program with prior approval by your advisor.

System Requirements: You should have a computer with Internet access and a Web browser (Netscape Navigator 4.05, Microsoft Internet Explorer 4.0, or America Online 4.0 or higher). Some courses have additional software requirements.

Example Course Titles: Some of the course titles in this program include Introduction to Information Systems, Introduction to Management and Organizational Behavior, Historical Studies, Introduction to Statistics, C Programming, and C++ Programming.

Program Contact: Advising Center
CSCE
One University Ave.
Lowell, MA 01854
(978) 934-2588
(978) 934-4006
continuing_education@uml.edu

Information Systems

Degree Offered: Bachelor of Science in Information Systems

Program Web Address: cybered.uml.edu

Online Program Started: 1996

Program Background: This program offers students the opportunity to learn skills vital for success in today's information age. Students can focus their studies on such specialized areas as UNIX, Information Technology, Multimedia Applications, Website Design and Development, or Data/Telecommunications.

Application Requirements: You must have your high school diploma or equivalency certificate (GED), as evidenced by your transcripts. The program operates on a rolling admissions basis and your application is reviewed when it is complete.

You need to submit an application, official transcripts and course descriptions from any college or university you've attended, and your high school transcripts or copy of your GED certificate.

Program Restrictions: If you have not yet completed 18 credit hours in your degree program, you may be admitted on a provisional basis.

Completion Requirements: You must successfully complete 120 hours for this degree.

On Campus Requirements: You may be required to attend some courses on-campus. You may be able to fulfill this requirement at a local institution and transfer them into the program with prior approval by your advisor.

System Requirements: You should have a computer with Internet access and a Web browser (Netscape Navigator 4.05, Microsoft Internet Explorer 4.0, or America Online 4.0 or higher). Some courses have additional software requirements.

Example Course Titles: Some of the course titles in this program include Introduction to Information Systems, College Writing I, PreCalculus Math I, C Programming, General Psychology, and Microeconomics.

Program Contact: Advising Center
CSCE
One University Ave.
Lowell, Massachusetts 01854
(978) 934-2588

(978) 934-4006
continuing_education@uml.edu

Information Technology

Degree Offered: Certificate in Fundamentals of Information Technology

Program Web Address: cybered.uml.edu

Program Background: This certificate is designed as an introductory program for those who want to explore information technology areas before deciding on a specialization.

Application Requirements: You must have your high school diploma or high school equivalency certificate (GED), and submit your most recent college transcripts.

Completion Requirements: You must successfully complete all of the required courses and electives with a C or better in order to receive this certificate.

On Campus Requirements: There are no on-campus requirements.

System Requirements: You should have a computer, Internet access, and a Web browser (Microsoft Internet Explorer 4.0 or higher, Netscape Navigator 4.05 or higher, or America Online 4.0 or higher). Some courses may have additional software requirements.

Example Course Titles: Some of the course titles in this program include Introduction to Information Systems, Introduction to Personal Computing and Microsoft Office, Visual Basic, C Programming, Relational Database Concepts, and Exploring the Internet.

Program Contact: Advising Center
CSCE
One University Ave.
Lowell, Massachusetts 01854
(978) 934-2588
(978) 934-4006
continuing_education@uml.edu

Intranet Development

Degree Offered: Certificate in Intranet Development

Program Web Address: cybered.uml.edu

Program Background: This program trains students in programming, as well as helps them gain a broader understanding of network topology, interface design, database interface, and other technology skills.

Application Requirements: You must have your high school diploma or high school equivalency certificate (GED), and submit any college transcripts.

Program Restrictions: You can transfer only one course from another institution of higher education into this certificate program.

Completion Requirements: You must successfully complete six courses with a C or better in order to receive this certificate.

On Campus Requirements: There are no on-campus requirements.

System Requirements: You need a personal computer with Internet access and a Web browser (Netscape Navigator 4.05 or higher, Microsoft Internet Explorer 4.0 or higher, or America Online 4.0 or higher). Some courses may have additional software requirements.

Example Course Titles: Some of the course titles in this program include Intranet Applications for the Organization, LAN/WAN Technologies, Java Programming, Introduction to Perl, TCP/IP and Network Architecture, and Relational Database Concepts.

Program Contact: Advising Center
CSCE
One University Ave.
Lowell, Massachusetts 01854
(978) 934-2588
(978) 934-4006
continuing_education@uml.edu

UNIX

Degree Offered: Certificate in UNIX

Program Web Address: cybered.uml.edu

Program Background: This certificate program is designed for students who are in the computer industry and who want to upgrade their skills, as well as for those who want to enter this field. The curriculum integrates theory and practice. Students learn skills that are immediately applicable in the workplace.

Application Requirements: You must have your high school diploma or equivalent, and submit official transcripts from any college or university you've attended.

Program Restrictions: You can transfer only one course to this certificate program.

Completion Requirements: You must successfully complete all five courses with a C or better in order to receive this certificate.

On Campus Requirements: There are no on-campus requirements.

System Requirements: You need a personal computer with Internet access and a Web browser (Netscape Navigator 4.05 or higher, Microsoft Internet Explorer 4.0 or higher, or America Online 4.0 or higher). Some courses may have additional software requirements.

Example Course Titles: Some of the course titles in this program include Introduction to Unix Operating System, C Programming, Unix Shell Programming, Introduction to Data Structures, C++ Programming, and Advanced C++.

Program Contact: Advising Center
CSCE
One University Ave.
Lowell, Massachusetts 01854
(978) 934-2588
(978) 934-4006
continuing_education@uml.edu

UNIVERSITY OF MINNESOTA, CROOKSTON

General Contact Information

4 Hill Hall
Crookston, Minnesota 56716-5001

WWW: www.crk.umn.edu/welcome.htm

Online Learning Information

Director of Continuing Education
217 Selvig Hall
2900 University Avenue
Crookston, Minnesota 56716

E-mail: klemmerm@mail.crk.umn.edu
WWW: www.crk.umn.edu/welcome.htm

Institution Background

Founded: 1966
Type of Institution: Public
Accreditation: North Central Association of Colleges and Schools

Programs
Applied Health

Degree Offered: Bachelor of Applied Health

Program Web Address: www.crk.umn.edu/academics/BAH/

Program Background: This program is designed for allied health personnel who seek professional advancement. Students gain the skill, knowledge, and experience to assume leadership roles in a variety of health care settings.

Example Course Titles: Some of the course titles in this program include Problem Solving in Complex Organizations, Small Group Behavior and Teamwork, Communicating for Results, Accessing and Using Information Effectively, Leadership in Global and Diverse Workplace, and Management and Human Resource Practices.

UNIVERSITY OF NEBRASKA-LINCOLN

General Contact Information

Alexander Building, 1410 Q Street
Lincoln, Nebraska 68588-0417

Phone: (402) 472-2023
FAX: (402) 472-0670
E-mail: nunusker@unl.edu
WWW: www.unl.edu

Online Learning Information

332 C NCCE
Lincoln, Nebraska 68583-9800

E-mail: mbarber2@unl.edu
WWW: www.unl.edu

Institution Background

The University of Nebraska-Lincoln (UNL) is Nebraska's only land grant and major comprehensive institution. With its four-part mission of teaching, research, service, and outreach, UNL offers a wide range of undergraduate, professional, and graduate programs including those leading to a doctorate.

Founded: 1869
Type of Institution: Public
Accreditation: North Central Association of Colleges and Schools

Online Course Background: UNL offers graduate degree sequences, certificates, and individ-

ual courses online at both the graduate and undergraduate levels. On-line courses are designed to meet the needs of many learners by providing interactive multimedia instructional environments.

Online Course Offered: 155

Online Students Enrolled: 2,897

Special Programs/Partnerships: UNL has partnerships with community colleges, state and private colleges, learning centers, and other system campuses; ADEC; the University of South Carolina, South Dakota, and Colorado in the delivery of high school curriculum; K-12 school districts and Educational Service Units; and the National Guard, Law Enforcement, and others in the delivery of courses.

Services Offered to Students: Students enrolled in online courses have access to the library, academic advising, bookstore, registration and record keeping, technical support, admissions and application support, laboratory, and other student services as needed.

Financial Aid: Financial aid is available to enrolled UNL students under the guidelines provided by the financial aid requirements. Students with questions about financial aid for distance learning students and programs should contact UNL's financial aid office.

Individual Undergraduate Courses: UNL has online courses in accounting, agricultural economics, art and art history, biological sciences, broadcasting, classics, curriculum and instruction, economics, English, family and consumer sciences, finance, geography, health and human performances, history, industrial and management systems engineering, journalism, management, marketing, mathematics and statistics, nursing, nutritional science and dietetics, philosophy, physics and astronomy, political science, psychology, real estate, and sociology.

Individual Graduate Courses: UNL has online courses in statistics, educational technology, distance education, agronomy, agricultural economics, music, and management.

Registration: You can register for courses via mail, phone, e-mail, and the World Wide Web.

Programs

Education

Degree Offered: Doctorate

Program Web Address: hou-edadone.unl. edu/welcome.htm

Online Program Started: 1995

Students Enrolled: 50

Program Background: Students in this program can specialize in administration, curriculum, or instruction. Students develop skills in educational leadership and higher education.

Completion Requirements: You must successfully complete 30 credit hours.

On Campus Requirements: You are required to participate in two ten-week summer sessions at the University of Nebraska-Lincoln.

System Requirements: You should have a personal computer with a 486 processor or faster running Windows 3.1/95, or a Macintosh 6800 or PowerPC, CD-ROM drive, minimum 55MB of hard drive space, 16MB of RAM, and a 28.8 baud modem.

Example Course Titles: Some of the course titles in this program include History and Philosophy of Higher Education, Issues in Educational Politics and Policies, Higher Education Environment, and Issues in Higher Education.

Program Contact: Dr. Al Seagren
University of Nebraska-Lincoln

P O Box 880638
Lincoln, Nebraska 68588-0638
(402) 472-0972
aseagren1@unl.edu

Interdepartmental Human Resources and Family Sciences

Degree Offered: Master of Science

Program Web Address: ianrwww.unl.edu/ ianr/chrfs/distihrf.htm

Students Enrolled: As of December 1998, 27 students were working on requirements for this degree.

Degrees Awarded: As of December 1998, 38 people received this degree.

Program Background: This Master's program gives students the opportunity for broad-based study in family and consumer sciences by integrating content areas and focusing on development of theoretical knowledge, communication skills, and professional application.

Application Requirements: You must be admitted to the University of Nebraska-Lincoln's Graduate Studies, which requires you to complete and submit an application for the program, submit three letters of recommendation, submit your GRE scores, and have an undergraduate grade point average of 3.0 or higher. Also you must have a minimum of 12 hours of undergraduate work related to your area of interest. And you must submit a written statement about yourself, your experiences, and your strengths, and describe why you're interested in this program and how it will benefit you. If you choose, you may submit a resume.

In addition to admittance to Graduate Studies, the Interdepartmental Human Resources and Family Services program requires you to have a Bachelor's degree in family or consumer sciences or its equivalent (with 24 hours in family and consumer sciences, and 20 hours in natural and social sciences).

You may be admitted to the program with full graduate standing, provisional status, or unclassified status. To be admitted with full graduate standing, you must meet all of the preceding requirements. Provisional status admittance means you have potential for the program, but you don't meet all of the admissions requirements. As a provisional student, you can't become a candidate for a degree until you are recommended for full graduate standing by a committee in consultation with your advisor. And unclassified status means you satisfy the minimum admission requirements, but don't wish to pursue a degree.

Program Restrictions: You need access to a research library. The University of Nebraska library allows online students to order research journal articles via e-mail and to receive photocopies by mail.

Completion Requirements: You must successfully complete 36 credit hours to earn this degree. Eighteen of the credit hours will be in Family and Consumer Sciences. The remaining 18 credit hours will be broken down as follows: six in Textiles, Clothing, and Design; six in Nutritional Science and Dietetics, three in Research Methods, and three in Statistics. You are also required to prepare a paper reflecting that you can think critically and solve problems, using what you've learned while earning this degree. And you must successfully pass a written, comprehensive examination.

Time for Completion: You can complete the degree requirements in four years if you enroll in one course per semester and one course during each summer session.

System Requirements: You need an Internet Service Provider as use of the Web is required for courses.

Example Course Titles: Some of the course titles in this program include Research Methods, Dress and Culture, Adolescent in the Family, Family Financial Management, Research Methods, Statistical Decision Making, Financial Counseling, Gerontology, Housing/Real Estate, Fashion Theory, Retirement Planning and Employee Benefits, and Insurance Planning for Families.

Program Contact: College of Human Resources and Family Sciences
University of Nebraska
105 Home Economics Building
P.O. Box 830800
Lincoln, Nebraska 68583-0800
(402) 472-9863
(402) 472-2895
EBOTTSFORD1@unl.edu

Journalism and Mass Communications

Degree Offered: Master of Arts in Journalism and Mass Communications

Program Web Address: www.unl.edu/ conted/telecom/index.html

Online Program Started: 1998

Students Enrolled: 4

Program Background: Students have two options in this Master's program through the College of Journalism and Mass Communications. The first option is to earn a standard Master's in Journalism, which focuses on professional knowledge, skills, and leadership in journalism and mass communications. This curriculum incorporates practical application and experience with the theoretical knowledge. Students in this area can select a specialization of advertising, broadcasting, or news-editorial.

The second option in this program is to earn a Master's in News-Editorial that is intended for middle- and high-school teachers. This curriculum focuses on skills needed by teachers who work on newspapers, yearbooks, and other publications with student staffs. It incorporates theory and practical experience directly related to teaching about and publishing projects.

Application Requirements: You must submit an application including a $35 application fee, resume, statement of goals, two copies of official transcripts from each college or university you've attended, work samples, and three letters of recommendation. If you are an international applicant, you must also submit your scores on the Test of English as a Foreign Language (TOEFL) and a Financial Resource Certification.

Completion Requirements: You must successfully complete 30 credit hours and a thesis or 36 credit hours for this degree.

Time for Completion: If you enroll in two courses per semester, you may complete either option in this program within three years.

System Requirements: You need a personal computer with a Pentium processor, 100 MHz minimum, and Windows 95 (or higher) or a Macintosh OS System 7.6. Your computer needs to have 16 MB of RAM if you have a personal computer or 24 MB of RAM if you have a Macintosh, 10 MB of hard disk space, a 28.8 Kbps modem, and an Internet connection.

Example Course Titles: Some of the course titles in the first option for this program include Mass Communication Theory, Methods of Mass Communication Research, and Mass Media and the Government.

Some of the course titles in the second option for this program include Creative Editing, School Publications, and Mass Media and Government.

Program Contact: Dr. Larry Walklin

University of Nebraska-Lincoln
P. O. Box 880131
Lincoln, Nebraska 68588-0131
(402) 472-3050
(402) 472-8597
lwalklin@unlserve.unl.edu

Textiles, Clothing, and Design

Degree Offered: Master of Science

Program Web Address: ianrwww.unl.edu/ianr/chrfs/TCDEXOVE.HTM

Program Background: This program provides students with general knowledge about textiles, clothing, and design. Students gain a broad understanding of the foundational perspectives, and learn to apply their knowledge of textile and apparel products in their work.

Application Requirements: You must submit an application and be admitted to the University's Graduate Studies. Along with your application, you should include your Graduate Record Examination scores, three letters of recommendation, and a written statement of your background, goals, experience, and strengths. You must have a minimum undergraduate grade point average of 3.0.

Completion Requirements: You must successfully complete 36 credit hours for this degree. Your coursework will be broken down as follows: at least 18 credit hours in textiles, clothing, and design courses; six credit hours in supporting work (family and consumer sciences, business, history, and so forth); three credit hours in research methods; three credit hours in statistics; and six credit hours in electives.

Time for Completion: If you enroll in one course per semester or summer session, you can complete this degree in four years and one semester.

Example Course Titles: Some of the course titles in this program include Research Methods, Dress and Culture, Adolescent in the Family, Family Financial Management, Research Methods, Contemporary Nutrition, Family Systems, Statistical Decision Making, Family Economics, and Nutrition Throughout the Life Cycle.

Program Contact: University of Nebraska Department of Textiles, Clothing and Design 206 Home Economics Building Lincoln, Nebraska 68583-0802 (402) 472-2913 krees1@unl.edu

UNIVERSITY OF NEVADA, RENO

General Contact Information

Independent Study, Mail Stop 050 Reno, Nevada 89557-0002

Phone: (775) 784-4652
FAX: (775) 784-1280
E-mail: istudy@scs.unr.edu
WWW: www.dce.unr.edu/istudy

Online Learning Information

Independent Study, Mail Stop 050 Reno, Nevada 89557

E-mail: istudy@scs.unr.edu
WWW: www.dce.unr.edu/istudy

Institution Background

Founded: 1869
Type of Institution: Public
Accreditation: Northwest Association of Schools and Colleges

Online Course Background: The University of Nevada, Reno (UNR), has courses in Math, English, Criminal Justice, and other subjects online. All of the syllabi for the courses are online for anyone to view at any time—no password is needed.

Online Course Offered: 17

Online Students Enrolled: 150

Services Offered to Students: Students enrolled in online courses have access to the library, tutoring, book ordering and enrollment, and financial aid.

Financial Aid: A few online students may be eligible for financial aid.

Registration: You can register for courses via mail, phone, e-mail, and the World Wide Web.

Programs

General Studies

Degree Offered: Bachelor of General Studies

Online Program Started: 1997

Application Requirements: You must have 60 credit hours to enter program, and not all of the courses can completed by distance.

Completion Requirements: You must successfully complete 124 credit hours.

Time for Completion: There is no specific amount of time in which you must complete this program.

On Campus Requirements: You are required to complete Western Tradition Capstone Courses on campus.

Program Contact: Judith Robertson University of Nevada, Reno Division of Continuing Education Reno, Nevada 89557 (775) 784-4046

UNIVERSITY OF NORTH DAKOTA

General Contact Information

Box 8135
Grand Forks, North Dakota 58202

E-mail: enrolser@sage.und.nodak.edu
WWW: www.und.nodak.edu

Online Learning Information

IVN Coordinator
Box 9021
Grand Forks, North Dakota 58202-9021

E-mail: dorine_houck@mail.und.nodak.edu

Institution Background

Founded: 1883
Type of Institution: Public
Accreditation: North Central Association of Colleges and Schools

Programs

Space Studies

Degree Offered: Bachelor of Science

Program Web Address: www.space.edu/info/distance/

Online Program Started: 1996

Program Background: This program is intended for aerospace professionals who want to expand their knowledge and those who are interested in a career in this field. By offering this program online, the University of North Dakota hopes to address the needs of those students with employment and family commitments that preclude them from attending on-campus.

Application Requirements: You need to complete an application and submit it with a $25 application fee, a statement of your goals and objectives, three letters of recommendation, and two official transcripts from each college or university you've attended.

Example Course Titles: Some of the course titles in this program include Observational Astronomy, Commercialization of Space, Soviet/Russian Space Program, Human Factors in Space, Space Treaties and Legislation, Space Studies Capstone, Life in the Universe, and Human Factors in Space.

Program Contact: Department of Space Studies
University of North Dakota
Box 9008
Grand Forks, North Dakota 58202-9008
(701) 777-2480
(701) 777-3711
bthompso@space.edu

UNIVERSITY OF NORTHERN IOWA

General Contact Information

124 SHC
Cedar Falls, Iowa 50614-0223

Phone: 1 (800) 772-1746 or (319) 273-2123
FAX: (319) 273-2872
E-mail: contined@uni.edu
WWW: www.uni.edu/contined/gcs

Online Learning Information

Continuing Education Credit Programs
124 SHC
Cedar Falls, Iowa 50614-0223

E-mail: kent.johnson@uni.edu
WWW: www.uni.edu/contined/gcs

Institution Background

Founded: 1876
Type of Institution: Public
Accreditation: North Central Association of Colleges and Schools

Online Course Background: The University of Northern Iowa's online courses are delivered via the World Wide Web using Web pages and a computer conference program called WebCT.

Online Course Offered: 12

Online Students Enrolled: 120

Services Offered to Students: Distance Learning students at the University of Northern Iowa have access to a broad range of library services.

Financial Aid: You should contact the school's financial aid office directly (319) 273-2700 to inquire about financial aid applications and eligibility.

Individual Undergraduate Courses: The University of Northern Iowa has online courses in education, music, geography, mathematics, health, and sociology.

Individual Graduate Courses: The University of Northern Iowa has online courses in education, health, and sociology.

Registration: You can register for courses via mail and the World Wide Web.

Programs

The University of Northern Iowa offers an online program of study in liberal studies.

UNIVERSITY OF PHOENIX

General Contact Information

WWW: www.uophx.edu/online

Online Learning Information

Enrollment Department
100 Spear Street, Suite 110
San Francisco, California 94105

E-mail: online@appollogrp.edu
WWW: www.uophx.edu/online

Institution Background

Founded: 1976
Type of Institution: Proprietary
Accreditation: North Central Association of Colleges and Schools

Programs

Business Administration

Degree Offered: Master of Business Administration

Program Web Address: www.uophx.edu/Allother_Campusesprograms/mba.html

Program Background: The MBA program is designed to meet the needs of working adult managers or supervisors who could benefit from a graduate business education. It is also an appropriate program for students whose career interests involve not-for-profit enterprise. The program requires a practical background in business, and the successful candidate will have at least three years of relevant experience.

Application Requirements: You should have at least three years of relevant experience, a Bachelor's degree from a regionally accredited college or university, and a cumulative grade point average of at least 2.5 (on a 4.0 scale). You need to complete and submit an application, official transcripts from any college or university you've attended, and verification of your three years professional experience and current employment. You are required to complete the University's Comprehensive Cognitive Assessment pre-test. If you are an international student whose native language is not English, you must take the Test of English as a Foreign Language (TOEFL) and score at least a 580.

Completion Requirements: You must successfully complete 51 credit hours for this degree.

Example Course Titles: Some of the course titles in this program include Executive Management in a Global Economy, Human Relations and Organizational Behavior, Legal Environment of Business, Statistics for Managerial Decision Making, Statistical Applications for Business, Operations Management for Total Quality, Applied Microeconomics, Financial Accounting, Advanced Managerial Accounting, Managerial Finance, Financial Analysis and Planning, Macroeconomics for Business Decision Making, Advanced Marketing Management, Strategy Formulation and Implementation, Managerial Ethics and Professional Responsibility, Applied Management Science Project Seminar, and Applied Management Science Project.

Program Contact: University of Phoenix Online
4605 E. Elwood St. 7th Floor
Phoenix, Arizona 85040
(800) 765-4922
(480) 894-2152

Business Administration— Global Management, Technology Management

Degree Offered: Master of Business Administration

Program Web Address: www.uophx.edu/ Allother_Campusesprograms/mbagm.html

Program Background: This program has two concentrations: Global Management and Technology Management. Students learn the skills necessary to manage multicultural and multi-

national workforces effectively in a rapidly-changing environment. The program is dedicated to linking technical and business cultures as integrated functions of the technology-based organization, and to establishing an innovative environment that will encompass technology development.

Application Requirements: You should have a Bachelor's degree from a regionally accredited college or university, and a cumulative grade point average of at least 2.5 (on a 4.0 scale). You need to complete and submit an application, official transcripts from any college or university you've attended, and verification of your three years professional experience and current employment. You are required to complete the University's Comprehensive Cognitive Assessment pre-test. If you are an international student whose native language is not English, you must take the Test of English as a Foreign Language (TOEFL) and score at least a 580.

Completion Requirements: You must successfully complete between 41 and 51 credit hours (depending upon area of concentration) for this degree.

Example Course Titles: Some of the course titles in this program include Cross-Cultural Considerations for International Managers, Global Management, International Human Resource Management, International Managerial Economics, International Financial Management, International Financial Management, Global Marketing, International Business Law, Project Management, Global Business Operations, International Business Systems, Special Topics: Global Village, and Global Business— Strategy Formulation and Implementation.

Program Contact: University of Phoenix Online
4605 E. Elwood St. 7th Floor
Phoenix, Arizona 85040
(800) 765-4922
(480) 894-2152

Business/Administration

Degree Offered: Bachelor of Science

Program Web Address: www.uophx.edu/ Allother_Campusesprograms/admin.html

Program Background: This program is designed for working adults employed in a business or public organization. It enables students to deal effectively with an increasingly complex business environment. The curriculum covers financial accounting, managerial finance, quantitative analysis, economics, marketing, and business-based research.

Application Requirements: You must be at least 23 years old, have a high school diploma or equivalent, and be employed. If you're not currently employed, you should have access to an organizational environment where you can apply the theoretical concepts that you're learning through courses. You must also complete the University of Phoenix proctored Comprehensive Cognitive Assessment. If you are an international student whose native language is not English, you must also have a minimum score of 580 on the Test of English as a Foreign Language (TOEFL).

Completion Requirements: You must successfully complete 33 credit hours for this degree.

Example Course Titles: Some of the course titles in this program include Critical Thinking and Decision Making, Business Law, Project Management, Financial Accounting, Managerial Finance, Economics for Business, Marketing, and Business Research Applications.

Program Contact: University of Phoenix Online
4605 E. Elwood St. 7th Floor
Phoenix, Arizona 85040
(800) 765-4922
(480) 894-2152

Business/Management

Degree Offered: Bachelor of Science

Program Web Address: www.uophx.edu/ Allother_Campusesprograms/mgt.html

Program Background: This program is for students who want to acquire or build knowledge and skills essential for management in private and public organizations. It emphasizes performance systems, employment law, marketing and public relations, financial analysis, global business strategies, and quality management.

Application Requirements: You must be at least 23 years old, have a high school diploma or equivalent, and be employed. If you're not currently employed, you should have access to an organizational environment where you can apply the theoretical concepts that you're learning through courses. You must also complete the University of Phoenix proctored Comprehensive Cognitive Assessment. If you are an international student whose native language is not English, you must also have a minimum score of 580 on the Test of English as a Foreign Language (TOEFL).

Example Course Titles: Some of the course titles in this program include Critical Thinking and Decision Making, Project Management, Human Resources Management, Employment Law, Marketing, Public Relations, Financial Analysis for Managers, Global Business Strategies, Quality Management and Productivity, and Business Research Applications.

Program Contact: University of Phoenix Online
4605 E. Elwood St. 7th Floor
Phoenix, Arizona 85040
(800) 765-4922
(480) 894-2152

Business/Marketing

Degree Offered: Bachelor of Science

Program Web Address: www.uophx.edu/

Allother_Campusesprograms/mkt.html

Program Background: Students enrolled in this program learn creative, analytical, and leadership abilities that they can use in managing the marketing function of the business enterprise. They learn how to identify customer needs, how to communicate information about products and services to customers and potential customers, where to market and how to price products and services, and how to respond to growing demands to markets in different countries and cultures.

Application Requirements: You must be at least 23 years old, have a high school diploma or equivalent, and be employed. If you're not currently employed, you should have access to an organizational environment where you can apply the theoretical concepts that you're learning through courses. You must also complete the University of Phoenix proctored Comprehensive Cognitive Assessment. If you are an international student whose native language is not English, you must also have a minimum score of 580 on the Test of English as a Foreign Language (TOEFL).

Example Course Titles: Some of the course titles in this program include Critical Thinking and Decision Making, Business Law, Economics for Business, Marketing, Financial Analysis for Managers, Buyer Behavior, Sales Management, Integrated Marketing Communications, Marketing Research, and International Marketing.

Program Contact: University of Phoenix Online
4605 E. Elwood St. 7th Floor
Phoenix, Arizona 85040
(800) 765-4922
(480) 894-2152

Business/Project Management

Degree Offered: Bachelor of Science

Program Web Address: www.uophx.edu/

Allother_Campusesprograms/bsbpm.html

Program Background: The Business/Project Management program focuses on real-world application of assignments that are designed so that students can to apply the new found skills and knowledge to the workplace. Students use practical study materials, and participate in team activities and presentations to the class. This program fosters teamwork and encourages students to develop critical thinking and self-confidence while applying technical and leadership skills on a real-time basis.

Application Requirements: You must be at least 23 years old, have a high school diploma or equivalent, and be employed. If you're not currently employed, you should have access to an organizational environment where you can apply the theoretical concepts that you're learning through courses. You must also complete the University of Phoenix proctored Comprehensive Cognitive Assessment. If you are an international student whose native language is not English, you must also have a minimum score of 580 on the Test of English as a Foreign Language (TOEFL).

Completion Requirements: You must successfully complete 33 hours for this degree.

Example Course Titles: Some of the course titles in this program include Business Law, Critical Thinking and Decision Making, Economics for Business, Marketing, Project Management, Strategic Management of Cross-Functional Projects, Financial Analysis for Managers, Contracting and Risk Management for Project Managers, Project Estimating and Control Techniques, and Project Management Capstone.

Program Contact: University of Phoenix Online
4605 E. Elwood St. 7th Floor
Phoenix, Arizona 85040
(800) 765-4922

(480) 894-2152

Computer Information Systems

Degree Offered: Master of Science

Program Web Address: www.uophx.edu/ Allother_Campusesprograms/mscis.html

Program Background: This degree program is designed for students who wish to integrate different disciplines of information technology in a business applications context. Students take courses that cover key concepts of information technology, information systems management, and interpersonal and organizational communications.

Application Requirements: You should have at least three years of relevant experience, a Bachelor's degree from a regionally accredited college or university, and a cumulative grade point average of at least 2.5 (on a 4.0 scale). You need to complete and submit an application, official transcripts from any college or university you've attended, and verification of your three years professional experience and current employment. You are required to complete the University's Comprehensive Cognitive Assessment pre-test. If you are an international student whose native language is not English, you must take the Test of English as a Foreign Language (TOEFL) and score at least a 580.

Completion Requirements: You must successfully complete 45 semester graduate credit hours with a minimum grade point average of B (3.0).

Example Course Titles: Some of the course titles in this program include CIS Business Communication, CIS Project Management, Operating Systems, Networks/DataCom, Database Concepts, Programming Management 3, CIS Business Financial Management, Software Engineering, CIS Strategic Planning, CIS Risk Management, CIS Contracts, Ethics and Intellectual Property, and CIS Organization and Management.

Program Contact: University of Phoenix Online
4605 E. Elwood St. 7th Floor
Phoenix, Arizona 85040
(800) 765-4922
(480) 894-2152

Education

Degree Offered: Master of Education

Program Web Address: www.uophx.edu/ Allother_Campusesprograms/mae.html

Program Background: This program is designed to meet the specific needs of educators through a variety of specializations. Courses in each area of specialization were developed to meet state licensing and content standards.

Application Requirements: You should have at least three years of relevant experience, a Bachelor's degree from a regionally accredited college or university, and a cumulative grade point average of at least 2.5 (on a 4.0 scale). You need to complete and submit an application, official transcripts from any college or university you've attended, and verification of your three years professional experience and current employment. You are required to complete the University's Comprehensive Cognitive Assessment pre-test. If you are an international student whose native language is not English, you must take the Test of English as a Foreign Language (TOEFL) and score at least a 580.

Completion Requirements: You must successfully complete 45 contact hours and 37 credits.

Program Contact: University of Phoenix Online
4605 E. Elwood St. 7th Floor
Phoenix, Arizona 85040

(800) 765-4922
(480) 894-2152

General Studies

Degree Offered: Associate of Arts

Program Web Address: www.uophx.edu/
Allother_Campusesprograms/aags.html

Program Background: The Associate of Arts degree in General Studies is designed to meet the needs of adult students who want to complete a general Associate's degree before entering a professional program. The curriculum provides a solid foundation and overview in communication arts, social sciences, mathematics, life sciences, and the humanities. Students develop skills in communication, critical thinking, and computing.

Application Requirements: You must be at least 23 years old, have a high school diploma or equivalent, and be employed. If you're not currently employed, you should have access to an organizational environment where you can apply the theoretical concepts that you're learning through courses. You must also complete the University of Phoenix proctored Comprehensive Cognitive Assessment. If you are an international student whose native language is not English, you must also have a minimum score of 580 on the Test of English as a Foreign Language (TOEFL).

Completion Requirements: You must successfully complete 60 credit hours.

On Campus Requirements: You are required to fulfill a residency for a minimum of 24 semester credits.

Example Course Titles: Some of the course titles in this program include Skills for Lifelong Learning, Contemporary Issues in American Business, Communication Skills for Career Growth, and Skills for Lifelong Learning.

Program Contact: University of Phoenix Online
4605 E. Elwood St. 7th Floor
Phoenix, Arizona 85040
(800) 765-4922
(480) 894-2152

Information Systems

Degree Offered: Bachelor of Science

Program Web Address: www.uophx.edu/
Allother_Campusesprograms/info.html

Program Background: This program is designed to enable students to effectively deal with information technology that is prevalent in today's complex business environment. It focuses on developing skills in technical areas of computer hardware and software architecture, file and data structures, systems analysis and design, programming, software engineering, and telecommunications.

Students must demonstrate their ability to integrate business and technical skills in problem solving by completing a major project that relates to their degree or professional responsibilities.

Application Requirements: You must be at least 23 years old, have a high school diploma or equivalent, and be employed in order to enroll in any University of Phoenix undergraduate program. If you're not employed, you should have access to an organization where you can apply the theoretical concepts that you'll learn through courses. You must also complete the University of Phoenix proctored Comprehensive Cognitive Assessment. If English is not your first language, you must have a minimum score of 580 on the Test of English as a Foreign Language (TOEFL).

You may wish to take advantage of the College Board's College Level Examination Program (CLEP) to earn up to 30 semester credits that you can transfer in toward a University of Phoenix Bachelor's degree. To find out more about CLEP, check out www.collegeboard.org.

Completion Requirements: Courses can be categorized as information technology courses, upper-division business courses, and business foundational courses. The goal of combining these courses is to provide students with the ability to apply information technology effectively in meeting business goals.

Example Course Titles: Some of the course titles in this program include Introduction to Software Engineering, Project Planning and Implementation, Computer Architecture, Data Design and Information Retrieval, Financial Analysis for Managers, Marketing, and Information Resource Management.

Program Contact: University of Phoenix Online
4605 E. Elwood St., 7th Floor
Phoenix, Arizona 85040
(800) 765-4922
(480) 894-2152

Information Technology

Degree Offered: Bachelor of Science

Program Web Address: www.uophx.edu/ Allother_Campusesprograms/bsit.htm

Program Background: The University of Phoenix's Bachelor of Science Information Technology (BSIT) Program focuses on acquiring and managing information technology. It also teaches students how to develop technology infrastructures and systems for organizational use. The core courses provide fundamental knowledge and practice in information technology function and system development. Specialty courses are extensions of the core courses and enable students to select an area of expertise.

The areas of expertise from which you can choose to specialize are Database Management, Networks and Communication, Programming and Operating Systems, Systems Analysis, and Web Management.

Application Requirements: You must be at least 23 years old, have a high school diploma or equivalent, and be employed in order to enroll in any University of Phoenix undergraduate program. If you're not employed, you should have access to an organization where you can apply the theoretical concepts that you'll learn through courses. You must also complete the University of Phoenix proctored Comprehensive Cognitive Assessment. If English is not your first language, you must have a minimum score of 580 on the Test of English as a Foreign Language (TOEFL).

You may wish to take advantage of the College Board's College Level Examination Program (CLEP) to earn up to 30 semester credits that you can transfer in toward a University of Phoenix Bachelor's degree. To find out more about CLEP, check out www.collegeboard.org.

Completion Requirements: To earn this degree, you must successfully complete at least 123 credit hours, which include a minimum number of upper division credits in your course of study, 54 credits in general education courses, 15 credits in interdisciplinary studies, and 3 credits in an integrating course. Also, you must maintain a cumulative grade point average of at least 2.0, pay all tuition and fees, and complete the University's Comprehensive Cognitive Assessment post-test. If you attend the Nevada campus, you're also required by the Nevada Regulatory Statute to complete coursework on the United States Constitution and the Nevada Constitution.

If you successfully complete the required courses in your area of study, you can acquire the remaining credits that you need for your degree in the following ways. You can fulfill the minimum requirements in other areas (general education or interdisciplinary). Or you can complete upper or lower division elective courses, take prerequisite courses, test-out of courses (by taking CLEP, ACT/PEP, or DAN-TES examinations), participate in the Prior Learning Assessment process (getting credits for life and work experience), or complete approved courses at another regionally accredited college or university. You should work closely with an Academic Counselor to ensure that you don't duplicate coursework.

On Campus Requirements: You are expected to earn 30 credit hours in-residence. These courses will be in your area of study. For more information about the on-campus requirements and which courses you are expected to take on-campus, please contact the school directly.

Example Course Titles: Some of the course titles for this program include Organizations and Technology, Organizational Communications, Ethics in Information Technology, Project Planning and Implementation, Computer and Information Processing, The Internet Concepts and Applications, Introduction to Operating Systems, Network and Telecommunication Concepts, Programming Concepts, and Introduction to Object Oriented Programming.

Program Contact: University of Phoenix Online
4605 E. Elwood St. 7th Floor
Phoenix, Arizona 85040
(800) 765-4922
(480) 894-2152

Nursing

Degree Offered: Bachelor of Science

Program Web Address: www.uophx.edu/ Allother_Campusesprograms/bsn.html

Application Requirements: You must have an Associate's degree or diploma in nursing, 56

transferable credit hours from a regionally accredited college or university (30 of which must be in nursing courses), a valid and unrestricted license as a registered nurse from the state in which you practice, and a cumulative grade point average of at least 2.0 (on a 4.0 scale). Additionally, you must have a minimum grade point average of 2.0 in all prior nursing courses. You need to complete an application and submit it with an application fee, official transcripts from each college or university you've attended, and official copies of test scores.

If you are an international student, you must score a 580 or higher on the Test of English as a Foreign Language (TOEFL).

Completion Requirements: You must successfully complete 126 credits for this degree, pay all tuition and fees, and pass the University's Comprehensive Cognitive Assessment.

Example Course Titles: Some of the course titles for this program include Theoretical Foundations for Professional Nursing, Pathophysiology and Health Assessment, Health Law and Ethics, Concepts of Family Nursing Theory, Clinical Integration: Nursing Management of Families, Issues and Strategies in Nursing Research Utilization, Dimensions of Community Nursing Practice, and Clinical Integration Partnerships in Community Practice.

Program Contact: University of Phoenix Online
4605 E. Elwood St. 7th Floor
Phoenix, Arizona 85040
(800) 765-4922
(480) 894-2152

Nursing

Degree Offered: Master of Science

Program Web Address: www.uophx.edu/ Allother_Campusesprograms/mn.html

Program Background: Registered nurses in this program develop and enhance their knowledge and skills, enabling them to pursue advanced positions in health care. The program integrates theory with practice.

Application Requirements: You must have an undergraduate nursing degree from a regionally accredited college or university or the international equivalent, or be a candidate for such a degree. You must also have a cumulative minimum grade point average of 2.5 (on a 4.0 scale) for your undergraduate work, a valid registered nurse's license from the state in which you practice, and three years of experience (within the past ten years) as a registered nurse. You need to complete an application and submit it with an application fee, official transcripts from each college or university you've attended, verification of your experience and current employment, two letters of recommendation, and proof of professional liability insurance of $1 million per occurrence, kept current and in effect throughout your coursework.

If you are an international student, you must score a 580 or higher on the Test of English as a Foreign Language (TOEFL).

Completion Requirements: You must successfully complete the curriculum with a minimum grade point average of a B, pass the University's Comprehensive Cognitive Assessment, complete a Nursing Research Project and Practicum, and pay all tuition and fees.

Example Course Titles: Some of the course titles in this program include Advanced Nursing Theory, Advanced Nursing Management: Individuals and Families, Health Care Infrastructure, Data Based Decision Making, Ethical Issues in Nursing, Nursing Research Project Orientation, Dynamics of Nursing Administration, Health Care Finance, Curriculum Development and Program Design, and Nursing Research Project.

Program Contact: University of Phoenix Online
4605 E. Elwood St. 7th Floor
Phoenix, Arizona 85040
(800) 765-4922
(480) 894-2152

Organizational Leadership

Degree Offered: Doctor of Management

Program Web Address: www.uophx.edu/ Allother_Campusesprograms/dm.html

Program Background: This degree program enables students to explore their personal readiness to become leaders in their professions. Students gain knowledge and skills in leadership literature and demonstrate their competence by applying what they learn in their work environments.

Application Requirements: You must have a Master's degree from a regionally accredited college or university, a minimum grade point average of 3.0, and a minimum of seven years work experience (post-Bachelor's degree). You need to submit an application with three letters of recommendation, and a ten-page personal statement. If you're an international student, you also need to submit official copies of your scores on the Test of English as a Foreign Language (TOEFL), on which you should score at least a 600.

Completion Requirements: You must successfully complete 60 semester credit hours with a minimum grade point average of 3.0. You also must successfully complete all residencies, a comprehensive examination, a comprehensive paper, the Learning Leader Journal, a doctoral project (which you must also present), and a graduation packet. You also need to pay all tuition and fees.

Time for Completion: You have up to six years to complete all degree requirements.

Example Course Titles: Some of the course titles for this program include Catalytic Leadership and Group Processes: A Skillshop, Finding Your Passion: Thinking About and Designing Your Doctoral Project, Learning Leader Journal I Orientation, A Philosophy of Knowledge, Inventing the World: How We Construct Meaning, Organization Theory: The Structural Conventions of the Industrial Paradigm, and Leadership Theory: The Human Conventions of the Industrial Paradigm.

Program Contact: University of Phoenix Online
4605 E. Elwood St. 7th Floor
Phoenix, Arizona 85040
(800) 765-4922
(480) 894-2152

Organizational Management

Degree Offered: Master of Arts

Program Web Address: www.uophx.edu/Allother_Campusesprograms/maom6.html

Program Background: Students in this program learn the skills necessary to manage effectively within private businesses, public agencies, and nonprofit organizations. The program focuses on managing human and fiscal resources. The curriculum covers executive management, budgeting, human resources management, conflict management, strategic planning, decision making, and other relevant topics.

Application Requirements: You must have a Bachelor's degree from a regionally accredited college or university, a minimum grade point average of 2.5 (on a 4.0 scale), currently be employed, and a minimum of three years of full-time, relevant work experience (post-high school). Also, you must complete the University's Comprehensive Cognitive Assessment pre-test. You need to submit an application with an application fee, official transcripts from each college or university you've attended, three letters of recommendation, and a ten-page personal statement. If you're an international student whose native language is not English, you also need to submit official copies of your scores on the Test of English as a Foreign Language (TOEFL), on which you should score at least a 580.

Completion Requirements: You must have 30 credit hours that you can transfer into this program, and you must successfully complete 39 credit hours through the University of Phoenix. Also you are required to maintain a minimum grade point average of 3.0, successfully complete a Capstone course, pay all tuition and fees, and complete the University's Comprehensive Cognitive Assessment post-test.

Example Course Titles: Some of the course titles in this program include Economics in the Marketplace, Marketing—The Quest for the Consumer, Managing Money—The Bottom Line, Technology and Organizations, Managing Change, The Learning Organization, and Advanced Human Relations Mangement.

Program Contact: University of Phoenix Online
4605 E. Elwood St. 7th Floor
Phoenix, Arizona 85040
(800) 765-4922
(480) 894-2152

UNIVERSITY OF WISCONSIN-MADISON

General Contact Information

750 University Avenue
Madison, Wisconsin 53706-1490

Phone: (608) 265-1234
E-mail: on.wisconsin@mail.admin.wisc.edu
WWW: www.dcs.wisc.edu

Online Learning Information

Outreach Program Manager
500 Lincoln Drive, 352 Bascom Hall
Madison, Wisconsin 53706

E-mail: steven.siehr@ccmail.adp.wisc.edu
WWW: www.dcs.wisc.edu

Institution Background

The University of Wisconsin-Madison provides complete student and technical support in all areas (application, registration, financial aid, progress notes, and content) 24-hours a day, seven days a week.

Founded: 1849
Type of Institution: Public
Accreditation: North Central Association of Colleges and Schools

Online Course Background: The University's courses are designed especially for online, interactive, asynchronous delivery. The content is specifically designed for practicing engineers, and the school has a synchronous component for each course via audioteleconferencing.

Online Course Offered: 20

Online Students Enrolled: about 50

Services Offered to Students: Graduate students in the University of Wisconsin-Madison's programs have full access to all student services—the library, writing center, bus passes for any on-campus visits, counseling, and technical support.

Financial Aid: Students enrolled in online programs may be eligible for Veterans benefits and federal student loans. Most of the students enrolled at the University of Wisconsin-Madison receive substantial support from their employers.

Individual Graduate Courses: The University of Wisconsin-Madison has online courses in engineering and Japanese.

Programs
Administrative Medicine

Degree Offered: Master of Science in Administrative Medicine

Program Web Address: www.medsch.wisc.edu/adminmed/

Online Program Started: 1996

Students Enrolled: 45

Degrees Awarded: 19

Program Background: This program is designed for health care professionals who have assumed major administrative responsibilities in their organizations and who want to make a career change from clinical practice to management. It focuses on issues that are central to the management of health care organizations, and its curriculum is based on sound business fundamentals. Students build upon their health care background to develop unique skills they can use on the job.

Application Requirements: You are required to meet the University of Wisconsin-Madison Graduate School entrance requirements, which include: having a minimum undergraduate grade point average of 3.0 (on a 4.0 scale); having a clinical degree (such as a M.D., D.O., or R.N.); and having a clinical or professional practice.

Completion Requirements: You must maintain satisfactory progress through the program, and complete an executive preceptorship with a senior health care executive.

Time for Completion: There are actually two programs available—one allows you up to two years for completion and the other gives you up to four years.

On Campus Requirements: You are required to begin and end each semester with a residency on the University's campus, for a total of approximately seven weeks of on-campus sessions during the program. The opening sessions provide in-depth introductions to each semester through lectures, seminars and laboratory exercises. The closing sessions are used to present final projects and integrate learning.

System Requirements: You should have a personal computer running Windows. You should also have access to the World Wide Web and e-mail, Netscape Communicator 4.61 or Netscape Communicator 4.X, and the Microsoft Office suite (Word, Excel, PowerPoint, Access).

Example Course Titles: Some of the course titles in this program include Organizational Behavior, Medical Informatics, Financial Management, Population Health, Health Economics, Statistics, Epidemiology, Ethics, Marketing, Health Law, Insurance/Managed Care, Quality of Health Care, Health Policy, Capital Finance, Strategic Planning, Assessment of Medical Technologies, and Capstone Seminar.

Program Contact: Heidi Wilde
Administrative Medicine Program
732 WARF Building
610 N. Walnut Street
Madison, Wisconsin 53705-2397
(608) 263-4889
(608) 263-4885
hwilde@facstaff.wisc.edu

Disaster Management

Degree Offered: Disaster Management Diploma

Program Web Address: epdwww.engr.wisc.edu/dmc/diploma/index.html

Online Program Started: 1996

Students Enrolled: 200

Degrees Awarded: 2

Application Requirements: You must be a high school graduate or have your GED.

Completion Requirements: You must successfully complete 60 Continuing Education Units (CEUs).

Time for Completion: You have up to five years to complete this program.

On Campus Requirements: There are no on-campus requirements.

Example Course Titles: Some of the course titles in this program include Aim and Scope of Disaster Management, Principles of Management, Natural Hazards:Causes and Effects, Disaster Preparedness, Damage and Needs Assessment, Disaster Response, Environmental Health Management after Natural Disaster, Health Service Organization after Natural Disaster, Emergency Health Management after Natural Disaster, Epidemiologic Surveillance after Natural Disaster, Emergency Vector Control after Natural Disaster, Health Education and Training of Refugee Health Workers, and Disasters and Development.

Program Contact: Disaster Management Center
432 N. Lake Street Room 701
Madison, Wisconsin 53706
(608) 262-5441
(608) 263-3160
dmc@engr.wisc.edu

Engineering

Degree Offered: Professional Development Degree

Program Web Address: epdwww.engr.wisc.edu

Students Enrolled: 70

Degrees Awarded: 6

Program Background: This program allows students to plan their own courses of study based on their professional career goals, and up to one-half of the credits a student needs to receive this degree can be transferred in from another school.

Application Requirements: You must have a Bachelor's degree in engineering from an ABET-approved program and have a minimum of four years professional experience as an engineer.

Completion Requirements: You must maintain satisfactory academic progress throughout the program.

Time for Completion: You have up to five years to complete this program.

On Campus Requirements: There are no on-campus requirements.

System Requirements: System requirements depend on the courses.

Example Course Titles: Courses are offered in engineering, management, foreign languages, and other enhancement study areas.

Program Contact: Karen Al-Ashkar
Engineering Professional Development
432 North Lake Street
Madison, Wisconsin 53706
(608) 262-0133
(608) 263-3160
karena@epd.engr.wisc.edu

Engineering in Professional Practice

Degree Offered: Master of Engineering

Program Web Address: epdwww.engr.wisc.edu/mepp/

Online Program Started: 1999

Students Enrolled: 25

Program Background: This program integrates an Engineering Management program with applications from a Business Administration program to address the needs of practicing engineers. The courses are asynchronous and delivered interactively to a cohort of up to 30 engineers.

Application Requirements: You must have a Bachelor's degree in engineering from an ABET program, a minimum grade point average of 3.0 (on a 4.0 scale), and a minimum of four years post-baccalaureate experience in engineering.

Completion Requirements: You must stay on track with the rest of your cohort and maintain a satisfactory grade point average (a 3.0 or better).

Time for Completion: You have two years to complete this program.

On Campus Requirements: You are required to attend a one-week residency on-campus during each August of the two-year program.

System Requirements: You need to have a personal computer with a Pentium II processor (or faster) running Windows 95 or higher, or a Macintosh equivalent running a Windows emulator. You should also have a stable Internet Service Provider and a 56.6 bps modem (or faster). Software requirements vary by course.

Example Course Titles: Some of the course titles for this program include Network Skills for Remote Learners, Engineering Economic Analysis and Management, Technical Project Management, Engineering Problem Solving with Computers, International Engineering Operations and Strategies, Engineering Application of Statistics, Communicating Technical Information, Quality Engineering, Quality Management, Engineering/Business Data

Communications, and the Virtual Engineering Office.

Program Contact: Karen Al-Ashkar
Engineering Professional Development
432 North Lake Street
Madison, Wisconsin 53706
(608) 262-0133
(608) 263-3160
karena@epd.engr.wisc.edu

Engineering in Technical Japanese

Degree Offered: Master of Engineering

Program Web Address: epdwww.engr.wisc.edu/metj/

Online Program Started: 1999

Students Enrolled: 12

Program Background: Students in this program learn the skills they need to deal with business and industry counterparts in Japan.

Application Requirements: You must have a Bachelor's degree in science or engineering from an accredited program, or a Bachelor's degree in another field with at least 16 credit hours in science or engineering. Also you must have a minimum undergraduate grade point average of 3.0 (on a 4.0 scale).

Completion Requirements: You must maintain satisfactory progress throughout the program.

Time for Completion: You have up to six years of part-time study to complete this program.

On Campus Requirements: There are no on-campus requirements for this program.

System Requirements: The hardware and software requirements vary by course.

Example Course Titles: Some of the course titles for this program include Japanese Language and Culture for Professionals, Basic Technical Japanese I and II, Intermediate Technical Japanese I and II, Science and Technology in Japan, Management of Technology in Japan, Technology Policy in Japan, Intellectual Property in Japan, and Japanese Business Sysetems.

Program Contact: Karen Al-Ashkar
Engineering Professional Development
University of Wisconsin-Madison
432 North Lake Street
Madison, Wisconsin 53706
(608) 262-0133
(608) 263-3160
karena@epd.engr.wisc.edu

UNIVERSITY OF WISCONSIN-PLATTEVILLE

General Contact Information

1 University Plaza
Platteville, Wisconsin 53818-3099

Phone: (800) 362-5460
FAX: (608) 342-1071
E-mail: disted@uwplatt.edu
WWW: www.uwplatt.edu/disted

Online Learning Information

506 Pioneer Tower
Platteville, Wisconsin 53818

E-mail: adams@uwplatt.edu
WWW: www.uwplatt.edu/disted

Institution Background

The Wisconsin Territorial Council charted the Platteville Academy in 1839, and the Pioneer Normal School at Platteville (the first teacher training institution in the state) was founded in 1866. The institution expanded its programs and services, and by 1923 it was offering only college-level courses. In 1927, the Normal School began awarding Bachelor's degrees, and was renamed the Platteville State Teachers College. In 1951, the school became Wisconsin State College, Platteville.

While the Normal School was growing and developing, the Wisconsin Legislature authorized the founding of the Wisconsin Mining Trade School in Platteville in 1907, and the school started operations the following year. It was established to train engineers for the mining industry, a vital link in the economic development of the entire area. It became the Wisconsin Mining School in 1917, and the addition of a fourth year of study to the curriculum in 1951 resulted in adopting the name Wisconsin Institute of Technology.

In 1959, the two Platteville institutions merged to form the Wisconsin State College and Institute of Technology at Platteville, which was renamed Wisconsin State University-Platteville in 1964. When the state university systems merged in 1971, the name University of Wisconsin-Platteville was adopted.

Founded: 1866
Type of Institution: Public
Accreditation: North Central Association of Colleges and Schools

Online Course Background: Each online course offered comes with the credibility of a University of Wisconsin-Platteville degree, and the online program is flexible. Although some courses are semester based, you choose your own learning times and set your own pace with most courses.

The University's online courses are geared towards practical degrees that meet the needs of a growing workforce. During 1993-94, FOCUS 2000 was introduced as an initiative to prepare and position the University of Wisconsin-Platteville for the next century. Departments, programs, and service areas were consolidated and became involved with the online courses.

Online Course Offered: 9

Online Students Enrolled: 20

Special Programs/Partnerships: The University of Wisconsin-Platteville is currently working on a partnership with other University of Wisconsin colleges to access their online courses. For more information about the program, please see www.uwcolleges.com.

Services Offered to Students: Students enrolled in online courses have the same basic services that are available to on-campus students. The main difference is that online students access the services in a different manner than on-campus students. These resources include financial aid, advising, tutoring, campus directory, policies and requirements, and career planning. Online students also have direct access to the Karrmann Library.

Financial Aid: Online students may be eligible for federal and state financial aid, including student loans. Financial aid for online courses is only available on a reimbursement basis at this time. You are required to pay for your tuition, fees, and course material, and then you will be reimbursed by financial aid, if you are eligible to receive it. As the area of financial aid is complex and requires a great deal of specialized knowledge and information, it's important for you to direct all of your questions to the financial aid office (608) 342-1836 or Reese@uwplatt.edu. For information about using Veterans benefits, call (608) 342-1321 or e-mail Deneen@uwplatt.edu.

Registration: You can register for courses via the World Wide Web.

Programs

Business

Degree Offered: Certificate in Business

Program Web Address: www.uwplatt.edu/

disted/online.html

Online Program Started: 1999

Students Enrolled: 5

Program Contact: Marge Karsten, Director
Extended Degree Program in Business
Administration
1 University Plaza
Platteville, Wisconsin 53818-3099
(608) 342-1468
(608) 342-1466
karsten@uwplatt.edu

Business Administration

Degree Offered: Bachelor of Science

Program Web Address: www.uwplatt.edu/
disted/online.html

Online Program Started: 1999

Students Enrolled: 5

Program Background: This program provides
students with a foundation in business basics.
Students can choose upper level courses that
are geared to their interests to add depth to the
degree.

Completion Requirements: You must successfully complete 120 hours for this degree.

Time for Completion: You have up to seven
years to complete this program.

System Requirements: You should have a personal computer with a 486 processor (or faster)
running Windows 95/NT or a Macintosh 100
MHz with OS 7.5.3 or later, 16 MB RAM, color
monitor capable of 256 colors, a CD-ROM
drive, a 28.8 kbps modem, a Web browser
(Netscape Navigator 4.x or newer or Microsoft
Internet Explorer 4.x or newer), and Lotus
Notes Client 4.51.

Example Course Titles: Some of the course titles in this program include Introduction to
American Business Enterprise, Leadership and
Management, Introduction to Marketing, Human Resource Management, The Legal Environment, Organizational Behavior, Quality
Management, Financial Management, Advertising, Labor-Management Relations, Marketing
Management, Business Policy/Strategy, Principles of Macroeconomics, Elementary Accounting I, Microcomputer Applications, and
Organizational Communication.

Program Contact: Marge Karsten, Director
Extended Degree Program in Business
Administration
1 University Plaza
Platteville, Wisconsin 53818-3099
(608) 342-1468
(608) 342-1466
karsten@uwplatt.edu

Criminal Justice

Degree Offered: Graduate Diploma

Program Web Address: www.uwplatt.edu/
disted/online.html

Online Program Started: 1999

Students Enrolled: 5

Program Background: This program is designed for professionals in criminal justice or
social service fields who need additional education for advancement.

Application Requirements: You must have a
Bachelor's degree from a nationally or regionally accredited institution recognized by the
council for Higher Education Accreditation
(CHEA). Your Bachelor's degree should be in
criminal justice, criminology, or a related field.
If your degree is in an unrelated field, you must
have three years of occupational experience in
the field of criminal justice.

Completion Requirements: You must successfully complete a set of five core graduate
courses.

Time for Completion: You have up to one year to complete this program

System Requirements: You should have a personal computer with a 486 processor (or faster) running Windows 95/NT or a Macintosh 100 MHz with OS 7.5.3 or later, 16 MB RAM, color monitor capable of 256 colors, a CD-ROM drive, a 28.8 kbps modem, a Web browser (Netscape Navigator 4.x or higher or Microsoft Internet Explorer 4.x or higher), and Lotus Notes Client 4.51.

Example Course Titles: Some of the course titles in this program include Criminal Justice Systems, Criminal Justice Research and Statistical Methods, Criminological Theory, and Law as Social Control.

Program Contact: Cheryl Banachowski-Fuller, Ph.D.
Director, Criminal Justice Distance Education Program
1 University Plaza
Platteville, Wisconsin 53818-3099
(608) 342-1652
(608) 342-1986
banachoc@uwplatt.edu

Criminal Justice

Degree Offered: Master of Science

Program Web Address: uwplatt.edu/disted/online.html

Students Enrolled: 5

Program Background: This program is designed for professionals working in criminal justice and social service fields who want a graduate education or who need additional skills and knowledge to advance in their careers.

Application Requirements: You must have a Bachelor's degree in criminal justice, criminology, or a related field from a nationally or regionally accredited college or university. If you

have a degree in an unrelated field, you must have a minimum of three years working in the field of criminal justice.

You can take courses through this program as a Special Student—a student who is not pursuing the Master's degree. Special students are allowed to take a maximum of 12 credit hours before you are required to apply for admission in the degree-seeking program.

Completion Requirements: You must successfully complete 30 credits for this degree—15 from required courses and 15 from electives.

Time for Completion: You must enroll in this program during traditional fall and spring registration dates, and you have up to one year to complete the program.

System Requirements: You need to have a personal computer with a 486 processor (or faster) running Windows 95/98/NT or a Macintosh running OS 7.5.3 or newer. Your computer should have 16 MB RAM, a VGA (or higher) monitor that can display 256-colors, a CD-ROM drive, a 28.8 kbps modem (or faster), and an Internet Service Provider. In terms of software, you'll need Netscape Navigator 4.0 or higher or Microsoft Internet Explorer 4.0 or higher, Lotus Notes Client 4.51 or higher, Adobe Acrobat, TechExplorer, Real Player, a text editor (a word processor will work), a sound player program, and e-mail software.

Example Course Titles: Some of the course titles for this program include Criminal Justice Systems, Criminal Justice Research and Statistical Methods, Criminological Theory, Law as Social Control, Advanced Research in Criminal Justice, Criminal Justice Theory, Criminal Justice Management, and Victim and Offender Services.

Program Contact: Cheryl Banachowski-Fuller, Ph.D.
Director, Criminal Justice Distance Education Program

1 University Plaza
Platteville, Wisconsin 53818-3099
(608) 342-1652
(608) 342-1986
banachoc@uwplatt.edu

Occupational Safety and Health

Degree Offered: Certificate in Occupational Safety and Health for General Industry

Program Web Address: www.uwplatt.edu/disted/online.html

Online Program Started: 1999

Students Enrolled: 5

Program Background: Students enrolled in this program are service practioners in industry who need to know the Occupational Safety and Health Act regulations.

Application Requirements: You must have a Bachelor's degree from an accredited institution that is recognized by the Council for Higher Education Accreditation (CHEA). International degrees will be evaluated on an individual basis. To be eligible for admission in full standing, you must have an overall undergraduate grade point average of 2.75 or above, or 2.90 on the last 60 credits of your undergraduate study.

Completion Requirements: You must successfully complete all required courses for the certificate, and you must have a grade point average of 3.0 or better.

Time for Completion: You have up to one year to complete this program.

System Requirements: You should have a personal computer with a 486 processor (or faster) running Windows 95/NT or a Macintosh 100 MHz with OS 7.5.3 or later, 16 MB RAM, color monitor capable of 256 colors, a CD-ROM drive, a 28.8 kbps modem, a Web browser (Netscape Navigator 4.x or newer or Microsoft Internet Explorer 4.x or newer), and Lotus Notes Client 4.51.

Example Course Titles: One of the course titles in this program is Safety and Health for General Industry.

Program Contact: Lisa A. Riedle, Director Engineering Distance Education Program
1 University Plaza
Platteville, Wisconsin 53818-3099
(608) 342-1686
(608) 342-1566
riedle@uwplatt.edu

Project Management

Degree Offered: Master of Science

Program Web Address: www.uwplatt.edu/disted/online.html

Students Enrolled: 8

Program Background: This program is designed for professionals who want to develop new skills in managing projects. Students learn how to manage projects, foster relationships between project teams and customers, and balance competing demands. It is a Web-based program, which enables students to pursue a degree without leaving their jobs. The core courses are in management and communications, and students get a well-rounded view of business in general.

Application Requirements: You must have a Bachelor's degree from a nationally or regionally accredited institution of higher education, and an overall undergraduate grade point average of 2.75 (or higher) or a minimum grade point average of 2.9 during the last 60 credit hours of your undergraduate study. The credentials of international students will be evaluated on an individual basis. If you don't qualify for full admission, you may be admitted on a trial enrollment.

You need to complete an application and submit it with official transcripts from any college or university you've attended and a current resume.

Completion Requirements: You must successfully complete 30-36 credit hours in business foundation courses, 15 credits in project management, and 9-15 credits of electives for this degree.

Time for Completion: You have up to one year to complete a course once you've enrolled in it. And you have up to seven years to complete all of the program requirements to complete your degree.

System Requirements: You need to have a personal computer with a 486 processor (or faster) running Windows 95/98/NT or a Macintosh running OS 7.5.3 or newer. Your computer should have 16 MB RAM, a VGA (or higher) monitor that can display 256-colors, a CD-ROM drive, a 28.8 kbps modem (or faster), and an Internet Service Provider. In terms of software, you'll need Netscape Navigator 4.0 or higher or Microsoft Internet Explorer 4.0 or higher, Lotus Notes Client 4.51 or higher, Adobe Acrobat, TechExplorer, Real Player, a text editor (a word processor will work), a sound player program, and e-mail software.

Example Course Titles: Some of the course titles in this program include Managerial Accounting, Organizational Behavior, Financial Management, Marketing Management, Advanced Quality Management, Organizational Communication, Industrial Operations and Management, and Industrial Psychology.

Program Contact: Donna Perkins, Director
Project Management Program
University of Wisconsin-Platteville
1 University Plaza
Platteville, Wisconsin 53818-3099
(608) 342-1547
(608) 342-1254
perkins@uwplatt.edu

UNIVERSITY OF WISCONSIN-STOUT

General Contact Information

124 Bowman Hall
Menomonie, Wisconsin 54751

E-mail: admissions@uwstout.edu
WWW: major.uwstout.edu

Online Learning Information

Continuing Education
Menomonie, Wisconsin 54751

E-mail: whites@uwstout.edu

Institution Background

James H. Stout, a lumber baron and one of the most progressive educators of his day, founded the University of Wisconsin-Stout (UW-Stout) in 1891 as an educational experiment. Today, UW-Stout is one of 13 universities in the University of Wisconsin System.

Founded: 1891
Type of Institution: Public
Accreditation: North Central Association of Colleges and Schools

Programs

Hospitality and Tourism

Degree Offered: Master of Science

Program Web Address: aln.uwstout.edu/global/

Completion Requirements: You must successfully complete 36 hours.

Example Course Titles: Some of the course titles in this program include Strategic Management in Hospitality, Managing Finance, Technology in the Business Environment—Communication and Marketing, Leadership and Personnel Management in the Hospitality Industry, Quality Assurance and Customer Service, Research Applications in Hospitality, and Hospitality Operational Systems.

Program Contact: Christine Clements
429 Home Economics Building
University of Wisconsin-Stout
Menomonie, Wisconsin 54751
(715) 232-2567
clementsc@uwstout.edu

Industrial Technology

Degree Offered: Bachelor of Science

Program Web Address: www.uwstout.edu/itde/

Program Background: The University of Wisconsin-Stout's Industrial Technology program is intended to give you managerial background as well as technical knowledge and communication skills so that you can effectively carry out your professional responsibilities. The program takes a hands-on approach to industry rather than just a theoretical one. And the program's basic requirements give you the foundation and management skills that you can use to advance your career.

This program's curriculum includes industrial management courses, general education and a variety of other technical and professional courses. The program draws upon various industrial advisory committees to provide feedback regarding skills that students need in their every day work. In this way, the program stays up to date with the changes in business and industry.

The Industrial Technology program is your opportunity to further your education and open doors without having to change your entire life. You no longer have to put off pursuing a Bachelor's degree because of your job schedule, family responsibilities, or lack of physical access to a college.

Application Requirements: You must have an Associate of Applied Science (A.A.S.) degree in a technical field, two or more years of technical work experience, a willingness to travel for teleconference courses, and Internet access at home, work, or a local institution. The campuses that participate in teleconference courses are the University of Wisconsin-Stout, Fox Valley Technical College in Appleton, North Central Technical College in Wausau, Western Wisconsin Technical College in La Crosse, Waukesha County Technical College in Waukesha, and Milwaukee Area Technical College.

Completion Requirements: You must successfully complete 124 credit hours to earn this degree. After you are enrolled in this program, you will begin working with an advisor to determine how your Associate's degree will be applied to program requirements.

Program Contact: Howard Lee
280 Technology Wing, Jarvis Hall
University of Wisconsin-Stout
Menomonie, Wisconsin 54751
(800) 991-5291
leeh@uwstout.edu

Technology Management

Degree Offered: Doctor of Philosophy

Program Web Address: web.indstate.edu:80/tech/acadprog/grad/cphd/cphd.html

Program Background: This degree program is geared toward technologists and combines traditional doctoral research with an innovative delivery system, a consortium of universities, and advanced technical specialization. It is a collaborative program that is administered by the School of Technology at Indiana State University. Other schools that participate include

Bowling Green State University, Central Connecticut State University, Central Missouri State University, East Carolina University, Eastern Michigan University, North Carolina A&T State University, Texas Southern University, and University of Wisconsin-Stout.

Application Requirements: You must apply to Indiana State University for admission to this doctoral program. You should have a Bachelor's degree from a regionally accredited college or university, a minimum undergraduate grade point average of 3.0 (on a 4.0 scale) and a minimum graduate grade point average of 3.5, two years of appropriate work experience, and a score of at least 500 on each section of the Graduate Record Examination. With your application, you should submit five letters of recommendation.

Completion Requirements: You must successfully complete a minimum of 90 semester hours of graduate study, with a majority of your coursework at the 600-level. Your program of study will be divided into five areas: Major Area of Specialization (24-30 semester hours), Internship (six semester hours), Research Core (27-33 semester hours), General Technology Core (12-18 semester hours), and Cognate Studies.

On Campus Requirements: You are required to complete two residencies for this program, but you have two options for fulfilling this requirement. You can complete two consecutive semesters at Indiana State University, or you can complete one semester at Indiana State University and one semester at the home university/consortium university where you're completing your specialization.

Example Course Titles: Some of the course titles in this program include Strategic Planning of Technological Processes, Internet Research Methods, Impacts of Technology, Legal Aspects of Industry, and Technological System, Assessment, and Innovation.

Program Contact: Len Sterry
224D Communication Technologies Bldg.
University of Wisconsin-Stout
Menomonie, Wisconsin 54751
(715) 232-1367
sterryl@uwstout.edu

UNIVERSITY OF WISCONSIN-WHITEWATER

General Contact Information

800 West Main Street
Whitewater, Wisconsin 53190-1791

E-mail: tam@uwwvax.uww.edu
WWW: www.uww.edu

Online Learning Information

Distance Education Coordinator
800 West Main Street
Whitewater, Wisconsin 53190-1790

E-mail: gibbsk@uwwvax.uww.edu
WWW: www.uww.edu

Institution Background

Founded: 1868
Type of Institution: Public
Accreditation: North Central Association of Colleges and Schools

Programs

Finance

Degree Offered: Master of Business Management

Program Web Address: academics.uww.edu/BUSINESS/onlinemba/

Program Background: This program is designed to provide students with an advanced understanding of how individual, team, and organization-level behavior affects organizational operations. Students learn from case studies, and develop skills in collecting, analyzing, and interpreting data.

Application Requirements: You must have a Bachelor's degree from a regionally accredited college or university. You also must have an overall undergraduate grade point average of 2.75 (on a 4.0 scale), at least a 2.90 during the last half of your undergraduate study, or at least 12 credit hours of graduate work at the University of Wisconsin-Whitewater with a 3.0 grade point average overall. In place of the grade point average requirement, you can have a graduate degree from another regionally accredited school, or meet these qualifications: have a 2.50 grade point average for your undergraduate program, a score of at least 570 on the Graduate Management Admission Test (GMAT), and five years or more of appropriate work experience.

If you're an international student, you should also have a score of 550 or higher on the Test of English as a Foreign Language (TOEFL). This is required for some programs and strongly recommended for others. You should have the Educational Testing Service (ETS) send your results directly to the University of Wisconsin-Whitewater.

Completion Requirements: You must maintain an overall grade point average of 3.0.

Time for Completion: You have up to seven years to complete this program.

System Requirements: You should have a personal computer with a Pentium processor, 16 MB RAM or more (32 MB are recommended), a standard 28.8k bps modem (or higher), a CD-ROM drive, 124 MB available space on hard drive, Windows 95, Internet access through an Internet Service Provider (ISP), and a Web browser.

Example Course Titles: Some of the course titles in this program include International Students Accounting Foundations, Profit Planning and Control, Management Cost Accounting, Economics Foundations, Financial Management, The Legal Environment of Business, Information System Foundations, Operations Management, Managerial and Organizational Behavior, Mathematics Foundations, Marketing, Business Conditions Analysis, Managerial Economics, Management and Organization Theory, Business Policy, Statistical Methods, and Financial Planning Process.

Program Contact: Online MBA
4033 Carlson Hall
College of Business and Economics
Whitewater, Wisconsin 53190
(414) 472-1945
gradbus@uwwvax.uww.edu

Management

Degree Offered: Master of Business Management

Program Web Address: academics.uww.edu/BUSINESS/onlinemba/

Program Background: Students enrolled in this program develop skills in collecting and analyzing data, conceptualizing, evaluating, and implementing solutions to complex business problems. The program gives students an advanced understanding of organizational operations, and how various individual and team behaviors affect them.

Application Requirements: You must have a Bachelor's degree from a regionally accredited college or university. You also must have an overall undergraduate grade point average of 2.75 (on a 4.0 scale), at least a 2.90 during the last half of your undergraduate study, or at least 12 credit hours of graduate work at the University of Wisconsin-Whitewater with a 3.0 grade point average overall. In place of the grade point average requirement, you can have a graduate degree from another regionally accredited school, or meet these qualifications: have a 2.50 grade point average for your undergraduate program, a score of at least 570 on the Graduate Management Admission Test (GMAT), and five years or more of appropriate work experience.

If you're an international student, you should also have a score of 550 or higher on the Test of English as a Foreign Language (TOEFL). This is required for some programs and strongly recommended for others. You should have the Educational Testing Service (ETS) send your results directly to the University of Wisconsin-Whitewater.

Time for Completion: You must complete this program within seven years.

System Requirements: You should have a personal computer with a Pentium processor, 16 MB RAM or more (32 MB are recommended), a standard 28.8k bps modem (or higher), a CD-ROM drive, 124 MB available space on hard drive, Windows 95, Internet access through an Internet Service Provider (ISP), and a Web browser.

Example Course Titles: Some of the course titles in this program include Accounting Foundations, Profit Planning and Control, Management Cost Accounting, Statistics Foundations, Financial Management, Information System Foundations, Operations Management, Managerial and Organizational Behavior, Marketing, and Management and Organization Theory.

Program Contact: Online MBA

College of Business and Economics
University of Wisconsin-Whitewater
4033 Carlson Hall
Whitewater, Wisconsin 53190
(414) 472-1945
gradbus@uwwvax.uww.edu

VATTEROTT COLLEGE

General Contact Information

501 N. 3rd St.
Quincy, IL 62301

Phone: (217) 224-0600
FAX: (217) 223-6771
E-mail: vattqcy@adams.net
WWW: www.vatterott-college.com

Institution Background

Founded: 1969
Accreditation: Accrediting Commission of Career Schools and Colleges of Technology

Programs

Computer Programming

Degree Offered: Associate

Program Web Address: www.vatterottglobal.com/New/ProgramsOfferedNew.htm

Program Background: This program prepares students for entry level employment as a Computer Programmer, Network Administrator, DatabaseTechnician, Database Administrator, Software Specialist, PC Desk Support, Computer Operator, Systems Consultant, and other similar positions in the Information Technology Field.

Completion Requirements: You must successfully complete 96 quarter hours.

Example Course Titles: Some of the course titles in this program include Introduction to Computer Programming, Integrated Software Applications, Programming in Visual Basic, Structured COBOL, Management Information Systems, Programming Language C—Windows, Programming Language C++—Windows, and Local Area Network.

Program Contact: Vatterott Global Online
3131 Frederick Avenue
St. Joseph, Missouri 64506
(888) 766-3601
(888) 546-3616
VGO@CCP.COM

WALDEN UNIVERSITY

General Contact Information

155 Fifth Avenue South
Minneapolis, Minnesota 55401

Phone: (800) 444-6795
FAX: (941) 498-4266
E-mail: request@waldenu.edu
WWW: www.waldenu.edu

Online Learning Information

Student Recruitment
24311 Walden Center Drive
Bonita Springs, Florida 34134

E-mail: request@waldenu.edu
WWW: www.waldenu.edu

Institution Background

Walden University is a pioneer in its field by blending a tradition of academic excellence with contemporary technology-enhanced delivery. Since its start, Walden has been delivering programs in places and at times convenient to the working professional. Its degrees have al-

ways been structured to provide students maximum benefits with minimal disruption.

Founded: 1970
Type of Institution: Private
Accreditation: North Central Association of Colleges and Schools

Online Course Offered: 200

Online Students Enrolled: 1400

Special Programs/Partnerships: Walden University has a partnership with Indiana University that gives students access to a research library and Walden's full-time Library Liaison Office at Indiana University, Bloomington. Indiana University, Bloomington, is also the site of Walden's annual summer session and commencement ceremonies.

Walden partners with institutions of higher learning to support the continuing education of their faculty and staff members through its Higher Education Professional Development Fellowship program. This institution-to-institution partnership requires a minimum of two student participants to qualify, and this fellowship provides the waiver of the application, orientation materials and commencement fees, and reduces tuition by ten percent.

Services Offered to Students: Students enrolled in online courses have access to technical support, assistance from the dissertaion editor, and access to the T.I.S. Bookstore in Bloomington, Indiana.

Financial Aid: Walden University offers financial assistance in the form of low-interest federally guaranteed and private sector student loans and extended payment plans. The financial aid office can assist students in securing tuition benefits from employers and other agencies. Several competitive fellowships providing partial tuition are available.

Individual Graduate Courses: Non-degree seeking students may enroll in psychology and education courses on a space-available basis. Individuals interested in taking courses should contact the Office of Admissions at 1-800-925-3368 for a Request for Courses/Non-Matriculation Status Form. Enrollment as a non-degree seeking student does not guarantee admission at any academic program at Walden.

Registration: You can register for courses via the World Wide Web.

Programs

Applied Management and Decision Sciences

Degree Offered: Doctor of Philosophy

Program Web Address: www.waldenu.edu/prospective/programs/amds/index.html

Program Background: This program is designed for students who are experienced decision-makers and mid-career professionals from public, nonprofit, and private organizations and who want to pursue a doctorate in a flexible and self-paced environment. Students learn knowledge in the areas of management, organizational leadership, strategic/operational planning, and finance.

Application Requirements: You must have a Master's degree from a regionally accredited institution, three years of professional experience related to the doctoral program, and demonstrated online capability and Web access.

Completion Requirements: You are required to successfully complete 128 quarter credit hours for this degree.

On Campus Requirements: You are required to fulfill an academic residency requirement. Academic residencies are dispersed throughout the calendar year and convene at various locations across the United States to provide you with a variety of choices and flexibility. You

fulfill the academic residency requirement by accumulating 32 residency units during your course of study. You begin fulfilling the residency requirement by attending a New Student Orientation Residency within the first 90 days of enrollment (60 days for doctoral psychology students). You are also required to complete a core residency within your first two years of study. Beyond these two guidelines, you may accumulate the remaining residency units by participating in any combination of core and continuing residencies.

Example Course Titles: Some of the course titles in this program include Theories of Societal Development, Current Research in Societal Development, Professional Practice and Societal Development, Principles of Human Development, Theories of Human Development, Current Research in Human Development, Professional Practice and Human Development, Principles of Organizational and Social Systems, Theories of Organizational and Social Systems, and Current Research in Organizational and Social Systems.

Program Contact: Student Recruitment
24311 Walden Center Drive
Bonita Springs, Florida 34134
request@waldenu.edu

Education

Degree Offered: Masters of Science

Program Web Address: www.waldenu.edu/prospective/programs/educ/mseduc.html

Program Background: This program is designed for K-12 classroom teachers and other K-12 practitioners who wish to study on a part-time basis in their work and home environment.

Application Requirements: You must have a Bachelor's degree from a regionally accredited institution, two years of relevant professional experience, and demonstrated online capability and Internet access.

Completion Requirements: You must successfully complete 45 quarter credit hours.

Example Course Titles: Some of the course titles in this program include Learning Theories, Motivation, and Relationship to Technology Curriculum, Curriculum Theory and Design, Evaluation and Assessment, Program Evaluation and Assessment Learning Organizations, Organizational Behavior and Systems Theory Technology, and Critical Survey of Technology.

Program Contact: Student Recruitment
24311 Walden Center Drive
Bonita Springs, Florida 34134
request@waldenu.edu

Education

Degree Offered: Doctor of Philosophy

Program Web Address: www.waldenu.edu/prospective/programs/educ/index.html

Program Background: This degree program is designed to meet the advanced and unique learning needs of educators from a wide range of practice fields and educational levels.

Application Requirements: You must have a Master's degree from a regionally accredited institution, three years of professional experience related to this program, and demonstrated online capability and Internet access.

Completion Requirements: You must successfully complete 128 quarter credit hours.

On Campus Requirements: You are required to fulfill a residency requirement. Doctoral students fulfill the academic residency requirement by accumulating 32 residency units during their course of study. You can begin fulfilling the residency requirement by attending a New Student Orientation Residency (NSOR)

within the first 90 days of enrollment (60 days for doctoral psychology students).

Example Course Titles: Some of the course titles in this program include Theories of Societal Development, Current Research in Societal Development, Professional Practice and Societal Development, Principles of Human Development, Theories of Human Development, Current Research in Human Development, Professional Practice and Human Development, Principles of Organizational and Social Systems, Theories of Organizational and Social Systems, and Current Research in Organizational and Social Systems.

Program Contact: Student Recruitment
24311 Walden Center Drive
Bonita Springs, Florida 34134
request@waldenu.edu

Health Services

Degree Offered: Doctor of Philosophy

Program Web Address: www.waldenu.edu/prospective/programs/hlth/index.html

Program Background: This program is designed for students who are experienced professionals in health services and who are committed to improving the delivery of health services. They include nurses, hospital administrators, pharmacists, physical and occupational therapists, environmental and public health specialists, and others who wish to advance their knowledge of the field and expand their circle of influence.

Application Requirements: You must have a Master's degree in psychology from a regionally accredited college or university and three years of professional experience in a mental health or social or behavioral science setting, and you must demonstrate online capability and Internet access.

Completion Requirements: You must successfully complete 128 quarter credit hours.

On Campus Requirements: You are required to complete 32 residency units at Walden University.

Example Course Titles: Some of the course titles in this program include Theories of Societal Development, Current Research in Societal Development, Professional Practice and Societal Development, Principles of Human Development, Theories of Human Development, Current Research in Human Development, Professional Practice and Human Development, Principles of Organizational and Social Systems, Theories of Organizational and Social Systems, and Current Research in Organizational and Social Systems.

Program Contact: Student Recruitment
24311 Walden Center Drive
Bonita Springs, Florida 34134
request@waldenu.edu

Human Services

Degree Offered: Doctor of Philosophy

Program Web Address: www.waldenu.edu/prospective/programs/humn/index.html

Program Background: This Ph.D. program is designed for experienced professionals who are committed to improving the delivery of human services, including social workers, counselors, administrators, criminal justice professionals, social policy analysts and planners, and others. The program allows and encourages exploring alternative models of human services practice and alternative strategies. Program faculty expect students to confront the challenges of personal, institutional, and social change in the 21st century.

Application Requirements: To be considered for admission in this Ph.D. program, you must have a Master's degree from a regionally accredited institution, three years of professional experience in a Human Services-related field, and demonstrate online capability and have access to the World Wide Web.

Completion Requirements: You must successfully complete 128 quarter-credit hours (KAM-based) to earn their Ph.D. in Human Services.

On Campus Requirements: Walden University requires doctoral students to fulfill an academic residency requirement that is unique and specific to the mission of the program. These residencies are dispersed throughout the calendar year, and convene at various locations across the United States to provide students with a variety of choices and flexibility. Doctoral students fulfill the academic residency requirement by accumulating 32 residency units during their course of study.

Doctoral students begin fulfilling the residency requirement by attending a New Student Orientation Residency (NSOR) within the first 90 days of enrollment. The NSOR is offered at all Continuing-4, Core-13, and Core-20 residencies. Doctoral students are also required to complete a core residency within their first two years of study. Beyond these two guidelines, students may accumulate the remaining residency units by participating in any combination of core and continuing residencies. This allows students maximum flexibility to choose residency experiences that best meet their needs and priorities, whether these be time, location, expense, or style of residency.

Example Course Titles: Some of the course titles for this program include Theories of Societal Development, Current Research in Societal Development, Professional Practice and Societal Development, Principles of Human Development, Theories of Human Development, Current Research in Human

Development, and Principles of Organizational and Social Systems.

Program Contact: Student Recruitment
Walden University
24311 Walden Center Drive
Bonita Springs, Florida 34134
request@waldenu.edu

Professional Psychology

Degree Offered: Doctor of Philosophy (Ph.D.)

Program Web Address: www.waldenu.edu/prospective/programs/psyc/index.html

Program Background: This Ph.D. program prepares practicing psychologists to address important societal problems that have impacts upon individuals, families, and organizations. It emphasizes theory and research-derived knowledge that guides professional practice.

Application Requirements: You must have a Master's degree in psychology from a regionally accredited college or university and three years of professional experience in a mental health or social or behavioral science setting, and you must demonstrate online capability and Internet access.

Completion Requirements: You must successfully complete 127 quarter credit hours for this degree.

On Campus Requirements: You are required to complete 32 residency units at Walden University. If you specialize in licensure-oriented areas of clinical counseling or school psychology, you are required to spend one academic year in residence.

Example Course Titles: Some of the course titles for this program include History and Systems of Psychology, Psychology and Social Psychology, Developmental Psychology, Biological Psychology, Psychology of Learning, So-cial Psychology, Tests and Measurements, and Quantitative Analyses.

Program Contact: Student Recruitment
24311 Walden Center Drive
Bonita Springs, Florida 34134
request@waldenu.edu

Psychology

Degree Offered: Master of Science

Program Web Address: www.waldenu.edu/prospective/programs/psyc/mspsyc.html

Program Background: This program is designed to address the needs of students who want to continue their education part-time from their own home or work. Students use e-mail and mailing lists to communicate with each other, and engage in discussions through online classrooms. All coursework is guided by instructor-prepared syllabi that specify course learning objectives, textbook and reading assignments, and methods for evaluation.

Application Requirements: You must have a Bachelor's degree from a regionally accredited college or university.

Completion Requirements: You must successfully complete 45 quarter credit hours for this degree.

On Campus Requirements: There are some courses at the Master's level that require brief residencies.

Example Course Titles: Some of the course titles include Physiology Psychology, History and Systems of Psychology, Statistics in Psychology, Advanced General Psychology, Cognitive Psychology, Human Motivation, Theories of Learning, Group Dynamics, and Theories of Personality.

Program Contact: Student Recruitment
24311 Walden Center Drive

Bonita Springs, Florida 34134
request@waldenu.edu

WEST TEXAS A & M UNIVERSITY

General Contact Information

2501 Fourth Avenue
Canyon, Texas 79016

Phone: (806) 651-2020
FAX: (806) 651-2071
E-mail: lilav@wtamu.edu
WWW: www.wtamu.edu

Institution Background

Founded: 1909
Type of Institution: Public
Accreditation: Southern Association of Colleges and Schools

Programs

Business Administration

Degree Offered: Master of Business Administration

Program Web Address: online.wtamu.edu/degree/mba.html

Program Background: This program is designed to prepare students for careers as professional managers, and is intended for students who desire an integrated program with limited concentration in one of the functional areas of business (management or marketing).

Application Requirements: You must have a Bachelor's degrees from an accredited institution. You should take the GMAT and have your scores sent to this school. You must score at least a 400 on the GMAT to be considered for admission. The school will use a score composed of your GMAT score and your overall undergraduate grade point average (or your grade point average during the last 60 hours of undergraduate study) to determine your admission status.

Completion Requirements: You must successfully complete 36 credit hours to earn this degree.

System Requirements: You should have a personal computer with a Pentium processor or a Macintosh PowerPC, 16 MB RAM (32 preferred), 1.44 floppy drive, CD-ROM, 16 bit sound card (preferred), 14″ color monitor (15″ preferred), keyboard, mouse, and 33.6 modem.

Program Contact: Master of Business Administration Online Advisor
West Texas A&M University
Canyon, Texas
(806) 651-2512
nterry@mail.wtamu.edu

Instructional Technology

Degree Offered: Master of Education

Program Web Address: online.wtamu.edu/degree/it.html

Program Background: Students in this program learn how to use technology effectively, design instruction using current technologies, implement technology, and facilitate networks of technology-aided learning environments.

Application Requirements: You must have a Bachelor's degree from an accredited institution, a satisfactory grade point average during your last 60 credit hours as an undergraduate, and a test score of 650 or higher on the GRE or a score of 400 or higher on the GMAT. If your score on the GRE or GMAT is less than the required minimum, you must retake the test and reapply for admission.

If your GRE or GMAT scores are satisfactory but you don't meet the other criteria for admission, you may petition for admittance on a probationary status. Probationary admission requires you to complete 12 to 15 credit hours of enrollment in graduate courses, earn a C or higher in each course, and submit a plan of study.

Should you need to complete prerequisite courses for the program, you'll have one semester of coursework to do so. Otherwise, West Texas A & M University will place an administrative hold on your registration.

Completion Requirements: You must successfully complete 36 credit hours to earn this degree.

System Requirements: You need a personal computer with a Pentium processor, 16 MB RAM (32 preferred), 1.44 floppy drive, CD-ROM (preferred), 16 bit sound card (preferred), 14" color monitor (15" or larger preferred), keyboard, mouse, 33.6 modem, and a Windows 95 operating system.

Example Course Titles: Some of the course titles in this program include Foundations of Instructional Technology, Local and Wide Area Networks in Instructional Settings, Planning for Technology, Multimedia: Application and Techniques of Design, and Principles and Practices of Distance Learning.

Program Contact: Distance Enrollment Coordinator
West Texas A&M University
Canyon, Texas 79016
(800) 99-WTAMU
wtonline@mail.wtamu.edu

WEST VIRGINIA NORTHERN COMMUNITY COLLEGE

General Contact Information

1704 Market Street

Wheeling, West Virginia 26003

Phone: (304) 233-5900 ext. 4214
FAX: (304) 232-0965
E-mail: tdanford@northern.wvnet.edu
WWW: www.northern.wvnet.edu

Online Learning Information

Distance Education
1704 Market Street
Wheeling, West Virginia 26003-3699

E-mail: tjenkins@northern.wvnet.edu
WWW: www.northern.wvnet.edu

Institution Background

West Virginia Northern Community College is a comprehensive, state asssisted community and technical college in the northern panhandle of West Virginia.

Founded: 1972
Type of Institution: Public
Accreditation: North Central Association of Colleges and Schools

Online Course Background: Northern Community College's online courses fall into two categories: Northern courses and SREC courses. Northern courses are designed and delivered by West Virginia Northern Community College faculty and SREC courses have additional review by the State of West Virginia and are listed on the SREC electronic campus.

Online Course Offered: 5

Online Students Enrolled: 80

Services Offered to Students: Students enrolled in online courses have access to library and computer resources.

Financial Aid: Online students may be eligible for any of the financial aid opportunities available at West Virginia Northern Community College.

Registration: You can register for courses via mail and the World Wide Web.

Programs
Business Administration

Degree Offered: Associate in Science

Program Web Address: www.northern.wvnet.edu

Online Program Started: 1997

Students Enrolled: 10

Program Background: This program is comparable to the traditional Associate in Science in Business Administration, but it is delivered via electronic and televised courses.

On Campus Requirements: Some courses may require minimal campus visits.

Example Course Titles: Some of the course titles in this program include Business Administration, Accounting, Economics, and General Studies.

Program Contact: Thomas R. Danford
WV Northern CC
1704 Market Street
Wheeling, West Virginia 26003-3699
(304) 233-5900
(304) 232-0965
tdanford@northern.wvnet.edu

WESTERN PIEDMONT COMMUNITY COLLEGE

General Contact Information

1001 Burkemont Avenue
Morganton, North Carolina 28655

Phone: (704) 438-6052
FAX: (704) 438-6015

WWW: www.wp.cc.nc.us

Institution Background

Founded: 1964
Type of Institution: Public
Accreditation: Southern Association of Colleges and Schools

Individual Undergraduate Courses: Western Piedmont Community College has online courses in art appreciation, computer information systems, English, geography, legal studies, mathematics, office technology, and psychology.

Programs
Paralegal Technology

Degree Offered: Associate of Applied Science

Program Web Address: www.wp.cc.nc.us/bustech/paralgl/paralgl.html

Program Background: This program prepares students to assist attorneys in private firms, government agencies, banks, insurance agencies, and other businesses, performing routine legal tasks and assisting with substantive legal work. It does not prepare students to practice law, give legal advice, or represent clients in a court of law. Students develop their knowledge in the areas of civil litigation, legal research and writing, real estate, family law, wills, estates, trusts, commercial law, and criminal law, as well as complete coursework in general subjects (such as English, mathematics, and computers).

Application Requirements: You must be 18 years or older and able to profit from formal education through Western Piedmont Community College to enroll. As a member of the North Carolina Community College System, Western Piedmont Community College has an open-door admissions policy.

You need to complete and submit an application to the Office of Admissions. You can print off an application at the school's Web page. You are required to meet application deadlines as posted. Along with your application, you need to include official transcripts from your high school and any college or university you've attended. You may be required to take placement tests before admission.

Completion Requirements: You must successfully complete 68 semester hours for this degree.

System Requirements: You should have access to a personal computer that has an Internet connection and Netscape Navigator/Communicator or Microsoft Internet Explorer. America Online, Compuserve, and Prodigy are not acceptable Internet Service Providers as they are not compatible with the school's course servers.

Example Course Titles: Some of the course titles in this program include Professional Research and Reporting, Survey of Mathematics, Introduction to Paralegal Study, Legal Research/Writing, Civil Injuries, Civil Litigation, Commercial Law, Family Law, and Wills, Estates, and Trusts.

Program Contact: Paralegal Technology Coordinator
1001 Burkemont Ave
Morganton, North Carolina 28655
(828) 438-6194
l.mckesson@wp.cc.nc.us

WYTHEVILLE COMMUNITY COLLEGE

General Contact Information

1000 East Main Street
Wytheville, Virginia 24382

Phone: (540) 223-4701
FAX: (540) 223-4860
E-mail: wcdixxs@wc.cc.va.us
WWW: www.wc.cc.va.us

Online Learning Information

Director of Continuing Education
1000 East Main Street
Wytheville, Virginia 24382

E-mail: wcjohnd@wc.cc.va.us
WWW: www.wc.cc.va.us

Institution Background

Wytheville Community College is small, supportive, and technologically advanced.

Founded: 1966
Type of Institution: Public
Accreditation: Southern Association of Colleges and Schools

Online Course Background: Wytheville Community College is strong in Information Systems Technology and most of their courses combine the Web, e-mail, and other technologies. They try to keep enrollment in online courses low and encourage the faculty to be very active in the course.

Online Course Offered: 25

Online Students Enrolled: approximately 500

Special Programs/Partnerships: Students can enroll in distance learning courses offered by any Virginia Community College and the courses will count toward a degree at Wytheville.

Services Offered to Students: Students enrolled in online courses have access to all of Wytheville's library databases and are given a free e-mail address.

Financial Aid: Online students may be eligible for any of the financial aid programs that Wytheville administers.

Registration: You can register for courses via the phone.

Programs

Web Page Design

Degree Offered: Certificate in Web Page Design

Program Web Address: www.wc.cc.va.us/webSiteDesign/

Online Program Started: 1999

Program Background: This certificate program takes students from a basic knowledge of using a computer to a solid grounding in the basics of Web site design.

Application Requirements: You must meet the general college admission requirements.

Completion Requirements: You must successfully complete 19 credits for this certificate.

On Campus Requirements: There are no on-campus requirements for this program.

System Requirements: You need to have a computer with an Internet connection.

Example Course Titles: Some of the course titles in this program include Web Page Design I, Internet Programming I (HTML), Internet Programming II (DHTML), and Database Management and File Structure.

Program Contact: Gary Laing
Wytheville Community College
1000 E. Main St.
Wytheville, Virginia 24382
(540) 223-4803
(540) 223-4778
wclaing@wc.cc.va.us

INDICES

ALPHABETICAL LISTING OF SCHOOLS

New School for Social Research
New York Institute of Technology
New York University
North Carolina A&T State University
Northwestern College
Norwich University
Nova Southeastern University
Ohio University
Oklahoma State University
Pennsylvania State University, University Park
  Campus
Regis University
Rochester Institute of Technology
Rogers State University
Rutgers University
Salt Lake Community College
Salve Regina University
Seton Hall University
Southwest Missouri State University
St. Petersburg Junior College
State University of New York Empire State
  College
Strayer University
Suffolk University
Texas Southern University
Thomas Edison State College
Troy State University-Florida Region
Ulster County Community College
Union Institute
United StateS Sports Academy
University of California, Davis—University
  Extension
University of Baltimore
University of Bridgeport
University of California Extension
University of California, Los Angeles
University of Central Florida
University of Colorado at Denver
University of Florida
University of Houston
University of Illinois at Chicago
University of Illinois at Springfield
University of Illinois at Urbana-Champaign
University of Maine at Fort Kent
University of Maine at Machias

University of Maryland—University College
University of Massachusetts Lowell
University of Minnesota, Crookston
University of Nebraska-Lincoln
University of Nevada, Reno
University of North Dakota
University of Northern Iowa
University of Phoenix
University of Wisconsin-Madison
University of Wisconsin-Platteville
University of Wisconsin-Stout
University of Wisconsin-Whitewater
Vatterott College
Walden University
West Texas A & M University
West Virginia Northern Community College
Western Piedmont Community College
Wytheville Community College

ALPHABETICAL LISTING OF AREAS OF STUDY

Aeronautics/Aviation
Accounting
Administration
Agribusiness/Agriculture
Anthropology
Arts and Science/General Studies
Audiology/Communicative Disorders/Speech
  Pathology
Automotive
Bookkeeping
Business/Management
Canadian Studies
Comparative Literature
Computer-Aided Design
Construction Technology
Criminal Justice
Dietary Management/Nutrition
Disaster/Emergency Management
Economics/Finance
Education

Engineering
English
Environmental Health and Safety
Facility Management
Fire Science
French
Gardening/Turfgrass Management
Geographic Information Systems
Gerontology
Hazardous Materials Management
History
Hospitality and Tourism/Travel
Human & Organization Development
Human Resource Development
Human Resources and Family Sciences
Humanities
Information Systems/Information Technology
International Relations
Journalism
Labor & Industrial Relations
Legal
Library & Information Science

Logistics/Purchasing
Medicine/Health/Opticianry
Military Science
Nursing
Occupational Safety and Health
Philosophy & Religious Studies
Physical Education/Sports Science
Physics
Political Science
Psychology/Counseling
Public Administration
Quantitative Studies
Resource Management
Sociology/Social Science
Space Studies
Statistics
Taxation
Textiles, Clothing, and Design
Theology
Veterinary Technology
Vocational Education
Women's Studies

MATRICES

Aeronautics/Aviation

Degree	Concentration	Institution	Requirements	Accreditation	Financial Aid	Description Page
Associate of Science	Aviation Business Administration	Embry-Riddle Aeronautical University	60 hours	Southern Association of Colleges and Schools	Yes	173
Associate of Science	Professional Aeronautics	Embry-Riddle Aeronautical University	Contact program administrator	Southern Association of Colleges and Schools	Yes	175
Bachelor of Science	Management of Technical Operations	Embry-Riddle Aeronautical University	120 hours	Southern Association of Colleges and Schools	Yes	174
Bachelor of Science	Professional Aeronautics	Embry-Riddle Aeronautical University	120 hours	Southern Association of Colleges and Schools	Yes	175
Master of Aeronautical Science	Aeronautical Science	Embry-Riddle Aeronautical University	36 semester credit hours	Southern Association of Colleges and Schools	Yes	173

Accounting

Degree	Concentration	Institution	Requirements	Accreditation	Financial Aid	Description Page
Certificate	Accounting	Algonquin College	12 courses	Government of Ontario	Contact program administrator	17
Certificate	Accounting	Athabasca University	Contact program administrator	Government of Alberta	Contact program administrator	33
Certificate	Accounting	Champlain College	5 courses	New England Association of Schools and Colleges	Contact program administrator	127
Certificate	Accounting	City University	45 credits	Northwest Association of Schools and Colleges	Yes	135
Certificate	Advanced Accounting	Athabasca University	Contact program administrator	Government of Alberta	Yes	34
Associate	Accounting	Champlain College	60 credits	New England Association of Schools and Colleges	Contact program administrator	127
Associate	Accounting	Northwestern College	108 hours	North Central Association of Colleges and Schools	Contact program administrator	244
Associate	Accounting	Strayer University	Contact program administrator	Middle States Association of Colleges and Schools	Contact program administrator	294

Degree	Concentration	Institution	Requirements	Accreditation	Financial Aid	Description Page
Associate of Applied Science	Accounting	Colorado Community College Online	60 credits	Accreditation dependent upon host institution	Contact program administrator	146
Associate of Applied Science	Accounting	Ivy Tech State College	60 credit hours	North Central Association of Colleges and Schools	Yes	211
Associate of Science	Accounting	Montgomery County Community College	60 credits	Middle States Association of Colleges and Schools	Yes	232
Bachelor	Accounting	Northwestern College	90 hours above Associate degree	North Central Association of Colleges and Schools	Contact program administrator	245
Bachelor of Arts/Bachelor of Science	Accounting	University of Maryland University College	120 semester hours	Middle States Association of Colleges and Schools	Yes	344
Bachelor of Science	Accounting	City University	180 credits	Northwest Association of Schools and Colleges	Yes	135
Master	Professional Accounting	Strayer University	Contact program administrator	Middle States Association of Colleges and Schools	Contact program administrator	299
Master of Accountancy	Accountancy	Golden Gate University	30 to 51 units	Western Association of Schools and Colleges	Contact program administrator	192

Administration

Degree	Concentration	Institution	Requirements	Accreditation	Financial Aid	Description Page
Associate	Administrative Assistant	Northwestern College	108 hours	North Central Association of Colleges and Schools	Contact program administrator	245
Associate	Word Processing Administrative Support	Northwestern College	108 hours	North Central Association of Colleges and Schools	Contact program administrator	250
Associate of Science	Office Administration	Eastern Oregon University	Contact program administrator	Northwest Association of Schools and Colleges	Contact program administrator	171
Master of Science	Administrative Studies	Southwest Missouri State University	36 hours	North Central Association of Colleges and Schools	Contact program administrator	288

Agribusiness/Agriculture

Degree	Concentration	Institution	Requirements	Accreditation	Financial Aid	Description Page
Associate	Agribusiness Marketing/Management Technology	Northwestern College	108 hours	North Central Association of Colleges and Schools	Contact program administrator	245

Degree	Concentration	Institution	Requirements	Accreditation	Financial Aid	Description Page
Associate of Applied Science	Agriculture Business	Colorado Community College Online	63 credit hours	Accreditation dependent upon host institution	Contact program administrator	147
Master of Agriculture	Agriculture	Colorado State University	Contact program administrator	North Central Association of Colleges and Schools	Contact program administrator	150
Master of Business Administration	Agriculture	Athabasca University	Contact program administrator	Government of Alberta	Yes	36
Master of Business Administration	Food and Agricultural Business	Purdue University	48 credits; nine weeks on-campus	North Central Association of Colleges and Schools	Contact program administrator	267
Master of Science	Agronomy	Iowa State University	30 credit hours	North Central Association of Colleges and Schools	Contact program administrator	210
Master of Science	Bioresource and Agricultural Engineering	Colorado State University	30 to 32 semester hours	North Central Association of Colleges and Schools	Contact program administrator	150

Anthropology

Degree	Concentration	Institution	Requirements	Accreditation	Financial Aid	Description Page
Bachelor of Arts	Anthropology	Athabasca University	120 credit hours	Government of Alberta	Yes	35

Arts and Science/General Studies

Degree	Concentration	Institution	Requirements	Accreditation	Financial Aid	Description Page
Certificate	Applied Sciences	Harvard University	Eight courses	New England Association of Schools and Colleges	Contact program administrator	198
Associate	General Studies	Strayer University	Contact program administrator	Middle States Association of Colleges and Schools	Contact program administrator	297
Associate of Applied Science	Applied Science	Community College of Aurora	Contact program administrator	North Central Association of Colleges and Schools	Contact program administrator	157
Associate in Applied Science	General Studies	Bladen Community College	Contact program administrator	Southern Association of Colleges and Schools	Yes	72
Associate of Arts	Arts	Brevard Community College	64 credit hours	Southern Association of Colleges and Schools	Contact program administrator	75
Associate of Arts	Arts	Chemeketa Community College	90 credit hours	Northwest Association of Schools and Colleges	Contact program administrator	132

Degree	Field	Institution	Credits	Accreditation	Residency	Page
Associate of Arts	Arts	Ohio University	Contact program administrator	North Central Association of Colleges and Schools	Contact program administrator	256
Associate of Arts	General Education	Colorado Community College Online	60 hours	Accreditation dependent upon host institution	Contact program administrator	148
Associate of Arts	General Studies	University of Phoenix	60 credit hours	North Central Association of Colleges and Schools	Contact program administrator	363
Associate of Arts	Liberal Arts	Atlantic Cape Community College	64 credits	Middle States Association of Colleges and Schools	Yes	53
Associate of Arts	Liberal Arts	Bucks County Community College	Contact program administrator	Middle States Association of Colleges and Schools	Contact program administrator	77
Associate of Arts	Liberal Arts	Cerro Coso Community College	60 units	Western Association of Schools and Colleges	Contact program administrator	126
Associate of Arts	Liberal Arts	Florence-Darlington Technical College	62 credit hours	Southern Association of Colleges and Schools	Contact program administrator	183
Associate of Arts	Liberal Arts	Lewis-Clark State College	64 credits	Northwest Association of Schools and Colleges	Yes	222
Associate of Arts	Liberal Arts	Rogers State University	60 credit hours	North Central Association of Colleges and Schools	Yes	278
Associate of Arts	Liberal Studies	Bemidji State University	64 semester credits	North Central Association of Colleges and Schools	Contact program administrator	71
Associate of Arts/ Associate of Science	Integrative Studies	Clayton College and State University	60 hours	Southern Association of Colleges and Schools	Contact program administrator	143
Associate of General Studies	General Studies	Barton County Community College	66 credit hours	North Central Association of Colleges and Schools	Contact program administrator	66
Associate of General Studies	General Studies	Chemeketa Community College	90 credit hours	Northwest Association of Schools and Colleges	Contact program administrator	132
Associate of General Studies	General Studies	Montgomery County Community College	60 credits	Middle States Association of Colleges and Schools	Yes	233
Associate of General Studies	General Studies	University of Nevada, Reno	124 credits; contact institution for on-campus requirements	Northwest Association of Schools and Colleges	Contact program administrator	356
Associate of Individualized Studies	Individualized Studies	Ohio University	Contact program administrator	North Central Association of Colleges and Schools	Contact program administrator	256
Associate of Science	General Education	Troy State University-Florida Region	92 hours	Southern Association of Colleges and Schools	Yes	303

Degree	Concentration	Institution	Requirements	Accreditation	Financial Aid	Description Page
Associate of Science	General Studies	Salt Lake Community College	63–83 credits	Northwest Association of Schools and Colleges	Yes	282
Associate of Science	Liberal Arts and Sciences	Ulster County Community College	30 credits	Middle States Association of Colleges and Schools	Yes	305
Associate of Science	Science	Brevard Community College	64 credit hours	Southern Association of Colleges and Schools	Contact program administrator	76
Associate of Science	Science	Ohio University	Contact program administrator	North Central Association of Colleges and Schools	Contact program administrator	256
Bachelor	General Studies	Strayer University	Contact program administrator	Middle States Association of Colleges and Schools	Contact program administrator	297
Bachelor of Arts	Arts	Athabasca University	90/120 credit hours	Government of Alberta	Yes	35
Bachelor of Arts	Arts	Jones International University	120 credit hours	North Central Association of Colleges and Schools	Yes	215
Bachelor of Arts	General Studies	City University	180 credits	Northwest Association of Schools and Colleges	Yes	138
Bachelor of Arts	General Studies	New School for Social Research	Contact program administrator	Middle States Association of Schools and Colleges	Contact program administrator	235
Bachelor of Arts	Liberal Studies	Norwich University	120 credit hours	New England Association of Schools and Colleges	Contact program administrator	251
Bachelor of Arts	Liberal Studies	University of Illinois at Springfield	60 semester hours	North Central Association of Colleges and Schools	Contact program administrator	332
Bachelor of Arts/Bachelor of Science	Integrative Studies	Clayton College and State University	120 hours	Southern Association of Colleges and Schools	Contact program administrator	143
Bachelor of Arts/Bachelor of Science	Liberal Studies	Eastern Oregon University	Contact program administrator	Northwest Association of Schools and Colleges	Contact program administrator	169
Bachelor of Arts/Bachelor of Science	Liberal Studies	University of Central Florida	45 semester hours	Southern Association of Colleges and Schools	Contact program administrator	319
Bachelor of Arts/Bachelor of Science/Bachelor of Professional Studies	Interdisciplinary Studies	New York Institute of Technology	120 credit hours	Middle States Association of Schools and Colleges	Yes	239
Bachelor of General Studies	General Studies	Athabasca University	90 credit hours	Government of Alberta	Yes	43
Bachelor of Integrated Studies	Integrated Studies	Emporia State University	124 semester hours	North Central Association of Colleges and Schools	Yes	177

Degree	Concentration	Institution		Accreditation		
Bachelor of Liberal Studies	Liberal Studies	University of Northern Iowa	124 semester hours	North Central Association of Colleges and Schools	Contact program administrator	358
Bachelor of Professional Arts	Professional Arts	Athabasca University	120 credit hours	Government of Alberta	Yes	35
Bachelor of Professional Studies	Professional Studies	Champlain College	120 credits	New England Association of Schools and Colleges	Contact program administrator	131
Bachelor of Science	Applied Arts and Science	Rochester Institute of Technology	Contact program administrator	Middle States Association of Colleges and Schools	Yes	272
Bachelor of Science	General Studies	City University	180 credits	Northwest Association of Schools and Colleges	Yes	138
Bachelor of Science	Interdisciplinary Studies	Lewis-Clark State College	128 credits; three weekend courses on-campus	Northwest Association of Schools and Colleges	Yes	221
Bachelor of Science	Science	Athabasca University	120 hours	Government of Alberta	Yes	35
Bachelor of Specialized Studies	Specialized Studies	Ohio University	Contact program administrator	North Central Association of Colleges and Schools	Contact program administrator	257
Master	General Studies	Strayer University	Contact program administrator	Middle States Association of Colleges and Schools	Contact program administrator	298
Master of Liberal Arts	Liberal Arts	Harvard University	40 units	New England Association of Schools and Colleges	Contact program administrator	199
Master of Science	Cross-Disciplinary Professional Studies	Rochester Institute of Technology	48 quarter credit hours	Middle States Association of Colleges and Schools	Yes	273

Audiology/Communicative Disorders/Speech Pathology

Degree	Concentration	Institution	Requirements	Accreditation	Financial Aid	Description Page
Master of Science	Communicative Disorders	California State University	Contact program administrator	Western Associations of Schools and Colleges	Contact program administrator	79
Master of Science	Speech Language Pathology	Florida State University	Contact program administrator	Southern Association of Schools and Colleges	Contact program administrator	189
Doctor of Audiology	Audiology	University of Florida	Completion of courses and qualifying exam	Southern Association of Schools and Colleges	Contact program administrator	322

Automotive

Degree	Concentration	Institution	Requirements	Accreditation	Financial Aid	Description Page
Associate	Automotive Management	Northwestern College	108 hours	North Central Association of Colleges and Schools	Contact program administrator	246

Bookkeeping

Degree	Concentration	Institution	Requirements	Accreditation	Financial Aid	Description Page
Certificate	Bookkeeping	Algonquin College	6 courses	Government of Ontario	Contact program administrator	18

Business/Management

Degree	Concentration	Institution	Requirements	Accreditation	Financial Aid	Description Page
Certificate	Applied Management	Algonquin College	6 courses	Government of Ontario	Contact program administrator	17
Certificate	Basic Supervisory Leadership	Pennsylvania State University, University Park	6 courses	Middle States Association of Colleges and Schools	Contact program administrator	259
Certificate	Business	Champlain College	Seven courses	New England Association of Schools and Colleges	Contact program administrator	128
Certificate	Business	University of Wisconsin-Platteville	Contact program administrator	North Central Association of Colleges and Schools	Yes	372
Certificate	Business Administration	Baker College	20 credit hours	North Central Association of Colleges and Schools	Contact program administrator	54
Certificate	Business Administration	University of California Extension	Contact program administrator	Western Association of Schools and Colleges	Contact program administrator	313
Certificate	Business Studies	Algonquin College	12 courses	Government of Ontario	Contact program administrator	18
Certificate	Communications Management	Rutgers University	12 credits	Middle States Association of Colleges and Schools	Contact program administrator	280
Certificate	Communications Technology Management	Capella University	20 quarter credits	North Central Association of Colleges and Schools	Yes	92

	Program	Institution	Credits/Courses	Accreditation		Page
Certificate	Customer Relationship Management	Pennsylvania State University, University Park	11 credits	Middle States Association of Colleges and Schools	Contact program administrator	260
Certificate	General Business Studies	University of California, Los Angeles	Nine courses	Western Association of Schools and Colleges	Contact program administrator	317
Certificate	General Management	Capella University	Five courses	North Central Association of Colleges and Schools	Yes	98
Certificate	Global Communication	Jones International University	Three courses	North Central Association of Colleges and Schools	Yes	216
Certificate	Industrial Management	Baker College	20 credit hours	North Central Association of Colleges and Schools	Contact program administrator	60
Certificate	International Business	Baker College	20 credit hours	North Central Association of Colleges and Schools	Contact program administrator	62
Certificate (Business Administration)	Leadership	Capella University	16 quarter credits	North Central Association of Colleges and Schools	Yes	106
Certificate	Leadership and Communication Skills for Managers and Executives	Jones International University	Two to four courses	North Central Association of Colleges and Schools	Yes	216
Certificate	Management	Champlain College	22 credit hours	New England Association of Schools and Colleges	Contact program administrator	130
Certificate	Management Studies	Algonquin College	12 courses	Government of Ontario	Contact program administrator	21
Certificate	Management Training	New York University	Contact program administrator	Middle States Association of Schools and Colleges	Contact program administrator	243
Certificate	Marketing	Algonquin College	Six courses	Government of Ontario	Contact program administrator	21
Certificate	Marketing	Baker College	20 credit hours	North Central Association of Colleges and Schools	Contact program administrator	64
Certificate	Marketing	University of California Extension	Contact program administrator	Western Association of Schools and Colleges	Contact program administrator	314
Certificate	Marketing Management	Algonquin College	Six courses	Government of Ontario	Contact program administrator	22
Certificate	Project Management	International School of Information Management	Three courses	Distance Education and Training Council	Contact program administrator	209
Certificate	Public Relations and Marketing	Jones International University	Three courses	North Central Association of Colleges and Schools	Yes	217

Degree	Concentration	Institution	Requirements	Accreditation	Financial Aid	Description Page
Certificate	Retail Management	Algonquin College	Six courses	Government of Ontario	Contact program administrator	23
Certificate	Starting and Operating Your Business	Algonquin College	Six courses	Government of Ontario	Contact program administrator	23
Advanced Graduate Diploma	Management	Athabasca University	Contact program administrator	Government of Alberta	Yes	48
Associate	Business	Champlain College	60 credits	New England Association of Schools and Colleges	Contact program administrator	128
Associate	Business	Lansing Community College	Contact program administrator	North Central Association of Colleges and Schools	Contact program administrator	219
Associate	Business Administration	Northwestern College	108 hours	North Central Association of Colleges and Schools	Contact program administrator	246
Associate	Business Administration	Strayer University	Contact program administrator	Middle States Association of Colleges and Schools	Contact program administrator	294
Associate	Management	Champlain College	60 credit hours	New England Association of Schools and Colleges	Contact program administrator	130
Associate	Marketing	Northwestern College	108 credit hours	North Central Association of Colleges and Schools	Contact program administrator	248
Associate	Marketing	Strayer University	Contact program administrator	Middle States Association of Colleges and Schools	Contact program administrator	298
Associate of Applied Science	Business	Colorado Community College Online	60 credit hours	Accreditation dependent upon host institution	Contact program administrator	147
Associate of Applied Science	Business Administration	Bladen Community College	71 hours	Southern Association of Colleges and Schools	Yes	72
Associate of Applied Science	Business Administration	Fayetteville Technical Community College	76 semester hours	Southern Association of Colleges and Schools	Contact program administrator	180
Associate of Applied Science	Business Administration	Ivy Tech State College	60 credit hours	North Central Association of Colleges and Schools	Yes	212
Associate of Arts	Business	Cerro Coso Community College	21 units	Western Association of Schools and Colleges	Contact program administrator	123
Associate of Arts	Business Administration	Bucks County Community College	62 credit hours	Middle States Association of Colleges and Schools	Contact program administrator	76
Associate of Arts	Business Administration	Rogers State University	Contact program administrator	North Central Association of Colleges and Schools	Yes	278
Associate of Arts	Business Management	Cerro Coso Community College	27 units	Western Association of Schools and Colleges	Contact program administrator	124

402

Degree	Major	Institution	Credit requirement	Accreditation	Transfer	Page
Associate of Business Administration	Business Administration	Baker College	96 quarter hours	North Central Association of Colleges and Schools	Contact program administrator	58
Associate of Science	Business	Salt Lake Community College	64 to 65 credit hours	Northwest Association of Schools and Colleges	Yes	281
Associate of Science	Business	State University of New York Empire State College	64 credits	Middle States Association of Colleges and Schools	Contact program administrator	291
Associate of Science	Business Administration	Cerro Coso Community College	26 units	Western Association of Schools and Colleges	Contact program administrator	123
Associate of Science	Business Administration	Montgomery County Community College	60 credits	Middle States Association of Colleges and Schools	Yes	232
Associate of Science	Business Administration	Troy State University-Florida Region	92 hours	Southern Association of Colleges and Schools	Yes	303
Associate of Science	Business Administration	West Virginia Northern Community College	Contact program administrator	North Central Association of Colleges and Schools	Yes	388
Associate in Science	Business Administration	Northwestern College	90 credit hours	North Central Association of Colleges and Schools	Contact program administrator	246
Bachelor	Business Administration	Strayer University	Contact program administrator	Middle States Association of Colleges and Schools	Contact program administrator	295
Bachelor of Administration	Administration	Athabasca University	90/120 credits	Government of Alberta	Yes	33, 36
Bachelor of Administration	Management	Athabasca University	90/120 credits	Government of Alberta	Yes	49
Bachelor of Administration	Organization	Athabasca University	21/120 credit hours	Government of Alberta	Yes	51
Bachelor of Arts	Commerce	City University	180 credits	Northwest Association of Schools and Colleges	Yes	137
Bachelor of Arts	Management	College of St. Scholastica	128 credit hours	North Central Association of Colleges and Schools	Contact program administrator	146
Bachelor of Arts	Management and Organizational Leadership	George Fox University	Contact program administrator	Northwest Association of Schools and Colleges	Yes	191
Bachelor of Arts/ Bachelor of Science	Business/Economics	Eastern Oregon University	Contact program administrator	Northwest Association of Schools and Colleges	Contact program administrator	169
Bachelor of Arts/ Bachelor of Science	Business and Management	University of Maryland University College	Contact program administrator	Middle States Association of Colleges and Schools	Yes	345
Bachelor of Arts/ Bachelor of Science	Communication Studies	University of Maryland University College	Contact program administrator	Middle States Association of Colleges and Schools	Yes	346

Degree	Concentration	Institution	Requirements	Accreditation	Financial Aid	Description Page
Bachelor of Arts and Sciences	Business Administration	Dallas Baptist University	126 semester hours	Southern Association of Colleges and Schools	Contact program administrator	160
Bachelor of Business Administration	Business Administration	Baker College	180 quarter hours	North Central Association of Colleges and Schools	Contact program administrator	54
Bachelor of Commerce	Commerce	Athabasca University	120 credit hours	Government of Alberta	Yes	38
Bachelor of Professional Arts	Communication Studies	Athabasca University	39 credit hours	Government of Alberta	Yes	38
Bachelor of Professional Studies	Business Administration	State University of New York Empire State College	128 credits	Middle States Association of Colleges and Schools	Contact program administrator	291
Bachelor of Professional Studies	Business Management	State University of New York Empire State College	128 credits	Middle States Association of Colleges and Schools	Contact program administrator	292
Bachelor of Professional Studies	Marketing	State University of New York Empire State College	128 credits	Middle States Association of Colleges and Schools	Contact program administrator	293
Bachelor of Science	Business/Administration	University of Phoenix	33 credit hours	North Central Association of Colleges and Schools	Contact program administrator	360
Bachelor of Science	Business/Management	University of Phoenix	33 credit hours	North Central Association of Colleges and Schools	Contact program administrator	360
Bachelor of Science	Business/Marketing	University of Phoenix	33 credit hours	North Central Association of Colleges and Schools	Contact program administrator	360
Bachelor of Science	Business/Project Management	University of Phoenix	33 credit hours	North Central Association of Colleges and Schools	Contact program administrator	361
Bachelor of Science	Business Administration	David N. Myers College	Contact program administrator	North Central Association of Colleges and Schools	Yes	161
Bachelor of Science	Business Administration	City University	180 credit hours	Northwest Association of Schools and Colleges	Yes	136
Bachelor of Science	Business Administration	New York Institute of Technology	120 credit hours	Middle States Association of Schools and Colleges	Yes	237
Bachelor of Science	Business Administration	Regis University	128 credit hours	North Central Association of Colleges and Schools	Contact program administrator	267
Bachelor of Science	Business Administration	State University of New York Empire State College	128 credits	Middle States Association of Colleges and Schools	Contact program administrator	291
Bachelor of Science	Business Administration	University of Wisconsin-Platteville	120 hours	North Central Association of Colleges and Schools	Yes	373
Bachelor of Science	Business Information Systems	Bellevue University	127 credit hours	North Central Association of Colleges and Schools	Contact program administrator	67

Degree	Major	Institution	Credits	Accreditation	Online/Residency	Page
Bachelor of Science	Business Management	State University of New York Empire State College	128 credits	Middle States Association of Colleges and Schools	Contact program administrator	292
Bachelor of Science	Communications	Endicott College	128 credits	New England Association of Schools and Colleges	Contact program administrator	179
Bachelor of Science	Global Business Management	Bellevue University	127 credit hours	North Central Association of Colleges and Schools	Contact program administrator	67
Bachelor of Science	Industrial Technology	East Carolina University	Contact program administrator	Southern Association of Colleges and Schools	Contact program administrator	164
Bachelor of Science	Industrial Technology	University of Wisconsin-Stout	124 credit hours	North Central Association of Colleges and Schools	Contact program administrator	377
Bachelor of Science	Management	Bellevue University	127 credit hours	North Central Association of Colleges and Schools	Contact program administrator	69
Bachelor of Science	Management	City University	180 credit hours	Northwest Association of Schools and Colleges	Yes	140
Bachelor of Science	Management	Marylhurst University	Contact program administrator	Northwest Association of Schools and Colleges	Yes	223
Bachelor of Science	Management of Information Systems	Bellevue University	127 credit hours	North Central Association of Colleges and Schools	Contact program administrator	69
Bachelor of Science	Marketing	City University	180 credit hours	Northwest Association of Schools and Colleges	Yes	140
Bachelor of Science	Organizational Communication	Marylhurst University	Contact program administrator	Northwest Association of Schools and Colleges	Yes	223
Bachelor of Science	Organizational Management	Hope International University	124 semester units	Western Association of Schools and Colleges	Contact program administrator	202
Master	Business Administration	Strayer University	Contact program administrator	Middle States Association of Colleges and Schools	Contact program administrator	295
Master of Arts	Business Communication	Jones International University	35 credit hours	North Central Association of Colleges and Schools	Yes	215
Master of Arts	Leadership	Bellevue University	36 credit hours	North Central Association of Colleges and Schools	Contact program administrator	68
Master of Arts	Organizational Design & Effectiveness	Fielding Institute	Three courses	Western Association of Schools and Colleges	Yes	182
Master of Arts	Organizational Management	University of Phoenix	39 semester credits	North Central Association of Colleges and Schools	Contact program administrator	367
Master of Arts	Strategic Communication and Leadership	Seton Hall University	36 credits	Middle States Association of Colleges and Schools	Contact program administrator	287

Degree	Concentration	Institution	Requirements	Accreditation	Financial Aid	Description Page
Master of Business Administration	Business Administration	Baker College	60 credit hours	North Central Association of Colleges and Schools	Contact program administrator	55
Master of Business Administration	Business Administration	Bellevue University	36 credit hours	North Central Association of Colleges and Schools	Contact program administrator	67
Master of Business Administration	Business Administration	California State University, Dominguez Hills	30 units	Western Associations of Schools and Colleges	Contact program administrator	80
Master of Business Administration	Business Administration	Capella University	52 credits	North Central Association of Colleges and Schools	Yes	88
Master of Business Administration	Business Administration	Colorado State University	36 credits	North Central Association of Colleges and Schools	Contact program administrator	151
Master of Business Administration	Business Administration	Dallas Baptist University	36 hours	Southern Association of Colleges and Schools	Contact program administrator	160
Master of Business Administration	Business Administration	Duke University	15 courses	Southern Association of Colleges and Schools	Contact program administrator	162
Master of Business Administration	Business Administration	Florida Institute of Technology	36 credit hours	Southern Association of Colleges and Schools	Contact program administrator	183
Master of Business Administration	Business Administration	Golden Gate University	48 units	Western Association of Schools and Colleges	Contact program administrator	192
Master of Business Administration	Business Administration	International School of Information Management	36 credits	Distance Education and Training Council	Contact program administrator	208
Master of Business Administration	Business Administration	University of Florida	48 credits	Southern Association of Colleges and Schools	Contact program administrator	324
Master of Business Administration	Business Administration	University of Maryland University College	Contact program administrator	Middle States Association of Colleges and Schools	Yes	345
Master of Business Administration	Business Administration	University of Phoenix	51 credit hours	North Central Association of Colleges and Schools	Contact program administrator	358
Master of Business Administration	Business Administration	Regis University	30 credit hours	North Central Association of Colleges and Schools	Contact program administrator	268
Master of Business Administration	Business Administration	Suffolk University	34 to 51 credits	New England Association of Schools and Colleges	Yes	299
Master of Business Administration	Business Administration	University of Baltimore	48 semester hour credits	Middle States Association of Colleges and Schools	Contact program administrator	310
Master of Business Administration	Business Administration	West Texas A & M University	36 credit hours	Southern Association of Colleges and Schools	Contact program administrator	386

Degree	Specialization	Institution	Credits	Accreditation	Admissions	Page
Master of Business Administration	Global Management	University of Phoenix	41 to 51 credit hours	North Central Association of Colleges and Schools	Contact program administrator	359
Master of Business Administration	Industrial Management	Baker College	50 credit hours	North Central Association of Colleges and Schools	Contact program administrator	60
Master of Business Administration	International Business	Baker College	50 credit hours	North Central Association of Colleges and Schools	Contact program administrator	63
Master of Business Administration	Leadership Studies	Baker College	50 credit hours	North Central Association of Colleges and Schools	Contact program administrator	64
Master of Business Administration	Management	Athabasca University	12 courses	Government of Alberta	Yes	49
Master of Business Administration	Marketing	Baker College	50 credit hours	North Central Association of Colleges and Schools	Contact program administrator	65
Master of Business Administration	Technology Management	University of Phoenix	41 to 51 credit hours	North Central Association of Colleges and Schools	Contact program administrator	359
Master of Business Administration Certificate	E-Business	Capella University	16 quarter credits	North Central Association of Colleges and Schools	Yes	94
Master of Business Management	Business Management	University of Wisconsin-Whitewater	Contact program administrator	North Central Association of Colleges and Schools	Contact program administrator	379
Master of Non-Profit Management	Non-Profit Management	Regis University	36 credit hours	North Central Association of Colleges and Schools	Contact program administrator	270
Master of Science	Business Education	Emporia State University	35 credit hours	North Central Association of Colleges and Schools	Yes	176
Master of Science	Communications Technology	Capella University	48 quarter units	North Central Association of Colleges and Schools	Yes	91
Master of Science	Direct Marketing Communications	New York University	Contact program administrator	Middle States Association of Schools and Colleges	Contact program administrator	240
Master of Science	Industrial Technology	East Carolina University	30 credits	Southern Association of Colleges and Schools	Contact program administrator	164
Master of Science	Management	Florida Institute of Technology	33 credit hours	Southern Association of Colleges and Schools	Contact program administrator	184
Master of Science	Management	Thomas Edison State College	36 credit hours	Middle States Association of Colleges and Schools	Contact program administrator	301
Master of Science	Management and Systems	New York University	36 credit hours	Middle States Association of Schools and Colleges	Contact program administrator	242
Master of Science	Management Information Systems	University of Illinois at Springfield	44 credit hours	North Central Association of Colleges and Schools	Contact program administrator	333

Degree	Concentration	Institution	Requirements	Accreditation	Financial Aid	Description Page
Master of Science	Marketing and Public Relations	Golden Gate University	45 units	Western Association of Schools and Colleges	Contact program administrator	194
Master of Science	Organization and Management	Capella University	48 quarter credits	North Central Association of Colleges and Schools	Yes	109
Master of Science	Project Management	University of Wisconsin-Platteville	30–36 credits	North Central Association of Colleges and Schools	Yes	375
Doctor of Management	Organizational Leadership	University of Phoenix	Contact program administrator	North Central Association of Colleges and Schools	Contact program administrator	366
Doctor of Philosophy	Applied Management & Decision Sciences	Walden University	128 quarter credit hour	North Central Association of Colleges and Schools	Yes	382
Doctor of Philosophy	Communications Technology	Capella University	Contact program administrator	North Central Association of Colleges and Schools	Yes	91
Doctor of Philosophy	Organization and Management	Capella University	64 quarter credits	North Central Association of Colleges and Schools	Yes	110

Canadian Studies

Degree	Concentration	Institution	Requirements	Accreditation	Financial Aid	Description Page
Bachelor of Arts	Canadian Studies	Athabasca University	120 credit hours	Government of Alberta	Yes	37

Comparative Literature

Degree	Concentration	Institution	Requirements	Accreditation	Financial Aid	Description Page
Associate of Arts	Comparative Literature	Cerro Coso Community College	18 units	Western Association of Schools and Colleges	Contact program administrator	124

Computer-Aided Design

Degree	Concentration	Institution	Requirements	Accreditation	Financial Aid	Description Page
Certificate	Computer Aided Design	Michigan State University	Contact program administrator	North Central Association of Colleges and Schools	Yes	227
Associate of Applied Science	Design Technology	Ivy Tech State College	64 credit hours	North Central Association of Colleges and Schools	Yes	213

Construction Technology

Degree	Concentration	Institution	Requirements	Accreditation	Financial Aid	Description Page
Associate of Applied Science	Construction Technology	Colorado Community College Online	61 credit hours	Accreditation dependent upon host institution	Contact program administrator	148

Criminal Justice

Degree	Concentration	Institution	Requirements	Accreditation	Financial Aid	Description Page
Graduate Diploma	Criminal Justice	University of Wisconsin-Platteville	Five courses	North Central Association of Colleges and Schools	Yes	373
Associate of Science	Administration of Justice	Cerro Coso Community College	21 units	Western Association of Schools and Colleges	Contact program administrator	123
Associate of Science	Criminal Justice	Bemidji State University	64 semester hours	North Central Association of Colleges and Schools	Contact program administrator	70
Bachelor of Professional Arts	Criminal Justice	Athabasca University	60 credit hours	Government of Alberta	Yes	40
Bachelor of Science	Criminal Justice	Bemidji State University	128 semester hours	North Central Association of Colleges and Schools	Contact program administrator	70
Bachelor of Science	Criminal Justice Administration	Bellevue University	127 credit hours	North Central Association of Colleges and Schools	Contact program administrator	68
Master	Criminal Justice Administration	Florida State University	36 hours	Southern Association of Colleges and Schools	Contact program administrator	185
Master of Arts	Education/Law Enforcement Leadership	Seton Hall University	36 semester hours; three weekend on-campus sessions	Middle States Association of Colleges and Schools	Contact program administrator	286
Master of Science	Criminal Justice	Michigan State University	Contact program administrator	North Central Association of Colleges and Schools	Yes	227
Master of Science	Criminal Justice	University of Wisconsin-Platteville	30 credits	North Central Association of Colleges and Schools	Yes	374

Dietary Management/Nutrition

Degree	Concentration	Institution	Requirements	Accreditation	Financial Aid	Description Page
Certificate	Dietary Manager	Pennsylvania State University, University Park	15–18 credits	Middle States Association of Colleges and Schools	Contact program administrator	261
Certificate	Dietetics and Aging	Pennsylvania State University, University Park	21 credits	Middle States Association of Colleges and Schools	Contact program administrator	262
Associate	Dietetic Technician	Pennsylvania State University, University Park	67 credits	Middle States Association of Colleges and Schools	Contact program administrator	261
Associate	School Food Service	Pennsylvania State University, University Park	67 credits	Middle States Association of Colleges and Schools	Contact program administrator	264
Master of Science	Human Nutrition	University of Bridgeport	31 credits	New England Association of Schools and Colleges	Yes	312

Disaster/Emergency Management

Degree	Concentration	Institution	Requirements	Accreditation	Financial Aid	Description Page
Diploma	Disaster Management	University of Wisconsin-Madison	60 continuing education units	North Central Association of Colleges and Schools	Yes	369
Certificate	Emergency Management and Planning	Colorado Community College Online	30 semester credits	Accreditation dependent upon host institution	Contact program administrator	148
Associate of Applied Science	Emergency Management and Planning	Colorado Community College Online	60 semester credits	Accreditation dependent upon host institution	Contact program administrator	148

Economics/Finance

Degree	Concentration	Institution	Requirements	Accreditation	Financial Aid	Description Page
Certificate	Economic Development	Baker College	20 credits	North Central Association of Colleges and Schools	Contact program administrator	57

Degree	Concentration	Institution	Requirements	Accreditation	Financial Aid	Description Page
Associate	Economics	Strayer University	Contact program administrator	Middle States Association of Colleges and Schools	Contact program administrator	296
Associate of Science	Economics	Cerro Coso Community College	22 units	Western Association of Schools and Colleges	Contact program administrator	125
Bachelor	Economics	Strayer University	Contact program administrator	Middle States Association of Colleges and Schools	Contact program administrator	297
Master of Business Management	Finance	University of Wisconsin-Whitewater	Contact program administrator	North Central Association of Colleges and Schools	Contact program administrator	378
Master of Science	Finance	Golden Gate University	51 units	Western Association of Schools and Colleges	Contact program administrator	193

Education

Degree	Concentration	Institution	Requirements	Accreditation	Financial Aid	Description Page
Certificate	Adult Education	Capella University	16 quarter credits	North Central Association of Colleges and Schools	Yes	86
Certificate	Career Development	Athabasca University	Contact program administrator	Government of Alberta	Yes	38
Certificate	Career Specialist Studies	University of Illinois at Springfield	12 semester hours	North Central Association of Colleges and Schools	Contact program administrator	331
Certificate	College Counseling	University of California, Los Angeles	23 units	Western Association of Schools and Colleges	Contact program administrator	316
Certificate	Cross-Cultural Language and Academic Development	University of California, Los Angeles	Five courses	Western Association of Schools and Colleges	Contact program administrator	316
Certificate	Distance Education	Capella University	16 quarter credits	North Central Association of Colleges and Schools	Yes	93
Certificate	Educational Administration	Capella University	16 quarter credits	North Central Association of Colleges and Schools	Yes	94
Certificate	Educational Psychology	Capella University	29 quarter credits	North Central Association of Colleges and Schools	Yes	96
Certificate	Educational Technology	McGill University	30 credits	Province of Quebec Ministry of Education	No	224
Certificate	Educational Technology Integration	Pennsylvania State University, University Park	18 credits	Middle States Association of Colleges and Schools	Contact program administrator	262
Certificate	Instructional Design	Capella University	16 quarter credits	North Central Association of Colleges and Schools	Yes	104

Degree	Concentration	Institution	Requirements	Accreditation	Financial Aid	Description Page
Certificate	Teachers and Trainers of Adults	Algonquin College	Five courses	Government of Ontario	Contact program administrator	24
Certificate	Teaching/Training Online	Capella University	16 quarter credits	North Central Association of Colleges and Schools	Yes	118
Certificate	Technology for Teachers	Goucher College	15 credit hours	Middle States Association of Colleges and Schools	Contact program administrator	197
Certificate	Using the Internet in Education	Jones International University	Two to three courses	North Central Association of Colleges and Schools	Yes	218
Advanced Graduate Diploma	Distance Education	Athabasca University	18 credits	Government of Alberta	Yes	41
Master of Arts	Education	Seton Hall University	36 semester hours; three weekends on-campus	Middle States Association of Colleges and Schools	Contact program administrator	284
Master of Arts	Education/Catholic School Leadership	Seton Hall University	36 semester hours; three weekends on-campus	Middle States Association of Colleges and Schools	Contact program administrator	285
Master of Arts/Master of Science	Student Affairs	Indiana State University	48 semester hours	North Central Association of Colleges and Schools	Contact program administrator	205
Master of Arts Education	Instructional Technology	East Carolina University	36 hours	Southern Association of Colleges and Schools	Contact program administrator	165
Master of Distance Education	Distance Education	Athabasca University	42 credit hours	Government of Alberta	Yes	40
Master of Education	Adult Education	Pennsylvania State University, University Park	33 credit hours	Middle States Association of Colleges and Schools	Contact program administrator	259
Master of Education	Curriculum, Technology, and Education Reform	University of Illinois at Urbana-Champaign	Eight units	North Central Association of Colleges and Schools	Yes	336
Master of Education	Education	Arizona State University	30 credit units	North Central Association of Colleges and Schools	Contact program administrator	31
Master of Education	Education	College of St. Scholastica	18 credits; two weekends on-campus	North Central Association of Colleges and Schools	Contact program administrator	145

Degree	Field	University	Credit Requirement	Accreditation	Online	Page
Master of Education	Education	University of Phoenix	37 credits	North Central Association of Colleges and Schools	Contact program administrator	362
Master of Education	Instructional Technology	West Texas A & M University	36 credit hours	Southern Association of Colleges and Schools	Contact program administrator	386
Master of Instructional Systems	Open and Distance Learning	Florida State University	36 credit hours	Southern Association of Colleges and Schools	Contact program administrator	188
Master of Science	Adult Education	Capella University	48 quarter credits; some courses have on-campus requirement	North Central Association of Colleges and Schools	Yes	87
Master of Science	Computing Technology in Education	Nova Southeastern University	36 credit hours	Southern Association of Colleges and Schools	Contact program administrator	255
Master of Science	Distance Education	Capella University	48 quarter credits	North Central Association of Colleges and Schools	Yes	93
Master of Science	Education	Walden University	45 credit hours	North Central Association of Colleges and Schools	Yes	382
Master of Science	Educational Administration	Capella University	48 quarter credits	North Central Association of Colleges and Schools	Yes	96
Master of Science	Educational Psychology	Capella University	60 quarter credits	North Central Association of Colleges and Schools	Yes	97
Master of Science	Instructional and Performance Technology	Boise State University	36 credits	Northwest Association of Schools and Colleges	Contact program administrator	73
Master of Science	Instructional Design	Capella University	48 quarter credits	North Central Association of Colleges and Schools	Yes	105
Master of Science	Language Education	Indiana University	36 credit hours	North Central Association of Colleges and Schools	Yes	207
Master of Science	Mathematics Education	Florida State University	33 semester hours	Southern Association of Colleges and Schools	Contact program administrator	188
Master of Science	Mathematics Education	Montana State University - Bozeman	30 semester hours	Northwest Association of Schools and Colleges	Contact program administrator	230
Master of Science	Science Education	Florida State University	Contact program administrator	Southern Association of Colleges and Schools	Contact program administrator	189
Master of Science	Science Education	Montana State University - Bozeman	30 semester hours	Northwest Association of Schools and Colleges	Contact program administrator	230

Degree	Concentration	Institution	Requirements	Accreditation	Financial Aid	Description Page
Master of Teacher Education	Teacher Education	Eastern Oregon University	Contact program administrator	Northwest Association of Schools and Colleges	Contact program administrator	172
Doctor of Education	Computing Technology in Education	Nova Southeastern University	64 credit hours	Southern Association of Colleges and Schools	Contact program administrator	255
Doctor of Philosophy	Adult Education	Capella University	120 quarter credits; some courses have on-campus requirement	North Central Association of Colleges and Schools	Yes	87
Doctor of Philosophy	Computing Technology in Education	Nova Southeastern University	64 credit hours	Southern Association of Colleges and Schools	Contact program administrator	255
Doctor of Philosophy	Education	Walden University	128 quarter credits	North Central Association of Colleges and Schools	Yes	383
Doctor of Philosophy	Educational Administration	Capella University	120 quarter credits	North Central Association of Colleges and Schools	Yes	95
Doctor of Philosophy	Educational Administration	Purdue University	60 semester hours	North Central Association of Colleges and Schools	Contact program administrator	266
Doctor of Philosophy	Educational Leadership and Change	Fielding Institute	Contact program administrator	Western Association of Schools and Colleges	Yes	181
Doctor of Philosophy	Educational Psychology	Capella University	120–124 quarter credits	North Central Association of Colleges and Schools	Yes	97
Doctor of Philosophy	Instructional Design	Capella University	120 quarter credits	North Central Association of Colleges and Schools	Yes	106
Doctorate	Education	University of Nebraska-Lincoln	30 credit hours; two 10-week on-campus sessions	North Central Association of Colleges and Schools	Yes	353

Engineering

Degree	Concentration	Institution	Requirements	Accreditation	Financial Aid	Description Page
Certificate	Noise Control Engineering	Pennsylvania State University, University Park	Three courses	Middle States Association of Colleges and Schools	Contact program administrator	264

Degree	Field	Institution	Credit Requirements	Accreditation	Online	Page
Bachelor of Science	Electrical/Mechanical Engineering Technology	Rochester Institute of Technology	193 credits	Middle States Association of Colleges and Schools	Yes	274
Bachelor of Science	Electrical Engineering	University of Florida	Contact program administrator	Southern Association of Colleges and Schools	Contact program administrator	323
Master of Electrical Engineering	Electrical Engineering	Colorado State University	30 semester hours	North Central Association of Colleges and Schools	Contact program administrator	152
Master of Engineering	Engineering	Arizona State University	Contact program administrator	North Central Association of Colleges and Schools	Contact program administrator	31
Master of Engineering	Engineering	University of Illinois at Chicago	35 semester hours	North Central Association of Colleges and Schools	Yes	326
Master of Engineering	Engineering in Professional Practice	University of Wisconsin-Madison	Contact program administrator	North Central Association of Colleges and Schools	Yes	370
Master of Engineering	Engineering in Technical Japanese	University of Wisconsin-Madison	Contact program administrator	North Central Association of Colleges and Schools	Yes	371
Master of Science	Civil Engineering	Colorado State University	Contact program administrator	North Central Association of Colleges and Schools	Contact program administrator	152
Master of Science	Electrical Engineering	Colorado State University	30 to 32 semester credits	North Central Association of Colleges and Schools	Contact program administrator	153
Master of Science	Electrical Engineering	University of Florida	Contact program administrator	Southern Association of Colleges and Schools	Contact program administrator	323
Master of Science	Electrical Engineering	University of Illinois at Urbana-Champaign	Eight units; thesis	North Central Association of Colleges and Schools	Yes	337
Master of Science	Engineering Management	Colorado State University	30 credits; thesis	North Central Association of Colleges and Schools	Contact program administrator	153
Master of Science	Engineering and Technology Management	Oklahoma State University	Contact program administrator	North Central Association of Colleges and Schools	Yes	258
Master of Science	Environmental Engineering	Colorado State University	Contact program administrator	North Central Association of Colleges and Schools	Contact program administrator	154
Master of Science	Mechanical Engineering	Colorado State University	Contact program administrator	North Central Association of Colleges and Schools	Contact program administrator	155
Master of Science	Theoretical and Applied Mechanics	University of Illinois at Urbana-Champaign	Eight units with thesis; Nine units without thesis	North Central Association of Colleges and Schools	Yes	341

Degree	Concentration	Institution	Requirements	Accreditation	Financial Aid	Description Page
Master of Science in Mechanical Engineering	Industrial Engineering	Colorado State University	Contact program administrator	North Central Association of Colleges and Schools	Contact program administrator	154
Doctor of Philosophy	Electrical Engineering	Colorado State University	42 credits	North Central Association of Colleges and Schools	Contact program administrator	153
Doctor of Philosophy	Mechanical Engineering	Colorado State University	Contact program administrator	North Central Association of Colleges and Schools	Contact program administrator	155

English

Degree	Concentration	Institution	Requirements	Accreditation	Financial Aid	Description Page
Certificate	English Language Studies	Athabasca University	Contact program administrator	Government of Alberta	Yes	42
Certificate	English Language Teaching	New School for Social Research	Contact program administrator	Middle States Association of Schools and Colleges	Contact program administrator	235
Associate of Arts	English	Cerro Coso Community College	30 units	Western Association of Schools and Colleges	Contact program administrator	125
Bachelor of Arts	English	Athabasca University	120 credit hours	Government of Alberta	Yes	42

Environmental Health and Safety

Degree	Concentration	Institution	Requirements	Accreditation	Financial Aid	Description Page
Bachelor of Science	Environmental Management and Technology	Rochester Institute of Technology	190 credits	Middle States Association of Colleges and Schools	Yes	275
Master of Science	Environmental Health and Safety Management	Rochester Institute of Technology	48 quarter credit	Middle States Association of Colleges and Schools	Yes	274

Facility Management

Degree	Concentration	Institution	Requirements	Accreditation	Financial Aid	Description Page
Certificate	Facility Management	Michigan State University	Four courses	North Central Association of Colleges and Schools	Yes	227

Fire Science

Degree	Concentration	Institution	Requirements	Accreditation	Financial Aid	Description Page
Associate of Applied Science	Fire Protection Technology	Chemeketa Community College	100 credit hours	Northwest Association of Schools and Colleges	Contact program administrator	133

French

Degree	Concentration	Institution	Requirements	Accreditation	Financial Aid	Description Page
Certificate	French	University of Illinois at Urbana-Champaign	Five courses	North Central Association of Colleges and Schools	Yes	337
Certificate	French Language Proficiency	Athabasca University	Contact program administrator	Government of Alberta	Yes	42
Bachelor of Arts	French	Athabasca University	120 credit hours	Government of Alberta	Yes	42

Gardening/Turfgrass Management

Degree	Concentration	Institution	Requirements	Accreditation	Financial Aid	Description Page
Certificate	Commercial Gardener	Algonquin College	18 courses	Government of Ontario	Contact program administrator	19
Certificate	Turfgrass Management	Pennsylvania State University, University Park	15–16 credit hours	Middle States Association of Colleges and Schools	Contact program administrator	265

Geographic Information Systems

Degree	Concentration	Institution	Requirements	Accreditation	Financial Aid	Description Page
Certificate	Geographic Information Systems	Pennsylvania State University, University Park	Four courses	Middle States Association of Colleges and Schools	Contact program administrator	263
Master of Engineering	Geographic Information Systems	University of Colorado at Denver	30 semester hours	North Central Association of Colleges and Schools	Yes	321

Gerontology

Degree	Concentration	Institution	Requirements	Accreditation	Financial Aid	Description Page
Certificate	Gerontology	Community College of Denver	30 credit hours	North Central Association of Colleges and Schools	Contact program administrator	157
Associate of Applied Science	Gerontology	Community College of Denver	60 credit hours	North Central Association of Colleges and Schools	Contact program administrator	158

Hazardous Materials Management

Degree	Concentration	Institution	Requirements	Accreditation	Financial Aid	Description Page
Certificate	Hazardous Materials Management	University of California Extension	Contact program administrator	Western Association of Schools and Colleges	Contact program administrator	314

History

Degree	Concentration	Institution	Requirements	Accreditation	Financial Aid	Description Page
Associate of Arts	History	Cerro Coso Community College	18 units	Western Association of Schools and Colleges	Contact program administrator	125
Bachelor of Arts	History	Athabasca University	120 credit hours	Government of Alberta	Yes	44

Hospitality and Tourism/Travel

Degree	Concentration	Institution	Requirements	Accreditation	Financial Aid	Description Page
Certificate	Customer Service Management for the Hospitality and Tourism Industries	New York University	12 credits	Middle States Association of Schools and Colleges	Contact program administrator	240
Certificate	Hotel-Restaurant Management	Champlain College	16 credits	New England Association of Schools and Colleges	Contact program administrator	129

Degree	Concentration	Institution	Requirements	Accreditation	Financial Aid	Description Page
Associate	Hospitality Supervision & Management	Champlain College	60 credits	New England Association of Schools and Colleges	Contact program administrator	130
Associate	Hotel, Restaurant, and Institutional Management	Pennsylvania State University, University Park	66–68 credits	Middle States Association of Colleges and Schools	Contact program administrator	263
Associate	Travel Management	Northwestern College	108 hours	North Central Association of Colleges and Schools	Contact program administrator	249
Associate of Applied Science	Hospitality and Tourism Management	Chemeketa Community College	96 credit hours	Northwest Association of Schools and Colleges	Contact program administrator	133
Bachelor of Professional Studies	Hospitality Management	New York Institute of Technology	120–122 credits	Middle States Association of Schools and Colleges	Yes	238
Bachelor of Science	Hotel and Restaurant Management	University of Houston	132 credits	Southern Association of Colleges and Schools	Contact program administrator	325
Master of Science	Hospitality and Industry Studies	New York University	39 credits	Middle States Association of Schools and Colleges	Contact program administrator	241
Master of Science	Hospitality and Tourism	University of Wisconsin-Stout	36 hours	North Central Association of Colleges and Schools	Contact program administrator	376

Human & Organization Development

Degree	Concentration	Institution	Requirements	Accreditation	Financial Aid	Description Page
Bachelor of Science	Human Development	Hope International University	124 semester units	Western Association of Schools and Colleges	Contact program administrator	202
Master of Arts	Human Development	Salve Regina University	Contact program administrator	New England Association of Schools and Colleges	Yes	283
Master of Arts in Cultural Anthropology & Social Transformation	Human & Organizational Transformation	California Institute of Integral Studies	Contact program administrator	Western Associations of Schools and Colleges	Contact program administrator	78
Doctor of Philosophy	Human & Organization Development	Fielding Institute	Eight curriculum areas	Western Association of Schools and Colleges	Yes	182

Human Resource Development

Degree	Concentration	Institution	Requirements	Accreditation	Financial Aid	Description Page
Certificate	Human Resource Management	Algonquin College	12 courses	Government of Ontario	Contact program administrator	20
Certificate	Training and Development	Capella University	20 quarter credits	North Central Association of Colleges and Schools	Yes	118
Master of Education	Human Resource Education	University of Illinois at Urbana-Champaign	Eight units	North Central Association of Colleges and Schools	Yes	338
Masters of Education in Education and Human Resource Studies	Human Resource Development	Colorado State University	Contact program administrator	North Central Association of Colleges and Schools	Contact program administrator	154
Master of Science	Human Resource Development	Indiana State University	33–36 hours	North Central Association of Colleges and Schools	Contact program administrator	204
Master of Science	Training and Development	Capella University	48 quarter credits	North Central Association of Colleges and Schools	Yes	119

Human Resources and Family Sciences

Degree	Concentration	Institution	Requirements	Accreditation	Financial Aid	Description Page
Master of Science	Human Resources and Family Services	University of Nebraska-Lincoln	36 credit hours	North Central Association of Colleges and Schools	Yes	353

Humanities

Degree	Concentration	Institution	Requirements	Accreditation	Financial Aid	Description Page
Associate of Arts	Literature	Cerro Coso Community College	18 units	Western Association of Schools and Colleges	Contact program administrator	126
Bachelor of Arts	Humanities	Athabasca University	120 credit hours	Government of Alberta	Yes	45
Bachelor of Arts	Humanities	City University	180 credits	Northwest Association of Schools and Colleges	Yes	139
Bachelor of Arts	Humanities	University of Maryland - University College	Contact program administrator	Middle States Association of Colleges and Schools	Yes	346
Master of Arts	Humanities	California State University, Dominguez Hills	30 units	Western Associations of Schools and Colleges	Contact program administrator	81

					Financial Aid	Description Page
Master of Arts	Humanities and Social Sciences	Norwich University	36 hours; one five-day on-campus colloquium	New England Association of Schools and Colleges	Contact program administrator	250
Doctor of Philosophy in Humanities	Transformative Learning and Change	California Institute of Integral Studies	Contact program administrator	Western Associations of Schools and Colleges	Contact program administrator	78

Information Systems/Information Technology

Degree	Concentration	Institution	Requirements	Accreditation	Financial Aid	Description Page
Certificate	C++ Programming	City University	45 credits	Northwest Association of Schools and Colleges	Yes	136
Certificate	Computer Information Systems	Algonquin College	14 courses	Government of Ontario	Contact program administrator	19
Certificate	Computer Information Systems	Baker College	20 credit hours	North Central Association of Colleges and Schools	Contact program administrator	56
Certificate	Computer Information Systems	University of California Extension	Contact program administrator	Western Association of Schools and Colleges	Contact program administrator	313
Certificate	Computer Programming	Champlain College	23 credits	New England Association of Schools and Colleges	Contact program administrator	129
Certificate	Computer Programming	University of California, Davis University Extension	30 units	Western Association of Schools and Colleges	Contact program administrator	308
Certificate	Computers and Management Information Systems	Athabasca University	Contact program administrator	Government of Alberta	Yes	39
Certificate	Computing and Information Systems	Athabasca University	Contact program administrator	Government of Alberta	Yes	39
Certificate	Database Technologies	Regis University	12 semester hours	North Central Association of Colleges and Schools	Contact program administrator	269
Certificate	Fundamentals of Information Technology	University of Massachusetts, Lowell	Contact program administrator	New England Association of Schools and Colleges	Yes	350

Degree	Concentration	Institution	Requirements	Accreditation	Financial Aid	Description Page
Certificate (Business Administration)	Information Technology	Capella University	16 quarter credits	North Central Association of Colleges and Schools	Yes	103
Certificate	Information Technology	New York University	16 credit hours	Middle States Association of Schools and Colleges	Contact program administrator	241
Certificate	Information Technology	Algonquin College	Six courses	Government of Ontario	Contact program administrator	20
Certificate	Internet Multimedia Software	Algonquin College	Ten courses	Government of Ontario	Contact program administrator	21
Certificate	Internetworking	City University	45 credit hours	Northwest Association of Schools and Colleges	Yes	139
Certificate	Intranet Development	University of Massachusetts, Lowell	Contact program administrator	New England Association of Schools and Colleges	Yes	350
Certificate	Management of Technology	Regis University	12 semester hours	North Central Association of Colleges and Schools	Contact program administrator	269
Certificate	Multimedia Technologies	Regis University	12 semester hours	North Central Association of Colleges and Schools	Contact program administrator	270
Certificate	Network / Telecommunications	City University	45 credit hours	Northwest Association of Schools and Colleges	Yes	140
Certificate	Networking Technologies	Regis University	12 semester hours	North Central Association of Colleges and Schools	Contact program administrator	270
Certificate	New Communications Technologies	Jones International University	Three courses	North Central Association of Colleges and Schools	Yes	217
Certificate	Object-Oriented Technologies	Regis University	12 semester hours	North Central Association of Colleges and Schools	Contact program administrator	271
Certificate	Telecommunications	Champlain College	23 credits	New England Association of Schools and Colleges	Contact program administrator	131
Certificate	UNIX	University of Massachusetts, Lowell	Contact program administrator	New England Association of Schools and Colleges	Yes	351
Certificate	Web Site Design	Wytheville Community College	19 credits	Southern Association of Colleges and Schools	Yes	390
Certificate	Web Site Development	University of California, Davis University Extension	23 units; only two courses currently online	Western Association of Schools and Colleges	Contact program administrator	309
Certificate	Webmaster	Pennsylvania State University, University Park	12 courses	Middle States Association of Colleges and Schools	Contact program administrator	265

Certificate	World Wide Web Page Design	New School for Social Research	Contact program administrator	Middle States Association of Schools and Colleges	Contact program administrator	236
Certificate in Applied Sciences	Computer Science	Harvard University	Eight courses	New England Association of Schools and Colleges	Contact program administrator	198
Certificate in Applied Sciences	Software Engineering	Harvard University	Eight courses	New England Association of Schools and Colleges	Contact program administrator	200
Certificate in Applied Sciences	Technical Writing and Multimedia	Harvard University	Eight courses	New England Association of Schools and Colleges	Contact program administrator	200
Advanced Graduate Diploma	Information Technology Management	Athabasca University	Contact program administrator	Government of Alberta	Yes	46
Associate	Computer Information Systems	Strayer University	Contact program administrator	Middle States Association of Colleges and Schools	Contact program administrator	295
Associate	Computer Programming	Champlain College	60 credits	New England Association of Schools and Colleges	Contact program administrator	129
Associate	Computer Programming	Vatterott College	96 quarter hours	Accrediting Commission of Career Schools and Colleges of Technology	Contact program administrator	380
Associate	Computer Technology	Northwestern College	108 hours	North Central Association of Colleges and Schools	Contact program administrator	247
Associate	Telecommunications	Champlain College	60 credits	New England Association of Schools and Colleges	Contact program administrator	131
Associate	Web Site Development and Management	Champlain College	60 credits	New England Association of Schools and Colleges	Contact program administrator	132
Associate of Applied Science	Computer Networking	Colorado Community College Online	60 credit hours	Accreditation dependent upon host institution	Contact program administrator	147
Associate of Science	Computer Information Systems	Cerro Coso Community College	Contact program administrator	Western Association of Schools and Colleges	Contact program administrator	124
Associate of Science	Computer Science	Rogers State University	Contact program administrator	North Central Association of Colleges and Schools	Yes	278
Associate of Science	Information Systems	University of Massachusetts, Lowell	33 semester credits	New England Association of Schools and Colleges	Yes	348
Bachelor	Computer Information Systems	Champlain College	120 credit hours	New England Association of Schools and Colleges	Contact program administrator	128

Degree	Concentration	Institution	Requirements	Accreditation	Financial Aid	Description Page
Bachelor	Computer Information Systems	Strayer University	Contact program administrator	Middle States Association of Colleges and Schools	Contact program administrator	296
Bachelor	Computer Networking	Strayer University	Contact program administrator	Middle States Association of Colleges and Schools	Contact program administrator	296
Bachelor of Arts	Computer Science	New Jersey Institute of Technology	Contact program administrator	Middle States Association for Colleges and Schools, Commission on Higher Education.	Yes	234
Bachelor of Arts	Information Systems	Athabasca University	120 credits	Government of Alberta	Yes	45
Bachelor of Arts	Information Systems	New Jersey Institute of Technology	Contact program administrator	Middle States Association for Colleges and Schools, Commission on Higher Education.	Yes	234
Bachelor of Arts/ Bachelor of Science	Computer and Information Science	University of Maryland University College	Contact program administrator	Middle States Association of Colleges and Schools	Yes	346
Bachelor of Arts/ Bachelor of Science	Technology and Management	University of Maryland University College	120 semester hours	Middle States Association of Colleges and Schools	Yes	347
Bachelor of Science	Computer and Information Science	Florida State University	60 hours	Southern Association of Colleges and Schools	Contact program administrator	185
Bachelor of Science	Computer Information Systems	Athabasca University	120 credits	Government of Alberta	Yes	38, 39
Bachelor of Science	Computer Information Systems	City University	180 credits	Northwest Association of Schools and Colleges	Yes	137
Bachelor of Science	Computer Science	American Institute for Computer Sciences	120 semester hours	Alabama State Department of Education; World Association of Colleges and Universities	Contact program administrator	26
Bachelor of Science	Computer Science	Colorado State University	Contact program administrator	North Central Association of Colleges and Schools	Contact program administrator	152
Bachelor of Science	Information Studies	Florida State University	60 credit hours	Southern Association of Colleges and Schools	Contact program administrator	186

Degree	Major	Institution	Credit Requirement	Accreditation	Transferable	Page
Bachelor of Science	Information Systems	American Institute for Computer Sciences	120 semester hours	Alabama State Department of Education; World Association of Colleges and Universities	Contact program administrator	27
Bachelor of Science	Information Systems	University of Phoenix		North Central Association of Colleges and Schools	Contact program administrator	363
Bachelor of Science	Information Systems	University of Massachusetts, Lowell	120 hours	New England Association of Schools and Colleges	Yes	349
Bachelor of Science	Information Technology	University of Phoenix	126 credit hours	North Central Association of Colleges and Schools	Contact program administrator	364
Master	Computer Science	Columbus State University	36 semester hours	Southern Association of Colleges and Schools	Contact program administrator	156
Master of Business Administration	Computer Information Systems	Baker College	50 credit hours	North Central Association of Colleges and Schools	Contact program administrator	57
Master of Business Administration	Information Technology Management	Athabasca University	Contact program administrator	Government of Alberta	Yes	47
Master of Liberal Arts	Information Technology	Harvard University	Ten courses	New England Association of Schools and Colleges	Contact program administrator	198
Master of Science	Computer Information Systems	Nova Southeastern University	36 credit hours	Southern Association of Colleges and Schools	Contact program administrator	253
Master of Science	Computer Information Systems	Regis University	36 credit hours	North Central Association of Colleges and Schools	Contact program administrator	268
Master of Science	Computer Information Systems	Southwest Missouri State	36 hours	North Central Association of Colleges and Schools	Contact program administrator	289
Master of Science	Computer Information Systems	University of Phoenix	45 semester credits	North Central Association of Colleges and Schools	Contact program administrator	362
Master of Science	Computer Science	American Institute for Computer Sciences	Contact program administrator	Alabama State Department of Education; World Association of Colleges and Universities	Contact program administrator	26

Degree	Concentration	Institution	Requirements	Accreditation	Financial Aid	Description Page
Master of Science	Computer Science	Colorado State University	Contact program administrator	North Central Association of Colleges and Schools	Contact program administrator	152
Master of Science	Computer Science	New Jersey Institute of Technology	Contact program administrator	Middle States Association for Colleges and Schools, Commission on Higher Education.	Yes	234
Master of Science	Computer Science	Nova Southeastern University	36 credit hours	Southern Association of Colleges and Schools	Contact program administrator	254
Master of Science	Computer Science	University of Illinois at Urbana-Champaign	Nine units	North Central Association of Colleges and Schools	Yes	335
Master of Science	Information Management	International School of Information Management	36 credits	Distance Education and Training Council	Contact program administrator	208
Master of Science	Information Systems	New Jersey Institute of Technology	36 credits	Middle States Association for Colleges and Schools, Commission on Higher Education.	Yes	234
Master of Science	Information Technology	New York University	40 credit hours	Middle States Association of Schools and Colleges	Contact program administrator	242
Master of Science	Information Technology	Rochester Institute of Technology	48 credit hours	Middle States Association of Colleges and Schools	Yes	276
Master of Science	Software Development and Management	Rochester Institute of Technology	48 quarter credits	Middle States Association of Colleges and Schools	Yes	277
Master of Science	Telecommunications Management	Golden Gate University	42 units	Western Association of Schools and Colleges	Contact program administrator	196
Master of Science	Telecommunications Management	Oklahoma State University	Contact program administrator	North Central Association of Colleges and Schools	Yes	258
Doctor of Philosophy	Computer Information Systems	Nova Southeastern University	64 credit hours	Southern Association of Colleges and Schools	Contact program administrator	253
Doctor of Philosophy	Computer Science	Nova Southeastern University	64 credit hours	Southern Association of Colleges and Schools	Contact program administrator	254
Doctor of Philosophy	Technology Management	Bowling Green State University	90 semester hours	North Central Association of Colleges and Schools	Contact program administrator	74

Degree	Concentration	Institution	Requirements	Accreditation	Financial Aid	Description Page
Doctor of Philosophy	Technology Management	Central Missouri State University	90 credit hours	North Central Association of Colleges and Schools	Contact program administrator	122
Doctor of Philosophy	Technology Management	East Carolina University	90 semester hours	Southern Association of Colleges and Schools	Contact program administrator	166
Doctor of Philosophy	Technology Management	Eastern Michigan University	90 semester hours	North Central Association of Colleges and Schools	Contact program administrator	168
Doctor of Philosophy	Technology Management	Indiana State University	90 semester hours	North Central Association of Colleges and Schools	Contact program administrator	205
Doctor of Philosophy	Technology Management	North Carolina A&T State University	90 semester hours	Southern Association of Colleges and Schools	Contact program administrator	243
Doctor of Philosophy	Technology Management	Texas Southern University	90 semester hours	Southern Association of Colleges and Schools	Contact program administrator	300
Doctor of Philosophy	Technology Management	University of Wisconsin-Stout	90 semester hours	North Central Association of Colleges and Schools	Contact program administrator	377

International Relations

Degree	Concentration	Institution	Requirements	Accreditation	Financial Aid	Description Page
Master of Arts	International Relations	Salve Regina University	36 credits	New England Association of Schools and Colleges	Yes	283
Master of Science	International Relations	Troy State University-Florida Region	10–12 courses	Southern Association of Colleges and Schools	Yes	303

Journalism

Degree	Concentration	Institution	Requirements	Accreditation	Financial Aid	Description Page
Certificate	Media Management	New School for Social Research	Contact program administrator	Middle States Association of Schools and Colleges	Contact program administrator	235
Master of Arts	Journalism and Mass Communications	University of Nebraska-Lincoln	30–36 credits	North Central Association of Colleges and Schools	Yes	354
Master of Arts	Media Studies	New School for Social Research	Contact program administrator	Middle States Association of Schools and Colleges	Contact program administrator	236

Labor & Industrial Relations

Degree	Concentration	Institution	Requirements	Accreditation	Financial Aid	Description Page
Certificate	Labour Relations	Athabasca University	Contact program administrator	Government of Alberta	Yes	47
Certificate	Labour Studies	Athabasca University	Contact program administrator	Government of Alberta	Yes	48
Bachelor of Administration	Industrial Relations	Athabasca University	90 credit hours	Government of Alberta	Yes	45
Bachelor of Arts	Labour Studies	Athabasca University	120 credit hours	Government of Alberta	Yes	48

Legal

Degree	Concentration	Institution	Requirements	Accreditation	Financial Aid	Description Page
Certificate	Paralegal Studies	City University	45 credit hours	Northwest Association of Schools and Colleges	Yes	141
Associate	Legal Assisting	Northwestern College	108 credit hours	North Central Association of Colleges and Schools	Contact program administrator	247
Associate	Legal Secretarial	Northwestern College	108 credit hours	North Central Association of Colleges and Schools	Contact program administrator	248
Associate of Applied Science	Paralegal Technology	Western Piedmont Community College	68 semester hours	Southern Association of Colleges and Schools	Contact program administrator	388

Library & Information Science

Degree	Concentration	Institution	Requirements	Accreditation	Financial Aid	Description Page
Associate of Science	Library Technical Assistant	Indian River Community College	48 semester hours	Southern Association of Colleges and Schools	Contact program administrator	203
Master of Library Science	Library Science	Connecticut State University System	36 credit hours	New England Association of Schools and Colleges	Contact program administrator	158
Master of Library Science	Library Science	Emporia State University	Contact program administrator	North Central Association of Colleges and Schools	Yes	178
Master of Science	Library and Information Science	University of Illinois at Urbana-Champaign	Ten units	North Central Association of Colleges and Schools	Yes	338

Master of Science	Library and Information Studies	Florida State University	Contact program administrator	Southern Association of Colleges and Schools	Contact program administrator	187
Master of Science	Library Studies	Florida State University	Contact program administrator	Southern Association of Colleges and Schools	Contact program administrator	187

Logistics/Purchasing

Degree	Concentration	Institution	Requirements	Accreditation	Financial Aid	Description Page
Certificate	Logistics and Supply Chain Management	Pennsylvania State University, University Park	Four courses	Middle States Association of Colleges and Schools	Contact program administrator	263
Certificate	Production and Inventory Control	California State University, Dominguez Hills	Five courses	Western Associations of Schools and Colleges	Contact program administrator	82
Certificate	Purchasing	California State University, Dominguez Hills	Four courses	Western Associations of Schools and Colleges	Contact program administrator	83
Master of Science	Materials Management	Algonquin College	13 courses	Government of Ontario	Contact program administrator	22
Master of Science	Quality Assurance	California State University, Dominguez Hills	33 units	Western Associations of Schools and Colleges	Contact program administrator	83

Medicine/Health/Opticianry

Degree	Concentration	Institution	Requirements	Accreditation	Financial Aid	Description Page
Certificate	Basic Opticianry	Durham Technical Community College	15 hours	Southern Association of Colleges and Schools	Contact program administrator	163
Certificate	Group Practice Management	New School for Social Research	Contact program administrator	Middle States Association of Schools and Colleges	Contact program administrator	235
Certificate	Health Care Administration	Capella University	16 quarter credits	North Central Association of Colleges and Schools	Yes	99
Certificate	Health Care Management	Baker College	20 credit hours	North Central Association of Colleges and Schools	Contact program administrator	59
Certificate	Health Development Administration	Athabasca University	Contact program administrator	Government of Alberta	Yes	43

429

Degree	Concentration	Institution	Requirements	Accreditation	Financial Aid	Description Page
Certificate	Health Information Management	University of Illinois at Chicago	Six courses	North Central Association of Colleges and Schools	Yes	328
Certificate	Integrated Health Care	Baker College	32 credit hours	North Central Association of Colleges and Schools	Contact program administrator	61
Associate	Medical Technology	Northwestern College	108 credit hours	North Central Association of Colleges and Schools	Contact program administrator	249
Associate	Medical Secretarial	Northwestern College	108 credit hours	North Central Association of Colleges and Schools	Contact program administrator	248
Associate	Pharmacy Assistant Technology	Northwestern College	108 credit hours	North Central Association of Colleges and Schools	Contact program administrator	249
Associate of Science	Emergency Medical Services	American College of Prehospital Medicine	60 semester hours	Distance Education and Training Council	Contact program administrator	25
Associate of Science	Health Physics	Lakeshore Technical College	64–67 credits	North Central Association of Colleges and Schools	Contact program administrator	218
Bachelor	Health Care Management	Northwestern College	90 credit hours	North Central Association of Colleges and Schools	Contact program administrator	247
Bachelor of Administration	Health Administration	Athabasca University	90 credits	Government of Alberta	Yes	36, 43
Bachelor of Applied Health	Applied Health	University of Minnesota, Crookston	Contact program administrator	North Central Association of Colleges and Schools	Contact program administrator	351
Bachelor of Professional Studies	Health Services Management	State University of New York Empire State College	128 credits	Middle States Association of Colleges and Schools	Contact program administrator	293
Bachelor of Science	Emergency Medical Services	American College of Prehospital Medicine	120 semester hours	Distance Education and Training Council	Contact program administrator	25
Bachelor of Science	Human Science	Athabasca University	120 hours	Government of Alberta	Yes	44
Bachelor of Science	Health Services Management	State University of New York Empire State College	128 credits	Middle States Association of Colleges and Schools	Contact program administrator	293
Master of Business Administration	Health Care Administration	Baker College	50 credit hours	North Central Association of Colleges and Schools	Contact program administrator	59
Master of Business Administration	Integrated Health Care	Baker College	60 credit hours	North Central Association of Colleges and Schools	Contact program administrator	62
Master of Health Professions Education	Health Professions Education	University of Illinois at Chicago	32 credit hours	North Central Association of Colleges and Schools	Yes	327

Degree	Field	University	Requirements	Accreditation	Contact program administrator	Page
Master of Healthcare Administration	Health Care Administration	Golden Gate University	36 units	Western Association of Schools and Colleges	Contact program administrator	193
Master of Science	Administrative Medicine	University of Wisconsin-Madison	Seven weeks on-campus	North Central Association of Colleges and Schools	Yes	368
Master of Science	Health, Physical Education and Recreation	Emporia State University	34–35 credit hours	North Central Association of Colleges and Schools	Yes	177
Master of Science	Health Care Administration	Capella University	48 quarter credits	North Central Association of Colleges and Schools	Yes	99
Master of Science/Health Care Administration	Health Care Administration	Seton Hall University	39 credits	Middle States Association of Colleges and Schools	Contact program administrator	286
Master of Science	Health Psychology	Capella University	60 quarter credits	North Central Association of Colleges and Schools	Yes	101
Master of Science	Health Sciences	Cleveland State University	36 credit hours	North Central Association of Colleges and Schools	Yes	144
Master of Science	Health Systems Administration	Rochester Institute of Technology	57 quarter credit hours	Middle States Association of Colleges and Schools	Yes	276
Master of Science	Human Services	Capella University	48 quarter credits	North Central Association of Colleges and Schools	Yes	102
Doctor of Pharmacy	Pharmacy	University of Illinois at Chicago	44 credit hours	North Central Association of Colleges and Schools	Yes	329
Doctor of Philosophy	Health Care Administration	Capella University	120 quarter credits	North Central Association of Colleges and Schools	Yes	100
Doctor of Philosophy	Health Psychology	Capella University	120 quarter credits	North Central Association of Colleges and Schools	Yes	101
Doctor of Philosophy	Health Services	Walden University	128 quarter credit hours	North Central Association of Colleges and Schools	Yes	383
Doctor of Philosophy	Human Services	Capella University	120 quarter credits	North Central Association of Colleges and Schools	Yes	102
Doctor of Philosophy	Human Services	Walden University	128 quarter credits; orientation residency	North Central Association of Colleges and Schools	Yes	384

Military Science

Degree	Concentration	Institution	Requirements	Accreditation	Financial Aid	Description Page
Bachelor of Arts	Military Studies	American Military University	120 semester hours	Distance Education and Training Council	Contact program administrator	29
Master of Arts	Military Studies	American Military University	36 semester hours	Distance Education and Training Council	Contact program administrator	29

Nursing

Degree	Concentration	Institution	Requirements	Accreditation	Financial Aid	Description Page
Certificate	Advanced Nursing Practice	University of Illinois at Chicago	Contact program administrator	North Central Association of Colleges and Schools	Yes	328
Advanced Graduate Diploma	Advanced Nursing Practice	Athabasca University	Contact program administrator	Government of Alberta	Yes	34
Bachelor of Arts/ Bachelor of Science	Nursing	Eastern Oregon University	Contact program administrator	Northwest Association of Schools and Colleges	Contact program administrator	170
Bachelor of Nursing	Nursing	Athabasca University	69 credits	Government of Alberta	Yes	50
Bachelor of Science	Nursing	California State University, Dominguez Hills	124 semester units	Western Associations of Schools and Colleges	Contact program administrator	82
Bachelor of Science	Nursing	Florida State University	Contact program administrator	Southern Association of Colleges and Schools	Contact program administrator	188
Bachelor of Science	Nursing	University of Central Florida	121 semester hours	Southern Association of Colleges and Schools	Contact program administrator	319
Bachelor of Science	Nursing	University of Maine at Fort Kent	Contact program administrator	New England Association of Schools and Colleges	Yes	342
Bachelor of Science	Nursing	University of Phoenix	Contact program administrator	North Central Association of Colleges and Schools	Contact program administrator	365
Master of Health Studies	Advanced Nursing Practice	Athabasca University	Contact program administrator	Government of Alberta	Yes	43

Occupational Safety and Health

Degree	Concentration	Institution	Requirements	Accreditation	Financial Aid	Description Page
Certificate	Occupational Health and Safety	Central Maine Technical College	Contact program administrator	New England Association of Schools and Colleges	Contact program administrator	120
Certificate	Occupational Safety	Colorado Community College Online	44 credit hours	Accreditation dependent upon host institution	Contact program administrator	159
Certificate	Occupational Safety and Health for General Industry	University of Wisconsin-Platteville	Contact program administrator	North Central Association of Colleges and Schools	Yes	375
Associate in Applied Science	Occupational Health and Safety	Central Maine Technical College	Contact program administrator	New England Association of Schools and Colleges	Contact program administrator	120
Associate in Applied Science	Occupational Safety	Colorado Community College Online	69 credit hours	Accreditation dependent upon host institution	Contact program administrator	149

Philosophy & Religious Studies

Degree	Concentration	Institution	Requirements	Accreditation	Financial Aid	Description Page
Bachelor of Arts/ Bachelor of Science	Philosophy, Politics, and Economics	Eastern Oregon University	Contact program administrator	Northwest Association of Schools and Colleges	Contact program administrator	171

Physical Education/Sports Science

Degree	Concentration	Institution	Requirements	Accreditation	Financial Aid	Description Page
Certificate	Sport Psychology	Capella University	20 quarter credits	North Central Association of Colleges and Schools	Yes	116
Bachelor of Science	Physical Education and Health	Eastern Oregon University	Contact program administrator	Northwest Association of Schools and Colleges	Contact program administrator	171
Master of Science	Sport Psychology	Capella University	60 quarter credits	North Central Association of Colleges and Schools	Yes	116
Master of Sport Science	Sport Coaching	United States Sports Academy	33 credit hours	Southern Association of Colleges and Schools	Contact program administrator	306
Master of Sport Science	Sports Medicine	United States Sports Academy	33 credit hours	Southern Association of Colleges and Schools	Contact program administrator	307

Degree	Concentration	Institution	Requirements	Accreditation	Financial Aid	Description Page
Master of Sport Science	Sport Management	United States Sports Academy	33 credit hours	Southern Association of Colleges and Schools	Contact program administrator	307
Doctor of Philosophy	Sport Psychology	Capella University	120 quarter credits	North Central Association of Colleges and Schools	Yes	117

Physics

Degree	Concentration	Institution	Requirements	Accreditation	Financial Aid	Description Page
Master of Science	Beam Physics	Michigan State University	30 credits; qualifying exam	North Central Association of Colleges and Schools	Yes	225
Doctor of Philosophy	Beam Physics	Michigan State University	qualifying exam	North Central Association of Colleges and Schools	Yes	226

Psychology/Counseling

Degree	Concentration	Institution	Requirements	Accreditation	Financial Aid	Description Page
Certificate	Addiction Psychology	Capella University	20 quarter credits	North Central Association of Colleges and Schools	Yes	84
Certificate	Chemical Dependency Counselor	Pennsylvania State University, University Park	18 credits	Middle States Association of Colleges and Schools	Contact program administrator	260
Certificate	Clinical Psychology	Capella University	20 quarter credits	North Central Association of Colleges and Schools	Yes	89
Certificate	Counseling Women	Athabasca University	Contact program administrator	Government of Alberta	Yes	39
Certificate	Marriage and Family Services	Capella University	16 quarter credits	North Central Association of Colleges and Schools	Yes	107
Certificate	Organizational Psychology	Capella University	20 quarter credits	North Central Association of Colleges and Schools	Yes	110
Certificate	Professional Counseling	Capella University	16 quarter credits	North Central Association of Colleges and Schools	Yes	112

Certificate	Social and Community Services	Capella University	16 quarter credits	North Central Association of Colleges and Schools	Yes	114
Bachelor of Arts/ Bachelor of Science	Behavioral and Social Sciences	University of Maryland University College	Contact program administrator	Middle States Association of Colleges and Schools	Yes	345
Bachelor of Arts	Behavioral Arts and Sciences	College of St. Scholastica	192 credits	North Central Association of Colleges and Schools	Contact program administrator	145
Bachelor of Arts	Behavioral Science	University of Maine at Machias	120 credit hours	New England Association of Schools and Colleges	Yes	343
Bachelor of Arts	Psychology	Athabasca University	120 credit hours	Government of Alberta	Yes	51
Bachelor of Science	Behavioral Sciences	New York Institute of Technology	128 credits	Middle States Association of Schools and Colleges	Yes	237
Bachelor of Science	Psychology	Endicott College	128 credits	New England Association of Schools and Colleges	Contact program administrator	179
Master of Arts	Counseling	Seton Hall University	48 credits	Middle States Association of Colleges and Schools	Contact program administrator	284
Master of Arts in Behavioral Science	Negotiation and Conflict Management	California State University, Dominguez Hills	Eight courses	Western Associations of Schools and Colleges	Contact program administrator	81
Master of Science	Addiction Psychology	Capella University	60 quarter credits	North Central Association of Colleges and Schools	Yes	85
Master of Science	Clinical Psychology	Capella University	60 quarter credits	North Central Association of Colleges and Schools	Yes	89
Master of Science	Marriage and Family Services	Capella University	48 quarter credits	North Central Association of Colleges and Schools	Yes	107
Master of Science	Organizational Psychology	Capella University	60 quarter credits	North Central Association of Colleges and Schools	Yes	111
Master of Science	Professional Counseling	Capella University	48 quarter credits	North Central Association of Colleges and Schools	Yes	113
Master of Science	Psychology	Walden University	45 credit hours	North Central Association of Colleges and Schools	Yes	385
Master of Science	Social and Community Services	Capella University	48 quarter credits	North Central Association of Colleges and Schools	Yes	115

Degree	Concentration	Institution	Requirements	Accreditation	Financial Aid	Description Page
Doctor of Philosophy	Addiction Psychology	Capella University	120 quarter credits; contact school for on-campus requirements	North Central Association of Colleges and Schools	Yes	85
Doctor of Philosophy	Clinical Psychology	Capella University	120 quarter credits; contact school for on-campus requirements	North Central Association of Colleges and Schools	Yes	90
Doctor of Philosophy	Clinical Psychology	Fielding Institute	Thirteen academic area components	Western Association of Schools and Colleges	Yes	181
Doctor of Philosophy	Marriage and Family Services	Capella University	120 quarter credits	North Central Association of Colleges and Schools	Yes	108
Doctor of Philosophy	Organizational Psychology	Capella University	120 quarter credits	North Central Association of Colleges and Schools	Yes	111
Doctor of Philosophy	Professional Counseling	Capella University	120 quarter credits	North Central Association of Colleges and Schools	Yes	113
Doctor of Philosophy	Professional Psychology	Walden University	127 quarter credit hours	North Central Association of Colleges and Schools	Yes	385
Doctor of Philosophy	Social and Community Services	Capella University	120 quarter credits	North Central Association of Colleges and Schools	Yes	115

Public Administration

Degree	Concentration	Institution	Requirements	Accreditation	Financial Aid	Description Page
Certificate	Public Administration	Athabasca University	Contact program administrator	Government of Alberta	Yes	51
Certificate	Public Administration	Indiana State University	12 semester hours	North Central Association of Colleges and Schools	Contact program administrator	205
Associate of Arts	Public Administration	Colorado Community College Online	60 credit hours	Accreditation dependent upon host institution	Contact program administrator	149
Bachelor of Administration	Public Administration	Athabasca University	90 credit hours	Government of Alberta	Yes	51

Degree	Concentration	Institution	Requirements	Accreditation	Financial Aid	Description Page
Bachelor of Public Administration	Public Administration	Golden Gate University	39 units	Western Association of Schools and Colleges	Contact program administrator	194
Bachelor of Science	Governmental Administration	Christopher Newport University	Contact program administrator	Southern Association of Colleges and Schools	Contact program administrator	134
Master of Public Administration	Public Administration	Golden Gate University	36 semester hours	Western Association of Schools and Colleges	Contact program administrator	195
Master of Public Administration	Public Administration	Troy State University-Florida Region	10–12 courses	Southern Association of Colleges and Schools	Yes	304

Quantitative Studies

Degree	Concentration	Institution	Requirements	Accreditation	Financial Aid	Description Page
Bachelor of Arts	Quantitative Studies	City University	180 credit hours	Northwest Association of Schools and Colleges	Yes	141

Resource Management

Degree	Concentration	Institution	Requirements	Accreditation	Financial Aid	Description Page
Bachelor of Applied Science	Resource Management	Troy State University-Florida Region	193 hours	Southern Association of Colleges and Schools	Yes	304

Sociology/Social Science

Degree	Concentration	Institution	Requirements	Accreditation	Financial Aid	Description Page
Associate of Arts	Social Science	Cerro Coso Community College	18 units	Western Association of Schools and Colleges	Contact program administrator	126
Bachelor of Arts	Social Science	City University	180 credits	Northwest Association of Schools and Colleges	Yes	142
Bachelor of Arts	Sociology	Athabasca University	120 credit hours	Government of Alberta	Yes	52
Master of Arts	Social Science	Norwich University	36 credit	New England Association of Schools and Colleges	Contact program administrator	252

Space Studies

Degree	Concentration	Institution	Requirements	Accreditation	Financial Aid	Description Page
Bachelor of Science	Space Studies	University of North Dakota	Contact program administrator	North Central Association of Colleges and Schools	Contact program administrator	357

Statistics

Degree	Concentration	Institution	Requirements	Accreditation	Financial Aid	Description Page
Master of Science	Applied Statistics	Rochester Institute of Technology	24 credits; oral examination	Middle States Association of Colleges and Schools	Yes	273
Master of Science	Statistics	Colorado State University	Contact program administrator	North Central Association of Colleges and Schools	Contact program administrator	155

Taxation

Degree	Concentration	Institution	Requirements	Accreditation	Financial Aid	Description Page
Master of Science	Taxation	Golden Gate University	41 units	Western Association of Schools and Colleges	Contact program administrator	195

Textiles, Clothing, and Design

Degree	Concentration	Institution	Requirements	Accreditation	Financial Aid	Description Page
Master of Science	Textiles, Clothing, and Design	University of Nebraska-Lincoln	36 credit hours	North Central Association of Colleges and Schools	Yes	355

Theology

Degree	Concentration	Institution	Requirements	Accreditation	Financial Aid	Description Page
Certificate	Christian Studies	Fuller Theological Seminary	Six courses	Western Association of Schools and Colleges	Contact program administrator	190

Degree	Concentration	Institution	Requirements	Accreditation	Financial Aid	Description Page
Certificate	Theological Studies	Eastern Mennonite University	Eight courses	Southern Association of Colleges and Schools and Association of Theological Schools	Contact program administrator	167
Certificate	Work-Life Ministry	Seton Hall University	15 credits	Middle States Association of Colleges and Schools	Contact program administrator	287
Bachelor of Arts	Christian Ministry	Crown College	Contact program administrator	North Central Association of Colleges and Schools	Contact program administrator	159
Bachelor of Arts	Christian Ministry	Lee University	130 hours	Southern Association of Colleges and Schools	Contact program administrator	220
Bachelor of Science	Christian Ministry	Hope International University	124 semester units	Western Association of Schools and Colleges	Contact program administrator	201
Master of Arts	Church Leadership	Crown College	Contact program administrator	North Central Association of Colleges and Schools	Contact program administrator	159

Veterinary Technology

Degree	Concentration	Institution	Requirements	Accreditation	Financial Aid	Description Page
Associate of Science	Veterinary Technology	St. Petersburg Junior College	73 credits	Southern Association of Colleges and Schools	Contact program administrator	290

Women's Studies

Degree	Concentration	Institution	Requirements	Accreditation	Financial Aid	Description Page
Bachelor of Arts	Women's Studies	Athabasca University	120 credit hours	Government of Alberta	Yes	52